GENERAL
ACCOUNTING

GENERAL ACCOUNTING

by

H. A. FINNEY, Ph.B., C.P.A.

Professor of Accounting, Northwestern University. Formerly Editor of the Students' Department of The Journal of Accountancy. Member of the Firm of Baumann, Finney & Co., Certified Public Accountants. Author of Principles of Accounting, Introductory; Principles of Accounting, Intermediate; and Principles of Accounting, Advanced.

NEW YORK: 1942

PRENTICE-HALL, INC.

First Printing.........January, 1941
Second Printing..........July, 1941
Third Printing........January, 1942

PRINTED IN THE UNITED STATES OF AMERICA

PREFACE

....

ACCOUNTING is the language of commerce—the language in which the history of a business is recorded, its operations are summarized, its financial condition is stated, and its budget forecasts are expressed.

Although accounting employs the familiar language in which all of our thoughts are expressed, it is like the language of contract bidding—conventions have given special significance to words and phrases. The accountant who prepares the reports and the layman to whom they are addressed too frequently are in the regrettable position of bridge partners of whom only one fully understands the language of the activity in which they are engaged.

Any language, to be fully useful, must be understood by both the speaker and the listener, by the writer and the reader. Unfortunately, this is not always the case with accounting. Business executives too often are unable to read their accounts and are not always able wholly to grasp the significance of the reports prepared for their guidance in making managerial decisions; professional men frequently are handicapped in their service to clients by their unfamiliarity with accounts; and many investors cannot adequately analyze the reports of companies in which they have placed their funds or contemplate placing them.

The responsibility for this state of affairs rests not with the laymen but with the accountants and educators. This book is for laymen and for students who, although not interested in accounting as a profession, realize the importance of a general familiarity with the subject.

The author expresses his sincere thanks to Professor Ralph C. Jones of Yale University, Professor Theodore Lang of New York University, and Professor I. B. Gritz of Alabama Polytechnic Institute, who read the manuscript and whose comments and suggestions were most helpful.

H. A. FINNEY

v

CONTENTS

GENERAL
ACCOUNTING

1

THE BALANCE SHEET

···

Assets, liabilities, and net worth.

Assets are things of value owned. Liabilities are creditors' claims. The net worth of a business is the excess of the value of its assets over its liabilities.

Nature of the balance sheet.

The balance sheet of a business is a statement of the assets, liabilities, and net worth of the business on a given date. It may be drawn up in the form illustrated below, which is an expression of the equation: Assets − Liabilities = Net Worth.

THE Y COMPANY

Balance Sheet—December 31, 1942

ASSETS:

Cash	$ 5,000.00
Accounts Receivable	8,000.00
Merchandise	12,000.00
Total Assets	$25,000.00

LIABILITIES:

Accounts Payable	7,000.00
NET WORTH	$18,000.00

It is obvious that the assets of a business are equalled by the claims of the creditors plus the equity of the owners. This relationship is expressed by the following restatement of the foregoing equation: Assets = Liabilities + Net Worth.

This form of the equation is the basis of the balance sheet illustrated below:

THE Y COMPANY

Balance Sheet—December 31, 1942

Assets		Liabilities and Net Worth	
Cash	$ 5,000	LIABILITIES:	
Accounts Receivable	8,000	Accounts Payable	$ 7,000
Merchandise	12,000	NET WORTH	18,000
	$25,000		$25,000

Series of illustrations.

The following illustrations are intended to show the general structure of the balance sheet and the nature of some of the more common elements thereof. A balance sheet is presented after each transaction or other assumed fact. (The illustrations are presented for the sole purpose of developing an understanding of the balance sheet; all considerations of natural continuity or completeness of business operations have been sacrificed to that purpose.) The reader is advised to compare each balance sheet with the immediately preceding one, and note carefully the changes caused by each transaction.

After issuance of stock. A corporation is organized and issues capital stock of $100,000.00 par value.

THE *A* COMPANY
Balance Sheet—June 1, 1941

Assets		Net Worth	
Cash	$100,000	Capital Stock	$100,000

After a bank loan. The company borrows $25,000.00 from a bank, giving a note for that amount. Observe how the captions "Liabilities" and "Net Worth" are used on the right side of the balance sheet for the purpose of more clearly separating the claims of creditors and the equity of the owners.

THE *A* COMPANY
Balance Sheet—June 2, 1941

Assets		Liabilities and Net Worth	
Cash	$125,000	LIABILITIES:	
		Notes Payable	$ 25,000
		NET WORTH:	
		Capital Stock	100,000
	$125,000		$125,000

After a cash purchase. The company buys merchandise for cash at a cost of $40,000.00.

THE *A* COMPANY
Balance Sheet—June 3, 1941

Assets		Liabilities and Net Worth	
Cash	$ 85,000	LIABILITIES:	
Merchandise	40,000	Notes Payable	$ 25,000
		NET WORTH:	
		Capital Stock	100,000
	$125,000		$125,000

After a purchase on account. The company buys merchandise on account at a cost of $30,000.00.

THE *A* COMPANY
Balance Sheet—June 5, 1941

Assets		Liabilities and Net Worth		
Cash	$ 85,000	LIABILITIES:		
Merchandise	70,000	Notes Payable	$25,000	
		Accounts Payable	30,000	$ 55,000
		NET WORTH:		
		Capital Stock		100,000
	$155,000			$155,000

After a purchase of real estate. The company pays $40,000.00 for real estate; the land cost $5,000.00, and the building cost $35,000.00. Observe that captions appear on the left side of the balance sheet to classify the assets; these captions are:

CURRENT ASSETS:
> Here are shown cash and other assets which normally will be converted into cash in the relatively near future through the regular operations of the business. "Relatively near future" is usually regarded as meaning one year.

FIXED ASSETS:
> Here is shown the relatively permanent property used in the operations of the business and not intended for sale.

THE *A* COMPANY
Balance Sheet—June 6, 1941

Assets			Liabilities and Net Worth		
CURRENT ASSETS:			LIABILITIES:		
Cash	$45,000		Notes Payable	$25,000	
Merchandise	70,000	$115,000	Accounts Payable	30,000	$ 55,000
FIXED ASSETS:			NET WORTH:		
Land	$ 5,000		Capital Stock		100,000
Building	35,000	40,000			
		$155,000			$155,000

After issuing a long-term note. The company borrows $15,-000.00 for ten years on a note secured by a mortgage on its real estate. New captions appear on the right side of the following balance sheet to classify the liabilities according to the immediacy of their maturity; these captions are:

CURRENT LIABILITIES:
> Here are shown the liabilities which mature in the relatively near future; this usually means within one year.

FIXED LIABILITIES:
> Here are shown the liabilities which mature in the relatively distant future.

THE *A* COMPANY
Balance Sheet—June 8, 1941

Assets			Liabilities and Net Worth		
CURRENT ASSETS:			CURRENT LIABILITIES:		
Cash	$60,000		Notes Payable	$25,000	
Merchandise	70,000	$130,000	Accounts Payable	30,000	$ 55,000
FIXED ASSETS:			FIXED LIABILITIES:		
Land	$ 5,000		Real Estate Mortgage		15,000
Building	35,000	40,000	NET WORTH:		
			Capital Stock		100,000
		$170,000			$170,000

After a sale for cash. Merchandise which cost $5,000.00 is sold for $7,500.00, and cash is received therefor. This transaction increases the cash $7,500.00 and decreases the merchandise $5,000.00; the $2,500.00 profit increases the net worth.

Observe that the following balance sheet shows two elements of net worth: capital stock, which is the portion of net worth contributed by the stockholders; and surplus, which is the increase in net worth resulting from profitable operations.

THE *A* COMPANY
Balance Sheet—June 9, 1941

Assets			Liabilities and Net Worth		
CURRENT ASSETS:			CURRENT LIABILITIES:		
Cash	$67,500		Notes Payable	$ 25,000	
Merchandise	65,000	$132,500	Accounts Payable	30,000	$ 55,000
FIXED ASSETS:			FIXED LIABILITIES:		
Land	$ 5,000		Real Estate Mortgage		15,000
Building	35,000	40,000	NET WORTH:		
			Capital Stock	$100,000	
			Surplus	2,500	102,500
		$172,500			$172,500

After sales on account. Merchandise which cost $30,000.00 is sold to various customers on account for $45,000.00.

THE *A* COMPANY
Balance Sheet—June 10, 1941

Assets			Liabilities and Net Worth		
CURRENT ASSETS:			CURRENT LIABILITIES:		
Cash	$67,500		Notes Payable	$ 25,000	
Accounts Receivable	45,000		Accounts Payable	30,000	$ 55,000
Merchandise	35,000	$147,500	FIXED LIABILITIES:		
FIXED ASSETS:			Real Estate Mortgage		15,000
Land	$ 5,000		NET WORTH:		
Building	35,000	40,000	Capital Stock	$100,000	
			Surplus	17,500	117,500
		$187,500			$187,500

After payment of expenses.   Various expenses totaling $5,000.00 are paid in cash, thus decreasing the cash and the net worth.   The decrease in net worth is reflected by a reduction in the surplus.

THE *A* COMPANY
Balance Sheet—June 11, 1941

Assets			Liabilities and Net Worth			
CURRENT ASSETS:			CURRENT LIABILITIES:			
Cash.............	$62,500		Notes Payable...	$ 25,000		
Accounts Receivable	45,000		Accounts Payable.	30,000	$ 55,000	
Merchandise......	35,000	$142,500	FIXED LIABILITIES:			
FIXED ASSETS:			Real Estate Mortgage......		15,000	
Land.............	$ 5,000		NET WORTH:			
Building.........	35,000	40,000	Capital Stock....	$100,000		
			Surplus.........	12,500	112,500	
		$182,500			$182,500	

Deferred expenses.   The company pays $300.00 for a one-year insurance policy, and $400.00 for coal.

For purposes of proper balance sheet presentation, expense payments should be divided into two classes:

> Payments for goods or services which should immediately be regarded as expenses; these should be deducted from Surplus, because they represent expenses already incurred.

> Payments for goods or services which will benefit a future period and therefore have an asset value to the business; these should be shown on the asset side of the balance sheet. The following balance sheet shows two such items of deferred expense: the unexpired insurance, which is the cost of future insurance protection; and the cost of the coal to be used in the future.

THE *A* COMPANY
Balance Sheet—June 30, 1941

Assets			Liabilities and Net Worth			
CURRENT ASSETS:			CURRENT LIABILITIES:			
Cash.............	$61,800		Notes Payable...	$ 25,000		
Accounts Receivable	45,000		Accounts Payable.	30,000	$ 55,000	
Merchandise.......	35,000	$141,800	FIXED LIABILITIES:			
FIXED ASSETS:			Real Estate Mortgage......		15,000	
Land.............	$ 5,000		NET WORTH:			
Building.........	35,000	40,000	Capital Stock....	$100,000		
DEFERRED EXPENSES:			Surplus.........	12,500	112,500	
Unexpired Insurance............	$ 300					
Fuel.............	400	700				
		$182,500			$182,500	

Deferred expenses are also called deferred charges.

Deferred income. Just as expenses may be paid in advance, so may income be collected in advance. To illustrate the effect upon the balance sheet, assume that the company leases a portion of its building to a tenant for an annual rental of $1,000.00, which is collected in advance. This transaction results in a $1,000.00 increase in cash. Although the rent income will eventually increase the net worth, surplus should not be immediately increased $1,000.00, because the rent will not be fully earned until the end of twelve months. Meanwhile the balance sheet should show a deferred income item on the right side.

THE *A* COMPANY
Balance Sheet—July 1, 1941

Assets			Liabilities and Net Worth		
CURRENT ASSETS:			CURRENT LIABILITIES:		
Cash	$62,800		Notes Payable	$ 25,000	
Accounts Receivable	45,000		Accounts Payable.	30,000	$ 55,000
Merchandise	35,000	$142,800	FIXED LIABILITIES:		
FIXED ASSETS:			Real Estate Mortgage		15,000
Land	$ 5,000		DEFERRED INCOME:		
Building	35,000	40,000	Rent Collected in Advance..		1,000
DEFERRED EXPENSES:			NET WORTH:		
Unexpired Insurance	$ 300		Capital Stock	$100,000	
Fuel	400	700	Surplus	12,500	112,500
		$183,500			$183,500

The right side of a balance sheet is headed "Liabilities and Net Worth"; a deferred credit is neither a liability nor a part of the net worth, but it has elements of both. It is not strictly a liability because it is not payable in cash; but its presence in a balance sheet does indicate the existence of an obligation; the deferred credit of Rent Collected in Advance represents an obligation to allow the tenant to occupy the leased premises. In a sense, also, a deferred credit is a sort of net worth item, because the net worth will be increased in the future when the service has been rendered and the income has been earned.

When the Sunday school teacher asked how many wanted to go to heaven, Johnny's hand did not go up. "No?" asked the teacher. "Not yet," said Johnny. He had some things to do yet. Deferred credits will be income by and by; but the addition to net worth must be deferred until the income has been earned by the rendition of the service for which the collection has been received in advance.

A Deferred Credits caption is often used instead of the Deferred Income caption illustrated in the foregoing balance sheet.

Other assets. In the following balance sheet, which shows the financial condition resulting from numerous transactions occurring prior to the close of the year, a new caption, "Other Assets," appears on the asset side. It is assumed that the company purchased vacant land in anticipation of a possible addition to its plant; this land is not a fixed asset because, according to the definition on page 3, fixed assets are used in the operations of the business; this land is not being so used. Also it is assumed that the company has made some permanent investments in stocks of other companies.

THE A COMPANY
Balance Sheet—December 31, 1941

Assets			Liabilities and Net Worth		
CURRENT ASSETS:			CURRENT LIABILITIES:		
Cash............	$50,000		Accounts Payable.	$ 34,000	
Accounts Receivable	35,000		Notes Payable...	35,000	$ 69,000
Notes Receivable..	25,000		FIXED LIABILITIES:		
Merchandise......	40,000	$150,000	Real Estate Mortgage......		15,000
FIXED ASSETS:			DEFERRED CREDIT:		
Land............	$ 5,000		Rent Collected in Advance..		1,000
Building..........	35,000	40,000	NET WORTH:		
OTHER ASSETS:			Capital Stock....	$100,000	
Vacant Land......	$10,000		Surplus..........	19,700	119,700
Investment in					
Stocks..........	4,000	14,000			
DEFERRED CHARGES:					
Unexpired Insurance............	$ 300				
Fuel.............	400	700			
		$204,700			$204,700

Accruals. The foregoing balance sheet was prepared without taking into consideration certain accrued assets and accrued liabilities which are usually given consideration in month-end or year-end balance sheets.

Interest in the amount of $375.00 has accrued on notes receivable but has not been collected; this accrued interest is an asset; and, since it has been earned, although it has not been collected, it is an item of income which is properly added to Surplus. Taking this accrual into the balance sheet will affect the Current Assets and Net Worth sections in the manner shown below:

CURRENT ASSETS:			NET WORTH:		
Cash............	$50,000		Capital Stock....	$100,000	
Accounts Receivable	35,000		Surplus..........	20,075	$120,075
Notes Receivable..	25,000				
Accrued Interest...	375				
Merchandise......	40,000	$150,375			

On the other hand, liabilities have accrued for the following expenses:

Interest on notes payable............................	$ 450.00
Unpaid wages......................................	250.00
Federal and state income taxes......................	3,375.00
Total..	$4,075.00

Taking these accruals into the balance sheet will involve increases in current liabilities and decreases in surplus, as indicated below:

CURRENT LIABILITIES:
Accounts Payable.	$ 34,000	
Notes Payable...	35,000	
Accrued Interest..	450	
Accrued Wages...	250	
Income Taxes....	3,375	$ 73,075

NET WORTH:
Capital Stock....	$100,000	
Surplus..........	16,000	116,000

The complete balance sheet, after adjustments for accruals have been made, appears below:

THE A COMPANY
Balance Sheet—December 31, 1941

Assets

CURRENT ASSETS:
Cash.............	$50,000	
Accounts Receivable	35,000	
Notes Receivable..	25,000	
Accrued Interest...	375	
Merchandise......	40,000	$150,375

FIXED ASSETS:
Land.............	$ 5,000	
Building.........	35,000	40,000

OTHER ASSETS:
Vacant Land......	$10,000	
Investment in Stocks..........	4,000	14,000

DEFERRED CHARGES:
Unexpired Insurance............	$ 300	
Fuel.............	400	700
		$205,075

Liabilities and Net Worth

CURRENT LIABILITIES:
Accounts Payable.	$ 34,000	
Notes Payable...	35,000	
Accrued Interest..	450	
Accrued Wages...	250	
Income Taxes....	3,375	$ 73,075

FIXED LIABILITIES:
Real Estate Mortgage......	15,000

DEFERRED CREDIT:
Rent Collected in Advance..	1,000

NET WORTH:
Capital Stock....	$100,000	
Surplus..........	16,000	116,000
		$205,075

Adjustments of deferred items. The item of $300.00 shown in the balance sheet as Unexpired Insurance represents the cost on June 30 of a one-year policy. Half of the year has expired; therefore half of the cost should be deducted from Surplus as an expense applicable to the expired period; and $150.00 should remain as a deferred charge representing an asset in the form of an expense prepayment for the next six months.

Of the fuel purchased at a cost of $400.00, approximately one fourth has been used; therefore $100.00 should be deducted from Surplus as an expense incurred, and the remaining $300.00 should be carried as a deferred charge.

The reductions in prepaid expenses affect the Deferred Charges and Net Worth sections of the balance sheet as follows:

DEFERRED CHARGES:			NET WORTH:		
Unexpired Insurance	$150		Capital Stock	$100,000	
Fuel	300	$450	Surplus	15,750	$115,750

On July 1, the company collected $1,000.00 as rental for twelve months. Half of this period has expired; therefore $500.00 has been earned and can be added to Surplus, and $500.00 remains as a deferred credit.

The complete balance sheet, after these adjustments of deferred charges and deferred credits have been made, appears as follows:

THE *A* COMPANY
Balance Sheet—December 31, 1941

Assets			Liabilities and Net Worth		
CURRENT ASSETS:			CURRENT LIABILITIES:		
Cash	$50,000		Accounts Payable.	$ 34,000	
Accounts Receivable	35,000		Notes Payable	35,000	
Notes Receivable	25,000		Accrued Interest	450	
Accrued Interest	375		Accrued Wages	250	
Merchandise	40,000	$150,375	Income Taxes	3,375	$ 73,075
FIXED ASSETS:			FIXED LIABILITIES:		
Land	$ 5,000		Real Estate Mortgage		15,000
Building	35,000	40,000	DEFERRED CREDITS:		
OTHER ASSETS:			Rents Collected in Advance.		500
Vacant Land	$10,000		NET WORTH:		
Investment in			Capital Stock	$100,000	
Stocks	4,000	14,000	Surplus	16,250	116,250
DEFERRED CHARGES:					
Unexpired Insurance	$ 150				
Fuel	300	450			
		$204,825			$204,825

Reserve for bad debts. The foregoing balance sheet shows accounts, notes, and interest receivable totaling $60,375.00. The balance sheet should show what portion of this total can probably be collected; in other words, the balance sheet should show the estimated value of the receivables after the estimated loss has been deducted. The reduction of the receivables to their estimated net collectible value causes a corresponding reduction in the net worth, as indicated by the following partial balance sheet in which a $1,000.00 deduction from the receivables causes a corresponding reduction in Surplus:

CURRENT ASSETS:				NET WORTH:		
Cash......................			$50,000	Capital Stock.............	$100,000	
Receivables:				Surplus..................	15,250	$115,250
Accounts Rec....	$35,000					
Notes Receivable.	25,000					
Accrued Interest.	375					
Total.......	$60,375					
Deduct Estimated						
Loss..........	1,000	59,375				
Merchandise...............		40,000	$149,375			

The amount deducted from the receivables as the estimated loss is usually called a "reserve." The reader should not allow himself to be disturbed by the introduction of accountants' fancy language; "Deduct Reserve for Bad Debts" means nothing more than "Deduct Amount that Probably Cannot Be Collected." The deduction of the reserve for bad debts is intended to reduce the balance sheet valuation of the receivables to the amount which it is estimated will be ultimately collected.

The complete balance sheet after the provision of a reserve for bad debts appears on the opposite page.

Reserve for depreciation. The building was shown in all of the foregoing balance sheets at its cost, $35,000.00. Let us assume that this building has an estimated life of 35 years from the date of its acquisition, and that it will have no value at the end of that time. Therefore the business will suffer a total depreciation expense, or loss, of $35,000.00 during the 35-year life of the building.

Years ago it was a rather general custom to ignore depreciation until the end of the life of the fixed asset, when the entire amount was deducted from Surplus. It is now recognized that depreciation takes place gradually and continuously throughout the life of the asset, and it is now customary to deduct the loss little by little over the asset's life. For instance, in dealing with depreciation of the building, which cost $35,000.00, the accountant's thinking would be as follows: If the building cost $35,000.00 and has an estimated life of 35 years with no scrap value, the annual depreciation (on an average or straight-line basis) is $1,000.00; the building was purchased six months ago; therefore the depreciation for the six months since acquisition is $500.00.

THE A COMPANY
Balance Sheet—December 31, 1941

Assets

CURRENT ASSETS:			
Cash			$50,000
Receivables:			
Accounts Receivable	$35,000		
Notes Receivable	25,000		
Accrued Interest	375		
Total		$60,375	
Deduct Reserve for Bad Debts		1,000	
Receivables—Net Book Value		59,375	
Merchandise		40,000	
Total Current Assets			$149,375
FIXED ASSETS:			
Land		$5,000	
Building		35,000	
Total Fixed Assets			40,000
OTHER ASSETS:			
Vacant Land		$10,000	
Investments in Stocks		4,000	
Total Other Assets			14,000
DEFERRED CHARGES:			
Unexpired Insurance		$ 150	
Fuel		300	
Total Deferred Charges			450
			$203,825

Liabilities and Net Worth

CURRENT LIABILITIES:		
Accounts Payable	$ 34,000	
Notes Payable	35,000	
Accrued Interest	450	
Accrued Wages	250	
Income Taxes	3,375	
Total Current Liabilities		$ 73,075
FIXED LIABILITIES:		
Real Estate Mortgage		15,000
DEFERRED CREDITS:		
Rent Collected in Advance		500
NET WORTH:		
Capital Stock	$100,000	
Surplus	15,250	
Total Net Worth		115,250
		$203,825

THE A COMPANY
Balance Sheet—December 31, 1941

Assets

CURRENT ASSETS:			
Cash			$50,000
Receivables:			
Accounts Receivable	$35,000		
Notes Receivable	25,000		
Accrued Interest	375		
Total	$60,375		
Deduct Reserve for Bad Debts	1,000		
Receivables—Net		59,375	
Merchandise		40,000	
Total Current Assets			$149,375
FIXED ASSETS:			
Land		$ 5,000	
Building:			
Cost	$35,000		
Less Reserve for Depreciation	500		
Depreciated Value		34,500	
Total Fixed Assets			39,500
OTHER ASSETS:			
Vacant Land	$10,000		
Investments in Stocks	4,000		
Total Other Assets			14,000
DEFERRED CHARGES:			
Unexpired Insurance	$ 150		
Fuel	300		
Total Deferred Charges			450
			$203,325

Liabilities and Net Worth

CURRENT LIABILITIES:		
Accounts Payable	$ 34,000	
Notes Payable	35,000	
Accrued Interest	450	
Accrued Wages	250	
Income Taxes	3,375	
Total Current Liabilities		$ 73,075
FIXED LIABILITIES:		
Real Estate Mortgage		15,000
DEFERRED CREDITS:		
Rent Collected in Advance		500
NET WORTH:		
Capital Stock	$100,000	
Surplus	14,750	
Total Net Worth		114,750
		$203,325

The estimated depreciation of the building could be shown in the balance sheet as follows:

FIXED ASSETS:
Land.. $ 5,000
Building:
Cost.................................. $35,000
Less Estimated Decrease in Value Resulting
from Depreciation.....................   500
Depreciated Value.............................. 34,500
Total Fixed Assets................................ $39,500

The amount deducted for depreciation is usually called a Reserve for Depreciation. The reader should clearly understand and always remember that a reserve for depreciation is not a fund of cash or other assets set aside to provide money for the eventual replacement of a fixed asset. A reserve for depreciation is merely a deduction representing a shrinkage in the value of a building or other fixed asset resulting from wear and tear and the action of the elements during the passage of time.

The balance sheet of The A Company after the provision of a reserve for depreciation of the building is shown on page 12. A comparison of this balance sheet with the one on page 11 shows that the provision for depreciation has caused a $500.00 reduction in the valuation of the building and in the surplus. No reserves are provided for depreciation of land, because land used as a building site does not suffer any decline in value as the result of wear and tear and the action of the elements.

2

OPERATING AND SURPLUS STATEMENTS

Operating statements.

The items of income and expense shown in a company's operating statement depend upon the nature of the company's operations and the elaborateness of its accounting system. A number of illustrations are given in this chapter.

Statements of a non-trading company.

As a first and extremely simple illustration, the statement of a company that operates a real estate agency and that records all of its income in one account and all of its expenses in one account is presented below:

THE BLACK REALTORS, INCORPORATED
Statement of Income and Expense
For the Year Ended December 31, 1941

Income from Commission	$10,000.00
Deduct Expenses	6,000.00
Net Income	$ 4,000.00

Assume that a similar company earns commissions from sales, fees for building management, insurance agency commissions, and brokerage for placing loans; assume, also, that it keeps a separate account with each class of income, but that it keeps only one expense account; its statement may appear as follows:

THE GREEN REALTORS, INCORPORATED
Statement of Income and Expense
For the Year Ended December 31, 1941

Income:	
Commissions on Sales	$15,000.00
Management Fees	8,000.00
Insurance Commissions	2,800.00
Brokerage on Loans	1,500.00
Total Income	$27,300.00
Deduct Expenses	19,600.00
Net Income	$ 7,700.00

Expenses may be detailed as follows:

THE GREEN REALTORS, INCORPORATED
Statement of Income and Expense
For the Year Ended December 31, 1941

Income:

Commissions on Sales	$15,000.00
Management Fees	8,000.00
Insurance Commissions	2,800.00
Brokerage on Loans	1,500.00
Total Income	$27,300.00

Deduct Expenses:

Office Rent	$1,200.00	
Heat and Light	400.00	
Office Salaries	6,000.00	
Stationery and Printing	950.00	
Miscellaneous Office Expense	525.00	
Advertising	1,375.00	
Telephone and Telegraph	725.00	
Postage	280.00	
Automobile Expense	1,125.00	
Insurance	115.00	
Taxes	1,280.00	
Executive Salaries	4,500.00	
Miscellaneous Expense	1,125.00	
Total Expenses		19,600.00
Net Income		$ 7,700.00

Statements of a trading company.

The gross profit of a merchandising company is the excess of its sales over the cost of goods sold. The net profit is the remainder after deduction of operating expenses from the gross profit.

THE OSBORNE COMPANY
Profit and Loss Statement
For the Year Ended December 31, 1941

Net Sales	$969,140.00
Deduct Cost of Goods Sold	615,460.00
Gross Profit on Sales	$353,680.00
Deduct Expenses	278,240.00
Net Profit	$ 75,440.00

Sales and returns.

Customers sometimes return merchandise that is unsatisfactory or was not ordered; or they may receive a credit allowance for goods not in conformity with the invoice, as to quantity or quality. The statement of a merchandising company therefore may show gross sales, returns and allowances, and net sales, as follows:

THE OSBORNE COMPANY
Profit and Loss Statement
For the Year Ended December 31, 1941

Gross Sales..	$982,400.00
Deduct Returned Sales and Allowances....................	13,260.00
Net Sales...	$969,140.00
Deduct Cost of Goods Sold..............................	615,460.00
Gross Profit on Sales...................................	$353,680.00
Deduct Expenses..	278,240.00
Net Profit...	$ 75,440.00

Cost of goods sold.

Some companies keep a record of the cost of each article sold. But such records are expensive to maintain and it is a rather general custom to compute the cost of goods sold by a procedure similar to Sir Walter Raleigh's method of weighing the smoke from a pipe of tobacco. He weighed the tobacco that went into the pipe, deducted the weight of the ashes and dottle remaining in the pipe, and called the remainder the weight of the smoke. Similarly, a merchant may add the inventory at the beginning and the purchases during the period; from this total he will deduct the inventory at the end of the period; the remainder he will call the cost of goods sold. Really, it is the cost of goods sold, lost, stolen, or otherwise disposed of during the period.

The foregoing profit and loss statement is expanded below to show such a computation of the cost of goods sold.

THE OSBORNE COMPANY
Profit and Loss Statement
For the Year Ended December 31, 1941

Gross Sales..			$982,400
Deduct Returned Sales and Allowances......................			13,260
Net Sales...			$969,140
Deduct Cost of Goods Sold:			
Inventory, December 31, 1940....................		$ 42,300	
Add Net Cost of Purchases:			
Purchases.........................	$625,479		
Deduct Returns and Allowances.......	5,826		
Net Purchases......................	$619,653		
Add Freight and Cartage In...........	4,217	623,870	
Total..		$666,170	
Deduct Inventory, December 31, 1941.............		50,710	
Remainder—Cost of Goods Sold..........................			615,460
Gross Profit on Sales..			$353,680
Deduct Expenses......................................			278,240
Net Profit..			$ 75,440

Expenses detailed.

The expenses, shown above in their total amount of $278,-240.00, are detailed and classified in the following statement.

THE OSBORNE COMPANY
Profit and Loss Statement
For the Year Ended December 31, 1941

Gross Sales			$982,400
Deduct Returned Sales and Allowances			13,260
Net Sales			$969,140
Deduct Cost of Goods Sold:			
Inventory, December 31, 1940		$ 42,300	
Add Net Cost of Purchases:			
Purchases	$625,479		
Deduct Returns and Allowances	5,826		
Net Purchases	$619,653		
Add Freight and Cartage In	4,217	623,870	
Total		$666,170	
Deduct Inventory, December 31, 1941		50,710	
Remainder—Cost of Goods Sold			615,460
Gross Profit on Sales			$353,680
Deduct Selling Expenses:			
Salesmen's Salaries		$ 49,890	
Traveling Expense		20,310	
Advertising		31,375	
Branch Office Expense		23,050	
Dealer Service		25,700	
Freight Out		20,080	
Miscellaneous		7,845	
Total Selling Expenses			178,250
Net Profit on Sales			$175,430
Deduct General Expenses:			
Officers' Salaries		$ 25,000	
Office Salaries		13,750	
Rent		4,000	
Stationery and Supplies		3,600	
Telephone and Telegraph		4,680	
Bad Debts		8,625	
Legal and Auditing		6,410	
Miscellaneous		4,645	
Total General Expenses			70,710
Net Profit on Operations			$104,720
Deduct Financial Expenses:			
Discount on Sales		$ 9,640	
Interest on Mortgage Payable		4,500	
Interest on Notes Payable		3,075	
Total Financial Expenses			17,215
Net Profit Before Federal Income Taxes			$ 87,505
Deduct Federal Income Taxes			12,065
Net Profit			$ 75,440

Statement with supporting schedules.

The following illustrations indicate the procedure of showing totals in the profit and loss statement and details in supporting schedules.

THE WHITCOMB COMPANY
Statement of Profit and Loss
For the Year Ended December 31, 1941

Gross Sales	$125,000.00
Deduct Returned Sales and Allowances	1,500.00
Net Sales	$123,500.00
Deduct Cost of Goods Sold—Schedule 1	70,675.00
Gross Profit on Sales	$ 52,825.00
Deduct Selling Expenses—Schedule 2	35,400.00
Net Profit on Sales	$ 17,425.00
Deduct General Expenses—Schedule 3	16,495.00
Net Profit on Operations	$ 930.00
Add Other Income—Schedule 4	3,385.00
Net Profit and Other Income	$ 4,315.00
Deduct Other Expenses—Schedule 4	1,125.00
Net Income	$ 3,190.00

THE WHITCOMB COMPANY　　　Schedule 1
Cost of Goods Sold
For the Year Ended December 31, 1941

Inventory, December 31, 1940		$19,740.00
Add Net Cost of Purchases:		
Purchases	$70,980.00	
Duty	2,110.00	
Warehousing	325.00	
Freight In	1,710.00	
Total	$75,125.00	
Deduct Returns and Allowances	1,210.00	73,915.00
Total Opening Inventory and Purchases		$93,655.00
Deduct Inventory, December 31, 1941		22,980.00
Cost of Goods Sold		$70,675.00

THE WHITCOMB COMPANY　　　Schedule 2
Selling Expenses
For the Year Ended December 31, 1941

Salesmen's Salaries	$15,000.00
Delivery Salaries	5,000.00
Salesmen's Traveling Expense	4,000.00
Depreciation—Delivery Equipment	50.00
Freight Out	2,600.00
Delivery Expense	2,750.00
Advertising	6,000.00
Total Selling Expenses	$35,400.00

THE WHITCOMB COMPANY   Schedule 3

General Expenses

For the Year Ended December 31, 1941

Office Salaries...	$ 1,300.00
Officers' Salaries.......................................	11,800.00
Depreciation—Furniture and Fixtures......................	50.00
Office Supplies..	300.00
Stationery and Printing..................................	125.00
Insurance...	35.00
Bad Debts...	1,250.00
Miscellaneous...	1,635.00
Total General Expenses...........................	$16,495.00

THE WHITCOMB COMPANY   Schedule 4

Other Income and Other Expenses

For the Year Ended December 31, 1941

Other Income:	
Discount on Purchases................................	$ 3,225.00
Interest Earned......................................	60.00
Delivery Income......................................	100.00
Total Other Income.............................	$ 3,385.00
Other Expenses:	
Discount on Sales....................................	$ 1,010.00
Interest on Notes Payable............................	115.00
Total Other Expenses...........................	$ 1,125.00

General remarks.

Profits are made by sales; other earnings, such as interest and dividends on investments or commissions and other forms of compensation for services, are not profits but income. Therefore the operating statement of a company engaged in selling purchased or manufactured goods is usually called a profit and loss statement, or statement of profit and loss, whereas the operating statement of a company making earnings other than profits on sales is more properly called a statement of income and expense.

It has seemed desirable in presenting the illustrations in this chapter to maintain a certain uniformity of pattern so as to avoid confusion. It should be understood, however, that anyone who has occasion to prepare an operating statement may avail himself of his constitutional right of freedom to draw it up in any manner which to him seems the clearest way of presenting the facts.

A balance sheet of a company shows the company's financial condition on a stated *date;* therefore the heading should show the date: e. g., "December 31, 1941." On the other hand, a profit and loss statement shows the results of operations during a stated *period;* therefore the heading of the statement should show the period: e. g., "For the Year Ended December 31, 1941." Do not head a balance sheet: "For the Year Ended December 31, 1941"; the financial condition of a business does not remain static during a year. Do not head a profit and loss statement: "December 31, 1941"; Rome was not built in a day. And do not head it: "For the Period Ended December 31, 1941"; what period?

Surplus statement.

The surplus statement for a given period should show the surplus at the beginning of the period, all increases and decreases during the period, and the balance at the end of the period. A simple illustration of a surplus statement is shown below:

THE OSBORNE COMPANY
Surplus Statement
For the Year Ended December 31, 1941

Surplus, December 31, 1940..................................		$132,610
Add Net Profit for the Year—Per Profit and Loss Statement....		75,440
Total...		$208,050
Deduct Dividends Paid:		
On Preferred Stock..............................	$ 7,000	
On Common Stock...............................	10,000	17,000
Surplus, December 31, 1941................................		$191,050

Dividend payments are not shown in the profit and loss statement, because they are not an expense; they are a distribution of profit. They are shown in the surplus statement because their payment results in a decrease in surplus.

Accountants have generally believed that the profit and loss statement (or income and expense statement) should show only the results of the regular operations of the business during a stated period of time.

If the profit and loss statement is to show only the results of *regular* operations, it must not include extraneous profits and losses. Extraneous profits or losses result from transactions or other events that are not a normal element of regular operations. For instance: a company that owned all of the stock of a subsidiary sold the stock at a profit; a part of a company's plant property was sold at a profit; a fire resulted in a loss. Extraneous profits and losses have usually been omitted from the profit and loss statement so that the reader of the statement will not get a confused idea of the company's normal operating results. Since they are omitted from the profit and loss statement, they must be included in the surplus statement.

If the profit and loss statement is to show the results of operations *during a stated period*, it should not include any profits or losses applicable to a prior period.   If, for example, an error in the computation of the 1940 profits was discovered in 1941, the correction should be shown in the surplus statement for 1941.   To include it in the profit and loss statement for 1941 would cause a misstatement of the operating results of that year also.

The elements of the surplus statement may be summarized as follows:

Balance at the beginning of the period.
Changes:
    Net profit or loss from regular operations of the period, as
        shown by the profit and loss statement.
    Extraneous profits or losses.
    Corrections of profits or losses of prior periods.
    Dividends.
Balance at the end of the period.

An illustrative statement containing these elements is shown below:

THE WHITCOMB COMPANY
Statement of Surplus
For the Year Ended December 31, 1941

Surplus, December 31, 1940		$22,650.00
Add:		
Net Income for the Year Ended December 31, 1941		3,190.00
Understatement of Inventory on December 31, 1940		1,000.00
Profit on Sale of Machinery		750.00
Total		$27,590.00
Deduct:		
Under-provision for 1940 Taxes	$ 320.00	
Fire Loss	1,725.00	
Dividends Paid	6,000.00	8,045.00
Surplus, December 31, 1941		$19,545.00

Inter-relation of statements.

The three principal statements customarily prepared at regular intervals are:

Balance sheet.
Statement of surplus.
Statement of profit and loss.

The following brief statements show the relationships existing among them:

THE *X* COMPANY   Exhibit A

Balance Sheet—December 31, 1941

Assets			Liabilities and Net Worth		
CURRENT ASSETS:			CURRENT LIABILITIES:		
Cash	$ 5,000		Accounts Payable...	$ 2,500	
Accounts Receivable	10,000	$15,000	Notes Payable	1,500	$ 4,000
FIXED ASSETS:			NET WORTH:		
Furniture	$ 2,000		Capital Stock	$10,000	
Automobile	1,500	3,500	Surplus—Exhibit B	4,500	14,500
		$18,500			$18,500

THE *X* COMPANY   Exhibit B

Statement of Surplus

For the Year Ended December 31, 1941

Surplus, December 31, 1940		$3,850.00
Add Net Income for the Year—Exhibit C		1,800.00
Total		$5,650.00
Deduct:		
Additional Income Tax—1940	$ 150.00	
Dividends Paid	1,000.00	1,150.00
Surplus, December 31, 1941		$4,500.00

THE *X* COMPANY   Exhibit C

Statement of Income and Expense

For the Year Ended December 31, 1941

Income from Fees	$2,975.00
Deduct Expenses	1,175.00
Net Income	$1,800.00

Observe that the statements are given identifying exhibit letters that are used for purposes of cross-reference.

The balance sheet shows the surplus at the end of the year and refers to Exhibit B, where further details regarding the surplus are found.

The surplus statement shows the changes in surplus during the year; the net income shown in this statement carries a reference to Exhibit C, where details of income and expense are found.

3

ACCOUNTS

....

Diversity of bookkeeping procedures.

This and the next fourteen chapters are intended to present only a general idea of the routine procedures of bookkeeping—enough to enable the general reader to understand the nature of debit and credit, the purposes of the ledger and of various books of original entry, and the processes of recording transactions, posting, taking a trial balance, preparing statements, and closing the books.

Some typical records are illustrated and discussed; the reader should understand that other records may be used for the same purposes. Bookkeeping methods in common use are described; the reader should remember that variations of these methods may be used to accomplish the same object. Furthermore, the reader should bear in mind that accounting records serve only one purpose: to provide information which someone is entitled to have. Hence no cut and dried procedures are applicable to every business; the procedures in each case should be those best adapted to serve the purposes of management.

It is hoped that the contents of these chapters will be sufficient to give one who seeks to obtain information from accounting records (as distinguished from one who records the information) a sufficient acquaintance with the basic principles and procedures of accounting to enable him to understand such records as he may have occasion to consult.

Use of accounting records.

To facilitate the preparation of the statements illustrated in the preceding chapters, it is desirable to keep records showing the changes in assets, liabilities, and net worth resulting from the transactions of the business. The changes in assets, liabilities, and net worth are recorded in accounts, which may be ruled in the form illustrated on the following page.

DATE	EXPLANATION	AMOUNT	DATE	EXPLANATION	AMOUNT

A separate account is kept with each asset, each liability, and each element of net worth. Each account has two sides, as indicated above, so that increases can be recorded on one side and decreases on the other.

The methods of recording changes in assets, liabilities, and net worth are explained in the remainder of this chapter, in which the illustrations are based on the operations of Benton Realty Company, which earns commissions for selling real estate.

Accounts with assets.

Changes in an asset are recorded in its account as follows:

> Increases are recorded on the left side.
> Decreases are recorded on the right side.

This procedure is illustrated by the following cash account, in which receipts are recorded on the left side and disbursements are recorded on the right side.

Cash

1941 Mar.		Explanation	Amount	1941 Mar.		Explanation	Amount
	1	Investment.......	10,000 00		3	Rent.............	200 00
	8	Commission......	300 00		12	White & Company.	500 00
	15	John Smith........	150 00		31	Wages............	375 00
	22	Commission.......	200 00		31	Dividends.........	200 00
	27	Fred Brown.......	175 00				

The receipts total $10,825.00; the disbursements total $1,-275.00; the difference, or balance, is $9,550.00.

The procedure of making entries in asset accounts is also illustrated by the following account which contains a record of the purchase of office equipment:

Office Equipment

1941 Mar.	5		1,200 00				

The following accounts contain entries on the left side charging clients with commissions for real estate sold for them; the entries on the right side represent reductions in the account receivable assets resulting from collections from the clients.

John Smith

1941				1941				
Mar.	10	Commission......		250|00	Mar.	15	Cash collection.....	150|00

Fred Brown

1941				1941				
Mar.	20	Commission......		375|00	Mar.	27	Cash collection.....	175|00

The balances on the left side of these accounts show the amounts still receivable from the debtors.

Accounts with liabilities.

Changes in a liability are recorded in its account as follows:

Increases are recorded on the right side.
Decreases are recorded on the left side.

This procedure is illustrated in the following account with the creditor from whom the company purchased the office equipment:

White & Company

1941				1941				
Mar.	12	Cash payment.....		500|00	Mar.	5	Equipment pur-chased..........	1,200|00

The balance on the right side of the account shows the amount still owed to the creditor.

Rules expressed graphically.

Observe that opposite procedures are applied in asset and liability accounts, as indicated by the following graphic expression of the rules for recording increases and decreases therein:

Asset Accounts

| Increases | Decreases |

Liability Accounts

| Decreases | Increases |

As a consequence of this difference in procedure, the balances in asset accounts are on the left side whereas the balances in liability accounts are on the right side.

Net worth accounts.

Liability and net worth accounts have this feature in common: they show claims against or interests in the assets of the business. Liability accounts show the interests of creditors; net worth accounts show the interests of the proprietors.

Consistency therefore dictates that net worth accounts should be kept like liability accounts, as follows:

Increases are recorded on the right side.
Decreases are recorded on the left side.

Separate accounts are kept with various increases and decreases in net worth, as illustrated below:

Capital Stock

			1941			
			Mar.	1	Investment........	10,000 00

Commission Income

			1941			
			Mar.	8	Collected in cash...	300 00
				10	Charged John Smith	250 00
				20	Charged Fred Brown	375 00
				22	Collected in cash...	200 00

Expense

1941					
Mar.	3	Rent.............	200 00		
	31	Wages...........	375 00		

Dividends Paid

1941				
Mar.	31	Paid stockholders...	200 00	

Debit and credit.

Heretofore we have referred to the two sides of an account as the left and right sides. Hereafter we shall refer to them as the debit and credit sides. These words are derived from the Latin: *debit* means "he owes"; *credit* means "he trusts." They were first used when the only accounts kept were accounts with debtors and creditors.

The entry on the left, or debit, side of the following account with John Smith shows that *he owed* the company $250.00 on March 10th.

John Smith

1941				
Mar.	10	Commission........	250 00	

And the entry on the right, or credit, side of the following account with White & Company shows that *they trusted* the company for $1,200.00 on March 5th.

White & Company

			1941				
			Mar.	5	Equipment pur- chased...........	1,200	00

Now that accounts are kept with such things as Cash, Office Equipment, Capital Stock, Commission Income, Expense, and Dividends Paid (none of which can owe or trust), the words debit and credit are no longer used in their original meaning. Debit means the left side of an account; credit means the right side.

Rules for debit and credit entries.

Using the words debit and credit, the rules for recording increases and decreases in assets, liabilities, and net worth may be restated as follows:

In ASSET accounts:
Increases are recorded by debits.
Decreases are recorded by credits.

In LIABILITY and NET WORTH accounts:
Increases are recorded by credits.
Decreases are recorded by debits.

Equality of debit and credit entries.

Double-entry bookkeeping derives its name from the fact that the complete record of each transaction requires debit and credit entries of equal amount. To illustrate this double-entry equality, let us again consider the transactions of Benton Realty Company (recorded in the foregoing accounts), and note the offsetting debit and credit entries for each transaction.

March 1—Capital stock of $10,000.00 par value was issued for cash.
Debit Cash (increase in asset).
Credit Capital Stock (increase in net worth).

Cash

1941									
Mar.	1	....	10,000	00					

Capital Stock

				1941				
				Mar.	1	....	10,000	00

March 3—Paid rent, $200.00.

> Debit Expense (decrease in net worth).
> Credit Cash (decrease in asset).

Expense

1941									
Mar.	3	Rent..........		200	00				

Cash

1941						1941			
Mar.	1	....	10,000	00	Mar.	3	....	200	00

March 5—Purchased office equipment at a cost of $1,200.00, from White & Company on account.

> Debit Office Equipment (increase in asset).
> Credit White & Company (increase in liability).

Office Equipment

1941								
Mar.	5	....	1,200	00				

White & Company

			1941				
			Mar.	5	....	1,200	00

March 8—Received $300.00 as a commission for selling a parcel of real estate.

> Debit Cash (increase in asset).
> Credit Commission Income (increase in net worth).

Cash

1941						1941			
Mar.	1	....	10,000	00	Mar.	3	....	200	00
	8	....	300	00					

Commission Income

			1941				
			Mar.	8	....	300	00

March 10—Charged John Smith a commission of $250.00, but made no collection at this time.

> Debit John Smith (increase in account receivable asset).
> Credit Commission Income (increase in net worth).

John Smith

1941								
Mar.	10	....	250	00				

Commission Income

			1941				
			Mar.	8	....	300	00
				10	....	250	00

March 12—Paid White & Company $500.00 on account.

        Debit White & Company (decrease in liability).
        Credit Cash (decrease in asset).

White & Company

1941			1941		
Mar. 12	....	500 00	Mar. 5	....	1,200 00

Cash

1941			1941		
Mar. 1	....	10,000 00	Mar. 3	....	200 00
8	....	300 00	12	....	500 00

March 15—Collected $150.00 from John Smith on account.

        Debit Cash (increase in cash asset).
        Credit John Smith (decrease in account receivable asset).

Cash

1941			1941		
Mar. 1	....	10,000 00	Mar. 3	....	200 00
8	....	300 00	12	....	500 00
15	....	150 00			

John Smith

1941			1941		
Mar. 10	....	250 00	Mar. 15	....	150 00

March 20—Charged Fred Brown a commission of $375.00, but collected nothing
at this time.

        Debit Fred Brown (increase in account receivable asset).
        Credit Commission Income (increase in net worth).

Fred Brown

1941					
Mar. 20	....	375 00			

Commission Income

			1941		
			Mar. 8	....	300 00
			10	....	250 00
			20	....	375 00

March 22—Received a $200.00 commission in cash.

        Debit Cash (increase in asset).
        Credit Commission Income (increase in net worth).

Cash

1941			1941		
Mar. 1	....	10,000 00	Mar. 3	....	200 00
8	....	300 00	12	....	500 00
15	....	150 00			
22	....	200 00			

Commission Income

			1941			
			Mar.	8	....	300 00
				10	....	250 00
				20	....	375 00
				22	....	200 00

March 27—Collected $175.00 from Fred Brown to apply on account.

        Debit Cash (increase in cash asset).

        Credit Fred Brown (decrease in account receivable asset).

Cash

1941				1941			
Mar.	1	....	10,000 00	Mar.	3	....	200 00
	8	....	300 00		12	....	500 00
	15	....	150 00				
	22	....	200 00				
	27	....	175 00				

Fred Brown

1941				1941			
Mar.	20	....	375 00	Mar.	27	....	175 00

March 31—Paid wages, $375.00.

        Debit Expense (decrease in net worth).

        Credit Cash (decrease in asset).

Expense

1941						
Mar.	3	Rent...........	200 00			
	31	Wages..........	375 00			

Cash

1941				1941			
Mar.	1	....	10,000 00	Mar.	3	....	200 00
	8	....	300 00		12	....	500 00
	15	....	150 00		31	....	375 00
	22	....	200 00				
	27	....	175 00				

March 31—Paid dividend to stockholders, $200.00.

        Debit Dividends Paid (decrease in net worth).

        Credit Cash (decrease in asset).

Dividends Paid

1941						
Mar.	31	....	200 00			

Cash

1941				1941			
Mar.	1	....	10,000 00	Mar.	3	....	200 00
	8	....	300 00		12	....	500 00
	15	....	150 00		31	....	375 00
	22	....	200 00		31	....	200 00
	27	....	175 00				

The ledger.

A group of accounts is called a ledger. Following is the complete ledger of Benton Realty Company at the end of March. The asset accounts are presented first; then the liability and net worth accounts.

Cash

1941				1941		
Mar.	1	10,000 00	Mar.	3		200 00
	8	300 00		12		500 00
	15	150 00		31		375 00
	22	200 00		31		200 00
	27	175 00				

John Smith

1941				1941		
Mar.	10	250 00	Mar.	15		150 00

Fred Brown

1941				1941		
Mar.	20	375 00	Mar.	27		175 00

Office Equipment

1941		
Mar.	5	1,200 00

White & Company

1941				1941		
Mar.	12	500 00	Mar.	5		1,200 00

Capital Stock

			1941		
			Mar.	1	10,000 00

Commission Income

		1941		
		Mar.	8	300 00
			10	250 00
			20	375 00
			22	200 00

Expense

1941			
Mar.	3	Rent	200 00
	31	Wages	375 00

Dividends Paid

1941		
Mar.	31	200 00

The trial balance.

The debit and the credit entries for each transaction are equal; therefore, if no bookkeeping errors are made, the total debit entries in the ledger will be equal to the total credit entries. The equality of the debits and the credits in the ledger of Benton Realty Company could be proved by listing the total debits and credits of each account, thus:

	Total Debits	Total Credits
Cash	$10,825.00	$ 1,275.00
John Smith	250.00	150.00
Fred Brown	375.00	175.00
Office Equipment	1,200.00	
White & Company	500.00	1,200.00
Capital Stock		10,000.00
Commission Income		1,125.00
Expense	575.00	
Dividends Paid	200.00	
	$13,925.00	$13,925.00

It is also possible to prove the equality of the debits and credits by listing merely the balances in the accounts, as illustrated below:

BENTON REALTY COMPANY
Trial Balance—March 31, 1941

Cash	$ 9,550.00	
John Smith	100.00	
Fred Brown	200.00	
Office Equipment	1,200.00	
White & Company		$ 700.00
Capital Stock		10,000.00
Commission Income		1,125.00
Expense	575.00	
Dividends Paid	200.00	
	$11,825.00	$11,825.00

Statements prepared from trial balance.

In the first paragraph of this chapter it was stated that accounting records facilitate the preparation of the statements illustrated in the first two chapters. The foregoing trial balance, showing the balances of all of the ledger accounts, provides the information required for the following statements.

BENTON REALTY COMPANY
Exhibit C
Statement of Income and Expense
For the Month of March, 1941

Commission Income	$1,125.00
Deduct Expense	575.00
Net Income	$ 550.00

BENTON REALTY COMPANY
Exhibit B

Statement of Surplus
For the Month of March, 1941

Net Income—Exhibit C.....................................	$	550.00
Deduct Dividends Paid....................................		200.00
Surplus, March 31, 1941..................................	$	350.00

BENTON REALTY COMPANY
Exhibit A

Balance Sheet—March 31, 1941

Assets			Liabilities and Net Worth		
CURRENT ASSETS:			CURRENT LIABILITIES:		
Cash...............	$9,550		Accounts Payable..........	$	700
Accounts Receivable.	300	$ 9,850	NET WORTH:		
FIXED ASSETS:			Capital Stock......	$10,000	
Office Equipment......		1,200	Surplus—Exhibit B.	350	10,350
		$11,050			$11,050

4
MERCHANDISE ACCOUNTS

....

Computing merchandise profits.

The following profit and loss statement of a merchandising company is repeated from page 17.

THE OSBORNE COMPANY
Profit and Loss Statement
For the Year Ended December 31, 1941

Gross Sales...			$982,400
Deduct Returned Sales and Allowances........................			13,260
Net Sales...			$969,140
Deduct Cost of Goods Sold:			
Inventory, December 31, 1940....................		$ 42,300	
Add Net Cost of Purchases:			
Purchases.......................... $625,479			
Deduct Returns and Allowances....... 5,826			
Net Purchases..................... $619,653			
Add Freight and Cartage In........... 4,217	623,870		
Total.. $666,170			
Deduct Inventory, December 31, 1941............. 50,710	615,460		
Gross Profit on Sales...			$353,680
Deduct Expenses...			278,240
Net Profit..			$ 75,440

Merchandise transactions and accounts.

On the following pages are presented certain typical merchandising transactions, together with the accounts in which they are recorded. The resulting ledger provides information required for a statement similar to that illustrated above. The accounts are presented in somewhat condensed form.

Aug. 1   The stockholders of a company invested $9,000.00 cash and merchandise worth $1,000.00, in exchange for capital stock of a par value of $10,000.00.

Debit Cash (asset acquired).
Debit Merchandise Inventory (asset acquired).
Credit Capital Stock (original net worth).

37

Cash	Capital Stock
Aug. 1 9,000.00|	Aug. 1 10,000.00

Merchandise Inventory
Aug. 1   1,000.00|

Aug. 2   Purchased store equipment for cash, $2,000.00.
   Debit Store Equipment (asset acquired).
   Credit Cash (decrease in cash asset).

Store Equipment	Cash	
Aug. 2 2,000.00|	Aug. 1 9,000.00| Aug. 2 2,000.00

Aug. 3   Purchased merchandise for cash, at a cost of $1,500.00.
   Debit Purchases (increase in merchandise asset; recorded in an
   account separate from the inventory, so as to provide information
   required for the profit and loss statement).
   Credit Cash (decrease in cash asset).

Purchases	Cash	
Aug. 3 1,500.00|	Aug. 1 9,000.00| Aug. 2 2,000.00
		3 1,500.00

Aug. 7   Purchased merchandise from George White on account, at a cost of
   $1,200.00.
   Debit Purchases (increase in merchandise asset).
   Credit George White (liability incurred).

Purchases	George White
Aug. 3 1,500.00|	Aug. 7 1,200.00
7 1,200.00|	

Aug. 10   Returned to George White defective merchandise that cost $100.00.
   Debit George White (decrease in liability).
   Credit Returned Purchases and Allowances (decrease in merchandise
   asset).

George White	Returned Purchases and Allowances
Aug. 10 100.00| Aug. 7 1,200.00	Aug. 10 100.00

Aug. 12   Paid George White $500.00 on account.
   Debit George White (decrease in liability).
   Credit Cash (decrease in asset).

George White	Cash	
Aug. 10 100.00| Aug. 7 1,200.00	Aug. 1 9,000.00| Aug. 2 2,000.00
12 500.00|		3 1,500.00
		12 500.00

Aug. 15   Paid freight on purchases, $50.00.

> Debit Freight and Cartage In (increase in cost of merchandise asset).
>
> Credit Cash (decrease in asset).

Freight and Cartage In			Cash			
Aug. 15	50.00		Aug. 1	9,000.00	Aug. 2	2,000.00
					3	1,500.00
					12	500.00
					15	50.00

Aug. 17   Sold merchandise for cash, $2,000.00.

> Debit Cash (increase in cash asset).
>
> Credit Sales (see explanation below).
>
> The rules for debits and credits on page 29 indicate that credits may record decreases in assets and increases in liabilities or net worth. What do credits to Sales represent?
>
> The selling price of merchandise includes two elements: the cost of goods sold and the profit on the sale. A credit to Sales account represents these two elements: a decrease in the merchandise asset (the cost of goods sold) and an increase in net worth (the gross profit). These two elements are entered together in the Sales account for two reasons: first, because it is difficult to determine the profit on each sale; second, so that the credit balance in the Sales account will give the information as to total sales required for the profit and loss statement. The profit element is ascertained later.

Cash				Sales	
Aug. 1	9,000.00	Aug. 2	2,000.00	Aug. 17	2,000.00
17	2,000.00	3	1,500.00		
		12	500.00		
		15	50.00		

Aug. 19   Sold merchandise to E. F. Bailey on account, $1,450.00.

> Debit E. F. Bailey (account receivable asset acquired).
>
> Credit Sales (decrease in merchandise and increase in net worth).

E. F. Bailey			Sales	
Aug. 19	1,450.00		Aug. 17	2,000.00
			19	1,450.00

Aug. 22   Merchandise sold to E. F. Bailey for $25.00 was returned by him.

> Debit Returned Sales and Allowances (a reduction of the amount credited to Sales).
>
> Credit E. F. Bailey (decrease in account receivable asset).

Returned Sales and Allowances			E. F. Bailey		
Aug. 22	25.00		Aug. 19	1,450.00	Aug. 22	25.00

Aug. 26   Collected $750.00 from E. F. Bailey to apply on account.
            Debit Cash (increase in cash asset).
            Credit E. F. Bailey (decrease in account receivable asset).

Cash				E. F. Bailey		
Aug. 1	9,000.00	Aug. 2	2,000.00	Aug. 19 1,450.00	Aug. 22	25.00
17	2,000.00	3	1,500.00		26	750.00
26	750.00	12	500.00			
		15	50.00			

Aug. 29   Paid expenses totaling $450.00.
            Debit Expense (decrease in net worth).
            Credit Cash (decrease in asset).

Expense		Cash			
Aug. 29 450.00		Aug. 1	9,000.00	Aug. 2	2,000.00
		17	2,000.00	3	1,500.00
		26	750.00	12	500.00
				15	50.00
				29	450.00

Aug. 31   Paid a cash dividend of $100.00 to the stockholders.
            Debit Dividends Paid (decrease in net worth).
            Credit Cash (decrease in asset).

Dividends Paid		Cash			
Aug. 31 100.00		Aug. 1	9,000.00	Aug. 2	2,000.00
		17	2,000.00	3	1,500.00
		26	750.00	12	500.00
				15	50.00
				29	450.00
				31	100.00

The ledger.

The ledger accounts constructed in the foregoing illustration are presented below.

Cash

Aug.	1	....	9,000	00	Aug.	2	....	2,000	00
	17	....	2,000	00		3	....	1,500	00
	26	....	750	00		12	....	500	00
						15	....	50	00
						29	....	450	00
						31	....	100	00

Merchandise Inventory

Aug.	1	....	1,000	00					

E. F. Bailey

Aug.	19	....	1,450	00	Aug.	22	....	25	00
						26	....	750	00

Store Equipment

| Aug. | 2 | .... | 2,000 00 | | | | | |

George White

| Aug. | 10 | .... | 100 00 | Aug. | 7 | .... | 1,200 00 |
| | 12 | .... | 500 00 | | | | |

Capital Stock

| | | | | Aug. | 1 | .... | 10,000 00 |

Sales

| | | | | Aug. | 17 | .... | 2,000 00 |
| | | | | | 19 | .... | 1,450 00 |

Returned Sales and Allowances

| Aug. | 22 | .... | 25 00 | | | | |

Purchases

| Aug. | 3 | .... | 1,500 00 | | | | |
| | 7 | .... | 1,200 00 | | | | |

Returned Purchases and Allowances

| | | | | Aug. | 10 | .... | 100 00 |

Freight and Cartage In

| Aug. | 15 | .... | 50 00 | | | | |

Expense

| Aug. | 29 | .... | 450 00 | | | | |

Dividends Paid

| Aug. | 31 | .... | 100 00 | | | | |

Trial balance.

Following is the trial balance drawn from the foregoing accounts.

	Debits	Credits
Cash..	$ 7,150.00	
Merchandise Inventory, August 1...............	1,000.00	
E. F. Bailey.................................	675.00	
Store Equipment.............................	2,000.00	
George White...............................		$ 600.00
Capital Stock...............................		10,000.00
Sales.......................................		3,450.00
Returned Sales and Allowances................	25.00	
Purchases...................................	2,700.00	
Returned Purchases and Allowances............		100.00
Freight and Cartage In.......................	50.00	
Expense.....................................	450.00	
Dividends Paid..............................	100.00	
	$14,150.00	$14,150.00

Statements.

The foregoing account balances provide all of the information required for the following statements, with one exception: the value of the inventory at the end of August must be determined by counting, weighing, or otherwise measuring the merchandise, and by pricing it; in other words, by taking a physical inventory. Let us assume that such an inventory discloses a valuation of $900.00 on August 31. With this information available, the following statements can be prepared:

THE WABASH COMPANY   Exhibit C
Profit and Loss Statement
For the Month of August, 1941

Gross Sales			$3,450
Deduct Returned Sales and Allowances			25
Net Sales			$3,425
Deduct Cost of Goods Sold:			
Inventory, August 1, 1941		$1,000	
Add Net Cost of Purchases:			
Purchases	$2,700		
Deduct Returned Purchases and Allowances	100		
Net Purchases	$2,600		
Add Freight and Cartage In	50	2,650	
Total		$3,650	
Deduct Inventory, August 31, 1941		900	2,750
Gross Profit on Sales			$ 675
Deduct Expenses			450
Net Profit			$ 225

THE WABASH COMPANY   Exhibit B
Statement of Surplus
For the Month of August, 1941

Net Profit—Exhibit C	$225.00
Deduct Dividends Paid	100.00
Surplus, August 31, 1941	$125.00

THE WABASH COMPANY   Exhibit A
Balance Sheet—August 31, 1941

Assets			Liabilities and Net Worth		
CURRENT ASSETS:			CURRENT LIABILITIES:		
Cash	$7,150		Accounts Payable	$	600
Accounts Receivable	675		NET WORTH:		
Merchandise Inventory	900	$ 8,725	Capital Stock	$10,000	
FIXED ASSETS:			Surplus—Exhibit B	125	10,125
Store Equipment		2,000			
		$10,725			$10,725

5

MISCELLANEOUS MATTERS

....

Expense accounts.

A single Expense account was used in the illustrations in Chapters 3 and 4. However, it is desirable to keep a number of expense accounts so that the people who are managing the business can easily see whether any particular expense is becoming excessive. The statements in Chapter 2 indicate the names of some expense accounts frequently kept.

Cash discounts.

Cash discount on sales is an expense incurred in inducing customers to pay their bills within a definite time. Assume that we have sold John Smith merchandise in the amount of $1,000.00 under the following terms: 1/10, n/30; these terms mean that Smith may deduct 1% of the invoice if he pays the bill within ten days from its date, and that payment in full is due in 30 days. If Smith takes advantage of the discount privilege, we should record the collection as follows:

> Debit Cash—$990.00 (increase in cash asset).
> Debit Discount on Sales—$10.00 (expense decreasing net worth).
> Credit John Smith—$1,000.00 (decrease in account receivable asset).

Cash discount on purchases is income earned by payment of bills within a definite time. If we pay Wilson & Company's $1,000.00 invoice in time to obtain a 1% discount, our record of the payment will include the following entries:

> Debit Wilson & Company—$1,000.00 (decrease in liability).
> Credit Cash—$990.00 (decrease in cash asset).
> Credit Discount on Purchases—$10.00 (income increasing net worth).

Notes receivable.

Whereas it is customary to keep a separate account with each debtor who owes the business an open account, notes receivable from all debtors may be recorded in one account, which may show details as to maker and maturity, thus:

Notes Receivable

1941					1941					
July	3	J. B. Gates. 60 da.	1,000	00	Aug.	1	J. F. Cole..........		750	00
	7	C. L. Peters. 30 da.	1,500	00						
	18	H. N. Burt. 30 da.	1,000	00						
	22	J. F. Cole.. 10 da.	750	00						

Each debit entry shows the name of the maker of the note and the time the note is to run. Credit entries are identified by name with the related debits.

Entries to be made when a note is received are indicated below:

(A) If a note is received from John Maker for a cash loan to him:

> Debit Notes Receivable (increase in note receivable asset).
> Credit Cash (decrease in cash asset).

(B) If a note is received from John Maker to apply on an account receivable owed by him:

> Debit Notes Receivable (increase in note receivable asset).
> Credit John Maker (decrease in account receivable asset).

Entries to be made when a note is collected are indicated below:

(A) If the note does not bear interest:

> Debit Cash (increase in cash asset).
> Credit Notes Receivable (decrease in note asset).

(B) If the amount collected includes the face of the note and interest:

> Debit Cash for the total collected (increase in cash asset).
> Credit Notes Receivable for the face of the note (decrease in note asset).
> Credit Interest Income (increase in net worth).

Notes payable.

Notes payable also are recorded in one account. Each credit entry shows the name of the payee to whom the note is given and the time the note runs. The debits recording payments are identified with the credits by the names of the payees, thus:

Notes Payable

1941					1941					
Sep.	5	C. E. Martin......	1,000	00	July	20	G. H. Doty..90 da.		2,500	00
					Aug.	6	C. E. Martin 30 da.		1,000	00

Entries to be made when a note is given are indicated below:

(A) If a note is given to James Payee for a cash loan:

> Debit Cash (increase in cash asset).
> Credit Notes Payable (increase in liability).

(B) If a note is given to James Payee to apply on an account payable to him:

> Debit James Payee (decrease in account payable liability).
> Credit Notes Payable (increase in note payable liability).

Entries to be made when a note payable is paid are indicated below:

(A) If the note does not bear interest:

> Debit Notes Payable (decrease in note liability).
> Credit Cash (decrease in cash asset).

(B) If the amount paid includes the face of the note and interest:

> Debit Notes Payable for the face of the note (decrease in liability).
> Debit Interest Expense (decrease in net worth).
> Credit Cash (decrease in cash asset).

Bad debts.

The first chapter contained a brief discussion of the reserve for bad debts and showed that, in the balance sheet, the reserve is deducted from the total receivables to reflect the estimated realizable value of the receivables.

At periodical intervals an estimate is made of probable losses and the following debit and credit entries are made:

> Debit Bad Debts—this is an expense account and the debit records a decrease in net worth.
> Credit Reserve for Bad Debts—this credit represents a deduction from the total debit balances of the receivables.

When an account receivable is determined to be uncollectible, the following entries are made:

> Debit Reserve for Bad Debts.
> Credit the account receivable that is uncollectible.

To illustrate in further detail, assume that a business began operations during 1941 and that, at the end of that year, the accounts receivable totaled $50,000.00 and the management estimated that the collection losses would total $1,000.00. The following debit and credit entries would be made:

Debit Bad Debts—$1,000.00 (this debit records an estimated decrease
in net worth represented by bad debt losses; it should be shown
among the expense items in the profit and loss statement).

Credit Reserve for Bad Debts—$1,000.00 (this credit records an esti-
mated decrease in the accounts receivable asset).

The reserve is shown as a deduction on the asset side of the
balance sheet, thus:

Accounts Receivable............................ $50,000.00
    Less Reserve for Bad Debts................   1,000.00 $49,000.00

If an account proves to be uncollectible, it should be "written
off." The entries to write off a $200.00 account receivable are:

Debit Reserve for Bad Debts—$200.00.
Credit the account receivable—$200.00.

The effect of writing off an account is indicated below. Assume
that, immediately before the account is written off, the total
accounts receivable and the reserve for bad debts are shown in the
balance sheet as follows:

Accounts Receivable............................ $25,000.00
    Deduct Reserve for Bad Debts.............   1,000.00 $24,000.00

After the $200.00 account is written off, the accounts and the
reserve are shown in the balance sheet as follows:

Accounts Receivable............................ $24,800.00
    Deduct Reserve for Bad Debts.............   800.00 $24,000.00

This illustration shows that writing off an uncollectible account
reduces both the total receivables and the reserve for estimated
uncollectible accounts, leaving unchanged the net amount estimated as collectible.

Depreciation.

The first chapter also contained a brief discussion of depreciation. Depreciation reserves are set up in the accounts at annual
or other intervals by the following debit and credit entries:

Debit Depreciation—this is an expense account; the debit records a
decrease in net worth and should be shown among the expenses in the
profit and loss statement.

Credit Reserve for Depreciation—this credit represents a deduction
from the debit balance in the asset account.

As an illustrative case, assume that a delivery truck is purchased at a cost of $1,000.00 and that it is expected to have a life

of five years with a scrap value of $100.00. The total depreciation is thus estimated at $900.00 and the annual depreciation at $180.00. Annual entries for depreciation would be:

> Debit Depreciation—Delivery Equipment—$180.00.
> Credit Reserve for Depreciation—Delivery Equipment—$180.00.

Each year's profit and loss statement would show a depreciation expense of $180.00. The balance sheet at the end of the first year would show the delivery equipment as follows:

> Delivery Equipment............................. $1,000.00
> Deduct Reserve for Depreciation................   180.00 $820.00

The balance sheet at the end of the fifth year would show the delivery equipment as follows:

> Delivery Equipment...................`.`........... $1,000.00
> Deduct Reserve for Depreciation................   900.00 $100.00

The truck is now carried in the accounts at a net value of $100.00. If it is sold for $100.00, the debit and credit entries to record the disposal will be:

> Debit Cash—$100.00 (increase in cash asset).
> Debit Reserve for Depreciation—Delivery Equipment—$900.00 (to eliminate the credit balance in the reserve).
> Credit Delivery Equipment—$1,000.00 (to eliminate the debit balance in the asset account).

If the truck is sold for only $60.00, instead of its carrying value of $100.00, there is a $40.00 loss, which should be charged to Surplus. The entries should be:

> Debit Cash—$60.00.
> Debit Surplus—$40.00.
> Debit Reserve for Depreciation—Delivery Equipment—$900.00.
> Credit Delivery Equipment—$1,000.00.

If the truck is sold for $125.00 (or $25.00 in excess of its carrying value), the entries should be:

> Debit Cash—$125.00.
> Debit Reserve for Depreciation—Delivery Equipment—$900.00.
> Credit Delivery Equipment—$1,000.00.
> Credit Surplus—$25.00.

Accruals.

Before a profit and loss statement and a balance sheet are prepared, at the end of the year or any other period, entries should be made to record accrued expenses and accrued income. Because these entries do not record transactions but merely adjust the accounts so that they will more truly reflect the condition at the end of the period, they are called adjusting entries.

As an illustration of an adjustment for accrued expense, assume that the taxes for the calendar year are $700.00 and that it is desired to prepare statements on June 30. The taxes are not payable until after the end of the year, but the profit and loss statement for the first half of the year should show a $350.00 tax expense, and the June 30 balance sheet should show an accrued liability of $350.00. The following adjusting entry should be made:

> Debit Taxes—$350.00 (an expense to be shown in the profit and loss statement).
> Credit Accrued Taxes—$350.00 (a liability to be shown in the balance sheet).

As an illustration of an adjustment for accrued income, assume that a company purchased 6% bonds of $100,000.00 par value on December 1. At the end of December, one month's interest, or $500.00, has been earned. The adjustment for this accrued income is:

> Debit Accrued Interest Receivable—$500.00 (an asset to be shown in the balance sheet).
> Credit Interest Income—$500.00 (an earning to be shown in the profit and loss statement).

Deferred charges and credits.

Before preparing statements at the close of any period, consideration should also be given to the propriety of making adjustments for deferred charges and deferred credits.

As an illustration of an adjustment for a deferred expense (or deferred charge), assume that, at the beginning of a year, a company purchased a three-year insurance policy at a cost of $900.00, which was charged to an Unexpired Insurance account, as follows:

Unexpired Insurance

1941								
Jan.	1	....	900 00					

At the date of purchase of the policy, the entire cost was properly regarded as an asset—insurance protection for three years. But on December 31, one third of the cost must be regarded as an expense of the year; this portion of the cost should therefore be transferred to an expense account by the following adjustment:

Debit Insurance Expense—$300.00 (an expense decreasing net worth).
Credit Unexpired Insurance—$300.00 (decrease in the asset).

The accounts will now appear as follows:

Unexpired Insurance

1941				900	00	1941				300	00
Jan.	1	....				Dec.	31	....			

The $600.00 debit balance in the Unexpired Insurance account
should appear under the Deferred Charges caption on the asset
side of the balance sheet.

Insurance Expense

1941				300	00				
Dec.	31	....							

The $300.00 debit balance in the Insurance Expense account
should appear among the expenses in the profit and loss statement.

As an illustration of a deferred income adjustment, assume that,
on October 1, 1941, a company collected $1,000.00 as rent in
advance for a full year on a portion of its building, and that a
deferred income account was credited as follows:

Rent Collected in Advance

						1941				1,000	00
						Oct.	1	....			

At the end of the year, one fourth of the rent has been earned
and should be transferred from the deferred income to an earned
income account, by the following adjustment:

Debit Rent Collected in Advance—$250.00.
Credit Rent Income—$250.00.

The accounts will now appear as follows:

Rent Collected in Advance

1941				250	00	1941				1,000	00
Dec.	31	....				Oct.	1	....			

The $750.00 credit balance in the Rent Collected in Advance
account should be shown under the Deferred Credits caption on
the right side of the balance sheet.

Rent Income

						1941				250	00
						Dec.	31	....			

The $250.00 credit balance in the Rent Income account should
appear in the profit and loss statement.

6

JOURNALIZING AND POSTING

The journal.

The preceding chapters may have led the reader to assume that transactions are recorded by making debit and credit entries *directly* in the ledger accounts. This, however, is not the customary procedure. Instead, it is customary first to record the transactions in a book of original entry.

A journal may be used as the only book of original entry; journal entries show the following facts with respect to each transaction:

The date.
The names of the accounts to be debited and credited.
The dollar amounts of the debit and credit entries.
An explanatory remark about the transaction.

Three journal entries are shown in the following illustration:

Journal   (Page 1)

1941						
June	1	Cash...	15,000	00		
		Inventory......................................	5,000	00		
		Capital Stock...............................			20,000	00
		Received cash and merchandise for stock of $20,-000.00 par value.				
	1	J. R. Walton..................................	1,200	00		
		Sales......................................			1,200	00
		Sale on account; invoice 1.				
	2	Notes Receivable..............................	1,200	00		
		J. R. Walton...............................			1,200	00
		Received a note from Walton due in 20 days, with 6% interest, for our invoice of yesterday.				

The names of accounts to be credited are indented slightly to distinguish them from accounts to be debited.

Posting.

Posting is the process of recording in the ledger accounts the debits and credits indicated by the journal entries.   Following are the ledger accounts produced by posting the entries for the first transaction:

Cash   (Page 1)

1941								
June	1	....	1	15,000	00			

Inventory   (Page 8)

1941								
June	1	....	1	5,000	00			

Capital Stock   (Page 20)

				1941					
				June	1	....	1	20,000	00

Observe that each ledger entry shows the date of the transaction, the number (1) of the journal page from which the entry was posted, and the dollar amount.

After each journal debit and each journal credit is posted, the ledger page number is entered in the journal, as illustrated below:

Journal   (Page 1)

1941						
June	1	Cash...	1	15,000	00	
		Inventory......................................	8	5,000	00	
		Capital Stock...............................	20			20,000 00
		Received cash and merchandise for stock of $20,-000.00 par value.				

Entering the journal page in the ledger and the ledger page in the journal produces a cross-reference between the two books. This is particularly helpful in tracing ledger entries back to the journal.

Purpose of journal and ledger.

The journal contains entries to record all transactions in their chronological order; the ledger classifies all these entries according to the accounts affected.

If one wishes to know what transactions occurred on a given date, he will look in the journal; if he wishes to know the total increases and decreases in cash during a period, he will look in the Cash account.

The journal has the added advantage of providing space where a comprehensive explanation of each transaction can be written.

Extended illustration—Journal.

A number of transactions are recorded in the following journal. It is suggested that each entry be carefully read to ascertain what facts it records. It will be helpful if each entry is interpreted on the basis of the rules for debits and credits stated in the preceding chapters. For example, in the first entry:

Cash is debited to record the acquisition of the cash asset; Inventory is debited to record the acquisition of the merchandise asset.

Capital Stock is credited to record the initial net worth.

Journal   **(Page 1)**

1941					
June	1	Cash...	1	15,000 00	
		Inventory.......................................	8	5,000 00	
		Capital Stock.............................	20		20,000 00
		Received cash and merchandise for stock of $20,-000.00 par value.			
	1	J. R. Walton....................................	3	1,200 00	
		Sales...	31		1,200 00
		Sale on account; invoice 1.			
	2	Notes Receivable...............................	7	1,200 00	
		J. R. Walton..............................	3		1,200 00
		Received a note from Walton due in 20 days, with 6% interest, for our invoice of yesterday.			
	3	F. B. White....................................	4	600 00	
		Sales...	31		600 00
		Sale on account; invoice 2.			
	4	Notes Receivable...............................	7	600 00	
		F. B. White...............................	4		600 00
		Received note due in 30 days at 6% for invoice of June 3.			
	4	Cash..	1	4,975 00	
		Interest Expense..............................	55	25 00	
		Notes Payable.............................	15		5,000 00
		Gave the bank our 30-day note. The bank charged discount at 6% and gave us cash for the proceeds.			
	4	Purchases.....................................	41	1,500 00	
		Brown & Green............................	11		1,500 00
		Purchase on account; invoice June 1.			
	4	J. R. Walton..................................	3	500 00	
		Sales...	31		500 00
		Sale on account; invoice 3.			

Journal   (Page 2)

1941						
June	5	Brown & Green................................	11	1,500 00		
		Notes Payable.............................	15		1,500 00	
		Gave Brown & Green note due in 20 days with 6%				
		interest, for purchase received June 4.				
	5	Purchases....................................	41	10,000 00		
		Cash......................................	1		10,000 00	
		Cash purchase.				
	5	F. B. White..................................	4	400 00		
		Sales.....................................	31		400 00	
		Sale on account; invoice 4.				
	5	Purchases....................................	41	300 00		
		Dalton & Company.........................	12		300 00	
		Purchase on account; invoice June 2.				
	6	Returned Sales and Allowances..................	32	50 00		
		F. B. White..............................	4		50 00	
		Issued White credit memo 1.				
	7	Cash..	1	2,000 00		
		Sales.....................................	31		2,000 00	
		Cash sale.				
	8	Dalton & Company............................	12	300 00		
		Notes Payable.............................	15		300 00	
		Gave note without interest, due in 30 days, for				
		invoice received June 5.				
	8	Purchases....................................	41	1,600 00		
		Brown & Green....................	11		1,600 00	
		Purchase on account; invoice June 4.				
	10	C. E. Magee.................................	5	480 00		
		Sales.....................................	31		480 00	
		Sale on account; invoice 5.				
	10	Brown & Green..............................	11	100 00		
		Returned Purchases and Allowances...........	42		100 00	
		Received their credit memo 75.				
	12	Cash..	1	100 00		
		J. R. Walton..............................	3		100 00	
		Collection on account.				
	12	Brown & Green..............................	11	1,000 00		
		Cash......................................	1		1,000 00	
		Payment on account.				
	13	Purchases....................................	41	2,000 00		
		Dalton & Company.........................	12		2,000 00	
		Purchase on account; invoice June 10.				

Journal (Page 3)

1941						
June	15	Expense..	53	250 00		
		Cash..	1		250 00	
		Paid store rent.				
	15	J. R. Walton...................................	3	300 00		
		Sales.......................................	31		300 00	
		Sale on account; invoice 6.				
	16	Returned Sales and Allowances..................	32	25 00		
		J. R. Walton..............................	3		25 00	
		Issued him our credit memo 2.				
	16	Purchases.....................................	41	1,850 00		
		E. R. Walker.............................	13		1,850 00	
		Purchase on account; invoice June 14.				
	17	E. R. Walker..................................	13	50 00		
		Returned Purchases and Allowances...........	42		50 00	
		Received his credit memo 139.				
	18	Cash...	1	1,200 00		
		Sales.......................................	31		1,200 00	
		Cash sale.				
	20	Cash...	1	350 00		
		F. B. White................................	4		350 00	
		Collection from him on account.				
	20	D. E. Bailey.................................	6	300 00		
		Sales.......................................	31		300 00	
		Sale on account; invoice 7.				
	22	Cash...	1	1,204 00		
		Notes Receivable...........................	7		1,200 00	
		Interest Income............................	54		4 00	
		Collected note received from J. R. Walton on June 2, with 20 days' interest at 6%.				
	22	Purchases....................................	41	300 00		
		Cash.......................................	1		300 00	
		Cash purchase.				
	24	Dalton & Company............................	12	2,000 00		
		Cash.......................................	1		2,000 00	
		Paid invoice of June 10.				
	24	Purchases....................................	41	1,750 00		
		Brown & Green.............................	11		1,750 00	
		Purchase on account; invoice June 22.				
	25	C. E. Magee.................................	5	400 00		
		Sales.......................................	31		400 00	
		Sale on account; invoice 8.				

Journal   (Page 4)

1941				
June 25	Notes Payable...............................	15	1,500 00	
	Interest Expense.............................	55	5 00	
	Cash.......................................	1		1,505 00
	Paid note given to Brown & Green on June 5, with 20 days' interest at 6%.			
28	Cash..	1	200 00	
	C. E. Magee...............................	5		200 00
	Collection on account.			
30	Cash..	1	500 00	
	Sales.....................................	31		500 00
	Cash sale.			
30	Expense...	53	150 00	
	Cash......................................	1		150 00
	Paid wages.			
30	D. E. Bailey....................................	6	290 00	
	Sales.....................................	31		290 00
	Sale on account; invoice 9.			
30	Returned Sales and Allowances....................	32	15 00	
	D. E. Bailey...............................	6		15 00
	Issued our credit memo 3.			
30	Purchases.......................................	41	750 00	
	O. L. Bates...............................	14		750 00
	Purchase on account; invoice June 27.			
30	O. L. Bates......................................	14	150 00	
	Returned Purchases and Allowances...........	42		150 00
	See our letter of June 30.			
30	Dividends Paid.................................	61	500 00	
	Cash.......................................	1		500 00
	Dividend to stockholders.			

Extended illustration—Ledger.

The accounts produced when the preceding journal entries are posted are presented below.

Cash   (Page 1)

1941					1941				
June	1	....	1	15,000 00	June	5	....	2	10,000 00
	4	....	1	4,975 00		12	....	2	1,000 00
	7	....	2	2,000 00		15	....	3	250 00
	12	....	2	100 00		22	....	3	300 00
	18	....	3	1,200 00		24	....	3	2,000 00
	20	....	3	350 00		25	....	4	1,505 00
	22	....	3	1,204 00		30	....	4	150 00
	28	....	4	200 00		30	....	4	500 00
	30	....	4	500 00						

J. R. Walton   (Page 3)

1941					1941				
June	1	....	1	1,200 00	June	2	....	1	1,200 00
	4	....	1	500 00		12	....	2	100 00
	15	....	3	300 00		16	....	3	25 00

F. B. White   (Page 4)

1941					1941				
June	3	....	1	600 00	June	4	....	1	600 00
	5	....	2	400 00		6	....	2	50 00
						20	....	3	350 00

C. E. Magee   (Page 5)

1941					1941				
June	10	....	2	480 00	June	28	....	4	200 00
	25	....	3	400 00					

D. E. Bailey   (Page 6)

1941					1941				
June	20	....	3	300 00	June	30	....	4	15 00
	30	....	4	290 00					

Notes Receivable   (Page 7)

1941					1941				
June	2	J. R. Walton. 20 da.	1	1,200 00	June	22	J. R. Walton.......	3	1,200 00
	4	F. B. White . . 30 da.	1	600 00					

Inventory   (Page 8)

1941									
June	1	....	1	5,000 00					

Brown & Green   (Page 11)

1941					1941				
June	5	....	2	1,500 00	June	4	....	1	1,500 00
	10	....	2	100 00		8	....	2	1,600 00
	12	....	2	1,000 00		24	....	3	1,750 00

Dalton & Company   (Page 12)

1941					1941				
June	8	....	2	300 00	June	5	....	2	300 00
	24	....	3	2,000 00		13	....	2	2,000 00

E. R. Walker   (Page 13)

1941					1941				
June	17	....	3	50 00	June	16	....	3	1,850 00

O. L. Bates   (Page 14)

1941					1941				
June	30	....	4	150 00	June	30	....	4	750 00

Notes Payable   (Page 15)

1941					1941				
June	25	Brown & Green....	4	1,500 00	June	4	Bank—30 da.......	1	5,000 00
						5	Brown & Green 20 da...........	2	1,500 00
						8	Dalton & Company 30 da...........	2	300 00

Capital Stock   (Page 20)

			1941				
			June	1	....	1	20,000 00

Sales   (Page 31)

			1941				
			June	1	....	1	1,200 00
				3	....	1	600 00
				4	....	1	500 00
				5	....	2	400 00
				7	....	2	2,000 00
				10	....	2	480 00
				15	....	3	300 00
				18	....	3	1,200 00
				20	....	3	300 00
				25	....	3	400 00
				30	....	4	500 00
				30	....	4	290 00

Returned Sales and Allowances   (Page 32)

1941				
June	6	....	2	50 00
	16	....	3	25 00
	30	....	4	15 00

Purchases   (Page 41)

1941				
June	4	....	1	1,500 00
	5	....	2	10,000 00
	5	....	2	300 00
	8	....	2	1,600 00
	13	....	2	2,000 00
	16	....	3	1,850 00
	22	....	3	300 00
	24	....	3	1,750 00
	30	....	4	750 00

Returned Purchases and Allowances   (Page 42)

			1941				
			June	10	....	2	100 00
				17	....	3	50 00
				30	....	4	150 00

Expense   (Page 53)

1941							
June	15	....	3	250	00		
	30	....	4	150	00		

Interest Income   (Page 54)

				1941				
				June	22	....	3	4	00

Interest Expense   (Page 55)

1941							
June	4	....	1	25	00		
	25	....	4	5	00		

Dividends Paid   (Page 61)

1941							
June	30	....	4	500	00		

Extended illustration—Trial balance.

Following is the trial balance drawn from the foregoing ledger:

Trial Balance—June 30, 1941

Cash......................................	$ 9,824.00	
J. R. Walton...............................	675.00	
C. E. Magee...............................	680.00	
D. E. Bailey..............................	575.00	
Notes Receivable...........................	600.00	
Inventory, June 1..........................	5,000.00	
Brown & Green.............................		$ 2,250.00
E. R. Walker..............................		1,800.00
O. L. Bates...............................		600.00
Notes Payable.............................		5,300.00
Capital Stock..............................		20,000.00
Sales.....................................		8,170.00
Returned Sales and Allowances..............	90.00	
Purchases.................................	20,050.00	
Returned Purchases and Allowances..........		300.00
Expense...................................	400.00	
Interest Income...........................		4.00
Interest Expense..........................	30.00	
Dividends Paid............................	500.00	
	$38,424.00	$38,424.00

7

BOOKS OF ORIGINAL ENTRY

Special purpose books.

A journal can be used as the only book of original entry, but labor can be saved by using special books designed for recording certain kinds of transactions. If a transaction is recorded in one of the special books of original entry, it is not also recorded in the journal. The advantages of special books can be illustrated by the transactions that were recorded in a journal in Chapter 6.

Sales book.

Each journal entry for a sale on account consists of a debit to some customer's account and a credit to Sales account. If these transactions are recorded in a book which contains *nothing but sales on account*, the names of the customers to be debited should be shown, as illustrated below; the credit to Sales is *implied*, because the entry is made in the sales book.

Sales Book (Page 1)

Date	L.F.	Name of Customer	Invoice No.	Amount
1941				
June 1	3	J. R. Walton...............................	1	1,200 00
3	4	F. B. White...............................	2	600 00
4	3	J. R. Walton...............................	3	500 00
5	4	F. B. White...............................	4	400 00
10	5	C. E. Magee...............................	5	480 00
15	3	J. R. Walton...............................	6	300 00
20	6	D. E. Bailey...............................	7	300 00
25	5	C. E. Magee...............................	8	400 00
30	6	D. E. Bailey...............................	9	290 00
30	31	Sales—credit...............................		4,470 00

The numbers in the L.F. (ledger folio) column are the numbers of the ledger pages to which the entries were posted. Each debit was posted to a customer's account; the total of all entries was posted to the credit of Sales account (ledger page 31).

The sales book saves labor in two ways: (1) the credit to Sales is written only once; (2) the credit to Sales is posted only once.

Returned sales and allowances book.

The following special book of original entry contains a record of the issuance of three credit memorandums.

Returned Sales and Allowances Book (Page 1)

Date	L.F.	Name of Customer	Credit Memo. No.	Amount	
1941					
June 6	4	F. B. White..................................	1	50	00
16	3	J. R. Walton.................................	2	25	00
30	6	D. E. Bailey.................................	3	15	00
30	32	Returned Sales and Allowances—debit..........		90	00

Three customers were credited, and the credits were posted to the customers' accounts. The total was posted to the debit of Returned Sales and Allowances.

Purchase book.

The entries in the following book are equivalent to seven journal entries debiting Purchases account and crediting the parties from whom the merchandise was purchased.

Purchase Book (Page 1)

Date	L.F.	Name of Creditor	Date of Creditor's Invoice	Amount	
1941					
June 4	11	Brown & Green..............................	June 1	1,500	00
5	12	Dalton & Company...........................	2	300	00
8	11	Brown & Green..............................	4	1,600	00
13	12	Dalton & Company...........................	10	2,000	00
16	13	E. R. Walker...............................	14	1,850	00
24	11	Brown & Green..............................	22	1,750	00
30	14	O. L. Bates................................	27	750	00
30	41	Purchases—debit...........................		9,750	00

The credits to the suppliers' accounts were posted individually; the total was posted to the debit of Purchases account.

Returned purchases and allowances book.

The three entries in the following book record debits to three creditors' accounts, resulting from returns of unsatisfactory merchandise.

Returned Purchases and Allowances Book　　　　(Page 1)

Date	L.F.	Name of Creditor	Explanation	Amount	
1941					
June 10	11	Brown & Green.............	Their cr. memo 75	100	00
17	13	E. R. Walker...............	Their cr. memo 139	50	00
30	14	O. L. Bates.................	See our letter 6/30	150	00
30	42	Returned Purchases and Allowances—credit		300	00

The debits to the personal accounts were posted individually; the total was posted to the credit of Returned Purchases and Allowances.

Cash receipts and disbursements books.

Each entry in the following cash receipts book shows the name of the account credited; the debit to Cash is implied.

Cash Receipts Book　　　　(Page 1)

Date	L.F.	Account Credited	Explanation	Amount	
1941					
June 1	20	Capital Stock...............	Investment	15,000	00
4	15	Notes Payable..............	Discounted at bank	5,000	00
7	31	Sales......................	Cash sale	2,000	00
12	3	J. R. Walton...............	On account	100	00
18	31	Sales......................	Cash sale	1,200	00
20	4	F. B. White................	On account	350	00
22	7	Notes Receivable...........	J. R. Walton	1,200	00
22	54	Interest Income............	On above note	4	00
28	5	C. E. Magee................	On account	200	00
30	31	Sales......................	Cash sale	500	00
30	1	Cash—debit..............		25,554	00

Each entry in the following cash disbursements book shows the name of the account debited; the credit to Cash is implied.

Cash Disbursements Book　　　　(Page 1)

Date	L.F.	Account Debited	Explanation	Amount	
1941					
June 4	55	Interest Expense...........	On discounted note	25	00
5	41	Purchases..................	Cash purchase	10,000	00
12	11	Brown & Green.............	On account	1,000	00
15	53	Expense....................	Store rent	250	00
22	41	Purchases..................	Cash purchase	300	00
24	12	Dalton & Company.........	Inv. June 10	2,000	00
25	15	Notes Payable..............	Brown & Green	1,500	00
25	55	Interest Expense...........	On above note	5	00
30	53	Expense....................	Wages	150	00
30	61	Dividends Paid.............	To stockholders	500	00
30	1	Cash—credit..............		15,730	00

The reader should determine the nature of the transaction recorded by each cash book entry. Three transactions may require explanation.

June 4—Note discounted at the bank.

>The entry in the receipts book credits Notes Payable $5,000.00; the entry in the disbursements book debits Interest Expense $25.00; the entries in the two books produce a net debit of $4,975.00 to Cash.

June 22—Note and interest collected.

>The two cash receipts book entries credit Notes Receivable $1,200.00 and Interest Income $4.00, and debit Cash $1,204.00.

June 25—Note and interest paid.

>Two cash disbursement entries are required.

The journal.

The following journal contains a record of the transactions which could not be recorded in the special books of original entry.

Journal (Page 1)

1941								
June	1	Inventory..	8	5,000	00			
		Capital Stock...............................	20			5,000	00	
		Issuance of capital stock for merchandise.						
	2	Notes Receivable...............................	7	1,200	00			
		J. R. Walton................................	3			1,200	00	
		Note due in 20 days, at 6%, for invoice of June 1.						
	4	Notes Receivable...............................	7	600	00			
		F. B. White................................	4			600	00	
		Note due in 30 days, at 6%, for invoice of June 3.						
	5	Brown & Green................................	11	1,500	00			
		Notes Payable..............................	15			1,500	00	
		Note due in 20 days, at 6%, for purchase received June 4.						
	8	Dalton & Company.............................	12	300	00			
		Notes Payable..............................	15			300	00	
		Note without interest, due in 30 days, for invoice received June 5.						

The ledger.

It is suggested that the reader trace the postings from the foregoing books of original entry to the following ledger accounts. These accounts are like those in Chapter 6, except:

The notations in the folio columns indicate the books from which the entries were posted; e. g., CR1 means cash receipts book page 1.

Because of the posting of column totals, fewer entries appear in the following accounts: Sales, Returned Sales and Allowances, Purchases, Returned Purchases and Allowances, and Cash.

Cash　　　　(Page 1)

1941						1941					
June	30	....	CR1	25,554	00	June	30	....	CD1	15,730	00

J. R. Walton　　　　(Page 3)

1941						1941					
June	1	....	S1	1,200	00	June	2	....	J1	1,200	00
	4	....	S1	500	00		12	....	CR1	100	00
	15	....	S1	300	00		16	....	RS1	25	00

F. B. White　　　　(Page 4)

1941						1941					
June	3	....	S1	600	00	June	4	....	J1	600	00
	5	....	S1	400	00		6	....	RS1	50	00
							20	....	CR1	350	00

C. E. Magee　　　　(Page 5)

1941						1941					
June	10	....	S1	480	00	June	28	....	CR1	200	00
	25	....	S1	400	00						

D. E. Bailey　　　　(Page 6)

1941						1941					
June	20	....	S1	300	00	June	30	....	RS1	15	00
	30	....	S1	290	00						

Notes Receivable　　　　(Page 7)

1941						1941					
June	2	J. R. Walton 20 da.	J1	1,200	00	June	22	J. R. Walton....	CR1	1,200	00
	4	F. B. White 30 da..	J1	600	00						

Inventory　　　　(Page 8)

1941											
June	1	....	J1	5,000							

Brown & Green　　　　(Page 11)

1941						1941					
June	5	....	J1	1,500	00	June	4	....	P1	1,500	00
	10	....	RP1	100	00		8	....	P1	1,600	00
	12	....	CD1	1,000	00		24	....	P1	1,750	00

Dalton & Company (Page 12)

1941					1941				
June	8	....	J1	300 00	June	5	....	P1	300 00
	24	....	CD1	2,000 00		13	....	P1	2,000 00

E. R. Walker (Page 13)

1941					1941				
June	17	....	RP1	50 00	June	16	....	P1	1,850 00

O. L. Bates (Page 14)

1941					1941				
June	30	....	RP1	150 00	June	30	....	P1	750 00

Notes Payable (Page 15)

1941					1941				
June	25	Brown & Green	CD1	1,500 00	June	4	Bank 30 da......	CR1	5,000 00
						5	Brown & Green 30 da.........	J1	1,500 00
						8	Dalton & Company 30 da....	J1	300 00

Capital Stock (Page 20)

					1941				
					June	1	....	CR1	15,000 00
						1	....	J1	5,000 00

Sales (Page 31)

					1941				
					June	7	....	CR1	2,000 00
						18	....	CR1	1,200 00
						30	....	CR1	500 00
						30	....	S1	4,470 00

Returned Sales and Allowances (Page 32)

1941									
June	30	....	RS1	90 00					

Purchases (Page 41)

1941									
June	5	....	CD1	10,000 00					
	22	....	CD1	300 00					
	30	....	P1	9,750 00					

Returned Purchases and Allowances (Page 42)

					1941				
					June	30	....	RP1	300 00

Expense (Page 53)

1941									
June	15	Store Rent.......	CD1	250 00					
	30	Wages..........	CD1	150 00					

Interest Income   (Page 54)

					1941				
·			·		June 22	.... CR1		4	00

Interest Expense   (Page 55)

1941							
June	4	.... CD1	25	00			
	25	.... CD1	5	00	·		

Dividends Paid   (Page 61)

1941							
June	30	.... CD1	500	00			

8

CONTROLLING ACCOUNTS

....

Division of labor.

To enable two or more bookkeepers to post at the same time, the ledger is frequently divided into the three following sections:

Accounts receivable ledger—containing accounts with customers.

Accounts payable ledger—containing accounts with trade creditors.

General ledger—containing all other accounts.

Controlling accounts and subsidiary ledgers.

When the ledger is divided into these three sections, the general ledger usually contains the two following accounts, which are obtained by posting the totals of certain columns of the books of original entry:

Accounts Receivable—The debit balance of this account is equal to the sum of the balances in the accounts receivable ledger.

Accounts Payable—The credit balance of this account is equal to the sum of the balances in the accounts payable ledger.

These two accounts are called *controlling* accounts; the two ledgers which contain the detailed accounts with debtors and creditors are called subsidiary ledgers.

Equality of debits and credits.

The illustration in this chapter is based on the same transactions as the illustration in Chapter 7. The general ledger illustrated in this chapter is the same as that in Chapter 7, except that the individual customers' and creditors' accounts have been removed to subsidiary ledgers; but, since they have been replaced by two controlling accounts, it will be possible to take a trial balance of the general ledger independently of the other ledgers.

Illustration.

The following books of original entry are the same as those in Chapter 7, except that special columns have been added where necessary to permit the posting of column totals to the controlling accounts.

Each book of original entry is followed by an explanation of the postings to the general ledger and to the subsidiary ledgers. The reader is advised to trace all of the postings from the various books of original entry to the ledgers, which appear on pages 74 to 77.

Sales book and Returned sales and allowances book.

Following is the illustrative sales book.

Sales Book   (Page 1)

Date	L.F.	Name of Customer	Invoice No.	Amount
1941				
June 1	√	J. R. Walton..	1	1,200 00
3	√	F. B. White..	2	600 00
4	√	J. R. Walton..	3	500 00
5	√	F. B. White..	4	400 00
10	√	C. E. Magee..	5	480 00
15	√	J. R. Walton..	6	300 00
20	√	D. E. Bailey..	7	300 00
25	√	C. E. Magee..	8	400 00
30	√	D. E. Bailey..	9	290 00
				4,470 00
				(2) (31)

General ledger postings:

Debit—Column total posted to Accounts Receivable controlling account —page 2.

Credit—Column total posted to Sales account—page 31.

(Note that the ledger page number at the foot of the column indicates that the column total has been posted.)

Subsidiary ledger postings:

Debit—Each entry posted to an account in the accounts receivable ledger.

(The customers' and creditors' accounts in the subsidiary ledgers are usually kept in loose-leaf binders or on cards, which are arranged alphabetically. Since these ledgers have no page numbers, book-keepers indicate that postings have been made by entering check marks in the L.F. columns of the books of original entry.)

Following is the returned sales and allowances book.

		Returned Sales and Allowances Book		(Page 1)
Date	L.F.	Name of Customer	Credit Memo No.	Amount
1941				
June 6	✓	F. B. White...	1	50 00
16	✓	J. R. Walton.......................................	2	25 00
30	✓	D. E. Bailey.......................................	3	15 00
				90 00
				(32) (2)

General ledger postings:

> Debit—Column total posted to page 32—Returned Sales and Allowances.
> Credit—Column total posted to page 2—Accounts Receivable controlling account.

Subsidiary ledger postings:

> Credit—Each entry posted to an account in the accounts receivable subsidiary ledger.

Purchase book and Returned purchases and allowances book.

Following is the purchase book.

		Purchase Book			(Page 1)
Date	L.F.	Name of Creditor	Date of Creditor's Invoice		Amount
1941					
June 4	✓	Brown & Green.............................	June	1	1,500 00
5	✓	Dalton & Company...........................		2	300 00
8	✓	Brown & Green.............................		4	1,600 00
13	✓	Dalton & Company...........................		10	2,000 00
16	✓	E. R. Walker...............................		14	1,850 00
24	✓	Brown & Green.............................		22	1,750 00
30	✓	O. L. Bates................................		27	750 00
					9,750 00
					(41) (10)

General ledger postings:

> Debit—Column total posted to page 41—Purchases.
> Credit—Column total posted to page 10—Accounts Payable controlling account.

Subsidiary ledger postings:

> Credit—Each entry posted to an account in the accounts payable subsidiary ledger.

Following is the returned purchases and allowances book.

Returned Purchases and Allowances Book   (Page 1)

Date	L.F.	Name of Creditor	Explanation	Amount	
1941					
June 10	✓	Brown & Green...............	Their credit memo 75	100	00
17	✓	E. R. Walker.................	Their credit memo 139	50	00
30	✓	O. L. Bates..................	See our letter June 30	150	00
				300	00
				(10) (42)	

General ledger postings:

> Debit—Column total posted to page 10—Accounts Payable controlling account.
> Credit—Column total posted to page 42—Returned Purchases and Allowances.

Subsidiary ledger postings:

> Debit—Each entry posted to an account in the accounts payable subsidiary ledger.

Cash receipts book.

All cash receipts books previously illustrated had only one money column; the following book has three. An Accounts Receivable credit column is provided so that the column total can be posted to the controlling account. This necessitates having another credit column in which to enter the amounts to be posted to other accounts in the general ledger, and the General Ledger credit column is provided for that purpose. The Cash debit column then becomes necessary to permit the posting of a column total to the Cash account.

Cash Receipts Book   (Page 1)

Date	Account Credited	Explanation	Credits				Debit Cash	
			General Ledger		Accounts Receivable			
			L.F.	Amount	L.F.	Amount		
1941								
June 1	Capital Stock..........	Investment	20	15,000 00			15,000 00	
4	Notes Payable..........	Discounted at bank	15	5,000 00			5,000 00	
7	Sales..................	Cash sale	31	2,000 00			2,000 00	
12	J. R. Walton...........	On account			✓	100 00	100 00	
18	Sales..................	Cash sale	31	1,200 00			1,200 00	
20	F. B. White............	On account			✓	350 00	350 00	
22	Notes Receivable.......	J. R. Walton	7	1,200 00			1,200 00	
22	Interest Income........	On above note	54	4 00			4 00	
28	C. E. Magee............	On account			✓	200 00	200 00	
30	Sales..................	Cash sale	31	500 00			500 00	
				24,904 00		650 00	25,554 00	
						(2)	(1)	

General ledger postings:

Debit—Column total posted to page 1—Cash account.
Credits—Individual items in the General Ledger column posted to the accounts named at the left, on the pages as numbered in the L.F. column.
Column total posted to page 2—Accounts Receivable controlling account.

Subsidiary ledger postings:

Credits—Each item in the Accounts Receivable column posted to an account in the accounts receivable ledger.

Cash disbursements book.

Special columns have been provided in the following cash disbursements book, for reasons similar to those explained in the preceding comments on the cash receipts book.

Cash Disbursements Book   **(Page 1)**

Date	Account Debited	Explanation	Debits				Credit Cash
			General Ledger		Accounts Payable		
			L.F.	Amount	L.F.	Amount	
1941							
June 4	Interest Expense..........	On discounted note	55	25 00			25 00
5	Purchases................	Cash purchase	41	10,000 00			10,000 00
12	Brown & Green..........	On account			✓	1,000 00	1,000 00
15	Expense.................	Store rent	53	250 00			250 00
22	Purchases................	Cash purchase	41	300 00			300 00
24	Dalton & Company.......	Invoice June 10			✓	2,000 00	2,000 00
25	Notes Payable............	Brown & Green	15	1,500 00			1,500 00
25	Interest Expense..........	On above note	55	5 00			5 00
30	Expense.................	Wages	53	150 00			150 00
30	Dividends Paid...........	To stockholders	61	500 00			500 00
				12,730 00		3,000 00	15,730 00
						(10)	(1)

General ledger postings:

Debits—Individual items in the General Ledger column posted to the accounts named at the left, on pages as numbered in the L.F. column.
Column total posted to page 10—Accounts Payable controlling account.
Credit—Column total posted to page 1—Cash account.

Subsidiary ledger postings:

Debits—Each item in the Accounts Payable column posted to an account in the accounts payable ledger.

Journal.

The following journal contains debit and credit columns to provide for posting column totals to the two controlling accounts, and a debit and a credit column for other general ledger accounts.

Journal (Page 1)

Debits						Credits		
Accounts Receivable	Accounts Payable	General Ledger	Date	L.F.		General Ledger	Accounts Payable	Accounts Receivable
			1941					
		5,000 00	June 1	8	Inventory			
				20	Capital Stock.......	5,000 00		
					Issuance of capital stock for merchandise.			
		1,200 00	2	7	Notes Receivable			
				✓	J. R. Walton........			1,200 00
					Note due in 20 days, at 6%, for invoice of June 1.			
		600 00	4	7	Notes Receivable			
				✓	F. B. White........			600 00
					Note due in 30 days, at 6%, for invoice of June 3.			
	1,500 00		5	✓	Brown & Green			
				15	Notes Payable.......	1,500 00		
					Note due in 20 days, at 6%, for purchase received June 4.			
	300 00		8	✓	Dalton & Company			
				15	Notes Payable.......	300 00		
					Note without interest, due in 30 days, for purchase received June 5.			
—	1,800 00	6,800 00				6,800 00	—	1,800 00
	(10)							(2)

General ledger postings:

> Debits—Column total posted to page 10—Accounts Payable control.
> Individual items in the General Ledger column posted to the accounts named, on the pages indicated in the L.F. column.
> Credits—Individual items in the General Ledger column posted to the accounts named, on the pages indicated in the L.F. column.
> Column total posted to page 2—Accounts Receivable control.

Subsidiary ledger postings:

> Debits—Items in the Accounts Payable column to accounts in the related subsidiary ledger.
> Credits—Items in the Accounts Receivable column to accounts in the related subsidiary ledger.

General ledger.

Following are the general ledger accounts resulting from the postings just explained.

Cash (Page 1)

1941				1941		
June 30	....	CR1	25,554 00	June 30	....	CD1	15,730 00

Accounts Receivable (Page 2)

1941					1941					
June	30	....	S1	4,470|00	June	30	....	RS1	90|00
						30	....	CR1	650	00
						30	....	J1	1,800	00

Notes Receivable (Page 7)

1941						1941				
June	2	J. R. Walton— 20 da..........	J1	1,200|00	June	22	J. R. Walton.....	CR1	1,200|00
	4	F. B. White— 30 da..........	J1	600	00					

Inventory (Page 8)

1941					
June	1	....	J1	5,000	00

Accounts Payable (Page 10)

1941						1941				
June	30	....	RP1	300|00	June	30	....	P1	9,750|00
	30	....	CD1	3,000	00					
	30	....	J1	1,800	00					

Notes Payable (Page 15)

1941						1941				
June	25	Brown & Green...	CD1	1,500|00	June	4	Bank—30 da.....	CR1	5,000|00
						5	Brown & Green— 20 da..........	J1	1,500	00
						8	Dalton & Company—30 da...	J1	300	00

Capital Stock (Page 20)

					1941				
				June	1	....	CR1	15,000	00
					1	....	J1	5,000	00

Sales (Page 31)

					1941				
				June	7	....	CR1	2,000	00
					18	....	CR1	1,200	00
					30	....	CR1	500	00
					30	....	S1	4,470	00

Returned Sales and Allowances (Page 32)

1941					
June	30	....	RS1	90	00

Purchases (Page 41)

1941					
June	5	....	CD1	10,000	00
	22	....	CD1	300	00
	30	....	P1	9,750	00

Returned Purchases and Allowances   (Page 42)

				1941				
				June	30	....	RP1	300 00

Expense   (Page 53)

1941								
June	15	....	CD1	250 00				
	30	....	CD1	150 00				

Interest Income   (Page 54)

				1941				
				June	22	....	CR1	4 00

Interest Expense   (Page 55)

1941								
June	4	....	CD1	25 00				
	25	....	CD1	5 00				

Dividends Paid   (Page 61)

1941								
June	30	....	CD1	500 00				

Accounts receivable ledger.

The accounts receivable ledger appears below:

J. R. Walton

1941					1941				
June	1	....	S1	1,200 00	June	2	....	J1	1,200 00
	4	....	S1	500 00		12	....	CR1	100 00
	15	....	S1	300 00		16	....	RS1	25 00

F. B. White

1941					1941				
June	3	....	S1	600 00	June	4	....	J1	600 00
	5	....	S1	400 00		6	....	RS1	50 00
						20	....	CR1	350 00

C. E. Magee

1941					1941				
June	10	....	S1	480 00	June	28	....	CR1	200 00
	25	....	S1	400 00					

D. E. Bailey

1941					1941				
June	20	....	S1	300 00	June	30	....	RS1	15 00
	30	....	S1	290 00					

Accounts payable ledger.

The subsidiary accounts payable ledger appears on the following page.

Brown & Green

1941					1941					
June	5	....	J1	1,500 00	June	4	....	P1	1,500 00
	10	....	RP1	100 00		8	....	P1	1,600 00
	12	....	CD1	1,000 00		24	....	P1	1,750 00

Dalton & Company

1941					1941					
June	8	....	J1	300 00	June	5	....	P1	300 00
	24	....	CD1	2,000 00		13	....	P1	2,000 00

E. R. Walker

1941					1941				
June	17	....	RP1	50 00	June	16	....	P1	1,850 00

O. L. Bates

1941					1941				
June	30	....	RP1	150 00	June	30	....	P1	750 00

Proving the ledgers.

Following is the trial balance of the general ledger:

General Ledger Trial Balance
June 30, 1941

Cash..	$ 9,824.00	
Accounts Receivable (control).................	1,930.00	
Notes Receivable.............................	600.00	
Inventory, June 1............................	5,000.00	
Accounts Payable (control)...................		$ 4,650.00
Notes Payable...............................		5,300.00
Capital Stock...............................		20,000.00
Sales.......................................		8,170.00
Returned Sales and Allowances................	90.00	
Purchases...................................	20,050.00	
Returned Purchases and Allowances............		300.00
Expense.....................................	400.00	
Interest Income.............................		4.00
Interest Expense............................	30.00	
Dividends Paid..............................	500.00	
	$38,424.00	$38,424.00

The subsidiary ledgers are proved when the following schedules of their balances are prepared and their totals are found to be in agreement with their respective controlling accounts in the general ledger.

Schedule of Accounts Receivable
June 30, 1941

J. R. Walton........................	$ 675.00
C. E. Magee...............................	680.00
D. E. Bailey..............................	575.00
	$1,930.00

Schedule of Accounts Payable
June 30, 1941

Brown & Green.. $2,250.00
E. R. Walker... 1,800.00
O. L. Bates.. 600.00
$4,650.00

General application.

The controlling account procedure can be applied whenever it is desired to eliminate details from the general ledger. For example, if accounts are carried in a number of banks, the general ledger may contain a controlling account called Cash in Banks, and a separate account with each bank may be kept in a subsidiary ledger. Or, if many parcels of real estate are owned, the general ledger may contain a controlling account with Real Estate, supported by a subsidiary ledger showing the cost of each parcel of land and each building. Or an Expense controlling account may be kept in the general ledger, with detailed expense accounts in a subsidiary ledger.

It is not necessary to do more here than to indicate that the controlling account procedure has many applications. If you ever have occasion to refer to a ledger to obtain desired information, remember that some of the accounts may be controlling accounts, and that additional detailed information can be obtained from the supporting subsidiary records.

9

SPECIAL COLUMNS IN BOOKS OF ORIGINAL ENTRY

....

Purposes of special columns.

Books of original entry often have many columns, and at first glance they may seem to be very complex.   Usually, however, it is not difficult to understand their nature if it is remembered that the entries in any book of original entry are intended to indicate debits and credits to be made in ledger accounts, and that special columns are introduced for the purpose of facilitating the accomplishment of this purpose.

Most special columns in books of original entry are intended to serve one or more of the following purposes:

To permit posting of column totals to controlling accounts.

To permit posting of column totals to accounts frequently debited or credited.

To provide for classification of data.

To avoid the use of more than one line to record one transaction.

To avoid the use of more than one book to record one transaction.

Columns for controlling accounts.

The use of controlling account columns in books of original entry was explained and illustrated in the preceding chapter.

Columns for accounts frequently debited or credited.

If numerous credits to one account appear in the cash receipts book, the posting work can be reduced by providing a special credit column for that account.   Entries can be made in the special column instead of in the General Ledger column, and the total of the special column can be posted at the end of the month.   The Sales credit column in the cash receipts book on page 80 is an illustration of a column for accounts frequently credited.

Cash Receipts Book

| Date | Account Credited | Explanation | Credits | | | | | | Debit Cash |
| | | | General Ledger | | Sales | Accounts Receivable | | | |
			L.F.	Amount		L.F.	Amount		
July 1	Sales.......				500 00				500 00
12	Sales.......				300 00				300 00
17	Sales.......				600 00				600 00
24	Sales.......				400 00				400 00

Similarly, if numerous debits to one account appear in the cash disbursements book, a special debit column may be provided for that account. The Purchases, Freight In, and Freight Out accounts in the following cash disbursements book are illustrations of columns for accounts frequently debited.

Cash Disbursements Book

| Date | Account Debited | Explanation | Debits | | | | | | | Credit Cash |
| | | | General Ledger | | Pur-chases | Freight In | Freight Out | Accounts Payable | | |
			L.F.	Amount				L.F.	Amount	
July 3	Purchases.....				1,000 00					1,000 00
7	Purchases.....				1,250 00					1,250 00
13	Freight......					60 00	25 00			85 00
20	Purchases.....				975 00					975 00
27	Purchases.....				1,260 00					1,260 00

Columns for classification.

As an illustration of columns to provide for classification of data, let us assume that a company operates two departments, and that it is desired to keep a record of the purchases and sales by departments. The cash receipts and cash disbursements books could be provided with departmental columns as shown in the following illustration. The sales book, the returned sales and allowances book, the purchases book, and the returned purchases and allowances book should have similar columns.

Cash Receipts Book

| Date | Account Credited | Explanation | Credits | | | | | | Debit Cash |
| | | | General Ledger | | Sales | | Accounts Receivable | | |
			L.F.	Amount	Dept. A	Dept. B	L.F.	Amount	
July 1	Sales........				500 00				500 00
12	Sales........					300 00			300 00
17	Sales........				250 00	350 00			600 00
24	Sales........				100 00	300 00			400 00

Cash Disbursements Book

| Date | Account Debited | Explanation | Debits | | | | | | | | Credit Cash |
| | | | General Ledger | | Purchases | | Freight In | Freight Out | Accounts Payable | | |
			L.F.	Amount	Dept. A	Dept. B			L.F.	Amount	
July 3	Purchases........				1,000 00						1,000 00
7	Purchases........				250 00	1,000 00					1,250 00
20	Purchases........				400 00	575 00					975 00
27	Purchases........					1,260 00					1,260 00

Columns to avoid entries on two lines.

The record of a cash receipt may require credits to two accounts. For instance, the collection of a note and interest is recorded as follows:

> Debit Cash for the total amount collected.
> Credit Notes Receivable for the face of the note.
> Credit Interest Income for the interest.

In the cash receipts books thus far illustrated, the record of such a transaction has required entries on two lines: one entry debiting Cash and crediting Notes Receivable for the face of the note, and an entry on the next line debiting Cash and crediting Interest Income. This procedure is illustrated in the cash receipts book on page 63.

If the cash receipts book is provided with an Interest Income credit column, the entire transaction can be recorded on one line; the credit to Notes Receivable can be entered in the General Ledger credit column, the credit for the interest can be entered in the Interest Income credit column, and the total collection can be recorded in the Cash debit column. This procedure is illustrated in the cash receipts book on page 83.

Special columns may be provided in the cash disbursements book similarly to simplify the recording of the payment of notes payable and interest, as shown by the illustration on page 83.

Columns to avoid entries in more than one book.

In all of the cash receipts books thus far illustrated, there has been only one debit column—Cash. Transactions frequently require debits to other accounts. Some transactions of this nature are described below:

> Discounted a 60-day $5,000.00 note at the bank; discount, $50.00; proceeds, $4,950.00. The record of this transaction requires the following entries:
>
> Debit Interest Expense.................................... $ 50.00
> Debit Cash... 4,950.00
> Credit Notes Payable..................................... 5,000.00

The cash receipts book on page 84 contains an Interest Expense debit column to facilitate the recording of this transaction.

The following transactions illustrate the use of other special columns in the cash receipts book on page 84.

Cash Receipts Book

Date		Account Credited	Explanation	Credits							Debit Cash
				General Ledger		Sales		Interest Income	Accounts Receivable		
				L.F.	Amount	Dept. A	Dept. B		L.F.	Amount	
July	9	Notes Receivable...........	J. O. Brown		1,000|00			10|00			1,010|00
	19	Notes Receivable...........	Black & Davis		5,000|00			25|00			5,025|00

Cash Disbursements Book

Date		Account Debited	Explanation	Debits								Credit Cash
				General Ledger		Purchases		Freight In	Freight Out	Interest Expense	Accounts Payable	
				L.F.	Amount	Dept. A	Dept. B				L.F.	Amount	
July	2	Notes Payable......	White & Co.		10,000|00					100|00			10,100|00
	11	Notes Payable......	E. G. McLean		2,000|00					200|00			2,200|00

Cash Receipts Book

Date	Account Credited	Explanation	General Ledger L.F.	General Ledger Amount	Sales Dept. A	Sales Dept. B	Interest Income	Accounts Receivable L.F.	Accounts Receivable Amount	Interest Expense	Discount on Sales	Freight Out	Coll. and Exch.	Cash
									Credits			Debits		
July 5	Notes Payable	Bank		5,000 00										4,950 00
13	C. J. Barnes	Invoice 216							1,000 00	50 00				980 00
15	Fred Barton	Invoice 236							700 00		20 00	25 00		675 00
22	John Holmes	Invoice 240							500 00				25	499 75
28	Henry Cotton	Invoice 261							1,000 00		20 00	15 00	50	964 50

Cash Disbursements Book

Date	Account Debited	Explanation	General Ledger L.F.	General Ledger Amount	Purchases Dept. A	Purchases Dept. B	Freight In	Freight Out	Interest Expense	Accounts Payable L.F.	Accounts Payable Amount	Discount on Purchases	Cash
						Debits						Credits	
July 16	Bacon & Co.	Inv. July 9									2,000 00	40 00	1,960 00
25	E. O. Dutton	Inv. July 18									3,500 00	35 00	3,465 00

84

Received a check for $980.00 from C. J. Barnes in settlement of an invoice of $1,000.00, less a cash discount of 2%.

Debit Discount on Sales (special column)................... $ 20.00
Debit Cash...   980.00
Credit C. J. Barnes.....................................   1,000.00

Goods were sold to Fred Barton, terms f.o.b. destination; the customer was requested to pay the freight and deduct the amount thereof when paying the invoice.   The invoice was $700.00 and the freight was $25.00; the net amount received was $675.00.

Debit Freight Out (special column)....................... $ 25.00
Debit Cash...   675.00
Credit Fred Barton.....................................   700.00

A check for $500.00 was received from John Holmes; when it was deposited, the bank charged $.25 exchange.

Debit Collection and Exchange (special column)............. $ .25
Debit Cash...   499.75
Credit John Holmes.....................................   500.00

Following is a transaction involving the use of three of the special debit columns mentioned above:

Amount of sale to Henry Cotton........................... $1,000.00
Deduct: Cash discount............................. $20.00
          Freight paid by customer and deducted by him 15.00   35.00
Check received from Cotton............................. $ 965.00
Exchange charged by bank..............................   .50
Net amount deposited................................... $ 964.50

Debit Discount on Sales....................... $ 20.00
Debit Freight Out.......................   15.00
Debit Collection and Exchange.................   .50
Debit Cash.....................................   964.50
Credit Henry Cotton.......................   1,000.00

The cash receipts book on page 84 contains special debit columns to facilitate the recording of these transactions.

A cash disbursements book with a special credit column for Discount on Purchases is also illustrated.

Saving labor in posting.

The primary purpose of most of the special columns illustrated in this chapter was something other than the saving of posting; however, this labor-saving feature is always an incidental benefit if a special column contains several entries, because column totals can be posted, as indicated by the ledger page numbers entered below the column totals in the cash receipts and cash disbursements books on page 86, which contain all of the illustrative entries given in this chapter.

Cash Receipts Book

Date	Account Credited	Explanation	Credits — General Ledger L.F.	Amount	Credits — Sales Dept. A	Sales Dept. B	Credits — Interest Income	Debits — Accounts Receivable L.F.	Amount	Debits — Interest Expense	Discount on Sales	Freight Out	Coll. and Exch.	Cash
July 1	Sales..........	Bank			500 00									500 00
5	Notes Payable......	J. O. Brown	12	5,000 00						50 00				4,950 00
9	Notes Receivable.....		3	1,000 00			10 00							1,010 00
12	Sales..........					300 00								300 00
13	C. J. Barnes.......	Invoice 216						✓	1,000 00		20 00			980 00
15	Fred Barton.......	Invoice 236						✓	700 00			25 00		675 00
17	Sales..........				250 00	350 00								600 00
19	Notes Receivable.....	Black & Davis	3	5,000 00			25 00							5,025 00
22	John Holmes........	Invoice 240			100 00	300 00		✓	500 00				25	499 75
24	Sales..........										20 00	15 00		400 00
28	Henry Cotton.......	Invoice 261						✓	1,000 00		20 00	40 00	50	964 50
				11,000 00	850 00	950 00	35 00		3,200 00	50 00	40 00	40 00	75	15,904 25
				(55)	(31)	(32)	(55)		(2)	(61)	(62)	(51)	(63)	(1)

Cash Disbursements Book

Date	Account Debited	Explanation	Debits — General Ledger L.F.	Amount	Debits — Purchases Dept. A	Purchases Dept. B	Freight In	Freight Out	Interest Expense	Credits — Accounts Payable L.F.	Amount	Credits — Discount on Purchases	Cash
July 2	Notes Payable.......	White & Co.	12	10,000 00					100 00				10,100 00
3	Purchases..........				1,000 00								1,000 00
7	Purchases..........				250 00	1,000 00							1,250 00
11	Notes Payable.......	E. G. McLean	12	2,000 00					200 00				2,200 00
13	Freight............						60 00	25 00					85 00
16	Bacon & Co........	Invoice July 9			400 00	575 00				✓	2,000 00	40 00	1,960 00
20	Purchases..........												975 00
25	E. O. Dutton.......	Invoice July 18				1,260 00				✓	3,500 00	35 00	3,465 00
27	Purchases..........												1,260 00
				12,000 00	1,650 00	2,835 00	60 00	25 00	300 00		5,500 00	75 00	22,295 00
				(✓)	(41)	(42)	(43)	(51)	(61)		(11)	(56)	(1)

86

General application.

It will of course be understood that the special columns illustrated in the cash books in this chapter are not the only ones that can be used. The object of the illustrations has been merely to indicate the general purposes of such columns. Those included in the books of any business should depend upon the nature of the business and the typical transactions to be recorded.

It will also be understood that special columns may be provided in books of original entry other than cash books if they will facilitate the work of recording transactions or will reduce the labor of posting.

10

THE VOUCHER SYSTEM

···

Purpose.

A voucher system is an accounting mechanism for recording all transactions which involve an immediate or prospective disbursement of cash. The essential elements of the system are a voucher, a voucher register, and a check register.

The voucher.

The following illustration indicates the essential features of a voucher; other features may be added as desired.

R. E. JOHNSON & COMPANY

2913 North Western Avenue

Chicago, Illinois

Voucher No. **1693**

Date **July 6, 1941**

Terms **1/10, n/30**

Payee **The Osborne Company**

Due **July 13**

215 West Canal Street

Chicago, Illinois

Check No.

Invoice Date	Invoice No.	Amount
July 3, 1941	2397	140.00
Cash Discount		1.40
Net		138.60

Approved *G. A. Oliver*

Passed for Payment

Controller

Treasurer

Voucher

89

Voucher Register

Voucher No.	Date	Payee	Explanation	Terms	Payment		Credit	Debit					
					Date Paid	Check No.	Vouchers Payable	Purchases		Freight In	Sundry Accounts		
								Dept. A	Dept. B		Acct.	L.F.	Amount
1693	July 6	The Osborne Company	Inv. July 3	1/10, n/30			140|00	140|00					

Assume that R. E. Johnson & Company purchased merchandise from The Osborne Company; the merchandise purchased was itemized on the vendor's invoice number 2397, dated July 3, 1941. When the goods were received they were checked against the invoice to see that the goods charged for were received; the invoice and the purchase order were checked against each other to see that they were in agreement; and the invoice was checked as to prices, extensions, and footings.

When all of these matters were found to be correct, R. E. Johnson & Company prepared the voucher on page 89.

It is not necessary to make a separate voucher for each invoice. Invoices from the same supplier can be accumulated in a voucher jacket, and be summarized on one voucher.

The controller has signed the voucher, thus indicating that the verification procedures mentioned above have been completed.

The treasurer has not yet signed the voucher to indicate approval of payment, because a check is not to be immediately issued; the period during which the 1% cash discount is available does not expire until July 13, ten days after the date of the invoice.

The voucher register.

All vouchers are recorded in the voucher register, whether they are to be paid immediately or at a later date. The voucher register serves as a book of original entry for purchases and other disbursements; also, as this chapter will show, it serves the purpose of the accounts payable subsidiary ledger.

In the voucher register illustrated at the left, the Voucher Number, Date, Payee, Explanation, and Terms columns provide for the recording of miscellaneous information about the voucher; the Date Paid and Check Number columns will be used when the voucher is paid; the money columns at the right contain the debit and credit entries.

The amount of each voucher is entered in the Vouchers Payable credit column and in a debit column. (The Vouchers Payable account takes the place of the Accounts Payable controlling account.) Special columns are provided for all accounts frequently debited. (A later illustration contains many more debit columns.) Debits to accounts for which special columns are not provided are indicated by entries in the Sundry Accounts debit section at the right of the register, where space is provided for writing the name of the account as well as the amount.

The entry in the voucher register on page 90 debits Purchases —Department A and credits Vouchers Payable.

Payment of the voucher.

If the voucher is not to be paid immediately, it is filed in a tickler, where it remains until the date on which it should be paid. When it is time to pay the voucher, it is presented to the person who is empowered to authorize disbursements; he signs the voucher on the line "Passed for Payment _____," and a check is drawn. To provide an internal check over disbursements, the voucher should be approved and the check drawn by different persons.

Following is the check register, showing an entry for the check issued to pay the voucher recorded in the register on page 90.

Check Register

Check No.	Date	Payee	Voucher No.	Debit Vouchers Payable	Credit Discount on Purchases	Cash
1668	July 13	The Osborne Company....................	1693	140 00	1 40	138 60

Since the issuance of each voucher is recorded by a credit to Vouchers Payable, the payment of each voucher is recorded by a debit to Vouchers Payable; the offsetting credit is to Cash. (Discount on Purchases also is credited if a discount is taken.)

After the check is recorded in the check register, notations are made in the Date Paid and Check Number columns of the voucher register, as illustrated below:

Voucher Register

Voucher No.	Date	Payee	Explanation	Terms	Payment Date Paid	Payment Check No.	Credit Vouchers Payable	Debit Purchases Dept. A	Debit Purchases Dept. B
1693	July 6	The Osborne Co.	Inv. July 3	1/10, n/30	July 13	1668	140 00	140 00	

After the entry in the check register and the notations in the Payment columns of the voucher register are made, the voucher is filed in a paid voucher file (usually in numerical order) where it and the supporting invoice or other documents are available as evidence of the propriety of the entries and the disbursement.

If a voucher is to be paid as soon as drawn, the procedure discussed above is followed except that there is no occasion to file the voucher in a tickler to await the payment date. Payment is made and recorded immediately.

Extended illustration.

The following check register and the voucher register on page 93, which represents two wide facing pages, contain the record of a month's transactions; it is suggested that the reader observe the entries for each transaction, noting the accounts debited and credited.

Check Register

Check No.	Date		Payee	Voucher No.	Debit Vouchers Payable	Credit Discount on Purchases	Credit Cash
1	1941 Aug.	3	C.N.W. Ry..............	2	18 00		18 00
2		4	Daily News.............	3	150 00		150 00
3		4	C.N.W. Ry..............	4	35 00		35 00
4		5	Davis Supply Co.........	5	105 00		105 00
5		7	G. E. Wilson...........	6	1,005 00		1,005 00
6		8	Barnard & Co...........	1	1,500 00	30 00	1,470 00
7		15	B. N. Haines...........	8	200 00		200 00
8		19	L. N. Whitely..........	7	3,500 00	35 00	3,465 00
9		23	Acme Garage............	10	25 00		25 00
10		26	F. R. Mason & Co........	9	2,600 00	52 00	2,548 00
11		28	Postmaster.............	12	25 00		25 00
12		31	Payroll................	14	850 00		850 00
					10,013 00	117 00	9,896 00
					(11)	(71)	(1)

Summary of August Transactions and Entries

1—Purchased merchandise from Barnard & Co.
    Entry in voucher register.

3—Paid freight on merchandise purchased.
    Entries in voucher and check registers.
    (Whenever an entry is made in the check register, notations are made in the Date Paid and Check Number columns of the voucher register; these notations will not hereafter be mentioned.)

4—Paid Daily News for advertising.
    Entries in voucher and check registers.

Voucher Register

Line No.	Voucher No.	Date	Payee	Explanation	Terms	Date Paid	Check No.	Credit Vouchers Payable	Purchases Dept. A	Purchases Dept. B	Freight In	Freight Out	Advertising
		1941 Aug.											
1	1		Barnard & Co.	Inv. July 31	2/10, n/30	Aug. 8	6	1,500 00	1,500 00				
2	2		C. N. W. Ry.			3	1	18 00			18 00		
3	3		Daily News	Bill dated Aug. 3	Cash	4	2	150 00					150 00
4	4		C. N. W. Ry.		Cash	5	3	35 00			20 00	15 00	
5	5		Davis Supply Co.	Invoice 317		5	4	105 00					
6	6		G. E. Wilson	Note dated July 8		7	5	1,005 00					
7	7		L. N. Whitely	Invoice Aug. 9	1/10, n/30	19	8	3,500 00	2,000 00	1,500 00			
8	8		B. N. Haines	Rent for August		15	7	200 00					
9	9		F. R. Mason & Co.	Inv. 2425	2/10, n/30	26	10	2,600 00	1,200 00	1,400 00			
10	10		Acme Garage	Rent for August		23	9	25 00					
11	11		George Martin	Inv. 1372	1/10, n/30	28	11	1,750 00	800 00	950 00			
12	12		Postmaster					25 00					
13	13		Dalton & Doane	Inv. 3639	2/10, n/30	31	12	1,875 00	600 00	1,275 00			
14	14		Payroll					850 00					
								13,638 00	6,100 00	5,125 00	38 00	15 00	150 00
								(11)	(31)	(32)	(35)	(41)	(42)

Line No.	Salesmen's Salaries	Delivery Expense	Miscellaneous Selling Expense	Office Salaries	Officers' Salaries	Office Supplies	Stationery and Printing	Postage	Notes Payable	Interest Expense	Sundry Accounts Debited — Account	L.F.	Amount	Remarks
1														
2														
3														
4														
5						30 00	75 00							
6									1,000 00	5 00				
7														
8											Store Rent	43	200 00	
9														
10		25 00												
11														
12								25 00						
13														
14	250 00	175 00		125 00	300 00									
	250 00	200 00		125 00	300 00	30 00	75 00	25 00	1,000 00	5 00			200 00	
	(44)	(45)		(51)	(52)	(53)	(54)	(55)	(12)	(61)				

93

4—Paid freight.
  Entries in voucher and check registers.

5—Paid Davis Supply Co. for office supplies and stationery.
  Entries in voucher and check registers.

7—Paid G. E. Wilson for note and interest.
  Entries in voucher and check registers.

8—Paid Barnard & Co. voucher 1.
  Entry in check register.

10—Purchased merchandise from L. N. Whitely.
  Entry in voucher register.

15—Paid store rent for the month.
  Entries in voucher and check registers.

17—Purchased merchandise from F. R. Mason & Co.
  Entry in voucher register.

19—Paid L. N. Whitely voucher 7.
  Entry in check register.

23—Paid Acme Garage for August rent.
  Entries in voucher and check registers.

26—Purchased merchandise from George Martin.
  Entry in voucher register.

26—Paid F. R. Mason & Co. voucher 9.
  Entry in check register.

28—Purchased postage stamps.
  Entries in voucher and check registers.

30—Purchased merchandise from Dalton & Doane.
  Entry in voucher register.

31—Paid salaries for the month.
  Entries in voucher and check registers.

Posting from the voucher and check registers.

The ledger page numbers entered below the column totals in the voucher and check registers, and in the L.F. column of the Sundry Accounts Debited section of the voucher register, indicate that the posting has been completed.

Voucher register postings:

  Credit—Total of Vouchers Payable column.
  Debits—Totals of all special debit columns and items in the Sundry column.

Check register postings:

  Debit—Total of Vouchers Payable column.
  Credits—Totals of Discount on Purchases and Cash columns.

Elimination of accounts payable ledger.

One of the advantages of the voucher system is the elimination of the subsidiary accounts payable ledger; the individual liabilities at any date can be determined by merely noting the "open" items in the voucher register—that is, the items without notations in the Date Paid and Check Number columns.

To illustrate, the posting of the totals of the Vouchers Payable columns in the voucher and check registers on the preceding pages produced the following controlling account with Vouchers Payable:

Vouchers Payable   (Page 5)

1941					1941				
Aug.	31	. . . .	ChR1	10,013	00	Aug.	31	. . . .	VR1	13,638	00

This account has a credit balance of $3,625.00. The open items making up this total are shown by the voucher register to be:

Voucher 11—George Martin. $1,750.00
Voucher 13—Dalton & Doane. 1,875.00
    Total. $3,625.00

Thus we see that the voucher register serves both as a book of original entry and as a subsidiary record supporting the controlling account of Vouchers Payable.

11

CLOSING THE BOOKS

....

Closing accounts showing changes in surplus.

When I was a boy a man in our town liked to know how much water fell when it rained. So he set out barrels at the corners of his house under the downspouts, and after each rain he measured the water in the barrels and emptied the barrels into the cistern.

Businessmen like to know the amounts of their income and expenses, so they set up barrels called accounts. After preparing operating statements at the end of a year or other period, they empty the accounts so that they can be used to measure the results of operations during the next period. The process of emptying the accounts is called closing the books or closing the ledger.

Illustration.

A ledger which appeared in Chapter 3 is repeated below. The entries are assumed to have been posted from pages 1 and 2 of a journal. The company is engaged in selling real estate on a commission basis.

Cash (Page 1)

1941				1941			
Mar.	1	1	10,000 00	Mar.	3	1	200 00
	8	1	300 00		12	1	500 00
	15	1	150 00		31	2	375 00
	22	2	200 00		31	2	200 00
	27	2	175 00				

John Smith (Page 2)

1941				1941			
Mar.	10	1	250 00	Mar.	15	1	150 00

Fred Brown (Page 3)

1941				1941			
Mar.	20	2	375 00	Mar.	27	2	175 00

Office Equipment (Page 4)

1941							
Mar.	5	1	1,200 00				

White & Company   (Page 5)

1941					1941					
Mar. 12	....	1	500	00	Mar. 5	....	1	1,200	00	

Capital Stock   (Page 6)

					1941					
					Mar. 1	....	1	10,000	00	

Commission Income   (Page 7)

					1941				
					Mar. 8	....	1	300	00
					10	....	1	250	00
					20	....	2	375	00
					22	....	2	200	00

Expense   (Page 8)

1941					
Mar. 3	Rent..............	1	200	00	
31	Wages............	2	375	00	

Dividends Paid   (Page 9)

1941				
Mar. 31	....	2	200	00

What accounts to close.

Remember that we are to close only the accounts with balances which show *changes in surplus during the period.*

The debit balances in the Cash, John Smith, Fred Brown, and Office Equipment accounts show the amounts of assets at the end of the period; therefore these accounts are not to be closed.

The credit balance in the account with White & Company shows a liability at the end of the period, and the credit balance in the Capital Stock account shows the par value of the stock outstanding at the end of the period; therefore these accounts are not to be closed.

The only accounts with balances showing changes in surplus during the period are: Commission Income, Expense, and Dividends Paid.

Closing income and expense accounts.

The income and expense accounts are closed by making and posting journal entries which transfer the balances in these accounts to a new account called Profit and Loss. All income for the period is thus shown on the credit side of the Profit and Loss account and all expenses are shown on the debit side. The credit balance of the Profit and Loss account then shows the net income for the period.

Journal entries to close the income and expense accounts are presented below; each journal entry is followed by the accounts affected.

Closing the income account.

<table>
<tr><td colspan="6" align="center">Journal</td><td colspan="2" align="right">(Page 3)</td></tr>
<tr><td>1941
Mar.</td><td>31</td><td>Commission Income.............................
Profit and Loss...............................
To close the Commission Income account and
transfer its credit balance to the credit of Profit
and Loss.</td><td>7
10</td><td>1,125</td><td>00</td><td>
1,125</td><td>
00</td></tr>
</table>

<table>
<tr><td colspan="6" align="center">Commission Income</td><td colspan="2" align="right">(Page 7)</td></tr>
<tr><td>1941
Mar.</td><td>31</td><td>To P. & L.........</td><td>3</td><td>1,125</td><td>00</td><td>1941
Mar.</td><td>8
10
20
22</td><td>...................
....
....
...................</td><td>1
1
2
2</td><td>300
250
375
200</td><td>00
00
00
00</td></tr>
<tr><td></td><td></td><td></td><td></td><td>1,125</td><td>00</td><td></td><td></td><td></td><td></td><td>1,125</td><td>00</td></tr>
</table>

<table>
<tr><td colspan="4" align="center">Profit and Loss</td><td colspan="2" align="right">(Page 10)</td></tr>
<tr><td></td><td></td><td></td><td>1941
Mar.</td><td>31</td><td>Commissions.......</td><td>3</td><td>1,125</td><td>00</td></tr>
</table>

The Commission Income account is now closed; that is, it has no balance. Its former credit balance of $1,125.00 has been transferred to the credit side of the Profit and Loss account.

Closing the expense account.

<table>
<tr><td colspan="8" align="center">Journal—*Continued*</td></tr>
<tr><td>1941
Mar.</td><td>31</td><td>Profit and Loss................................
Expense....................................
To close the Expense account and transfer its debit
balance to the debit of Profit and Loss.</td><td>10
8</td><td>575</td><td>00</td><td>
575</td><td>
00</td></tr>
</table>

<table>
<tr><td colspan="6" align="center">Expense</td><td colspan="2" align="right">(Page 8)</td></tr>
<tr><td>1941
Mar.</td><td>3
31</td><td>Rent..............
Wages.............</td><td>1
2</td><td>200
375</td><td>00
00</td><td>1941
Mar.</td><td>31</td><td>To P. & L.........</td><td>3</td><td>575</td><td>00</td></tr>
<tr><td></td><td></td><td></td><td></td><td>575</td><td>00</td><td></td><td></td><td></td><td></td><td>575</td><td>00</td></tr>
</table>

This account is now closed; its former debit balance has been transferred to the debit of Profit and Loss.

<table>
<tr><td colspan="4" align="center">Profit and Loss</td><td colspan="2" align="right">(Page 10)</td></tr>
<tr><td>1941
Mar.</td><td>31</td><td>Expense...........</td><td>3</td><td>575</td><td>00</td><td>1941
Mar.</td><td>31</td><td>Commissions.......</td><td>3</td><td>1,125</td><td>00</td></tr>
</table>

The credit balance in this account now shows the net income for the month.

Closing the Profit and Loss and the Dividends Paid accounts.

During March the surplus was increased by the net income (now shown by the credit balance of the Profit and Loss account) and was decreased by the dividends paid (shown by the debit in the Dividends Paid account); the balances in these two accounts are transferred to Surplus by the two journal entries shown below. The effect of posting these journal entries is shown by the ledger accounts.

Closing the Profit and Loss account.

Journal—*Continued*

1941						
Mar.	31	Profit and Loss...............................	10	550	00	
		Surplus.................................	11			550	00
		To close the Profit and Loss account and transfer its credit balance, representing the net income for the month, to Surplus.				

Profit and Loss (Page 10)

1941						1941					
Mar.	31	Expense...........	3	575	00	Mar.	31	Commissions.......	3	1,125	00
	31	To Surplus.........	3	550	00						
				1,125	00					1,125	00

Surplus (Page 11)

					1941					
					Mar.	31	Net Income........	3	550	00

Closing the Dividends Paid account.

Journal—*Continued*

1941						
Mar.	31	Surplus..	11	200	00	
		Dividends Paid...........................	9			200	00
		To close the Dividends Paid account and transfer its balance to the debit of Surplus.				

Dividends Paid (Page 9)

1941						1941					
Mar.	31	....	2	200	00	Mar.	31	To Surplus.........	3	200	00

Surplus (Page 11)

1941						1941					
Mar.	31	Dividends.........	3	200	00	Mar.	31	Net Income........	3	550	00

The balance in this account now shows the surplus at the end of March.

Effect of closing the books.

To indicate more fully the effect of closing the books, trial balances of the accounts before and after closing are presented below.

Trial Balances—March 31, 1941

	Before Closing		After Closing	
Cash...................	$ 9,550.00		$ 9,550.00	
John Smith............	100.00		100.00	
Fred Brown...........	200.00		200.00	
Office Equipment.......	1,200.00		1,200.00	
White & Company......		$ 700.00		$ 700.00
Capital Stock..........		10,000.00		10,000.00
Commission Income.....		1,125.00		—
Expense...............	575.00		—	
Dividends Paid........	200.00		—	
Profit and Loss........	—		—	
Surplus...............		—		350.00
	$11,825.00	$11,825.00	$11,050.00	$11,050.00

Subsequent closing.

The trial balance at the end of the next month is as follows:

Trial Balance—April 30, 1941

Cash.......................................	$10,035.00	
John Smith.................................	275.00	
Fred Brown.................................	150.00	
George Whitely.............................	500.00	
Office Equipment...........................	1,200.00	
McGee & Company...........................		$ 900.00
DuPont and Son.............................		500.00
Capital Stock..............................		10,000.00
Commission Income..........................		1,250.00
Expense....................................	640.00	
Dividends Paid.............................	200.00	
Surplus....................................		350.00
	$13,000.00	$13,000.00

The journal entries to close the books are shown below.

Journal   (Page 6)

1941						
Apr.	30	Commission Income.............................	7	1,250 00		
		Profit and Loss................................	10		1,250 00	
		To close the income account.				
	30	Profit and Loss.................................	10	640 00		
		Expense....................................	8		640 00	
		To close the expense account.				

Journal—*Continued*

1941						
Apr.	30	Profit and Loss..................................	10	610	00	
		Surplus....................................	11			610	00
		To close the net income to the Surplus account.				
	30	Surplus.....................................	11	200	00	
		Dividends Paid............................	9			200	00
		To close the dividends account.				

Following are the accounts affected by the closing entries.

Commission Income (Page 7)

1941						1941					
Mar.	31	To P. & L.........	3	1,125	00	Mar.	8	....	1	300	00
							10	....	1	250	00
							20	....	2	375	00
							22	....	2	200	00
				1,125	00					1,125	00
Apr.	30	To P. & L.........	6	1,250	00	Apr.	6	....	4	450	00
							15	....	4	175	00
							22	....	5	300	00
							29	....	5	325	00
				1,250	00					1,250	00

Expense (Page 8)

1941						1941					
Mar.	3	....	1	200	00	Mar.	31	To P. & L.........	3	575	00
	31	....	2	375	00						
				575	00					575	00
Apr.	1	....	4	200	00	Apr.	30	To P. & L.........	6	640	00
	30	....	5	400	00						
	30	....	5	40	00						
				640	00					640	00

Dividends Paid (Page 9)

1941						1941					
Mar.	31	....	2	200	00	Mar.	31	To Surplus.........	3	200	00
Apr.	30	....	5	200	00	Apr.	30	To Surplus.........	6	200	00

Profit and Loss (Page 10)

1941						1941					
Mar.	31	Expense...........	3	575	00	Mar.	31	Commissions......	3	1,125	00
	31	To Surplus.........	3	550	00						
				1,125	00					1,125	00
Apr.	30	Expense...........	6	640	00	Apr.	30	Commissions......	6	1,250	00
	30	To Surplus.........	6	610	00						
				1,250	00					1,250	00

Surplus (Page 11)

1941						1941					
Mar.	31	Dividends.........	3	200	00	Mar.	31	Net Income........	3	550	00
Apr.	30	Dividends.........	6	200	00	Apr.	30	Net Income........	6	610	00

rial balances.

The effect of the closing at the end of April is shown by the ollowing trial balances.

Trial Balances—April 30, 1941

	Before Closing		After Closing	
Cash.....................	$10,035.00		$10,035.00	
John Smith.............	275.00		275.00	
Fred Brown............	150.00		150.00	
George Whitely.........	500.00		500.00	
Office Equipment.......	1,200.00		1,200.00	
McGee & Company.....		$ 900.00		$ 900.00
DuPont and Son........		500.00		500.00
Capital Stock...........		10,000.00		10,000.00
Commission Income.....		1,250.00		—
Expense................	640.00		—	
Dividends Paid.........	200.00		—	
Profit and Loss.........	—	—	—	—
Surplus................		350.00		760.00
	$13,000.00	$13,000.00	$12,160.00	$12,160.00

nsult to intelligence.

"Dear Sir: It is the end of the month.   You owe me $100.00. Please remit, so that I can close my books."

CLOSING THE BOOKS—Continued

Basis of illustration.

The following accounts will serve as the basis of an illustration of the procedure of closing the books of a merchandise company.

	Cash						(Page 1)	
1941 Sep. 1	....	1	4,000 00	1941 Sep. 3	....	1	1,500 00	
18	....	1	2,000 00	26	....	1	500 00	
27	....	1	750 00	28	....	1	200 00	
				30	....	1	250 00	

	E. F. Bailey						(Page 2)
1941 Sep. 25	....	1	1,350 00	1941 Sep. 27	....	1	750 00

	Inventory					(Page 3)
1941 Sep. 1	....	1	1,000 00			

	George White						(Page 4)
1941 Sep. 26	....	1	500 00	1941 Sep. 7	....	1	1,200 00

	Capital Stock					(Page 5)
			1941 Sep. 1	....	1	5,000 00

	Purchases				(Page 6)
1941 Sep. 3	....	1	1,500 00	
7	....	1	1,200 00	

	Sales					(Page 7)
		1941 Sep. 18	....	1	2,000 00
		25	....	1	1,350 00

	Expense				(Page 8)
1941 Sep. 28	Store Rent........	1	200 00	

	Dividends Paid				(Page 9)
1941 Sep. 30	....	1	250 00		-

The inventory at the end of September cost $1,150.00.

Statements.

The following statements were prepared from the foregoing accounts.

THE MORTON COMPANY
Statement of Profit and Loss

For the Month of September, 1941

Sales..		$3,350.00
Deduct Cost of Goods Sold:		
Inventory, September 1, 1941...................	$1,000.00	
Purchases.....................................	2,700.00	
Total....................................	$3,700.00	
Deduct Inventory, September 30, 1941...........	1,150.00	
Remainder—Cost of Goods Sold........................		2,550.00
Gross Profit on Sales....................................		$ 800.00
Deduct Expenses...		200.00
Net Profit for the Month.................................		$ 600.00

THE MORTON COMPANY
Statement of Surplus
For the Month of September, 1941

Net Profit for the Month....................................	$600.00
Deduct Dividends Paid......................................	250.00
Balance, September 30, 1941................................	$350.00

THE MORTON COMPANY
Balance Sheet
September 30, 1941

Assets		Liabilities and Net Worth		
Cash......................	$4,300.00	Accounts Payable...........		$ 700.00
Accounts Receivable.........	600.00	Net Worth:		
Inventory.................	1,150.00	Capital Stock..	$5,000.00	
		Surplus........	350.00	5,350.00
	$6,050.00			$6,050.00

Closing the books.

Closing the books of a merchandising company accomplishes two things:

(1) All accounts used in determining the net income for the period, and any other accounts (such as Dividends Paid) showing changes in surplus during the period, are closed.

(2) The inventory at the end of the period is entered in the books as an asset.

The journal entries to close the foregoing ledger appear below; each journal entry is followed by the ledger accounts affected.

Closing the Inventory account. The first entry closes the Inventory account by transferring its balance (representing the cost of the opening inventory) to the debit of Profit and Loss.

Journal   (Page 2)

```
1941
Sep. 30  Profit and Loss...........................  1,000.00
              Inventory.............................             1,000.00
         To charge Profit and Loss with the inventory
         at the beginning of the period.
```

Inventory   (Page 3)

1941						1941					
Sep.	1	....	1	1,000	00	Sep.	30	To P. & L.........	2	1,000	00

Profit and Loss   (Page 10)

1941					
Sep.	30	Inventory, Sep. 1...	2	1,000	00

Closing the Purchases account. The second entry closes the Purchases account by transferring its balance to the debit of Profit and Loss.

```
Sep. 30  Profit and Loss...........................  2,700.00
              Purchases.............................             2,700.00
         To close the Purchases account.
```

Purchases   (Page 6)

1941						1941					
Sep.	3	....	1	1,500	00	Sep.	30	To P. & L.........	2	2,700	00
	7	....	1	1,200	00						
				2,700	00					2,700	00

Profit and Loss   (Page 10)

1941					
Sep.	30	Inventory, Sep. 1...	2	1,000	00
	30	Purchases..........	2	2,700	00

The debit balance in the Profit and Loss account now shows the cost of goods which were available for sale during the month.

Inventory at end of period. The third entry places the September 30 inventory on the books as an asset, with an offsetting credit to Profit and Loss. The credit to Profit and Loss represents a deduction from the opening inventory and purchases costs which were debited to that account.

Sep. 30 Inventory.................................. 1,150.00
    Profit and Loss........................   1,150.00
     To place the September 30 inventory on the
     books as an asset, and to credit Profit and
     Loss with the amount thereof.

Inventory (Page 3)

1941					1941				
Sep.	1	....	1	1,000|00	Sep.	30	To P. & L.........	2	1,000|00
Sep.	30	....	2	1,150|00					

Profit and Loss (Page 10)

1941					1941				
Sep.	30	Inventory, Sep. 1...	2	1,000|00	Sep.	30	Inventory, Sep. 30..	2	1,150|00
	30	Purchases..........	2	2,700|00					

The debit balance in the Inventory account shows the valuation of the goods on hand at the end of September.

The debit balance of $2,550.00 in the Profit and Loss account is the cost of goods sold during September.

Closing the Sales account.

Sep. 30 Sales..................................... 3,350.00
    Profit and Loss........................   3,350.00
     To close the Sales account.

Sales (Page 7)

1941					1941				
Sep.	30	To P. & L.........	2	3,350|00	Sep.	18	....	1	2,000|00
						25	....	1	1,350|00
				3,350|00					3,350|00

Profit and Loss (Page 10)

1941					1941				
Sep.	30	Inventory, Sep. 1...	2	1,000|00	Sep.	30	Inventory, Sep. 30..	2	1,150|00
	30	Purchases..........	2	2,700|00		30	Sales..............	2	3,350|00

All accounts used in determining the gross profit on sales have now been closed, and the Profit and Loss account has a credit balance of $800.00, the gross profit shown by the profit and loss statement.

Closing the Expense account.

Sep. 30 Profit and Loss........................... 200.00
    Expense...............................   200.00
     To close the Expense account.

Expense   (Page 8)

1941					1941				
Sep.	28	Store Rent.........	1	200|00	Sep.	30	To P. & L..........	2	200|00

Profit and Loss   (Page 10)

1941					1941				
Sep.	30	Inventory, Sep. 1...	2	1,000|00	Sep.	30	Inventory, Sep. 30..	2	1,150|00
	30	Purchases..........	2	2,700|00		30	Sales..............	2	3,350|00
	30	Expense...........	2	200|00					

The Profit and Loss account now has a credit balance of $600.00, the net profit for the month.

Closing the Profit and Loss account.

Sep. 30 Profit and Loss............................ 600.00
             Surplus...............................   600.00
         To transfer the net profit to Surplus.

Profit and Loss   (Page 10)

1941					1941				
Sep.	30	Inventory, Sep. 1...	2	1,000|00	Sep.	30	Inventory, Sep. 30..	2	1,150|00
	30	Purchases..........	2	2,700|00		30	Sales..............	2	3,350|00
	30	Expense...........	2	200|00					
	30	To Surplus........	2	600|00					
				4,500|00					4,500|00

Surplus   (Page 11)

					1941				
					Sep.	30	Net Profit..........	2	600|00

The net profit for the month has now been transferred to the credit of Surplus.

Closing the Dividends Paid account.

Sep. 30 Surplus.................................... 250.00
             Dividends Paid.......................   250.00
         To close the Dividends Paid account.

Dividends Paid   (Page 9)

1941					1941				
Sep.	30	....	1	250|00	Sep.	30	To Surplus........	2	250|00

Surplus   (Page 11)

1941					1941				
Sep.	30	Dividends Paid.....	2	250|00	Sep.	30	Net Profit..........	2	600|00

The Surplus account now has a credit balance of $350.00, the surplus at the end of September.

Ledger accounts.

The ledger accounts after the closing of the books appear on the following pages.

Accounts affected by closing entries.

Inventory (Page 3)

1941						1941					
Sep.	1	....	1	1,000	00	Sep.	30	To P. & L.........	2	1,000	00
Sep.	30	....	2	1,150	00						

Purchases (Page 6)

1941						1941					
Sep.	3	....	1	1,500	00	Sep.	30	To P. & L.........	2	2,700	00
	7	....	1	1,200	00						
				2,700	00					2,700	00

Sales (Page 7)

1941						1941					
Sep.	30	To P. & L.........	2	3,350	00	Sep.	18	....	1	2,000	00
							25	....	1	1,350	00
				3,350	00					3,350	00

Expense (Page 8)

1941						1941					
Sep.	28	Store Rent.........	1	200	00	Sep.	30	To P. & L.........	2	200	00

Dividends Paid (Page 9)

1941						1941					
Sep.	30	....	1	250	00	Sep.	30	To Surplus.........	2	250	00

Profit and Loss (Page 10)

1941						1941					
Sep.	30	Inventory, Sep. 1...	2	1,000	00	Sep.	30	Inventory, Sep. 30..	2	1,150	00
	30	Purchases..........	2	2,700	00		30	Sales..............	2	3,350	00
	30	Expense...........	2	200	00						
	30	To Surplus.........	2	600	00						
				4,500	00					4,500	00

Surplus (Page 11)

1941						1941					
Sep.	30	Dividends Paid.....	2	250	00	Sep.	30	Net Profit.........	2	600	00

Accounts not affected by closing entries.

Cash (Page 1)

1941						1941					
Sep.	1	....	1	4,000	00	Sep.	3	....	1	1,500	00
	18	....	1	2,000	00		26	....	1	500	00
	27	....	1	750	00		28	....	1	200	00
							30	....	1	250	00

E. F. Bailey (Page 2)

1941						1941					
Sep.	25	....	1	1,350	00	Sep.	27	....	1	750	00

George White   (Page 4)

| 941 | | | | 500 | 00 | 1941 | | | | 1 | 1,200 | 00 |
| Sep. | 26 | .... | 1 | | | Sep. | 7 | .... | 1 | | |

Capital Stock   (Page 5)

| | | | | | | 1941 | | | | 1 | 5,000 | 00 |
| | | | | | | Sep. | 1 | .... | | | |

Trial balances.

The effect of closing the books of a merchandise company is shown by the following trial balances.

Trial Balances—September 30, 1941

	Before Closing		After Closing	
Cash.....................	$4,300.00		$4,300.00	
Inventory.................	1,000.00		1,150.00	
E. F. Bailey...............	600.00		600.00	
George White..............		$ 700.00		$ 700.00
Capital Stock..............		5,000.00		5,000.00
Purchases.................	2,700.00		—	
Sales.....................		3,350.00	—	
Expense...................	200.00		—	
Dividends Paid............	250.00		—	
Surplus...................		—		250.00
	$9,050.00	$9,050.00	$6,050.00	$6,050.00

13

CLOSING THE BOOKS—Continued

Basis of illustration.

The following trial balance indicates the accounts which will serve as the basis of an illustration showing a somewhat more complex closing procedure.

THE WATSON CORPORATION
Trial Balance—December 31, 1941

Cash..	$ 18,325.00	
Accounts Receivable........................	25,500.00	
Notes Receivable...........................	6,000.00	
Inventory—December 31, 1940..............	25,000.00	
Delivery Equipment........................	3,000.00	
Vouchers Payable...........................		$ 7,375.00
Notes Payable.............................		4,000.00
Capital Stock..............................		35,000.00
Surplus—December 31, 1940................		27,361.00
Sales......................................		103,500.00
Returned Sales and Allowances..............	1,500.00	
Purchases.................................	65,000.00	
Returned Purchases and Allowances..........		1,000.00
Freight In.................................	2,000.00	
Store Rent.................................	6,000.00	
Advertising................................	3,000.00	
Salesmen's Salaries.........................	8,000.00	
Freight Out................................	4,000.00	
Insurance..................................	300.00	
Taxes.....................................	100.00	
Office Salaries.............................	3,000.00	
Office Expenses............................	3,625.00	
Delivery Income...........................		1,200.00
Discount on Purchases......................		900.00
Interest Income............................		24.00
Discount on Sales..........................	975.00	
Interest Expense...........................	35.00	
Dividends Paid.............................	5,000.00	
	$180,360.00	$180,360.00

Working papers.

As an aid in the preparation of the statements at the end of the period and the closing journal entries, accountants sometimes make working papers in a form similar to the following illustration.

All balances shown in the trial balance are classified according to the statements in which they will be used.

The inventory at the end of the year does not appear in the trial balance; but it is entered, below the trial balance figures, in the columns for the profit and loss statement and the balance sheet, because it will appear in both of these statements.

The net income for the year is shown as the balancing figure in the Profit and Loss columns, and is extended to the credit Surplus column.

The surplus at the end of the year is shown as the balancing figure in the Surplus columns, and is extended to the credit Balance Sheet column.

THE WATSON CORPORATION
Working Papers
For the Year Ended December 31, 1941

	Trial Balance		Profit and Loss Statement		Surplus Statement		Balance Sheet	
Cash....................	$ 18,325						$18,325	
Accounts Receivable......	25,500						25,500	
Notes Receivable.........	6,000						6,000	
Inventory, Dec. 31, 1940...	25,000		$ 25,000					
Delivery Equipment.......	3,000						3,000	
Vouchers Payable.........		$ 7,375						$ 7,375
Notes Payable............		4,000						4,000
Capital Stock............		35,000						35,000
Surplus, Dec. 31, 1940.....		27,361				$27,361		
Sales....................		103,500		$103,500				
Ret'd Sales and Allowances.	1,500		1,500					
Purchases................	65,000		65,000					
Ret'd Purchases and Allow.		1,000		1,000				
Freight In................	2,000		2,000					
Store Rent...............	6,000		6,000					
Advertising..............	3,000		3,000					
Salesmen's Salaries........	8,000		8,000					
Freight Out..............	4,000		4,000					
Insurance................	300		300					
Taxes....................	100		100					
Office Salaries............	3,000		3,000					
Office Expenses...........	3,625		3,625					
Delivery Income..........		1,200		1,200				
Discount on Purchases.....		900		900				
Interest Income..........		24		24				
Discount on Sales.........	975		975					
Interest Expense..........	35		35					
Dividends Paid...........	5,000				$ 5,000			
	$180,360	$180,360						
Inventory, Dec. 31, 1941...				26,000			26,000	
Net Income—To Surplus...			10,089		10,089			
			$132,624	$132,624				
Surplus, Dec. 31, 1941.....					32,450			32,450
					$37,450	$37,450	$78,825	$78,825

Statements.

The statements prepared at the end of the year are shown on the next page.

THE WATSON CORPORATION   Exhibit C
Statement of Profit and Loss
For the Year Ended December 31, 1941

Gross Sales			$103,500
Deduct Returned Sales and Allowances			1,500
Net Sales			$102,000
Deduct Cost of Goods Sold:			
Inventory, December 31, 1940		$25,000	
Purchases	$65,000		
Deduct Ret'd. Purchases and Allowances	1,000		
Net Purchases	$64,000		
Add Freight In	2,000		
Total		66,000	
Total Opening Inventory and Purchases		$91,000	
Deduct Inventory, December 31, 1941		26,000	65,000
Gross Profit on Sales			$ 37,000
Deduct Selling Expenses:			
Store Rent		$ 6,000	
Advertising		3,000	
Salesmen's Salaries		8,000	
Freight Out		4,000	
Total Selling Expenses			21,000
Net Profit on Sales			$ 16,000
Deduct General Expenses:			
Insurance		$ 300	
Taxes		100	
Office Salaries		3,000	
Office Expenses		3,625	
Total General Expenses			7,025
Net Profit on Operations			$ 8,975
Add Other Income:			
Delivery Income		$ 1,200	
Discount on Purchases		900	
Interest Income		24	
Total Other Income			2,124
Net Profit on Operations and Other Income			$ 11,099
Deduct Other Expenses:			
Discount on Sales		$ 975	
Interest Expense		35	
Total Other Expenses			1,010
Net Income			$ 10,089

THE WATSON CORPORATION   Exhibit B
Statement of Surplus
For the Year Ended December 31, 1941

Balance, December 31, 1940	$27,361
Add Net Income, per Exhibit C	10,089
Total	$37,450
Deduct Dividends Paid	5,000
Balance, December 31, 1941	$32,450

THE WATSON CORPORATION   Exhibit A
Balance Sheet, December 31, 1941

Assets		Liabilities and Net Worth		
Cash	$18,325	LIABILITIES:		
Accounts Receivable	25,500	Accounts Payable	$ 7,375	
Notes Receivable	6,000	Notes Payable	4,000	$11,375
Inventory	26,000	NET WORTH:		
Delivery Equipment	3,000	Capital Stock	$35,000	
		Surplus, per Exhibit B	32,450	67,450
	$78,825			$78,825

Closing entries.

Following are the journal entries to close the books at the end of the year.

```
Profit and Loss............................... 25,000.00
    Inventory..................................          25,000.00
    To charge Profit and Loss with the inventory at the
    beginning of the year.


Profit and Loss............................... 67,000.00
    Purchases..................................          65,000.00
    Freight In.................................           2,000.00
    To close the two last-named accounts.


Returned Purchases and Allowances.............. 1,000.00
    Profit and Loss...........................           1,000.00
    To close the Returned Purchases and Allowances
    account.
```

After these entries are posted, the Profit and Loss account has a debit balance of $91,000.00, representing the cost of goods available for sale during the year.

```
Inventory..................................... 26,000.00
    Profit and Loss...........................          26,000.00
    To put the December 31, 1941, inventory on the
    books.
```

After this entry is posted, the Profit and Loss account has a debit balance of $65,000.00, representing the cost of goods sold during the year.

```
Sales......................................... 103,500.00
    Profit and Loss...........................          103,500.00
    To close the Sales account.


Profit and Loss............................... 1,500.00
    Returned Sales and Allowances.............           1,500.00
    To close the last-named account.
```

After these entries are posted, the Profit and Loss account has a credit balance of $37,000.00, representing the gross profit on sales, as shown by the profit and loss statement on page 115.

Profit and Loss.................................	21,000.00	
Store Rent.................................		6,000.00
Advertising.................................		3,000.00
Salesmen's Salaries.........................		8,000.00
Freight Out...............................		4,000.00
To close the selling expense accounts.		
Profit and Loss.................................	7,025.00	
Insurance.................................		300.00
Taxes		100.00
Office Salaries.............................		3,000.00
Office Expenses............................		3,625.00
To close the general expense accounts.		
Delivery Income.............................	1,200.00	
Interest Income.............................	24.00	
Discount on Purchases......................	900.00	
Profit and Loss...........................		2,124.00
To close the other income accounts.		
Profit and Loss.................................	1,010.00	
Interest Expense...........................		35.00
Discount on Sales..........................		975.00
To close the miscellaneous expense accounts.		

After these entries are posted, the Profit and Loss account has a credit balance of $10,089.00, representing the net income for the year.

Profit and Loss.................................	10,089.00	
Surplus...................................		10,089.00
To transfer the net income to Surplus.		
Surplus.......................................	5,000.00	
Dividends Paid............................		5,000.00
To close the dividends account.		

Condensed entries.

Some accountants prefer to reduce the number of closing journal entries by combining related items. The extent to which such condensation is carried is a matter of personal preference. An illustration of such a procedure is given below:

Inventory (December 31, 1941).................	26,000.00	
Sales..	103,500.00	
Returned Purchases and Allowances..............	1,000.00	
Inventory (December 31, 1940)..............		25,000.00
Purchases.................................		65,000.00
Freight In.................................		2,000.00
Returned Sales and Allowances..............		1,500.00
Profit and Loss............................		37,000.00
To set up the inventory at the end of the year and to close to Profit and Loss all accounts with balances used in the determination of gross profit on sales.		

```
Profit and Loss.............................   29,035.00
    Store Rent..............................                 6,000.00
    Advertising.............................                 3,000.00
    Salesmen's Salaries.....................                 8,000.00
    Freight Out.............................                 4,000.00
    Insurance...............................                   300.00
    Taxes...................................                   100.00
    Office Salaries.........................                 3,000.00
    Office Expenses.........................                 3,625.00
    Interest Expense........................                    35.00
    Discount on Sales.......................                   975.00
        To close the expense accounts.

Delivery Income............................    1,200.00
Interest Income............................       24.00
Discount on Purchases......................      900.00
    Profit and Loss........................                 2,124.00
        To close the miscellaneous income accounts.

Profit and Loss............................   10,089.00
    Surplus................................                10,089.00
        To transfer the net income to Surplus.

Surplus....................................    5,000.00
    Dividends Paid.........................                 5,000.00
        To close the dividends account.
```

Profit and Loss and Surplus accounts.

The Profit and Loss and Surplus accounts appear below.

Profit and Loss

1941						1941					
Dec.	31	Inv. Dec. 31, 1940.	J4	25,000	00	Dec.	31	Rtd. P. & A.......	J4	1,000	00
	31	Purchases.........	J4	65,000	00		31	Inv., Dec. 31, 1941	J4	26,000	00
	31	Freight In........	J4	2,000	00		31	Sales............	J4	103,500	00
	31	Rtd. S. & A.......	J4	1,500	00		31	Delivery Income ..	J4	1,200	00
	31	Store Rent........	J4	6,000	00		31	Interest Income....	J4	24	00
	31	Advertising.......	J4	3,000	00		31	Discount on			
	31	Salesmen's Salaries.	J4	8,000	00			Purchases.......	J4	900	00
	31	Freight Out.......	J4	4,000	00						
	31	Insurance........	J4	300	00						
	31	Taxes...........	J4	100	00						
	31	Office Salaries.....	J4	3,000	00						
	31	Office Expenses....	J4	3,625	00						
	31	Interest Expense ..	J4	35	00						
	31	Discount on Sales..	J4	975	00						
	31	Net Income—									
		To Surplus......	J4	10,089	00						
				132,624	00					132,624	00

Surplus

1941						1940					
Dec.	31	Dividends Paid....	J4	5,000	00	Dec.	31	Balance...........		27,361	00
						1941					
						Dec.	31	Net Income.......	J4	10,089	00

edger after closing.

The condition of the ledger accounts after the books are closed t the end of 1941 is indicated below.

The following accounts were not affected:

	Debit Balance	Credit Balance
Cash..	$18,325.00	
Accounts Receivable..........................	25,500.00	
Notes Receivable.............................	6,000.00	
Delivery Equipment..........................	3,000.00	
Vouchers Payable............................		$ 7,375.00
Notes Payable...............................		4,000.00
Capital Stock...............................		35,000.00

The following accounts were closed:

Sales
Returned Sales and Allowances
Purchases
Returned Purchases and Allowances
Freight In
Store Rent
Advertising
Salesmen's Salaries
Freight Out
Insurance
Taxes
Office Salaries
Office Expenses
Delivery Income
Interest Income
Discount on Purchases
Interest Expense
Discount on Sales
Dividends Paid

The balances in the following accounts were changed by the closing entries:

Inventory—Before the books were closed, the Inventory account had a balance of $25,000.00, representing the inventory at the end of 1940; it now has a balance representing the inventory at the end of 1941, in the amount of..........	26,000.00	
Surplus—Before the books were closed, the Surplus account had a balance of $27,361.00, representing the surplus at the end of 1940. It now has a balance representing the surplus at the end of 1941, in the amount of..........................		32,450.00
	$78,825.00	$78,825.00

14

ADJUSTING AND CLOSING THE BOOKS

•••

Basis of illustration.

The following trial balance indicates the accounts which will serve as the basis of the illustration in this chapter.

THE MONTGOMERY COMPANY
Trial Balance, December 31, 1941

Cash....................................	$ 300.00	
Accounts Receivable......................	25,000.00	
Reserve for Bad Debts....................		$ 800.00
Notes Receivable.........................	5,000.00	
Inventory, December 31, 1940.............	35,000.00	
Land....................................	10,000.00	
Store Building...........................	40,000.00	
Reserve for Depreciation—Store Building......		8,000.00
Store Fixtures...........................	4,000.00	
Reserve for Depreciation—Store Fixtures......		1,200.00
Delivery Equipment.......................	3,000.00	
Reserve for Depreciation—Delivery Equipment.		900.00
Office Equipment.........................	2,000.00	
Reserve for Depreciation—Office Equipment...		400.00
Unexpired Insurance......................	700.00	
Accounts Payable........................		16,000.00
Mortgage on Real Estate..................		25,000.00
Rental Collected in Advance..............		600.00
Capital Stock............................		50,000.00
Surplus, December 31, 1940...............		26,250.00
Sales...................................		200,000.00
Returned Sales and Allowances.............	500.00	
Purchases...............................	170,000.00	
Returned Purchases and Allowances..........		1,200.00
Salesmen's Salaries.......................	9,000.00	
Advertising..............................	5,000.00	
Delivery Expense.........................	2,150.00	
Miscellaneous Selling Expense..............	800.00	
Taxes...................................	450.00	
Office Salaries...........................	3,500.00	
Office Expense...........................	2,000.00	
Interest Expense.........................	1,200.00	
Discount on Sales........................	1,750.00	
Dividends Paid...........................	9,000.00	
	$330,350.00	$330,350.00

Inventory, December 31, 1941, $46,500.00

Adjustments.

Before the books are closed, adjusting entries must be made for deferred and accrued items, and for bad debt and depreciation reserves, by the methods described in Chapter 5.

(a) Insurance Expense.................................. 375
　　　　Unexpired Insurance............................ 375
　　To transfer expired insurance premiums to an expense account.

(b) Rental Collected in Advance........................ 400
　　　　Rent Income.................................... 400
　　To transfer earned rent to an income account.

(c) Accrued Interest Receivable 150
　　　　Interest Income................................ 150
　　To record the accrued interest on the notes receivable.

(d) Interest Expense 300
　　　　Accrued Interest Payable....................... 300
　　To record the accrued interest on the mortgage.

(e) Bad Debts 700
　　　　Reserve for Bad Debts......................... 700
　　To increase the bad debt reserve to $1,500.00.

(f) Depreciation—Store Building........................ 2.000
　　　　Reserve for Depreciation—Store Building......... 2.000
　　To provide depreciation—5% of $40,000.00.

(g) Depreciation—Store Fixtures........................ 300
　　　　Reserve for Depreciation—Store Fixtures......... 300
　　To provide depreciation—7½% of $4,000.00.

(h) Depreciation—Delivery Equipment.................... 600
　　　　Reserve for Depreciation—Delivery Equipment.... 600
　　To provide depreciation—20% of $3,000.00.

(i) Depreciation—Office Equipment...................... 150
　　　　Reserve for Depreciation—Office Equipment....... 150
　　To provide depreciation—7½% of $2,000.00.

Working papers and statements.

On page 123 is a work sheet showing the trial balance before adjustments, the application of the adjusting entries, the trial balance after adjustments, and the distribution of the adjusted balances to columns indicative of the statements in which the balances should appear. Such working papers are frequently prepared by accountants as an aid in the preparation of statements and closing entries. The statements appear on pages 124 and 125.

Working Papers—Year Ended December 31, 1941

Account	TB Before Adj. Dr	TB Before Adj. Cr	Adjustments Dr	Adjustments Cr	TB After Adj. Dr	TB After Adj. Cr	Profit and Loss Dr	Profit and Loss Cr	Surplus Dr	Surplus Cr	Balance Sheet Dr	Balance Sheet Cr
Cash	$ 300				$ 300						$ 300	
Accounts Receivable	25,000				25,000						25,000	
Reserve for Bad Debts		$ 800		700e		$ 1,500						$ 1,500
Notes Receivable	5,000				5,000						5,000	
Accrued Interest Receivable			150c		150						150	
Inventory, December 31, 1940	35,000				35,000		$ 35,000					
Land	10,000				10,000						10,000	
Store Building	40,000				40,000						40,000	
Reserve for Depreciation—S. B.		8,000		2,000f		10,000						10,000
Store Fixtures	4,000				4,000						4,000	
Reserve for Depreciation—S. F.		1,200		300g		1,500						1,500
Delivery Equipment	3,000				3,000						3,000	
Reserve for Depreciation—D. E.		900		600h		1,500						1,500
Office Equipment	2,000				2,000						2,000	
Reserve for Depreciation—O. E.		400		150i		550						550
Unexpired Insurance	700			375a	325						325	
Accounts Payable		16,000				16,000						16,000
Accrued Interest Payable				300b		300						300
Mortgage on Real Estate		25,000				25,000						25,000
Rental Collected in Advance		600	400d			200						200
Capital Stock		50,000				50,000						50,000
Surplus, December 31, 1940		26,250				26,250				$26,250		
Sales		200,000				200,000		$200,000				
Returned Sales and Allowances	500				500		500					
Purchases	170,000				170,000		170,000					
Returned Purchases and Allowances		1,200				1,200		1,200				
Salesmen's Salaries	9,000				9,000		9,000					
Advertising	5,000				5,000		5,000					
Delivery Expense	2,150				2,150		2,150					
Depreciation—Store Building			2,000f		2,000		2,000					
Depreciation—Store Fixtures			300g		300		300					
Depreciation—Delivery Equipment			600h		600		600					
Miscellaneous Selling Expense	800				800		800					
Taxes	450				450		450					
Office Salaries	3,500				3,500		3,500					
Office Expense	2,000				2,000		2,000					
Insurance Expense			375a		375		375					
Depreciation—Office Equipment			150i		150		150					
Bad Debts			700e		700		700					
Interest Expense	1,200		300b		1,500		1,500					
Discount on Sales	1,750				1,750		1,750					
Rent Income				400d		400		400				
Interest Income				150c		150		150				
Dividends Paid	9,000				9,000				$ 9,000			
	$330,350	$330,350	$4,975	$4,975	$334,550	$334,550						
Inventory, December 31, 1941								46,500			46,500	
Net Income							12,475			12,475		
							$248,250	$248,250				
Surplus, December 31, 1941									29,725			29,725
									$38,725	$38,725	$136,275	$136,275

123

THE MONTGOMERY COMPANY ·   Exhibit C
Statement of Profit and Loss
For the Year Ended December 31, 1941

Gross Sales			$200,000
Deduct Returned Sales and Allowances			500
Net Sales			$199,500
Deduct Cost of Goods Sold:			
Inventory, December 31, 1940		$ 35,000	
Purchases	$170,000		
Deduct Returned Purchases and Allowances	1,200		
Net Purchases		168,800	
Total Opening Inventory and Purchases		$203,800	
Deduct Inventory, December 31, 1941		46,500	157,300
Gross Profit on Sales			$ 42,200
Deduct Selling Expenses:			
Salesmen's Salaries		$ 9,000	
Advertising		5,000	
Delivery Expense		2,150	
Depreciation:			
Store Building		2,000	
Store Fixtures		300	
Delivery Equipment		600	
Miscellaneous Selling Expense		800	
Total Selling Expenses			19,850
Net Profit on Sales			$ 22,350
Deduct General Expenses:			
Taxes		$ 450	
Office Salaries		3,500	
Office Expense		2,000	
Insurance Expense		375	
Depreciation—Office Equipment		150	
Bad Debts		700	
Total General Expenses			7,175
Net Profit on Operations			$ 15,175
Add Other Income:			
Rent Income		$ 400	
Interest Income		150	550
Net Profit on Operations and Other Income			$ 15,725
Deduct Other Expenses:			
Interest Expense		$ 1,500	
Discount on Sales		1,750	3,250
Net Income			$ 12,475

THE MONTGOMERY COMPANY   Exhibit B
Statement of Surplus
For the Year Ended December 31, 1941

Surplus, December 31, 1940	$26,250.00
Add Net Income—Exhibit C	12,475.00
Total	$38,725.00
Deduct Dividends Paid	9,000.00
Surplus, December 31, 1941	$29,725.00

THE MONTGOMERY COMPANY   Exhibit A

Balance Sheet—December 31, 1941

Assets

CURRENT ASSETS:

Cash..		$ 300	
Accounts Receivable......................	$25,000		
Deduct Reserve for Bad Debts..........	1,500	23,500	
Notes Receivable...............................		5,000	
Accrued Interest Receivable......................		150	
Inventory.......................................		46,500	
Total Current Assets.............:..........................			$ 75,450

FIXED ASSETS:

Land.......................................		$10,000	
Store Building...........................	$40,000		
Deduct Reserve for Depreciation.........	10,000		
Depreciated Value........................		30,000	
Store Fixtures...........................	$ 4,000		
Deduct Reserve for Depreciation.........	1,500		
Depreciated Value........................		2,500	
Delivery Equipment......................	$ 3,000		
Deduct Reserve for Depreciation.........	1,500		
Depreciated Value........................		1,500	
Office Equipment........................	$ 2,000		
Deduct Reserve for Depreciation.........	550		
Depreciated Value........................		1,450	
Total Fixed Assets—Depreciated Value................		45,450	

DEFERRED CHARGES:

Unexpired Insurance.....................................	325	
	$121,225	

Liabilities and Net Worth

CURRENT LIABILITIES:

Accounts Payable...........................	$16,000.00		
Accrued Interest Payable...................	300.00		
Total Current Liabilities..........................		$ 16,300.00	

FIXED LIABILITIES:

Mortgage Payable.....................................		25,000.00

DEFERRED CREDITS:

Rental Collected in Advance...........................		200.00

NET WORTH:

Capital Stock..............................	$50,000.00	
Surplus—Exhibit B........................	29,725.00	
Total Net Worth................................		79,725.00
		$121,225.00

Closing entries.

Following are the journal entries to close the books.

Profit and Loss...............................	35,000.00	
Inventory.................................		35,000.00
To charge P. & L. with the inventory at the beginning of the year.		

Profit and Loss................................ 168,800.00
Returned Purchases and Allowances............ 1,200.00
  Purchases.................................   170,000.00
  To close the two last-named accounts and charge
  P. & L. with the net purchases.

Inventory..................................... 46,500.00
  Profit and Loss...........................   46,500.00
  To place on the books as an asset the inventory
  at the end of the year.

Sales... 200,000.00
  Returned Sales and Allowances.............   500.00
  Profit and Loss...........................   199,500.00
  To close the two first-named accounts and credit
  P. & L. with the net sales.

Profit and Loss............................... 19,850.00
  Salesmen's Salaries.......................   9,000.00
  Advertising...............................   5,000.00
  Delivery Expense..........................   2,150.00
  Depreciation—Store Building...............   2,000.00
  Depreciation—Store Fixtures...............   300.00
  Depreciation—Delivery Equipment...........   600.00
  Miscellaneous Selling Expense.............   800.00
  To close the selling expense accounts.

Profit and Loss...............................   7,175.00
  Taxes.....................................   450.00
  Office Salaries...........................   3,500.00
  Office Expense............................   2,000.00
  Insurance Expense.........................   375.00
  Depreciation—Office Equipment.............   150.00
  Bad Debts.................................   700.00
  To close the general expense accounts.

Rent Income...................................   400.00
Interest Income...............................   150.00
  Profit and Loss...........................   550.00
  To close the miscellaneous income accounts.

Profit and Loss...............................   3,250.00
  Interest Expense..........................   1,500.00
  Discount on Sales.........................   1,750.00
  To close the miscellaneous expense accounts.

Profit and Loss............................... 12,475.00
  Surplus...................................   12,475.00
  To transfer the net income to Surplus.

Surplus.......................................   9,000.00
  Dividends Paid............................   9,000.00
  To close the dividends account.

After-closing trial balance.

Following is a trial balance of the ledger after the adjusting and
closing entries have been posted. Observe that the only accounts

pen after the books have been closed are those with balances
which appear in the balance sheet.

THE MONTGOMERY COMPANY
Trial Balance After Closing—December 31, 1941

Cash.....................................	$ 300.00	
Accounts Receivable........................	25,000.00	
Reserve for Bad Debts......................		$ 1,500.00
Notes Receivable...........................	5,000.00	
Accrued Interest Receivable.................	150.00	
Inventory, December 31, 1941...............	46,500.00	
Land......................................	10,000.00	
Store Building.............................	40,000.00	
Reserve for Depreciation—Store Building......		10,000.00
Store Fixtures.............................	4,000.00	
Reserve for Depreciation—Store Fixtures......		1,500.00
Delivery Equipment........................	3,000.00	
Reserve for Depreciation—Delivery Equipment		1,500.00
Office Equipment..........................	2,000.00	
Reserve for Depreciation—Office Equipment....		550.00
Unexpired Insurance........................	325.00	
Accounts Payable...........................		16,000.00
Accrued Interest Payable....................		300.00
Mortgage Payable..........................		25,000.00
Rental Collected in Advance.................		200.00
Capital Stock..............................		50,000.00
Surplus...................................		29,725.00
	$136,275.00	$136,275.00

15

MANUFACTURING ACCOUNTS

....

Manufacturing costs.

A merchandising concern buys its goods ready for resale, and its books contain a Purchases account which shows the cost of merchandise purchased. A manufacturing concern buys raw materials, but the process of manufacture also involves expenditures for labor and for a great variety of manufacturing expenses; its books therefore must contain accounts in which all of these manufacturing costs can be recorded.

There are three principal elements of manufacturing cost: materials, direct labor, and manufacturing expense.

Materials (sometimes called direct materials) include only those things which enter into and become part of the finished product. Supplies used in the operation of the factory do not become part of the finished product; therefore they are classified as indirect materials, and are regarded as a manufacturing expense.

The nature of direct labor can best be shown by contrast with indirect labor. Employees who work on the product with tools, or who operate machines in the process of production, are direct laborers; but superintendents and foremen who supervise the work of production, and engineers and janitors whose services are incidental to the process of production, are indirect laborers.

Manufacturing expense, or manufacturing overhead, includes all cost incurred in production which cannot be classed as material or direct labor. Manufacturing expense includes, among other things, indirect labor; depreciation of the factory building and equipment; cost of power; supplies; taxes and insurance on the assets used in manufacture; and repairs and upkeep of the factory.

One cannot determine the cost of finished goods manufactured during a given period, however, by merely adding the expenditures during the period for materials, direct labor, and manufacturing expense. There may be unfinished goods, called goods in process, on hand at the end of the period, and one must deduct the cost of these unfinished goods to determine the cost of the goods finished. Similarly, there may have been goods in process at the beginning of the period, and these must also be taken into consideration.

The following statement shows the elements included in the computation of the cost of goods manufactured:

THE *A B C* COMPANY   Exhibit D

Statement of Cost of Goods Manufactured

Year Ended December 31, 1941

Materials:			
Inventory, December 31, 1940			$ 12,000
Purchases	$94,000		
Less Returned Purchases and Allowances	1,500		
Net Purchases	$92,500		
Freight In	800		
Total		93,300	
Total Inventory and Purchases		$105,300	
Less Inventory, December 31, 1941		9,000	
Remainder—Cost of Materials Used			$ 96,300
Direct Labor			80,750
Manufacturing Expenses:			
Indirect Labor		$ 9,125	
Heat, Light, and Power		3,500	
Building and Machinery Repairs		300	
Depreciation:			
Buildings		3,500	
Machinery and Equipment		6,000	
Insurance		950	
Taxes		1,400	
Factory Supplies		3,500	
Miscellaneous Factory Expense		2,500	
Total Manufacturing Expenses			30,775
Total Materials, Labor, and Manufacturing Expenses			$207,825
Add Goods in Process Inventory, December 31, 1940			15,000
Total			$222,825
Deduct Goods in Process Inventory, December 31, 1941			11,000
Cost of Goods Manufactured			$211,825

Profit and loss and surplus statements.

The profit and loss statement and the surplus statement of a manufacturing company do not necessarily differ from those of a trading company except in one particular: the profit and loss statement of a manufacturing company shows the cost of goods *manufactured* (as determined by the statement of cost of goods manufactured), while the profit and loss statement of a trading company shows the cost of goods *purchased*.

THE *A B C* COMPANY
Exhibit C
Statement of Profit and Loss
For the Year Ended December 31, 1941

Gross Sales..		$300,000
Less Returned Sales and Allowances.........................		2,000
Net Sales..		$298,000
Less Cost of Goods Sold:		
Finished Goods Inventory, December 31, 1940......	$ 20,000	
Cost of Goods Manufactured, per Exhibit D........	211,825	
Total...	$231,825	
Less Finished Goods Inventory, December 31, 1941.	17,000	
Remainder—Cost of Goods Sold........................		214,825
Gross Profit on Sales...		$ 83,175
Less Selling Expenses:		
Advertising.......................................	$ 9,000	
Salesmen's Salaries...............................	20,360	
Salesmen's Traveling Expense......................	8,000	
Miscellaneous Selling Expense....................	2,500	39,860
Net Profit on Sales...		$ 43,315
Less General Expenses:		
Office Salaries...................................	$ 3,040	
Officers' Salaries................................	18,000	
Stationery and Printing...........................	400	
Office Supplies...................................	300	
Depreciation of Furniture and Fixtures............	750	
Bad Debts...	800	
Miscellaneous General Expense....................	700	23,990
Net Profit on Operations..		$ 19,325
Less Net Financial Expense:		
Discount on Sales.................................	$ 2,500	
Less Discount on Purchases........................	1,200	1,300
Net Income..		$ 18,025

THE *A B C* COMPANY
Statement of Surplus
For the Year Ended December 31, 1941

Balance, December 31, 1940...............................	$71,450.00
Net Income for the Year, per Exhibit C....................	18,025.00
Total..	$89,475.00
Less Dividends...	6,000.00
Balance, December 31, 1941...............................	$83,475.00

Balance sheet.

The balance sheet of a manufacturing company usually differs from that of a trading company in that the former includes fixed assets required for manufacturing operations, and inventories of materials, goods in process, and finished goods instead of a single merchandise inventory.

THE *A B C* COMPANY
Balance Sheet, December 31, 1941

Assets

CURRENT ASSETS:

Cash		$25,000	
Accounts Receivable	$40,000		
Less Reserve for Bad Debts	1,000	39,000	
Inventories:			
Finished Goods	$17,000		
Goods in Process	11,000		
Raw Materials	9,000	37,000	
Total Current Assets			$101,000

FIXED ASSETS:

Land		$10,000	
Factory Buildings	$70,000		
Less Reserve for Depreciation	15,500	54,500	
Machinery and Equipment	$60,000		
Less Reserve for Depreciation	21,000	39,000	
Furniture and Fixtures	$ 5,000		
Less Reserve for Depreciation	2,250	2,750	
Total Fixed Assets—Depreciated Value			106,250

DEFERRED CHARGES:

Unexpired Insurance			300
			$207,550

Liabilities and Net Worth

CURRENT LIABILITIES:

Accounts Payable	$ 22,800	
Accrued Salaries and Wages	1,275	
Total Current Liabilities		$ 24,075

NET WORTH:

Capital Stock	$100,000	
Surplus, per Exhibit B	83,475	
Total Net Worth		183,475
		$207,550

Closing the books.

There appear below the trial balance and end-of-year inventories from which the foregoing statements were prepared. The trial balance was taken after the posting of adjusting entries for deferred and accrued items and for bad debt and depreciation reserve provisions. For the sake of clarity, the account balances have been classified according to the statements in which they appear and have been arranged in the sequence in which they appear in these statements.

The journal entries to close the books of this manufacturing company are shown immediately after the trial balance.

Trial Balance

December 31, 1941

ACCOUNTS USED FOR STATEMENT OF COST OF
GOODS MANUFACTURED:

Raw Material Inventory—12/31/40.........	$ 12,000.00	
Purchases—Raw Material..................	94,000.00	
Returned Purchases and Allowances........		$ 1,500.00
Freight In...............................	800.00	
Direct Labor............................	80,750.00	
Indirect Labor...........................	9,125.00	
Heat, Light, and Power...................	3,500.00	
Building and Machinery Repairs...........	300.00	
Depreciation of Buildings.................	3,500.00	
Depreciation of Machinery and Equipment...	6,000.00	
Insurance...............................	950.00	
Taxes...................................	1,400.00	
Factory Supplies.........................	3,500.00	
Miscellaneous Factory Expense............	2,500.00	
Goods in Process Inventory—12/31/40......	15,000.00	

ACCOUNTS USED FOR STATEMENT OF PROFIT AND
LOSS:

Sales....................................		300,000.00
Returned Sales and Allowances............	2,000.00	
Finished Goods Inventory—12/31/40.......	20,000.00	
Advertising..............................	9,000.00	
Salesmen's Salaries.......................	20,360.00	
Salesmen's Traveling Expense.............	8,000.00	
Miscellaneous Selling Expense.............	2,500.00	
Office Salaries...........................	3,040.00	
Officers' Salaries........................	18,000.00	
Stationery and Printing...................	400.00	
Office Supplies...........................	300.00	
Depreciation of Furniture and Fixtures......	750.00	
Bad Debts...............................	800.00	
Miscellaneous General Expense............	700.00	
Discount on Sales........................	2,500.00	
Discount on Purchases....................		1,200.00
Totals forward...........................	$321,675.00	$302,700.00

Trial Balance—*Continued*

Totals brought forward......................	$321,675.00	$302,700.00
ACCOUNTS USED FOR STATEMENT OF SURPLUS:		
Surplus—12/31/40........................		71,450.00
Dividends...............................	6,000.00	
ACCOUNTS USED FOR BALANCE SHEET:		
Cash....................................	25,000.00	
Accounts Receivable......................	40,000.00	
Reserve for Bad Debts....................		1,000.00
Land....................................	10,000.00	
Factory Buildings........................	70,000.00	
Reserve for Depreciation—F. B............		15,500.00
Machinery and Equipment.................	60,000.00	
Reserve for Depreciation—M. & E..........		21,000.00
Furniture and Fixtures....................	5,000.00	
Reserve for Depreciation—F. & F..........		2,250.00
Unexpired Insurance......................	300.00	
Accounts Payable.........................		22,800.00
Accrued Salaries and Wages...............		1,275.00
Capital Stock............................		100,000.00
	$537,975.00	$537,975.00

Inventories, December 31, 1941:		
Finished Goods..............	$17,000.00	
Goods in Process.............	11,000.00	
Raw Materials...............	9,000.00	

Manufacturing account entries.

The accounts showing elements of manufacturing cost are closed to a Manufacturing account instead of to Profit and Loss. The following entries produce a balance in the Manufacturing account representing the cost of goods manufactured.

Goods in process at the beginning of the year:

Manufacturing Account..........................	15,000.00	
Goods in Process Inventory..................		15,000.00

To charge Manufacturing account with the cost of goods in process at the beginning of the year.

Materials used during the year:

Manufacturing Account..........................	12,000.00	
Raw Material Inventory.....................		12,000.00

To charge Manufacturing account with the cost of raw materials on hand at the beginning of the year.

Manufacturing Account..........................	94,800.00	
Purchases—Raw Material...................		94,000.00
Freight In................................		800.00

To close the Purchases and Freight accounts.

Returned Purchases and Allowances...............	1,500.00	
Manufacturing Account......................		1,500.00

To close the Returned Purchases and Allowances account.

Manufacturing Account

1941			1941		
Dec. 31	Goods in Process Inventory, Dec. 31, 1940	15,000 00	Dec. 31	Returned Purchases and Allowances	1,500 00
31	Raw Material Inventory, Dec. 31, 1940	12,000 00	31	Raw Material Inventory, Dec. 31, 1941	9,000 00
31	Raw Material Purchases	94,000 00	31	Goods in Process Inventory, Dec. 31, 1941	11,000 00
31	Freight In	800 00	31	Cost of Goods Mfd.—To Profit and Loss	211,825 00
31	Direct Labor	80,750 00			
31	Indirect Labor	9,125 00			
31	Heat, Light, and Power	3,500 00			
31	Building and Machinery Repairs	300 00			
31	Insurance	950 00			
31	Taxes	1,400 00			
31	Factory Supplies	3,500 00			
31	Miscellaneous Factory Expense	2,500 00			
31	Depreciation of Buildings	3,500 00			
31	Depreciation of Machinery and Equipment	6,000 00			
		233,325 00			233,325 00

Raw Material Inventory...................... 9,000.00
    Manufacturing Account....................   9,000.00
    To set up the inventory of raw materials at the end
    of the year.

Direct labor costs:

Manufacturing Account....................... 80,750.00
    Direct Labor............................   80,750.00
    To charge Manufacturing account with the cost
    of direct labor.

Manufacturing expenses:

Manufacturing Account....................... 30,775.00
    Indirect Labor...........................   9,125.00
    Heat, Light, and Power..................   3,500.00
    Building and Machinery Repairs...........   300.00
    Insurance...............................   950.00
    Taxes...................................   1,400.00
    Factory Supplies........................   3,500.00
    Miscellaneous Factory Expense............   2,500.00
    Depreciation of Buildings...............   3,500.00
    Depreciation of Machinery and Equipment..   6,000.00
    To close the manufacturing expense accounts.

Goods in process at end of period:

Goods in Process Inventory.................. 11,000.00
    Manufacturing Account...................   11,000.00
    To set up the goods in process inventory at the
    end of the year.

The balance in the Manufacturing account represents the cost of goods manufactured during the year; the account is closed by an entry shown on the following page, transferring its balance to Profit and Loss.

Profit and loss and surplus entries.

The remaining entries are similar to those with which the reader is already familiar in closing the books of a trading company.

Entries to credit Profit and Loss with net sales:

Sales....................................... 300,000.00
    Profit and Loss.........................   300,000.00
    To close the Sales account.

Profit and Loss............................. 2,000.00
    Returned Sales and Allowances............   2,000.00
    To close the Returned Sales and Allowances
    account.

Entries to debit Profit and Loss with the cost of goods sold:

Profit and Loss..............................	20,000.00	
Finished Goods Inventory..................		20,000.00
To charge Profit and Loss with the inventory of finished goods at the beginning of the year.		
Profit and Loss..............................	211,825.00	
Manufacturing Account...................		211,825.00
To close the Manufacturing account, and to charge Profit and Loss with the cost of goods manufactured during the year.		
Finished Goods Inventory.....................	17,000.00	
Profit and Loss...........................		17,000.00
To set up the inventory of finished goods at the end of the year.		

Entry for selling expenses:

Profit and Loss..............................	39,860.00	
Advertising...............................		9,000.00
Salesmen's Salaries........................		20,360.00
Salesmen's Traveling Expense...............		8,000.00
Miscellaneous Selling Expense.............		2,500.00
To close the selling expense accounts.		

Entry for general expenses:

Profit and Loss..............................	23,990.00	
Office Salaries............................		3,040.00
Officers' Salaries.........................		18,000.00
Stationery and Printing...................		400.00
Office Supplies............................		300.00
Miscellaneous General Expense.............		700.00
Bad Debts.................................		800.00
Depreciation of Furniture and Fixtures......		750.00
To close the general expense accounts.		

Entries for financial income and expense:

Discount on Purchases........................	1,200.00	
Profit and Loss...........................		1,200.00
To close.		
Profit and Loss..............................	2,500.00	
Discount on Sales........................		2,500.00
To close.		

Entries in Surplus:

Profit and Loss..............................	18,025.00	
Surplus...................................		18,025.00
To transfer the net income to Surplus.		
Surplus......................................	6,000.00	
Dividends.................................		6,000.00
To charge Surplus with dividends paid during the year.		

Profit and Loss

1941				1941			
Dec.	31	Returned Sales and Allowances..........	2,000 00	Dec.	31	Sales............	300,000 00
	31	Finished Goods Inventory, Dec. 31, 1940....	20,000 00		31	Finished Goods Inventory, Dec. 31, 1941....	17,000 00
	31	Cost of Goods Manufactured............	211,825 00		31	Discount on Purchases...........	1,200 00
	31	Advertising.................	9,000 00				
	31	Salesmen's Salaries.............	20,360 00				
	31	Salesmen's Traveling Expense...........	8,000 00				
	31	Miscellaneous Selling Expense...........	2,500 00				
	31	Office Salaries...............	3,040 00				
	31	Officers' Salaries.............	18,000 00				
	31	Stationery and Printing............	400 00				
	31	Office Supplies...............	300 00				
	31	Miscellaneous General Expense...........	700 00				
	31	Bad Debts................	800 00				
	31	Depreciation of Furniture and Fixtures....	750 00				
	31	Discount on Sales.............	2,500 00				
	31	Net Income—To Surplus.............	18,025 00				
			318,200 00				318,200 00

16

NUMERICAL CHART OF ACCOUNTS

Illustration.

Few companies now use bound ledgers. Most ledgers are kept on cards or in loose-leaf binders; each account is given a number, and the cards or sheets are kept in numerical order. It is customary to indicate the relationships of groups of accounts by a system of numbers similar to that illustrated below. Numbering systems differ, but the following chart of accounts illustrates the general principle.

Chart of Accounts

ssets and Related Reserves—1 to 99:

Current Assets—1 to 39:
  Cash assets—1 to 9:
    1 —Cash in Bank.
    3 —Cash on Hand.
  Receivables—10 to 19:
    10 —Accounts Receivable.
    10R—Reserve for Bad Debts.
    12 —Notes Receivable.
    15 —Accrued Interest Receivable.
  Inventories—20 to 29:
    21 —Finished Goods.
    23 —Goods in Process.
    25 —Materials.

Other Assets—40 to 49:
    41 —Investments in Bonds.
    42 —Investments in Stocks.

Fixed Assets—50 to 79:
    51 —Land.
    53 —Buildings.
    53R—Reserve for Depreciation—Buildings.
    55 —Machinery and Equipment.
    55R—Reserve for Depreciation—Machinery and Equipment.
    57 —Tools.
    57R—Reserve for Depreciation—Tools.
    61 —Delivery Equipment.

61R—Reserve for Depreciation—Delivery Equipment.
65 —Furniture and Fixtures.
65R—Reserve for Depreciation—Furniture and Fixtures.
70 —Patents.
70R—Reserve for Patent Expiration.
75 —Goodwill.

Deferred Charges—80 to 89:
81 —Unexpired Insurance.
82 —Prepaid Interest.
86 —Coal Inventory.
87 —Supplies Inventory.

LIABILITY AND DEFERRED CREDIT ACCOUNTS—100 to 199:

Current Liabilities—100 to 139:
101 —Vouchers Payable.
102 —Notes Payable.
111 —Accrued Payroll.
112 —Accrued Interest on Notes Payable.
113 —Accrued Taxes.
120 —Accrued Mortgage Interest.
130 —Dividends Payable—Common.
131 —Dividends Payable—Preferred.

Fixed Liabilities—150 to 179:
151 —Mortgage Payable.

Deferred Credits—180 to 199:
181 —Interest Collected in Advance.

NET WORTH ACCOUNTS—200 to 299:
201 —Capital Stock—Common.
202 —Capital Stock—Preferred.
211 —Surplus.
221 —Dividends.

MANUFACTURING ACCOUNTS—300 to 499:

Raw Materials—300 to 309:
301 —Purchases—Raw Materials.
303 —Freight In.
304 —Returned Purchases and Allowances.

Direct Labor—310 to 319:
311 —Direct Labor.

Manufacturing Expenses—400 to 499:
401 —Indirect Labor.
402 —Superintendence.
410 —Depreciation—Buildings.
411 —Depreciation—Machinery, Equipment, and Tools.
412 —Patent Expiration Expense.
420 —Factory Supplies.
430 —Insurance.
440 —Taxes.
450 —Factory Rent.
460 —Heat, Light, and Power.
481 —Repairs to Buildings.

482 —Repairs to Machinery and Equipment.
490 —Miscellaneous Factory Expense.

SALES ACCOUNTS—500 to 599:
501 —Sales.
502 —Returned Sales and Allowances.

SELLING EXPENSES—600 to 699:
601 —Salesmen's Salaries.
602 —Delivery Salaries.
603 —Commissions.
604 —Salesmen's Traveling Expense.
610 —Depreciation—Delivery Equipment.
662 —Freight Out.
663 —Delivery Expense.
665 —Freight on Returned Sales.
670 —Advertising.
690 —Miscellaneous Selling Expenses.

GENERAL EXPENSES—700 to 799:
701 —Office Salaries.
703 —Officers' Salaries.
710 —Depreciation—Furniture and Fixtures.
720 —Office Supplies.
721 —Stationery and Printing.
730 —Insurance.
740 —Taxes.
764 —Bad Debts.
771 —Postage.
773 —Collection and Exchange.
790 —Miscellaneous General Expense.

OTHER INCOME—800 to 849:
801 —Interest Income.
802 —Discount on Purchases.
803 —Delivery Income.

OTHER EXPENSES—850 to 899:
851 —Interest Expense.
852 —Discount on Sales.
860 —Mortgage Interest.

CLOSING ACCOUNTS—900 to 999:
901 —Manufacturing Account.
902 —Profit and Loss.

Use of account numbers instead of names.

The use of account numbers instead of account names saves space in the books of original entry, and saves time and effort in recording transactions.

The convenience of Account Number (instead of name) columns in the books of original entry is indicated below. The check registers previously illustrated had only three money columns, as shown in the register on the following page.

Check Register

Check No.	Date	Payee	Voucher No.	Debit Vouchers Payable	Credit	
					Discount on Purchases	Cash
1668	July|13	The Osborne Company.....	1693	140|00	1|40	13860

It is occasionally necessary, when paying vouchers, to debit or credit other accounts than those for which columns were provided in the foregoing check register. Therefore it is desirable to provide a Sundry Accounts debit column and a Sundry Accounts credit column in the check register. (Similar columns are also often desirable in other books of original entry.)

The illustration of the cash disbursements book on page 143 shows how such columns may be used. The facts recorded are:

Amount of voucher being paid................................. $400.00
Less cash discount.. 8.00
Net.. $392.00
Exchange charged by bank for a bank draft to be sent to the creditor .20
Amount of check issued to the bank in payment of the draft..... $392.20

The entry in the cash disbursements book contains the following debits and credits. The account numbers are those shown by the foregoing chart of accounts.

Debits:
   101—Vouchers Payable.................................... $400.00
   773—Collection and Exchange............................ .20
Credits:
   802—Discount on Purchases.............................. $ 8.00
     1—Cash.. 392.20

Controlling accounts.

In Chapter 8, "Controlling Accounts," it was stated that controlling accounts are introduced into the accounting system when the work becomes so heavy that it must be divided.

In a very large business the controlling account procedure may find extensive application. For instance, controlling accounts with various classes of expense can be kept in the general ledger, and the details can be kept in subsidiary records.

Referring to the foregoing chart of accounts, the general ledger might contain the following controlling accounts:

        400—Manufacturing Expense.
        600—Selling Expense.
        700—General Expense.

Cash Disbursements Book

Check No.	Date	Payee	Voucher No.	Debits				Credits				
				Vouchers Payable (101)	Sundry Accounts			Sundry Accounts			Discount on Purchases (802)	Cash (1)
					Acct. No.	✓	Amount	Acct. No.	✓	Amount		
357	Dec. 15	R. L. Peterson.........	348	400|00	773	✓	|20				8|00	392|20

(Purpose of columns headed ✓: A check mark is entered at the right of the account number after the amount is posted.)

143

The detailed accounts shown in the chart could be kept in a subsidiary ledger.

The subsidiary expense ledgers may be kept in the usual account form, or a columnar expense record may be kept in the following form:

Selling Expense Analysis Record

Date	Vo. No.	Ref.	601	602	604	610	662	663	670	690
1941										
July 3	4								200.00	
5	7						25.00			
7	13		100.00							
8	21						45.00			
9	28							50.00		
11	39				127.00					
15	46		250.00	200.00						
19	71		225.00							
23	82							240.00		
26	91						32.00			
28	99				138.00					
31	115		228.00	200.00						
31		J2				25.00				
	Total		803.00	400.00	265.00	25.00	102.00	290.00	200.00	

All of the entries in this subsidiary record came from the voucher register, except the last one, which is an entry for depreciation of delivery equipment; this last entry was posted from the journal. The "Ref." (reference) column is intended to show the source of all entries not posted from the voucher register.

Numbered statement forms.

Many companies have printed forms prepared for the periodical statements, so that the bookkeeper can prepare the statements by merely entering the ledger balances. These printed statements are usually not worth while if statements are prepared only once a year, but they may save a good deal of time and labor if statements are prepared monthly. Reference to the chart of accounts and the illustrations on pages 145 to 148 will show that the accounts have been arranged in the ledger in the order in which their balances appear in the statements. The statements are therefore much more easily prepared than they would be if the accounts were arranged in the ledger in, say, alphabetical order.

The notations at the left of the statements show the numbers of the accounts from which the amounts were obtained, or indicate

that the amounts shown in the statements were determined by
taking physical inventories (Inv.), or that they were brought over
from some other statement (Exhibit B, C, or D).

NAME OF COMPANY

Balance Sheets—1941

Exhibit A

ACCT. No.	Assets	JAN- UARY 31	FEB- RUARY 28	ETC.
	CURRENT ASSETS:			
	Cash:			
1	In Bank............................	$ 20,000.00		
3	On Hand...........................	1,000.00		
	Total...........................	$ 21,000.00		
	Receivables:			
10	Accounts Receivable..................	$ 25,000.00		
10R	Less Reserve for Bad Debts...........	1,000.00		
	Net...............................	$ 24,000.00		
12	Notes Receivable.....................	10,000.00		
15	Accrued Interest Receivable...........	50.00		
	Total............................	$ 34,050.00		
	Inventories:			
(Inv.)	Finished Goods.......................	$ 20,000.00		
(Inv.)	Goods in Process.....................	3,500.00		
(Inv.)	Raw Materials.......................	5,000.00		
	Total............................	$ 28,500.00		
	Total Current Assets.................	$ 83,550.00		
	FIXED ASSETS:			
51	Land.................................	$ 8,000.00		
53	Buildings............................	$ 50,000.00		
53R	Less Reserve for Depreciation..........	10,000.00		
	Depreciated Value....................	$ 40,000.00		
55	Machinery and Equipment...............	$ 35,000.00		
55R	Less Reserve for Depreciation..........	15,000.00		
	Depreciated Value....................	$ 20,000.00		
61	Delivery Equipment....................	$ 3,000.00		
61R	Less Reserve for Depreciation..........	500.00		
	Depreciated Value....................	$ 2,500.00		
65	Furniture and Fixtures.................	$ 3,050.00		
65R	Less Reserve for Depreciation..........	300.00		
	Depreciated Value....................	$ 2,750.00		
	Total Fixed Assets...................	$ 73,250.00		
	DEFERRED CHARGES:			
81	Unexpired Insurance....................	$ 300.00		
82	Prepaid Interest......................	25.00		
	Total Deferred Charges...............	$ 325.00		
		$157,125.00		

Balance Sheets—1941—*Continued*

Acct. No.	Liabilities and Net Worth	January 31	February 28	Etc.
	CURRENT LIABILITIES:			
101	Vouchers Payable..........................	$ 20,000.00		
102	Notes Payable............................	10,000.00		
111	Accrued Payroll..........................	375.00		
112	Accrued Interest Payable.................	60.00		
113	Accrued Taxes...........................	150.00		
	Total Current Liabilities..............	$ 30,585.00		
	FIXED LIABILITIES:			
151	Mortgage Payable.......................	$ 25,000.00		
	Total Liabilities.....................	$ 55,585.00		
	DEFERRED CREDITS:			
181	Interest Collected in Advance............	$ 15.00		
183	Delivery Income Collected in Advance.....	100.00		
	Total Deferred Credits...............	$ 115.00		
	NET WORTH:			
201	Capital Stock...........................	$ 75,000.00		
Ex. B	Surplus................................	26,425.00		
	Total Net Worth..................	$101,425.00		
		$157,125.00		

NAME OF COMPANY   Exhibit B

Statements of Surplus—1941

Acct. No.		January	February Etc.
211	Balance, Beginning of Period..............	$ 23,985.00	
Ex. C	Net Income............................	3,190.00	
	Total.............................	$ 27,175.00	
221	Dividends.............................	750.00	
	Balance, End of Period..................	$ 26,425.00	

NAME OF COMPANY   Exhibit C

Statements of Profit and Loss—1941

Acct. No.		January	February Etc.
501	Sales....................................	$125,000.00	
502	Deduct Returned Sales and Allowances.......	1,500.00	
	Net Sales...............................	$123,500.00	
	Deduct Cost of Goods Sold:		
21	Finished Goods Inventory, Beginning......	$ 19,000.00	
Ex. D	Cost of Goods Manufactured..............	71,675.00	
	Total.................................	$ 90,675.00	
(Inv.)	Deduct Finished Goods Inventory, End of Period...............................	20,000.00	
	Cost of Goods Sold.................	$ 70,675.00	
	Gross Profit on Sales (Forward)............	$ 52,825.00	

Statements of Profit and Loss—1941—*Continued*

CCT. No.		JANUARY	FEBRUARY
	Gross Profit on Sales (Brought forward)......	$ 52,825.00	
	Deduct Selling Expenses:		
601	Salesmen's Salaries......................	$ 15,000.00	
602	Delivery Salaries........................	5,000.00	
604	Salesmen's Traveling Expense............	4,000.00	
610	Depreciation—Delivery Equipment........	50.00	
662	Freight Out............................	2,600.00	
663	Delivery Expense.......................	2,750.00	
670	Advertising............................	6,000.00	
	Total Selling Expenses...............	$ 35,400.00	
	Net Profit on Sales.......................	$ 17,425.00	
	Deduct General Expenses:		
701	Office Salaries.........................	$ 1,300.00	
703	Officers' Salaries.......................	11,800.00	
710	Depreciation—Furniture and Fixtures......	50.00	
720	Office Supplies.........................	300.00	
721	Stationery and Printing.................	125.00	
730	Insurance..............................	35.00	
764	Bad Debts.............................	1,250.00	
790	Miscellaneous General Expense...........	1,635.00	
	Total General Expenses...............	$ 16,495.00	
	Net Profit on Operations..................	$ 930.00	
	Add Other Income:		
801	Interest Income........................	60.00	
802	Discount on Purchases..................	3,225.00	
803	Delivery Income........................	100.00	
	Net Profit and Other Income...............	$ 4,315.00	
	Deduct Other Expenses:		
851	Interest Expense.......................	$ 115.00	
852	Discount on Sales......................	1,010.00	
	Total Other Expenses...............	$ 1,125.00	
	Net Income.............................	$ 3,190.00	

NAME OF COMPANY   Exhibit D

Statements of Cost of Goods Manufactured—1941

CCT. No.		JANUARY	FEBRUARY ETC.
	Materials:		
25	Inventory, Beginning....................	$ 7,000.00	
301	Purchases..............................	30,000.00	
303	Freight In.............................	1,200.00	
	Total................................	$38,200.00	
304	Deduct: Returned Purchases..............	$ 800.00	
nv.)	Inventory, End of Period.........	5,000.00	
	Total Deductions................	$ 5,800.00	
	Materials Used......................	$32,400.00	
311	Direct Labor............................	$26,000.00	
	Total Materials and Direct Labor (Forward)...	$58,400.00	

Statements of Cost of Goods Manufactured—1941—*Continued*

ACCT.
No.   JANUARY   FEBRUARY

Total Materials and Direct Labor............. $58,400.00

Manufacturing Expenses:
401	Indirect Labor...........................	$ 6,500.00
402	Superintendence.........................	1,200.00
410	Depreciation—Buildings..................	200.00
411	Depreciation—Machinery, Equipment, and Tools...................................	300.00
420	Factory Supplies.........................	850.00
430	Insurance...............................	325.00
440	Taxes...................................	250.00
460	Heat, Light, and Power..................	2,000.00
490	Miscellaneous Factory Expense............	1,350.00
	Total Manufacturing Expenses........	$12,975.00
	Total.............................	$71,375.00
23	Add Goods in Process, Beginning.............	3,800.00
	Total.............................	$75,175.00
(Inv.)	Deduct Goods in Process, End of Period.......	3,500.00
	Cost of Goods Manufactured	$71,675.00

17

OPERATING PROFITS

....

Accounting for operating profits.

The profit and loss statement is intended to show the operating profit or loss for a stated period of time. The profit and loss statement is almost never a statement of absolute fact; usually it is only an expression of the opinion of one or more persons, because, in the preparation of the statement, it is necessary to make many estimates, such as the proper valuation of the inventory and the provisions to be made for bad debts, depreciation, and other losses. Since these estimates are largely matters of opinion, and since opinions may honestly differ, conditions often arise in which widely different statements of profits may be defended by different individuals. In such instances of doubt it is conservative to make estimates that, if wrong, err on the side of understating the profits rather than overstating them. If the estimates are later found to be wrong, the stockholders will be pleasantly surprised rather than disappointed, and the creditors will have no reason to claim that they have been injured.

On the other hand, ultra-conservatism understates the book value of the net assets and the earnings of the company; such understatements may depress the value of the company's securities and possibly work an injustice upon their holders.

Thus we find that the accountant is obliged to sail a careful course between the Scylla of inflated profits and the Charybdis of overconservatism, and at many points in the course he must steer according to his opinion. His opinions, however, should be determined by certain established rules which are known as accounting principles. The following are among the most important of these rules:

(1) Distinguish between operating and extraneous profits.
(2) Take up income and expense in the proper period.
(3) Distinguish between profits and savings.

(4) Distinguish between capital and revenue expenditures.
(5) Value all assets as correctly as possible.
(6) Anticipate no profit and provide for all losses.
(7) Avoid unwarranted conservatism.
(8) Maintain, in successive periods, a consistency in the bases of computing profits.

Distinguish between operating and extraneous profits.

Operating profits are made by sales of the commodity in which the business deals; extraneous profits are made by sales of assets not regularly dealt in by the business. Profits on sales of merchandise are operating profits; profits on sales of buildings, equipment, and securities are extraneous profits unless the business deals regularly in these commodities.

When the books are closed and the statements are prepared at the end of the period, operating profits and losses should be clearly distinguished from extraneous profits and losses. Operating items should be closed to the Profit and Loss account and shown in the profit and loss statement; extraneous items should be closed directly to Surplus and shown in the surplus statement. This distinction should be maintained in order that the Profit and Loss account and statement will show the results of regular operations, unaffected by unusual and extraordinary transactions extraneous to operations.

The following illustration may perhaps make the reason for this distinction better understood:

	This Year	Last Year
Net profit from regular operations	$ 40,000.00	$50,000.00
Profit from sale of factory	100,000.00	
Total	$140,000.00	$50,000.00

If the company reported that it made a profit of $140,000.00 this year and $50,000.00 last year, the statement would be true but misleading. It would suggest an expansion of business wholly at variance with the facts. The company's profit and loss statements should show a profit of $40,000.00 this year and a profit of $50,000.00 last year, both resulting from regular operations. And its surplus statement should show that this year it also made an extraneous profit of $100,000.00 from the sale of fixed assets.

The same rule also holds with respect to extraneous losses; they should be shown in the surplus statement rather than in the profit and loss statement. But this very proper rule is subject to abuse. A concern desiring to show a good operating income may omit many losses and expenses from its profit and loss statement, charge them directly to Surplus, and insist that they are extraneous items. There are many border-line situations. For instance, assume that a department was closed during the year, and that severe losses were incurred in the disposition of its inventories. Does the fact that this department's operations were a part of the regular operations in the past require the loss from liquidation of the department to be charged to Profit and Loss? Or do the department's operations become extraneous when the decision to discontinue is reached? These questions are not answered here; the reader's attention is merely called to the fact that, because such conditions may be taken advantage of in an attempt to make a good statement of operating income, no one should rely on the profit and loss statement alone in determining the total profit or loss of a company during a stated period; the surplus statement should also be examined.

Although accountants understand this distinction between operating profits and losses, shown in the profit and loss statement, and extraneous profits and losses, shown in the surplus statement, there is a danger that the public may not be familiar with the distinction and may think that the profit and loss statement tells the whole story and fail to refer also to the surplus statement. For this reason there has recently been some tendency to combine the two statements, and to show extraneous profits and losses, as well as other surplus adjustments, below the net operating income, in some form similar to the following illustration.

THE *A* COMPANY

Statement of Profit and Loss and Surplus

For the Year Ended December 31, 1941

Sales		$100,000.00
Deduct Cost of Goods Sold		70,000.00
Gross Profit on Sales		$ 30,000.00
Deduct Expenses		20,000.00
Net Income		$ 10,000.00
Add Profit on Sale of Abandoned Plant		15,000.00
Total		$ 25,000.00
Deduct:		
Additional Assessment of Income Tax—1939	$1,500.00	
Fire Loss	4,000.00	5,500.00
Increase in Surplus, before Dividends		$ 19,500.00
Deduct Dividends Paid		5,000.00
Increase in Surplus		$ 14,500.00
Surplus, December 31, 1940		25,000.00
Surplus, December 31, 1941		$ 39,500.00

Take up income and expense in the proper period.

Since the profit and loss statement purports to show the net income from operations *during a stated period of time*, it should:

(1) Include all income applicable to the period; therefore:
   (a) Adjustments should be made to take up income that has accrued but has not been entered in the accounts because it has not been collected.
   (b) If goods have been sold but not delivered, the sale should be recorded and the profit taken, provided that title has passed to the purchaser. The goods remain in the vendor's possession, but they are held by him as a bailee.
(2) Include all expenses applicable to the period; therefore:
   (a) Adjustments should be made to take up expenses that have accrued but have not been entered in the accounts.
   (b) All purchases made and expenses incurred prior to the close of the period should be included, even though the invoices may not be received until some time after the close of the period.
(3) Exclude income applicable to a future or prior period.
   (a) Income collected in advance is applicable to a future period and should be deferred by setting up a deferred credit account.
   (b) Income applicable to a prior period but which was overlooked when the profit and loss statement for that period was prepared, should not be included in the profit and loss statement for the current period because the income for the current period would thus be overstated. It should be credited to Surplus, as a correction of the profits of the prior period.
(4) Exclude expenses applicable to another period.
   (a) Prepaid expenses should be deferred to a future period.
   (b) Expenses overlooked in preparing the profit and loss statement of a prior period should be charged to Surplus and not included in the profit and loss statement of the current period.

If any operating transaction applicable to the period is omitted from the books, and gains or losses are thereby ignored, it is evident that the operating profits will be incorrectly stated—so evident, in fact, that the point may scarcely be worth mentioning. But there are two reasons why attention should be called to this fact.

The first reason is that the point is often overlooked. Expenses are not entered in the books because they have not been paid; income is not entered because it has not been collected; purchases are not recorded because time is required to pass the invoices through the office routine, and they do not come through for vouching until the beginning of the next period.

A second reason is that some doubt oftentimes exists concerning the period to which the transaction properly belongs.

Distinguish between profits and savings.

A saving, but not a profit, results from manufacturing a thing at a price less than that at which it could be purchased. Companies sometimes construct their own fixed assets, and when this is done at a cost lower than the price at which they could be purchased, there is often an inclination to value the fixed assets at a theoretical purchase price and to take up a so-called profit. There is a subtle semblance of fairness in such a procedure; why should a company utilize its manufacturing facilities to make fixed assets for its own use and thus forego the opportunity of manufacturing merchandise that could be sold at a profit? The answer is that, even if the manufacture of fixed assets curtailed the manufacture of salable merchandise (which is unlikely), the profit and loss statement must show what really happened instead of what might have happened. The manufacture of the fixed assets may increase future profits by reducing the depreciation charges, but a present saving with a prospect of increased future profits must not be taken as a present, realized profit.

Distinguish between capital and revenue expenditures.

An expenditure is the payment, or the assumption of an obligation to make a future payment, for a benefit received. There are two classes of expenditures, known as capital expenditures and revenue expenditures. Capital expenditures result in benefits of a permanent nature, such as land, buildings, and machinery; such expenditures should be capitalized by charges to asset accounts. Revenue expenditures are in the nature of expenses, and should be charged to expense accounts.

If the bookkeeping records are to furnish an accurate record of profits and of assets, liabilities, and capital, it is essential that a careful distinction be made between these two classes of expenditures.   If a machine is purchased, a capital expenditure is made; it must not be charged to an expense account, or the assets will be undervalued and the profits understated.   On the other hand, if the machine is repaired, a revenue expenditure is made; the expenditure must not be capitalized by being charged to an asset account, or the assets will be overvalued and the profits overstated.

It is not always easy to distinguish between capital and revenue expenditures, and so many principles are involved that a complete discussion must be postponed until later chapters.   Just now the point of interest is that the distinction must be made in accordance with sound principles of accounting, or the profits will be incorrectly stated.

Value all assets as correctly as possible.

So many questions are involved in the correct valuation of assets that several chapters are devoted to this subject.   At this point it is desired merely to state the following general principles:

(1) *Current assets.*   Adequate reserves should be provided for losses on receivables, and the inventories should be valued at the lower of cost or market.   Any losses taken on current assets in compliance with these requirements of good accounting should be charged against current operations.

(2) *Investments.*   Temporary investments in stocks and bonds should be valued at the lower of cost or market, and any losses thus taken up should be charged against current operations. Minor fluctuations in the market value of permanent investments may be ignored, because realization at current values is not contemplated; but material decreases in market values of permanent investments should be provided for by the establishment of a reserve; the reserve may be created by a charge to Surplus rather than to Profit and Loss, to distinguish such losses from those resulting from regular operations.

(3) *Fixed assets.*   Operations should be charged with depreciation, depletion, and amortization applicable to fixed assets; upward or downward fluctuations in the market value of fixed assets may be ignored.

Anticipate no profit and provide for all losses.

This all-inclusive rule of conservatism should govern the accountant in all matters pertaining to the determination of profits.

The requirement that profits shall not be anticipated may be expressed thus: do not credit operations with any unrealized profits. Profits are realized by sales or exchanges in which the value received is greater than the cost (or book value) of the thing parted with. It is not necessary that the profit be realized in cash; profits are regarded as realized if cash or property is received in the transaction, or if the transaction creates a valid claim against a solvent debtor. Profits and income may be anticipated in many ways, a few of which are mentioned below:

By valuing inventories in excess of cost.

By taking up profits on consignments, on shipments to branches, or on transfers of merchandise from one department to another.

By writing up fixed assets or investments with offsetting credits to Profit and Loss.

By failing to defer income collected in advance.

The admonition to "provide for all losses" is to some extent a rhetorical exaggeration and needs some clarification. It is not necessary to provide for *all* losses. For instance, there is no obligation to record a decrease in the market value of fixed assets. Fixed assets are not intended for sale; they are intended for use, and declines in market value presumably do not affect their usefulness.   Or, assume that a company is a defendant in a law suit; the contingency of an adverse decision may be too remote to justify an immediate charge for any loss.

Also it should be remembered that some losses should be charged to Surplus and not against current operations; these include losses which should have been charged to operations in a prior period but were overlooked, and extraneous (i. e., non-operating) losses.

The rule to provide for losses may, therefore, be modified as follows: Some losses should be provided for by charges to operations; some losses should be provided for by charges to Surplus; and some possible losses, because of the remote probability of realization, may be ignored.

Avoid unwarranted conservatism.

A plea of conservatism will not justify an understatement of income that results in an evasion of income taxes. Moreover, the understatement of income may be prejudicial to the interests of stockholders or of the holders of other securities who, believing that the company is less prosperous than it really is, may sell their holdings for less than they are really worth.

Ultra-conservatism produces secret reserves. To illustrate, let us assume that a company's inventory is worth $100,000.00, but that it is valued at only $75,000.00. The profits for the year are understated $25,000.00, and the assets and net worth are similarly understated in the balance sheet. This understatement may be known only to the directors or officials who authorized the write-down.

Or, assume that forty years would be a fair estimate of the life of a company's buildings. A $2\frac{1}{2}\%$ depreciation rate would, therefore, be adequate. If the company provides depreciation at 5% per annum, the profits are understated each year, and the assets and net worth are also understated. A secret reserve is thus created. Although it is true that the depreciation reserve is shown on the balance sheet, the fact that the reserve is excessive may be known only to those in intimate control of the business.

In one sense secret reserves are a source of strength to a company, because, in the event of unusual or excessive losses, the surplus can be protected. That is to say, after the loss has been charged off, an entry can be made restoring an understated asset to a fair value, with an offsetting credit to Surplus. But it is a serious ethical question whether directors have any right to create secret reserves when the understatement of the company's profits and net worth may cause uninformed stockholders to dispose of their holdings at prices lower than they would accept if the profits and net worth were correctly stated.

Maintain consistency.

There are some alternative procedures to which accounting authorities give equal, or essentially equal, sanction.

For instance, there are the so-called "cash" and "accrual" bases of accounting. Under the cash basis all consideration of accrued and deferred expense and income may be ignored; under the accrual basis adjustments are made for all such matters. Although each basis is acceptable, a change from one basis to another may materially affect the statement of operations of the period in which the change is made.

The rule for inventory valuation regarded as most conservative is "cost or market, whichever is lower." But valuation at cost is sometimes also recognized as acceptable. If the inventory at the end of a given year has a value of $100,000.00 at cost and

$90,000.00 at market, it is obvious that a change from the cost or market basis to the cost basis of inventory valuation for profit and loss statement purposes, will cause an addition of $10,000.00 to the profits.

A change from one accepted basis to another accepted basis should never be made merely for the purpose of affecting the profit or loss. If a change is made for some legitimate reason, the amount of the effect should be determined, if possible, and stated in a footnote or comment on the profit and loss statement.

Changes are sometimes made from an acceptable to an unacceptable or less acceptable basis (or vice versa) for no other reason than to increase or decrease the stated profits. For instance, inventories may be deliberately undervalued or overvalued, provisions for depreciation and bad debts may be increased or decreased, and expenditures for advertising may be unjustifiably carried forward as deferred charges.

For the reasons indicated in the preceding paragraphs, it is becoming increasingly the custom for accountants to include in the opinion (certificate) of their audit reports words similar to the following: "In accordance with accepted principles of accounting consistently maintained during the current and the prior year. . . ."

Let the chips fly where they will.

Human nature being what it is, one should not be surprised to find that business management often injects an artificial control over the amount of profit shown in the income statement.

Such control may be exercised with the deliberate purpose of increasing or decreasing the stated profit. Inventory valuations may be fixed with the desired net income figure in mind—not necessarily by falsification of quantities or the use of obviously incorrect prices, but by devices which can be more readily concealed or defended because they are matters of opinion, such as the cost accounting methods to be used, or the market prices to apply (the market may be unstable, or quotations applicable to the inventory quantities may not be available), or the amount of the deduction which should be made for obsolete merchandise. Or the amounts charged to operations and credited to reserves for depreciation, for bad debts, and for other losses and contingencies may be determined, not with an eye single to the reserve requirements, but with a major thought to the effect of the charges on the final figure in the profit and loss statement. Or there may be manipulation of the balances carried forward as deferred charges and deferred credits. Or there may be items of income and expense of a nature close enough to the border line between operating and extraneous operations to provide an arguable choice of classification. Or losses properly chargeable against income may be charged to reserves not provided for such losses, or to reserves set up out of surplus.

Such control may also be exercised with a belief in the desirability of stabilizing the reported periodical earnings and leveling, to some extent at least, the peaks and valleys incident to business activity. If the volume of business has been low, reduce the charge for depreciation and defend the procedure on the ground that the plant has been relatively inactive and, therefore, that relatively less depreciation has been suffered. Or adopt a standard cost system, price the goods sold and the inventory at the standard cost, and carry forward as a deferred charge any excess of actual costs over the standards. If the capital stock is closely held, reduce the salaries paid to stockholding officers; the difference can be made up in additional dividends.

Stabilizing procedures are frequently applied, not with the deliberate purpose of changing an unsatisfactory showing, but with a sincere belief that such procedures are proper and in conformity with good accounting principles. For instance, businesses are subject to fire, casualty, and other insurable hazards. If insurance is carried, the premiums are proper operating expense charges. But some businesses believe that, because of geographical distribution or other reasons, the losses will be less than the premium costs, and they therefore adopt a so-called self-insurance procedure by setting up reserves against which losses can be charged if and when they occur. It certainly cannot be said that there is anything improper in a company assuming its own risks; of course, it is not "self-insurance" nor insurance of any kind; it is merely taking chances, but experience has convinced many companies that the chances are in their favor. The question of impropriety arises only from the periodical charge to operations and the subsequent charging of a loss to the reserve. These produce a stabilized appearance which is contrary to the facts. The periodical charge to operations (for the amounts credited to the reserve) is defended on the ground that there would be a similar charge if insurance were purchased, and that the company's accounts should be on a comparable basis with other companies that do carry insurance; the answer seems to be that, since there is a difference in operating procedure, the accounts should be kept in such a way as to disclose the difference instead of concealing it, and that no charge to Profit and Loss is justified unless and until a loss is incurred. Making a periodical operating charge for a theoretical premium not paid, and charging an incurred loss to a reserve, produces a stabilized appearance at variance with the facts; some periods suffer charges when there are no losses, and other periods are relieved of charges for losses that do occur.

Growing emphasis on the profit and loss statement.

For many years the balance sheet was regarded as the statement of major importance for purposes of investigation of a company's affairs and the profit and loss statement was given less consideration. The importance of the profit and loss statement is now being more fully recognized. This increasing emphasis on the profit and loss statement imposes on accountants a further responsibility to adhere to proper accounting principles and procedures. The decision as to the treatment of some debatable matter may have relatively little effect on the balance sheet but a relatively important effect on the profit and loss statement. Assume that a company's balance sheet shows a working capital of $100,000.00, a net worth of $150,000.00, and deferred charges of $10,000.00, and that its profit and loss statement shows a net profit of $4,000.00; an addition of $5,000.00 to the deferred charges would have no effect on the working capital and would cause only a small per cent of overstatement of net worth, but the increase in the stated profit from $4,000.00 to $9,000.00 would be a major distortion.

The increasing reliance of credit analysts, investors, and others upon the profit and loss statement increases the accountant's responsibility not only with respect to matters which can be denounced as deliberate misrepresentations but also with respect to matters which can be more or less plausibly defended as questions of judgment, and with respect to stabilizing procedures which tend to conceal existing fluctuations in operations.

Cum grano salis.

After having stated several rules for the guidance of accountants in the preparation of profit and loss statements (and incidentally of the related balance sheets), perhaps one rule should be given to the reader of the statements: Take them with a grain of salt.

In the first place, you must remember that they are, to a very considerable extent, matters of opinion based on estimates. Inventories, depreciation and bad debt reserve provisions, and the propriety of deferring expense and income items, are often matters impossible of exact determination. Two equally able and equally honest accountants may differ widely with respect to them and the resultant net profit.

Second, some men are liars.

18

CORPORATE NET WORTH–CAPITAL STOCK

....

Elements of net worth.

The net worth of a corporation, as shown by its balance sheet, may consist of the following elements:

> Capital stock.
> Surplus.
> Capital surplus.
> Reserves for unrealized profits.

In this chapter we shall consider some matters relative to the nature of capital stock and the proper methods of accounting for it.

Stock certificates.

Investments in the capital stock of a corporation are evidenced by stock certificates. Blank stock certificates are bound in books with stubs, like check books. The stock certificate shown on page 162, which is still attached to its stub, has been filled out for issuance to George Tuttle, as evidence of his investment of $800.00 in The Marquis Corporation.

The certificate has been signed by the secretary and the president of the corporation, and is ready to be detached, stamped with the corporation's seal, and given to Tuttle. The stub, which will remain in the certificate book, shows the essential facts about the certificate.

The important facts shown by the certificate and the stub are:

	Shown by Certificate	Shown by Stub
Certificate number	3	3
Number of shares.....................	8	8
Authorized capital...................	$5,000.00	
Number of authorized shares..........	50	
Par value per share...................	$100.00	
Issued to............................	George Tuttle	George Tuttle
Name of corporation..................	The Marquis Corporation	
Date of issuance of certificate..........	July 1, 1941	July 1, 1941

Certificate No. 3   8   Shares

CAPITAL STOCK $5,000.00
50 Shares of $100.00 Par Value

THIS CERTIFIES That   George Tuttle   is the

owner of   Eight   Shares of the Capital Stock of

THE MARQUIS CORPORATION

transferable only on the books of the Corporation by the holder hereof in person or by attorney upon the surrender of this Certificate properly endorsed.

IN WITNESS WHEREOF, the said Corporation has caused this Certificate to be signed by its duly authorized officers, and to be sealed with the seal of the Corporation at Chicago, Illinois this 1st day of   July   , 1941

F. K. Patterson
Secretary

J. E. White
President

Certificate No. 3

For   8   Shares

Issued to

George Tuttle

Transferred from

Original

Date _____ 19___

Original Certificate No.	Number of Original Shares	Number of Shares. Transferred

Received Certificate No. 3

For   8   Shares

this 1st day of July, 1941

George Tuttle

Stock Certificate with Stub

162

Stock certificate stubs do not always contain the receipt form shown at the bottom of the stub in the illustration.

The use of the blank spaces under the words *Transferred from* will be explained in the next section.

Transfer of shares.

One of the advantages of the corporate form of business organization is that each stockholder has a right to transfer all or a portion of his interest in the capital stock. Suppose, for instance, that Tuttle wishes to sell two shares of his stock to Henry Reid. Tuttle fills in the endorsement form which is printed on the back of the certificate, as follows:

For Value Received,_____ I _____hereby sell,

transfer and assign to_____ Henry Reid _____

- - - - - - - - - - - Two - - - - - - - - - - - -

Shares of stock within mentioned and hereby authorize

_____ F. K. Patterson _____

to make the necessary transfer on the books of the Corporation.

WITNESS my hand and seal this__3rd__day of

_____August,_____, 19_41_

Witnessed by:

F. C. Finch   George Tuttle (Seal)

Endorsement Form on Back of Certificate

When the stock certificate is presented to the corporation for transfer of the stock, the certificate is canceled and attached to the stub from which it was originally taken. The open stubs (stubs to which no unissued or canceled certificates are attached) indicate the certificates still outstanding.

In accordance with the terms of Tuttle's endorsement, two new certificates are issued: one certificate to Henry Reid for the two shares which Tuttle sold to him, and another certificate to Tuttle for the six shares which he retained. The following is the stub of the new certificate issued to Reid; the stub of the certificate for six shares issued to Tuttle would be similarly filled in.

Certificate No. 5

For 2 Shares

Issued to

Henry Reid

Transferred from

George Tuttle

Date August 3, 1941

Original Certificate No.	Number of Original Shares	Number of Shares Transferred

Received Certificate No. 5

For 2 Shares

this 3rd day of Aug. 1941

Henry Reid

Stub

Rights inherent in stock.

Subject to the modifications discussed hereafter, the ownership of a share of stock confers the following rights upon its owner:

(1) The right to subscribe to additional shares of the same stock.

(2) The right to share in the management by voting at the stockholders' meetings.

(3) The right to share in the profits.

(4) The right to share in the distribution of the assets of the corporation in the event of its dissolution and liquidation.

If a corporation has only one class of stock, the four above-mentioned rights are enjoyed proportionately, share and share alike, by all stockholders. However, the pre-emptive right to subscribe to additional shares may be restricted or entirely eliminated, particularly with respect to non-voting stock. Different classes of stock are created by differences in the rights to vote, to share in the profits, or to share in the assets in liquidation.

Preferred stock.

Stock which is preferred as to dividends gives its holders certain special rights with respect to profits—usually the right to receive dividends at a certain rate (or of a stipulated amount, in the case of no-par stock) before any dividends are paid on the common stock. Preferred dividends should not be understood to be guaranteed dividends, however, because the payment of dividends on preferred stock as well as on common stock depends, first, on the earning of profits, and, second, on the declaration of dividends by the directors. The holders of stock which is preferred as to dividends may receive no dividends because the corporation has no surplus or because the directors have withheld the dividends on the ground that the funds are needed in the business.

The special preference right to receive a dividend before one is paid to the common stockholders may be non-cumulative or cumulative. In the latter case, unpaid dividends for any period become a claim against profits and surplus in future periods, and all preferred dividends in arrears must be paid before any dividends can be paid on the common stock.

Stock which is preferred as to assets entitles its holders to payment in liquidation before any payments are made to the common stockholders. This preference extends only to the par of the stock unless some larger liquidation value is specified. Dividends in arrears ordinarily are not payable at liquidation unless the stock is cumulative and a surplus exists sufficient to cover the dividends in arrears.

The preferred stockholders' right to vote has frequently been abridged or eliminated; in some states it cannot legally be withheld.

Giving one class of stock a special preference with respect to one of the fundamental rights does not inferentially give it any preference with respect to the other fundamental rights. Thus, stock which is preferred as to dividends is not also preferred as to assets unless that right has been specifically conferred upon it.

Also, a class of stock which has been given a special right continues to enjoy the four basic rights unless some right is removed. However, there is some difference of opinion as to whether stock which is preferred as to dividends without being specifically stated to be participating still retains the right to participate with the common stock in dividends above the preference rate.

One must not jump to the conclusion that preferred stock is common stock plus certain rights. It may be common stock plus certain rights and minus others. It is necessary to read the charter stipulations printed on the certificate, and it may be necessary to refer to the charter itself. In examining the charter provisions to determine the rights of the stock, one should start with the assumption that the stock entitles the holder to the four basic rights mentioned, and correct this assumption by adding the special rights specifically mentioned, and by eliminating those basic rights which are specifically withdrawn.

For instance, if the stock is indicated to be 6% cumulative non-voting preferred, the analysis of its rights will be as follows:

(1) Right to subscribe to new stock:
No restriction.
(2) Right to share in the management:
Specifically withdrawn.
(3) Right to share in the profits:
Special right to receive 6% cumulative dividends before any dividends are paid on the common.
No specific restriction of the basic right to share proportionately in all dividends.
(4) Right to assets in liquidation:
No special right given; hence, the common and preferred are entitled to share ratably.

Stock designated by letters.

Companies issuing more than one class of stock frequently use letters to designate the various classes—as Class A, Class B, and Class C stock. One of these classes must necessarily be common stock; the others enjoy some special privilege, or are subject to some curtailment, with respect to one or more of the basic rights: to share in the management, in the profits, in additional stock issues, and in the distribution of assets in liquidation.

Letters have no inherent significance whatever. The designation of a stock issue by a letter necessitates the determination of the rights appertaining to the stock by reference to the stock certificate or possibly to the charter.

Capital stock in the balance sheet.

The balance sheet should indicate the par value of the stock (or state that it is without par value) and should present information with respect to the amounts of stock authorized, unissued (if any), and outstanding. Some illustrations of adequate balance sheet presentation are given below:

NET WORTH:
    Capital Stock—$100.00 par value; Authorized and outstanding, 1,000 shares................................ $100,000.00

If some of the shares have not been issued, the condition may be shown as follows:

NET WORTH:
    Capital Stock—$100.00 par value:
      Authorized,   1,000 shares................ $100,000.00
      Unissued,   250 shares................ 25,000.00
      Outstanding, 750 shares............................ $75,000.00

A somewhat more modern method of presenting the same facts is illustrated below:

NET WORTH:
    Capital Stock—$100.00 par value; Authorized, 1,000 shares;
      unissued, 250 shares; outstanding, 750 shares........... $75,000.00

If there is more than one class of stock, complete data should be shown with respect to each class.

NET WORTH:
    Capital Stock—$100.00 par value:
      Preferred—6% cumulative, participating; authorized, 1,000
        shares; outstanding, 500 shares........................ $ 50,000
      Common—authorized, 2,000 shares; outstanding, 1,250 shares   125,000

Uncollected subscriptions.

Let us assume the following facts with respect to a corporation's stock issue:

    Only one class of stock.
    Par value per share, $100.00.
    Shares authorized, 1,000.
    Shares subscribed, 1,000.
    Shares for which subscriptions have been fully collected, 600.
    Uncollected subscriptions, $25.00 per share on 400 shares.

Let us also assume that 1,000 shares have been issued, although (as indicated above) 400 of them have not been fully paid for by the subscribers. The balance sheet may be drawn up as follows:

Balance Sheet
Assets

Cash..	$ 90,000	
Subscriptions to Stock......................................	10,000	
	$100,000	

Net Worth

Capital Stock—$100.00 par value:
Authorized—1,000 shares.

Issued—600 shares..............................	$60,000	
Subscribed—400 shares..........................	40,000	$100,000
		$100,000

Showing the uncollected subscriptions as an asset is permissible if it is presumed that they are to be collected. (Of course they should be shown separately from ordinary accounts receivable.) However, if there appears to be no intention to require the stockholders to pay in the balance of their subscriptions, the uncollected balances should be deducted on the right side of the balance sheet, to determine the true net worth, thus:

Balance Sheet
Assets

Cash...	$90,000
	$90,000

Net Worth

Capital Stock—$100.00 par value:
Authorized—1,000 shares.

Issued—600 shares..............................		$60,000	
Subscribed—400 shares....................	$40,000		
Less Uncollected Subscriptions..............	10,000	30,000	$90,000
			$90,000

Stock premium and discount.

Assume that all of the stock of a company, of a par value of $50,000.00, is issued at 110. The facts could be shown in the balance sheet as follows:

Balance Sheet

Cash.......................	$55,000	NET WORTH:	
		Capital Stock—$100.00 par value; Authorized and issued, 500 shares.........	$50,000
		Premium on Stock..........	5,000
	$55,000		$55,000

On the other hand, assume that stock of a par value of $50,000.00 is issued at a discount of $5,000.00. One sometimes sees a balance sheet in which the stock discount appears on the asset side, under the caption of Deferred Charges, as in the following illustration:

Balance Sheet

CURRENT ASSETS:		NET WORTH:
Cash..................... $45,000		Capital Stock—$100.00 par value; Authorized and issued, 500 shares.......... $50,000
DEFERRED CHARGES:		
Discount on Stock.......... 5,000		
$50,000		$50,000

This is not the best practice; the stock discount should be recognized as a deduction from the stock in determining the net worth, and the balance sheet should appear as follows:

Balance Sheet

Assets

CURRENT ASSETS:
Cash.. $45,000

Liabilities and Net Worth

NET WORTH:
Capital Stock—$100.00 par value:
Authorized and issued, 500 shares................. $50,000
Less Stock Discount.............................. 5,000
Net Worth....................................... $45,000

Something will be said in a later chapter about including stock premiums in Surplus and deducting stock discount from Surplus. At present it is merely desired to point out that a stock premium is an addition to the net worth, that a stock discount is a deduction, and that they should be treated as such in the balance sheet.

Organization expense.

The expenses of organization, such as incorporation fees and legal fees, are usually set up in an Organization Expense account. This account may be shown in the balance sheet as a deferred charge or as a deduction in the Net Worth section. It should be written off as rapidly as possible by charges to Surplus. Not infrequently such expenses are charged to a Goodwill account, where they remain permanently capitalized; this is improper.

Stock issued for property.

When stock is issued for property other than cash, the question arises whether the property is really worth the par value of the stock issued. If it is not worth the par of the stock, a Discount on Stock account should appear on the books. Such an account is not likely to appear, however, because directors are disposed to value the property at the par of the stock. And in so doing they are acting within their legal rights, for the law allows directors great latitude in exercising their discretion as to the value of property taken for stock. The general rule of law has been that courts will not overrule the directors' valuation, even when creditors are trying to prove that the stock was, in reality, issued at a discount, unless valuations have been grossly excessive and unless fraud is apparent. There is, however, a growing tendency for the courts to scrutinize more carefully the valuations of assets taken for stock when creditors are attempting to prove that stock was issued for property at a discount.

Accounts used.

Following are some of the accounts which might appear in a corporation's ledger as a result of transactions in capital stock:

	Debit Balance	Credit Balance
Capital Stock Authorized.....................		$100,000.00

The credit balance in this account shows the par value of the stock authorized.

| Unissued Stock............................. | $40,000.00 | |

The debit balance in this account shows the par value of the stock that has not been issued.

The difference between the balances of the two accounts is the par value of the issued stock.

| Capital Stock Subscribed.................... | | 15,000.00 |
| Subscriptions to Capital Stock................ | 10,000.00 | |

The first account is credited and the second account is debited with the amount which subscribers agree to pay for stock. The second account is credited with the collections received on subscriptions; its debit balance represents the balance receivable from the subscribers.

| Discount on Stock........................... | 1,000.00 | |

The debit balance in this account shows the excess of the par value of stock over its subscription price.

| Premium on Stock........................... | | 2,000.00 |

The credit balance in this account shows the excess of the subscription price of stock over its par value.

To indicate further the nature of these accounts, we shall assume a few typical transactions and give the entries (in journal form) to record them.

(a) The company obtains a charter authorizing it to issue 1,000 shares of stock, of $100.00 par value per share:

Unissued Stock..........................	100,000.00	
Capital Stock Authorized...............		100,000.00

(b) Subscriptions are received to 250 shares at par:

Subscriptions to Capital Stock............	25,000.00	
Capital Stock Subscribed...............		25,000.00

(c) Collections of $10,000.00 are received in full payment of certain subscriptions, and the stock is issued:

Cash....................................	10,000.00	
Subscriptions to Capital Stock..........		10,000.00
Capital Stock Subscribed................	10,000.00	
Unissued Stock........................		10,000.00

(d) Partial collections, totaling $5,-000.00, are received on the other subscriptions:

Cash....................................	5,000.00	
Subscriptions to Capital Stock..........		5,000.00

(e) 250 shares of stock are issued for cash at a discount of $1,000.00:

Cash....................................	24,000.00	
Discount on Stock.......................	1,000.00	
Unissued Stock........................		25,000.00

(f) 250 shares of stock are issued for cash at a premium of $2,000.00:

Cash....................................	27,000.00	
Unissued Stock.........................		25,000.00
Premium on Stock......................		2,000.00

Watered stock.

Stock is said to be watered when the company's assets are overvalued; that is, when the net assets are, in reality, not worth as much as the capital shown in the Net Worth section of the balance sheet minus any obvious deductions, such as Stock Discount, that may be carried on the asset side of the balance sheet. Water is injected into stock if stock is issued in excess of the value of the assets received, and if these assets are overstated in the accounts. Plant and other property accounts may be grossly overstated or goodwill may be written into the accounts at a figure that is not warranted by past profits. Water is also injected into the stock if an asset is written up and a stock dividend is declared against the surplus thus created.

The water may be eliminated by a scaling down of the outstanding stock, which is effected by reduction of either the number of shares or the par value of each share. If each stockholder suffers a pro-rata reduction, his proportionate interest in the corporation is not affected. Or stock may be donated and resold, thus increasing the assets without increasing the stock outstanding; the credit for the donation should be passed to the overvalued asset accounts and not to surplus. Or assets may be written down by charges to surplus, or capital expenditures may be charged off as expenses. The latter method is not advisable, however, as it corrects one error by committing another, namely, the misstatement of operating profits.

Corporation requirements ignored.

Stockholders and directors, particularly in small companies, often fail to realize that many things which can be done in a partnership cannot legally be done in a corporation, and that many things are required of corporations which are not required of partnerships. This is especially true when a business that has been conducted as a partnership is changed to a corporation.

The old, informal conferences of the partners must in many instances be superseded by formal directors' meetings, and minutes of these meetings must be kept. Profits can no longer be distributed in an arbitrary ratio but must be divided in accordance with the stockholdings. Moreover, they can be distributed only after a formal declaration of dividends, and not in the free and easy manner of drawings. Distributions of dividends must not impair the capital. Salaries of officers must be authorized by the board of directors. The capital stock must not be increased or decreased without authorization.

19

CORPORATE NET WORTH—Continued
CAPITAL STOCK WITHOUT PAR VALUE

....

History.

The first American law permitting the issuance of stock without par value was enacted in 1912 in New York, upon recommendation of the New York Bar Association, which believed that the issuance of stock without par value would eliminate some of the evils attendant upon the issuance of par value stock.

Other states have followed the example of New York; unfortunately, the laws of the various states differ in many particulars. All allow the issuance of common stock without par value, and some also permit the issuance of preferred stock without par value. Some laws make no requirement as to a minimum issuing price; others establish a minimum price. Some provide that the issuing price may be divided by the directors into two elements: stated value, or fixed capital (usually a fixed minimum amount per share) which shall be credited to Capital Stock, and the remainder, which may be credited to Surplus.

These variations in state laws have created some confusion with respect to the accounting procedures applicable to no-par value stock, and this confusion has been considerably augmented by the variation in state laws applicable to the payment of dividends on such stock.

Advantages of no-par stock.

Some of the principal objections to par value stock and theoretical advantages of no-par stock are mentioned below:

(1) The par value printed on a share of stock is not a true indication of its real value. Even if the shares are issued for cash at par, they may immediately have a market value

greater than par because of the prospects of large profits. The value of a share of stock depends upon the value of the corporation's net assets and the amount of its earnings—not upon the figures printed on the certificate.

(2) Printing a par value on a certificate has not infrequently resulted in making it easy for promoters to extract money from the uninformed and the unsuspecting. There is an inevitable attraction about a hundred-dollar share of stock offered for fifty dollars which many people find impossible to withstand. The early advocates of no-par stock expressed the belief that, if a stock certificate carried no dollar value but showed only the total number of shares authorized and the number of shares represented by it, a prospective purchaser would be more likely to make inquiries as to the matters which affect the value of the stock, namely, the net assets and the earnings of the corporation. Experience does not seem to have shown that this is necessarily true.

(3) The use of no-par stock relieves the stockholders of liability for stock discount. The liability for discount results from the purchase of stock at less than par. If there is no par, there can of course be no discount.

(4) The use of no-par stock reduces the incentive for the overvaluation of assets in order to balance the books at the time of organization. Properties can be put on the books at a fair value, and capital stock can be credited at the same value.

For instance, the use of no-par stock permits the issuance of stock for patents, franchises, goodwill, and other intangibles at any fair value instead of at an arbitrary par value which may be grossly excessive. Assume that A and B form a corporation in which A is to invest patents and B is to invest $100,000.00 in cash. It is desired that they shall have equal interests in the capital and profits. Under the par value stock system, A might receive stock of a par value of $100,000.00 to equal the amount issued to B for his cash. This would encumber the balance sheet with an excessive proportion of intangibles and would impose large patent amortization charges against income. Under the no-par value system, 1,000 shares might be issued to B for his cash and recorded at a value of $100,000.00, while another 1,000 shares might be issued to A for his patents and recorded at any fair value—say $5,000.00.

(5) No-par stock is peculiarly suited for use in reorganizations where several companies are to be combined and stock is to be issued for goodwill. If par value stock is issued and if the amount is based on the future earnings, the capitalized value of the excess earnings, to be set up as goodwill, may be a very considerable amount and entirely disproportionate to the other assets. If no-par value stock is used, any desired number of shares may be issued, and the goodwill may still be placed on the books at a reasonable figure.

(6) No-par stock also has advantages when new capital is being sought to put a financially embarrassed company on its feet again. Assume, for the sake of illustration, that a company which has suffered losses until its stock is worth only 80 desires to obtain additional capital by selling shares at 80 or below. Par value stock probably could not be sold at 80 because the purchasers would incur a discount liability. With no-par stock, sales could be made at any figure which would be equitable and attractive, without imposing on the purchasers the risk of a discount liability.

Disadvantages of no-par stock.

Transfer fees, organization fees, stock taxes, fees for the privilege of operating in foreign states, and other taxes may be based on an arbitrary figure very much in excess of the fair value of the stock.

Laws not uncommonly provide that no-par shares shall be assumed to have a par of $100.00 for tax purposes, which would entail a very unreasonable expense if the shares were sold at, say, $5.00.

Issuance of no-par stock.

Logically it would appear that the total amount received by a corporation on the issuance of its no-par stock should be credited to Capital Stock, that the entire amount should be regarded as permanent capital, and that no portion of it should be credited to Surplus and become available for dividends. Unfortunately, the laws of many states do not make any such requirement, and the directors of corporations therefore have assumed that they were permitted to divide the issuing price into two portions for purposes of bookkeeping, one portion being credited to Capital Stock and the other portion being credited to Surplus.

Some state laws expressly permit the directors to divide the issuing price into capital stock and surplus elements. Other state laws make no mention of a stated value but prescribe a minimum (such as $5.00 per share) below which stock of no-par value may not be issued; some corporations subject to this requirement have recorded as capital stock the required minimum per share and have recorded the remainder of the issuing price as Surplus; others have credited the entire issuing price to Capital Stock.

Because of the diversity of laws and the diversity of practice, the amount shown in a balance sheet as the value assigned to no-par stock has no definite meaning. It may represent the entire amount received for the stock; it may represent a stated value permitted by the law or a fixed minimum required by the law; or it may represent almost any amount arbitrarily arrived at by the directors.

Entries for issuances.

The first entry made in connection with par value capital stock is a debit to Unissued Stock and a credit to Capital Stock Authorized. Such an entry usually is impossible in connection with no-par value stock, as there is no value to assign to it.. The number of shares authorized may be indicated by a memorandum in the Capital Stock account, as follows:

Capital Stock

	(1,000 shares authorized)

If stock is issued for full payment, without the necessity of opening accounts for subscriptions, the entries are:

```
Cash.......................................  100,000.00
    Capital Stock.............................            100,000.00
    To credit Capital Stock with full amount re-
    ceived upon issuance of 1,000 shares.
```

If only a portion of the proceeds of the stock is to be regarded as fixed capital, the foregoing entry may be modified as follows:

```
Cash.......................................  100,000.00
    Capital Stock.............................             75,000.00
    Surplus (or Capital Surplus)...............             25,000.00
    To record the issuance of 1,000 shares, and the
    allocation of the proceeds in accordance with the
    directors' authorization.
```

If subscriptions are not fully collected when received, entries may be made as follows:

```
Subscriptions to Capital Stock.................. 100,000.00
     Capital Stock Subscribed..................         100,000.00
     To record subscriptions to 1,000 shares of stock.

Cash......................................  40,000.00
     Subscriptions to Capital Stock.............         40,000.00
     To record collections in full of subscriptions to
     400 shares.

Capital Stock Subscribed......................  40,000.00
     Capital Stock.............................         40,000.00
     To record issuance of 400 fully paid shares.

Cash......................................  30,000.00
     Subscriptions to Capital Stock.............         30,000.00
     To record 50% collections on remaining sub-
     scriptions.
```

Changing from a par to a no-par basis.

The laws permit corporations organized on a par basis to change the stock to a no-par basis. This *may* be done without in any way changing the amounts previously shown as capital stock and surplus. However, changing from a par basis to a no-par basis has been found to be a most convenient method of eliminating an embarrassing deficit. Let us assume that a company's balance sheet contains the following Net Worth section:

```
NET WORTH:
     Capital Stock—par value, $100.00 per share; authorized and
          outstanding, 1,000 shares............................... $100,000
     Less Deficit............................................   35,000
          Net Worth..........................................  $ 65,000
```

By obtaining a charter amendment authorizing a change from a par value to a no-par value basis, the old shares can be called in, an equal number of no-par shares can be issued in their place, and the following net worth picture can be presented:

```
NET WORTH:
     Capital Stock—No-par value; authorized and outstanding,
          1,000 shares........................................... $65,000
```

By dividing the issuing price of the new no-par stock into two portions, a still more pleasing net worth picture may be painted, such as the following:

```
NET WORTH:
     Capital Stock—No-par value; authorized and out-
          standing, 1,000 shares............................ $50,000
     Surplus (or Capital Surplus)......................   15,000 $65,000
```

Preferred stock of no-par value.

When preferred stock is issued without par value, a fixed price is usually stated at which the preferred stock may be redeemed by the company, or which represents its liquidating value in the event of the dissolution of the company. This redemption or liquidation value may be, and often is, different from the price at which the stock was issued. At what amount, then, should such preferred stock be shown in the balance sheet?

To illustrate, assume that 1,000 shares of preferred stock were issued at $40.00 per share, and that its liquidating or redemption value was fixed at $50.00 per share. At the same time, 1,000 shares of common stock were issued at $40.00 per share.

If the two classes of stock are shown in the balance sheet at their issuing price, the Net Worth section will appear as follows:

```
Capital Stock—No-par value:
    Preferred—authorized and outstanding, 1,000 shares........... $40,000
    Common—authorized and outstanding, 1,000 shares...........   40,000
```

Such a balance sheet presentation does not indicate the liquidating value of the preferred stock. But if the preferred stock were shown at its liquidating value of $50.00 per share, the stated value of the common stock would have to be correspondingly reduced, thus:

```
Capital Stock—No-par value:
    Preferred—authorized and outstanding, 1,000 shares at liquidat-
        ing value of $50.00 per share.............................. $50,000
    Common—authorized and outstanding, 1,000 shares...........   30,000
```

Such a method of presentation destroys the record of the amount received for each class of stock. It is desirable to retain this information in the balance sheet, and to show the liquidating value parenthetically, thus:

```
Capital Stock—No-par value; Stated at issuing price:
    Preferred—Authorized and outstanding, 1,000 shares (Liquidat-
        ing value, $50.00 per share).............................. $40,000
    Common—Authorized and outstanding, 1,000 shares..........   40,000
```

Units of preferred and common.

A peculiar difficulty arises if preferred and common shares without par value are sold in units, with no separation of the price between the two classes, or if preferred and common shares are issued together in acquisition of a business. In such cases the accountant will have great difficulty in showing separate valuations for the common and preferred stock in the balance sheet unless a directors' resolution states a value for each of the two classes of stock.

To illustrate, assume that 1,000 shares of preferred stock and 1,000 shares of common stock, both without par value, are issued in acquisition of a business. The charter provides a liquidating value of $50.00 per share for the preferred. The business acquired is valued at $90,000.00.

Let us assume, first, that the directors establish a stated value of $50.00 for the preferred, and a stated value of $40.00 for the common. The accountant can then show the facts in the balance sheet as follows:

Capital Stock—No-par value:
    Preferred—issued and outstanding, 1,000 shares at stated and
        liquidating value of $50.00 per share...................... $50,000
    Common—issued and outstanding, 1,000 shares at stated value
        of $40.00 per share..................................... 40,000

If no stated values are fixed by the directors, the mere fact that the preferred stock has a liquidating value of $50.00 per share is not sufficient to justify the accountant in preparing a balance sheet in which the total capital is divided between the two classes of stock in the amounts shown above. The liquidating value will apply only at such future date as may be determined upon for the retirement of the preferred stock or the liquidation of the company. Therefore, it does not necessarily represent a present equity which the accountant has the right to insist upon showing. Unless the directors will assent to some apportionment, the accountant may be obliged to prepare a balance sheet in which the total capital is shown in the following manner:

Capital Stock—No-par value................................. $90,000
    Represented by 1,000 shares of preferred stock with a liquidating
    value of $50.00 per share, and 1,000 shares of common stock.

20

CORPORATE NET WORTH–Continued
TREASURY STOCK

Definition.

Treasury stock is a corporation's own stock, once issued and fully paid, and later reacquired. It will be noted that there are three important elements in this definition:

(1) Treasury stock must be the company's own stock; holdings of the stock of other companies should not be called treasury stock.

(2) The stock must have been issued; unissued stock should not be called treasury stock.

(3) When originally issued, the stock must have been paid for in full. This is a very important element of the definition.

Original stock sold at a discount carries with it a personal liability for the payment of corporate debts; if such stock is reacquired by the corporation and reissued, the liability still attaches to it, if purchased with a knowledge of the original issuance at a discount.

But if, when originally issued, the stock was paid for in full, it may be reacquired as treasury stock and reissued at a discount without any liability being imposed upon the purchaser.

Methods of acquisition.

Treasury stock may be reacquired by donation, by purchase, or in settlement of an account. Donations may be made to provide stock that may be resold to furnish working capital, or to eliminate the water from the stock, or to wipe out a deficit, or to provide common stock to be given as a bonus to the purchasers of a new issue of preferred stock, or for other reasons. It may be purchased to buy out a stockholder, or to create a market demand for the stock and thus retard a downward tendency in the market value.

Treasury stock in the balance sheet.

Treasury stock is not an asset; the acquisition of treasury stock merely reduces the amount of stock outstanding. Therefore, holdings of treasury stock should be shown in the balance sheet as deductions in the Net Worth section. Two methods are illustrated below:

First method:

NET WORTH:
  Capital Stock—$100.00 par value:
    Authorized and issued, 1,000 shares.............. $100,000
    Less Treasury Stock, 50 shares...................   5,000
    Outstanding... $95,000

Second method:

NET WORTH:
  Capital Stock—$100.00 par value; authorized and issued, 1,000
    shares; in treasury, 50 shares; outstanding, 950 shares....... $95,000

Treasury stock is not an asset.

Public accountants are sometimes requested to show treasury stock on the asset side of the balance sheet. Although the stock may have a ready marketability, the purchase of treasury stock does not result in the acquisition of an asset but causes a reduction of the corporation's net worth. It is true that the treasury stock subsequently may be sold, but so may unissued stock be sold; it seems evident that treasury stock, like unissued stock, is not an asset but is merely a source of possible additional capital.

Recording transactions—par value stock.

In the first illustration under the heading "Treasury stock in the balance sheet," the par value of the treasury stock is deducted from the par value of the issued stock to show the par value of the stock outstanding. To facilitate such a deduction, treasury stock should be carried in the accounts at its par value, regardless of the price at which it was acquired. The premium and discount on treasury stock purchases and sales should be recorded in some account other than Treasury Stock. Accountants hold various inions as to the proper account to use for that purpose. It was rmerly the general custom to record such premiums and discunts in Surplus; there is a growing preference for the use of a pital Surplus account. In some states it is illegal to pay vidends from discount on treasury stock purchases until the scount has been realized by subsequent resale of the stock; in ch states it is advisable to use some special account such as iscounts and Premiums on Treasury Stock. To make the present scussion of treasury stock entries as simple as possible, discounts id premiums will be recorded in Capital Surplus. Entries are ven below for several illustrative transactions; the stock has a r value of $100.00 per share.

(1) Ten shares of stock are purchased at 90:

Treasury Stock	1,000.00	
Cash		900.00
Capital Surplus		100.00

(2) Ten shares are purchased at 101:

Treasury Stock	1,000.00	
Capital Surplus	10.00	
Cash		1,010.00

(3) Two shares are donated to the company:

Treasury Stock	200.00	
Capital Surplus		200.00

(4) Five shares are sold at 92:

Cash	460.00	
Capital Surplus	40.00	
Treasury Stock		500.00

(5) One share is sold at 103:

Cash	103.00	
Treasury Stock		100.00
Capital Surplus		3.00

If a company has more than one class of stock, the treasury ock accounts should indicate the classes, thus: Treasury Stock— 'ommon, or Treasury Stock—Preferred.

ecording transactions—no-par value stock.

Assume that a company originally issued its no-par stock for 25.00 per share and that, after the passage of some time, the ompany's net worth was as follows:

NET WORTH:
 Capital Stock—No par value—authorized and issued.
  1,000 shares.................................... $25,000
  Surplus.. 15,000
   Total...................................... $40,000

Assume that the company repurchases 100 shares at $35.00 per share; the $3,500.00 cost reduces the net worth to $36,500.00. Accountants hold different opinions as to the proper method of recording such purchases. Two methods are shown below.

First method. The purchase price may be divided into two parts: $2,500.00 representing the price ($25.00 per share) at which the stock was issued, and $1,000.00 representing the excess of the reacquisition cost over the issuing price. This division is indicated in the following entry recording the purchase.

 Treasury Stock................................. 2,500.00
 Surplus....................................... 1,000.00
  Cash.......................................   3,500.00
  To record the purchase of 100 shares of treasury stock.

The net worth could be shown in the balance sheet in the following manner:

NET WORTH:
 Capital Stock—No par value:
  Authorized and issued, 1,000 shares.............. $25,000
  In treasury, 100 shares......................... 2,500
  Outstanding, 900 shares......................... $22,500
 Surplus... 14,000
  Total.. $36,500

Or merely thus:

NET WORTH:
 Capital Stock—No par value: Authorized and issued,
  1,000 shares; in treasury, 100 shares; outstanding,
  900 shares..................................... $22,500
 Surplus... 14,000
  Total.. $36,500

Second method. Because such a division of the purchase price would be extremely difficult and perhaps impracticable if the stock originally had been sold at various times and at different prices, some accountants favor charging the entire cost to the Treasury Stock account, thus:

 Treasury Stock................................. 3,500.00
  Cash.......................................   3,500.00
  To record the cost of 100 shares of treasury stock.

The net worth would be shown in the balance sheet as follows:

NET WORTH:
  Capital Stock—No par value: Authorized and issued,
    1,000 shares.................................... $25,000
  Surplus... 15,000
    Total....................................... $40,000
  Deduct Treasury Stock—100 shares, at cost.......... 3,500
    Remainder... $36,500

Treasury stock and dividends.

It has been facetiously said that the first corporation in England was created by royal decree upon application by a number of noble lords who previously had met and decided how much of their debts they were willing to pay. The right to incorporate is no longer a matter of special privilege available only to the influential; the benefit of limited liability is now open to all.

The history of corporate laws indicates that there has been some difficulty in giving stockholders the advantage of limited liability and at the same time safeguarding the creditors. Corporate laws generally have attempted to do so by provisions intended to prevent the payment of dividends except out of profits. Thus, for example, if a corporation had capital stock of $100,000.00 par value and a surplus of $25,000.00, dividends could be paid to stockholders only to the extent of the $25,000.00 surplus.

But such a limitation upon dividends did not act as a restriction upon the purchase of treasury stock; consequently, if the stockholders of the corporation mentioned in the preceding paragraph wished to take $50,000.00 out of the corporate treasury, they could do so by taking a $25,000.00 dividend out of surplus and also selling the company treasury stock for $25,000.00. And the poor creditors, who may have thought that their debtor's net worth could not be reduced below $100,000.00, would find that it had been reduced to $75,000.00.

It thus became evident that laws restricting dividends are not an adequate safeguard to creditors. Recently, therefore, corporation laws in some states have set up a concept of fixed or stated capital and have provided that the combined dividends and treasury stock purchases shall not impair this stated capital. In other words, it seems to be the intent of such legislation, however expressed, to limit the combined dividends and cost of treasury stock purchases to the amount of the surplus.

If a corporation is subject to such a law, it may have a surplus but have no legal right to pay a dividend because the surplus is restricted by reason of a treasury stock purchase. Such a condition should, of course, be reflected by the balance sheet. Several methods have been used to indicate the restriction. A clear presentation is:

NET WORTH:
    Capital Stock—Par value, $100.00:
        Authorized and issued, 1,000 shares; in treasury, 250 shares;
           outstanding, 750 shares............................. $ 75,000
    Surplus (Restricted as to dividends to the extent of $25,000.00
        by reason of the purchase of treasury stock).............. 40,000
        Total.. $115,000

Sometimes the restriction is indicated by deduction of the treasury stock from the surplus, thus:

NET WORTH:
    Capital Stock—Par value, $100.00: Authorized and
        issued, 1,000 shares........................... $100,000
    Surplus:
        Total....................................... $40,000
        Restricted—Cost of 250 shares of treasury stock... 25,000
        Available for dividends........................   15,000
        Total................................... $115,000

And sometimes the restriction is indicated merely by deduction of the treasury stock from the total issued stock and surplus, thus:

NET WORTH:
    Capital Stock—Par value, $100.00: Authorized and issued, 1,000
        shares.. $100,000
    Surplus... 40,000
        Total.. $140,000
    Deduct cost of treasury stock—250 shares.................. 25,000
    Remainder—Net Worth................................. $115,000

The last method does not seem to be a sufficiently clear presentation to give adequate notice of the dividend restriction to a reader of the balance sheet who is not thoroughly familiar with the legal limitations resulting from the purchase of treasury stock.

CORPORATE NET WORTH–Continued
SURPLUS

Sources of net worth.

Let us assume the following facts relative to the growth of the net worth of a company during the first year of its existence:

The company issued stock of a par value of.........	$1,000,000.00
The stock was issued at a premium of..............	25,000.00
The city where the company was located made a donation of land for a plant site; the land was worth....	20,000.00
Purchases and sales of treasury stock resulted in a profit of......................................	5,000.00
Of the land, building, and equipment purchased by the company, a portion was found not to be required and was sold at a profit of...........................	20,000.00
The remainder was appraised at the end of the year and was found to have a value in excess of cost; this appraisal "profit" amounted to..................	50,000.00
The net operating profit for the year was.............	100,000.00
Total......................................	$1,220,000.00

It is probable that, until rather recently, the net worth of this company usually would have been shown in its balance sheet as follows:

NET WORTH:
Capital Stock.............................	$1,000,000	
Surplus...................................	220,000	
Total...		$1,220,000

During recent years, however, there has been a growing belief among accountants that increments in net worth of so diverse a nature as those included in the stated surplus of $220,000.00 should not be shown in a balance sheet in one amount.

Classification of increments in net worth.

The above-mentioned increments in net worth belong to several classes, which are briefly defined below:

    (I) Realized increments:
        (A) Operating profits:
            Operating profits are those produced by the regular operations of the business, such as sales of merchandise and services.
        (B) Extraneous profits:
            Extraneous profits are those produced by unusual or exceptional transactions which are not a part of regular operations, such as disposals of fixed assets and sales of treasury stock. (A few accountants believe that entries in surplus should be made only in connection with unusual disposals of major portions of fixed assets, and that profits or losses on normal disposals should be regarded as operating items.)
        (C) Contributions to surplus:
            (1) By stockholders; these include, among others:
                (a) Premiums on par value stock.
                (b) The excess of the amount received for no-par value stock over the amount credited to the Capital Stock account.
                (c) Donations of stock or assets at dates subsequent to organization, usually to eliminate a deficit.
            (2) By outsiders.
                For example—the gift of a plant site to induce a company to locate in the donor city.
    (II) Unrealized increments:
        (D) Unrealized profits:
            Profits are realized by closed transactions in which the value received is greater than the value at which the assets disposed of were carried in the accounts. Unrealized profits, or "paper profits," are increases in the value of assets which have not been disposed of.

The expression "unrealized profit" is really a contradiction in terms; an increase in the value of an asset should not be called a profit until it has been realized.

The increments in net worth mentioned in the foregoing lustration fall into the above classification as follows:

Operating profits:		
Net profit for the year..................................		$100,000.00
Extraneous profits:		
Profit on sale of fixed assets..................	$20,000.00	
Profit on sales of treasury stock..............	5,000.00	25,000.00
Contributions to surplus:		
Premium on issuance of stock................	$25,000.00	
Donation of plant site......................	20,000.00	45,000.00
Unrealized profits:		
From appraisal of plant.................................		50,000.00
Total...		$220,000.00

Classification in the balance sheet.

Although, as stated above, there is a growing belief among accountants that the various classes of surplus should be separated n the balance sheet, there unfortunately seems to be no unanimity of opinion as to how this should be done. Three varying opinions are stated below:

Opinion I:
   All operating profits, realized extraneous profits, and contributions to surplus may be shown as Surplus.
   Unrealized profits from appraisals should be shown as Capital Surplus.

Opinion II:
   Surplus should be credited with operating profits only.
   Capital Surplus should be credited with extraneous profits, contributions, and unrealized profits from appraisals.

Opinion III:
   Surplus should include operating profits only.
   Capital Surplus should comprise realized extraneous profits and contributions.
   A Reserve for Unrealized Profit on Appraisal should show the amount of such unrealized profits.

To emphasize the differences in the balance sheets which would be prepared by accountants holding the three above-described opinions, a summary is presented on the following page.

Surplus, Capital Surplus, and Unrealized Profit Reserves

	Opinion I		Opinion II		Opinion III		
	Surplus	Capital Surplus	Surplus	Capital Surplus	Surplus	Capital Surplus	Reserve for Unrealized Profit
Operating profit	$100,000		$100,000		$100,000		
Profit on sale of fixed assets...	20,000			$ 20,000		$20,000	
Profit on sales of treasury stock	5,000			5,000		5,000	
Premium on stock........	25,000			25,000		25,000	
Donation of plant site....	20,000			20,000		20,000	
Appraisal of plant........		$50,000		50,000			$50,000
Total......	$170,000	$50,000	$100,000	$120,000	$100,000	$70,000	$50,000

In other words, the net worth might be shown in the balance
sheet in three different ways, as follows:

```
(I) Net Worth:
     Capital Stock.................... $1,000,000.00
     Surplus.........................      170,000.00
     Capital Surplus.................       50,000.00
          Total.....................................  $1,220,000.00
(II) Net Worth:
     Capital Stock.................... $1,000,000.00
     Surplus.........................      100,000.00
     Capital Surplus.................      120,000.00
          Total.....................................   1,220,000.00
(III) Net Worth:
     Capital Stock.................... $1,000,000.00
     Surplus.........................      100,000.00
     Capital Surplus.................       70,000.00
     Unrealized Profit on Appraisal....     50,000.00
          Total.....................................   1,220,000.00
```

So what is Capital Surplus?

Because of the diversity of opinion and treatment illustrated
above, a Capital Surplus balance in a balance sheet has no univer-
sal and definite significance.   Until accountants themselves agree
as to what can properly be called Surplus (sometimes referred to as
Earned Surplus) and what should be classified as Capital Surplus,
laymen certainly cannot be expected to have a very definite idea of
what these words mean in any given balance sheet.

The reader of a balance sheet in which a Capital Surplus
appears should understand that the accountant who prepared it is

making what he regards as a significant classification. Beyond this, the reader of the balance sheet can usually only guess. He cannot know, by an examination of the balance sheet alone, whether the capital surplus includes paid-in surplus, extraneous profits, unrealized profits from asset write-ups, or a miscellany of all.

Effect of dividends.

Even if the accountants could unanimously agree upon rules for the classification of operating profits, extraneous profits, and other increments in net worth, the layman should remember that the laws relative to the payment of dividends may allow the directors virtually to nullify any attempt by the accountant to indicate, by a classification in the balance sheet, the sources of the surplus.

In many states it is legal to pay dividends from extraneous profits and paid-in surplus as well as from operating profits, and in some states it is permissible to pay dividends from unrealized profits arising from appraisals. Therefore some may feel that it is scarcely worth while to classify meticulously the various increments in net worth by setting up Surplus, Capital Surplus, and unrealized profit reserves if the directors can order that dividends be deducted from any of these amounts according to their pleasure. Thus, if a company earns $25,000.00 of operating profits and makes a $10,000.000 profit on an extraneous transaction such as the sale of fixed assets, and the accountant classifies these earnings as

Surplus..	$25,000.00
Capital Surplus..	10,000.00

what ultimate benefit is derived if the directors authorize the charging of a $10,000.00 dividend against capital surplus? The balance sheet will show only the earned surplus of $25,000.00. The accountant might about as well have thrown the operating profit and the extraneous profit together in the first place and deducted the dividend from the total.

However, one definite advantage is obtained from a surplus and capital surplus classification: the surplus statement for each year (prepared in the second form illustrated below) will more clearly show the various increments of net worth during the year, and will show what classes of surplus were charged with dividends during the year. A person who has access to a company's statements for a series of years will thus be able to obtain an idea of the sources of the surplus remaining on any date.

Surplus statement illustrated.

Following are two illustrative surplus statements. In one, no attempt has been made to distinguish between the various elements of surplus; in the second, a distinction has been made.

THE *A B* COMPANY

Statement of Surplus

For the Year Ended December 31, 1941

Balance, December 31, 1940		$115,000.00
Add:		
Net Income for the Year	$35,000.00	
Donation of Land	4,500.00	
Total Additions		39,500.00
Total		$154,500.00
Deduct:		
Provision for Additional Tax Accrual for 1940	$ 1,000.00	
Dividends	20,000.00	
Total Deductions		21,000.00
Balance, December 31, 1941		$133,500.00

THE *A B* COMPANY

Statement of Surplus Accounts

For the Year Ended December 31, 1941

	Earned Surplus	Capital Surplus	Total
Balances, December 31, 1940	$ 90,000.00	$25,000.00	$115,000.00
Add:			
Net Income for the Year	35,000.00	—	35,000.00
Donation of Land	—	4,500.00	4,500.00
Total	$125,000.00	$29,500.00	$154,500.00
Deduct:			
Provision for Additional Tax Accrual for 1940	$ 1,000.00	$ —	$ 1,000.00
Dividends	15,000.00	5,000.00	20,000.00
Total	$ 16,000.00	$ 5,000.00	$ 21,000.00
Balances, December 31, 1941	$109,000.00	$24,500.00	$133,500.00

Note that the surplus statements contain items of the following nature:

> Opening balances.
> Net income for the period—this is the final
> figure of the profit and loss statement.
> Extraneous profits.
> Corrections of profits of prior periods.
> Dividends.
> Closing balances.

Capital stock and surplus in the balance sheet.

Although the net worth is customarily divided in the balance sheet into capital stock and surplus elements (with a possible subdivision of the surplus along the lines already discussed in this chapter), it is not always possible to tell exactly what the stock and surplus elements mean.

It is often assumed that the amount shown as capital stock represents the stockholders' original investment in the company. This assumption may be wrong, for the following reasons:

Par value stock may have been sold at a premium; the amount shown in the balance sheet as capital stock will then be less than the original investment.

Par value stock may have been issued at a discount; the par value shown in the balance sheet will then be more than the original investment.

If the stock has no par value, a portion of the proceeds of its sale may have been credited to Capital Stock and the remainder may have been credited to Surplus.

A stock dividend may have been issued in the past and recorded by a debit to Surplus and a credit to Capital Stock; thus a portion of the surplus is converted into capital stock.

The company may have incurred a deficit and obtained donations of stock to eliminate the deficit. For instance, assume a net worth condition as follows:

NET WORTH:
Capital Stock Outstanding................ $100,000.00
Less Deficit.............................   35,000.00 $65,000.00

If the stockholders donate half of their stock to the company, the net worth condition may be changed to the following:

NET WORTH:
Capital Stock Outstanding................. $50,000.00
Surplus...................................   15,000.00 $65,000.00

Sometimes it is assumed that the amount shown as capital stock represents the permanent capital not distributable to the stockholders until the discontinuance and liquidation of the company. This may not be the case; the company may have the right, or even be under obligation, to retire preferred stock. And, subject to certain statutory limitations, it may reduce its capital by the acquisition of treasury stock.

It is frequently assumed that the amount shown in the balance sheet as surplus represents accumulated earnings. This also may not be the case. As pointed out above, part of the surplus may have arisen from premiums on par value stock, or from donations, or from the writing up of assets, or from an arbitrary treatment of a portion of the proceeds of the issuance of no-par stock as surplus.

It is also rather frequently assumed that the amount shown as surplus represents the amount available for dividends. This very frequently is not the case. The laws relative to dividends are so varied and complex that accountants should not presume to indicate, in a balance sheet or elsewhere, the amount which the company can legally pay in dividends; and the reader of a balance sheet should not assume that the amount shown as surplus represents the amount which the accountant believes can be so distributed.

From the foregoing discussion it should be apparent that the amounts shown in the balance sheet as capital stock and surplus do not necessarily have any definite significance. The combined amounts should represent the net worth, but the meaning of the individual amounts cannot be known unless one knows the history of the Capital Stock and Surplus accounts from the beginning of the life of the company, and a good bit of corporation law.

Does the net worth section show the net worth?

Not only is it impossible to know with certainty what is represented by the capital stock and surplus elements shown in the balance sheet, but it is also unwise to assume unquestioningly that the amount shown in the balance sheet as net worth really represents the net worth. Some of the reasons are stated below.

(1) The net worth may be misstated by a deliberate or ignorant violation of accounting principles, the result being improper statements of the amounts of assets and liabilities.

(2) Certain items may be carried on the asset side of the balance sheet which should be treated as net worth deductions. Among these are:

    (a) Discount on stock.

        In some balance sheets discount on stock is shown on the asset side under the Deferred Charge caption. It should be deducted from the stated net worth to determine the true net worth.

(b) Uncollected subscriptions.

> Uncollected subscriptions to capital stock are frequently shown on the asset side of the balance sheet. Unless they are to be currently collected, the reader of the balance sheet should regard them as a proper deduction from the stated net worth.

(c) Treasury stock.

> Treasury stock should not be classified as an asset but should be treated as a deduction in the net worth section. Unfortunately, when treasury stock is included among the assets in the balance sheet, it may be merged with stock investments so that the amount cannot be ascertained.

(d) Overvalued intangible assets such as goodwill.

> Goodwill, patents, franchises, copyrights, and other intangible assets are sometimes extremely valuable, and sometimes are worth even more than the amounts at which they appear in the balance sheet. But also they are sometimes grossly overvalued. In general such intangibles do not usually have much value unless the company is making good profits. Therefore, if such items appear in the balance sheet, the reader should at least wonder whether they should be deducted from the stated net worth.

(3) A portion of the surplus may have been transferred to an appropriated surplus reserve. (Such reserves are further discussed in the next chapter.) Appropriated surplus reserves still represent surplus, but surplus which temporarily, at least, is not to be used for dividends. Such appropriations of surplus should. be included in the net worth section of the balance sheet; however, they are shown sometimes as liabilities and sometimes under a special reserve caption, either with the intent to understate the net worth or from a failure to understand their nature.

CORPORATE NET WORTH–Continued
SURPLUS AVAILABLE FOR DIVIDENDS

lassification of dividends.

Dividends distributed by corporations to their stockholders ay be classified as follows:

(A) Dividends out of surplus.

    (1) Decreasing net worth.

        Such dividends are usually paid in cash; other assets may be distributed; or scrip or other evidences of indebtedness may be given to the stockholders.

    (2) Not affecting net worth.

        In this classification belong stock dividends, which merely transfer a portion of the net worth from surplus to capital stock. A stock dividend does not change the net worth of the issuing corporation; it merely reduces the portion of the net worth represented by surplus, and equally increases the portion of net worth represented by capital stock. Nor does it change the individual stockholder's interest in the net worth; it merely increases the number of shares by which his interest is represented.

(B) Dividends out of capital. These are also called liquidating dividends; they return to the stockholders all or a portion of the capital invested.

They may be classified as follows:

    (1) Dividends *intended* to return the capital to the stockholders because the corporation is discontinuing operations; or dividends intended to return a portion of the capital to the stockholders

because the scope of the business is being reduced and the total capital is no longer required.

(2) Returns of capital resulting from the payment of dividends which, though intended to be dividends out of surplus, exceed the surplus legally available for dividends.

The following discussion deals with the subject of dividends out of surplus.

Legality of dividends.

Since corporations are entities apart from their stockholders, and since the stockholders are, generally, not liable for the debts of the corporation, the statutes place limitations upon the payment of dividends, the object of the limitations being to preserve a capital fund as a safeguard to creditors. In general it may be said that the laws seek to prohibit the impairment of capital by the payment of dividends; that the legality of a dividend payment depends upon the company's profits and surplus, and not upon its cash balance; and that realized profits from extraneous as well as from operating transactions are available for dividends. Aside from these, few general rules, applicable to the country as a whole, can be stated. To illustrate some of the many variations in the corporation laws of the different states, the following matters may be mentioned:

(1) In some states dividends can be paid from paid-in surplus represented by premiums on par value stock, or the excess of the paid-in value of no-par stock over the declared value thereof. In other states, such dividends are illegal. In at least one state, dividends from paid-in surplus can be paid to preferred stockholders but not to common stockholders.

(2) In some states dividends may be paid from profits before any discount on the issuance of stock is written off; in other states dividends cannot be paid until the company has written off the stock discount and has accumulated a surplus.

(3) If losses have impaired the capital, most states prohibit the payment of dividends until the capital is restored and a surplus is accumulated; a few states permit the payment of dividends from current profits regardless of the existence of an accumulated deficit.

(4) Some states prohibit the payment of any dividends from unrealized appreciation of assets; others permit the distribution of stock dividends from a surplus thus created; and at least one state permits the distribution of either cash or stock dividends from such a source.

(5) In some states, when treasury stock is purchased at less than par, the discount is regarded as a profit which is immediately available for dividends; in other states the discount does not produce surplus available for dividends unless and until the stock is resold at par. And in some states the purchase of treasury stock never produces a surplus available for dividends, regardless of the purchase price, but makes surplus previously available for dividends unavailable to the extent of the purchase price of the stock.

(6) In at least one state, dividends on preferred stock can be paid from surplus from any source, while dividends on common stock can be paid from earned surplus only.

(7) In some states a reduction of capital stock will not be permitted to produce a surplus available for dividends; in other states dividends may be paid from surplus thus produced; and in at least one state a scaling down of the common stock may create a surplus available for dividend payments on the preferred stock.

(8) In most states the surplus available for dividends may be determined without deduction for depletion; in some states, however, dividends cannot be paid from surplus thus determined if the rights of creditors are jeopardized; and in a few states the rights of preferred stockholders are similarly safeguarded.

(9) In addition to the usual requirement that dividends shall not impair the capital, some statutes include specific limitations based upon the amount of liabilities. For instance, the laws of some states provide that no dividends shall be paid if the liabilities exceed the assets; in one state no dividends may be paid if the liabilities exceed two-thirds of the assets; and in certain states no dividends may be paid unless the assets exceed the liabilities and the preferred stock.

Because of these and other diversities in the corporation statutes, accountants cannot be expected to assume the responsibility of determining the amount of surplus which is legally available for dividends; consequently, the reader of a balance sheet should not assume that the amount shown therein as surplus is so available.

Restricted surplus.

Surplus which normally would be available for dividends may become temporarily or permanently not so available. Such restrictions upon surplus may be imposed by law or may result from contracts.

A legal restriction results in some states from the purchase of treasury stock. The purpose and nature of this restriction were discussed in Chapter 20.

Surplus which is legally available for dividends may become temporarily not so available by reason of contracts with creditors. The sinking fund reserve discussed in Chapter 37 is an illustration of a surplus appropriation required by a contract.

Appropriated surplus.

The directors of a corporation may consider it inexpedient to pay dividends to the full amount of the accumulated surplus because funds produced by profits have been, or are to be, used for other purposes, such as plant additions; they may therefore desire to reduce the surplus balance so as to indicate that large dividends cannot be expected. To this end they may direct that a portion of the surplus be transferred to a reserve by debiting Surplus and crediting an account with some title such as Reserve for Plant Additions.

The creation of such a reserve does not reflect a legal restriction upon the payment of dividends; it is merely an accounting device to indicate that a portion of the surplus, although legally available for dividends, will not be used for that purpose because it would be financially inexpedient to do so. The directors can at any time transfer the reserve balance back to surplus. Meanwhile it should be regarded as an element of the net worth and should be shown in the net worth section of the balance sheet.

Declared dividends a liability.

After a legal dividend has been declared and notice of the declaration has been given to the stockholders, the unpaid dividend ranks as an outside liability and should be shown as such in the balance sheet. If the corporation becomes insolvent before the dividend is paid, the stockholders will be entitled to share pro

rata with outside creditors in the payment of declared dividends
and debts. For instance, if there are liabilities of $45,000.00,
unpaid dividends of $5,000.00, and assets of $40,000.00, distribution should be made as follows:

To creditors:	⅘ of $45,000.00............................	$36,000.00
To stockholders:	⅘ of 5,000.00............................	4,000.00

So positive is this rule that, if a corporation while solvent sets
aside a fund for the payment of the dividend and becomes insolvent
before the fund is used for the designated purpose, the fund will
be considered a trust fund for the stockholders, and will not be
available for the payment of creditors.

But the rule will not hold if the corporation was insolvent when
the dividend was declared, or if the dividend was illegal, or if
notice of the declaration was not given to the stockholders before
the company became insolvent.

Preferred dividends in arrears.

Preferred dividends in arrears, even though cumulative, do
not constitute a liability until they have been declared. This is
true even though there may be sufficient surplus to provide for
their payment.

However, the balance sheet should indicate the amount of the
cumulative preferred dividends in arrears because they constitute
a claim against corporate earnings having precedence over the
common stockholders' rights. The facts are usually stated in a
balance sheet footnote, worded somewhat as follows: "Dividends
on the preferred stock are in arrears since . . . ," or "No dividends have been paid on the preferred stock since . . . ," or
"Preferred dividends in the amount of $ . . . were in arrears on
[the balance sheet date]."

23

CASH

....

What is current cash?

Cash consists of legal tender, checks, bank drafts, money orders, and demand deposits in banks. Deposits in savings accounts are usually classified in the balance sheet as cash, notwithstanding the legal right of the bank to demand a certain notice before withdrawal. Demand certificates of deposit may be classified as cash, but time certificates should not be so classified.

The practice of carrying due bills in the cash in place of money advanced to individuals should be discouraged; if such due bills are found in the cash, they should be shown in the balance sheet as amounts receivable from officers, employees, and so forth, and not as cash.

When a petty cash fund is carried in the office, it is customary to postpone recording expenditures until the fund is nearly exhausted and then to record all of the expenditures at one time. Before a balance sheet is prepared, all of the disbursements should be recorded, so that the cash will not be overstated in the balance sheet.

Bonds, stocks, and other investments should not be shown as cash in the balance sheet, even though they may have been purchased as temporary investments of excess funds and may be readily convertible into cash without loss.

A distinction should be made in the balance sheet between cash available for general operating purposes and cash tied up in special-purpose funds. If a fund is to be used for the payment of a current liability, as is the case with money deposited with a trustee for the payment of mortgage interest and taxes on mortgaged property, it may be shown, as a separate item, under the Current Assets caption. Special funds not available for current needs should be shown under some caption other than current assets.

Whether paper left at the bank for collection should be shown in the balance sheet as cash or as a receivable depends on whether the bank took the paper as a deposit or merely for collection. If the bank credited the depositor's account with the paper, the item may properly be included in the cash; otherwise not.

Internal check.

An adequate system of internal check to safeguard the cash requires a control over both receipts and disbursements. The methods of effecting this control vary greatly in different organizations, and the system described below should be understood to be indicative of the objects to be attained, rather than a procedure to be invariably followed.

The danger of misappropriation of cash is reduced if collusion is made necessary to conceal an abstraction of cash receipts; therefore it is desirable to divide the work of handling cash receipts among several people, whose records must agree, as indicated below:

(1) All mail receipts and the totals of cash register receipts should be listed and totaled by a trusted employee; the letters accompanying the mail receipts should be marked by the employee with the amount of the remittance, initialed by him, and turned over to the bookkeeper. The cash should be turned in to the cashier.

(2) The cashier, after making up the deposit, should submit the deposit slip to the employee mentioned in (1), who should compare the amount of the deposit with the amount of cash received as shown by his own list. All cash received should be deposited daily. When the bank's statement is received at the end of the month, it should be checked by the cashier, and the deposits shown by it should be compared by the employee mentioned in (1) with the daily lists prepared by him.

(3) The bookkeeper who makes up the cash book should not be the same as the cashier.

With such a system of internal check, fraud with respect to collections from debtors cannot be practiced and concealed even for a day, without the collusion of three persons. The first employee has no access to the books and cannot falsify the records to conceal a misappropriation; he cannot expect to withhold funds received from debtors without detection, because the debtors will receive statements or letters from the credit department and will report their remittances. If the cashier withholds any cash, his daily deposit will not agree with the first employee's list or with the bookkeeper's cash receipts record made from the remittance letters and other sources of information. The bookkeeper, having no access to the cash, has no opportunity to misappropriate any of it, and therefore has no incentive to falsify his records unless he is participating in a three-party collusion.

Since all receipts are deposited daily in the bank, all disbursements must be made by check. The person authorized to sign checks should have no authority to make entries in the cash book; thus a fraudulent disbursement by check could not be concealed without the collusion of two persons. The collusion of a third person can be made necessary:

(1) Either by requiring that all checks shall be signed by one person and countersigned by another.

(2) Or by installing the voucher system, allowing the checks to be signed by one person, but only upon authorization evidenced by a voucher signed by some other person.

All checks should be prenumbered. All spoiled, mutilated, or voided checks should be preserved. Some companies even go so far as to require that such checks be recorded in their proper sequence in the cash disbursements record, without entry in the money column, but with a notation to the effect that the check is void.

Lapping.

Unless the cash receipts are safeguarded by a proper system of internal check, the cashier may easily conceal a shortage by "lapping." This is particularly true if the functions of bookkeeper and cashier are exercised by one person. Lapping consists of a series of postponements of entries debiting Cash and crediting Accounts Receivable or some other account.

To illustrate, assume that $100.00 in currency is received from A on account. The cashier pockets the money and makes no entry. But it is dangerous to leave A's account uncredited for any length of time, since A may receive a statement and make a protest, which will bring the facts to light. Therefore, within a day or two, when $110.00 is collected from B, the cashier turns in $100.00 of the cash, debits Cash and credits A with $100.00, and pockets the extra $10.00. This process may be carried on indefinitely, the cashier being short all the time, but the credit to each customer's account being delayed only a few days.

Non-cash credits to customers.

Another method of covering a shortage consists of taking money received from a customer and passing a non-cash credit through the books, usually for some item such as returns and allowances. The system of safeguarding receipts already discussed will make this practice difficult; but, in addition, it is desirable to have all non-cash credits supported by duplicate credit memorandums, which should be initialed by someone in authority other than the cashier.

Petty cash fund.

In the discussion of the system of internal check, it was stated that all disbursements should be made by check. How is this possible when certain disbursements of trifling amounts, for carfares and lunches, for instance, must be made in cash? While such petty disbursements may not actually be made by check, their total can be represented by checks if a petty, sometimes called imprest, cash fund is operated.

A check is drawn for an amount which will provide for petty disbursements for a reasonable time, and cashed; the cash is held in the office. The drawing of the check is recorded by a debit to Petty Cash and a credit to the general Cash account. As disbursements are made from the petty cash fund, receipts and other memoranda are retained as evidence of their propriety. When the fund is nearly exhausted, another check is cashed for the amount of the expenditures; this check is recorded by a credit to the general Cash account and a debit to various expense (or other) accounts indicated by the receipts and other memoranda.

Reconciliation of bank account.

The balance shown by the bank's statement at the end of the month rarely agrees with the balance shown by the depositor's books. Almost invariably checks are outstanding; deposits mailed to the bank on the last day of the period may not have been received and credited by the bank; and the proceeds of notes and drafts left with the bank for collection may have been credited by the bank but not taken up on the depositor's books.

Before the balance sheet is prepared, therefore, the bank account should be reconciled. If the differences consist entirely of items on the depositor's books but not on the bank's books, the reconciliation may be prepared as follows:

Bank Reconciliation—December 31, 1941

Balance per bank statement..................................		$ 862.57
Add deposit, December 31, not recorded by bank until January		216.31
Total..		$1,078.88
Deduct checks outstanding:		
No. 965...	$31.53	
No. 971...	15.31	46.84
Balance per books..		$1,032.04

If, in addition, items appear on the bank statement which have not been recorded on the company's books, the true balance is not shown by either the bank statement or the books, and both balances must be reconciled to the correct balance; for example:

Bank Reconciliation—December 31, 1941

Balance per bank statement..................................		$2,500.00
Items shown by company's books, but not yet taken up by the bank:		
Add deposit mailed December 31.........................		1,000.00
Total..		$3,500.00
Deduct checks outstanding:		
No. 79...	$200.00	
No. 83...	50.00	250.00
Correct balance..		$3,250.00
Balance per books..		$2,450.85
Items shown by bank statement, but not yet recorded on company's books:		
Add proceeds of paper collected by bank:		
Sight draft on James Brown..........................		500.00
Note receivable from J. C. Kent......................		300.00
Total..		$3,250.85
Deduct collection charges..............................		.85
Correct balance..		$3,250.00

After the reconciliation has been completed, entries should be made in the books for any items shown by the bank statement but not yet recorded by the company, so that the cash balance will be shown correctly by the books and in the balance sheet.

Distorted cash balances.

To make a better showing in its balance sheet, a company may resort to the practice of "holding its cash book open" for a few days after the close of the period. This means that remittances received from debtors after the close of the year are recorded as additions to cash and deductions from accounts receivable as of the last day of the year. This has the effect of overstating the most current asset, cash, and understating the less current asset of accounts receivable.

The company may then go a step further by drawing checks after the close of the period for the payment of current liabilities, and recording such payments as of the last day of the period.

To show how this practice misstates the current position, let us assume that the following transactions actually occurred in January, 1942, but were recorded as having taken place on December 31, 1941:

Cash collections on accounts receivable..................... $25,000.00
Cash payments on accounts payable........................   20,000.00

The true working capital condition on December 31, 1941 is shown below in the first column; the misstated condition is shown in the second column.

	Correct	Distorted
Current assets:		
Cash..	$ 5,000.00	$10,000.00
Accounts receivable.....................................	50,000.00	25,000.00
Inventories...	30,000.00	30,000.00
Total current assets.................................	$85,000.00	$65,000.00
Current liabilities:		
Accounts payable.....................................	50,000.00	30,000.00
Net current assets....................................	$35,000.00	$35,000.00
Working capital ratio—or dollars of current assets per dollar of current liabilities..............	1.70	2.17
Dollars of cash per dollar of current liabilities...	.10	.33

By this artful dodge, the company shows a working capital ratio of 2.17 to 1 instead of 1.70 to 1, and considerably overstates its cash balance and the ratio of cash to current liabilities.

ACCOUNTS RECEIVABLE

edger rulings.

Accounts with debtors can be kept on ledger sheets ruled in
ie form of all preceding illustrations.   Such an account is shown
elow.

Fred White

41					1941					
ne	21	....	S2	500|00	June	25	....	CR1	300|00
	27	....	S3	425|00	July	9	....	CR2	200|00

This form has one distinct disadvantage: there is no column in
hich to show the balance of the account.   Such a column is
·ovided in the following ruling:

Fred White

)ate		Explanation	Folio	Debit	Credit	Balance
41						
ne	21	....	S2	500|00		500|00
	25	....	CR1		300|00	200|00
	27	....	S3	425|00		625|00
ly	9	....	CR2		200|00	425|00

In accounts with debtors, the amount shown in the Balance
lumn is assumed to be a debit balance; if, for any reason, the
count develops a credit balance, this fact may be indicated by
riting the balance in red ink or by following the balance with
·e letters *Cr.*

bdivided subsidiary ledgers.

In a large business there may be so many customers' accounts
at the subsidiary ledger cannot be kept by one bookkeeper.   In
ch cases, the subsidiary ledger may be divided into sections, as:

Accounts Receivable—A to H.
Accounts Receivable—I to P.
Accounts Receivable—Q to Z.

One controlling account with Accounts Receivable may control all of the subsidiary ledgers, but it is much better to have a separate controlling account for each ledger, so that each subsidiary bookkeeper's work can be verified independently. It then becomes desirable to have a separate controlling account column for each subsidiary ledger in the various books of original entry, as illustrated below:

Sales Book

Date	√	Invoice No.	Name	Debit Accounts Receivable			Credit Sales
				A-H	I-P	Q-Z	

Ledger headings.

The headings of the ledger sheets or cards used for accounts receivable usually are provided with spaces in which to enter certain general information relating to the debtor which may be useful for credit or sales purposes. The data varies in different businesses, but provision usually is made to show the information indicated by the following illustration representing the heading of a customer's account.

Sheet No._____   Name_____
Rating_____   Address_____
Credit Limit_____   _____
Salesman_____   Business_____

The Sheet Number space is needed on active accounts extending over several pages kept in a loose-leaf binder; if the current sheet is number 7, it is known that six other sheets must be found, either in the current binder or in the transfer binder, to include the entire account.

The Rating space is used to show the credit rating given the customer by rating agencies, such as Dun & Bradstreet.

The Credit Limit space shows the maximum fixed by the credit department.

The salesman's name may be desired on the account so that the sales manager can see whether the salesman appears to be neglecting his sales opportunity with the customer, and so that the credit and collection department can see which salesmen are making sales on accounts that become delinquent.

Account and statement at one impression.

Many concerns which make a practice of sending monthly statements to their customers use bookkeeping machines to keep their accounts receivable. The machines type the entries and compute and enter the balance after each entry. Such concerns generally use the three-column ledger ruling with debit, credit, and balance columns at the right side.

At the beginning of the month, a statement form is inserted in the binder with each customer's ledger sheet, and a carbon is used so that the ledger account and the statement are duplicates. At the end of the month the statement is removed from the binder and mailed to the customer.

Lettering and checking entries.

The following illustration shows how entries in accounts with Balance columns may be checked and lettered to indicate offsetting items.

J. H. Boyce

Date		Explanation	Folio	Debit	Credit	Balance
1941						
Sep.	15	....	S1	a 250 00		250 00
Oct.	3	....	S2	b 500 00 ✓		750 00
	9	....	CR1		b 500 00 ✓	250 00
	15	....	S2	c 800 00 ✓		1,050 00
	20	Note Receivable...............	J2		c 500 00 ✓	550 00
	20	....	CR2		c 300 00 ✓	250 00
	22	....	S3	d 750 00 ✓		1,000 00
	25	....	S3	d 200 00 ✓		1,200 00
	31	....	CR3		d 950 00 ✓	250 00
Nov.	5	....	S4	e 600 00 ✓		850 00
	7	....	S4	f 250 00		1,100 00
	9	....	CR4		e 200 00 ✓	900 00
	10	Note Receivable...............	J3		e 400 00 ✓	500 00
	11	....	S4	g 375 00		875 00
	16	....	CR5		f 100 00	775 00

The components of the $775.00 balance of this account can be quickly ascertained. The checked items can be ignored; they represent offsetting items which do not enter into the balance. The balance consists of:

(a) September 15 debit.. $250.00
(f) November 7 debit............................... $250.00
    Less credit of November 16 applicable to it....... 100.00   150.00
(g) November 11 debit...................................... 375.00
    Total.. $775.00

Current and non-current accounts receivable.

Certain kinds of receivables are not likely to be collected in the relatively near future and in the regular order of business; such receivables should not be shown in the balance sheet under the Current Assets caption.   Some receivables of this nature are mentioned below.

Amounts receivable from officers, directors, and stockholders (unless the accounts arose from sales which are collectible in accordance with the regular credit terms) are not likely to be collected with any promptness, and should not be classified as current assets.

Advances to subsidiary or affiliated companies, if of a more or less permanent nature, should not be included with customers' accounts in the balance sheet.   However, if a corporation sells merchandise to a related company and receives collections as regularly and promptly as from other customers, such receivables (as distinguished from permanent advances) may properly be included among the accounts receivable under the Current Assets caption.

In most businesses, the terms of sale require payment within 30, 60, or 90 days; therefore, the reader of a balance sheet has the right to assume that the accounts receivable are relatively quick assets.   But in some lines of business the accounts receivable are collectible in installments over a long period of time; the author has in mind cases where the installments extend over a period as long as three years.   To include the total of such receivables under the current caption would produce a grossly misleading ratio of current assets to current liabilities.   In such cases the balance sheet may show the total of the currently collectible installments under the Current Assets caption and the total of the non-current installments below the current caption.   Or the issue may be dodged by the omission of all side captions from the balance sheet; thus no claim is made that the receivables are current, but the reader of such a balance sheet should be on notice that the omission of the current captions may mean that the receivables are not all current and may be collectible over a long period of time.

Credit balances in customers' accounts.

The individual accounts in the accounts receivable ledger normally have debit balances; some accounts may run into credit balances because of overpayments, because of credits for returns and allowances after the account has been collected in full, or for other reasons.

If there are credit balances in the subsidiary ledger, the balance in the controlling account will be equal to the total debit balances minus the total credit balances in the subsidiary ledger. For instance:

Debit balances in subsidiary ledger	$6,500.00
Credit balances in subsidiary ledger	175.00
Debit balance in controlling account	$6,325.00

The debit balance of the controlling account should not be shown in the balance sheet; that would indicate that there are receivables of $6,325.00. Actually there are receivables of $6,500.00 and payables of $175.00. The balance sheet should show as receivables the total debit balances in the subsidiary ledger, and as liabilities the total credit balances.

CURRENT ASSETS:
   Accounts Receivable.......... $6,500

CURRENT LIABILITIES:
   Credit Balances in Customers' Accounts................... $175

Accounts receivable assigned.

Some businesses finance their current operations to some extent by selling or assigning their accounts receivable to discount companies. These discount companies advance funds under so many different kinds of contracts that it is impossible to discuss the subject thoroughly here. To illustrate one form of contract, assume that:

A company assigns accounts receivable totaling	$10,000.00
And receives from the discount company cash amounting to	8,000.00
Remainder	$ 2,000.00
The discount company charges a commission of	500.00
Leaving the company an equity in the assigned accounts of	$ 1,500.00

The discount company is entitled to the first $8,500.00 collected; the company that sold the accounts is entitled to the $1,500.00 remainder, less interest charges.

Assume that the company also has $20,000.00 of accounts which it did not assign and that it shows its accounts receivable in the balance sheet as follows:

CURRENT ASSETS:
   Accounts Receivable.................................... $21,500.00

This is a misleading statement because it does not disclose the important fact that $1,500.00 of the $21,500.00 is an equity in assigned accounts. This fact is shown in the following statement:

CURRENT ASSETS:
Accounts Receivable......................... $20,000.00
Equity in Assigned Accounts................   1,500.00 $21,500.00

But even such a presentation of the facts is not adequate, because a company assigning its accounts receivable is usually obliged to guarantee them, and thus assumes a contingent liability for their payment to the discount company. The balance sheet should disclose this contingent liability, either by a footnote to the effect that "The company was contingently liable on December 31, 1941, in the amount of $8,500.00 as guarantor of assigned accounts receivable," or by showing the receivables in the balance sheet thus:

CURRENT ASSETS:
Accounts Receivable......................... $20,000.00
Equity in $10,000.00 of Accounts Receivable
Assigned under Guarantee.................   1,500.00 $21,500.00

25

NOTES AND ACCEPTANCES RECEIVABLE

....

Promissory notes.

The following definition is quoted from the Uniform Negotiable Instruments Act:

A negotiable promissory note within the meaning of this act is an unconditional promise in writing made by one person to another, signed by the maker, engaging to pay on demand or at a fixed or determinable future time a sum certain in money to order or bearer.

The original parties to a note are the maker and the payee. If the payee transfers the note by endorsement, he becomes an endorser; the party to whom the note is transferred is the endorsee.

Endorsements.

Paper which is payable to a named payee *or order* must be endorsed to be transferred. Paper which is payable *to bearer* can legally be transferred by delivery without endorsement; however, the party to whom the paper is to be transferred may require that it be endorsed, in order to make the transferor contingently liable for its payment.

Endorsements are classified and illustrated below. F. K. Hamilton was the original payee of the note.

(1) *Unqualified endorsements* (the transferor assumes the full contingent liability imposed by law upon an endorser):

    (a) In full (shows name of party to whom the paper is transferred):

Pay to the order of
John Smith
F. K. Hamilton

    The paper is still payable *to order*; that is, Smith must endorse it in order to transfer it.

(b) In blank (does not show name of party to whom the paper is transferred):

F. K. Hamilton

The paper is now payable to bearer and can legally be transferred by subsequent holders without endorsement.

One who endorses unqualifiedly may be held for the payment of the paper if it is presented to the maker at maturity and dishonored by him, and if the endorser is given notice of the dishonor in accordance with the legal requirements.

(2) *Qualified endorsement* (the endorser limits his contingent liability by inserting the words *Without Recourse*):

(a) In full:
Pay to the order of
John Smith
Without Recourse
F. K. Hamilton

(b) In blank:
Without Recourse
F. K. Hamilton

One who endorses *without recourse* materially lessens his contingent liability as an endorser. He warrants that the paper is valid and that he has a good title to it, but he does not assume a legal obligation to pay merely because the maker does not do so.

(3) *Restrictive endorsement* (which must be in full):

(a) To prevent further transfers:
Pay to John Smith only
F. K. Hamilton

(b) To make the endorsee an agent for a special purpose:
Pay to the order of
First National Bank
For collection
F. K. Hamilton

Purpose of endorsements.

Endorsements are made for two purposes:

(1) To transfer negotiable instruments.
(2) To lend one's credit (accommodation endorsements).

As an illustration of an endorsement for the latter purpose, ssume that John Brown wishes to borrow $1,000.00 from the ank, and that the bank will not make the loan unless some person f good financial standing will endorse the note. Fred White grees to accommodate Brown in this way. Brown makes a note ayable to the bank, and White endorses it, thus assuming a contingent liability to pay the note if Brown dishonors it at its naturity.

Notes without interest.

The following entries, stated in journal form, record certain ransactions in non-interest-bearing notes:

```
Notes Receivable................................  1,000.00
    Cash........................................            1,000.00
    60-day note from John Maker for cash loan to him.

Notes Receivable................................  2,000.00
    John Maker..................................            2,000.00
    90-day note received from Maker to apply on his
    account.

Cash............................................  1,000.00
    Notes Receivable............................            1,000.00
    Collected note from John Maker.
```

Notes with interest.

Following are entries for transactions involving notes bearing unning interest:

```
Notes Receivable................................  2,000.00
    John Maker..................................            2,000.00
    90-day note received from Maker to apply on his
    account.

Cash............................................  2,030.00
    Notes Receivable............................            2,000.00
    Interest Income.............................              30.00
    Collected 90-day note from John Maker, with 6%
    interest.
```

Dishonor at maturity.

If a note received from a debtor to apply on account cannot be collected at maturity, it should be charged back to the account eceivable from the debtor so that the debtor's account will show, or purposes of credit information, that the note was dishonored. Cases involving dishonored notes are illustrated on the following page.

(1) We were unable to collect a non-interest-bearing note from the maker

```
John Maker................................ 1,500.00
    Notes Receivable........................         1,500.00
    To charge back dishonored note.
```

(2) We were unable to collect a 60-day interest-bearing note. The maker's account should be charged with the interest because he owes the interest as well as the principal.

```
John Maker................................ 1,515.00
    Notes Receivable........................         1,500.00
    Interest Income.........................           15.00
    To charge back dishonored note and accrued
    interest.
```

(3) Maker dishonors his 60-day, 6% note for $5,000.00, but gives us a new note for the principal and interest.

```
John Maker................................ 5,050.00
    Notes Receivable........................         5,000.00
    Interest Income.........................           50.00
    To charge back dishonored note.

Notes Receivable.......................... 5,050.00
    John Maker.............................         5,050.00
    To record new note received.
```

(4) At the maturity of a 60-day, 6% note for $1,000.00, we collect the interest and $300.00 on the principal, and receive a new note for the balance of the principal.

```
Cash...................................... 310.00
    Notes Receivable........................         300.00
    Interest Income.........................          10.00
    Partial collection of John Maker note.

John Maker................................ 700.00
    Notes Receivable........................         700.00
    Dishonored portion of note charged to him.

Notes Receivable.......................... 700.00
    John Maker.............................         700.00
    New note received.
```

Discounting notes receivable—Computing proceeds.

If we wish to borrow money at the bank, we may issue our own note to the bank, or we may endorse and discount at the bank any notes receivable held by us which are acceptable to the bank. The proceeds of discounted notes are computed as follows:

First, determine the value of the note at maturity (i.e., the amount which the bank will be entitled to collect at maturity):

On non-interest-bearing notes, this value is the face.

On interest-bearing notes, the value at maturity is the face plus interest for the full period of the note.

Second, determine the discount period, or time from the date of discount to maturity.

Third, compute the discount at the bank's rate, on the value at maturity, for the discount period.

Fourth, deduct the discount from the value at maturity.

To illustrate, let us compute the proceeds of two notes:

	B. Bates	C. Cole
Maker..	B. Bates	C. Cole
Date of note...................................	August 1	August 1
Time from date of note to maturity..............	60 days	60 days
Date of discount...............................	August 11	August 11
Discount period—or time from date of discount to maturity.....................................	50 days	50 days
Rate of interest borne by the note................	None	5½%
Rate of discount charged by the bank............	6%	6%
Computation of proceeds:		
Face of note.................................	$6,000.00	$6,000.00
Add interest from date of note to maturity:		
The Bates note is non-interest-bearing.		
Interest on the Cole note at 5½% for 60 days is..		55.00
Value at maturity............................	$6,000.00	$6,055.00
Deduct discount at 6% for 50 days:		
50 days' interest on $6,000.00................	50.00	
50 days' interest on $6,055.00................		50.46
Proceeds....................................	$5,950.00	$6,004.54

ecording the discounting of notes.

To transfer the Bates and Cole notes to the bank, we must ndorse them, thus rendering ourselves contingently liable for eir payment. This contingent liability should be shown in our counts. Therefore, in recording the discount transaction, we all credit an account called Notes Receivable Discounted, as lustrated by the following entries:

Bates note—for which we receive less than the face:

Cash..	5,950.00	
Interest Expense..................................	50.00	
Notes Receivable Discounted..................		6,000.00
Note of B. Bates discounted at bank.		

Cole note—for which we receive more than the face:

Cash..	6,004.54	
Notes Receivable Discounted..................		6,000.00
Interest Income..............................		4.54
Note of C. Cole discounted at bank.		

The $50.00 charge to Interest Expense in the entry for the discounting of the Bates note represents the expense incurred for the use of money from August 11 to September 30, or for fifty days. If statements are prepared or the books are closed at the end of August, only $20.00 of the interest charge should be regarded as an expense of August, and the $30.00 expense applicable to September should be treated as a deferred charge.

On the other hand, the $4.54 credit to Interest Income in the entry for the discounting of the Cole note is the amount earned during the ten-day period from August 1 to August 11, while the note was held. The entire $4.54 is therefore an earning of the month of August, and no portion thereof should be deferred at the end of that month.

Ledger accounts.

Assume that, after the foregoing entries have been posted, the Notes Receivable account and the Notes Receivable Discounted account appear as follows:

Notes Receivable

1941						1941				
July	1	A. Arnold 30 da.....	J1	a5,000	00	July	31	A. Arnold..........	J1	a5,000	00
Aug.	1	B. Bates 60 da......	J2	b6,000	00					
	1	C. Cole 60 da. 5½%	J2	c6,000	00					
	5	D. Dale 60 da. 6%..	J3	d2,000	00					

Notes Receivable Discounted

						1941				
						Aug.	11	B. Bates...........	J4	b6,000	00
							11	C. Cole............	J4	c6,000	00

These two accounts give the following information with respect to the notes receivable:

The Arnold note has been collected, as indicated by the credit in the Notes Receivable account.

The Bates and the Cole notes have been discounted; the debits in the Notes Receivable account are offset by the credits in the Notes Receivable Discounted account. So far as these two notes are concerned, we have no asset and no actual liability, but the contingent liability is indicated by the Notes Receivable Discounted account.

The Dale note is still owned.

alance sheet presentation.

The balance sheet should indicate that our asset of notes ceivable amounts to $2,000.00, and that we have a contingent ability on notes receivable discounted in the amount of $12,- 00.00. There are several ways of showing these facts on the alance sheet; the method most in favor among public accountants illustrated below:

Balance Sheet, August 31, 1941

Assets	Liabilities
Notes Receivable....... $2,000.00	

Note: The company was contingently liable, on August 31, 1941, on notes receivable discounted in the amount of $12,000.00.

This method may be stated as follows:

On the asset side of the balance sheet show the excess of the debit balance of the Notes Receivable account over the credit balance of the Notes Receivable Discounted account; this net amount represents the notes receivable on hand. (In the illustration, the $2,000.00 represents the Dale note, which is the only one still held.)

State the contingent liability on notes receivable discounted by a footnote below the balance sheet totals.

iscounted note receivable paid by maker.

Assume that B. Bates paid his note to the bank at maturity; e no longer have any contingent liability on his note and can nerefore make the following journal entry:

Notes Receivable Discounted......................	6,000.00	
Notes Receivable............................		6,000.00
Bates note paid to bank by maker at maturity		

The accounts now appear as follows:

Notes Receivable

41					1941				
uly	1	A. Arnold 30 da.....	J1	a5,000 00	July	31	A. Arnold.........	J1	a5,000 00
ug.	1	B. Bates 60 da.....	J2	b6,000 00	Sep.	30	B. Bates..........	J8	b6,000 00
	1	C. Cole 60 da. 5½%	J2	c6,000 00					
	5	D. Dale 60 da. 6%..	J3	d2,000 00					

Notes Receivable Discounted

41					1941				
p.	30	B. Bates..........	J8	b6,000 00	Aug.	11	B. Bates..........	J4	b6,000 00
						11	C. Cole..........	J4	c6,000 00

Discounted note dishonored by maker.

An endorser cannot be held for the payment of a discounted note unless the holder has presented it to the maker at maturity, demanded and not received payment, and given proper notice of dishonor to the endorser. In some cases, notice of dishonor can be given informally, either orally or in writing. In other cases, notably those of *foreign* paper (that is, paper originating in one state and payable in another), protest and formal notice of dishonor are necessary. Notice may in any case be given in this manner if the holder of the paper desires to do so.

Protest is a formal declaration in writing by a notary public to the effect that he has presented an instrument to the person primarily liable thereon and demanded payment, and that the instrument has been dishonored. Notice of protest is sent by the notary public to the maker and to all of the endorsers.

The holder of the paper engages the services of the notary public and pays his fee, which he may charge back to the endorser.

To illustrate the entries to be made in the event that a discounted note receivable is not paid by the maker at maturity, let us assume that C. Cole (in our previous illustration) dishonored his note at maturity, and that it was protested by the bank. We are obliged to make the following payment to the bank:

Face of note...	$6,000.00
Interest at 5½% for 60 days.............................	55.00
Protest fee...	2.04
Total...	$6,057.04

In the following entry recording the payment of the note, interest, and protest fee, the entire disbursement is charged to C. Cole because we are entitled to reimbursement of the whole amount from him.

C. Cole..	6,057.04	
Cash.......................................		6,057.04
Payment of dishonored note, interest, and protest fee.		

There is no longer any contingent liability on this note; it developed into a real liability, which was paid. Therefore the following entry should also be made:

Notes Receivable Discounted......................	6,000.00	
Notes Receivable.............................		6,000.00
To eliminate contingent liability on Cole note discounted, and paid by us at maturity. See cash disbursement entry.		

Bills of exchange.

The following definition is quoted from the Uniform Negotiable Instruments Act:

A bill of exchange is an unconditional order in writing addressed by one person to another, signed by the person giving it, requiring the person to whom it is addressed to pay on demand or at a fixed or determinable future time a sum certain in money to order or bearer.

The parties to a bill of exchange are:

The drawer—the person signing the order.
The drawee—the person to whom the bill is addressed and who is ordered to make the payment.
The payee—the person to whom payment is to be made.

Bank and commercial bills.

A check is a bill of exchange; it is a written order in which the depositor (as drawer) orders the bank (as drawee) to pay a certain sum of money to a named person or to bearer. A bank draft is a bill of exchange drawn by a bank against its deposit in some other bank. A cashier's check is an order drawn by a bank against itself. Bank bills have the status of cash, and consequently will not be considered in this chapter.

Three-party bills.

In early days, before the development of bank facilities, three-party drafts were not infrequently used. If A, living in New York, had on his books an account receivable from B and an account payable to C, both in San Francisco, he might effect a settlement with both parties by drawing a draft on B ordering him to pay C, thus avoiding the transfer of funds from B in San Francisco to New York and back again to C. With the bank facilities which are now generally available, such drafts are rarely used. In this chapter, therefore, we shall be concerned only with two-party drafts.

Two-party sight draft.

A two-party sight draft, or demand draft, is illustrated on the following page. J. K. Graf & Co. is both drawer and payee.

Although the drawee is ordered to pay the draft immediately upon presentation to him, he is under no obligation to do so unless he has agreed to honor the draft.

```
$100.00              Chicago, Illinois,  July 20,  1941

At sight                          Pay to the order of OURSELVES

One Hundred - no/100 - - - - - - - - - - - - Dollars

   To   C. V. Olander

        Decatur, Illinois        J. K. Graf & Co.
```

Two-Party Sight Draft

Two-party sight draft for collection of an account.

Two-party sight drafts are sometimes used in an attempt to obtain collection of a past-due account. To illustrate, assume that Olander owed J. K. Graf & Co. $100.00 on open account and paid no attention to letters requesting payment. J. K. Graf & Co. drew the above draft, endorsed it as follows:

Pay to the order of
First National Bank of Chicago
For Collection
J. K. Graf & Co.

and left it with the First National Bank. This bank in turn endorsed it to some bank in Decatur, preferably the bank in which Olander keeps his account. The Decatur bank then presented it to Olander for payment. While Olander was under no greater obligation to pay the draft than he was to respond to the collection letters, he might do so in order to preserve his credit standing with his bank.

If Olander pays the draft to his local bank, that bank will remit the proceeds to the First National Bank of Chicago, after deduction of a collection fee. The Chicago bank may also charge a collection fee.

J. K. Graf & Co. should make no entry at the time of drawing the draft, as it may not be collected. If they receive notice from the Chicago bank that the draft has been collected, and that their account has been credited with the net proceeds (say $99.70), they should make entries which may be expressed in journal form as follows:

```
Cash....................................................  99.70
Collection and Exchange................................    .30
     C. V. Olander.....................................           100.00
```

Two-party sight draft for C.O.D. sale.

When the seller of merchandise which is to be shipped by freight wishes to make the sale on C.O.D. terms, he obtains an order bill of lading from the railroad.   When an order bill of lading is used, the purchaser cannot obtain the merchandise from the carrier without presenting the bill of lading.   When an order bill of lading is used, the purchaser cannot obtain the merchandise from the carrier without presenting the bill of lading.

The seller attaches the bill of lading to a sight draft payable to himself.   He endorses the bill of lading and the draft, and leaves them with his bank.   The bank sends the draft, with bill of lading attached, to a bank in the purchaser's city; this bank notifies the purchaser that it holds the sight draft and the bill of lading. The purchaser goes to the bank, pays the draft, and obtains the bill of lading.   The bank returns the proceeds to the shipper's bank, which credits the shipper's account.   Either or both of the banks may charge a collection fee.

At the time of shipping the merchandise, the seller will debit the customer and credit Sales; when the proceeds of the draft are received, he will debit Cash (and Collection and Exchange if such a charge is made) and credit the customer.

Two-party time draft.

A two-party time draft is illustrated below:

$100.00	Chicago, Illinois, July 20, 19 41

Thirty days after date Pay to the order of OURSELVES

One Hundred - no/100 - - - - - - - - - - - - Dollars

To C. V. Olander

Decatur, Illinois   J. K. Graf & Co.

Two-Party Time Draft

Acceptance.

A time draft should be presented to the drawee to obtain his agreement to pay it at maturity.   This agreement is called *acceptance* of the draft and is expressed by the following words written across the face of the draft:

Accepted

[Drawee's signature]

After a time draft has been accepted by the drawee, it is called an acceptance. Thus the word "acceptance" has two meanings: the act of accepting, and an accepted draft.

Time drafts may be payable:

(1) A certain period after the date of the paper, thus:

> "Thirty days after date, pay to the order of (. . .)."

A draft drawn on June 15, payable thirty days after date, will be due on July 15, regardless of the date on which it is accepted. Since the date of acceptance has no bearing on the maturity of the draft, the date of acceptance need not be shown.

(2) A certain period after the date of the acceptance, thus:

> "Thirty days after sight, pay to the order of (. . .)," or
> "At thirty days' sight, pay to the order of (. . .)."

A draft drawn on June 15, payable thirty days after sight, and accepted on June 20, will be due on July 20. Since the date of acceptance of such a draft determines the date of its maturity, the date of acceptance should be shown thus:

> Accepted
> June 20, 1941
> [Drawee's signature]

Accounts with notes and acceptances.

An accepted time draft, like a promissory note, is a debtor's written agreement to pay a certain sum of money at a fixed or determinable future date. Therefore, most accountants record acceptances receivable in the Notes Receivable account, and acceptances payable in the Notes Payable account.

Two-party time draft for collection purposes.

Occasionally two-party time drafts are used to reduce a past-due account to a written promise to pay. If a debtor will not pay his account, he may consent to give a promissory note or accept a time draft. If a time draft is to be used, it will be drawn by the creditor and sent to the debtor for acceptance. If the drawee accepts the draft, the drawer should record the fact by debiting Notes Receivable and crediting the drawee. When the draft is collected, the collection should be recorded by a debit to Cash and a credit to Notes Receivable.

Two-party time draft per terms of sale.

Frequently the terms of sale require the purchaser of merchandise to accept a time draft for the amount of the invoice. This is desirable from the seller's standpoint for two reasons: first, the debtor's obligation is reduced to writing and has a definite maturity; second, the seller can discount the acceptance.

If the purchaser has established a credit standing with the seller, the merchandise is shipped on a straight bill of lading and the draft is sent to the purchaser for acceptance. If the purchaser has not established a credit standing, a draft with an order bill of lading attached may be sent to a bank in the purchaser's city. The purchaser must accept the draft before the bank will release the bill of lading.

The seller should record the sale in the customary manner by a debit to the customer and a credit to Sales. When the draft comes back to him accepted, he should debit Notes Receivable and credit the customer. When the acceptance is collected at maturity, he should debit Cash and credit Notes Receivable.

If the seller discounts the acceptance at his bank, he will make the entries at the date of discount and at the date of maturity that were described earlier in this chapter in connection with notes receivable discounted.

Trade acceptance.

A trade acceptance is a draft or a bill of exchange, drawn by the seller on the purchaser of goods sold, accepted by such purchaser, and bearing on its face the evidence that it arose from a sale of merchandise. Trade acceptances are used in connection with transactions of the nature just described.

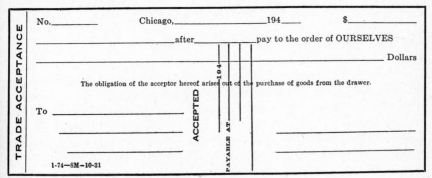

Trade Acceptance

Notes receivable register.

The space available in a ledger account for the description of notes and acceptances is so small that it is advisable to keep a supplementary register to show all explanatory data.

The customary debits and credits for note transactions are posted to the ledger account, which might appear as follows:

Notes Receivable

1941							1941						
Aug.	15	....	J1	a2,400	00		Aug.	25	....	CR1	a2,400	00
	15	....	J1	b4,000	00			27	....	CR1	b4,000	00
	20	....	J1	c6,000	00							
	26	....	J1	d4,500	00							

The related register appears on the opposite page.

The first three items in the register represent notes receivable; the fourth represents an acceptance. All of the entries in the note register are self-explanatory with the possible exception of the figures in the narrow columns headed J, F, M, and so forth. These columns represent the different months of the year, and the numbers in the columns show the day of the month on which the paper matures.

Notes and acceptances receivable in the balance sheet.

Only currently collectible notes and acceptances receivable should be included under the current asset caption in the balance sheet. Notes receivable from officers, employees, subsidiaries, or others from whom collections cannot be expected currently, may be shown as notes receivable, but not under the current caption.

Past-due notes, theoretically, should not be shown in the balance sheet with other notes receivable; a past-due note has lost one of the principal characteristics of a negotiable promissory note, for it is no longer payable at a fixed or determinable future date. However, in most cases, past-due notes are included with other notes, and the fact that they are past due is disclosed in the comments of the auditor's report.

If the reserve for bad debts provides for losses on notes and acceptances receivable as well as for losses on accounts receivable, the reserve may be deducted from the total of the accounts, notes, and acceptances. Or a separate reserve may be established for the notes and acceptances.

The contingent liability on notes or acceptances discounted should be disclosed on the balance sheet in the manner indicated earlier in the chapter.

Notes Receivable Register

Date Recd.	Date of Paper	Maker or Drawee	Drawer or Endorser	Where Payable	Time Mo.	Da.	Int. Rate	Year	When Payable							A	S				Amount	Date Paid	Remarks
									J	F	M	A	M	J	J	A	S	O	N	D			
1941 Aug. 15	Aug. 15	J. B. Lakin............		Our office	10		6%	1941								25					2,400 00	Aug. 25	
15	15	C. E. Weldon..........		First Natl.	12		6%	1941								27					4,000 00	27	
20	20	C. M. White...........			30		6%	1941									19				6,000 00		
26	26	F. M. Miller (accept.)........		Our office	30			1941									25				4,500 00		Disc. Aug. 29 at First Natl.

26

VALUATION RESERVES AGAINST RECEIVABLES

Reserves required.

The accounts receivable and the notes receivable should be valued in the balance sheet at the total thereof, less certain reserves. A reserve for bad debts should almost always be provided, and sometimes there should also be reserves for returned sales and allowances, freight, and cash discounts which will be deducted by customers.

Reserve for bad debts.

Two objects are sought by the creation of a reserve for bad debts:

(1) To charge the loss against the period that caused the loss by the sale of goods to customers whose accounts proved to be uncollectible.
(2) To show the estimated realizable value of the customers' accounts.

It is not always possible, however, to accomplish both of these results, as will be shown in the following discussion of the various methods of estimating the amounts to be credited periodically to the reserve.

The amount to be credited to the reserve is usually determined in one of three ways:

(1) By aging the receivables and considering supplementary data.
(2) By setting up in the reserve a percentage of the accounts open at the end of the period.
(3) By crediting the reserve with a percentage of the sales for the period.

Aging the receivables.

A schedule of the accounts receivable ledger is drawn off on columnar paper, with columns headed to indicate various ages, such as 1 to 30 days, 31 to 60 days, 61 to 90 days, 3 to 6 months, and over 6 months. The balance of each debtor's account is analyzed to determine the age of the component elements, and the aging schedule is filled out by entries such as the following (which is based on the account with J. H. Boyce on page 211):

Accounts Receivable Aging, November 30, 1941

Name	Total	1–30 Days	31–60 Days	61–90 Days	3–6 Months	Over 6 Months
J. H. Boyce..........	775|00	525|00		250|00		

By reference to Boyce's account on page 211, it will be seen that the method of lettering and checking the entries in the accounts receivable is very helpful in preparing the aging schedule.

There are four unchecked items in the account, and these are, therefore, the only ones which enter into the balance:

Date		Debit	Credit
1941			
Sept. 15.....................................	(a)	$250.00	
Nov. 7.....................................	(f)	250.00	
11.....................................	(g)	375.00	
16.....................................	(f)		$100.00

The $775.00 balance in the account consists of the $250.00 September item (which is between 61 and 90 days old on November 30), and two November debits and one November credit in a net amount of $525.00 (which is between 1 and 30 days old on November 30).

After all of the balances have been aged, the columns are totaled and the reserve is estimated on the basis of the total amounts of various ages. Supplementary information must also be considered; some accounts which are not old may be known to be doubtful, while there may be good reason to believe that accounts long past due will be collected.

The amount to be added to the reserve is recorded by a journal entry debiting Bad Debts and crediting Reserve for Bad Debts.

A schedule showing the age of the receivables is not only helpful in estimating probable bad debt losses; it furnishes a good idea of the condition of the receivables, and therefore is informative to anyone interested in the financial condition of the business. For this reason such a schedule is frequently included in an audit report. It should be accompanied by information as to the terms

which sales are made, and its informative value is enhanced if
is prepared on a comparative basis showing the condition on two
tes.   Such a schedule is illustrated below.

| | December 31, 1941 | | December 31, 1940 | |
	Amount	Per Cent of Total	Amount	Per Cent of Total
t due	$15,000.00	30.93%	$20,000.00	41.67%
to 30 days past due	12,000.00	24.74	16,000.00	33.33
to 60 days past due	8,000.00	16.50	5,000.00	10.42
to 90 days past due	6,000.00	12.37	4,500.00	9.38
to 120 days past due	4,000.00	8.25	1,000.00	2.08
re than 120 days past due	2,000.00	4.12	1,000.00	2.08
nkrupt or with attorneys	1,500.00	3.09	500.00	1.04
Total	$48,500.00	100.00%	$48,000.00	100.00%
s reserve for bad debts	2,000.00	4.12	2,000.00	4.17
Net book value	$46,500.00	95.88%	$46,000.00	95.83%

This analysis shows (by comparison of amounts and per cents)
at the accounts are relatively less current on December 31,
41, than they were at the close of the preceding year; and
at, notwithstanding this fact, the reserve for bad debts is a
aller percentage of the total accounts.

This method has the advantage of accomplishing the second
the two objects stated above, since it results in a fairly accurate
luation of the accounts on the books.   However, it may easily
sult in a failure to distribute losses to the periods during which
ey were caused.   To illustrate, assume monthly closings, with
les, estimated uncollectibles, and ascertained losses as follows:

	January	February	March	April	May
es	$10,000	$10,000	$10,000	$10,000	$10,000
timated uncollectibles at end of month	100	110	125	130	150
sses ascertained during month	0	75	100	130	170

Since the sales are uniform month by month, it is to be assumed
at losses are caused in equal amounts by these sales; hence,
om the profit and loss standpoint, the charge for bad debts should
an equal amount monthly.   If the estimate of $150.00 for
collectible accounts at the end of May is correct, the average loss
r the five months is:

Actual losses ascertained in February	$ 75.00
" " " " March	100.00
" " " " April	130.00
" " " " May	170.00
Estimated uncollectibles at end of May	150.00
Total	$625.00
Average—per month	$125.00

The actual charges, month by month, are as follows:

January:	Charge to P. & L. to set up reserve	$100.00
February:	Bad debts charged to reserve	75.00
	Balance of reserve, end of February (before addition)	$ 25.00
	Charge to P. & L. to raise reserve to desired amount	85.00
	Balance—end of February	$110.00
March:	Bad debts charged to reserve	100.00
	Balance of reserve, end of March (before addition)	$ 10.00
	Charge to P. & L. to raise reserve to desired amount	115.00
	Balance—end of March	$125.00
April:	Bad debts charged to reserve	130.00
	Balance of reserve, end of April (before addition)	$ 5.00
	Charge to P. & L. to raise reserve to desired amount	135.00
	Balance—end of April	$130.00
May:	Losses ascertained during month	170.00
	Balance of reserve, end of May (before addition)	$ 40.00
	Charge to P. & L. to raise reserve to desired amount	190.00
	Balance—end of May	$150.00

* (Instead of throwing the reserve into a debit balance, the excess of losses over the available reserve could, and probably would, be charged direct to Bad Debts, but the net charge to Profit and Loss for the month would be the same.

Now this method does not produce an equitable distribution of the expense among the months, if it can be assumed that the losses are proportionate to sales, which is probably a fair assumption in most cases. The fact that an inequitable distribution of expense is made month by month is shown by the following comparative statement:

	Average Loss Proportionate to Sales	Actual Charge to Profit & Loss
January	$125.00	$100.00
February	125.00	85.00
March	125.00	115.00
April	125.00	135.00
May	125.00	190.00
Totals	$625.00	$625.00

Percentage of open accounts.

One can compute the required balance of the reserve by multiplying the total of the receivables open at the end of the period by a per cent, on the assumption that a certain per cent of the receivables will not be collected.

Assume that a company has accounts receivable of $40,000.00 and a reserve balance (resulting from former credits) of $1,000.00.

ssume, also, that the company's experience shows that about
per cent of the accounts on the books at any time will prove
ncollectible.   Then the total loss may be estimated at 8 per cent
$40,000.00, or $3,200.00.   Since the reserve already has a credit
alance of $1,000.00, only $2,200.00 need be added to the reserve;
his may be done by the following journal entry:

```
Bad Debts.......................................  2,200.00
    Reserve for Bad Debts........................            2,200.00
        To increase the reserve to the total estimated loss.
```

This method is not to be recommended, partly because of the
sadvantage pointed out in connection with the method of aging
e receivables, and partly because of the difficulty of making an
ccurate percentage estimate.   If the method is used, the rate
ould be determined by dividing the average losses during several
st periods by the average amount of receivables carried during
ose periods.

Moreover, after a rate has been decided upon, careful considera-
on must be given to the matter of a uniform policy with respect
write-offs.   To illustrate, let us assume that the rate in use was
etermined from the experience of a five-year period in which the
mpany has followed the policy of promptly writing off accounts
soon as they become extremely doubtful of collection.   Assume
at a 5 per cent rate is thus established.   At the end of 1941,
ere are $200,000.00 of accounts on the books; of these, $10,000.00
e of extremely doubtful collectibility, and there presumably
ill be losses on the remaining $190,000.00.   If the extremely
oubtful accounts are not written off before the addition is made to
e reserve, the reserve will be computed as 5 per cent of $200,-
00.00, and the accounts will be shown in the balance sheet as
llows:

```
Accounts Receivable........................ $200,000.00
    Less Reserve for Bad Debts...............   10,000.00 $190,000.00
```

If the extremely doubtful accounts are written off before the
serve is computed, the condition will be shown in the balance
eet as follows:

```
Accounts Receivable........................ $190,000.00
    Less Reserve for Bad Debts...    .......    9,500.00 $180,500.00
```

ercentage of sales.

Assume, for example, that the company mentioned above has
ound by experience that its bad debt losses average about 1 per

cent of its sales; on this basis, the reserve will be credited each period (month or year) with 1 per cent of the sales for the period.

From the profit and loss standpoint, this method probably produces the most equitable distribution of bad debt losses among periods. However, if the reserve credit is made only once a year, the result may be a very inaccurate statement of the estimated collectible value of the receivables shown in balance sheets prepared during the year.

To illustrate, if the reserve at the end of 1941 is in a reasonable amount to absorb losses on the receivables open at that date, charge-offs during 1942 (for losses on receivables open at the beginning of 1942 and on receivables arising from sales in 1942), without additional credits to the reserve, will so reduce the reserve that, by the latter part of 1942, it will no longer contain an adequate provision for losses on receivables then open. On the other hand, if the reserve at the beginning of 1942 was large enough to absorb all 1942 write-offs and still leave an adequate reserve against receivables open toward the end of that year, it surely was excessive at the beginning of the year, and the balance sheet then prepared understated the collectible value of the receivables.

For this reason, reserve provisions based on sales should be made monthly.

Writing off bad accounts.

When an account is finally regarded as uncollectible, it should be written off by an entry similar to the following:

```
Reserve for Bad Debts.................................  75.00
     P. K. Lane.....................................          75.00
     To write off the uncollectible account.
```

Recoveries.

Assume that Lane's account was finally collected. The collection might be recorded as follows:

```
Cash................................................  75.00
     Collections on Accounts Previously Written Off.........     75.00
     To show collection of P. K. Lane's account.
```

Since the debit to the reserve, to write off the account, proved to be erroneous, some accountants credit the reserve with the amount collected, thus:

```
Cash................................................  75.00
     Reserve for Bad Debts............................          75.00
     To record collection of P. K. Lane's account, previously
     written off.
```

But this procedure is not wholly satisfactory because the entry previously made in Lane's account, writing off the balance to the bad debt reserve, leaves a bad credit record in his account. For this reason it seems preferable to reverse the write-off entry and then record the collection in the debtor's account, as follows:

```
P. K. Lane.................................................... 75.00
     Reserve for Bad Debts................................          75.00
     To reverse entry writing off Lane's account.


Cash........................................................... 75.00
     P. K. Lane.............................................          75.00
     To record collection.
```

Reserves for returns and allowances, cash discounts, and freight.

Let us assume that a company has total accounts receivable of $20,000.00 on December 31, 1941, and has provided a reserve of $1,000.00 for bad debts. This reserve may be an adequate provision for bad debt losses, but it does not necessarily follow that the company will collect $19,000.00 from the accounts. Customers may demand credits for returned merchandise and allowances on defective goods; many of the debtors will take the cash discounts to which they are entitled; and, if the goods are sold on terms which require the customers to pay the freight but allow them to deduct such payments in remitting for the merchandise, deductions will be taken for such freight.

Theoretically, all of these prospective deductions should be provided for by reserves, so that the accounts receivable will be stated in the balance sheet at the estimated net amount which will be collected after all such deductions have been allowed. However, reserves for returns and allowances, cash discounts, and freight are rarely provided.

27

INVENTORIES

....

Kinds of inventories.

The inventory of a concern that buys its goods in condition for sale is usually called merely the merchandise inventory; in a manufacturing concern there are inventories of finished goods, goods in process, raw materials, and supplies. Whether supplies should be classified in the balance sheet as a current asset or a deferred charge is a debatable question.

Detailing the inventories.

The balance sheet should show the inventories of finished goods, goods in process, and raw materials in detail. To illustrate why this should be done, let us assume that a company shows merely the total of the three inventories in its balance sheet, and that the balance sheets at two dates showed the following:

On December 31, 1941....................................... $75,000.00
On December 31, 1940....................................... 70,000.00

No significant changes are disclosed. But suppose that, upon analysis, the following facts are shown:

	December 31, 1941		December 31, 1940	
	Amount	Per Cent of Total	Amount	Per Cent of Total
Finished goods...........	$10,000.00	13.33%	$20,000.00	28.57%
Goods in process.........	30,000.00	40.00	35,000.00	50.00
Raw materials...........	35,000.00	46.67	15,000.00	21.43
Total.................	$75,000.00	100.00%	$70.000.00	100.00%

The percentage of raw materials has greatly increased, and the percentage of finished goods has materially decreased. Since the raw materials cannot be converted into cash until they have been manufactured (which will require time and the incurring of manufacturing costs), the inventories were relatively much less current at the end of 1941 than they were at the end of 1940.

Essentials of inventory determination.

A correct determination of inventories involves questions of quantity, quality, ownership, and pricing. Quantities may be determined by physical count, measurement, or weighing; considerations of quality may necessitate the entire elimination or a scaling down of values of obsolete or shop-worn articles; questions of ownership involve such matters as the inclusion of all purchases to which title has been received, whether or not the goods have been received, the inclusion of goods out on consignment, and the exclusion of goods held on consignment; the problem of pricing is often a matter of so serious importance, in its relation to asset valuation and profit determination, that extensive consideration is given to it in the immediately following paragraphs. Although the principles can be easily stated, their application often involves practical difficulties.

Cost or market.

The standard rule for the valuation of inventories is "cost or market, whichever is lower." The cost or market rule is in conformity with the general accounting principle of anticipating no profits and providing for all losses.

Assume that the market purchase price at the end of the period is less than the cost of the merchandise on hand. Since purchase prices have declined, selling prices will presumably decline with them. Reducing the inventory from cost to the lower market price takes up the loss in the period when the price declined; in other words, it applies the rule: provide for all losses.

If the market purchase price has increased, selling prices may increase also and an increased profit may be realized. But this increased profit is not realized until the merchandise is sold at an increased price. Pricing the inventory at a value in excess of cost would anticipate a profit; to do so is contrary to conservative accounting.

The cost or market rule should be applied to each item in the inventory, thus:

Stock Number	Cost	Market	Inventory Value
A3615	$1,000.00	$ 800.00	$ 800.00
A3616	500.00	600.00	500.00
Total	$1,500.00	$1,400.00	$1,300.00

Effect of cost or market rule on gross profit.

Although the *cost or market* rule is a conservative one, and is generally accepted, the application of the rule misstates the gross profit of a period in which the market purchase prices decline.

To illustrate, assume that a company buys goods at a cost of $10,000.00 and sells one half of them for $7,500.00. The true gross profit is determined as follows:

Sales...	$7,500.00
Less Cost of Goods Sold (½ of $10,000.00)..................	5,000.00
Gross Profit on Sales......................................	$2,500.00

But assume that the inventory valuation of the remaining half at the lower of cost or market is only $4,000.00. The profit and loss statement would usually be prepared thus:

Sales...		$7,500.00
Less Cost of Goods Sold:		
Purchases.....................................	$10,000.00	
Less Inventory at End of Period..............	4,000.00	6,000.00
Gross Profit on Sales.......................................		$1,500.00

A more nearly correct statement of facts would be:

Sales...		$7,500.00
Less Cost of Goods Sold:		
Purchases.....................................	$10,000.00	
Less Inventory—at Cost......................	5,000.00	5,000.00
Gross Profit on Sales.......................................		$2,500.00
Less Inventory Shrinkage...................................		1,000.00
Gross Profit Less Inventory Shrinkage......................		$1,500.00

But, to prepare a statement in the last form illustrated, it would be necessary to value the inventory at both the cost ($5,000.00) and the lower of cost or market ($4,000.00) in order to determine the shrinkage. Computing the value of the inventory on two bases would involve so much work that it is usually regarded as impracticable.

What is market?

Market value is defined by the Treasury Department for tax purposes as follows: "Under ordinary circumstances, 'market' means the current bid price prevailing at the date of the inventory for the particular merchandise in the volume in which ordinarily purchased by the taxpayer." The restriction as to quantity is important; if it were omitted, wholly inapplicable market values might be used.

What is cost?

It is easy enough to speak of the cost of goods, but it is not always easy to determine the cost.   The problem of ascertaining costs is complicated by a number of difficult points, among which may be mentioned:

> Incidental costs.
> Manufacturing costs.
> Relation of interest to cost.
> Numerous purchases.
> Widely fluctuating costs.
> Cash discounts.
> Apportioned costs.

Incidental costs.

Cost includes not only the purchase price but also all incidental costs, such as duties, freight, drayage, and storage, necessary to place the goods in the market.   The total of these items is clearly an addition to the total cost of purchases, but it is not a simple matter to apportion these incidental costs among individual purchases and to determine what portion of the incidental costs is applicable to the goods in the inventory.

Manufacturing costs.

The purchase cost of the merchandise of a trading company and the raw material of a manufacturing company can be determined from invoices.   But the cost of a manufacturing company's goods in process and finished goods, including material, labor, and overhead, can be determined only if adequate cost records are maintained.   Moreover, the valuations determined by cost systems are usually only estimates, of varying degrees of accuracy.

Relation of interest to cost.

Should interest on plant investment be included in manufacturing cost?   Some years ago this question received a good deal of attention from accountants.   Those who advocated including interest as a cost maintained that the cost of the fixed assets used in manufacturing affects the cost of the article manufactured; that, other things being equal, an article manufactured with the aid of an expensive machine in an expensive building costs more than an article manufactured with inexpensive fixed assets; and, therefore, that the cost shown by the books should include interest on the investment in fixed assets.

Those who opposed including interest in costs admitted that the cost of fixed assets affects the cost of the manufactured product, but they maintained that the effect of varying fixed asset costs is reflected in the depreciation charges. They further maintained that, if manufacturing is charged with a theoretical interest on capital invested in plant assets, the offsetting credit for interest will be taken into income; the costs will thus be overstated, by the inclusion of an element of income therein, and profits will be anticipated unless all of the manufactured goods are sold.

A few accountants still adhere to the theory that interest on plant investment should be included in manufacturing cost, but most accountants and associations of accountants regard the inclusion of interest as incorrect in theory and impractical in application.

Another question with respect to interest as an element of cost arises if the process of manufacture requires aging or seasoning of the product. Under such circumstances, should interest on the inventory value for the aging period be added to cost?

Some accountants consider it permissible to make such an addition if the total inventory value thus determined does not exceed the price at which similar goods could be purchased. The approval of such an addition is, however, a departure from conservative accounting. It is well recognized that the use of capital in the manufacture of goods does not result in the production of income unless the manufactured goods are sold. But the addition of interest to a seasoning inventory requires an offsetting credit to income and results in a taking up of profit before the sale of goods.

Numerous purchases.

There is also the problem of which cost to use if several invoices are purchased during the period at different prices, or if goods are manufactured during the year at various costs. Four methods are illustrated below, all of which are considered correct; it is significant that, even when purchase prices are definitely known, there are several possible costs for inventory purposes.

Assume that purchases have been made during the period, as follows:

1st purchase	100 units @ $1.00	....	$100.00
2nd purchase	200 units @ 1.10	....	220.00
3rd purchase	250 units @ 1.20	....	300.00
4th purchase	100 units @ 1.25	....	125.00

There are 150 units in the inventory.

First-in, first-out method. The goods on hand are considered to have been acquired by the most recent purchases; therefore the inventory is composed of:

From 4th purchase:	100 units @ $1.25........................	$125.00
From 3rd purchase:	50 units @ 1.20........................	60.00
Cost of inventory...		$185.00

Last-in, first-out method. The sales are assumed to consist of the last goods purchased, and the inventory at the end of the period is assumed to consist of any opening inventory and the earliest purchases. Therefore the inventory is composed of:

From the 1st purchase:	100 units @ $1.00....................	$100.00
From the 2nd purchase:	50 units @ 1.10	55.00
Cost of inventory...		$155.00

This method has been proposed only recently, and has not yet been generally accepted. One criticism raised against it is the fact that the inventory valuation at the end of a period may depend upon the dates and frequency of previous inventory-takings. To illustrate, assume that an inventory was taken after the second purchase, and that 200 units were found to be on hand; they were valued as follows:

From the 1st purchase:	100 units @ $1.00....................	$100.00
From the 2nd purchase:	100 units @ 1.10....................	110.00
Cost of inventory (@ $1.05)..................................		$210.00

At the time of taking the later inventory, the records would show:

Opening inventory	200 units @ $1.05........................	$210.00
3rd purchase	250 units @ 1.20........................	300.00
4th purchase	100 units @ 1.25........................	125.00

The 150 units now in the inventory would be regarded as appertaining to the opening inventory, and would be valued at $1.05 per unit, or $157.50, instead of at $155.00, which was the valuation determined on the assumption that there had been no intervening inventory.

Those who advocate this method point out that it has a stabilizing effect on profits in periods of rising or falling prices, by applying recent costs against current selling prices and letting the inventory valuation absorb the effect of the stabilization of profits. The critics of the method say that, since artificial stabilization of profits is improper (see page 157), the method is improper.

Weighted average method. The total cost of the opening inventory and purchases is divided by the total units in the inventory and the purchases, and a weighted average cost is thus determined:

> Total units purchased 650
> Total cost $745.00
> Unit cost = $745.00 ÷ 650 = $1.14615
> Inventory valuation = $1.14615 × 150 = $171.92

Moving average method. Assume that purchases and sales have been made in the following order and amounts:

> First purchase, 100 units at $1.00
> First sale, 50 units
> Second purchase, 200 units at $1.10
> Second sale, 100 units
> Third purchase, 250 units at $1.20
> Third sale, 200 units
> Fourth purchase, 100 units at $1.25
> Fourth sale, 150 units

Computation of Inventory

1st Purchase	100	@ $1.00	$100.00	$1.00 each
1st Sale	50		50.00	
	50		$ 50.00	1.00
2nd Purchase	200	@ 1.10	220.00	
	250		$270.00	1.08
2nd Sale	100		108.00	
	150		$162.00	1.08
3rd Purchase	250	@ 1.20	300.00	
	400		$462.00	1.155
3rd Sale	200		231.00	
	200		$231.00	1.155
4th Purchase	100	@ 1.25	125.00	
	300		$356.00	1.186
4th Sale	150		178.00	
Inventory	150		$178.00	1.186

Widely fluctuating costs.

A modification of the moving average cost computation illustrated in the preceding section is peculiarly suited for the determination of monthly inventory values when unit costs vary widely from month to month because of differences in the quantity of production. To illustrate, let us assume that a company manufactures a product which sells heavily in warm months and poorly in cold months, and that its production fluctuates with sales. The quantities and the monthly costs of production during two years are shown on the next page.

	1942			1943		
	Units Pro-duced	Total Cost	Unit Cost	Units Pro-duced	Total Cost	Unit Cost
January	100	$ 1,660	$16.600	90	$ 1,705	$18.944
February	115	1,738	15.113	75	1,688	22.507
March	220	2,232	10.145	250	2,195	8.780
April	3,200	8,745	2.733	3,720	10,503	2.823
May	4,600	11,935	2.595	4,360	11,700	2.683
June	5,950	13,665	2.297	6,325	15,260	2.413
July	6,300	15,060	2.390	6,720	16,800	2.500
August	6,750	15,855	2.349	7,310	18,215	2.492
September	5,200	13,470	2.590	6,205	16,225	2.615
October	850	4,170	4.906	960	4,515	4.703
November	300	2,475	8.250	412	2,925	7.100
December	140	1,940	13.857	125	2,025	16.200
Totals and Averages	33,725	$92,945	2.756	36,552	$103,756	2.839

High unit costs appear in the months of low production because a large fixed overhead is distributed over a small number of units of production.

The inventories at the close of the year can be valued at the average costs for the year: $2.756 at the end of 1942, and $2.839 at the close of 1943. But what basis can be used for the valuation of monthly inventories, if monthly statements are desired? Obviously, the monthly unit costs would not be appropriate, because of their wide fluctuation. Nor would it be entirely correct to use, in the 1943 monthly statements, the average cost for 1942 ($2.756), since 1943 costs appear to be on a higher level, as evidenced by the higher average for the year ($2.839).

A progressive average cost, computed in the manner illustrated below, appears suitable for such a situation.

	Units			Cost			
	This Year (Add)	Last Year (Deduct)	Twelve Months	This Year (Add)	Last Year (Deduct)	Twelve Months	Pro-gressive Average
Year 1942			33,725			$ 92,945	$2.756
Year 1943:							
January	90	100	33,715	$ 1,705	$ 1,660	92,990	2.758
February	75	115	33,675	1,688	1,738	92,940	2.760
March	250	220	33,705	2,195	2,232	92,903	2.756
April	3,720	3,200	34,225	10,503	8,745	94,661	2.766
May	4,360	4,600	33,985	11,700	11,935	94,426	2.778
June	6,325	5,950	34,360	15,260	13,665	96,021	2.795
July	6,720	6,300	34,780	16,800	15,060	97,761	2.811
August	7,310	6,750	35,340	18,215	15,855	100,121	2.833
September	6,205	5,200	36,345	16,225	13,470	102,876	2.831
October	960	850	36,455	4,515	4,170	103,221	2.831
November	412	300	36,567	2,925	2,475	103,671	2.835
December	125	140	36,552	2,025	1,940	103,756	2.839

ash discounts.

The treatment of cash discounts on merchandise purchases
as some bearing upon the inventory valuation and hence upon the
etermination of profits.   The questions involved require con-
deration of the nature of discounts and, incidentally, of their
roper treatment in the profit and loss statement.   And, since a
onsistent treatment should be accorded to discounts on purchases
id discounts on sales, the present discussion, although concerned
rincipally with discounts on purchases, will necessarily give con-
deration to discounts on sales.

Four different opinions are held by accountants with respect
o the nature of cash discounts, their proper presentation in
ie profit and loss statement, and their relation to inventory
aluations.

(1) Discounts are financial items like interest, and should be
milarly treated.   The following condensed profit and loss state-
ent so treats them:

THE WATSON CORPORATION
Statement of Profit and Loss
For the Year Ended December 31, 1941

Gross Sales			$103,500
Deduct Returned Sales and Allowances			1,500
Net Sales			$102,000
Deduct Cost of Goods Sold:			
Inventory, December 31, 1940		$25,000	
Purchases	$65,000		
Deduct Returned Purchases and Allowances.	1,000		
Net Purchases	$64,000		
Add Freight In	2,000	66,000	
Total Opening Inventory and Purchases		$91,000	
Deduct Inventory, December 31, 1941		26,000	65,000
Gross Profit on Sales			$ 37,000
Deduct Selling and General Expenses			28,025
Net Profit on Operations			$ 8,975
Add Other Income:			
Delivery Income		$ 1,200	
Discount on Purchases		900	
Interest Income		24	2,124
Net Profit on Operations and Other Income			$ 11,099
Deduct Other Expenses:			
Discount on Sales		$ 975	
Interest Expense		35	1,010
Net Income			$ 10,089

In support of this view of the nature of cash discounts, it may
e said that, since they are contingent upon payment within a

definite period, their financial and time elements give them a close relation to interest. This relation is increased by reason of the fact that discounts on sales may be offered to obtain funds for current needs without borrowing; and that, on the other hand, money may be borrowed and interest may be paid to provide funds with which to take discounts on purchases. If discounts are regarded as financial income and expense, the gross invoice price should be used as cost for inventory valuation purposes.

(2) Cash discounts are a deduction from the price; therefore, discounts on sales should be deducted from sales in the profit and loss statement, discounts on purchases should be deducted from purchases, and the merchandise cost for inventory purposes should be regarded as the gross invoice price less discounts taken. The following profit and loss statement is based on this point of view.

THE WATSON CORPORATION
Statement of Profit and Loss
For the Year Ended December 31, 1941

Gross Sales			$103,500
Deduct:			
Returned Sales and Allowances		$ 1,500	
Discount on Sales		975	2,475
Net Sales			$101,025
Deduct Cost of Goods Sold:			
Inventory, December 31, 1940		$24,750	
Purchases	$65,000		
Deduct:			
Returned Purchases and Allowances	$1,000		
Discount on Purchases	900	1,900	
Net Purchases		$63,100	
Add Freight In		2,000	65,100
Total Opening Inventory and Purchases		$89,850	
Deduct Inventory, December 31, 1941		25,650	64,200
Gross Profit on Sales			$ 36,825
Deduct Selling and General Expenses			28,025
Net Profit on Operations			$ 8,800
Add Other Income:			
Delivery Income		$ 1,200	
Interest Income		24	1,224
Net Profit on Operations and Other Income			$ 10,024
Deduct Interest Expense			35
Net Income			$ 9,989

In support of this point of view, it may be said that cash discounts on purchases should not be treated as an immediate income, because a profit should not be taken directly or indirectly on a purchase; there is no profit realization until the goods are sold.

In other words, if an invoice of $1,000.00 is purchased subject to a 2% cash discount, the discount is merely a saving in the cost; the purchase should be recorded at $980.00, and that valuation should be used as inventory cost; if the $20.00 is taken as an immediate income and the goods are included in the inventory at $1,000.00, an anticipated profit is taken on the purchase. Although no similar anticipation of profit results from not treating discounts on sales as a deduction from the selling price, a consistent procedure should be followed.

Although the treatment of purchase discounts as income may result in an anticipation of profit, this will presumably be the case only if the inventory at the end of the period is greater than that at the beginning, or if a larger proportion of discounts was taken during the current period than during the prior one. Business management, therefore, is sometimes disposed to feel that the greater degree of theoretical accuracy may not be sufficient (a) to warrant the trouble involved in determining what portion of the inventory should be valued at the net price (because discounts were availed of) and what portion should be valued at the gross price (because discounts were not taken), and (b) to justify the omission from the profit and loss statement of significant information relative to the company's discount-taking policy and ability.

(3) There is a certain element of inconsistency in the theory that cash discounts taken on purchases are a deduction from the price. Those who advocate it sometimes say that its propriety would become more apparent if trade practices were changed and merchandise were billed at the net price (say $980.00) and a penalty (say $20.00) were exacted if payment was postponed beyond a certain period; the $980.00 would then obviously be the purchase cost and the $20.00 would be a sort of interest charge. This is rather conclusive, but it also seems to indicate that consistency would require the deduction-from-price advocates to treat all *available* purchase discounts as a deduction from the price (and not merely the discounts taken) and to show as an expense all discounts not taken. This theory is, in fact, advocated by some accountants, not so much, perhaps, for the purposes of consistency, as to furnish management with information as to the amounts of discounts lost. A condensed profit and loss statement is presented on the following page, prepared on the assumption that $1,300.00 of purchase discounts was available during the year, and that only $900.00 was taken.

THE WATSON CORPORATION
Statement of Profit and Loss
For the Year Ended December 31, 1941

Gross Sales...			$103,500
Deduct:			
Returned Sales and Allowances...........................		$ 1,500	
Discount on Sales..		975	2,475
Net Sales..			$101,025
Deduct Cost of Goods Sold:			
Inventory, December 31, 1940............................		$24,500	
Purchases.....................................	$65,000		
Deduct:			
Returned Purchases and Allowances.......	$1,000		
Purchase Discounts Available.............	1,300	2,300	
Net Purchases.................................		$62,700	
Add Freight In................................		2,000	64,700
Total Opening Inventory and Purchases..................		$89,200	
Deduct Inventory, December 31, 1941..................		25,480	63,720
Gross Profit on Sales...			$ 37,305
Deduct Selling and General Expenses.................................			28,025
Net Profit on Operations...			$ 9,280
Add Other Income:			
Delivery Income..		$ 1,200	
Interest Income...		24	1,224
Net Profit on Operations and Other Income.........................			$ 10,504
Deduct Other Expenses:			
Interest Expense..		$ 35	
Purchase Discounts Lost.................................		400	435
Net Income...			$ 10,069

(4) It has been advocated (formerly more than at present) that cash discounts at a normal rate should be treated as financial items, and that discounts at an abnormal rate should be treated as deductions from the price. A 2% rate has been mentioned, rather arbitrarily, as the highest rate at which discounts can be regarded as financial items.

Apportioned costs.

A special problem arises when a whole, acquired at a lump price, is divided into parts which, because of differences in nature or in quality, are sold at different prices. To determine a cost for the parts sold and a cost for the parts remaining in the inventory, it is necessary to make an apportionment of the lump-sum price.

To illustrate, assume that land is purchased, developed, and subdivided into cemetery lots. The total cost, assumed to be $60,000.00, may be apportioned to individual lots in the ratio of selling price, as shown on the following page.

Apportionment of Cost of Lots

Selling Price Per Lot	Number of Lots	Product	Per Cent of Total	Apportioned Cost	
				Total	Per Lot
$200.00	40	$ 8,000.00	8%	$ 4,800.00	$120.00
500.00	60	30,000.00	30	18,000.00	300.00
600.00	80	48,000.00	48	28,800.00	360.00
700.00	20	14,000.00	14	8,400.00	420.00
Total...............		$100,000.00	100%	$60,000.00	

Omissions from inventory.

All unsold goods that were purchased before the end of the period should be included in the inventory at the end of the period. Two general types of errors may be made by a failure to include all purchased goods in the inventory.

In the first place, the purchase may be recorded, but the goods may be omitted from the inventory. This omission, of course, results in an understatement of the profits.

In the second place, no entry may be made for the purchase, and the goods may be omitted from the inventory. This omission does not result in an understatement of the profits, since the purchases (debited to Profit and Loss) and the closing inventory (credited to Profit and Loss) are equally understated. The practice is to be condemned, however, both because it results in an incorrect showing of purchases and inventory in the profit and loss statement, and because it understates the current assets and current liabilities in the balance sheet. Thus, a financial condition is shown more favorable than really exists, partly because the working capital ratio is overstated, and partly because, in many instances, the accounts payable will have to be paid before the merchandise is sold and converted into cash.

Consignments.

Consignments are sometimes incorrectly recorded as sales. The fundamental distinction between a sale and a consignment is this: In a sale the title to the goods passes from a vendor to a vendee, whereas in a consignment the consignor retains title to goods not sold by the consignee. This distinction must be borne in mind for three reasons:

First, since the consignor retains title to the goods, he can recover them if the consignee becomes insolvent.

Second, since a consignment is not a sale, no profit results from the transaction, and none should be taken up until the goods have been sold by the consignee.

Third, when the consignor prepares statements or closes his books, any goods out on consignment should be included in his inventory. The cost of such goods, for inventory purposes, may include any expenses incurred in placing the goods with the consignee.

Profit on uncompleted work.

In an ordinary manufacturing business it is always considered improper to take up any profit on work in process; no profit should be taken up until the goods are completed and sold. A special problem arises, however, in the contracting business, if the completion of a contract requires a considerable period of time, and if the books are closed before the contract is completed.

If the contract is on a cost-plus basis, there is no objection to taking up profits earned on the work done; but if the contract is on a flat price basis, it is always dangerous to take up profit on uncompleted work, because of the possibility that unforeseen costs may turn a probable profit into a much smaller profit or into an actual loss.

Although, from the standpoint of a going concern, it is always conservative to defer the taking of a profit until the contract is completed, situations sometimes arise when a partner or a stockholder is to retire before the completion of a contract and is to sell his interest to the remaining partners or stockholders. In such instances, it is usually customary to estimate the profit to be earned on the contract, and to take up such a proportion of the profit as the cost of the work done up to the date of retirement bears to the total estimated cost.

To illustrate, assume that a contract is taken at a flat price of $50,000.00. The work done to date has cost $25,000.00, and it is estimated that $15,000.00 will complete the work. The portion of profit earned on the uncompleted contract may be estimated as follows:

Contract price		$50,000.00
Less estimated cost:		
Cost to date	$25,000.00	
Estimated cost to complete	15,000.00	40,000.00
Estimated total profit		$10,000.00
Portion of estimated profit earned to date:		
$25/40$ of $10,000.00		$ 6,250.00

Determining the inventory value.

The inventory value may be determined, with varying degrees of accuracy, by four methods:

(a) Physical inventory.
(b) Perpetual inventory.
(c) Gross-profit method.
(d) Retail method.

Physical inventory.   A physical inventory is taken by listing the quantities and applying costs shown by invoices, or lower market values.   This is the most accurate of all methods.

Perpetual inventory.   A perpetual inventory is a record showing quantities (or quantities and cost) of items going into and out of stock.   A separate record is kept with each kind of article.   A form for recording quantities only is illustrated below:

	NAME OF ARTICLE		
		Quantity	
Date	Into Stock	Out of Stock	Balance
June 1	500	—	500
10	200	—	700
15	—	400	300
20	—	110	190

The inventory value can be determined by the application of cost or market prices to the quantities shown in the Balance column. With a perpetual inventory it is possible to determine the inventory from the records, without the inconvenience of taking a physical inventory; it is customary, however, to take physical inventories (of either the entire stock or portions thereof) at intervals, as a check on the accuracy of the perpetual inventories and to determine that none of the stock is mysteriously disappearing.

Gross-profit method.   This method is often used to estimate the value of merchandise which has been destroyed by fire or otherwise. It is based on the assumption of a uniform rate of gross profit; since this assumption may not be warranted by the facts, the estimated value of the inventory may be inaccurate.

To illustrate the method, assume that a company made 25% gross profit on its sales during 1941; an inventory was taken at the end of 1941, and a fire occurred on May 25, 1942. The estimated value of the inventory at the date of the fire could be computed in the manner shown on the next page.

```
Inventory, December 31, 1941 (physical inventory)............. $ 10,000
Purchases, January 1 to May 25, 1942.......................     94,000
        Total............................................... $104,000
Less estimated cost of goods sold, January 1 to May 25:
    Sales.......................................... $124,000
    Less estimated gross profit—25% of $124,000.00....   31,000
    Remainder, estimated cost of goods sold...................   93,000
Estimated cost of goods on hand, May 25, 1942............... $ 11,000
```

This method may also be used to estimate the inventory if it is desired to prepare a balance sheet as of a date when no physical inventory was taken.

Retail method. This method, which is frequently used by department stores and chain stores, enables the management to determine the estimated cost of the merchandise on hand at the close of each day. The general theory of the method is indicated by the following illustration.

Records are required showing:

(1) Sales at selling price.
(2) Purchases and returned purchases at cost and also at selling price.

From such records, daily summaries can be built up as follows:

	Cost	Selling Price
Inventory, June 30...........................	$55,900.00	$86,000.00
July 1:		
Purchases................................	3,300.00	5,000.00
Total...................................	$59,200.00	$91,000.00
Returned purchases.......................	700.00	1,000.00
Goods available for sale................	$58,500.00	$90,000.00
Sales (at selling price only)...................		8,000.00
Inventory, July 1, at selling (or retail) price.....		$82,000.00

This inventory may now be valued on an estimated cost basis as follows:

Ratio of cost to selling price, of goods available for sale—$58,500.00 ÷ $90,000.00 = 65%.
Then the estimated cost of the inventory is 65% of $82,000.00, or $53,300.00.

Estimated inventories at subsequent dates can be determined by continuing the record.

This illustration indicates the general procedure followed, but the practical application of the procedure is usually much more complicated because of mark-ups and mark-downs in selling price, which have been ignored in the illustration.

28

TANGIBLE FIXED ASSETS

....

Fixed assets.

Fixed assets are assets of a relatively permanent nature used in the operation of the business and not intended for sale.

A building used as a factory is a fixed asset because it complies with the three elements of the definition: It is relatively permanent property, it is used in the operation of the business, and it is not intended for sale.

Land held as a prospective site for a future plant is not a fixed asset. It is permanent property and it is not intended for sale, but it is not used in the operation of the business. Therefore it should not be classified under the Fixed Assets caption in the balance sheet.

A factory building once used for operations but no longer so used is not a fixed asset. It is relatively permanent property; it may or may not be for sale; but it is not used in the operation of the business.

Tangible and intangible fixed assets.

The term *tangible* means having bodily substance. Strictly speaking, therefore, an asset is intangible if its value resides, not in the physical properties of the asset itself, but in the rights which its possession confers upon its owner. Tangible fixed assets include land, buildings, machinery, tools, patterns, delivery equipment, furniture and fixtures, and other similar property having physical substance. Intangible assets include goodwill, patents, copyrights, trademarks, franchises, and other similar assets having no bodily substance but having value because of the rights which their ownership confers.

Depreciation, depletion, and amortization.

Fixed assets do not last forever; wear and tear and the action of the elements result in an impairment of their operating effectiveness and eventually make replacements necessary. For this reason the cost of a fixed asset is a sort of deferred charge to be absorbed as an expense during the life of the asset. This expiration of invested costs is called depreciation.

Depletion is the reduction in value of natural resources, such as timber tracts, oil wells, and mines, caused by their conversion into inventories.

Amortization is the reduction in value of intangible fixed assets, such as patents, copyrights, and leaseholds, resulting from the lapse of time.

Classification of fixed assets.

Fixed assets may be classified, with respect to their nature and the decreases in value to which they are subject, as follows:

(A) Tangible:
  (1) Plant property.
      (a) Not subject to depreciation.
          Example: Land.
      (b) Subject to depreciation.
          Examples: Buildings, machinery, tools and equipment, delivery equipment, furniture and fixtures.
  (2) Natural resources, subject to depletion.
      Examples: Timber tracts, mines, oil wells.

(B) Intangible:
  (1) Subject to amortization.
      Examples: Patents, copyrights, franchises, leasehold improvements.
  (2) Not subject to amortization.
      Examples: Trademarks, goodwill.

Valuation of fixed assets.

It is considered good accounting to show fixed assets in the balance sheet at cost less proper deductions for depreciation, depletion, and amortization.

Certain matters incident to the determination of the cost of fixed assets are discussed in this chapter under the following captions:

Incidental costs.
Capital and revenue expenditures.

Interest during construction.
Assets purchased with securities.
Fixed assets manufactured.
Cash discounts.

Incidental costs.

The cost of a fixed asset includes the original purchase price
plus incidental expenditures. For instance, the cost of land
includes the purchase price, broker's commission, fees for examining
and recording title, taxes accrued at the date of purchase, taxes
assessed against the land during the period of construction of the
building, and expenditures for local improvements such as sewers
and pavements.

If an old building is purchased, its total cost includes the
purchase price, the costs incurred in making repairs necessitated
by depreciation prior to purchase, and costs of alterations and
improvements. If a building is constructed, the cost includes
payments for permits, architects' fees and superintendents'
salaries, premiums on workmen's liability insurance, and taxes
and insurance during the construction period.

The cost of machinery includes the purchase price, freight,
and installation charges. If it is necessary to operate the machinery unproductively for a while, in order to break it in or test it,
the costs of such operation may be capitalized—that is, regarded
as part of the cost of the machinery rather than as an expense.

Capital and revenue expenditures.

Expenditures incident to the ownership of fixed assets are of
two classes:

Capital expenditures, which should be recorded by an increase
   in the book value of the assets.   In most cases this is done by
   debits to the asset accounts; in some cases it is done by
   debits to the depreciation reserves.
Revenue expenditures, which should be charged to expense
   accounts.

A careful distinction must be made between capital and revenue
expenditures if a correct accounting for fixed assets and for profits
is to be maintained. If a capital expenditure is charged to an
expense account, the book value of the fixed assets will be understated, and the net profits and net worth will also be understated.

On the other hand, if a revenue expenditure is charged to an asset account instead of to an expense account, the book value of the fixed assets will be overstated and the net profits and net worth will also be overstated.

The proper treatment of some of the more common types of expenditures is indicated below:

Particulars	Revenue Expenditures Charged to Expense Accounts	Capital Expenditures	
		Book Value of Assets Increased by Charges to	
		Asset Account	Depreciation Reserve
Acquisition cost:			
A company purchased three second-hand machines; charge the fixed asset account.........		$3,000.00	
Expenditures to make good depreciation which took place prior to acquisition:			
Before the machines were put into use, they were thoroughly overhauled. This was a capital expenditure..............................		400.00	
Installation cost:			
This is a capital expenditure...................		50.00	
Betterment:			
Additional accessories were purchased for use with the machines; this expenditure is chargeable to the asset account.........................		75.00	
Ordinary repair:			
At the end of the first month of operations, a repair bill was paid; this was a revenue expenditure or expense...........................	$18.00		
Extraordinary repair:			
After three years of use the machines were again thoroughly reconditioned at a cost of $400.00. This was a capital expenditure because it made good some of the accrued depreciation; it should not be recorded by a charge to the asset account because it is not an addition to cost; it should be recorded by a charge to the depreciation reserve because it is a reduction of accrued depreciation.			$400.00

Reinstallation expense:

The first cost of installing machinery in a factory is a proper charge to the asset account. If machinery is rearranged in the factory for the purpose of improving the routing or otherwise reducing the time and cost of production, the reinstallation expense cannot properly be charged to the property account, because that account has already been debited with one installation charge. On the other hand, to charge off the expenditure as an expense of the period would scarcely be equitable, particularly if the expenditure is large. The best procedure, therefore, seems to be to carry forward the expense as a deferred charge to be written off over future periods which will be benefited by the reinstallation.

Interest during construction.

Utility commissions permit utility companies to include interest paid during the construction period in the cost of fixed assets. This is done because no income is earned during construction to offset the interest; when operations begin, rates and earnings are fixed on the basis of investment; since the interest cannot be recovered before operations begin, the utility is permitted to recover it after operations have begun by including it in the property valuation which will determine the rate for service.

There is no similar justification for allowing industrials to capitalize interest during the construction period. But the sanction of utility commissions has been carried over into the field of accounting for industrials without consideration of the difference in conditions. Interest paid, either by a utility or by an industrial, is not a necessary cost of construction; it could be avoided by the use of funds obtained through the issuance of stock. But, because it is permissible practice in utility accounting, industrials are accustomed to capitalize interest during construction; the practice is now so well established that it is no longer challenged, although it is doubtful whether it can be defended logically.

Assets purchased with securities.

If fixed assets were acquired by an issue of 1,000 shares of stock of a par value of $100.00 per share, did the fixed assets cost $100,-000.00? This is an important question for two reasons: (1) if the assets were worth less than $100,000.00, the stock was really issued at a discount and the stockholders may be liable to creditors for the amount of the discount; (2) if the $100,000.00 valuation cannot be established for tax purposes, the company will not be allowed, in its tax returns, to deduct depreciation on that valuation.

One way of establishing the valuation is by showing that similar securities were issued for cash at par at about the same time. But even this may not be conclusive evidence. Assume, for instance, that A takes 10 shares of stock at par for cash, and 1,000 shares at par for a building; the 10-share sale may be merely a subterfuge to establish a value, and may be challenged as such. Sales to third parties are more conclusive evidence.

When creditors of an insolvent company have come into court claiming that property was not worth the par value of the stock issued for it, that the stock was, therefore, issued at a discount, and that the stockholders should be held for the payment of the company's debts to an amount equal to the discount, courts have been reluctant to find for them, because the law allows the directors of a corporation considerable discretion in determining the value of property taken in payment for stock.

The question is considerably more important from the tax standpoint, as the valuation of the property must be established by evidence of the fair market value of the property itself or of the stock issued in acquiring it; otherwise, the stated cost may not be accepted as a basis for depreciation. A company issued a large number of common shares for a patent, charged the Patents account with a cost based on the par value of the stock issued, and, in its tax return, deducted amortization of the patent on the basis of this cost. Shortly after the issuance of the common stock for the patent, the company issued preferred stock and gave common stock with it as a bonus. The patent valuation was attacked for tax purposes because the issuance of the common stock as a bonus indicated that the common stock issued for the patent was not worth par.

Fixed assets manufactured.

The cost of finished goods manufactured includes materials, labor, and factory overhead; if a company uses its factory for the manufacture of fixed assets for its own use, should the cost of the fixed assets include these three elements? There is no question about the material and labor costs; they should be included in the cost of the fixed assets manufactured. There is less certainty about the factory overhead.

Assume that a company used its plant in 1940 for the manufacture of merchandise only, that in 1941 it also constructed some fixed assets, and that the following data are determinable:

| | 1940 | | 1941 | |
	Finished Goods Only	Total	Finished Goods	Fixed Assets
Materials................	$ 50,000.00	$ 75,000.00	$ 50,000.00	$25,000.00
Direct labor..............	50,000.00	75,000.00	50,000.00	25,000.00
Manufacturing expense....	50,000.00	50,000.00	?	?
Total................	$150,000.00	$200,000.00	?	
Selling price..............	200,000.00		200,000.00	
Gross profit..............	$ 50,000.00		$?	

Assume that the same quantity of finished goods was manufactured in 1941 as in 1940 and sold at the same price. If we charge part of the factory overhead in 1941 to finished goods and part to fixed assets (in the ratio of the direct labor, for instance), we produce the following results:

| | 1940 | 1941 | |
	Finished Goods	Finished Goods	Fixed Assets
Materials............................	$ 50,000.00	$ 50,000.00	$25,000.00
Direct labor.........................	50,000.00	50,000.00	25,000.00
Factory overhead (apportioned on basis of direct labor)......................	50,000.00	33,333.00	16,667.00
Total............................	$150,000.00	$133,333.00	$66,667.00
Selling price of finished goods............	200,000.00	200,000.00	
Gross profit.........................	$ 50,000.00	$ 66,667.00	

The gross profit in 1941 is shown to be $16,667.00 more than that in 1940, although the same quantity of merchandise was manufactured and sales were made at the same price. This $16,667.00 is the amount of overhead charged to fixed assets. Therefore, if the total overhead was not increased because of the construction of fixed assets, and if we charge the fixed assets with a part of the overhead, it is evident that the charge to fixed assets is in effect offset by an addition to the net profit, and that the company is in reality taking a profit on work done for itself and not sold.

Perhaps the best procedure is to charge the fixed assets with only such increase in factory overhead as can reasonably be attributed to the construction of fixed assets.

Cash discounts.

If cash discounts are taken on purchases of fixed assets, should the discount be recorded as a financial income or as a reduction in the cost of the property? This is a question on which some difference of opinion exists among accountants.

Chapter 27 contains a discussion of the nature of cash discounts on merchandise purchases, and it is there pointed out that to regard cash discounts on purchases as a financial income immediately earned and to value the inventory at the gross invoice price result in an anticipation of income, because a profit is taken on a purchase whereas profits are realized only by sales. It was pointed out, however, that no serious distortion of profits results if the inventories at both the beginning and the end of the period are valued on the same basis, and if there has been no material change in the inventory amounts or in the ratios of discounts taken to purchases.

To record fixed asset purchases at the gross invoice price and to take the discount as an immediate earning also results in an anticipation of profits.   Moreover, the anticipation is more serious. The inventories at the beginning and end of the period exercise an immediate modifying influence upon the anticipation of profits applicable to merchandise purchases; any discount earning taken on the purchase of a fixed asset is offset only gradually by the slightly higher depreciation charges over the life of the asset.

The only argument against treating discounts on fixed assets as a deduction from the price is a possible one of consistency. If discounts on merchandise purchases are treated as a financial income, whereas discounts on capital expenditures are treated as a deduction from cost, an inconsistency is introduced into the accounts, and this inconsistency results in a distortion of what is regarded as financial income.   However, if discounts on merchandise purchases are treated as deductions from cost, it is not inconsistent to apply a similarly conservative procedure to the purchases of fixed assets.

Donated assets.

Corporations sometimes receive gifts of fixed assets, either from their stockholders or from cities which make a policy of attracting industries by providing them with plants or with plant sites. If the rule of valuation at cost were strictly applied, such assets could be put on the books only at the amount of any incidental costs involved in the acceptance of the gifts.   Since this rule might result in an injustice to a business by requiring it to present a balance sheet in which its assets were grossly undervalued, the rule is modified to permit the placing of such gifts on the books at a fair valuation.   The debit to the fixed asset account may be offset by a credit to Surplus; or, if a distinction is to be maintained in the accounts between operating and extraneous profits, the credit should be made to Capital Surplus.

Accounts and records.

Land and buildings should not be carried in a single account called Real Estate.   Separate accounts should be opened for the land and the buildings, because land does not depreciate and need not be insured, whereas buildings do depreciate and are insured. The statement that land does not depreciate applies, of course, to land used as a building site.   Land used for farming and deposits of natural resources are subject to depletion.

If any real estate is owned which is not used in operations (for instance an abandoned factory, property held as a speculation, or land awaiting plant extensions), it should not be included in the balance sheet under the Fixed Assets caption. The amounts shown under that caption should indicate the investment in fixed property used in the business operations.

It is also desirable to keep a separate record with each parcel of land and each building, so that, if one is disposed of, the cost, depreciation, and resulting profit or loss can be ascertained.

If numerous machines are owned, a machinery record should be kept, with a page or card for each machine, containing the following information:

> Name of machine.
> Number (to identify the machine).
> Location.
>
> Manufacturer.
> From whom purchased.
> Date of installation.
>
> Purchase price.
> Cost of installation.
> Other elements of original cost.
>
> Service and depreciation data:
>   Estimated life.
>   Actual life.
>
>   Estimated residual value.
>   Actual residual value.
>
> Depreciation rate.
> Periodical depreciation provision, and accumulated amount provided
>   to date.
>
> Ordinary and extraordinary repairs, with information as to date, cost,
>   and nature.
>
> Information as to abnormal operating conditions, such as overtime
>   work, affecting depreciation and operating life.

Such records provide information desirable for insurance purposes, and are extremely helpful in proving a claim for loss. The service information is valuable as a guide to future purchases, and the information as to actual life and actual residual value realized upon the disposal of the asset is helpful in making future estimates of depreciation rates to be applied to similar equipment.

TANGIBLE FIXED ASSETS—Continued
DEPRECIATION AND OTHER
DECREASES IN VALUE

Change in business attitude.

The income tax law has changed the attitude of many business-men with respect to depreciation. Before the passage of the law, the attitude was frequently: "How little depreciation can I take to make as good a profit showing as possible?" Since the passage of the law, the attitude in many cases has become: "How much depreciation can I take to reduce my taxable income?"

Early accountants were confronted with the task of convincing businessmen that depreciation was an expense which should be recognized regardless of the profits; their clients preferred to write off little or no depreciation in years of poor profits or of losses, with compensatingly large provisions in years of good profits.

As accountants began to press home the argument that depreciation was an expense which must be provided for in bad years as well as good, they were met by several arguments. One was that depreciation had been offset by an increase in the market value of the property, so that the assets, even after a number of years of use, were worth as much as they cost. This was merely an attempt to offset an operating expense against an unrealized extraneous profit.

Another argument was that depreciation provisions were unnecessary because repairs kept the asset as good as new. It is difficult to find a better answer to this argument than Professor Hatfield's much-quoted and now almost classic sentence: "All machinery is on an irresistible march to the junk heap, and its progress, while it may be delayed, cannot be prevented by repairs."

But all that is changed now, and businessmen willingly deduct charges for depreciation and would also gladly make a deduction for the contingency of obsolescence if they were permitted to deduct contingent obsolescence in their tax returns.

The nature of depreciation.

If a machine costs $100.00 and will last for five years, the $100.00 cost is an expense of the five-year period. Each year's operations should be charged with a portion of the cost, and the asset should be regarded as having a decreased value at the end of each year.

Textbooks usually state that depreciation should be determined by a computation involving the cost, the estimated life, and the estimated residual or scrap value to be realized when the asset is no longer usable. In practice the scrap value is usually ignored, and the annual depreciation is computed by multiplying the cost by a rate which is acceptable for income tax purposes.

Computing depreciation.

There are a large number of theoretical methods of computing depreciation, some of which involve actuarial computations. Four methods are mentioned below:

(1) *The straight-line method.* A percentage rate is determined on the basis of estimated life (for instance, 20% for a 5-year life, 10% for a 10-year life) and the annual depreciation is computed by multiplying the cost by the depreciation rate. This method is acceptable for tax purposes.

(2) *The diminishing-value or diminishing-charge method.* The depreciation rate is applied the first year to cost, and thereafter to cost less the increasing reserve. The depreciation charge thus decreases each year; this is theoretically desirable because repair charges will presumably increase as the asset ages. Decreasing the depreciation charge to offset the increase in repair charges will tend to produce a more uniform annual total charge. This method is not generally accepted for tax purposes.

(3) Various methods by which *the charge is made proportionate to the use.* A rate per hour may be used, thus making the depreciation charge in any year dependent upon the hours of use during the year; a rate per mile may be used for depreciating automobile equipment, thus making the depreciation charge proportionate to the mileage. Use methods are generally acceptable for tax purposes.

(4) Utility companies usually create their depreciation reserves by *setting up a percentage of their gross revenue.* At first thought this appears entirely illogical, as it would seem that the amount of depreciation depends upon the cost and life of the assets rather than upon the amount of revenue produced by them. But, on the other hand, the life of a fixed asset is influenced by the extent to which it is used, so that the gross-revenue basis of computing depreciation may be defended by this reasoning: the more gross revenue, the more use; the more use, the more depreciation. For tax purposes, however, the depreciation must be computed on the basis of the cost and life of the property.

The straight-line method.

As stated above, most companies provide depreciation on the straight-line basis. This method has two things to recommend it: it is relatively simple to apply, and it is acceptable for tax purposes. It accomplishes the desired result of spreading the cost of the asset over its estimated life by periodical charges to expense, and of reducing the book value of the asset to zero at the end of the estimated life.

It may be contended that this method is not theoretically correct from the standpoint of the profit and loss statement. The amount of use may not be the same each year, and it may be argued that a larger charge to expense should be made in a year of much use than in a year of little use. But it is not always convenient to measure these differences, and the equal annual charge is, therefore, made notwithstanding the theoretical inaccuracy.

What is represented by the depreciated book value of a fixed asset? If a machine cost $100.00 and is depreciated by the straight-line method over an estimated life of five years, the depreciated book values will be $100.00, $80.00, $60.00, $40.00, $20.00, $0.00. But an engineer would probably say that the machine suffers relatively little physical deterioration the first year, and that it goes to pieces rapidly toward the end of its life. The book values resulting from the equal annual depreciation charge, and the values fixed by an engineer on the basis of actual physical deterioration, might therefore be somewhat as follows:

Book values—accounting basis......	$100.00	$80.00	$60.00	$40.00	$20.00	$0.00
Depreciated values—engineer's basis	100.00	90.00	80.00	65.00	40.00	0.00

Nor do the depreciated values shown by the books represent the realizable market values of the assets. It is well known that, from a resale standpoint, fixed assets suffer most heavily during the first year of use, because only a little use makes them second-hand. The book values on a theoretical depreciation basis, the values on an engineering basis, and the values on a second-hand market basis might, therefore, be somewhat as follows:

Book values—straight-line accounting basis	$100.00	$80.00	$60.00	$40.00	$20.00	$0.00
Depreciated values—engineer's basis	100.00	90.00	80.00	65.00	40.00	0.00
Second-hand market values	100.00	70.00	65.00	50.00	35.00	0.00

The theory of equal depreciation provisions may be summarized as follows:

(a) The total cost (minus any residual value) of a depreciating fixed asset should be written off as an expense over the estimated life of the asset.

(b) Each year should be made to bear a portion of this total expense by entries debiting Depreciation (expense account) and crediting a Reserve for Depreciation.

(c) Since the exact amount of expense properly chargeable to each year cannot be definitely determined, an arbitrary equal charge may be made each year.

(d) The depreciated value shown by the books merely represents the portion of the asset not yet written off to expense, and may not correspond with a value fixed by an appraiser on either a physical condition basis or a second-hand market value basis.

Bookkeeping entries.

We shall now briefly consider entries to be made with respect to periodical depreciation, fully depreciated assets, sales and abandonments, and trades.

Periodical depreciation.

Depreciation is recorded periodically by a journal entry debiting an expense account and crediting a reserve. For example, annual depreciation of a machine which cost $1,000.00 and which had an estimated life of ten years, with no residual value, would be recorded by the following journal entry:

Depreciation—Machinery	100.00	
Reserve for Depreciation—Machinery		100.00

The depreciation expense account would be closed to Profit and Loss; the reserve would accumulate.

It seems desirable to reiterate that the creation of a depreciation reserve does not mean that a fund of assets is being set aside to replace the fixed asset at the end of its useful life. The creation of a depreciation reserve means only that a book entry has been made, resulting in an expense deduction in the profit and loss statement and a reduction in the asset carrying value from cost to a lower amount.

Fully depreciated assets.

Assume that a Machinery account and its related depreciation reserve have the following balances:

Machinery.................................. $100,000.00
Reserve for Depreciation—Machinery.......... $36,000.00

Assume, also, that depreciation has been provided at the rate of 10% per annum, and that the above amounts represent the cost and depreciation provisions applicable to two units of machinery, as follows:

| | | Depreciation | Net |
Cost	Age	Provided	Book Value
$20,000.00	10 years	$20,000.00	—
80,000.00	2 years	16,000.00	$64,000.00

The machinery which cost $20,000.00 has been fully depreciated. Since no further depreciation is allowable on this machinery, its cost may be removed from the asset account by the following entry:

Reserve for Depreciation—Machinery............ 20,000.00
   Machinery.................................   20,000.00
   Reversal to eliminate from the accounts the cost of,
   and the accumulated depreciation on, fully depreciated machinery.

Objection may be raised to this procedure because the balance sheet will not disclose the fact that the company owns machinery which is in use, although it is not carried at any value in the accounts, and that a secret reserve or undervaluation of net assets exists as a result of the adoption of too high a depreciation rate.

Some accountants therefore contend that, since the depreciation charges to operations were excessive in the past, the reserve should be reduced by a credit to Surplus, and that credits to the reserve should be continued during the remaining useful life of the asset.

Other accountants merely advocate transfers, as indicated by the following journal entries:

```
Machinery—Fully Depreciated..................  20,000.00
    Machinery...............................              20,000.00
    To set up a separate account for the fully depre-
    ciated machinery.

Reserve for Depreciation—Machinery............  20,000.00
    Reserve for Depreciation—Fully Depreciated
    Machinery...............................              20,000.00
    To set up a separate reserve for depreciation of
    fully depreciated assets.
```

The accounts would then contain the following balances:

```
Machinery.....................................  $80,000
Reserve for Depreciation—Machinery............           $16,000
Machinery—Fully Depreciated...................   20,000
Reserve for Depreciation—Fully Depreciated
    Machinery................................            20,000
```

The balance sheet would show, under the Fixed Assets caption:

```
Machinery.....................................  $80,000
Less Reserve for Depreciation.................   16,000  $64,000
```

and the cost of the fully depreciated machinery still in use could be mentioned in a balance sheet footnote.

Sales and abandonments.

When a depreciated fixed asset is disposed of, an entry should be made crediting the asset account with the cost of the asset and debiting the depreciation reserve with the depreciation provided. Cash will be debited for the amount received.

If the amount realized is more or less than the book value, an entry will also be made in the Surplus account for the difference between the book value at the date of disposal and the amount received. Three illustrations are given:

(1) *Price equal to book value.* Assume that, at the date of disposal of a fixed asset, the asset and the reserve accounts had the following balances:

```
Asset account.................................  $2,500.00
Reserve for Depreciation......................            $2,200.00
```

The asset had a net book value of $300.00 and was disposed of for $300.00. The following debits and credit should be made:

```
Cash (amount received)........................   300.00
Reserve for Depreciation (to relieve the reserve of the
    depreciation provided)....................  2,200.00
    Asset account (to relieve the asset account of the
    cost)...................................             2,500.00
```

(2) *Price less than book value.* Assume that the accounts had the following balances:

Asset account.................................... $2,500.00
Reserve for Depreciation........................ $1,760.00

The asset had a net book value of $740.00 and was disposed of for $400.00; hence there was a loss of $340.00; the following debits and credit should be made:

Cash..   400.00
Reserve for Depreciation........................ 1,760.00
Surplus..   340.00
    Asset account..............................   2,500.00

(3) *Price more than book value.* Assume that the accounts had the following balances:

Asset account.................................... $2,500.00
Reserve for Depreciation........................ $2,200.00

The asset had a net book value of $300.00 and was disposed of for $500.00; hence there was a profit of $200.00. The following debits and credits should be made:

Cash..   500.00
Reserve for Depreciation........................ 2,200.00
    Asset account..............................   2,500.00
    Surplus...................................   200.00

To illustrate the entries for the abandonment of a fixed asset without any recovery value, assume that the asset cost $2,500.00 and that the balance in the depreciation reserve was $2,200.00. The entire net book value must be charged to Surplus:

Reserve for Depreciation........................ 2,200.00
Surplus..   300.00
    Asset account..............................   2,500.00

Trades.

If fixed assets are acquired by exchange, two questions arise: (1) the valuation of the asset acquired and (2) any gain or loss on the disposal of the old asset. The answers to these questions depend upon the available information.

To illustrate, assume that the old asset is carried at a gross value of $1,000.00, with a depreciation reserve of $400.00. A new asset is acquired by exchange of the old asset plus a cash payment of $750.00.

If we assume that the new asset has an ascertainable market cost value of $1,100.00, it can be put on the books at that value, and the loss on the disposal of the old asset can be computed as follows:

```
Net book value of old asset:
    Property account..........................................  $1,000.00
    Less depreciation reserve.................................      400.00
    Net book value............................................  $  600.00
Amount allowed for old asset:
    Gross value of new asset.....................  $1,100.00
    Cash payment.................................     750.00
    Amount allowed on trade-in................................      350.00
Loss..........................................................  $  250.00
```

The exchange may be recorded as follows:

```
Debit:   Property account—valuation of new asset.............  1,100.00
         Depreciation reserve—provision on old asset..........    400.00
         Surplus—loss on old asset...........................    250.00
Credit:      Property account—cost of old asset..............            1,000.00
             Cash—amount of payment..........................              750.00
```

If, however, the new asset has no ascertainable market value, no profit or loss on the exchange can be determined, and the new asset should be put on the books at the book value of the old asset plus the amount of the cash payment; the entries are:

```
Debit:   Property account—to value the new asset at the $600.00
         net book value of the old asset plus the $750.00 cash
         payment...............................................  1,350.00
         Depreciation reserve.................................    400.00
Credit·      Property account—cost of old asset..............            1,000.00
             Cash.............................................              750.00
```

Depreciation and depletion.

Depletion and depreciation both represent reductions in the value of fixed assets, but they differ from each other in two important particulars:

First, as to their nature.

Depreciation is a matter of physical deterioration; depletion is a matter of reduction in quantity. A machine depreciates, but the depreciation causes little if any reduction in its weight. On the other hand, the coal in a mine, the oil in a well, and the timber in a forest are depleted by their conversion from fixed assets into merchandise.

Second, as to their relation to dividends.

Although both depreciation and depletion must be provided for before the net profits are known, depletion on such wasting assets as mines, oil wells, and timber lands need not be deducted to determine the amount of dividends which may legally be paid. The theory of the law is that stockholders and creditors, knowing the nature of the business, should realize that the receipts from sales are in part profits and in part a return of investment. If the return of investment were not legally distributable among the stockholders, the corporation would be obliged to hold the funds until the exhaustion of the property. This might be advisable if the corporation expected to acquire and operate another similar piece of property, but not otherwise.   The law, therefore, allows the corporation to follow the financial policy best suited to its plans, assuming that the creditors are not injured, because of their knowledge of the nature of the business.

After setting up a depletion reserve in order to compute the net profit, the corporation may pay a dividend equal to the profits and the depletion.

Depletion methods.

Depletion is usually computed by dividing the cost of the wasting asset by the estimated number of tons, barrels, thousand feet, or other units in the asset, thus determining a unit depletion charge.   The total depletion charge for each period is then computed by multiplying the unit charge by the number of units converted during the period from a fixed nature into merchandise.

To illustrate, assume that $90,000.00 is paid for a mine which is estimated to contain 300,000 tons of available deposit.   The unit depletion charge is:

$$\$90,000.00 \div 300,000 = \$.30$$

If 20,000 tons are mined in a given year, the depletion charge for that year will be $.30 × 20,000, or $6,000.00.

Depletion is recorded by a journal entry similar to the following:

```
Depletion.......................................  6,000.00
     Reserve for Depletion.......................            6,000.00
```

Depreciation of plant on wasting asset.

Depreciation must, of course, be provided on buildings and machinery located on a wasting asset.   If the life of the wasting asset is estimated to be less than the life of the plant, it is customary to accept the life of the wasting asset as the life of the plant for depreciation purposes.   This is done on the theory that the plant will have only a scrap value when it is no longer needed for operations in its present location. As the life of the wasting asset is contingent upon the amount of annual operations, the depreciation of the plant may be computed on the same basis that is used for depletion; that is:

$$\text{Annual Depreciation} = (\text{Cost} - \text{Scrap}) \times \frac{\text{Units Extracted During Year}}{\text{Total Estimated Units}}$$

Contingent decreases in the value of fixed assets.

Depreciation and depletion of tangible fixed assets and amortization of intangible fixed assets are decreases in value which are definitely known to have occurred, although the amounts thereof may have to be estimated. Provision for these decreases in value must, therefore, be made if the balance sheet and operating statement are to conform to accepted accounting principles.

There are certain other possible decreases in fixed asset values which are contingent in nature and for which reserves are not imperative, but for which reserves may be established out of considerations of conservatism. These contingent losses include:

(1) *Obsolescence.* A fixed asset may become obsolete from two general causes:
  (a) A new asset may be perfected which operates so cheaply that it is advantageous to discard the old one and install the new. Such obsolescence is also called supersession.
  (b) The product produced by the asset may have a sale which is dependent upon a fad or a fashion, or it may be replaced by some other product. If the fixed asset is capable of producing only the one product, a cessation of the demand for that product will make the fixed asset obsolete.

(2) *Inadequacy.* Business expansion may make an asset, while still perfectly capable of carrying its old load, unequal to the increased service required.

(3) *Declines in market value.* As long as the fixed assets are used in operations, and as long as it is expected that they will be retained for that purpose, declines in market value need not be provided for by reserves. If the assets are not to be disposed of, the market declines are not prospective losses.

30

INTANGIBLE FIXED ASSETS

Classification of intangible fixed assets.

Intangible fixed assets were classified in a preceding chapter as follows:

(1) Subject to amortization, or the decrease in value caused by the lapse of time. *Examples:* Patents, copyrights, franchises, leaseholds, and leasehold improvements.
(2) Not subject to amortization. *Examples:* Trademarks and goodwill.

Intangible Fixed Assets Subject to Amortization

Valuation of patents.

If a patent is acquired by purchase, its cost is the purchase price. If it is obtained by the inventor, its cost is the total of the experimental expense, costs of working models, and expenses of obtaining the patent, including drawings, attorney's fees, and filing fees. A patent has no proven worth until it has stood the test of an infringement suit; therefore the cost of a successful suit may be added to the book value of the patent.

Writing off patents.

A patent is issued for seventeen years; hence the cost of the patent should usually be written off during that period. Of course, if the patent is purchased some time after it was granted, the purchaser will have to write it off in less than seventeen years.

Although seventeen years is the theoretical period for writing off a patent, practical considerations often make it desirable to write off the cost in less than that time. When the patent covers an article which will be marketable only during the duration of a fad, it is advisable to write off the patent during the probable continuance of the fad.

If the owner of a patent finds that the product manufactured under it is not in demand and cannot be marketed profitably, the patent is evidently valueless even though its legal life has not expired; in such cases it should be written off.

Copyrights.

A copyright is issued for twenty-eight years with a possibility of renewal for an additional twenty-eight years. Publications rarely have any considerable market for so long a period, and it is usually considered advisable to write off the copyright cost as a deduction from the income from the first edition.

Franchises.

Franchises should not appear on the books unless a payment, either direct or indirect, was made in obtaining them. Franchises may be perpetual, in which case the cost need never be written off. They may be granted for a definite period of time, in which case the cost should be written off over that period. They may be revocable at the option of the city or other governmental body which granted them, in which case it is advisable to write them off rapidly, although there is a tendency to look upon such franchises as perpetual and to make no provision for writing off their cost.

Leaseholds.

A leasehold is an estate for years. It should not be entered on the books as an asset unless rentals have been paid in advance, in which case such payments may be written off to expense over the life of the lease. The possession of a long-time lease to property in a neighborhood where rents are rapidly advancing may be a very great advantage, but that is not sufficient justification for arbitrarily placing a value on such a lease and including it as an asset in the balance sheet.

Leasehold improvements.

Leases frequently provide that the lessee shall pay the costs of any alterations or improvements of the leased real estate, such as new fronts, partitions, and built-in shelving. Such improvements become a part of the property and revert to the owner of the real estate at the expiration of the lease; but the lessee obtains the right to benefit by the improvements during the life of the lease and this right is an intangible asset which can properly appear in the lessee's balance sheet as leasehold improvements. However, it should be amortized over the life of the lease.

Intangible Fixed Assets Not Subject to Amortization

Trademarks.

Trademarks may be registered, but they are valid under the common law even though not registered if the claimant is able to prove his prior use of the mark. As trademarks do not expire, it is not necessary to write off any cost which may have been incurred in obtaining them.

Goodwill.

The following is quoted from a court decision:

When an individual or a firm or a corporation has gone on for an unbroken series of years conducting a particular business, and has been so scrupulous in fulfilling every obligation, so careful in maintaining the standard of the goods dealt in, so absolutely fair and honest in all business dealings that customers of the concern have become convinced that their experience in the future will be as satisfactory as it has been in the past, while such customers' good report of their own experience tends continually to bring new customers to the concern, there has been produced an element of value quite as important—in some cases, perhaps, far more important—than the plant or machinery with which the business is carried on. That it is property is abundantly settled by authority, and, indeed, is not disputed. That in some cases it may be very valuable property is manifest. The individual who has created it by years of hard work and fair business dealing usually experiences no difficulty in finding men willing to pay him for it if he be willing to sell it to them.

With all deference to the learned jurist, a company may be scrupulous in fulfilling every obligation, it may maintain a high standard of goods dealt in, it may be absolutely fair and honest in all its business dealings, it may do all of the things mentioned in the decision quoted, and yet may have no goodwill. The existence of a goodwill depends upon the earning of excess profits, or the relation of earnings to net assets.

Relation of earnings to net assets.

Goodwill may be defined as the capitalized value of the profits of a business which are in excess of a normal or basic return on the net assets exclusive of goodwill. To illustrate, let us assume the following conditions:

	Co. *A*	Co. *B*
Net income earned........................... ...	$10,000.00	$15,000.00
Each concern has net assets of $100,000.00. If 10% be accepted as a basic rate, the basic return on the net assets is 10% of $100,000.00 or...........................	10,000.00	10,000.00
And the excess earnings are...........................	$ —	$ 5,000.00

Company *A* apparently has no goodwill; Company *B*, with excess earnings, apparently has a goodwill.

Valuation of goodwill.

If a business is to be sold, the price to be paid for the goodwill, if any, may be agreed upon by the purchaser and the seller. It may be an arbitrary sum arrived at without formal computations, or it may be more or less carefully computed by:

(1) A careful estimate of the probable future profits, and
(2) Application of one of several methods of estimating goodwill on the basis of the probable future profits.

Probable future profits.

When the purchaser of a business pays a price for goodwill, he is not paying for the excess profits of the past, but for the probable excess profits of the future. The accomplishments of the past, however, furnish the best evidence of the probable accomplishments in the future, and hence it is customary to estimate the future profits on the basis of past profits. In making a statement of past profits which are to be used as the basis for computing the goodwill, consideration should be given to the following points:

(1) All extraneous and non-operating profits and losses should be excluded. These are unusual in nature and not likely to be repeated; hence they should not be included in a statement which is to be used in estimating future profits.
(2) If any known facts point to a difference between past and future profits, these facts should be given consideration. For instance, if management salaries have not been deducted by the vendor, or if the salaries have been merely nominal, deductions should be made for the management salaries to be paid by the purchaser, provided these salaries are reasonable.

If the success of the business in the past has been due largely to the personality or business ability of the old management, and if those who are responsible for this success are not to go with the business to the new management, the profits and the goodwill should be recognized as largely personal, and consideration should be given to this fact in estimating future profits.

If the fixed assets of the business are to be transferred to the purchaser at a higher price than that at which they have been carried on the seller's books, recognition should be given to the fact that higher depreciation charges will be required in the future, and that future profits will be correspondingly diminished.

No one should pay for goodwill on the basis of average past profits without considering the *trend* of those profits. To emphasize how the trend of past profits is indicative of probable future profits, let us consider four companies whose profits have averaged $20,000.00 for five years:

	Co. *A*	Co. *B*	Co. *C*	Co. *D*
1937	$ 25,000.00	$ 19,100.00	$ 30,000.00	$ 10,000.00
1938	40,000.00	19,800.00	25,000.00	15,000.00
1939	19,000.00	20,400.00	20,000.00	20,000.00
1940	2,000.00*	20,200.00	15,000.00	25,000.00
1941	18,000.00	20,500.00	10,000.00	30,000.00
Total	$100,000.00	$100,000.00	$100,000.00	$100,000.00
Average	$ 20,000.00	$ 20,000.00	$ 20,000.00	$ 20,000.00

* Denotes loss.

Net assets, exclusive of goodwill, amount to $150,000.00 in each case.

Although each of these concerns has made an average annual net profit of $20,000.00, it is evident that it would be unwise to pay the same amount for the goodwill of each business.

Company *A*'s profits show a wide fluctuation, from a profit of $40,000.00 in 1938 to a loss of $2,000.00 in 1940. Such a history furnishes very poor assurance of dependable profits in the future.

Company *B*'s profits, on the other hand, are very uniform year by year, and show a slight tendency to increase.

Company *C* has no goodwill (assuming that 10% is a fair basic rate); its profits are steadily declining; the profit for the last year was less than 10% of the net assets exclusive of goodwill; and, if the declining curve of profits is projected for two more years, the company will have no profits.

Company *D* seems to have the most goodwill of all, for its profits are steadily increasing. In fact, just as it would be unwise for a purchaser to pay C anything for goodwill, because of its declining profits, so also it would probably be unfair to D to base its goodwill on the average profits. Because D's profits are steadily increasing, it appears likely that its future profits will be considerably more than the past average.

Methods of computation.

Six methods of computing goodwill are illustrated in the following sections. All of these illustrations are based on the following assumed facts: the purchaser and seller of a business have agreed that the net assets, other than goodwill, shall be valued at $100,- 000.00; the profits for the five years next preceding the date of sale were $19,000.00, $19,500.00, $19,000.00, $21,500.00, and $21,000.00, or an annual average of $20,000.00.

(1) *Years' purchase of past annual profits.* Assume that the goodwill is to be valued at an amount equal to the total profits of the last preceding two years; the payment to be made for goodwill is called a two years' purchase of past profits. The amount is computed as follows:

Profits of second preceding year	$21,500.00
Profits of first preceding year	21,000.00
Total, and price to be paid for the goodwill	$42,500.00

This is an illogical method of computing goodwill because it fails to recognize the fact that the goodwill is not dependent upon total profits, no matter how large, but upon the relation of the profits to the investment, and that no goodwill exists unless the profits are in excess of a normal income on the net assets other than goodwill.

(2) *Years' purchase of average past profits.* This method differs from the preceding one in only one particular: average profits are used. Assume that the goodwill is to be valued at two years' purchase of the average profits of the past five years; the computation of the goodwill value is made as follows:

Average profits of last five years (as stated above)	$20,000.00
Multiply by number of years of purchase	2
Goodwill	$40,000.00

This method is as illogical as the preceding one since it ignores the fact that goodwill is dependent upon excess profits rather than on total profits. The use of an average profit does not correct this error.

(3) *Years' purchase of excess profits.* Assume that the goodwill is to be valued at three years' purchase of the past profits in excess of 12½% of the $100,000.00 agreed value of the net assets other than goodwill. The amount to be paid for the goodwill is computed as follows:

Year Preceding Sale	Profits	12½% of Net Assets	Excess
Third...........................	$19,000.00	$12,500.00	$ 6,500.00
Second..........................	21,500.00	12,500.00	9,000.00
First............................	21,000.00	12,500.00	8,500.00
Total payment for goodwill...........................			$24,000.00

(4) *Years' purchase of average excess profits.* Assume that the goodwill is to be valued at three years' purchase of the average profits of the past five years in excess of 12½% of the $100,000.00 agreed value of the net assets. This method is similar to the preceding one except that average profits are used instead of actual annual profits. The valuation of the goodwill is computed as follows:

Average profits of past five years...........................	$20,000.00
Deduct 12½% of $100,000.00...............................	12,500.00
Excess..	$ 7,500.00
Multiply by number of years of purchase....................	3
Goodwill..	$22,500.00

(5) *Capitalized profits, minus net assets.* Assume that the purchaser and seller agree upon 12½% as a normal or basic rate, and agree to base the valuation of the business upon a capitalization, at that rate, of the average income for the past five years. The goodwill is computed as follows:

Capitalized value of average net profits—or total value of business: $20,000.00 ÷ 12½%...........................	$160,000.00
Deduct agreed value of net assets other than goodwill.......	100,000.00
Goodwill.....................................	$ 60,000.00

(6) *Excess profits capitalized.* A serious theoretical objection can be raised against the last preceding method. This objection may be made apparent by dividing the total purchase price into two parts and noting what the purchaser of the business obtains in return for each portion of the purchase price.

	Net Assets	Profits
For the first $100,000.00 of the purchase price, the purchaser receives:		
Net assets of..	$100,000.00	
Prospective profits of 12½% thereof................		$12,500.00
For the remaining $60,000.00 of the purchase price, the purchaser receives:		
An intangible asset of goodwill.....................	60,000.00	
Prospective profits of 12½% thereof................		7,500.00

But the $60,000.00 intangible asset of goodwill has no value apart from the $7,500.00 of profits. Therefore, it may be more exactly stated that:

> For the first $100,000.00, the purchaser receives net assets and prospective profits;
> For the remaining $60,000.00, the purchaser receives only prospective profits.

It therefore appears that, if 12½% is a fair rate for the capitalization of the first $12,500.00 of profits (which are accompanied by assets), a higher rate should be used for the capitalization of the $7,500.00 of profits which are not accompanied by assets. The use of two rates is illustrated by the following computation of goodwill, it being assumed that the purchaser and seller have agreed that 12½% is a fair rate for the capitalization of profits accompanied by assets, and that the remaining profits should be capitalized at 25%.

Average profits of past five years..........................	$20,000.00
Deduct profits regarded as applicable to net assets acquired— 12½% of $100,000.00..................................	12,500.00
Remaining profits, regarded as indicative of goodwill........	$ 7,500.00
Goodwill = $7,500.00 ÷ 25%.............................	$30,000.00

This method is probably the most theoretically correct of all.

Goodwill in the balance sheet.

Goodwill should appear in the balance sheet at not more than the amount actually paid for it in acquiring a going business. The amount shown in the balance sheet should represent the amount paid for goodwill, not its value at the date of the balance sheet. If profits have increased, the goodwill has increased; but the amount shown in the balance sheet as goodwill should not be increased. If profits have decreased, there is no obligation to write off part or all of the goodwill.

If goodwill appears in the balance sheet, the reasonableness of the value assigned to it can be tested by one of the "capitalization of income" procedures described in the preceding sections, preferably the following:

Multiply the value of the net assets other than goodwill, as shown by the balance sheet (in other words, the net worth stated in the balance sheet minus the goodwill stated therein) by a reasonable income rate to cover a return on investment (8%, for instance);

Deduct the product thus obtained from the net income shown by the profit and loss statement;

Capitalize the remaining earnings, as thus determined, by dividing by a relatively high rate (20%, for instance) to determine the goodwill or capitalized value of the excess earnings;

Compare the goodwill valuation thus determined with the goodwill valuation shown in the balance sheet.

If the reader of a balance sheet could be sure that the amount shown therein as goodwill represented the amount actually paid for goodwill in connection with the acquisition of a profitable going business, the term would not suffer from its present disrepute. Unfortunately, many balance sheets have shown as goodwill the amounts of expenditures for organization expenses (which should have been deducted from surplus), or advertising expenditures (which should have been deducted from the operating profits), or operating losses of a development period, or the amounts of stock issued in excess of the fair value of the assets received.

31

APPRAISALS OF FIXED ASSETS

....

Purpose of appraisals.

Appraisals may be made for various purposes, among which are determinations of values for tax, sale, consolidation, and credit purposes. During a period of rising costs, the depreciated value based on reproduction cost is likely to exceed the depreciated value based on original cost. For instance, an appraisal and the books might show the following values of machinery:

	Per Appraisal	Per Books	Excess per Appraisal
Cost:			
Reproduction cost new—per appraisal....	$140,000.00		
Original cost—per books................		$100,000.00	
Excess of reproduction cost new over original cost...........................			$40,000.00
Depreciation:			
On reproduction cost—per appraisal......	35,000.00		
On original cost—per books............		25,000.00	
Excess of depreciation on reproduction cost over depreciation on original cost.......			10,000.00
Depreciated value:			
Sound value—per appraisal..............	$105,000.00		
Net book value.......................		$ 75,000.00	
Excess of sound value per appraisal over net book value......................			$30,000.00

Change in accountants' attitude.

For many years, accountants took the position that fixed assets should be carried on the books and shown in the balance sheet at cost less depreciation, regardless of higher appraised values, because writing up the assets to appraised values would involve credits to Surplus which would be unwarranted because the appraisal increment would be an unrealized profit. However, they were confronted with situations of this sort:

Cost of property, less depreciation—per books..............	$ 75,000.00
Reproduction cost new, less depreciation—per appraisal......	105,000.00
Note payable, secured by a mortgage on the property........	60,000.00

285

If the accountant insisted upon showing the property in the balance sheet at original cost less depreciation, he indicated that a liability of $60,000.00 was secured by property worth only $75,-000.00. If the appraisal was reliable, the balance sheet was obviously unfair.

To meet such a situation, the accountant might show the facts in the balance sheet thus:

Balance Sheet—December 31, 1941

Asset Side

Machinery (Reproduction Cost New, Less Depreciation, Per Appraisal by The Blank Appraisal Company, as of December 31, 1941, $105,000.00):

Cost	$100,000.00	
Less Depreciation on Cost	25,000.00	$75,000.00

Liability Side

Mortgage Payable..................................... $60,000.00

Such a balance sheet, in which the appraised value of the fixed assets is merely shown parenthetically, is obviously much less satisfactory from the company's standpoint than one in which the appraised values appear in the money columns, as follows:

Balance Sheet—December 31, 1941

Asset Side

Machinery—Per Appraisal by The Blank Appraisal Company as of December 31, 1941:

Reproduction Cost New	$140,000	
Less Depreciation	35,000	105,000

Liability Side

Mortgage Payable.. $ 60,000

Accountants therefore reconsidered their position, and rather generally reached the conclusion that it is permissible to record appraisals in the accounts if the write-up is not credited to Surplus and if depreciation subsequent to the appraisal is properly computed.

Recording appraisals: first method.

Referring to the foregoing illustration, the asset and depreciation reserve accounts before the appraisal was recorded were:

Machinery	$100,000.00	
Reserve for Depreciation—Machinery		$25,000.00

These accounts might be adjusted to agree with the appraisal by the journal entry on the following page.

```
Machinery.....................................  40,000.00
    Reserve for Depreciation—Machinery..........                10,000.00
    Reserve for Unrealized Increment per Appraisal..            30,000.00
```

The $40,000.00 debit to Machinery is the excess of the replacement cost new over the original cost; the $10,000.00 credit to the reserve is the excess of the depreciation per appraisal over the depreciation per books. And the $30,000.00 credit to the Reserve for Unrealized Increment is the net increase; crediting this reserve accomplishes the accountant's desire to keep the unrealized profit out of the Surplus account.

The adjusted balances of the accounts would be shown in the balance sheet as follows:

Balance Sheet—December 31, 1941

Assets

FIXED ASSETS:
Machinery—Per Appraisal by The Blank
Appraisal Company as of December 31, 1941:

```
    Reproduction Cost New........................  $140,000
    Less Depreciation............................    35,000  $105,000
```

Liabilities and Net Worth

NET WORTH:

```
    Capital Stock................................  $xxx,xxx
    Surplus......................................    xx,xxx
    Reserve for Unrealized Increment per Appraisal....  30,000
    Total Net Worth..............................          $xxx,xxx
```

Recording appraisals: second method.

It is probable that entries recording appraisals are usually made in the manner illustrated above; this method, however, is subject to a very definite criticism: namely, a clear distinction between actual costs and appraisal write-ups is not maintained. To maintain such a distinction, it is desirable to:

(1) Open a separate property account which will be charged with the excess of reproduction cost new over original cost; and

(2) Open a separate depreciation reserve which will be credited with the excess of the depreciation on reproduction cost over the depreciation on original cost.

If this method is used, the journal entry to take up the appraisal will be:

```
Machinery—Appraisal Increase...................  40,000.00
    Reserve   for   Depreciation—Machinery—Ap-
        praisal Increase.........................                10,000.00
    Reserve for Unrealized Increment per Appraisal.            30,000.00
```

After the appraisal has been thus recorded, the accounts will contain the following balances:

Machinery (original cost)........................ $100,000.00
Machinery—Appraisal Increase................ 40,000.00
Reserve for Depreciation (on cost)............ $25,000.00
Reserve for Depreciation—Appraisal Increase...   10,000.00
Reserve for Unrealized Increment per Appraisal.   30,000.00

The two asset accounts have a combined balance of $140,-000.00, as above; the two depreciation reserves have a combined balance of $35,000.00; and the unrealized profit is set up in a reserve, as before.

Adjustment of depreciation on cost.

It will be noted that, in the preceding illustration, the books and the appraisal each reflected depreciation equal to 25% of the gross value, as follows:

	Per Books	Per Appraisal
Gross value	$100,000.00	$140,000.00
Depreciation	25,000.00	35,000.00
Net value	$ 75,000.00	$105,000.00
Per cent of accrued depreciation	25%	25%

But assume that the appraisal disclosed a per cent of accrued depreciation different from that shown by the books; for example:

	Per Books	Per Appraisal
Gross value	$100,000.00	$140,000.00
Depreciation	25,000.00	28,000.00
Net value	$ 75,000.00	$112,000.00
Per cent of accrued depreciation	25%	20%

The fact that the appraisal shows only 20% accrued depreciation appears to indicate that the depreciation provided in the accounts on a cost basis has been excessive, and that the total reserve on cost should be only 20% of $100,000.00, or $20,000.00, instead of $25,000.00.

It may be in order to adjust the accounts with respect to this apparent overdepreciation. However, it should be understood that a difference in the degrees of depreciation shown by the books and by the appraisal does not necessarily, or even usually, indicate that the depreciation reserve based on cost should be adjusted. The book provisions for depreciation are not intended to equal depreciation on an engineering or appraisal basis; they are intended merely to extinguish the invested cost over the life of the asset by appropriate charges to operations. The difference between the per cent of depreciation per the appraisal and the per cent of depreciation provided on an accounting basis 'may be ignored unless, at the time of the appraisal, it is practically certain that the original estimate of the life of the asset, on which the book depreciation was based, was in error, and unless the consequences of the error are of such serious magnitude as to make adjustments to a new estimated life basis of material importance.

Continuing the illustration, and assuming that an adjustment is regarded as in order, the entry is:

Reserve for Depreciation—Machinery............ 5,000.00
    Surplus...................................   5,000.00
    To reduce the depreciation reserve from $25,000.00
    (25% of cost) to $20,000.00 (20% of cost) and
    credit Surplus with the adjustment.

Surplus is credited with the amount of the excess depreciation, because the excess provision reduced the profits of prior years and hence reduced the Surplus balance.

After this entry is posted, the accounts will have balances which are compared below with those shown by the appraisal:

	Per Books	Per Appraisal
Cost and replacement cost new..............	$100,000.00	$140,000.00
Depreciation (20%)........................	20,000.00	28,000.00
Net value.................................	$ 80,000.00	$112,000.00

The accounts now can be adjusted to reflect the appraisal by the following entry:

Machinery—Appraisal Increase.................. 40,000.00
    Reserve for Depreciation—Machinery—Ap-
      praisal Increase........................   8,000.00
    Reserve for Unrealized Increment per Appraisal   32,000.00

After this entry is posted, the accounts will contain the following amounts:

Machinery (original cost)..................... $100,000.00
Machinery—Appraisal Increase.................   40,000.00
Reserve for Depreciation (adjusted to 20% of the
    cost of machinery)....................... $20,000.00
Reserve for Depreciation—Appraisal Increase
    (20% of the $40,000.00 increase in gross value).   8,000.00
Reserve for Unrealized Increment per Appraisal.   32,000.00
Surplus (credit for excess depreciation in prior
    periods)..................................   5,000.00

On the other hand, assume that the appraisal discloses a degree of depreciation higher than that reflected by the books; for example:

	Per Books	Per Appraisal
Cost and replacement cost new.............	$100,000.00	$140,000.00
Depreciation..............................	25,000.00	42,000.00
Net value.................................	$ 75,000.00	$ 98,000.00
Per cent of accrued depreciation............	25%	30%

If the depreciation provided in the past is inadequate because of an overestimate of the life of the asset, and if it is desired to adjust the accounts, the adjustment may be made by the following journal entry:

```
Surplus........................................  5,000.00
    Reserve for Depreciation—Machinery.........            5,000.00
    To increase the depreciation reserve from $25,000.00
    (25% of cost) to $30,000.00 (30% of cost—basis
    shown by appraisal) and to charge Surplus with the
    amount of the adjustment of prior years' deprecia-
    tion.
```

The book values (after this adjustment has been posted) are compared below with the appraisal values:

	Per Books	Per Appraisal
Cost and replacement cost new.............	$100,000.00	$140,000.00
Depreciation (30%).......................	30,000.00	42,000.00
Net value................................	$ 70,000.00	$ 98,000.00

The accounts can now be adjusted to reflect the appraisal values as follows:

```
Machinery—Appraisal Increase................... 40,000.00
    Reserve for Depreciation—Machinery—Ap-
        praisal Increase........................          12,000.00
    Reserve for Unrealized Increment per Appraisal        28,000.00
```

After this entry is posted, the accounts will contain balances as follows:

```
Machinery (original cost)............................ $100,000.00
Machinery—Appraisal Increase........................  40,000.00
Reserve for Depreciation—Machinery (adjusted to 30% of
    the cost of the machinery)...........................          $30,000.00
Reserve for Depreciation—Machinery—Appraisal Increase
    (30% of the $40,000.00 increase in gross value).........          12,000.00
Reserve for Unrealized Increment per Appraisal.........          28,000.00
Surplus (charge for inadequate depreciation in prior
    periods)........................................  5,000.00
```

Subsequent depreciation.

Assume that the accounts, after an appraisal has been recorded, contain the following balances:

Machinery (original cost).............................	$100,000.00	
Machinery—Appraisal Increase........................	40,000.00	
Reserve for Depreciation—Machinery (on cost)..........		$25,000.00
Reserve for Depreciation—Machinery—Appraisal Increase		10,000.00
Reserve for Unrealized Increment per Appraisal..........		30,000.00

The machinery had an estimated original life of twenty years; a 5% depreciation rate was used prior to the appraisal; the annual depreciation charge was therefore $5,000.00; five years of the asset's life have expired, and hence the accumulated reserve based on cost is $25,000.00; fifteen years of estimated life remain. Should Profit and Loss be charged during each of these fifteen years with depreciation based on cost or with depreciation based on the appreciated value? There has been a difference of opinion among accountants on this question.

Entries based on cost.

Probably the majority of accountants have held the opinion that, since the cost of a fixed asset is a sort of deferred charge to be written off against operations during the life of the asset, depreciation charges after an appraisal should be based, as before, on cost, so that operations during the life of the asset will be charged with the invested cost—no more, no less. According to this opinion, the depreciation provision to be closed to Profit and Loss would be recorded by the following journal entry:

Depreciation—Machinery.........................	5,000.00	
Reserve for Depreciation—Machinery (on cost)...		5,000.00

To provide depreciation of 5% of the original cost of $100,000.00 (or $\frac{1}{15}$ of the $75,000.00 remaining undepreciated cost at the date of the appraisal).

At the date of the appraisal, the net appraisal value was $30,000.00 in excess of the net book value based on cost, and this excess was set up in an unrealized profit reserve. But fifteen years hence the property will presumably have no value, and the unrealized increment will have disappeared. For this reason, the Reserve for Unrealized Increment should disappear also. It can be made to disappear by fifteen annual entries as follows:

Reserve for Unrealized Increment per Appraisal.......	2,000.00	
Reserve for Depreciation Machinery—Appraisal Increase		2,000.00

Depreciation of appreciation—$\frac{1}{15}$ of $30,000.

At the end of fifteen years the accounts will contain the following balances:

Machinery (original cost)............................ $100,000.00
Machinery—Appraisal Increase....................... 40,000.00
Reserve for Depreciation—Machinery (on cost)......... $100,000.00
Reserve for Depreciation—Machinery—Appraisal Increase 40,000.00
Reserve for Unrealized Increment per Appraisal......... —

Since the asset is fully depreciated, the accounts can be eliminated by a journal entry debiting the two depreciation reserves and crediting the two asset accounts.

Entries based on replacement value.

Although depreciation based on replacement value is of course not permitted for income tax computations, many accountants have believed that depreciation for general accounting purposes should be based on replacement value (if it is in excess of cost), on the theory that a manufacturer operating low-cost, long-ago acquired fixed assets places himself ultimately in a bad position by basing his depreciation on cost. For the time being his manufacturing costs may be lower than those of another manufacturer operating newer and more expensive machinery, and he may be disposed to make his selling prices correspondingly low. This gives him a temporary advantage in meeting competition; but what shall it profit a manufacturer if he gain all the business, but at a price which will not enable him to replace his fixed assets at the new and higher costs? To avoid such an eventual calamity, it has been contended that depreciation should be based on the costs which would be incurred in replacing the machinery, so that manufacturing costs would be computed at a higher figure, and selling prices would therefore be set at a higher figure, and the manufacturer would thereby take pains to get enough for his products to enable him to replace his fixed assets.

Accountants holding this view advocate that annual entries should be made in some manner similar to the following:

Depreciation—Machinery (to be closed to P. & L.).......... 7,000
    Reserve for Depreciation—Machinery (on cost)......... 5,000
    Reserve for Depreciation—Machinery—Appraisal Increase 2,000
    To charge operations with depreciation on replacement value.

Reserve for Unrealized Increment per Appraisal............ 2,000
    Surplus.. 2,000
    Adjustment for depreciation of appreciation.

The second entry is required for two reasons: (1) the debit is required to extinguish gradually the Unrealized Increment account of $30,000.00, because the unrealized profit will have disappeared at the end of the life of the asset; and (2) Surplus should be credited $2,000.00 to offset the fact that charging operations with $7,000.00 depreciation instead of $5,000.00 resulted in showing a theoretical profit (closed to Surplus) which was $2,000.00 less than the true profit.

At the end of fifteen years, the accounts would contain the same balances as those shown in the preceding section illustrating entries based on cost, and the same journal entry could be made to close them.

To the proponents of depreciation-on-replacement-value, the advocates of the cost basis could reply: A good businessman knows that his selling prices must be high enough to enable him to buy new equipment when the old is worn out; he can remember this without keeping his accounts in such a manner as to distort his true costs. Depreciation charges are intended to spread the cost of a fixed asset over the asset's life as an expense; the total depreciation expense cannot be greater than the cost; while the low-cost asset is still in use the depreciation expense should be based on its cost; when it is replaced by a higher-cost asset, the depreciation will have to be based on the new cost.

Perhaps the point can be made clearer by analogy. A merchant buys an article for $1.00 and marks it to sell for $1.50. Before it is sold, the market purchase price goes up from $1.00 to $1.35; the merchant then advances his selling price to $1.85 so that he can buy another article for $1.35 and still have $.50 for operating expenses and dividends. But he does not say that the first article cost $1.35; he does not consider it necessary to misstate the cost and profit on the first article merely to assure his ability to replace his merchandise.

The Institute's pronouncement.

The preceding sections of this chapter indicate the general opinions long held by accountants relative to appraisals and subsequent depreciation. Under date of April 1940, the Committee on Accounting Procedure of the American Institute of Accountants issued a bulletin containing two pronouncements:

(1) That fixed assets should normally be carried in the accounts at cost, and that any other basis of valuation is "impracticable and inexpedient."

(2) That if, nevertheless, a corporation should record the appreciation of its fixed assets disclosed by an appraisal, operations should thereafter be charged with depreciation computed on the basis of the appraised value.

Entries for subsequent depreciation, if made in accordance with this expression of opinion, would presumably take the form illustrated in the preceding section "Entries based on replacement value." However, the Committee's reason for this opinion appears to be wholly different from the arguments formerly presented by accountants who have advocated basing depreciation on replacement values. The reason offered by the Committee in support of its proposal as to subsequent depreciation can be summarized as follows: A company must be consistent; if the balance sheet says the replacement value of the property is $150,000.00, a cost valuation of $100,000.00 should not be used for purposes of computing the depreciation charges shown in its profit and loss statement; in other words, if one valuation appears in the balance sheet, nothing inconsistent with it should appear in the income statement.

There is much to be said in support of this point of view, and it is in line with two recent trends of major importance in the theory and practice of accounting: a tendency to give increasing consideration to the statement of earnings, and an emphasis upon accounting consistency.

In support of the principle of consistency, it can be contended that if a company abandons the cost basis of accounting for fixed assets in order to make a good balance sheet showing, it should not be permitted to escape the concomitant penalty in the form of additional depreciation charges against earnings. It may also be said that a company which writes down its fixed assets does not hesitate to base its subsequent depreciation charges on the lower values; consistency seems to require that an accountant who sanctions this procedure should insist upon a comparable procedure if fixed assets are written up.

At the present writing it is impossible to forecast the extent to which the Committee's pronouncement will alter current practice. The Committee is clothed with no authority to impose its findings upon the profession; it must rely upon their general acceptability. It is possible that accountants may be impressed with the soundness of the doctrine of consistency; it is also possible that they may continue to regard it as proper to show appraised values in the books and in the balance sheet, for reasons that have seemed adequate in the past, and may fail to see any glaring inconsistency between a balance sheet in which, although the fixed assets are stated at appraised values, there is an unrealized profit reserve showing the amount of the appreciation, and an income statement in which depreciation is based on cost.

Revaluations downward.

For many years the trend of prices was upward, and appraisals generally disclosed increases in fixed asset valuations; appraisals were then frequently made and recorded to establish increased valuations for purposes incident to the issuance of securities.

During the depression which began in 1929, the downward trend in fixed asset values developed another point of view, and not a few concerns adopted the policy of writing down fixed assets to low values. In many instances, no doubt, the fixed assets were written down so that a more conservative picture of the financial condition would be shown by the balance sheet. In many other instances, however, it appears that the write-off to Surplus was made for the purpose of relieving future operations of large depreciation charges, in order that more favorable operating results could be shown in the income statement.

There is some doubt as to the propriety of making a large charge to Surplus when the effect is to relieve future periods of a portion of the depreciation charges which would otherwise be charged as operating expenses. Many accountants, however, have regarded this as permissible if the write-down was made by charge to Earned Surplus.

Accounting authorities do not sanction creating a capital surplus by having stockholders turn in a part of their stock, or by changing from a par to a no-par stock basis, or otherwise, and then reducing the carrying values of fixed assets by charges against such capital surplus credits. In other words, relieving future periods of operating charges for depreciation by writing down fixed assets may be permissible if the reduction in value is charged against a Surplus account created by operating profits of prior periods, but it is not permissible if the charge is made to a surplus created in some other way.

32

INVESTMENTS IN STOCKS

....

Valuation of stock investments.

At what valuation should stock investments be carried? The answer to this question depends upon whether the stock is held by:

(1) A dealer.
(2) An investor or speculator.
(3) A parent or holding company.

Accounting methods applicable to these classes of owners are discussed in the remainder of this chapter.

Securities owned by dealers.

To a dealer in securities, stocks owned are merchandise; under the tax regulations, dealers are permitted to value securities owned on any one of three bases, namely: at cost, at market, or at the lower of cost or market. But a consistent basis must be followed year after year unless permission to change the basis is received from the Commissioner. The lower of cost or market is, of course, the conservative basis of valuation, for the reasons stated in the chapter dealing with the valuation of merchandise.

Securities owned by investors.

Investors are required, for purposes of computing income taxes, to value securities owned at cost. A decrease in market value cannot be deducted as a loss until the securities are sold, nor is there any tax on a paper profit represented by an increase in market value not realized by a sale.

Although a decline in market value is not a deductible loss for tax purposes, it should under some circumstances, but not always, be regarded as a loss for general accounting purposes. Slight decreases in the market value of permanent investments can usually be ignored; the market may recover before the securities are sold. But serious declines in the market value of long-term investments should be taken up in the accounts as losses. And any market declines in the value of temporary investments should be immediately recorded as losses.

Entries to record a loss resulting from a decline in market value should be made in such a way as to preserve a record of the cost of the securities; if the securities are sold at a later date, it will be necessary to know the cost in order to compute the difference between cost and selling price, which is the taxable profit or deductible loss. If a company owns securities which cost $100,-000.00 and which have a market value of only $90,000.00, the journal entry to record the loss in value should be:

```
Market Loss on Securities....................... 10,000.00
      Reserve to Reduce Securities to Market........          10,000.00
```

The debit balance in the Market Loss on Securities account will be closed to Profit and Loss (or possibly Surplus) when the books are closed. The asset and related reserve accounts will have balances as follows:

```
Investments in Stocks....................... $100,000.00
Reserve to Decrease Securities to Market.......          $10,000.00
```

The investment may be shown on the asset side of the balance sheet thus:

```
Stocks Owned:
    Cost.................................... $100,000.00
    Less Reserve to Reduce to Market........  10,000.00 $90,000.00
```

or merely thus:

```
Stocks Owned—At Market Value....................... $90,000.00
```

Profits and losses on sales of stock.

For tax purposes an investor's or speculator's taxable income or deductible loss from dealings in stocks is the difference between the value received and the cost of the stock. If stocks are bought for cash and later sold for cash, there is no question as to the cost and the value received. The difficulty comes in determining the cost of stock acquired in exchange for property other than cash, and the value received for stock parted with in exchange for property other than cash.

When stock is exchanged for other property, the parties to the exchange may place a value on the property or on the stock. For instance, a value is placed on the property if the contract states that A agrees to buy B's real estate for $20,000.00, payable in so many shares of such and such stock.   Or a value is placed on the stock if the contract states that B agrees to buy A's stock for $20,000.00, and pay for it with such and such real estate.

Placing a value on the property automatically places a value on the stock, and vice versa.   In either of the above cases:

A will compute his profit or loss as follows:

Selling price of stock.................................... $20,000.00
Deduct cost of stock.....................................   ?

B will compute his profit or loss as follows:

Selling price of real estate.............................. $20,000.00
Deduct cost of real estate...............................   ?

and each party will put his newly acquired asset on his books at a valuation of $20,000.00 for purposes of computing any profit or loss on its subsequent disposal.

But the $20,000.00 value stated in the contract is tentative only and may not be accepted by the Bureau of Internal Revenue because it does not represent a fair market value for either the stock or the real estate.   If a market value for either the stock or the real estate is established at, say, $25,000.00, A's and B's taxes on the transaction will be changed.   It will then be desirable for each of them to adjust the book value of his newly acquired asset from $20,000.00 to $25,000.00, because taxes on any subsequent disposal of the asset will be computed on the basis of a cost of $25,000.00.

If the exchange is not made at a stated price, as in the foregoing illustration, the transaction should be recorded on the basis of the fair market value of the stock or the fair market value of the other property at the time of the exchange.

If it is impossible to establish a fair market value for either the stock or the property, A and B may be permitted to report no taxable profit or deductible loss; in that case, A should take the real estate onto his books at the amount which the stock had cost him, and B should take the stock onto his books at the price which he had paid for the real estate.

If property is turned into a corporation for shares of its stock, the person thus acquiring the stock should place it on his books at its fair market value, or, if this is not determinable, at the fair market value of the property given for it.   If neither value is determinable, the government may set the value at the par of the stock and place upon the taxpayer the burden of proof that par is not a fair valuation.

If a man buys ten shares of stock at $50.00 per share and ten more at $75.00 per share, and later sells ten shares at $60.00 per share, has he made a profit or a loss? For tax purposes (and the tax rule is satisfactory for general accounting purposes also) the answer depends upon whether the shares sold can be identified; if they cannot be identified, the first shares purchased will be assumed to be the first ones sold. Therefore, if the taxpayer desires to obtain a deductible loss, he will take care to transfer to the purchaser the certificate for the second purchase (which cost $75.00 per share), thus taking a loss of the difference between $750.00 and $600.00. If, after the two purchases, the 20 shares had been merged in a single certificate so that the shares sold could not be identified, the 10 shares sold would be assumed to be the first ones purchased; the cost would thus be established at $50.00 per share, and a profit of $10.00 per share would have to be reported.

Stock rights.

A stock right or subscription right is a privilege extended by a corporation to its stockholders to subscribe for additional stock at a stated price. To make the stock right attractive, the stated subscription price must be below the market price.

The announcement of the granting of the right states the date on which the stock records will be closed to determine the stockholders of record to whom the warrants will be issued, and also the later date when subscriptions will be payable. Between the date of the announcement and the date of the issuing of the warrants, the stock and the rights are inseparable, and the stock is dealt in "rights-on." During this period no special accounting problems arise, for the stock and the rights are carried at the cost of the stock, and, if the stock is sold "rights-on," the profit on the sale of the stock and rights is the excess of the amount received over the cost of the stock.

After the warrants are issued, the stock is dealt in "ex-rights"; that is, the rights may be sold separately. If the rights are sold, two accounting questions arise:

(1) What is the profit or loss on the sale of the rights?
(2) What adjustment, if any, should be made in the valuation of the stock?

One can determine the profit or loss on the sale of a right by apportioning the original cost of the stock between the stock and the right on the basis of the market value of the right and the market value of the stock "ex-rights" at the time of the issuance of the right. To illustrate, assume that a share of stock cost $100.00; some time subsequent to the acquisition of this share of stock, the holder received a right to subscribe to an additional share. (The subscription price is immaterial to the illustration.) At the time of the issuance of the right, the right had a market value of $30.00 and the stock "ex-rights" had a market value of $120.00. The right was sold at its market value of $30.00. What was the profit?

```
Apportionment of cost of stock between stock and right:
  Market value of stock..............................  $120.00    80%
  Market value of right..............................    30.00    20
      Total..........................................  $150.00   100%

  Selling price of right..............................  $ 30.00
  Cost of right—on basis of above apportionment:
    20% of $100.00 (original cost of stock)...........    20.00
  Profit on sale of right.............................  $ 10.00
```

The stock investment account should be adjusted to reduce the valuation of the share of stock from $100.00, the original cost, to $80.00, which is the portion of the cost regarded, under the foregoing apportionment, as applicable to the stock.

Or the entire amount received for the right *may* be regarded as profit for tax purposes; on this basis, no apportionment of cost (between the stock and the right) is necessary, and no adjustment of the carrying value of the stock is required.

Investments in subsidiaries.

If one corporation owns all, or a controlling portion, of the stock of another company, the relation of parent and subsidiary exists, and some special problems arise with respect to the valuation at which the parent company should carry the investment in the subsidiary stock and the proper treatment to be accorded by the parent company to its share of the profits of the subsidiary.

In this chapter we shall consider these problems from the standpoint of the parent company's books and statements; consideration will be given later (in Chapters 47 to 49) to the preparation of consolidated statements of the parent company and the subsidiary.

Let us assume that Company P (parent company) organized Company S (subsidiary) and acquired its entire authorized stock at its par value of $100,000.00. Its balance sheet immediately after the acquisition would show among the assets:

Investment in Stock of Subsidiary Company S—100%...... $100,000.00

Subsidiary profits, losses, and dividends.

What entries should be made by the parent company with respect to profits, losses, and dividends of the subsidiary? And how should these matters, as well as the stock investment, be dealt with in the parent company's statements?

There are two different procedures, based on two very different concepts which may be called, for purposes of identification:

(1) The economic concept; and
(2) The legal concept.

Procedure based on the economic concept.

Let us assume that, during the first year of its operation, the subsidiary made a profit of $30,000.00, thus increasing its net assets from the $100,000.00 invested to $130,000.00.

It seems rather obvious that, if the subsidiary's net assets have increased from $100,000.00 to $130,000.00, the value of the parent company's investment, based on underlying net assets, has increased the same amount. It also seems obvious that, since the subsidiary is owned by the parent company, the subsidiary's operations are conducted for the benefit of the parent company, and the $30,000.00 profit made by the subsidiary is really a profit for the parent company. In other words, it appears that the parent company is justified in making the following entry:

Investment in Stock of Subsidiary Company S..... 30,000.00
    Income from Operations of Subsidiary S.......   30,000.00

If statements are prepared by the parent company after this entry is made, the investment will be shown in the balance sheet at a valuation of $130,000.00, and the $30,000.00 will be shown as income in the profit and loss statement.

Continuing the illustration, let us assume that the subsidiary pays a dividend of $5,000.00. Since the parent company has taken up as income the net profit made by the subsidiary, it cannot also regard as income the dividend received from the subsidiary.   The parent company should recognize that the receipt of the dividend merely converts a part of its subsidiary investment into cash, and should record this fact as follows:

```
Cash.........................................    5,000.00
       Investment in Stock of Subsidiary Company S.            5,000.00
```

Further continuing the illustration, let us assume that, during the second year, the subsidiary suffers a loss of $15,000.00 but nevertheless pays the parent company a dividend of $5,000.00 from the profits of the prior year.

The parent company will now record the loss and the resulting decrease in the valuation of the investment by the following entry:

```
Loss from Operations of Subsidiary S.............. 15,000.00
       Investment in Stock of Subsidiary Company S.           15,000.00
```

And it will record the receipt of the dividend as follows:

```
Cash.........................................    5,000.00
       Investment in Stock of Subsidiary Company S.            5,000.00
```

These entries are summarized as follows:

	Investment	Profit or Loss
Cost of investment........................	$100,000.00	
First year:		
Profit.................................	+30,000.00	+30,000.00
Dividend..............................	− 5,000.00	
Carrying value of investment..............	$125,000.00	
Second year:		
Loss...................................	−15,000.00	−15,000.00
Dividend..............................	− 5,000.00	
Carrying value of investment.............	$105,000.00	

By the end of the second year, the parent company will have taken up a net profit of $15,000.00 and will be carrying the investment at $105,000.00, which is equal to the net assets of the subsidiary: $100,000.00 invested + $15,000.00 profits − $10,000.00 distributed as dividends.

Procedure based on the legal concept.

From a strictly legal standpoint a parent and its subsidiary are separate corporate entities, and the profits earned by the subsidiary are not profits to the parent company until they are realized by the parent company through the receipt of dividends.   If this position be accepted as the proper basis for parent and subsidiary accounting, the investment will always be carried at cost and the

parent company will take up as income only the dividends received.
Referring to the preceding illustration:

At the end of the first year, the parent company's profit and
loss statement will show as income the $5,000.00 dividend
received, instead of the $30,000.00 net profit earned by the
subsidiary; and its balance sheet will show the investment
at its cost of $100,000.00 instead of at $125,000.00, the
amount of the subsidiary's net assets.

At the end of the second year, the parent company's profit and
loss statement will show the $5,000.00 dividend received as
income, although the subsidiary lost $15,000.00; and its
balance sheet will still show the investment at its cost of
$100,000.00.

Can these concepts be reconciled?

The two procedures just discussed appear to present an irrecon-
cilable conflict of opinion.

If one is governed only by legal considerations of separate corporate entities, he must admit that profits earned by a subsidiary
do not become surplus available for the payment of dividends by
the parent company until they have been realized by the parent
company through the receipt of dividends from the subsidiary.

But if the accountant carries the investment at cost, and takes
up dividends as income regardless of the results of the subsidiary's
operations, the parent company's statements may reflect all sorts
of absurdities, such as:

Showing in the profit and loss statement a $5,000.00 income
from dividends in a year when the subsidiary made $30,-
000.00 of profit for the benefit of the parent company;

Showing in the profit and loss statement a $5,000.00 income
from dividends in a year when the subsidiary lost $15,000.00;

Showing in the balance sheet the cost of the investment regardless of increases and decreases in underlying net asset values.

It is somewhat regrettable that the two bases of accounting
described above exist. For one reason, one cannot safely under-
take to interpret the statements of a parent company unless he
knows which basis of accounting has been used. And for another
reason, cases are known where a company has jumped from one
basis to another in succeeding years, in order to make the best
picture: showing subsidiary earnings as parent company income

in a year when the earnings exceeded the dividends, and showing dividends as income in a year when they exceeded the subsidiary's earnings.

The author personally feels that the method of accounting based on what (for want of a better name) we have called the economic concept more truly reflects the parent company's income and the underlying value of its investments. Its only fault seems to be that the parent company's surplus is credited with subsidiary earnings not transferred to the parent company in the form of dividends; in other words, the parent company's surplus contains amounts not legally available for the payment of parent company dividends.

It would seem that a fair and desirable compromise between the two methods could be effected by entries similar to the following:

Investment in Stock of Subsidiary Company S............ 30,000
    Earnings of Subsidiary S (closed to Restricted Surplus)   30,000
    (This entry takes up the subsidiary's profits of the first
    year by addition to the investment account, but by credit
    to a restricted surplus account to show that these profits
    are not available for the payment of parent company
    dividends.)

Cash... 5,000
    Investment in Stock of Subsidiary Company S........   5,000
    (This entry records the collection of a dividend.)

Restricted Surplus.................................... 5,000
    Surplus..   5,000
    (This entry transfers from restricted surplus to free surplus
    the portion of the subsidiary's earnings now realized by
    the parent company through the collection of a dividend,
    and therefore now available for the payment of dividends
    by the parent company.)

The surplus can be shown in the parent company's balance sheet in two amounts, as illustrated below. It is assumed that the parent company's free surplus includes $50,000.00 realized by its own operations.

Surplus:
    Restricted—Subsidiary earnings not received in divi-
        dends $25,000
    Free... 55,000 $80,000

This compromise procedure seems to have the following merits: it enables the parent company to take up true economic earnings and losses; it results in adjustment of the carrying value of the stock investment to reflect changes in the underlying net assets; and yet, by the separation of the surplus into two elements, it indicates the portion not legally available for parent company dividends.

Partial ownership.

The illustrations in this chapter are based on conditions of complete subsidiary ownership by the parent company. If the ownership is less than 100% but still sufficient to effect a control by the parent company, the procedures discussed in this chapter may still be applied, affected only by the fact that the amounts will be determined on the basis of the percentage of parent company ownership.

33

INVESTMENTS IN BONDS

....

Classes of bonds.

There are so many kinds of bonds, carrying so many different kinds of rights, that a general definition can be stated only in the broadest terms. A bond is a promise to pay the principal of and interest on a loan. It differs from a note in that it is more formal, and is under seal. In corporate financing, notes are usually given for short-time loans, and bonds for long-time loans; this is a matter of expediency and is not a necessary characteristic of a note or a bond.

It is impossible to give a complete list of the various types of bonds, but the following outline includes some of the most common classifications.

As to nature of business of obligor:
    Governments.
    Municipals: cities and other governmental subdivisions.
    Public utilities: gas companies, street railways, railroads, etc.
    Industrials: manufacturing and trading concerns.
    Real estate: apartments, hotels, office buildings, etc.

As to nature of obligation:
    Mortgage bonds.
    Collateral trust bonds.
    Guaranteed bonds.
    Debenture bonds.
    Income bonds.
    Participating bonds.
    Convertible bonds.

As to evidence of ownership and method of collecting interest:
    Registered bonds.
    Coupon bonds.

Mortgage bonds.

A mortgage is a transfer of title to property, usually made by a borrower to a lender, subject to the condition that, upon due payment of the debt, the title to the property is to revest in the borrower. Formerly, a mortgage was considered as an actual though conditional conveyance of title; if the debt was not paid, the title to the mortgaged property then vested in the mortgagee absolutely.

The modern theory of a mortgage is that it is primarily a security device. Although the mortgage deed does purport to convey to the mortgagee title to the pledged property, actually it serves only to create a lien on the property to secure payment of the debt.

Mortgages may be used with either notes or bonds. If the debtor is able to find a person who is willing to loan the entire amount desired, the note and mortgage may be used; the note recites the terms of the obligation, and the mortgage serves as the security.

If it is necessary to borrow the money from a number of persons, the bond and mortgage or trust deed are used. The bond issue creates a number of obligations, all of equal rank and all equally secured by the mortgage. However, since there are a number of lenders, since these lenders are not known when the bond issue is being arranged, and since they will change with each transfer of a bond, the mortgage cannot name the lenders personally as the transferees of the pledged property. Therefore a trust deed, rather than a mortgage deed, is used. Corporations, when borrowing funds on long-time bond issues, generally use the trust deed. In such deeds the borrower conveys the property to a third person, usually a bank or a trust company, as trustee. Upon final payment of the bonds, the trustee executes and delivers a release deed, whereby the lien on the property, created by the trust deed, is removed. In the event of a default in payment of the bonds, the trustee may commence foreclosure proceedings for the benefit of the bondholders. Thus the issuance of bonds secured by a trust deed is, for all practical purposes, a mortgage transaction and is so considered by law.

Bonds may be secured by first, second, third, or even more mortgages. If the obligations are not met and foreclosure ensues the proceeds of the property must go first to the satisfaction of the first mortgage bondholders, any residue to the satisfaction of the second mortgage bondholders, and so on. Bonds secured by prior liens are called underlying bonds; the others are called junior bonds

The mere fact that a bond is called a first mortgage bond does not necessarily mean that it has a lien prior to all others.   To illustrate, assume that three companies, *A*, *B*, and *C*, each have two mortgages on their property.   A consolidation is effected by which the three companies are combined, and a new issue of bonds is marketed, secured by a mortgage on all of the property.   This issue might be called First Consolidated Bonds, but it is really secured by a third mortgage.   On the other hand, assume that first, second, and third mortgage bonds have been issued, and that the first and second have been paid; the third mortgage bonds really have a first lien on the pledged property.

Collateral trust bonds.

Collateral trust bonds are similar to collateral notes in that they are secured by pledged collateral.   To illustrate the use of these bonds, assume that a corporation holds stocks and bonds of several subsidiaries.   The tangible property of the holding company and the subsidiaries may be mortgaged to the point where junior issues cannot be marketed; therefore the holding company issues its own bonds and places the stocks and bonds of the subsidiaries in the hands of a trustee as collateral.

Guaranteed bonds.

A corporation cannot guarantee to pay the principal and interest of its own bonds, although it obligates itself to do so.   If a guarantee is made, it must be made by a third party.   Sometimes a holding company guarantees the principal and interest of the bonds of its subsidiaries, and sometimes a company leasing the property of another company guarantees the bonds of that company.

Debenture bonds.

A debenture bond, or debenture, is merely an unsecured bond.   It is similar to an unsecured note, in that it rests on the general credit of the debtor and is a general lien on all of the unpledged assets of the debtor.   It may or may not be a safe investment, depending upon the financial condition of the issuing company.

Income bonds.

The peculiar feature of an income bond is that the payment of interest is conditional upon the earning of income.   If the debtor company's income is not sufficient to pay the interest, there is no obligation to pay interest. The bond may be cumulative or non-cumulative. If cumulative, any interest not paid in one year becomes a lien against future profits; if non-cumulative, any interest lost in one year is lost forever. The principal may or may not be secured.

Participating bonds.

These are sometimes called profit-sharing bonds because, in addition to assuring the holder a definite rate of income regardless of profits or losses, they entitle him to participate with the stockholders in profits. The bondholders may participate pro rata, under the same rules which apply to participating preferred stock, or the extent of the participation may be limited.

Convertible bonds.

A convertible bond gives its holder the right to exchange the bond for some other security, usually common stock, of the issuing company. The bond stipulates the terms on which the transfer can be made: that is, par for par; or par for the bond, and book value for the stock; or par and accrued interest for the bond, and par and accrued dividends for the stock; or par for the bond, par and a premium for the stock, and interest and dividends to be adjusted; or any other arrangement. Such bonds give the holder an assured income and a secured principal during the development period of the issuing company, with a right to become a stockholder if the operations of the company are successful.

Registered and coupon bonds.

Bonds may be divided into three general types, on the basis of registry:

(1) Registry as to principal and interest.

The name of the owner of the bond is registered on the books of the issuing company or its fiscal agent, and interest is paid by check, drawn to the order of the bondholder. This method has the advantage of safeguarding the owner against loss or theft, because a transfer of the bond could be accomplished only by a forgery. It has two disadvantages, however: (1) a sale and transfer can be made only by assignment and

registry, instead of by delivery; and (2) the check
method of paying interest is burdensome.
(2) Registry as to principal only.
     If the bond is registered as to principal only, and coupons
     are attached for the interest, the owner is safeguarded
     against loss or theft, while the debtor company is
     relieved of the burden of issuing interest checks.
(3) No registration.
     Such a bond is transferable by delivery, and without
     endorsement; the interest coupons are clipped and
     presented at a bank for deposit or collection.

Valuation and profits.

All that was said in the preceding chapter with respect to
the valuation of stock on the books of investors and dealers,
the determination of cost of securities acquired for property, the
valuation of property acquired for securities, profits on sales,
profits on exchanges, profits on sales when purchases were made at
different prices, and reserve provisions for decreases in market
values, applies equally to investments in bonds.

Interest and amortization of premium.

If I buy a $1,000.00 four-year 6% bond for $1,035.85, hold it
to maturity, and collect it at par, my net earning is:

Interest for 4 years at 6%...		$240.00
Less premium lost:		
Cost of bond..................................	$1,035.85	
Amount collected at maturity.....................	1,000.00	35.85
Net earning..		$204.15

For income tax purposes, I must report as income each year
the interest collected, and will report the premium lost as a deduction in the year when the bond matures. Although this is the
tax rule, it is not regarded as the best accounting procedure. If
a bond is purchased at a premium, its value tends to decrease to
par as its maturity approaches; therefore, for balance sheet purposes, it appears proper to amortize (write off) the premium over
the life of the bond, and thus gradually to reduce the carrying
value of the bond; and from the income statement standpoint,
it seems better to spread the premium loss over the life of the bond
as a deduction from the interest income, instead of taking the
entire amount as a loss when the bond matures.

The premium may be amortized in equal periodical amounts; for example, referring to the foregoing illustration and assuming that the bond bears eight semiannual coupons, the semiannual premium amortization could be $35.85 ÷ 8, or $4.48 (actually seven of $4.48 and one of $4.49) and the entry at each semiannual interest date would be:

```
Cash...................................................  30.00
   Interest Income......................................          25.52
   Bond Investment (for premium amortized).............           4.48
```

After the first of these entries is posted, the bond account will appear as follows:

Bond Investment

Jan.| 1‖ Cost.............‖ ‖ 1,035‖85‖June‖30 ‖Amortization.......‖ ‖ 4‖48

At the maturity of the bond, the balance in the bond investment account will have been reduced to par.

The carrying values of the investment, and the periodical income during the life of the bond, are shown below on the tax basis and on the amortization basis of accounting:

	Tax Basis		Amortization Basis	
	Investment Account	Income	Investment Account	Income
Cost..............................	$1,035.85		$1,035.85	
After collection of coupon:				
1................................	1,035.85	$ 30.00	1,031.37	$ 25.52
2................................	1,035.85	30.00	1,026.89	25.52
3................................	1,035.85	30.00	1,022.41	25.52
4................................	1,035.85	30.00	1,017.93	25.52
5................................	1,035.85	30.00	1,013.45	25.52
6................................	1,035.85	30.00	1,008.97	25.52
7................................	1,035.85	30.00	1,004.49	25.52
8................................	1,035.85	5.85*	1,000.00	25.51
Total earning.................		$204.15		$204.15

*The $5.85 loss in the eighth period is the amount of the premium minus the interest coupon.

Interest and amortization of discount.

If I buy a $1,000.00, four-year, 6% bond for $965.63, hold it to maturity, and collect it at par, my total earning is:

```
Interest for 4 years at 6%....................................  $240.00
Add discount gained:
   Amount collected at maturity.................... $1,000.00
   Cost of bond....................................    965.63     34.37
Net earning..............................................     $274.37
```

On my income tax return for the first three years I will report as income the $60.00 interest collected; in my return for the fourth year I will report as income the interest plus the discount realized.

But a proper accounting for the investment and the income thereon requires a recognition of the fact that a bond purchased at a discount tends to increase in value as its maturity approaches. For balance sheet purposes, therefore, it appears proper to amortize the discount over the life of the bond, thus gradually increasing the carrying value of the bond. And from the income statement standpoint, it seems proper to regard a portion of the discount as earned periodically.

If the discount is amortized in equal semiannual installments of $34.37 ÷ 8, or $4.30 (actually seven installments of $4.30 and one of $4.27), the entry for the collection of the interest and the amortization of the discount at each semiannual interest date will be:

```
Cash.............................................  30.00
Bond Investment (discount amortized)..............   4.30
    Interest Income...................................       34.30
```

After the first of these semiannual entries is posted, the bond account will appear as follows:

Bond Investment

| Jan. | 1 | Cost............. | 965 | 63 | | | | | | | |
| June | 30 | Amortization....... | 4 | 30 | | | | | | | |

At the maturity of the bond, the balance in the investment account will have been increased to par.

The carrying values of the investment, and the periodical income during the life of the bond, are shown below on the tax basis and on the amortization basis of accounting:

| | Tax Basis | | Amortization Basis | |
	Investment Account	Income	Investment Account	Income
Cost................................	$965.63		$ 965.63	
After collection of coupon:				
1................................	965.63	$ 30.00	969.93	$ 34.30
2................................	965.63	30.00	974.23	34.30
3................................	965.63	30.00	978.53	34.30
4................................	965.63	30.00	982.83	34.30
5................................	965.63	30.00	987.13	34.30
6................................	965.63	30.00	991.43	34.30
7................................	965.63	30.00	995.73	34.30
8................................	965.63	64.37	1,000.00	34.27
Total earning....................		$274.37		$274.37

Amortization of premium—effective rate method.

The nominal interest rate is that stated by the bond; the effective rate is that actually earned on the investment.

When a bond is bought at a premium, the effective rate is less than the nominal rate, for two reasons: (1) the investment is more than par; and (2) the income is the coupon minus a portion of the premium. Referring to the foregoing illustration of a $1,000.00, four-year, 6% bond purchased at a price of $1,035.85, the nominal rate is 6%, but the effective rate is only 5%—or 2½% each six months.

The approximate or equal-installment method of amortizing bond premiums or discounts, as described on the preceding pages, is sufficiently accurate for most purposes. However, the theoretically ideal method of computing the amortization requires the use of the effective interest rate. The semiannual interest and amortization entries for a bond bought at a premium are as follows:

> Debit Cash with the amount of the coupon.
> Credit Interest Income with an amount computed by multiplying the carrying value of the investment at the beginning of the interest period by the effective semiannual interest rate.
> Credit the bond account with the remainder of the coupon.

If this procedure is applied to the bond purchased for $1,035.85, the entry at the end of the first six months is:

> Debit Cash—for amount of semiannual coupon................... $30.00
> Credit Interest Income—2½% of $1,035.85..................... 25.90
> Credit Bond Investment account—premium amortized........... $ 4.10

After this entry is posted the bond investment account will have a balance of $1,031.75, as indicated below:

Bond Investment

| Jan. | 1 | Cost............... | | | 1,035 | 85 | June | 30 | Amortization....... | | | 4 | 10 |

The entry at the end of the second six months is:

> Debit Cash... $30.00
> Credit Interest Income—2½% of new balance of $1,031.75........ 25.79
> Credit Bond Investment account—premium amortized........... $ 4.21

This method of premium amortization is regarded as theoretically ideal because the amount credited to income decreases each six months proportionately with the decrease in the carrying value of the investment.

The interest and amortization entries, and the reducing book value of the investment, during the four-year life of the bond, are summarized below:

	Semiannual Entries			Investment
		Credit		Investment
	Debit Cash	Interest Income	Bond Investment	Account Balance
Original investment...............				$1,035.85
End of semiannual period:				
1...............................	$ 30.00	$ 25.90	$ 4.10	1,031.75
2...............................	30.00	25.79	4.21	1,027.54
3...............................	30.00	25.69	4.31	1,023.23
4...............................	30.00	25.58	4.42	1,018.81
5...............................	30.00	25.47	4.53	1,014.28
6...............................	30.00	25.36	4.64	1,009.64
7...............................	30.00	25.24	4.76	1,004.88
8...............................	30.00	25.12	4.88	1,000.00
	$240.00	$204.15	$35.85	

Amortization of discount—effective rate method.

When a bond is bought at a discount, the effective rate is greater than the nominal rate, for two reasons: (1) the investment is less than par; and (2) the income is the coupon plus a portion of the discount. The $1,000.00 four-year 6% bond bought at $965.63 (see page 312) was bought on a 7% basis—that is, to yield an effective rate of 7%.

The semiannual interest and amortization entries on the effective rate basis for a bond bought at a discount, are:

Credit Interest Income with an amount computed by multiplying the carrying value of the investment at the beginning of each semiannual period by the effective semiannual interest rate.

Debit Cash with the amount of the coupon.

Debit the bond account with the amount of the discount amortization, or the excess of the interest income credit over the cash debit.

Applying this procedure to the bond purchased for $965.63, the entry at the end of the first six months is:

Credit Interest Income—3½% of $965.63....................... $33.80
Debit Cash—for amount of coupon........................... 30.00
Debit Bond Investment account—discount amortized............ $ 3.80

The posting of the discount amortization entry of $3.80 to the debit of the investment account will increase the balance of that account from $965.63 to $969.43. Therefore the entry at the end of the second six months will be:

Credit Interest Income—3½% of $969.43....................... $33.93
Debit Cash.. 30.00
Debit Bond Investment account.............................. $ 3.93

The interest and amortization entries, and the increasing book value of the nvestment, during the four-year life of the bond, are summarized below.

	Semiannual Entries			
	Credit	Debit		Investment
	Interest		Bond	Account
	Income	Cash	Investment	Balance
Original cost......................				$ 965.63
End of semiannual period:				
1...............................	$ 33.80	$ 30.00	$ 3.80	969.43
2...............................	33.93	30.00	3.93	973.36
3...............................	34.07	30.00	4.07	977.43
4...............................	34.21	30.00	4.21	981.64
5...............................	34.36	30.00	4.36	986.00
6...............................	34.51	30.00	4.51	990.51
7...............................	34.67	30.00	4.67	995.18
8...............................	34.82	30.00	4.82	1,000.00
	$274.37	$240.00	$34.37	

Use of bond tables.

The price to be paid for a bond to net a stated rate depends upon (1) the difference between the nominal rate and the effective rate, and (2) the life of the bond. Thus:

(a) As to bonds bought to yield more than the nominal rate:
   (1) The greater the excess of the effective rate over the nominal rate, the greater the discount for each six-month period; and,
   (2) The longer the life of the bond, the more interest periods, and consequently the more aggregate discount.

(b) As to bonds bought to yield less than the nominal rate:
   (1) The greater the excess of the nominal over the effective rate, the greater the premium for each six months; and,
   (2) The longer the life of the bond, the more interest periods, and consequently the more aggregate premium.

The price to be paid for a bond to yield a stated rate is shown by bond tables; since the total premium or discount depends upon the life of the bond, bond tables usually contain a page showing values for bonds maturing in six months, a page for bonds maturing in a year, a page for bonds maturing in a year and half, and so on. And, since the price also depends upon the difference between the nominal and effective rates, the bond tables contain columns for various nominal rates, each column containing values at different effective rates shown in the first column. The following is from the four-year page of such a bond table.

4 Years
Interest Payable Semiannually

Effective Rate Per Annum	Nominal Rates						
	3%	3½%	4%	4½%	5%	6%	7%
4.00	96.34	98.17	100.00	101.83	103.66	107.33	110.99
4.10	95.98	97.81	99.63	101.46	103.29	106.94	110.60
4.125	95.89	97.72	99.54	101.37	103.20	106.85	110.50
4.20	95.62	97.45	99.27	101.09	102.92	106.56	110.21
Etc.							
4.90	93.17	94.97	96.77	98.56	100.36	103.95	107.54
5.00	92.83	94.62	96.41	98.21	100.00	103.59	107.17
5.10	92.49	94.26	96.06	97.85	99.64	103.22	106.80
5.125	92.40	94.19	95.98	97.77	99.55	103.13	106.70
5.20	92.15	93.93	95.72	97.50	99.29	102.86	106.43
5.25	91.98	93.76	95.54	97.33	99.11	102.67	106.24
5.30	91.81	93.59	95.37	97.15	98.93	102.49	106.06
5.375	91.55	93.33	95.11	96.89	98.67	102.22	105.78
5.40	91.47	93.25	95.02	96.80	98.58	102.13	105.69
5.50	91.13	92.91	94.68	96.45	98.23	101.77	105.32
5.625	90.71	92.48	94.25	96.02	97.79	101.33	104.86
5.75	90.30	92.06	93.83	95.59	97.35	100.88	104.41
5.875	89.88	91.64	93.40	95.16	96.92	100.44	103.96
6.00	89.47	91.23	92.98	94.74	96.49	100.00	103.51

Determining the price to yield a desired rate. What price can be paid for a 6% bond for $100.00, due in 4 years, to yield 5%?

Find 5% in the first column, which is a column of effective rates; glance across the 5% line to the 6% nominal rate column; at the intersection of the 5% line and the 6% column, the price is shown to be $103.59.

Determining the yield rate at a given price. What effective rate would be earned on a four-year 7% bond bought at $105.78? Glance down the 7% nominal rate column until the $105.78 value is found; it appears on the 5.375% line. The yield or effective rate is, therefore, 5⅜%.

What effective rate would be earned on a four-year 5% bond bought at 99? Look down the 5% column for the 99 value. It does not appear. The nearest values are:

5.25%.............................. 99.11
5.30%.............................. 98.93

The effective rate is, therefore, between 5.25% and 5.30%.

34

FUNDS

....

Funds and reserves distinguished.

Although funds and reserves are wholly different in nature, there seems to be an inclination to confuse them.

Funds are assets, usually set aside for particular purposes and generally consisting of cash and securities held by the company or by a trustee. Fund accounts, therefore, always* have debit balances, always represent assets, and always appear on the asset side of the balance sheet.

Reserves, on the other hand, always have credit balances, and therefore never represent assets. Just what they do represent is fully discussed in Chapter 37. At present it is desired merely to emphasize one fact: namely, fund accounts always represent assets, and reserves never do.

The term *reserve fund* has no well-defined meaning, and its use is not recommended. It is sometimes applied to a fund and sometimes to a reserve, and for this reason its use is likely to be confusing.

Valuation of fund assets.

The discussion in preceding chapters with respect to the valuation of stocks and bonds held as general investments applies equally to securities held in special funds. All such securities should be valued at cost, except that (1) decreases in market values may require the creation of reserves, and (2) premiums and discounts on bonds in special funds may be amortized.

Sinking funds.

A sinking fund, strictly defined, consists of assets set aside and accumulated at compound interest for the payment of a liability at its maturity.

---

* This is true so far as general industrial accounting is concerned; terminology is different in municipal and institutional accounting.

Strictly speaking, therefore, a fund created for the retiremen of preferred stock is not a sinking fund, because preferred stock i not a liability.

Also, strictly speaking, a fund from which periodical expendi tures are made for the purchase and cancellation of bonds is no a sinking fund, because the liability is paid in installments before maturity instead of in total at maturity. Such a fund would more properly be called a redemption fund.

The distinction between a stock retirement fund, a bond redemption fund, and a true sinking fund is interesting as a matter of precision in terminology. However, usage modifies meanings and commercial usage is fast sanctioning the extension of the term "sinking fund" to include funds for the retirement of stock and for the redemption of liabilities in installments before maturity.

Sinking fund contributions.

The amounts of the periodical contributions to a sinking fund may be determined on several bases, among which are the following:

(a) An equal annual amount computed by dividing the total required fund by the number of years of the life of the bonds. For instance, if a fund of $200,000.00 is to be provided in ten years, the annual addition to the fund will be $20,000.00. As the contributions alone will be sufficient to retire the entire indebtedness, interest earned on the sinking-fund assets can go into the general cash.

(b) An equal annual amount computed on a compound-interest basis. For instance, contributions of $15,900.92 made at the end of each of ten years will create a fund of $200,000.00 at the end of the tenth year if compound interest at 5% per annum is earned on all fund assets.

(c) A certain number of cents per unit of output. This method is often used when the bonds are secured by a mortgage on wasting assets such as mines or timber tracts, the intention being to increase the fund as the property security is diminished.

(d) A percentage of the profits. This method has been used frequently in connection with so-called preferred-stock sinking funds, the theory being that the profits are used to retire the preferred stock instead of for dividends on the common stock.   There seems to be a tendency to extend its use to funds for the payment of liabilities.

Sinking fund entries.

The operations of a sinking fund consist of contributions to the fund, investments in securities, the collection of income, the payment of expenses, and the eventual retirement of the bonded indebtedness.   The entries for these transactions are considered below.

Contributions of cash:

Sinking Fund Cash............................	xx,xxx.xx	
Cash......................................		xx,xxx.xx

Purchase of securities:

Sinking Fund Securities—*A B* Bonds............. xx,xxx.xx
    Sinking Fund Cash........................   xx xxx.xx
    (This entry should be for the cost of the bonds purchased regardless of whether they are purchased at par or at a premium or a discount. Any premium or discount may be amortized in the income entries.)

Collection of income:

Sinking Fund Cash............................ xxx.xx
    Sinking Fund Income......................   xxx.xx
    (Entry for interest on bonds purchased at par.)

Sinking Fund Cash............................ xxx.xx
S. F. Securities—*A B* Bonds.................... xx.xx
    Sinking Fund Income......................   xxx.xx
    (Entry for interest on bonds purchased at a discount.)

Sinking Fund Cash............................ xxx.xx
    S. F. Securities—*C D* Bonds................   xx.xx
    Sinking Fund Income......................   xxx.xx
    (Entry for interest on bonds purchased at a premium.)

Payment of expenses:

Sinking Fund Expense......................... xxx.xx
    Sinking Fund Cash........................   xxx.xx
    (Entry if expenses are paid from fund cash.)

Sinking Fund Expense......................... xxx.xx
    Cash....................................   xxx.xx
    (Entry if expenses are paid from general cash.)

Cancellation of bonds at maturity:

Sinking Fund Cash............................ xxx,xxx.xx
Loss on Sinking Fund Securities................. xx.xx
    Sinking Fund Securities....................   xxx,xxx.xx
    (Entry if securities are sold at a loss.)

Sinking Fund Cash........................... xxx,xxx.xx		
Sinking Fund Securities....................	xxx,xxx.xx	
Profit on Sinking Fund Securities...........	xx.xx	
(Entry if securities are sold at a profit.)		

Sinking Fund Cash........................... xxx.xx

Cash...................................... xxx.xx

(Entry if sinking fund is insufficient to pay bonds, and additional payment is made into fund from general cash.)

Bonds Payable,............................. xxx,xxx.xx

Sinking Fund Cash........................ xxx,xxx.xx

(Entry for payment of the bonds.)

Cash.. xxx.xx

Sinking Fund Cash........................ xxx.xx

(Entry if any residue of cash remains in the fund and is returned to the general cash.)

The Sinking Fund Income and Sinking Fund Expense accounts should be closed at the end of each period to Profit and Loss. The account showing the profit or loss on the final sale of sinking fund securities should be closed to Surplus as an extraneous profit or loss.

Holding bonds alive in the sinking fund.

Assume that the sinking fund trustee uses the cash deposits for the purchase of the very bonds intended to be paid off; what should be done with the bonds thus acquired from time to time?

To answer this question, let us assume that a company borrows $200,000.00 on a ten-year bond issue, agreeing to establish a sinking fund for the retirement of the bonds:

(a) If the company is obligated to pay the trustee $20,000.00 per annum, the trustee is not dependent upon earning any interest on the sinking fund assets to make up the required fund; therefore, the trustee can use each deposit for the retirement of bonds.

(b) But, if the contribution is computed on the assumption that compound interest is to be earned on the sinking fund securities, and that the periodical contributions plus compound interest will produce a fund at the maturity of the liability sufficient to retire it at that date, the trustee must invest the periodical contributions in income-producing securities.

If he buys the company's own bonds, he must treat them as he would the bonds of other companies which he might buy for the fund. That is, he must "hold them alive" in the fund. They will be regarded both as an asset and as a liability; they will be included in the sinking fund on the asset side of the balance sheet and in the bonds payable liability on the other side of the balance sheet. The company will continue to pay the interest on the bonds to the sinking fund trustee; the amount of the interest payments to the trustee will be included in the total bond interest shown as an expense in the profit and loss statement, and will also be included in the sinking fund income shown in that statement.

Deposit with trustee is not payment of debt.

The deposit of funds with a trustee for the payment of debt principal or interest, or both, does not constitute payment of the principal or interest; the total funds on deposit with the trustee should be shown on the asset side of the balance sheet, and the liability for accrued interest as well as for the principal should be shown on the liability side of the balance sheet. The liability on principal and interest cannot be eliminated from the balance sheet until the trustee has applied the funds to the payment of the liability.

Stock redemption funds.

The redemption fund method has long been used for the retirement of bonds in installments, and is becoming a popular method of retiring preferred stock. The provisions of the stock issue may require that a definite amount of stock shall be retired annually, but it is doubtful whether this requirement could be enforced against the corporation if profits were inadequate and creditors' rights were jeopardized. More frequently the amount of stock to be retired annually is made dependent upon the profits of the preceding year; it may be a fixed percentage of the profits, or it may be determined by a sliding scale of rates.

Other funds.

Funds for the payment of contingent liabilities are encountered occasionally. A deposit by a contractor to guarantee the performance of work in accordance with specifications, and a fund for the payment of damages which may result from an adverse decision of a pending patent infringement suit, are illustrations of funds for the payment of contingent liabilities.

Funds may be provided for liabilities which do not yet exist but which will accrue as a consequence of the provisions of existing agreements. For example, leases frequently contain clauses requiring the immediate deposit of cash to be applied in payment of the rent of subsequent (often the last) years of the lease. Cemeteries frequently sell lots under an agreement that a certain portion of the sale price shall be deposited with a trustee as a fund to provide for perpetual care.

Sometimes the directors of a corporation adopt the policy of reducing dividends and establishing a fund for the acquisition of plant assets. A building fund, machinery fund, or similar fund may then make its appearance on the asset side of the balance sheet.

Funds in the balance sheet.

Although special funds may consist of cash and readily marketable securities, they usually should not appear in the balance sheet under the Current Assets caption. Ordinarily they should appear either under a separate caption devoted to them alone or under some non-current caption such as Other Assets.

Occasionally a fund is created for use for some current purpose such as the payment of bond interest; such a fund can properly be included among the current assets in the balance sheet.

Fund installments in arrears.

As indicated in the preceding paragraphs, some funds are created by voluntary action of the corporate management; others are created in accordance with the terms of mortgage indentures or other contracts.

If a delinquency exists with respect to an obligatory fund and the amount thereof is less than it should be to conform with the requirements of the obligation, this fact should be disclosed by the balance sheet. The disclosure is made if a portion of the cash is earmarked as required for fund purposes, thus:

CURRENT ASSETS:
Cash...................................... $25,000.00
　Less sinking fund contribution in arrears..... 5,000.00
　Available current balance............................ $20,000.00
SINKING FUND:
Balance on deposit with trustee............... $13,000.00
Contribution required from current cash....... 5,000.00
　Total required fund................................ 18,000.00

Or a footnote may be appended to the balance sheet stating the condition in somewhat the following words: "A sinking fund contribution payable to the trustee in cash prior to December 31, 1941 (the assumed date of the balance sheet), had not been made at that date."

35

CURRENT AND CONTINGENT LIABILITIES

....

Problems in accounting for liabilities.

The problems incident to accounting for liabilities are much more simple than those which concern assets. The problem of valuation, often so difficult in accounting for assets, does not arise in dealing with liabilities, except in cases of contingent and accrued liabilities of undeterminable amount.

The two principal matters to be considered in connection with liabilities are:

(1) The classification of liabilities in the balance sheet.
(2) The inclusion of all liabilities in the balance sheet.

Classification of liabilities.

Liabilities may be classified as follows:

(1) Current.
(2) Deferred.
(3) Fixed.
(4) Contingent.

Current and fixed liabilities.

There is no unanimity of opinion among accountants as to a rule to be followed in differentiating between current and fixed liabilities. Some accountants have held that only liabilities maturing within ninety days from the balance sheet date should be regarded as current; however, it generally is held that a year should be considered the current period.

Liabilities can usually be classified as current and non-current without a definitely established dividing line, because liabilities for purchases, wages, and other operating expenses usually should be regarded as current liabilities, and liabilities on bonds and mortgages maturing in the distant future are fixed liabilities.

Deferred liabilities.

Sometimes, by special credit arrangements, liabilities arising in the regular order of trade do not have to be paid within even a year from the balance sheet date. It may not be proper to include these liabilities under the Current Liabilities caption; to take care of such special conditions, a caption "Deferred Liabilities" sometimes (though very rarely) appears in the balance sheet between the current and fixed liabilities.

Omission of current liabilities from the balance sheet.

Balance sheets prepared soon after the close of the period rarely include all of the current liabilities existing at the balance sheet date. Some of the liabilities frequently omitted are:

(1) *Accounts payable for goods purchased before the close of the accounting period.* This omission may result from two causes:

   (a) Delays in recording purchases. In most concerns it is the custom to make no record of the liability for purchases until the goods are received. But there may be some delay in getting the record on the books, so that purchases of goods received at the end of one accounting period may not be recorded until the beginning of the following period. This is an extremely serious error if the goods are included in the inventory, because the merchandise is included on the asset side of the balance sheet although the liability is not included on the other side of the balance sheet. As a result, the current ratio is misstated. Moreover, the omission of the cost of the purchases results in an overstatement of the profits; and this overstatement of profits results in an overstatement of surplus. To illustrate, assume that $10,000.00 of merchandise has been included in the inventory although no record has been made of the purchase and the liability. The profits for the period are overstated $10,000.00 and there are errors in the balance sheet as indicated below:

	Current Assets	Current Liabilities	Current Ratio	Surplus
Company's balance sheet	$70,000.00	$20,000.00	3½ to 1	$100,000.00
Correct balance sheet........	70,000.00	30,000.00	2⅓ to 1	90,000.00

It is less serious if the goods are not included in the inventory; in that case the surplus and profits are not overstated. But the balance sheet does not show all of the merchandise owned, nor all of the liabilities owed; and these omissions may seriously affect the ratio between the current assets and the current liabilities. To illustrate. assume the following conditions:

	Current Assets	Current Liabilities	Current Ratio	Surplus
Company's balance sheet..	$60,000.00	$20,000.00	3 to 1	$90,000.00
Correct balance sheet.........	70,000.00	30,000.00	2⅓ to 1	90,000.00

(b) A policy of not recording merchandise purchases until the goods are received, instead of recording them at a prior date when title to the merchandise passed. A liability exists as soon as title to the goods passes to the purchaser; and, according to the legal rules relative to sales, title may pass to the purchaser before the goods have been shipped. Therefore, it would seem that, if the books are to record and the balance sheet to reflect all liabilities, entries for purchases should be made when title passes according to the law, whether this be before the goods are shipped or when they are received.

(2) *Miscellaneous liabilities for services rendered to the business prior to the balance sheet date but not billed until after that date.* One illustration will probably suffice to show the point in mind. An attorney rendered service during 1940 to a company involved in some legal difficulties; he did not render his bill until March 1941, and the liability was not considered when the balance sheet was prepared at the end of 1940.

(3) *Accrued liabilities for such expenses as wages, interest, and taxes.* These may be overlooked because the accountant preparing the balance sheet has not had sufficient training to appreciate the importance of taking up all such accruals.

(4) *Liabilities to be liquidated in merchandise, arising from the issuance of due bills, merchandise coupon books, trading stamps, etc.* It is often the custom to make no entry at the time of issuing such evidences of liabilities because there is no certainty that they will ever be presented for redemption. Good accounting requires that the liability be set up, in an estimated amount based upon the company's experience as to the percentage of such obligations presented for redemption.

Classification of current liabilities in the balance sheet.

The extent to which current liabilities will be detailed in the balance sheet, and the sub-captions which will be used for classifying liabilities in the current group, will depend somewhat upon the purpose for which the balance sheet is to be used. The present attitude is that banks and other prospective creditors are entitled to much more information than need be given general publicity in the published balance sheet.

The requirements of current practice are satisfied if a balance sheet for general use contains the following classification of current liabilities:

Accounts payable. (These, unless otherwise indicated, should include only amounts payable to trade creditors for merchandise or raw materials purchased.)
Trade notes payable.
Other notes payable. (There is no uniformity of practice with respect to indicating whether or not any of the notes are past due.)
Accounts payable to officers, stockholders, and employees.
Notes payable to officers, stockholders, and employees.
Accrued liabilities.
Other current liabilities.

It is highly important that amounts payable to trade creditors for merchandise and raw material purchases be shown separately from other current debts. In the analysis of a balance sheet and a profit and loss statement, it is significant to note the ratio between the purchases for the period (shown in the profit and loss statement) and the notes and accounts payable liability for such purchases existing at the end of the period (shown by the balance sheet). This ratio gives some indication as to whether liabilities for purchases are being paid within the credit period prevailing in the trade.

To illustrate, assume that a company is purchasing merchandise under terms specifying payment within thirty days. Its profit and loss statements and balance sheets show the following facts:

	1940	1941
Purchases for the year ended December 31	$100,000.00	$100,000.00
Trade accounts and notes payable at end of year	10,000.00	15,000.00
Per cent of purchases unpaid at end of year	10%	15%

One month's purchases, on the assumption of uniform business throughout the year, would be $8\frac{1}{3}\%$ of the total purchases for the year. Seasonal business may account for the fact that more than this percentage of the year's purchases was unpaid at the end of each year; but why should the ratio have increased from 10% to 15%?

If liabilities not arising from the purchase of merchandise or raw materials are combined in the balance sheet with merchandise liabilities, the ratio will indicate a more unfavorable condition than really exists.

The balance sheet should indicate which current liabilities are secured and which are unsecured. This information may be given on the liability side of the balance sheet, thus:

Notes payable (secured by pledge of inventories valued at
  $30,000.00)... $20,000.00

Or the information may be given on the asset side, thus:

Inventories:
  Pledged as security to notes payable of
    $20,000.00............................. $30,000.00
  Not pledged............................. 70,000.00 $100,000.00

Long-term liabilities maturing currently.

A special problem of classification arises when long-time liabilities approach their maturity and are due within, say, a year. Should they be included among the current liabilities in the balance sheet although, in preceding balance sheets, they were included among the fixed liabilities? The proximity of the maturity date is not the sole determining factor. If bonds maturing in, say, nine months are to be retired with the proceeds of a refinancing, the inclusion of the bonds among the current liabilities would be improper, as it would convey the impression that the bonds were to be paid out of current assets, and would so distort the ratio of current assets and current liabilities as to give an entirely erroneous idea of the concern's working capital. It appears that all necessary facts are shown if the bonds are left among the fixed liabilities with a statement as to the maturity.

The situation is somewhat different, however, when an installment on a serial bond issue is shortly to become due. The natural assumption is that the installment will be paid out of working capital, and it seems proper to show the condition as follows:

Balance Sheet—December 31, 1940

CURRENT LIABILITIES:
Accounts Payable...................................... $35,000.00
Serial Bonds Payable—Installment due April 1, 1941....... 10,000.00
FIXED LIABILITIES:
Serial Bonds Payable, 6%—Payable in Equal Annual Install-
ments Beginning April 1, 1942........................ 90,000.00

A slightly less satisfactory method is illustrated below:

CURRENT LIABILITIES (Exclusive of Current Installment of
Bonds Payable):
Accounts Payable..................................... $ 35,000.00
FIXED LIABILITIES:
Serial Bonds Payable, 6%—Maturing in Ten Equal Annual
Installments Beginning April 1, 1941................. 100,000.00

Of course, if a fund has been established for the payment of the bonds, the current installment will presumably be paid from the fund instead of from the current assets; therefore the current installment need not be shown among the current liabilities.

Contingent liabilities.

A contingent liability is a possible debt. It is important to note the distinction between contingent liabilities and contingent losses. A few illustrations may clarify this distinction:

A lawsuit is pending which may require the payment of damages for a patent infringement; in this instance there is both a contingent liability and a contingent loss.

Dividends are in arrears on cumulative preferred stock; in this instance there is a contingent liability, but no contingent loss.

There is a possibility that accidents may destroy property; in this instance there is a contingent loss, but no contingent liability.

Contingent liabilities may be shown by balance sheet footnotes, on the right side of the balance sheet under a Contingent abilities caption, but with the amounts shown "short"—that not extended to the money columns included in the balance eet totals. If the contingency seems likely to become a reality, reserve may be required.

ustrations.

Among the more common forms of contingent liabilities are:

(1) *Notes discounted.* The proper procedure for recording the discounting of notes receivable was discussed in Chapter 25. If there is a likelihood that discounted notes may have to be paid, and that collections cannot be obtained from the makers, provision for the loss should be made in the Reserve for Bad Debts or in a separate reserve.

(2) *Accounts assigned.* The procedure for showing assigned accounts receivable was discussed in Chapter 24. Provisions for losses should be made in the Reserve for Bad Debts.

(3) *Accommodation paper.* A person may become an accommodation party on a promissory note either as a maker or as an indorser. The contingent liability may be shown by a footnote appended to the balance sheet; or the facts may be shown short as follows:

Contingent Liabilities:
  Accommodation Notes Payable.............. $1,000.00

This procedure shows the contingent liability but does not include the amount among the liabilities.

(4) *Guarantees.* Goods are often sold with guarantees regarding quality or performance. Experience will show the probable expense of making good on such guarantees, and a reserve should be set up by a charge against Profit and Loss.

(5) *Lawsuits.* If a lawsuit is pending and if there is a probability that the suit will be lost, a reserve should be set up to record the contingency. If it is not desired to

show too clearly the nature of the reserve, and thus perhaps to indicate the fact that the management expects to lose the suit, the reserve may be called a Reserve for Contingencies.

(6) *Additional Federal taxes.* If there is a possibility that Federal taxes in excess of the amount shown by the tax return may have to be paid, the additional contingent liability may be set up in a reserve.

(7) *Cumulative dividends in arrears.* No entry should be made for preferred dividends until they are declared. The methods of showing the arrears of dividends in the balance sheet were discussed in Chapter 22.

(8) *Guarantees of liabilities of other companies.* One company may guarantee the interest, or both the principal and the interest, of the bonds of another company, which may or may not be a subsidiary. If there is a probability that payments will have to be made under the guarantee, and that the claim for compensation arising out of the payments will not be collectible in full, a reserve may be set up for the estimated loss.

(9) *Purchase commitments.* If goods are ordered for future delivery, the commitment represents a contingent liability either for the full purchase price or for such an amount as must be paid in the event of cancellation. In a rising market, these commitments may be ignored, as there is no probability of loss, or, at most, they may be mentioned in a footnote. In a falling market, however, there is a likelihood of a loss equal to the difference between the commitment price and the market price at the date of delivery. Although the total price of the order should not be put on the books, it would be conservative and desirable to set up a reserve for any loss likely to result from falling market prices.

36

FIXED LIABILITIES

....

Advantages and disadvantages of bonds.

When a corporation desires to raise additional funds, the question arises as to whether the funds should be obtained by the issuance of short-time notes, bonds, or stock. Short-time paper is properly used when funds are required for current operations; funds for plant extensions or other permanent investments should be raised by the issuance of long-time securities.

One advantage of a bond issue over a stock issue is that the bondholders have no vote and the stockholders therefore do not have to share the management with them. Another advantage is that the funds can usually be obtained at a lower money cost. If common stock is issued, the contributors of new capital will share pro rata with the old stockholders in all earnings; if preferred stock is issued, it may be participating, in which case the new stockholders will share pro rata with the old; or it may be non-participating, but in that case it will usually be found necessary to give the preferred stock a dividend rate higher than the rate at which bonds could be floated, because bonds are a secured liability with a definite maturity, and because the bond interest is payable unconditionally whereas preferred dividends are dependent upon earnings.

Disadvantages of the bond issue lie in the fact that the principal is due at a definite date and the interest is a fixed charge. If either the principal or the interest is not paid when due, foreclosure may take place and the loss on liquidation may leave a very small equity for the stockholders.

Bonds in the balance sheet.

The balance sheet should reflect all of the important facts with respect to the bonds or other fixed liabilities. It is not sufficient to show merely:

Bonds Payable... $500,000.00

The special features of the bonds should be shown, and the interest rate and maturity should be stated. For instance, thus:

First Mortgage, Real Estate, Sinking Fund, 6% Bonds, Due
December 31, 1950................................. $500,000.00

If the bonds mature serially, the balance sheet should contain a sufficiently extensive statement of the facts to enable the reader to determine the maturities exactly, thus:

First Mortgage, Real Estate, Sinking Fund, 6% Bonds,
Maturing Serially; $25,000.00 Annually, from December
31, 1941 to 1949, Inclusive, and the Remainder on December 31, 1950.. $500,000.00

Treasury or unissued bonds.

Very frequently a larger amount of bonds will be authorized than are be issued immediately. To illustrate, assume that the fixed property of the corporation is ample in value to secure an issue of $500,000.00 of first mortgage bonds. Only $300,000.00 of funds are now required, but there may be later requirements of $200,000.00. If the first issue is made for only $300,000.00, a subsequent issue can be secured only by a second mortgage, which will perhaps necessitate a higher interest rate, and will undoubtedly involve greater marketing difficulties. By authorizing $500,000.00 of bonds and issuing $300,000.00, the corporation puts itself in a position to market the remaining $200,000.00 at a future date without incurring the disadvantages incident to a second mortgage bond issue. Such an issue should be recorded as follows:

Treasury Bonds............................... 200,000.00
Cash.. 300,000.00
    Bonds Payable.......'...................... 500,000.00

If any bonds are unissued, the balance sheet should reflect that fact in some manner. One way is illustrated below:

First Mortgage, 6%, Real Estate, Mortgage Bonds Payable,
Due December 30, 1950; Authorized, $500,000.00; Issued. $300,000.00

Bonds issued at a discount.

Assume that bonds with a par value of $100,000.00, due in five years, with interest at 4% per annum payable semiannually, are issued for $95,623.97. The entry to record the issuance is:

Cash.. 95,623.97
Bond Discount............................... 4,376.03
    Bonds Payable........................... 100,000.00

The bond discount will appear on the balance sheet as a deferred charge; it is in reality an additional interest cost, paid in advance, and it should be amortized by semiannual entries in which the Bond Interest expense account is debited and the Bond Discount account is credited.

Writing off bond discount immediately.

Some companies, following what they seem to regard as a conservative policy, eliminate the bond discount immediately from the balance sheet by writing it off against Surplus.

This procedure is conservative to this extent: it gets the deferred charge off the balance sheet. But the operations of future periods will be relieved of the necessity of absorbing the discount amortization as an expense; hence the interest costs will be understated and the net income will be overstated. Most accountants do not consider it proper thus to "clean the balance sheet" when the result is an overstatement of the earnings of subsequent periods. To charge Surplus with any expense which should be deducted from annual income is not good accounting.

Amortization of bond discount.

In Chapter 33, dealing with investments in bonds, it was stated that the amortization of discount or premium on bonds owned was good accounting but was not recognized for income tax purposes. The amortization of discount or premium on bonds issued is permitted for tax purposes.

If the bond discount of $4,376.03 is written off in ten equal semiannual installments during the five-year life of the bonds, the semiannual interest and discount entries will be:

```
Bond Interest.....................................  2,000.00
    Cash.........................................              2,000.00
        To record the payment of bond interest.
```

```
Bond Interest.....................................    437.60
    Bond Discount................................               437.60
        Semiannual amortization of bond discount.
```

Or the two charges to the interest expense account may be combined, as in the following entry:

```
Bond Interest.....................................  2,437.60
    Cash.........................................              2,000.00
    Bond Discount................................               437.60
        To record the semiannual interest payment and dis-
        count amortization.
```

The discount may be amortized by the scientific effective interest rate method described in Chapter 33. The bonds mentioned in the foregoing example bear a nominal rate of 4%; they were issued at a sufficient discount to place them on an effective rate basis of 5% per year, or 2½% semiannually. The following table shows the interest and amortization entries on the effective interest rate basis. To compute the semiannual charges to Bond Interest (shown in the first column), the increasing net carrying values of the bond liability (bonds minus unamortized discount, as shown in the last column) were multiplied by 2½%.

Semiannual Interest and Discount Amortization Entries
4% Five-Year Bond Issue Sold to Net 5%

Period	Debit Bond Interest	Credit Cash	Credit Bond Discount	Bonds Minus Discount
				$ 95,623.97
1	$ 2,390.60	$ 2,000.00	$ 390.60	96,014.57
2	2,400.36	2,000.00	400.36	96,414.93
3	2,410.37	2,000.00	410.37	96,825.30
4	2,420.63	2,000.00	420.63	97,245.93
5	2,431.15	2,000.00	431.15	97,677.08
6	2,441.93	2,000.00	441.93	98,119.01
7	2,452.98	2,000.00	452.98	98,571.99
8	2,464.30	2,000.00	464.30	99,036.29
9	2,475.91	2,000.00	475.91	99,512.20
10	2,487.80	2,000.00	487.80	100,000.00
	$24,376.03	$20,000.00	$4,376.03	

Bonds issued at a premium.

Assume that $100,000.00 par value of bonds due in five years, with interest at 6% per annum payable semiannually, are issued for $104,376.03. The entry to record the issuance is:

```
Cash.......................................  104,376.03
    Bonds Payable...........................            100,000.00
    Bond Premium............................              4,376.03
```

The bond premium will appear on the balance sheet under the Deferred Credits caption. Since the premium received at the time of issuance reduces the net interest cost, the premium should be amortized. If the premium is written off in ten equal semiannual installments, the entries will be:

```
Bond Interest..................................  3,000.00
    Cash......................................            3,000.00
    To record the payment of bond interest.

Bond Premium..................................    437.60
    Bond Interest.............................              437.60
    Semiannual amortization of bond premium.
```

Or the two entries may be combined, as follows:

```
Bond Interest....................................  2,562.40
Bond Premium...................................    437.60
    Cash.......................................              3,000.00
```

These bonds were issued on a 5% effective interest basis. The following table shows the interest and amortization entries on the effective interest rate basis. The semiannual charges to Bond Interest were computed as 2½% of the decreasing amounts shown in the last column.

Semiannual Interest and Premium Amortization Entries
6% Five-Year Bond Issue Sold to Net 5%

Period	Debit Bond Interest	Debit Bond Premium	Credit Cash	Bonds Plus Premium
				$104,376.03
1	$ 2,609.40	$ 390.60	$ 3,000.00	103,985.43
2	2,599.64	400.36	3,000.00	103,585.07
3	2,589.63	410.37	3,000.00	103,174.70
4	2,579.37	420.63	3,000.00	102,754.07
5	2,568.85	431.15	3,000.00	102,322.92
6	2,558.07	441.93	3,000.00	101,880.99
7	2,547.02	452.98	3,000.00	101,428.01
8	2,535.70	464.30	3,000.00	100,963.71
9	2,524.09	475.91	3,000.00	100,487.80
10	2,512.20	487.80	3,000.00	100,000.00
	$25,623.97	$4,376.03	$30,000.00	

Equal installment and scientific methods.

The scientific method of amortizing bond discount and premium results in an interest charge conforming to the effective rate at which the bonds were issued. For this reason it is theoretically ideal. The equal installment method is usually regarded, however, as producing, with relatively little effort, results which are sufficiently accurate for all practical purposes.

Amortization of premium or discount on serial bonds.

Assume that $500,000.00 of 6% bonds are issued, maturing in five equal annual installments beginning at the end of the sixth year; the bonds are sold for $490,000.00. What amount of discount should be amortized each year?

Bond discount is virtually interest paid in advance; the cash interest payments will decrease after the sixth year; the discount charges should decrease similarly; both the cash interest and the discount amortization should be proportionate to the bonds outstanding. Amortization by the effective interest rate method is ideal, but is usually so difficult to compute as to be impracticable. The following illustration of the "bonds outstanding" method of amortization shows how such cases are usually handled:

Year	Bonds Outstanding		Discount Amortized* for the Year	Cash Interest	Total Charge to Interest
	Amount	Ratio to Total			
1........	$ 500,000.00	12.5%	$ 1,250.00	$ 30,000.00	$ 31,250.00
2........	500,000.00	12.5	1,250.00	30,000.00	31,250.00
3........	500,000.00	12.5	1,250.00	30,000.00	31,250.00
4........	500,000.00	12.5	1,250.00	30,000.00	31,250.00
5........	500,000.00	12.5	1,250.00	30,000.00	31,250.00
6........	500,000.00	12.5	1,250.00	30,000.00	31,250.00
7........	400,000.00	10.0	1,000.00	24,000.00	25,000.00
8........	300,000.00	7.5	750.00	18,000.00	18,750.00
9........	200,000.00	5.0	500.00	12,000.00	12,500.00
10........	100,000.00	2.5	250.00	6,000.00	6,250.00
	$4,000,000.00	100.0%	$10,000.00	$240,000.00	$250,000.00

* Amounts in this column were computed by multiplying the total discount of $10,000.00 by the per cents shown in the Ratio to Total column.

Bond retirements.

When a bond issue is retired at its maturity, any discount or premium on the issuance presumably will have been fully amortized. Therefore, the only entries required to record the retirement are a debit to the bond liability account and a credit to Cash.

If a bond issue is retired before maturity, any unamortized premium or discount may be written off to surplus. This has been the customary procedure in the past; the Committee on Accounting Procedure of the American Institute of Accountants recently published an opinion that, although the write-off to surplus is still to be regarded as permissible, the unamortized discount may be carried forward and written off over the period ending at the original maturity of the bonds.

If a bond issue is retired by a refinancing program in which the old issue is replaced by a new one, it has, in the past, been regarded as good accounting to write off any unamortized premium or discount on the old issue over the period of the new issue. The report of the Committee mentioned above advocates the discontinuance of this procedure and either an immediate write-off to surplus or an amortization procedure which will eliminate the unamortized discount on the old issue over not more than the remaining period of the original life of the old issue.

37

RESERVES

....

What reserves represent.

Probably no other term used by accountants is required to do duty in so many capacities as the word "reserve." A reserve may represent:

(1) A deduction from an asset.
(2) A liability.
(3) A contingent liability or a contingent reduction in the value of an asset.
(4) A part of the net worth:
    (a) Appropriations of surplus.
    (b) Unrealized profits.

Since reserves represent so many different things, it is small wonder that they sometimes prove confusing to the reader of a balance sheet.

Reserves against assets.

Decreases in the value of assets are recorded by credit entries. If the decrease in value is definitely determinable, it may be recorded by a credit to the asset account. If the decrease is merely estimated, it may be recorded by a credit to a reserve. Thus, a reserve for bad debts, a reserve for depreciation, and a reserve for depletion represent estimated decreases in the value of the related asset. These are known as valuation reserves, or valuation accounts, and should be shown on the balance sheet as deductions from the assets.

Reserves are sometimes set up to record decreases in asset values which are exactly measurable. To illustrate, assume that a company leases property for a period of ten years, and makes leasehold improvements which will revert to the owner of the real estate at the expiration of the lease. The asset of leasehold improvements decreases in value each year by exactly one tenth

of the cost.   Although some accountants might set up a reserve
by annual credits of one tenth of the cost of the improvements,
it is usually considered preferable to write down the asset.

In some instances it is considered proper to set up a reserve,
instead of writing down the asset, even though the amount of the
decrease in value is definitely ascertainable.   A reserve for the
decrease in the market value of securities owned is a good example.
It is desirable, for general accounting and income tax purposes,
to maintain a record of the cost of the securities; this record
would be confused if the asset account were credited with market
decreases as well as with sales; to avoid this confusion, a reserve
is created.   The reserve is also justified in such a situation because,
whereas the market decrease at a given date is determinable, the
ultimate loss (or possible gain) is not determinable.

Reserves for liabilities.

Accrued expenses may have created liabilities which are certain
in amount or uncertain in amount.   Liabilities both certain and
uncertain in amount are sometimes shown as reserves, but it
appears preferable to use reserve accounts for only those liabilities
that are not exactly measurable, and to set up accrued liability
accounts for those that are definite in amount.   Thus, Accrued
Interest and Accrued Wages are better titles than Reserve for
Interest and Reserve for Wages, because the amounts of these
accruals should be definitely determinable.   But Reserve for
Property Taxes may be preferable to Accrued Taxes, if the amount
of the probable assessment cannot be closely estimated.

Reserves for contingencies.

Reserves may be provided for contingencies which, if they
become realities, may create liabilities or reduce the value of
assets.

As an illustration of reserves for contingent liabilities, assume
that a concern operating a factory does not carry workmen's
compensation insurance; since workmen may be injured and
liabilities for damages may be incurred thereby, a reserve for the
contingency may be established.   Or assume that a company
has been made defendant in a patent infringement suit; an adverse
decision may result in a liability for damages, and the contingency
may be provided for by the creation of a reserve.

To illustrate contingent reserves for losses in assets, assume
that a company, because its tangible assets are distributed in
relatively small amounts in a large number of locations, decides

upon a policy of self-insurance. No insurance is carried, but a reserve is created against which fire losses may be charged if and when they occur; such a reserve provides for a contingency which may result in a decrease in asset values. Or assume that, after valuing the inventory at the end of the year at the lower of cost or market at that date, it appears desirable to make a provision for possible further market declines during the ensuing year; a reserve for such a contingency might be created.

Reserves representing net worth.

Reserves which may be regarded as representing a part of the net worth may be classified as follows:

(1) Appropriations of surplus.
  (a) Required by contracts.
      Example: Sinking fund reserve.
  (b) Created by authorization of management.
      Example: Reserve for plant extension.
(2) Unrealized profit.
      Example: Reserve for unrealized profit on appraisal.

Net worth reserves—Obligatory appropriations of surplus.

A company may be required under the terms of a contract to set apart some of its surplus under the title of a reserve.

As an illustration, assume that a company borrows $100,000.00 on bonds, and that it is required to make cash deposits of $10,-000.00 a year to create a sinking fund for the payment of the bonds. If the company is permitted to pay dividends to the full amount of the profits, such dividend payments plus the sinking fund deposits may drain the cash to such an extent as to impair the working capital and make it difficult for the company to earn the profits necessary to provide for the sinking fund deposits. The indenture may therefore provide that a portion of the surplus shall not be available for dividends, and that the portion not so available shall be set up in a reserve. Such a reserve is created by a debit to Surplus and a credit to Sinking Fund Reserve. It should be clearly understood that such a reserve is still a part of the net worth, and it should be shown under the Net Worth caption in the balance sheet.

Net worth reserves—Voluntary appropriations of surplus.

Although the directors of a corporation may have the legal right to pay dividends equal to the entire accumulated surplus,

they may consider it financially inexpedient to do so.   They may
believe that the best interests of the company will be served if
part of the funds are used for other purposes; for example, they may
desire eventually to build a new plant, or to spend considerable
sums for advertising, or to "plow profits back into the business"
for various other purposes.   Of course, the directors can limit the
payment of dividends without dividing the surplus into two parts
on the balance sheet, but they may feel that it is desirable to reduce
the amount shown as surplus in the balance sheet, and set up such
items as Reserve for Plant Extension, Reserve for Advertising,
and Reserve for Contingencies in order to indicate a restriction
upon the payment of dividends and thus avoid the clamor for
dividends which might otherwise come from the stockholders.

Such reserves should be definitely understood to represent
surplus and should appear under the Net Worth caption of the
balance sheet.   Sometimes, apparently with the intention of
deliberately understating the net worth, such reserves are shown
in the balance sheet under a special caption of Reserves.

One objection to setting up such surplus reserves is the difficulty
of getting rid of them.   If a reserve for plant extension is established, it cannot be charged with the cost of any additional plant
acquired; the new plant must be charged to the asset accounts.
A reserve for advertising, created as an appropriation of surplus,
cannot be charged with advertising expenditures; these must
be charged to the expense accounts.   A reserve for contingencies
can be charged with only such extraneous losses as might be debited
directly to Surplus.

Therefore, setting up appropriated surplus reserves to reduce
the surplus balance to the amount which the directors feel may
be distributed in dividends, has its disadvantages.   Setting up
such reserves merely temporizes with the situation, because there
is usually no way of getting rid of the reserves except by returning
them to surplus.   The stock dividend is a way out; it gives the
stockholders something without giving them the current funds
needed by the business, and it disposes, once and for all, of the
embarrassing surplus balance by merely converting it into another
element of net worth.

Net worth reserves—Unrealized profits on appraisals.

If it is desired to show fixed assets in the balance sheet at an
appraised value which is in excess of cost less depreciation, the

addition to the asset value will have to be accompanied by a corresponding increase on the right side of the balance sheet.

Although this increase in the value of an asset represents an increase in the net worth, the increase should not be added to the surplus, as it ordinarily is not available for dividends. It may be shown as a separate net worth element, in a manner illustrated later in this chapter.

How are reserves created?

Credits to reserves may be offset by debits to:

(A) *Profit and Loss,* or expense accounts chargeable to Profit and Loss.

Such reserves provide for losses and expenses which can be regarded as proper charges to current operations. Reserves for depreciation, bad debts, and liabilities incurred for operating costs and expenses come under this classification.

(B) *Surplus.*

Reserves set up by charges to Surplus may be classified as follows:

(1) To provide for losses and expenses not regarded as proper charges to current operations.

(a) To supplement inadequate past charges to Profit and Loss. For instance, if insufficient provisions for depreciation or bad debts were made in the past, the inadequacy may be remedied by a debit to Surplus as a correction of the profits of past periods.

(b) To provide for losses incurred during the period but not properly chargeable to operations. To illustrate, assume that a manufacturing company holds large permanent investments in securities, the market value of which has greatly decreased. The loss need not be regarded as an operating loss, and the reserve for the market decline may be created by a charge to Surplus.

(c) To create conservative provisions for contingent losses. If the reserve provides for a loss which, when ultimately incurred, is chargeable to Surplus because of its extraneous nature, the debit for the establishment of the reserve obviously should be made to Surplus. But the charge may also be made to Surplus even though the loss, if and when ultimately incurred, should be charged to operations, provided that, at the time of the creation of the reserve, the loss is so problematical and contingent that an ultimate charge to operations may never be required.

(2) To appropriate surplus to indicate that it is not available for dividends. Such appropriations may be made:

(a) In fulfillment of contracts with creditors, as in the case of a sinking fund reserve.

(b) At the volition of the management, as in the case of a reserve for extension of plant.

(C) *Fixed asset accounts.*

Such reserves reflect so-called unrealized profits disclosed by appraisals.

Charges to reserves.

Before a loss or an expense is charged against a reserve, two questions should be asked:

Is the loss or expense of such a nature that it constitutes an operating charge, or is it an extraneous item properly chargeable to Surplus?

Was the reserve set up by charges to Profit and Loss or to Surplus?

If the charge represents an operating expense, and if the reserve was set up by charges to operations, the loss may be written off against the reserve. For example, depreciated assets and uncollectible accounts are written off against the depreciation and bad debt reserves because such losses are operating costs and the reserves were set up by charges to operations.

If the expense or loss is of a non-operating or extraneous nature, it may be charged against a reserve set up out of Surplus. For example, if a reserve has been created out of Surplus to reduce the book value of permanent security investments from cost to market, the loss ultimately realized on the disposal of the securities may be charged against the reserve.

However, operating expenses or losses should not be charged against reserves created out of Surplus. Thus, a Reserve for Advertising is merely an appropriation of surplus to show that dividends are being restricted for a definite purpose. Advertising expenditures, when made, should be charged to operations. Or if, after the inventory has been valued at the lower of cost or market, a conservative provision for possible subsequent market declines is set up out of Surplus, losses incurred because of such further declines should be absorbed in the Profit and Loss account and the reserve should be restored to Surplus. If operating expenses or losses were charged against reserves created out of Surplus, the results of operations would be incorrectly stated in the Profit and Loss account.

Reserves in the balance sheet.

Since reserves represent so many different things, they should be carefully classified in the balance sheet to assist the reader in understanding their nature. The proper marshalling of reserves in the balance sheet is indicated by the following classification:

(1) *Valuation reserves against assets.* Reserves for bad debts, reserves for depreciation and depletion, and other valuation reserves should be deducted from the gross values of the related assets. Sometimes, in an attempt to improve the asset side of the balance sheet, such reserves are improperly shown on the right side of the balance sheet under a caption of reserves, below the liabilities.

(2) *Reserves representing actual liabilities.* If a reserve represents an actual liability, as distinguished from a conservative provision for a possible or contingent liability, it should be shown under a liability caption. As such reserves usually represent current liabilities, they should generally be shown under the current liability caption.

(3) *Reserves for contingencies.* Such reserves are often very difficult to classify in the balance sheet because the proper classification depends upon the degree of probability of the contingency becoming a reality. Three different conditions may be found:

    (a) If there is a very strong probability that the contingency will become a reality resulting in a decrease in an asset or the creation of a liability, the reserve should be deducted from the asset or included among the liabilities.

(b) If the loss is merely a possible one, but not definitely probable, the reserve should appear on
the right side of the balance sheet under a
Reserve caption.

(c) If the contingency is so remote as to be distinctly
improbable, the reserve constitutes a voluntary
appropriation of surplus, to be shown in the
Net Worth section.

(4) *Reserves representing net worth:*

(a) Appropriations of surplus. Reserves representing
appropriations of surplus, whether required by
contract or established voluntarily, should be
shown under the Surplus caption, thus:

```
Surplus:
    Reserve for Sinking Fund..... $50,000.00
    Reserve for Plant Extension...  75,000.00
    Reserve for Contingencies.....  25,000.00
    Free Surplus.................   40,000.00 $190,000.00
```

The treatment of the reserve for contingencies
illustrated above is based on the assumption that
no real contingency exists and that the reserve
was set up by the directors because of their intention to curtail dividends and because of their
desire to convey to stockholders the impression
that less surplus is available for dividends than is
really the case. To aid the deception, the directors probably would want the reserve shown under
a Reserve caption with, or close to, the liabilities.
It should be shown under the Surplus caption,
although the directors may object to such a
classification as defeating the very purpose for
which the reserve was created.

(b) Unrealized profit reserves. Some accountants
believe that reserves for unrealized profits placed
on the books in connection with an appraisal
should be shown under a Reserve caption. However, if the fixed assets have actually increased in
value it appears obvious that the net worth has
also increased, although there has been no increase
in surplus available for dividends. If the net
worth has increased, there seems to be no good
reason why the reserve should not be included

under the Net Worth caption, provided it is clearly differentiated from realized surplus. This may be accomplished as follows:

NET WORTH:
Capital Stock.....................		$1,000,000
Surplus:		
Reserve for Sinking Fund.	$50,000	
Reserve for Plant Extension.................	75,000	
Reserve for Contingencies	25,000	
Free Surplus............	40,000	190,000
Reserve for Unrealized Profit on Appraisal of Plant..........		50,000
Total Net Worth....		$1,240,000

Secret reserves.

A secret reserve exists whenever the net worth shown in the balance sheet is understated. It is, in a sense, the exact opposite of water in the stock. A secret reserve may be created by any device which understates assets or overstates liabilities. Capital expenditures may be charged to revenue, income may be credited to the account with the asset which produced the income, excessive depreciation or bad debt provisions may be made, liabilities may be deliberately overstated, assets may be written off to Surplus, and an almost innumerable variety of other devices may be employed.

The creation of secret reserves is not so common now as it was before the income tax rendered inexpedient the misstatement of income. In the old days, corporations frequently wrote down assets arbitrarily on the theory that it was conservative, and directors often deliberately created secret reserves on the theory that such reserves made it possible to equalize profits and thus to maintain a uniformity and stability which was advantageous to the corporation.

The theory and operation of the secret reserve was somewhat as follows: In a prosperous year, when profits were above normal, it was wise to conceal the company's prosperity, partly to avoid attracting competition and partly to avoid creating in the stockholders' minds an expectation of similarly abnormal profits in the future. The directors therefore wrote off excessive depreciation or resorted to some other method of overstating the expenses. In a subsequent year, when profits were subnormal, and when a disclosure of this fact might adversely affect the standing and stability of the corporation, the assets formerly written down were written up to make a Surplus or Profit and Loss credit, and an appearance of uniformity was thereby maintained.

Secret reserves are now generally recognized to be improper. Aside from the tax phases of the subject, it may be said that any deliberate misstatement in the profit and loss statement or in the balance sheet should be discouraged. Stockholders have a right to receive true statements, in order that they may judge for themselves the advisability of retaining or disposing of their investments. If stock sales are made by stockholders on the basis of understated book values as shown by the balance sheet of a company which has created secret reserves, stockholders may suffer losses which they would not have suffered if they had known the facts.

Secret reserves may be deliberate or unintentional. Provisions for depletion, depreciation, bad debts, and other expenses must be based on estimates. If the estimate is excessive, the expenses are overstated, the profits and net worth are understated, and a secret reserve is thereby created. When the reserves are estimated in the most careful manner possible, the creation of the secret reserve is unavoidable. But, when the overprovision is discovered, the secret reserve should be eliminated by a transfer to surplus of enough of the reserve for depreciation or for bad debts to correct the provision.

38

DEFERRED CHARGES AND CREDITS; INSTALLMENT SALES

....

Cash and accrual bases of accounting.

The principal difference between the cash basis and the accrual basis of accounting lies in the fact that, on the accrual basis, recognition is given to accrued expenses and income and to deferred charges and credits, whereas on the cash basis such recognition is not given. To illustrate briefly, let us assume the facts discussed below:

(A) Accrued expense—At the end of 1941, wages were accrued in the amount of $500.00; these wages were paid in 1942.

On the accrual basis of accounting, the $500.00 would be included in the expenses of 1941, and a liability of $500.00 would be included in the balance sheet at the end of 1941.

On the cash basis of accounting, no liability would be included in the balance sheet at the end of 1941, and the $500.00 would be included in the expenses of 1942, the year in which it was paid.

(B) Accrued income—At the end of 1941, interest in the amount of $75.00 had accrued on notes receivable; this interest was collected in 1942.

On the accrual basis, the $75.00 would be included in the income of 1941, and an item with some name such as Accrued Interest on Notes Receivable would appear on the asset side of the balance sheet.

On the cash basis, this accrual would be ignored at the end of 1941, and it would be included in the income of 1942, the year in which it was collected.

(C) Deferred charge—On October 1, 1941, a one-year insurance policy was purchased at a premium cost of $1,200.00.

On the accrual basis, the expenses shown in the 1941 profit and loss statement would include only three months' (October, November, and December) proportion of the premium, or $300.00. The remaining $900.00 would be shown in the balance sheet at the end of 1941 as a deferred charge.

On the cash basis, the entire $1,200.00 would be included in the expenses of 1941.

(D) Deferred credit—On October 1, 1941, there was collected $2,400.00 as a year's rent on a portion of the building.

On the accrual basis, the 1941 profit and loss statement would include as income only three months' proportion of the $2,400.00, or $600.00; the remaining $1,800.00 would be shown in the balance sheet as a deferred credit.

On the cash basis, the entire $2,400.00 would be included in the income of 1941 because it was collected during that year.

Which is the more accurate basis?

Although the cash basis of accounting is accepted by the Bureau of Internal Revenue for purposes of reporting income for taxes, accountants generally regard the accrual basis as more accurate—at least from a theoretical standpoint.

It seems obvious from the foregoing illustrations that the year in which the cash is collected or disbursed may not be the year in which all of the income is earned or all of the expense is incurred. And it seems equally obvious that the cash basis cannot reflect the results of operations during a given period on the basis of income earned and expenses incurred during that period.

But on the other hand, one should be aware that the accrual basis may be only theoretically more accurate than the cash basis. Actually, a profit and loss statement prepared on the accrual basis may very inaccurately reflect the results of operations, because of uncertainties and even abuses to which it is subject. Whenever uncertainties make estimates necessary, the door is opened for errors of judgment and for deliberate misrepresentations defended by plausible arguments.

As a general rule, accruals do not open this door as frequently as it is opened by deferred charges and credits. Therefore no further consideration will be given to accruals in this chapter, other than to say that many accruals can be accurately computed, others must be estimated and therefore are subject to innocent misstatement, and all can be deliberately misstated or entirely omitted.

Some further consideration will be given to deferred charges and credits, as any such items appearing in a balance sheet should be the subject of special scrutiny.

Deferred charges.

Amounts shown under the Deferred Charge caption in the balance sheet may be of two classes:

Deferred charges to surplus. For example, discount on stock and organization expenses. Anyone finding such items in a balance sheet is usually justified in immediately deducting them from the net worth as stated on the right side of the balance sheet, in order to adjust the net worth to a correct basis.

Deferred charges to operations. For example, unexpired insurance, prepaid interest, and supplies. The reader of a balance sheet usually cannot tell, unless he is well informed about the business, whether all such items appearing in the statement are of a nature which makes it proper to defer them, and, if so, whether the amount deferred has been correctly computed.

The amount to be deferred may be subject to definite computation on the basis of expired time; for example, the portion of insurance premiums unexpired, or the amount of interest prepaid on a bank loan. The amount to be deferred for some other items, such as fuel and supplies, may be determined with varying degrees of accuracy by actual or estimated inventories.

If the nature of the item is such that a deferring program is correct in theory, any errors in the determination of amounts to be deferred are likely to be insignificant. The really serious misrepresentations occur when the management of a business deliberately sets about to juggle the profit and loss statement to its liking by adopting a deferred charge policy which will show a desired profit and which can be supported by reasons, however specious.

A company was going through a period of business expansion involving the opening of numerous branch offices and the expenditure of considerable amounts for radio and other advertising. The nature of the business was such that each new branch office usually went through a period of considerable promotion costs and operating losses, but as soon as an office was established on a profitable basis it was possible (although not intended) to dispose of it at a price which would involve a profit or payment for goodwill. Shortly before December 31st, the president of the company announced to some prospective sources of additional capital that the profit for the year would be at least so many thousand dollars. But, after the close of the year, the auditors submitted a profit and loss statement which showed earnings somewhat less than the amount forecast by the president. A proposal was immediately made by the president to defer considerable charges of two classes: (1) the operating losses of all offices which were still "in the red"; this was defended by the management on the ground that these offices were in the development period; and (2) portions of the advertising expenditures; this was defended on the ground that the effect of a radio advertising campaign is cumulative and that the expenditures during the early part of such a campaign do not immediately become fully effective. The total of these two classes of proposed deferred charges was sufficient to restore the earnings to the amount which the president had stated would be earned.

The reader of a balance sheet cannot always detect such manipulations. However, there are certain things he can do. He can note the deferred items, and raise in his own mind the question as to whether it seems reasonable and proper to postpone charging them to operations. If he has access to one or more previously rendered balance sheets, he can compare the deferred charges shown in all balance sheets available and see whether a consistent policy appears to have been followed. And he can read the auditor's report and see what comments or qualifications have been made therein relative to the deferred items.

Deferred credits.

A deferred credit usually represents an item of *gross* income which is to be credited to Profit and Loss in a future period. Emphasis has been given to the fact that the credit represents a gross income, because the reader of a balance sheet should understand that, before the deferred credit can be taken into income, some costs and expenses probably will be incurred.

The following questions should arise in the mind of a reader of a balance sheet with respect to each deferred credit included therein:

(1) Will the ultimate net profit probably be a large or a small percentage of the deferred credit?

(2) Has the deferred credit been set up because there exists an obligation to furnish goods or services to some other party, or has it been set up merely as a conservative bookkeeping device?

(3) Before the deferred credit can be taken into earnings, will it be necessary to make considerable expenditures from working capital; in other words, should a considerable portion of the deferred credit be regarded as a sort of quasi-current liability?

(4) Is the nature of the deferred credit such that the company management is able to exercise a choice as to the procedure of taking it into income, and is it thus enabled to determine somewhat arbitrarily the amount shown as earned income during any given period?

These four matters are discussed below:

(1) The percentage of probable profit contained in a deferred credit usually cannot be estimated with much accuracy by a person not intimately acquainted with the business, because the amounts of the costs and expenses to be incurred cannot be estimated.

(2) Has the deferred credit been set up because there exists an obligation to furnish goods or services to some other party, or has it been set up merely as a conservative bookkeeping device? Examples illustrating different conditions are presented below:

A company has rented a portion of its building and has collected rent in advance; there is an obligation to permit the tenant to occupy the building.

A magazine publisher collects a year's subscription in advance; there is an obligation to send magazines to the subscriber during the year.

A company sells merchandise and makes collections on the installment plan; since the merchandise has been delivered, the seller has no further obligation to the purchaser. Nevertheless, he may set up the gross profit in a deferred credit account and take it into income gradually over the period required for the collection of the receivable, as a conservative accounting procedure—partly to postpone the taking of profit because losses are relatively heavy in installment selling, and partly to provide future periods with a portion of the profit because they will be required to stand accounting, collection, and other carrying charges arising from the sale.

(3) Should a considerable portion of the deferred credit be regarded as a quasi-current liability? The nature of the deferred credit may give some indication of the answer.

A deferred credit of Rent Collected in Advance presumably contains only a small requirement for future expenditures from working capital. Some of the building expenses, such as depreciation, require no current expenditures; others are relatively fixed charges which would be incurred even if a portion of the space were not rented.

A deferred credit of Subscriptions Collected in Advance presumably includes a large proportionate element of requirements for future expenditures to service the subscriptions.

A deferred credit of Deferred Gross Profit on Installment Sales implies no obligation to make expenditures for the benefit of the purchaser, because the goods have been made and delivered. Any required expenditures will arise out of the carrying of the accounts.

(4) Can the transfers from deferred income to earned income be arbitrarily controlled by the management, with plausible supporting reasons? Some deferred credits, such as rent and interest collected in advance, should usually be taken into income on a pro rata basis over the periods for which the advance collections are received, and any departure from this procedure normally would be regarded as indefensible. With respect to some other types of deferred credits, two companies with similar operations may defend different procedures. For instance, one company engaged in buying real estate mortgages at a discount takes 25% of the discount into earnings in the period when the paper is purchased, and takes the remaining 75% of the discount into earnings over the years during which the paper is carried; the immediate taking of 25% is defended on the ground that it is an offset against acquisition costs. Another company spreads the entire 100% over the life of the paper. If there is room for reasonable difference of opinion as to the proper basis for transferring deferred income to earnings, the reader of the statements should be aware that the stated earnings can be arbitrarily affected by the choice of methods; he should seek to determine whether the method chosen appears reasonable and proper; he should be sure that the procedure has been maintained on a consistent basis from one period to another; and, if the method has been changed, he should try to determine the dollar effect upon the stated profits.

Installment sales.

The deferring of profit on installment sales involves accounting procedures which require some special consideration.

Because losses and expenses incident to installment selling are incurred in large amounts in periods subsequent to the period of sale, considerable difficulty has been encountered in taking up profits in a logical and conservative way.   Two methods may be used:

(1) Take up all of the profit in the period of sale, and set up reserves for losses on bad debts, collection expenses, and costs of reconditioning repossessed merchandise.   Such a method is theoretically correct, but it has two practical disadvantages: (a) it is difficult to estimate the amounts of the required reserves; and (b) reserves for collection and reconditioning expenses are not deductible for Federal income tax purposes.

(2) Take up the profit in installments on a basis of cash collections.   The following basis is permitted for tax purposes: Each collection is regarded as including profit and a return of cost in the same proportion that these two elements were included in the total selling price.   Thus, if a sale price of $150.00 included $100.00 cost of merchandise and $50.00 profit, a collection of $15.00 would be regarded as including a $10.00 return of cost and a $5.00 profit.

Illustration—Single sale.

As a simple illustration of the accounting procedure applied in taking up profits on the basis of the profit element included in each collection, let us assume the following facts:

Sale: July 15:
```
  Selling price.........................................  $15,000.00
  Cost..................................................   10,000.00
  Profit................................................    5,000.00
  Ratio of profit to total selling price, 33⅓%
Collections:
  Down payment..........................................    3,000.00
  Monthly payment.......................................    1,500.00
```

The sale is recorded by the following entry:

```
A Customer.................................. 15,000.00
    Installment Sales..........................         15,000.00
```

The collections are recorded by debits to Cash and credits to the customer. Assuming that installments are collected regularly on the first of each month during the remainder of the year, the customer's account will appear as follows:

Customer

July 15	Sale..............	15,000.00	July 15	Cash..............	3,000.00
			Aug. 1	Cash..............	1,500.00
			Sep. 1	Cash..............	1,500.00
			Oct. 1	Cash..............	1,500.00
			Nov. 1	Cash..............	1,500.00
			Dec. 1	Cash..............	1,500.00

Since $10,500.00 has been collected, and since the ratio of profit to selling price was 33⅓%, the profit regarded as realized is one third of $10,500.00, or $3,500.00.

The accounting procedure at the end of the year may be summarized by a continuance of the foregoing illustration as follows:

(1) Set up the entire gross profit on the installment sale by a credit to an account called Deferred Gross Profit on Installment Sales, or some similar title.

The exact procedure for closing the gross profit into this account will depend upon whether the company operates a trading or a manufacturing business, upon whether all or only part of the sales are made on an installment basis, and upon the general procedure followed in the closing of the books.

In a trading business we might, for example, find the following entries:

Cost of Installment Sales.....................	10,000.00	
Purchases..............................		10,000.00
To set up an account showing the cost of goods sold on installments.		

Installment Sales............................	15,000.00	
Cost of Installment Sales.................		10,000.00
Deferred Gross Profit on Installment Sales..		5,000.00
To set up the entire gross profit on the installment sales.		

(2) Transfer the realized portion of the gross profit from the Deferred Profit account to Profit and Loss, thus:

Deferred Gross Profit on Installment Sales......	3,500.00	
Profit and Loss...........................		3,500.00
To take up as income the portion of the gross profit on installment sales realized by collections.		

The accounts will then appear as follows:

Installment Sales

To close............	15,000.00	Sales...............	15,000.00

Cost of Installment Sales

Cost...............	10,000.00	To close............	10,000.00

Deferred Gross Profit on Installment Sales

To Profit and Loss.....	3,500.00	Total gross profit.......	5,000.00

After the remaining installments have been collected, the balance in the Deferred Gross Profit account may be closed to Profit and Loss.

Illustration—Numerous sales.

When numerous installment sales are made, it is impracticable to attempt to compute the rate of gross profit on each sale and to apply a separate rate of gross profit to the collections from each sale. Instead, an average rate of gross profit on all installment sales for a year may be applied to the collections on receivables resulting from the sales of that year. To illustrate, assume the following facts for the year 1939:

Installment sales.......................................	$150,000.00
Cost of installment sales................................	100,000.00
Gross profit...	50,000.00
Ratio of gross profit to selling price......'...............	$33\frac{1}{3}\%$
Collections during 1939.................................	$105,000.00
Gross profit realized, $33\frac{1}{3}\%$ of $105,000.00...............	35,000.00

The controlling account with installment receivables may be summarized as follows:

Installment Accounts Receivable

Sales...................	150,000.00	Collections...............	105,000.00

And the Deferred Gross Profit account, after the books are closed at the end of the year in the manner previously explained, will appear as follows:

Deferred Gross Profit on Installment Sales

To Profit and Loss..........	35,000.00	Total gross profit...........	50,000.00

Operations for a series of years.

Let us now assume that installment sales operations are conducted over a series of years, and that the transactions during three years were as summarized on the following page.

Summary of Facts

	1939	1940	1941
Sales...	$150,000	$200,000	$250,000
Cost of goods sold.............................	100,000	120,000	125,000
Gross profit....................................	$ 50,000	$ 80,000	$125,000
Rate of gross profit............................	33⅓%	40%	50%
Cash collections:			
On 1939 accounts...........................	$105,000	$ 30,000	$ 15,000
On 1940 accounts...........................		125,000	50,000
On 1941 accounts...........................			175,000
Gross profits realized by collections:			
33⅓% of collections on 1939 accounts..........	$ 35,000	$ 10,000	$ 5,000
40 % of collections on 1940 accounts..........		50,000	20,000
50 % of collections on 1941 accounts..........			87,500

To distinguish clearly the collections applicable to different years and subject to different gross profit rates, the cash receipts book may contain columns headed:

Accounts Receivable—1939

Accounts Receivable—1940

Accounts Receivable—1941

Separate deferred profit accounts may be kept by years, and transfers from these accounts to Profit and Loss may be made on the basis of the collections shown by the several accounts receivable columns in the cash receipts book. Entries for taking up the realized portions of the gross profit, computed on the basis of cash collections as shown in the foregoing summary of facts, would be:

At the end of 1939:

> Deferred Gross Profit on Installment Sales—1939......... 35,000
>   Profit and Loss.................................... 35,000
>   Gross profit equal to 33⅓% of collections.

At the end of 1940:

> Deferred Gross Profit on Installment Sales—1939......... 10,000
> Deferred Gross Profit on Installment Sales—1940......... 50,000
>   Profit and Loss.................................... 60,000
>   33⅓% of collections on 1939 accounts, and 40% of collections on 1940 accounts.

At the end of 1941:

> Deferred Gross Profit on Installment Sales—1939......... 5,000
> Deferred Gross Profit on Installment Sales—1940......... 20,000
> Deferred Gross Profit on Installment Sales—1941......... 87,500
>   Profit and Loss.................................... 112,500
>   33⅓% of collections on 1939 accounts, 40% of collections on 1940 accounts, and 50% of collections on 1941 accounts.

By the end of 1941, the deferred gross profit accounts would appear as follows:

Deferred Gross Profit on Installment Sales—1939

To P. & L. in 1939.......	35,000.00	Total gross profit.........	50,000.00
To P. & L. in 1940.......	10,000.00		
To P. & L. in 1941.......	5,000.00		
	50,000.00		50,000.00

Deferred Gross Profit on Installment Sales—1940

To P. & L. in 1940......	50,000.00	Total gross profit.........	80,000.00
To P. & L. in 1941......	20,000.00		

Deferred Gross Profit on Installment Sales—1941

To P. & L. in 1941.......	87,500.00	Total gross profit........	125,000.00

Profit and loss statement.

The gross profit on regular and installment sales may be shown in the profit and loss statement in the manner illustrated below, with a supporting schedule showing the computation of the gross profit realized on installment sales.

Profit and Loss Statement
For the Year Ended December 31, 1941

Sales—Other than Installment Sales...............................		$ 60,000.00
Deduct Cost Thereof..		40,000.00
Gross Profit...		$ 20,000.00
Realized Gross Profit on Installment Sales (Schedule 1):		
On 1939 Sales......................................	$ 5,000.00	
On 1940 Sales......................................	20,000.00	
On 1941 Sales......................................	87,500.00	
Total Gross Profit Realized on Installment Sales..............		112,500.00
Total Gross Profit...		$132,500.00

Schedule of Realized Gross Profit
on Installment Sales   Schedule 1

	Year of Sale		
	1939	1940	1941
Installment Sales......................	$150,000.00	$200,000.00	$250,000.00
Cost of Goods Sold....................	100,000.00	120,000.00	125,000.00
Gross Profit..........................	$ 50,000.00	$ 80,000.00	$125,000.00
Per Cent of Gross Profit................	33⅓%	40%	50%
Collections in 1941....................	$ 15,000.00	$ 50,000.00	$175,000.00
Profit Applicable to Collections........,,,,,	$ 5,000.00	$ 20,000.00	$ 87,500.00

Defaults.

If a customer defaults in the payment of installments and if no further collections can be expected, both his account and the deferred profit applicable to the uncollectible installments should be written off. To illustrate, let us assume the following facts:

	Account Receivable	Gross Profit
Sale...	$150.00	
Gross profit, at 33⅓%.............................		$50.00
Collections.......................................	90.00	
Gross profit realized by collections, 33⅓%............		30.00
Balances..	$ 60.00	$20.00

The balances in these accounts indicate that the $60.00 still due from the customer includes $20.00 of unrealized profit and $40.00 of unrecovered cost. If the property sold cannot be recovered or if it has no value, the unrecovered cost, $40.00, is a loss. In such a situation the entry for the default should be:

Defaults..	40.00	
Deferred Gross Profit on Installment Sales.................	20.00	
A Customer..		60.00

A default register may be used, in which entries will be made as illustrated below:

Default Register

Date	Name	1939 Accounts (33⅓%)	1940 Accounts (40%)	1941 Accounts (50%)
1941				
July 5	A Customer.............................	60 00		
11	B Customer.............................		100 00	
12	C Customer.............................			150 00
	(Etc.).................................			
	Credit Accounts Receivable...............	360 00	700 00	350 00
	Debit Deferred Profit....................	120 00	280 00	175 00
	Debit Defaults........................	240 00	420 00	175 00

The customers' accounts in the subsidiary ledgers are written off by crediting them with the amounts shown opposite their names. At the end of the month, the columns of the register are footed and the totals are posted to the credit of the Accounts Receivable controlling accounts by years. The deferred gross profit lost is computed by multiplying the total of each column by the gross profit rate for the year, and the resulting products are posted to the debit of the Deferred Gross Profit accounts. The differences between the uncollectible receivables and the deferred profits are the losses from unrecovered costs, to be charged to Defaults.

Defaults and repossessions.

A default by a customer usually results in a repossession of the merchandise by the seller, and the loss on the uncollectible account is reduced to the extent of the value of the property.

Three methods of accounting for repossessed merchandise are discussed below:

(1) Do not take up the repossessed merchandise as an asset at the time it is repossessed; when the merchandise is resold, credit the selling price to Sales of Repossessed Property, and regard the entire selling price as income.

This method is sometimes used if the repossessed property has little value, or if its realizable value cannot be determined with a reasonable degree of accuracy. But it should be understood that, if this method is used, and if repossessed property of value is not taken into the accounts until sold, statements prepared before the disposal of the property will misstate the profits or losses on repossession and will understate the net assets.

(2) Take up the repossessed merchandise at the unrecovered cost, with the result that no gain or loss is shown until the merchandise is resold.

This method has little justification, since it places a wholly arbitrary value on the property and frequently results in postponing the taking of a loss.

(3) Take up the repossessed merchandise at a depreciated value. This may be difficult to determine, but experience may enable a company to establish repossession values at amounts which will allow a fair profit on resale.

This method is to be recommended, because it should result in the most nearly correct statement of repossession losses, of inventory values, and of profits on resales.

Referring to the first illustration in the section on Defaults, and assuming that the repossessed property is considered to be worth $35.00, the entry for the repossession will be:

```
Repossessed Merchandise.............................  35.00
Defaults............................................   5.00
Deferred Gross Profit on Installment Sales..........  20.00
    A Customer......................................          60.00
```

If the repossessed property is given a value of $75.00, the entry will be:

Repossessed Merchandise	75.00	
Deferred Gross Profit on Installment Sales	20.00	
A Customer		60.00
Defaults		35.00

To provide for recording repossessions, the default register previously illustrated may be modified by the inclusion of a column in which to record the estimated value of repossessed merchandise. The total of this column should be posted to the debit of a merchandise (purchase or inventory) account and should be applied in reduction of the debit to Defaults.

Expenses and bad debt losses.

Two questions arise with respect to expenses, namely:

(1) Since gross profits are deferred and taken into income on the basis of collections, should expenses of the period of sale be similarly deferred and charged to income on the basis of collections?

It might appear that such a procedure would be justifiable, since there is a certain element of inconsistency in deferring the profits from sales and not deferring the expenses incurred in making the sales. The inconsistency is justified, however, because the realization of the profits is contingent upon the collection of the accounts, but the same contingency does not exist with respect to the expenses already incurred.

(2) Expenses will be incurred in periods subsequent to the period in which the sale is made. For example, collection expenses will be incurred and sales commissions may be payable on the basis of amounts collected. Should reserves be provided for such expenses?

To set up such reserves by charges against the profits of the period in which the sales were made appears a little severe; such a procedure would mean that the sale period would be deprived of the deferred portion of the gross profit but would, nevertheless, be charged with all past and prospective expenses connected with the sale. For this reason, current practice sanctions charging the sale period with the expenses incurred in that period, and subsequent periods with the expenses incurred in such sub-

sequent periods.   But reserves for bad debt losses and
future expenses may be created by charges against the
deferred profit.   This subject is discussed later.

Installment receivables in the balance sheet.

Installment accounts receivable usually should be shown in the
balance sheet by years of maturity, and the installments that
mature beyond one year from the balance sheet date should be
excluded from the Current Assets section.   Often this is impracticable, and in some lines of business custom sanctions the inclusion
of the entire amount of the receivables under the current caption.

Although reserves for the estimated future expenses and for
bad debts should not be set up by charges to Profit and Loss, there
is no objection to setting them up by charges against the Deferred
Gross Profit account.   In fact, such a procedure may be desirable.
If the reserves are created, a clearer and more complete picture is
presented by the balance sheet; and, since the reserves are set up
out of the deferred profit rather than by charges to Profit and Loss,
the portion of the profit regarded as realized during the sale period
is not subjected to charges for subsequent expenses.

The deferred gross profit should be sufficient to cover bad debt
losses and future expenses applicable to past sales, and still leave
a margin of net profit.   Therefore, if estimates can be made, the
deferred gross profit should be divided into three elements for
balance sheet presentation.   For example, assume that a deferred
gross profit balance of $50,000.00 is estimated to contain the follow-
ing elements:

Losses on bad debts...................................... $10,000.00
Future expenses applicable to past sales.....................   15,000.00
Deferred net profit..   25,000.00

The three elements may be classified in the balance sheet as
follows:

Reserve for Bad Debts.................................... $10,000.00
    (To be deducted from the accounts receivable, to reduce the
    net balance to the estimated realizable value of the install-
    ment receivables.)
Reserve for Installment Sales Expenses.....................   15,000.00
    (In the author's opinion, this reserve should appear under a
    Reserve caption and should not be included among the
    liabilities because no liabilities for the estimated subsequent
    expenses exist at the balance sheet date.)
Estimated Net Profit on Installment Sales...................   25,000.00
    (This portion of the deferred gross profit should be shown in
    the balance sheet under the caption of Deferred Credits.)

It should be understood that, if the deferred gross profit is thus apportioned, the apportionment is made *for balance sheet purposes only*; reserves need not be set up in the ledger. The deferred gross profit should be transferred to income when the profit is realized, and bad debts and expenses should be charged to income.

39

REVIEW

Purpose of the chapter.

A number of chapters have been devoted to a consideration of accounting principles governing correct statements of assets, liabilities, profits, surplus, and net worth. This chapter contains:

A trial balance prepared by the company's bookkeeper at the end of 1940.

A balance sheet, surplus statement, and profit and loss statement prepared by the company's bookkeeper.

Comments relative to a number of violations of accounting principles assumed to have been disclosed by the auditor.

The adjustments made by the auditor (some of these would be made only in auditor's working papers and not on the company's books).

The balance sheet, surplus statement, and profit and loss statement prepared by the auditor.

The object of the illustration is to review and to emphasize the importance of the accounting principles discussed in the preceding chapters. The emphasis lies in the fact that the company's statements, affected by many violations of accounting principles, indicate a satisfactory financial condition and good operating results, whereas the auditor's statements, conforming with good accounting principles, present a far less flattering picture.

Company's trial balance and statements.

To shorten the trial balance and thus simplify the illustration, it is assumed that, before the trial balance was taken, the books were partially closed by entries in a Cost of Goods Sold account, as follows:

Accounts with the inventories on December 31, 1939, purchases, direct labor, and manufacturing expenses were closed to Cost of Goods Sold.

The inventories on December 31, 1940, were placed on the books by debit to an Inventories account and credit to Cost of Goods Sold.

A summary of the Cost of Goods Sold account appears below:

Debits:

Inventories, December 31, 1939		$ 70,000
Purchases		306,300
Freight In		7,400
Direct Labor		143,000
Manufacturing Expenses:		
Indirect Labor	$48,000	
Heat, Light, and Power	21,500	
Repairs	6,450	
Depreciation	8,917	
Taxes	3,000	
Insurance Expense	3,600	91,467
Total Debits		$618,167
Credits:		
Returned Purchases and Allowances	$ 8,500	
Inventories, December 31, 1940	85,000	
Total Credits		93,500
Cost of Goods Sold		$524,667

THE *X Y Z* COMPANY
Trial Balance—December 31, 1940

Cash	$ 4,650	
Accounts Receivable	103,150	
Notes Receivable	10,000	
Inventories, December 31, 1940	85,000	
Investments in Stocks and Bonds	103,850	
Land and Buildings	140,000	
Machinery and Equipment	40,000	
Delivery Equipment	10,000	
Leasehold	20,000	
Goodwill	25,000	
Discount on Bonds	6,000	
Discount on Common Stock	7,500	
Accounts Payable		$ 64,000
Notes Payable		30,000
Bonds Payable		60,000
Reserve for Doubtful Accounts		3,000
Reserve for Depreciation		29,000
Capital Stock—Common		140,000
Capital Stock—Preferred		60,000
Surplus		95,700
Sales		707,987
Returned Sales and Allowances	9,620	
Cost of Goods Sold	524,667	
Salesmen's Salaries	23,200	
Delivery Expense	4,900	
Freight Out	8,300	
Totals Forward	$1,125,837	$1,189,687

Trial Balance—*Continued*

Totals Brought Forward	$1,125,837	$1,189,687
Office Salaries	18,200	
Officers' Salaries	32,000	
Bad Debts	3,200	
Miscellaneous Expense	3,410	
Interest Income		800
Discount on Purchases		4,310
Bond Interest Expense	3,600	
Interest on Notes Payable	900	
Discount on Sales	7,650	
	$1,194,797	$1,194,797

THE *X Y Z* COMPANY   Exhibit A
Balance Sheet—December 31, 1940

Assets

CURRENT ASSETS:

Cash	$ 4,650.00	
Accounts Receivable	103,150.00	
Notes Receivable	10,000.00	
Inventories	85,000.00	
Investments in Stocks and Bonds	103,850.00	
Total Current Assets		$306,650.00

FIXED ASSETS:

Land and Buildings	$140,000.00	
Machinery and Equipment	40,000.00	
Delivery Equipment	10,000.00	
Leasehold	20,000.00	
Goodwill	25,000.00	
Total Fixed Assets		235,000.00

DEFERRED CHARGES:

Discount on Bonds	$ 6,000.00	
Discount on Common Stock	7,500.00	
Total Deferred Charges		13,500.00
		$555,150.00

Liabilities and Net Worth

CURRENT LIABILITIES:

Accounts Payable	$ 64,000.00	
Notes Payable	30,000.00	
Total Current Liabilities		$ 94,000.00

FIXED LIABILITIES:

Bonds Payable		60,000.00

RESERVES:

Reserve for Doubtful Accounts	$ 3,000.00	
Reserve for Depreciation	29,000.00	
Total Reserves		32,000.00

NET WORTH:

Capital Stock—Common	$140,000.00	
Capital Stock—Preferred	60,000.00	
Surplus	169,150.00	
Total Net Worth		369,150.00
		$555,150.00

This balance sheet shows a net worth of $369,510.00 and liabilities of only $154,000.00, or $2.40 of net worth per dollar of liabilities. It also shows current assets of $306,650.00 and current liabilities of $94,000.00, or a working capital of $212,650.00, or $3.26 of current assets per dollar of current liabilities.

THE *X Y Z* COMPANY   Exhibit B

Surplus Statement

For the Year Ended December 31, 1940

Balance, December 31, 1939............................	$ 80,700.00
Add:	
Net Profit from Operations..........................	73,450.00
Profit on Manufacture of Machinery..................	2,000.00
Goodwill...	25,000.00
Total...	$181,150.00
Deduct Dividends Paid on Common Stock...............	12,000.00
Balance, December 31, 1940..........................	$169,150.00

THE *X Y Z* COMPANY   Exhibit C

Profit and Loss Statement

For the Year Ended December 31, 1940

Sales...			$707,987.00
Less Returned Sales and Allowances....................			9,620.00
Net Sales...			$698,367.00
Deduct Cost of Goods Sold.............................			524,667.00
Gross Profit on Sales.................................			$173,700.00
Deduct Selling Expenses:			
Salesmen's Salaries.......................		$23,200.00	
Delivery Expense..........................		4,900.00	
Freight Out...............................		8,300.00	
Total Selling Expenses............................			36,400.00
Net Profit on Sales...................................			$137,300.00
Deduct General Expenses:			
Office Salaries...........................		$18,200.00	
Officers' Salaries........................		32,000.00	
Bad Debts.................................		3,200.00	
Miscellaneous Expense.....................		3,410.00	
Total General Expenses...........................			56,810.00
Net Profit on Operations..............................			$ 80,490.00
Deduct Net Financial Expenses:			
Bond Interest Expense...........	$3,600.00		
Interest on Notes Payable........	900.00		
Discount on Sales...............	7,650.00		
Total..............................		$12,150.00	
Less:			
Interest Income..............	$ 800.00		
Discount on Purchases.........	4,310.00	5,110.00	7,040.00
Net Income..............................			$ 73,450.00

Auditor's adjustments.

Following are the various matters discovered by the auditor which required adjustment. Each adjusting journal entry is given a letter for purposes of cross-reference with the auditor's working papers, which appear on pages 379 to 385.

(a) It was the company's practice when leaving notes receivable at the bank for collection to make entries immediately debiting Cash and crediting Notes Receivable, as if the notes had been collected. The bank, however, did not give the company credit in its checking account until it received the collection. At the balance sheet date, notes of $2,500.00 left with the bank had not been collected. The following adjustment is required to reverse the entry made by the company with respect to these uncollected notes:

```
Notes Receivable...............................  2,500.00
     Cash......................................             2,500.00
```

(b) In accordance with the requirements of the indenture, the company has established a sinking fund for the payment of the bonds payable. On December 31, 1940, the sinking fund included uninvested cash in the amount of $150.00. This cash is not available for general purposes, and should be shown as part of the sinking fund. The following adjustment is required:

```
Sinking Fund Cash.............................   150.00
     Cash......................................             150.00
```

(c) The cash book was held open at the end of 1940, and receipts from customers in the amount of $9,000.00, received during January 1941, were recorded as of December 31, 1940. Thus the cash as of December 31, 1940, was overstated and the accounts receivable were understated. Required correction:

```
Accounts Receivable...........................  9,000.00
     Cash......................................             9,000.00
```

(d) January 1941 payments to creditors, totaling $8,000.00, were recorded as of December 31, 1940, by debits to Accounts Payable and credits to Cash. Required correction:

```
Cash..........................................  8,000.00
     Accounts Payable..........................             8,000.00
```

(e) The company's balance sheet includes as accounts receivable the $103,150.00 balance of the Accounts Receivable controlling account; it should include the following details shown by the subsidiary ledger:

Debit balances (receivables)............................... $105,150.00
Credit balances (payables)................................   2,000.00

The following adjustment increases the receivables and sets up the credit balances as a liability:

Accounts Receivable...........................   2,000.00
    Credit Balances in Customers' Accounts.......   2,000.00

(f) Most of the company's finished goods are disposed of by direct sale, but some are sent out on consignment. Such consignments have been recorded as sales, thus incorrectly reducing the inventory, overstating the cost of goods sold, overstating the accounts receivable, and taking up a profit before the goods have been sold. On December 31, 1940, there were unsold goods on consignment which cost $10,000.00, which had been consigned at selling prices of $15,000.00, and on which a profit of $5,000.00 therefore had been anticipated. Required correcting entries:

Sales....................................... 15,000.00
    Accounts Receivable......................   15,000.00
    To reverse improper entry for consignments.

Finished Goods................................ 10,000.00
    Cost of Goods Sold.........................   10,000.00
    To take unsold goods out of Cost of Sales and add
    them to inventory.

(g) The accounts receivable include accounts with officers amounting to $5,000.00. This amount was outstanding throughout the entire year 1940, and cannot be regarded as a current asset. It should be taken out of the current accounts receivable from trade debtors and set up as a separate item. Correction:

Accounts Receivable—Officers...................   5,000.00
    Accounts Receivable (current)...............   5,000.00

(h) The amount shown in the balance sheet as accounts receivable also includes common stock subscriptions amounting to $20,000.00. These should be eliminated from the current receivables. Adjustment:

Stock Subscriptions—Common................... 20,000.00
    Accounts Receivable.......................   20,000.00

(i) The amount shown as accounts receivable also includes an equity of $1,500.00 in assigned accounts totaling $10,000.00. This equity should be shown in the balance sheet as a separate item, and hence the following adjusting journal entry is required:

```
Accounts Receivable Assigned—Equity............  1,500.00
    Accounts Receivable......................            1,500.00
```

The contingent liability of $8,500.00 for advances received on the assigned accounts should be mentioned in a balance-sheet footnote.

(j) The amount shown as accounts receivable also includes permanent advances of $8,000.00 to a subsidiary. These should not be included with the regular receivables from trade debtors.

```
Advances to Subsidiary........................  8,000.00
    Accounts Receivable......................            8,000.00
```

(k) Accrued interest amounting to $200.00, earned on notes receivable but not collected, was ignored.

```
Accrued Interest Receivable...................   200.00
    Interest Income..........................             200.00
```

(l) The $85,000.00 shown in the company's balance sheet in one total as Inventories should be detailed as indicated in the following adjusting entry:

```
Finished Goods................................  60,000.00
Goods in Process..............................   5,000.00
Raw Materials.................................  20,000.00
    Inventories..............................           85,000.00
```

(m) Prior to the close of the year, the company purchased $10,000.00 worth of raw materials which were in transit on December 31. Title had passed, but (because the goods had not been received) no entry was made to record the purchase and the liability, and the goods were not included in the inventory. The cost of goods sold was not affected, because the $10,000.00 was omitted both from the purchases during the year and from the inventory at the end of the year. But the balance sheet does not include all of the merchandise owned, nor all of the accounts payable owned. Correction:

```
Raw Materials.................................  10,000.00
    Accounts Payable.........................           10,000.00
```

(n) Raw materials costing $4,000.00 were received before the end of the year and were included in the inventory. But the entry recording the purchase and the liability was not made. Therefore, (1) the cost of the goods sold was understated because the goods were included in the inventory without being included in the cost of purchases, and (2) the liabilities at the end of the year were understated. Correction:

```
Cost of Goods Sold...........................  4,000.00
    Accounts Payable.........................            4,000.00
```

(o) The market value of raw materials on December 31, 1940, was less than the cost. Therefore the raw material inventory valuation should be decreased to the market price. Moreover, since the goods in process and the finished goods include materials, the inventories of goods in process and finished goods should be reduced to the extent of the market decline in the value of the material elements thereof. Since the closing inventories were overvalued, the cost of goods sold was understated. Correction:

```
Cost of Goods Sold...........................  4,500.00
    Finished Goods...........................            3,000.00
    Goods in Process.........................              500.00
    Raw Materials............................            1,000.00
```

(p) The company has taken a so-called manufacturing profit on all finished goods. That is, the finished goods are valued above cost to reflect the profit which the company considers that it makes by manufacturing instead of buying its merchandise. The finished goods inventory includes $8,000.00 of such unrealized and anticipated profit, and the cost of goods sold is understated by a like amount. Correction:

```
Cost of Goods Sold...........................  8,000.00
    Finished Goods...........................            8,000.00
```

(q) The $103,850.00 shown in the balance sheet as Investments in Stocks and Bonds should be detailed as indicated in the following adjusting entry:

```
Sinking Fund Securities.......................  23,850.00
Investment in Stock of Subsidiary (wholly owned). 50,000.00
Preferred Treasury Stock......................  11,500.00
Stock Investments (not readily marketable).......  10,000.00
Investments in Bonds (not readily marketable)....   8,500.00
    Investments in Stocks and Bonds...........           103,850.00
```

(r) The amount shown as Land and Buildings includes:

```
Land used as a plant site.....................  $ 10,000.00
Factory buildings.............................   100,000.00
Land acquired in settlement of an account (being
    held until a sale can be made)..............    10,000.00
Improvements to a leased building used as a sales
    office....................................    20,000.00
        Total..................................  $140,000.00
```

Reclassification is required as shown by the following entry:

Land...   10,000.00
Factory Buildings...........................   100,000.00
Land Held for Resale........................   10,000.00
Leasehold Improvements......................   20,000.00
    Land and Buildings......................   140,000.00

(s) The amount shown as Reserve for Depreciation should be detailed as follows:

Reserve for Depreciation......................   29,000.00
    Reserve for Dep'n.—Buildings..............   15,000.00
    Reserve for Dep'n.—Machinery & Equipment   8,000.00
    Reserve for Dep'n.—Delivery Equipment....   4,000.00
    Reserve for Amortization—Leasehold Improve-
      ments..................................   2,000.00

These reserves should be deducted from the related asset balances instead of being shown on the right side of the balance sheet.

The depreciation item included as a manufacturing expense in the Cost of Goods Sold account consists of the following details:

    Depreciation—Buildings........................... $2,500.00
    Depreciation—Machinery and Equipment............   3,750.00
    Depreciation—Delivery Equipment.................   2,000.00
    Amortization—Leasehold Improvements.............   667.00
      Total....................................... $8,917.00

The depreciation provisions for buildings and for machinery and equipment are manufacturing expenses and should remain a part of the cost of goods sold; the depreciation of delivery equipment and the amortization of leasehold improvements should be included in the selling expenses.   Correction:

Depreciation—Delivery Equipment..............   2,000.00
Amortization—Leasehold Improvements.........   667.00
    Cost of Goods Sold......................   2,667.00

(t) The buildings cost $75,000.00 six years ago.   One year ago the asset account was written up to $100,000.00 by crediting Surplus $25,000.00.   The valuation was supported by an appraisal by independent appraisers, and it is allowed to remain.   But the credit should be transferred from Surplus to a reserve.

Surplus......................................   25,000.00
    Reserve for Unrealized Profit on Appraisal...   25,000.00

(u) The buildings had an estimated life of 30 years when new and an estimated life of 25 years after the appraisal.   One year has elapsed since the appraisal; therefore, $\frac{1}{25}$ of the unrealized profit from the appraisal should be written off by transfer to the reserve for depreciation. Adjustment:

```
Reserve for Unrealized Profit on Appraisal...........  1,000.00
     Reserve for Depreciation—Buildings.............             1,000.00
```

(v) The company manufactured some of its own machinery and equipment at a cost of $4,000.00, but put it into the fixed asset account at $6,000.00, the estimated cost at which it could have been purchased. The $2,000.00 "manufacturing profit" was credited to Surplus. This unrealized profit should be eliminated from the Surplus account, and the machinery valuation should be reduced to cost. This is accomplished by the following adjusting entry:

```
Surplus..........................................  2,000.00
     Machinery and Equipment.....................             2,000.00
```

(w) The company sold some of its machinery for $2,000.00, and recorded the transaction by debiting Cash and crediting the Machinery and Equipment account for that amount. The complete facts were as follows:

```
Cost of machinery sold............................. $5,000.00
Less depreciation provided in the reserve.............  1,000.00
Net book value of the machinery sold................ $4,000.00
Cash received......................................  2,000.00
Loss on sale....................................... $2,000.00
```

There are shown below, in parallel columns, the entry which the company made and the entry which it should have made.

	Entry Made		Proper Entry	
	Debit	Credit	Debit	Credit
Cash..............................	2,000.00		2,000.00	
Reserve for Depreciation—M. & E.....			1,000.00	
Surplus............................			2,000.00	
Machinery and Equipment..........		2,000.00		5,000.00

The required adjustment includes the debit and credit entries that should have been made but were not:

```
Reserve for Depreciation—M. & E.................  1,000.00
Surplus...........................................  2,000.00
     Machinery and Equipment.....................             3,000.00
```

(x) The company purchased some machinery for $3,000.00, agreeing to pay for it in installments. Up to December 31, 1940, it had paid only $1,000.00. It has debited the Machinery and Equipment account with only the installments paid, and has not set up any liability for the unpaid installments, all of which mature within the next six months.

```
Machinery and Equipment.........................  2,000.00
    Machinery Purchase Obligation.................          2,000.00
    To charge the Machinery account with the remaining
    cost of the machinery purchased, and to set up the
    liability for the unpaid installments.
```

(y) Machinery repairs totaling $3,000.00, which should have been included in manufacturing expenses, have been charged to the Machinery account. In other words, revenue expenditures have been capitalized. The cost of goods sold is understated because these expenses have not been charged to it, and the fixed asset account is correspondingly overstated.

```
Cost of Goods Sold...............................  3,000.00
    Machinery and Equipment.....................          3,000.00
    Adjustment for revenue expenditures capitalized.
```

(z) Because adjustments have been made reducing the balance in the Machinery and Equipment account, corresponding adjustments must be made in the related Reserve for Depreciation. Too much depreciation has been provided, because the asset value was overstated, as indicated below:

```
Overstatements of asset value:
    (v)  Unrealized profit on manufacture of machinery..  $2,000.00
    (w)  Inadequate credit for machinery sold..........    3,000.00
    (y)  Revenue expenditures capitalized..............    3,000.00
        Total...................................        $8,000.00
Understatement of asset value:
    (x)  Unpaid installments of purchase price..........    2,000.00
Net overstatement................................      $6,000.00
```

The preceding adjustments reduce the balance in the Machinery and Equipment account $6,000.00. We shall assume that the excess depreciation of machinery and equipment (provided on the $6,000.00 overstatement in the balance in the asset account) is $500.00. This excess provision overstated the reserve and overstated the depreciation charged to Cost of Goods Sold.

```
Reserve for Depreciation—M. & E..................  500.00
    Cost of Goods Sold...........................          500.00
    To eliminate the excessive depreciation provision.
```

(aa) The leasehold was put on the books three years ago by credit to Surplus. There was no authority for the valuation except the directors' estimate. While the valuation may be allowed to remain and the leasehold may be shown as an asset on the balance sheet, the item should be qualified to show that it is based solely on the directors' estimate. Moreover, the credit should be transferred from surplus to a reserve.

```
Surplus.........................................  20,000.00
    Reserve for Unrealized Profit on Leasehold.....          20,000.00
    To transfer the unrealized profit from surplus to a
    reserve.
```

(bb) When the $20,000.00 valuation was placed on the leasehold, the lease had ten years to run. Three years have expired. Therefore, three tenths of the valuation should be written off.

```
Reserve for Unrealized Profit on Leasehold.........   6,000.00
    Leasehold..................................          6,000.00
    Amortization of leasehold valuation.
```

(cc) Amortization of leasehold improvements was provided at the rate of $3\frac{1}{3}\%$ (the same rate that was applied to buildings owned by the company). But the lease was for ten years; therefore, the leasehold improvements should have been written off over a ten-year life. Three years have expired; therefore, the company should have written off three tenths, or 30%, of the cost of the improvements. Instead, it has written off $3\frac{1}{3}\%$ for 3 years, or a total of only 10%. An additional 20% should be amortized; two thirds of the additional amortization is an adjustment of prior years' profits and should be charged to Surplus; the remaining third should be charged to the current year's amortization expense.

```
Amortization—Leasehold Improvements...........   1,333.00
Surplus........................................   2,667.00
    Reserve for Amortization—Leasehold Improve-
    ments....................................          4,000.00
    To provide an additional 20% amortization on the
    $20,000.00 cost of leasehold improvements.
```

(dd) The goodwill was written onto the books by credit to Surplus. It should be written off by debit to Surplus.

```
Surplus........................................  25,000.00
    Goodwill..................................          25,000.00
    To write off the goodwill.
```

(ee) It will be remembered that the company owns all of the stock of a subsidiary. The subsidiary has lost $10,000.00 since the company acquired its stock ($1,000.00 during the current year). This loss has not been taken up.

```
Loss from Subsidiary's Operations.................   1,000.00
Surplus........................................   9,000.00
    Investment in Stock of Subsidiary.............          10,000.00
    To take up subsidiary loss.
```

(ff) The cost of the preferred treasury stock ($11,500.00) includes a premium of $500.00. This premium should be written off.

```
Surplus........................................  500.00
     Preferred Treasury Stock....................          500.00
     To write off premium.
```

(gg) The "other stock investments," which cost $10,000.00, have an estimated market value of only $7,000.00. A reserve should be set up for the decrease in value.

```
Surplus........................................ 3,000.00
     Reserve for Securities Owned.................        3,000.00
     To provide for decrease in market value.
```

(hh) The bonds payable ($60,000.00) were issued at 90; the discount of $6,000.00 remains in the accounts. The bonds were ten-year bonds, and half of their life has expired. Therefore, half of the discount should have been amortized. Four fifths is applicable to prior years and should be charged to Surplus, and one fifth should be charged to the current Bond Interest Expense account.

```
Surplus........................................ 2,400.00
Bond Interest Expense..........................  600.00
     Discount on Bonds...........................        3,000.00
     Amortization of discount.
```

(ii) Unexpired insurance premiums amounting to $1,200.00 were not deferred, and the cost of goods sold is overstated by the amount of the excess insurance charged as a manufacturing expense.

```
Unexpired Insurance............................ 1,200.00
     Cost of Goods Sold...........................        1,200.00
     To set up unexpired premiums as a deferred charge
```

(jj) The following accrued expenses have been ignored.

```
Accrued wages (Salesmen's salaries)................ $1,800.00
Accrued property taxes (A manufacturing expense).... 2,500.00
Accrued interest on notes payable.................. 1,000.00
     Total....................................... $5,300.00
```

They are set up by the following entry:

```
Salesmen's Salaries............................. 1,800.00
Cost of Goods Sold.............................. 2,500.00
Interest on Notes Payable....................... 1,000.00
     Accrued Wages.............................         1,800.00
     Accrued Property Taxes.....................         2,500.00
     Accrued Interest on Notes Payable..........         1,000.00
     Accrued expenses.
```

(kk) Accounts payable for miscellaneous expenses totaling $2,100.00 were not recorded because the bills had not been received prior to the end of the year.

Miscellaneous Expenses......................... 2,100.00
    Other Accrued Expenses....................   2,100.00
    Accrued unpaid expenses.

(ll) One thousand dollars should be added to the reserve for doubtful accounts to make an adequate provision for probable losses.

Bad Debts.................................... 1,000.00
    Reserve for Doubtful Accounts..............   1,000.00
    To increase the reserve.

(mm) A reserve of $1,500.00 should be provided for freight to be paid by customers and deducted by them in settling their accounts.

Freight Out.................................. 1,500.00
    Reserve for Freight to be Deducted.........   1,500.00

(nn) The trust indenture requires the creation of a sinking fund reserve in connection with the bond issue. An amount equal to one tenth of the total bond issue ($60,000.00) should have been transferred from Surplus to the reserve annually. Five years of the life of the bonds have expired, and no transfer has been made to the reserve.

Surplus...................................... 30,000.00
    Sinking Fund Reserve......................   30,000.00
    To show restriction of dividends in accordance with
    the trust indenture.

(oo) A 6% dividend was declared on the preferred stock prior to December 31, 1940, payable after that date. No entry was made to set up the liability created by the declaration of this dividend. The outstanding stock is $49,000.00 ($60,000.00 total less $11,000.00 treasury stock), and a 6% dividend, therefore, amounts to $2,940.00.

Surplus...................................... 2,940.00
    Preferred Dividends Payable................   2,940.00

Auditor's adjustment working papers.

The following working papers show the balances appearing in the company's trial balance, the adjustments (or postings of the adjusting journal entries) mentioned on the preceding pages, and the adjusted balances.

Auditor's Adjustment Working Papers
December 31, 1940

	Company's Trial Balance		Adjustments		Adjusted Trial Balance	
	Debit	Credit	Debit	Credit	Debit	Credit
Cash	$ 4,650					
a Uncollected notes				$ 2,500		
b Sinking fund cash				150		
c 1941 receipts				9,000		
d 1941 disbursements			$ 8,000			
Adjusted balance					$ 1,000	
Accounts Receivable	103,150					
c 1941 collections			9,000			
e Credit balances			2,000			
f Consignment				15,000		
g Receivables from officers				5,000		
h Stock subscriptions				20,000		
i Equity in assigned accounts				1,500		
j Advances to subsidiary				8,000		
i Adjusted balance					64,650	
Accounts Receivable Assigned—Equity			1,500		1,500	
Reserve for Doubtful Accounts		$ 3,000				
ll Additional provision				1,000		
Adjusted balance						$ 4,000
mm Reserve for Freight to be Deducted				1,500		1,500
Notes Receivable	10,000					
a Uncollected notes			2,500			
Adjusted balance					12,500	
k Accrued Interest Receivable			200		200	
Inventories	85,000					
l Classified in detail				85,000		
Finished Goods:						
l Inventory total detailed			60,000			
f Cost of consigned goods			10,000			
Totals forwarded	$ 202,800	$ 3,000	$ 93,200	$148,650	$ 79,850	$ 5,500

379

Auditor's Adjustment Working Papers—*Continued*
December 31, 1940

	Company's Trial Balance		Adjustments		Adjusted Trial Balance	
	Debit	Credit	Debit	Credit	Debit	Credit
Totals brought forward	$202,800	$3,000	$93,200	$148,650	$79,850	$5,500
o Market value adjustment				3,000		
p Manufacturing profit				8,000		
Adjusted balance					59,000	
Goods in Process:						
l Inventory total detailed			5,000			
o Market value adjustment				500		
Adjusted balance					4,500	
Raw Materials:						
l Inventory total detailed			20,000			
m Purchases omitted from inventory			10,000			
o Market value adjustment				1,000		
Adjusted balance					29,000	
g Accounts Receivable—Officers			5,000		5,000	
Investments in Stocks and Bonds	103,850					
g Reclassification entry				103,850		
Sinking Fund for Bonds Payable:						
b Cash			150		150	
q Securities			23,850		23,850	
Investments and Advances—Subsidiary:						
q Investment in stock			50,000			
ee Loss since acquisition				10,000		
Adjusted balance					40,000	
j Advances			8,000		8,000	
q Other Stock Investments			10,000		10,000	
gg Reserve for Securities Owned				3,000		3,000
q Investments in Bonds			8,500		8,500	
Land and Buildings	140,000					
r Reclassification entry				140,000		
Totals forwarded	$446,650	$3,000	$233,700	$418,000	$267,850	$8,500

Auditor's Adjustment Working Papers—*Continued*

December 31, 1940

	Company's Trial Balance		Adjustments		Adjusted Trial Balance	
	Debit	Credit	Debit	Credit	Debit	Credit
Totals brought forward	$ 446,650	$ 3,000	$233,700	$418,000	$ 267,850	$ 8,500
r Land			10,000		10,000	
r Land Held for Resale			10,000		10,000	
r Factory Buildings			100,000		100,000	
Reserve for Depreciation		29,000	29,000			
s Reclassification						
Reserve for Depreciation—Buildings:						
s Reclassification				15,000		
u Depreciation of appreciation				1,000		
Adjusted balance						16,000
Machinery and Equipment	40,000					
v Manufacturing profit				2,000		
w Adjustment for sale				3,000		
x Unrecorded purchase installments			2,000			
y Repairs capitalized				3,000		
Adjusted balance					34,000	
Reserve for Depreciation—Machinery and Equipment:						
s Reclassification				8,000		
w Accrued depreciation on assets sold			1,000			
z Reduction of provision			500			
Adjusted balance						6,500
Delivery Equipment	10,000				10,000	
Reserve for Depreciation—Delivery Equipment:						
s Reclassification				4,000		4,000
Leasehold:						
Directors' valuation	20,000					
bb Amortization				6,000		
Adjusted balance					14,000	
r Leasehold Improvements			20,000		20,000	
Totals forwarded	$ 516,650	$ 32,000	$406,200	$460,000	$ 465,850	$ 35,000

Auditor's Adjustment Working Papers—*Continued*
December 31, 1940

	Company's Trial Balance		Adjustments		Adjusted Trial Balance	
	Debit	Credit	Debit	Credit	Debit	Credit
Totals brought forward	$516,650	$32,000	$406,200	$460,000	$465,850	$35,000
Reserve for Amortization—Leasehold Improvements:						
s Reclassification				2,000		
cc Adjustment for under-provision				4,000		
Adjusted balance						6,000
Discount on Bonds	6,000					
hh Amortization				3,000		
Adjusted balance					3,000	
ii Unexpired Insurance			1,200		1,200	
Goodwill	25,000					
dd Write-off				25,000		
Accounts Payable—Trade		64,000				
d 1941 payments				8,000		
m Material purchases in transit				10,000		
n Unrecorded purchases in inventory				4,000		
Adjusted balance						86,000
Notes Payable		30,000				30,000
x Machinery Purchase Obligation				2,000		2,000
jj Accrued Wages				1,800		1,800
jj Accrued Property Taxes				2,500		2,500
jj Accrued Interest on Notes Payable				1,000		1,000
kk Other Accrued Expenses				2,100		2,100
e Credit Balances in Customers' Accounts				2,000		2,000
oo Preferred Dividends Payable				2,940		2,940
Bonds Payable		60,000				60,000
Capital Stock—Preferred		60,000				60,000
Deferred Treasury Stock:						
q Cost of stock			11,500			
ff Premium written off				500		
Adjusted balance					11,000	
Totals forwarded	$547,650	246,000	$418,900	$530,840	$481,050	$291,340

Auditor's Adjustment Working Papers—*Continued*
December 31, 1940

	Company's Trial Balance		Adjustments		Adjusted Trial Balance	
			Debit	Credit		
Totals brought forward	$ 547,650	$ 246,000	$418,900	$530,840	$ 481,050	$ 291,340
Capital Stock—Common		140,000				140,000
Discount on Common Stock	7,500				7,500	
Stock Subscriptions—Common:						
h Reclassification			20,000		20,000	
Reserve for Unrealized Profit on Leasehold:						
aa Transfer credit from surplus				20,000		
bb Write-off for amortization			6,000			
Adjusted balance						14,000
Reserve for Unrealized Profit on Appraisal of Buildings:						
t Transfer credit from surplus				25,000		
u Depreciation of appreciation			1,000			
Adjusted balance						24,000
Sinking Fund Reserve:						
nn Appropriation from surplus				30,000		30,000
Surplus		95,700				
t Unrealized profit on appraisal of building—To a reserve			25,000			
v Manufacturing profit on machinery			2,000			
w Loss on sale of machinery			2,000			
aa Unrealized profit on leasehold—To a reserve			20,000			
cc Additional amortization of leasehold improvements for prior years			2,667			
dd Write-off goodwill			25,000			
ee Subsidiary loss from date of acquisition to December 31, 1939			9,000			
ff Premium on treasury stock			500			
gg Reduce stock investments to market			3,000			
Totals forwarded	$ 555,150	$ 481,700	$535,067	$605,840	$ 508,550	$ 499,340

Auditor's Adjustment Working Papers—*Continued*
December 31, 1940

	Company's Trial Balance		Adjustments		Adjusted Trial Balance	
			Debit	Credit		
Totals brought forward..................	$ 555,150	$ 481,700	$535,067	$605,840	$ 508,550	$ 499,340
hh Amortization of bond discount from date of issuance to December 31, 1939...................			2,400			
mn Appropriation to sinking fund reserve.......			30,000			
oo Dividend payable on preferred stock.........			2,940			
Adjusted balance.........					28,807	
Sales.......................		707,987	15,000			
f Goods consigned, not sold.....						692,987
Adjusted balance........						
Returned Sales and Allowances.........	9,620				9,620	
Cost of Goods Sold...................	524,667					
f Cost of goods consigned, not sold.........				10,000		
n Unrecorded purchases in inventory..........			4,000			
o Reduce inventories to market...............			4,500			
p Manufacturing profit on finished goods.......			8,000			
s Depreciation applicable to selling expense...				2,667		
y Machinery repairs capitalized...........			3,000			
z Excess depreciation—machinery........				500		
ii Unexpired insurance.........				1,200		
jj Accrued property taxes......			2,500			
Adjusted balance....					532,300	
Salesmen's Salaries......	23,200					
jj Accrued wages..........			1,800			
Adjusted balance......					25,000	
Delivery Expense........	4,900				4,900	
s Depreciation—Delivery Equipment........			2,000		2,000	
Freight Out........	8,300					
mm Provision for reserve...........			1,500			
Adjusted balance........					9,800	
Totals forwarded...................	$1,125,837	$1,189,687	$612,707	$620,207	$1,120,977	$1,192,327

Auditor's Adjustment Working Papers—*Concluded*
December 31, 1940

	Company's Trial Balance		Adjustments		Adjusted Trial Balance	
	Debit	Credit	Debit	Credit	Debit	Credit
Totals brought forward	$1,125,837	$1,189,687	$612,707	$620,207	$1,120,977	$1,192,327
s Amortization—Leasehold Improvements			667			
cc Additional amortization			1,333			
Adjusted balance					2,000	
Office Salaries	18,200				18,200	
Officers' Salaries	32,000				32,000	
Bad Debts	3,200					
ll Additional provision			1,000			
Adjusted balance					4,200	
Miscellaneous Expense	3,410					
kk Unrecorded expenses			2,100			
Adjusted balance					5,510	
Bond Interest Expense	3,600					
hh Amortization of discount for 1940			600			
Adjusted balance					4,200	
Interest on Notes Payable	900					
jj Accrued interest			1,000			
Adjusted balance					1,900	
Discount on Sales	7,650				7,650	
ee Loss from Subsidiary's Operations			1,000		1,000	
Interest Income		800				
k Accrued interest ignored				200		
Adjusted balance						1,000
Discount on Purchases		4,310				4,310
	$1,194,797	$1,194,797	$620,407	$620,407	$1,197,637	$1,197,637

Trial balance after adjustment.

The adjusted trial balance serves as the basis of the auditor's profit and loss statement and balance sheet. To avoid further reference to the complete working papers, the following is presented:

Adjusted Trial Balance
December 31, 1940

Cash..	$ 1,000	
Accounts Receivable................................	64,650	
Accounts Receivable Assigned—Equity................	1,500	
Reserve for Doubtful Accounts......................		$ 4,000
Reserve for Freight to be Deducted.................		1,500
Notes Receivable..................................	12,500	
Accrued Interest Receivable........................	200	
Finished Goods....................................	59,000	
Goods in Process..................................	4,500	
Raw Materials.....................................	29,000	
Accounts Receivable—Officers......................	5,000	
Sinking Fund Cash.................................	150	
Sinking Fund Securities............................	23,850	
Investment in Subsidiary...........................	40,000	
Advances to Subsidiary.............................	8,000	
Other Stock Investments............................	10,000	
Reserve for Securities Owned.......................		3,000
Investments in Bonds..............................	8,500	
Land..	10,000	
Land Held for Resale..............................	10,000	
Factory Buildings.................................	100,000	
Reserve for Depreciation—Buildings.................		16,000
Machinery and Equipment...........................	34,000	
Reserve for Depreciation—Machinery and Equipment....		6,500
Delivery Equipment................................	10,000	
Reserve for Depreciation—Delivery Equipment.........		4,000
Leasehold...	14,000	
Leasehold Improvements............................	20,000	
Reserve for Amortization—Leasehold Improvements......		6,000
Discount on Bonds.................................	3,000	
Unexpired Insurance...............................	1,200	
Accounts Payable—Trade............................		86,000
Notes Payable.....................................		30,000
Machinery Purchase Obligation......................		2,000
Accrued Wages.....................................		1,800
Accrued Property Taxes.............................		2,500
Accrued Interest on Notes Payable..................		1,000
Other Accrued Expenses............................		2,100
Credit Balances in Customers' Accounts.............		2,000
Preferred Dividends Payable........................		2,940
Bonds Payable.....................................		60,000
Capital Stock—Preferred...........................		60,000
Preferred Treasury Stock...........................	11,000	
Capital Stock—Common.............................		140,000
Discount on Common Stock..........................	7,500	
Stock Subscriptions—Common........................	20,000	
Totals Forward...................................	$ 508,550	$ 431,34

Trial Balance—*Continued*

Totals Brought Forward...........................	$ 508,550	$ 431,340
Reserve for Unrealized Profit on Leasehold..............		14,000
Reserve for Unrealized Profit on Appraisal of Buildings....		24,000
Sinking Fund Reserve................................		30,000
Surplus..	28,807	
Sales..		692,987
Returned Sales and Allowances........................	9,620	
Cost of Goods Sold..................................	532,300	
Salesmen's Salaries.................................	25,000	
Delivery Expense....................................	4,900	
Depreciation—Delivery Equipment....................	2,000	
Freight Out..	9,800	
Amortization—Leasehold Improvements................	2,000	
Office Salaries.....................................	18,200	
Officers' Salaries...................................	32,000	
Bad Debts..	4,200	
Miscellaneous Expenses..............................	5,510	
Bond Interest Expense...............................	4,200	
Interest on Notes Payable............................	1,900	
Discount on Sales...................................	7,650	
Loss from Subsidiary's Operations.....................	1,000	
Interest Income.....................................		1,000
Discount on Purchases		4,310
	$1,197,637	$1,197,637

Auditor's profit and loss statement.

The following statement was prepared from balances shown in the adjusted trial balance.

THE *X Y Z* COMPANY
Profit and Loss Statement
For the Year Ended December 31, 1940

Exhibit C

Sales...		$692,987
Less Returned Sales and Allowances.........................		9,620
Net Sales...		$683,367
Deduct Cost of Goods Sold................................		532,300
Gross Profit on Sales.....................................		$151,067
Deduct Selling Expenses:		
Salesmen's Salaries..............................	$25,000	
Delivery Expense................................	4,900	
Depreciation—Delivery Equipment.................	2,000	
Freight Out.....................................	9,800	
Amortization—Leasehold Improvements.............	2,000	
Total Selling Expenses.............................		43,700
Net Profit on Sales.......................................		$107,367
Deduct General Expenses:		
Office Salaries..................................	$18,200	
Officers' Salaries...............................	32,000	
Bad Debts......................................	4,200	
Miscellaneous Expense...........................	5,510	
Total General Expenses............................		59,910
Net Profit on Operations (Forward).........................		$ 47,457

Profit and Loss Statement—*Continued*

Net Profit on Operations (Brought Forward).................			$ 47,457
Deduct Net Financial Expense:			
Bond Interest Expense.....................	$4,200		
Interest on Notes Payable.................	1,900		
Discount on Sales........................	7,650		
Loss from Subsidiary's Operations..........	1,000		
Total...............................		$14,750	
Less:			
Interest Income........................	$1,000		
Discount on Purchases..................	4,310	5,310	9,440
Net Profit...			$ 38,017

Auditor's surplus statement.

The following statement was prepared from data shown by the bookkeeper's surplus statement, the Surplus section of the working papers, the trial balance after adjustments, and the auditor's profit and loss statement.

THE *X Y Z* COMPANY   Exhibit B

Surplus Statement

For the Year Ended December 31, 1940

Balance, December 31, 1939:			
Surplus Before Adjustment..			$80,700
Deduct:			
Unrealized Profits—Transferred to Reserves:			
Buildings...	$25,000		
Leasehold...	20,000		
Amortization of Leasehold Improvements—Prior Years......	2,667		
Subsidiary's Loss in Prior Years..........................	9,000		
Amortization of Bond Discount—Prior Years...............	2,400		
Transfers to Sinking Fund Reserve—Prior Years............	24,000	83,067	
Deficit After Adjustment...			$ 2,367
Changes During the Year:			
Credit—Net Income (Exhibit C)...........................		$38,017	
Charges:			
Loss on Sale of Machinery.........................	$ 2,000		
Premium on Preferred Treasury Stock.............	500		
Reserve for Market Decline in Stocks..............	3,000		
Transfer to Sinking Fund Reserve.................	6,000		
Dividends:			
Paid on Common Stock........................	12,000		
Declared on Preferred Stock...................	2,940	26,440	
Net Credit...			11,577
Surplus, December 31, 1940..			$ 9,210

Auditor's balance sheet classification of working papers.

The following working papers indicate the captions under which the items are grouped in the auditor's balance sheet. Comments on the working papers appear on page 391.

Auditor's Classification Working Papers—Asset Sheet

	Adjusted Balances	Classification in Auditor's Balance Sheet				
		Current Assets	Investments and Sundry Assets	Fixed Assets	Deferred Charges	Deducted Contra
Cash	$ 1,000.00	$ 1,000.00				
Accounts Receivable—Trade	64,650.00	64,650.00				
Accounts Receivable—Officers	5,000.00		$ 5,000.00			
Accounts Receivable Assigned—Equity	1,500.00	1,500.00				
Notes Receivable	12,500.00	12,500.00				
Accrued Interest Receivable	200.00	200.00				
Finished Goods	59,000.00	59,000.00				
Goods in Process	4,500.00	4,500.00				
Raw Materials	29,000.00	29,000.00				
Sinking Fund Securities	23,850.00		23,850.00			
Sinking Fund Cash	150.00		150.00			
Investment in Subsidiary	40,000.00		40,000.00			
Advances to Subsidiary	8,000.00		8,000.00			
Preferred Treasury Stock	11,000.00					$11,000.00
Other Stock Investments	10,000.00		10,000.00			
Investments in Bonds	8,500.00		8,500.00			
Land	10,000.00			$ 10,000.00		
Factory Buildings	100,000.00			100,000.00		
Land Held for Resale	10,000.00		10,000.00			
Leasehold Improvements	20,000.00			20,000.00		
Machinery and Equipment	34,000.00			34,000.00		
Delivery Equipment	10,000.00			10,000.00		
Leasehold—Directors' Valuation—Less Amortization	14,000.00			14,000.00		
Discount on Bonds	3,000.00				$3,000.00	
Discount on Common Stock	7,500.00					7,500.00
Unexpired Insurance	1,200.00				1,200.00	
Stock Subscriptions—Common	20,000.00					20,000.00
	$508,550.00	$172,350.00	$105,500.00	$188,000.00	$4,200.00	$38,500.00

389

Auditor's Classification Working Papers—Liability and Net Worth Sheet

	Adjusted Balances	Classification in Auditor's Balance Sheet			
		Current Liabilities	Fixed Liabilities	Net Worth	Deducted Contra
Accounts Payable—Trade	$ 86,000.00	$ 86,000.00			
Notes Payable	30,000.00	30,000.00			
Machinery Purchase Obligation	2,000.00	2,000.00			
Accrued Wages	1,800.00	1,800.00			
Accrued Property Taxes	2,500.00	2,500.00			
Accrued Interest on Notes Payable	1,000.00	1,000.00			
Other Accrued Expenses	2,100.00	2,100.00			
Credit Balances in Customers' Accounts	2,000.00	2,000.00			
Deferred Dividends Payable	2,940.00	2,940.00			
Bonds Payable	60,000.00		$60,000.00		
Reserve for Doubtful Accounts	4,000.00				$ 4,000.00
Reserve for Freight to be Deducted	1,500.00				1,500.00
Reserves for Depreciation:					
Buildings	16,000.00				16,000.00
Machinery and Equipment	6,500.00				6,500.00
Delivery Equipment	4,000.00				4,000.00
Reserve for Amortization—Leasehold Improvements	6,000.00				6,000.00
Reserve for Securities Owned	3,000.00				3,000.00
Reserves for Unrealized Profit:					
On Leasehold	14,000.00			$ 14,000.00	
Appraisal of Buildings	24,000.00			24,000.00	
Sinking Fund Reserve	30,000.00			30,000.00	
Capital Stock—Common	140,000.00			140,000.00	
Capital Stock—Preferred	60,000.00			60,000.00	
Surplus	9,210.00			9,210.00	
	$508,550.00	$130,340.00	$60,000.00	$277,210.00	$41,000.00

390

A number of errors of grouping or classification appear in the company's balance sheet. The company included the sinking fund ecurities, the subsidiary stock, the preferred treasury stock, and he other investments in stocks and bonds under the Current Assets caption. These items are not included under the Current Assets caption in the auditor's balance sheet. The preferred reasury stock is deducted from the capital stock in the Net Worth ection, and the other stocks and bonds are shown under an Investments and Sundry Assets caption. The miscellaneous stock and bond investments might have been left in the current asset group except for the specific information that they had no ready marketability.

In the company's balance sheet, the land held for resale was ncluded with other land in the fixed asset group. Since the land held for resale is not used in operations, the auditor's balance sheet shows it under the Investments and Sundry Assets caption rather han as a fixed asset.

In the company's balance sheet the discount on stock was ncluded among the deferred charges; in the auditor's balance sheet t is deducted from the capital stock to show the paid-in capital. Similarly, the uncollected subscriptions are deducted in the Net Worth section, instead of being shown as an asset, because there s no apparent intention to call for collections from the subscribers.

In the company's balance sheet the valuation reserves (for doubtful accounts and depreciation) are shown on the liability side; in the auditor's balance sheet they are deducted from the related assets.

Balance sheet footnotes.

Adjustment (i) referred to accounts receivable assigned; the company had an equity of $1,500.00 in $10,000.00 of assigned accounts. The equity has been separated from the other accounts receivable in the auditor's balance sheet. It is also necessary to mention the contingent liability in a footnote.

The company was also contingently liable in the amount of $20,000.00 on customers' notes discounted. This contingent liability requires a balance sheet footnote.

The company has not made the sinking fund deposit of $6,-000.00 required as of December 31, 1940. This fact is mentioned n a footnote.

The company was obligated on purchase commitments amounting to $75,000.00 for raw materials which had a market purchase value of $73,000.00 on December 31, 1940. Also on that date the company was defendant in a suit charging it with a patent infringement.

THE *X Y Z* COMPANY Exhibit A

Balance Sheet—December 31, 1940

ASSETS

CURRENT ASSETS:

Cash			$ 1,000
Accounts Receivable—Trade (Including $1,500.00 equity in assigned accounts)		$ 66,150	
Less:			
Reserve for Doubtful Accounts	$4,000		
Reserve for Freight to be Deducted	1,500	5,500	60,650
Notes Receivable			12,500
Accrued Interest Receivable			200
Inventories:			
Finished Goods		$ 59,000	
Goods in Process		4,500	
Raw Materials		29,000	92,500
Total Current Assets			$166,850

INVESTMENTS AND SUNDRY ASSETS:

Accounts Receivable—Officers		$ 5,000
Sinking Fund for First Mortgage Bonds Payable:		
Securities	$ 23,850	
Cash	150	24,000
Investment in and Advances to Wholly-owned Subsidiary:		
Investment in Stock—Adjusted to Agree with Net Assets of Subsidiary	$ 40,000	
Advances	8,000	48,000
Other Stock Investments—At Market Value		7,000
Investments in Bonds—At Cost		8,500
Land Held for Resale		10,000
Total Investments and Sundry Assets		102,500

FIXED ASSETS:

Land		$10,000
Factory Buildings—Based on Appraisal by (name of appraiser)—as of December 31, 1939	$100,000	
Less Reserve for Depreciation	16,000	84,000
Machinery and Equipment	$ 34,000	
Less Reserve for Depreciation	6,500	27,500
Delivery Equipment	$ 10,000	
Less Reserve for Depreciation	4,000	6,000
Leasehold Improvements—Less Amortization		14,000
Leasehold—Directors' Valuation—Less Amortization		14,000
Total Fixed Assets		155,500

DEFERRED CHARGES:

Discount on Bonds		$ 3,000
Unexpired Insurance		1,200
Total Deferred Charges		4,200
		$429,050

THE *X Y Z* COMPANY
Balance Sheet—December 31, 1940—*Continued*

LIABILITIES AND NET WORTH

CURRENT LIABILITIES:

Accounts Payable—Trade		$ 86,000	
Notes Payable		30,000	
Machinery Purchase Obligation		2,000	
Credit Balances in Customers' Accounts		2,000	
Preferred Dividends Payable		2,940	
Accrued Wages		1,800	
Accrued Property Taxes		2,500	
Accrued Interest on Notes Payable		1,000	
Other Accrued Expenses		2,100	
Total Current Liabilities			$130,340

FIXED LIABILITIES:

First Mortgage, 6%, Sinking Fund Bonds Payable—
Due December 31, 1945...................................... 60,000

NET WORTH:

Capital Stock—$100.00 par value per share:

Preferred—Authorized, 1,000 shares; unissued, 400 shares; in treasury, 110 shares; outstanding, 490 shares		$ 49,000	
Common—Authorized, 1,500 shares; unissued, 100 shares; issued and outstanding, 1,400 shares	$140,000		
Less:			
Uncollected Subscriptions	$20,000		
Discount	7,500	27,500	112,500
Total		$161,500	

Surplus:

Sinking Fund Reserve	$ 30,000		
Free and Available for Dividends	9,210	39,210	
Reserve for Unrealized Profit on Appraisal of Buildings		24,000	
Reserve for Unrealized Profit on Directors' Valuation of Leasehold		14,000	238,710
			$429,050

NOTES:

The Company was contingently liable on December 31, 1940, in the amount of $20,000.00 on customers' notes discounted; in the amount of $8,500.00 on customers' accounts assigned; and in an undeterminable amount on pending patent infringement litigation.

Commitments in the amount of $75 000.00 for purchases of raw materials having a market value of $73,000.00 on December 31, 1940, were outstanding at that date. No provision has been made for the difference between the commitment and market prices.

A $6,000.00 sinking fund deposit, required as of December 31, 1940, had not been made at that date.

Comparison of company's and auditor's balance sheets.

The comparisons on the following page indicate the major differences between the company's balance sheet and the adjusted balance sheet prepared by the auditor.

Summarized Balance Sheets

	Company's Balance Sheet		Auditor's Balance Sheet		Ratio Auditor's to Company's
	Amount	Per Cent	Amount	Per Cent	
Current Assets..............	$306,650	55.24%	$166,850	38.89%	.54
Investments and Sundry Assets	—	—	102,500	23.89	—
Fixed Assets................	235,000	42.33	155,500	36.24	.66
Deferred Charges...........	13,500	2.43	4,200	.98	.31
	$555,150	100.00%	$429,050	100.00%	
Current Liabilities...........	$ 94,000	16.93%	$130,340	30.38%	1.39
Fixed Liabilities.............	60,000	10.81	60,000	13.98	1.00
Valuation Reserves...........	32,000	5.76	—	—	—
Net Worth.................	369,150	66.50	238,710	55.64	.65
	$555,150	100.00%	$429,050	100.00%	

Working Capital

	Company	Auditor
Current Assets...........................	$306,650.00	$166,850.00
Current Liabilities.......................	94,000.00	130,340.00
Working Capital.........................	$212,650.00	$ 36,510.00
Working Capital Ratio....................	3.26	1.28

Quick Assets and Current Liabilities

	Company	Auditor
Cash...................................	$ 4,650.00	$ 1,000.00
Accounts Receivable—Net................	100,150.00	60,650.00
Notes Receivable and Interest.............	10,000.00	12,700.00
Total...............................	$114,800.00	$ 74,350.00
Current Liabilities.......................	94,000.00	130,340.00
Excess of Quick Current Assets Over Current Liabilities.............................	$ 20,800.00	$ 55,990.00*
Acid Test Ratio.........................	1.22	.57

* Deficiency

Ratio of Worth to Debt

	Company	Auditor
NET WORTH:		
Capital Stock:		
Preferred............................	$ 60,000.00	$ 49,000.00
Common.............................	140,000.00	112,500.00
Surplus:		
Free................................	169,150.00	9,210.00
Sinking Fund Reserve.................		30,000.00
Reserves for Unrealized Profit:		
On Buildings..........................		24,000.00
On Leasehold.........................		14,000.00
Total...............................	$369,150.00	$238,710.00
LIABILITIES:		
Current...............................	$ 94,000.00	$130,340.00
Fixed.................................	60,000.00	60,000.00
Total...............................	$154,000.00	$190,340.00
Ratio of Worth to Debt..................	2.40	1.25

ANALYTICAL AND COMPARATIVE STATEMENTS

....

mounts and analytical per cents.

The expression "analytical per cents" is intended to describe ch ratios as the per cent of each balance sheet item to the total, ch profit and loss statement item to the net sales, and each ele-ent of manufacturing cost to the total. Amounts and analytical r cents appear in the following statements.

Balance Sheet
December 31, 1940

	Amount	Per Cent of Total
Assets		
Cash...	$ 4,000.00	7%
Receivables.....................................	12,000.00	22
Inventory.......................................	22,000.00	41
Fixed Assets....................................	16,000.00	30
	$54,000.00	100%
Liabilities and Net Worth		
Accounts Payable................................	$17,000.00	31%
Capital Stock...................................	30,000.00	56
Surplus...	7,000.00	13
	$54,000.00	100%

Profit and Loss Statement
Year Ended December 31, 1940

	Amount	Per Cent of Net Sales
Sales...	$200,000.00	100%
Cost of Sales...................................	150,000.00	75
Gross Profit....................................	$ 50,000.00	25%
Expenses..	40,000.00	20
Net Profit......................................	$ 10,000.00	5%

omparison of amounts and analytical per cents.

Following are a comparative balance sheet as of two dates and a ndensed comparative profit and loss statement for two years, ith comparisons of amounts and analytical per cents.

THE OSBORNE COMPANY
Comparative Balance Sheets
December 31, 1941 and 1940

	December 31, 1941		December 31, 1940		Increase-Decrease*	
Assets	Amount	Per Cent of Total	Amount	Per Cent of Total	In Amount	In Per Cent
CURRENT ASSETS:						
Cash...............................	$ 22,360.00	2.92%	$ 21,085.00	3.03%	$ 1,275.00	.11%*
Accounts Receivable...............	$215,420.00		$168,845.00		$46,575.00	
Notes Receivable..................	34,050.00		41,600.00		7,550.00*	
Total Receivables.............	$249,470.00		$210,445.00		$39,025.00	
Less Reserve for Bad Debts.....	11,065.00		15,430.00		4,365.00*	
Net Receivables...............	$238,405.00	31.18%	$195,015.00	27.99%	$43,390.00	3.19%
Inventories:						
Finished Goods..................	$ 50,710.00	6.63%	$ 42,300.00	6.07%	$ 8,410.00	.56%
Goods in Process................	30,260.00	3.96	24,860.00	3.57	5,400.00	.39
Raw Materials...................	33,430.00	4.37	37,050.00	5.32	3,620.00*	.95*
Total Inventories.............	$114,400.00	14.96%	$104,210.00	14.96%	$10,190.00	—
Total Current Assets........	$375,165.00	49.06%	$320,310.00	45.98%	$54,855.00	3.08%
FIXED ASSETS:						
Land.............................	$ 30,500.00	3.99%	$ 30,500.00	4.38%	$ —	.39%*
Building.........................	$222,050.00		$193,000.00		$29,050.00	
Less Reserve for Depreciation....	65,480.00		59,320.00		6,160.00	
Net............................	$156,570.00	20.47%	$133,680.00	19.19%	$22,890.00	1.28%
Machinery and Equipment..........	$372,510.00		$349,515.00		$22,995.00	
Less Reserve for Depreciation....	188,310.00		153,615.00		34,695.00	
Net............................	$184,200.00	24.09%	$195,900.00	28.12%	$11,700.00*	4.03%*
Total Fixed Assets..........	$371,270.00	48.55%	$330,080.00	51.69%	$11,190.00	3.14%*

Comparative Balance Sheets—*Continued*

	December 31, 1941		December 31, 1940		Increase-Decrease*	
	Amount	Per Cent of Total	Amount	Per Cent of Total	In Amount	In Per Cent
Assets—*Continued*						
DEFERRED CHARGES:						
Unexpired Insurance	$ 7,270.00	.95%	$ 6,540.00	.94%	$ 730.00	.01%
Supplies Inventories	10,995.00	1.44	9,710.00	1.39	1,285.00	.05
Total Deferred Charges	$ 18,265.00	2.39%	$ 16,250.00	2.33%	$ 2,015.00	.06%
	$764,700.00	100.00%	$696,640.00	100.00%	$68,060.00	—%
Liabilities and Net Worth						
CURRENT LIABILITIES:						
Bank Loans	$ 30,000.00	3.92%	$ 50,000.00	7.18%	$20,000.00*	3.26%*
Accounts Payable	68,215.00	8.92	51,350.00	7.37	16,865.00	1.55
Accrued Salaries and Expenses	25,435.00	3.33	22,680.00	3.26	2,755.00	.07
Total Current Liabilities	$123,650.00	16.17%	$124,030.00	17.81%	$ 380.00*	1.64%*
FIRST MORTGAGE 6% BONDS	150,000.00	19.62	150,000.00	21.53	—	1.91 *
Total Liabilities	$273,650.00	35.79%	$274,030.00	39.34%	$ 380.00*	3.55%*
NET WORTH:						
7% Preferred Stock	$100,000.00	13.08%	$ 90,000.00	12.92%	$10,000.00	.16%
Common Stock	250,000.00	32.69	200,000.00	28.71	50,000.00	3.98
Surplus	141,050.00	18.44	132,610.00	19.03	8,440.00	.59 *
Total Net Worth	$491,050.00	64.21%	$422,610.00	60.66%	$68,440.00	3.55%
	$764,700.00	100.00%	$696,640.00	100.00%	$68,060.00	—%

THE OSBORNE COMPANY

Condensed Comparative Profit and Loss Statements

For the Years Ended December 31, 1941 and 1940

| | Year Ended December 31 | | | | Increase-Decrease* | |
| | 1941 | | 1940 | | | |
	Amount	Per Cent of Net Sales	Amount	Per Cent of Net Sales	In Amount	In Per Cent
Net Sales...................	$969,140.00	100.00%	$715,900.00	100.00%	$253,240.00	—%
Cost of Goods Sold........	615,460.00	63.51	435,640.00	60.85	179,820.00	2.66
Gross Profit on Sales......	$353,680.00	36.49%	$280,260.00	39.15%	$ 73,420.00	2.66%*
Selling Expenses..........	178,250.00	18.39	162,440.00	22.69	15,810.00	4.30*
Net Profit on Sales........	$175,430.00	18.10%	$117,820.00	16.46%	$ 57,610.00	1.64%
General Expenses..........	70,710.00	7.30	53,215.00	7.43	17,495.00	.13*
Net Profit on Operations...	$104,720.00	10.80%	$ 64,605.00	9.03%	$ 40,115.00	1.77%
Net Financial Expense......	17,215.00	1.77	21,600.00	3.02	4,385.00*	1.25%*
Net Profit before Federal Income Tax....	$ 87,505.00	9.03%	$ 43,005.00	6.01%	$ 44,500.00	3.02%
Federal Income Tax†.......	12,065.00	1.25	5,700.00	.80	6,365.00	.45
Net Profit................	$ 75,440.00	7.78%	$ 37,305.00	5.21%	$ 38,135.00	2.57%

† Tax rates for 1940 and 1941 are unknown at the time of writing; arbitrary amounts, too small to imply estimates, therefore are used.

Per cents of increase and decrease.

Following are comparative statements with per cents of increase and decrease.

THE OSBORNE COMPANY
Comparative Balance Sheets
December 31, 1941 and 1940

	December 31 1941	December 31 1940	Increase-Decrease* Amount	Increase-Decrease* Per Cent
Assets				
CURRENT ASSETS:				
Cash	$ 22,360	$ 21,085	$ 1,275	6.05%
Accounts Receivable	$215,420	$168,845	$46,575	27.58
Notes Receivable	34,050	41,600	7,550*	18.15*
Total Receivables	$249,470	$210,445	$39,025	18.54
Less Reserve for Bad Debts	11,065	15,430	4,365*	28.29*
Net Receivables	$238,405	$195,015	$43,390	22.25
Inventories:				
Finished Goods	$ 50,710	$ 42,300	$ 8,410	19.88
Goods in Process	30,260	24,860	5,400	21.72
Raw Materials	33,430	37,050	3,620*	9.77*
Total Inventories	$114,400	$104,210	$10,190	9.78
Total Current Assets	$375,165	$320,310	$54,855	17.13
FIXED ASSETS:				
Land	$ 30,500	$ 30,500	$ —	—
Building	$222,050	$193,000	$29,050	15.05
Less Reserve for Depreciation	65,480	59,320	6,160	10.38
Net	$156,570	$133,680	$22,890	17.12
Machinery and Equipment	$372,510	$349,515	$22,995	6.58
Less Reserve for Depreciation	188,310	153,615	34,695	22.59
Net	$184,200	$195,900	$11,700*	5.97*
Total Fixed Assets	$371,270	$360,080	$11,190	3.11
DEFERRED CHARGES:				
Unexpired Insurance	$ 7,270	$ 6,540	$ 730	11.16
Supplies Inventories	10,995	9,710	1,285	13.23
Total Deferred Charges	$ 18,265	$ 16,250	$ 2,015	12.40
	$764,700	$696,640	$68,060	9.77
Liabilities and Net Worth				
CURRENT LIABILITIES:				
Bank Loans	$ 30,000	$ 50,000	$20,000*	40.00*
Accounts Payable	68,215	51,350	16,865	32.84
Accrued Salaries and Expenses	25,435	22,680	2,755	12.15
Total Current Liabilities	$123,650	$124,030	$ 380*	.31*
FIRST MORTGAGE 6% BONDS	$150,000	$150,000	$ —	—
NET WORTH:				
7% Preferred Stock	$100,000	$ 90,000	$10,000	11.11
Common Stock	250,000	200,000	50,000	25.00
Surplus	141,050	132,610	8,440	6.36
Total Net Worth	$491,050	$422,610	$68,440	16.19
	$764,700	$696,640	$68,060	9.77

THE OSBORNE COMPANY

Condensed Comparative Profit and Loss Statements

For the Years Ended December 31, 1941 and 1940

| | Year Ended December 31 | | Increase-Decrease* | |
	1941	1940	Amount	Per Cent
Net Sales................	$969,140.00	$715,900.00	$253,240.00	35.37%
Less Cost of Goods Sold....	615,460.00	435,640.00	179,820.00	41.28
Gross Profit on Sales.......	$353,680.00	$280,260.00	$ 73,420.00	26.20
Selling Expenses...........	178,250.00	162,440.00	15,810.00	9.73
Net Profit on Sales........	$175,430.00	$117,820.00	$ 57,610.00	48.90
General and Administrative Expense.................	70,710.00	53,215.00	17,495.00	32.88
Net Profit on Operations....	$104,720.00	$ 64,605.00	$ 40,115.00	62.09
Net Financial Expense......	17,215.00	21,600.00	4,385.00*	20.30*
Net Profit for the Year, before Federal Income Tax	$ 87,505.00	$ 43,005.00	$ 44,500.00	103.48
Federal Income Tax........	12,065.00	5,700.00	6,365.00	111.67
Net Income..............	$ 75,440.00	$ 37,305.00	$ 38,135.00	102.22

Computing increases and decreases, and per cents thereof.

In the preparation of comparative statements and the determination of increases and decreases, accountants are frequently required to deal with positive and negative amounts of a related nature. For example, a bank balance may exist at one date and a bank overdraft at another; the bank balance may be shown on the asset side of one balance sheet, and the overdraft may be shown on the liability side of the other; or, the overdraft may be shown on the asset side in red ink, or in black ink with an asterisk.

Or, the purchase and sales discounts may be shown net in a condensed profit and loss statement; in one statement the purchase discounts may exceed the sales discounts while in another statement the sales discounts exceed the purchase discounts.

When a positive and a negative amount appear on the same line, care must be exercised in determining whether the difference should be shown as an increase or as a decrease. Some typical cases are illustrated below:

	This Year	Last Year	Increase Decrease*
Expenses:			
A............................	$3,000.00	$2,800.00	$ 200.00
B............................	500.00	800.00	300.00*
C............................	200.00*	1,000.00	1,200.00*
D............................	200.00	300.00*	500.00
E............................	1,000.00*	800.00*	200.00*
F............................	500.00*	800.00*	300.00
	$2,000.00	$2,700.00	$ 700.00*

The change in A is obviously an increase, and the change in B is obviously a decrease. In C, the change from an expense of $1,000.00 to an income of $200.00 is equivalent to a $1,200.00 decrease in expense. In D, the change from an income of $300.00 to an expense of $200.00 is equivalent to a $500.00 increase in expense. In E, the $200.00 increase in income is equivalent to a $200.00 decrease in expense. In F, the $300.00 decrease in income is equivalent to a $300.00 increase in expense.

Following are illustrations of some peculiar problems which arise in the determination of per cents of increase and decrease:

	This Year	Last Year	Increase-Decrease Amount	Per Cent
Positive amounts last year:				
A...........................	$1,500.00	$1,000.00	$ 500.00	50%
B...........................	500.00	1,000.00	500.00*	50*
C...........................	—	1,000.00	1,000.00*	100*
D...........................	500.00*	1,000.00	1,500.00*	150*
No amount last year:				
E...........................	1,500.00	—	1,500.00	—
F...........................	500.00*	—	500.00*	—
Negative amounts last year:				
G...........................	1,500.00*	1,000.00*	500.00*	—
H...........................	500.00	1,000.00*	1,500.00	—
I...........................	—	1,000.00*	1,000.00	—

The computations of the per cents in A, B, C, and D are obvious. No per cents can be computed in the second group; no base exists, because no amounts are shown in the Last Year column. In the third group, no per cents are shown because the Last Year amounts were negative quantities. Per cents might be computed and positive or negative signs determined on an algebraic basis, thus:

$$G \quad \frac{-\ 500}{-1,000} = +50\%$$

$$H \quad \frac{+1,500}{-1,000} = -150\%$$

$$I \quad \frac{+1,000}{-1,000} = -100\%$$

But such per cents obviously would be misleading, since the $+50\%$ accompanies a $500.00 decrease, and the -150% and the -100% accompany increases of $1,500.00 and $1,000.00. For this reason no per cents are shown when the base is a negative quantity.

Ratios.

The relation of one amount to another in a comparative statement may be shown by ratios computed by dividing the amount for the later date or period by the amount for the earlier date or period. Such ratios are illustrated below:

| | December 31 | | Ratio |
	1941	1940	1941 to 1940
Cash..........................	$ 4,000.00	$ 6,000.00	.67
Receivables...................	12,000.00	11,000.00	1.09

Such ratios are less commonly used than per cents of increase. However, ratios expressed decimally have certain advantages, as shown by the following brief illustration:

| | December 31 | | Increase-Decrease* | | Ratio |
	1941	1940	Amount	Per Cent	1941 to 1940
A................... $	—	$100.00	$ 100.00*	100*%	0
B...................	150.00	100.00	50.00	50	1.50
C...................	50.00	100.00	40.00*	50*	.50
D...................	1,500.00	100.00	1,400.00	1,400	15.00

In the first place, the Per Cent of Increase and Decrease column requires the use of red ink (or asterisks) and black ink, whereas the Ratio column requires black ink only.

In the second place, some of the figures in the Per Cent of Increase and Decrease column show increases and others show decreases (hence the significance of the asterisk or the red ink must be constantly recognized); the figures in the Ratio column are all on a common basis, expressing the ratios of the 1941 amounts to the 1940 amounts.

Finally, it is probably difficult for many persons to grasp quickly the significance of large per cents, such as 1,400%; it is much easier to understand that one item is 15 times as large as the other item.

On a previous page it was shown that per cents of increase and decrease are not stated if the base (or the amount for the preceding date or period) was zero or a minus quantity. The same rule is true of ratios.

A comparative profit and loss statement with comparisons expressed in ratios appears on the following page.

Mind the base.

When reading a statement similar to the following, in which ratios or per cents of increase and decrease are computed on two

THE OSBORNE COMPANY
Comparative Profit and Loss Statements
For the Years Ended December 31, 1941, 1940, and 1939

	Year Ended December 31				
	1941		1940		1939
	Amount	Ratio to 1940	Amount	Ratio to 1939	Amount
Gross Sales.........................	$982,400	1.35	$727,650	.78	$932,645
Returned Sales and Allowances.........	13,260	1.13	11,750	.41	28,600
Net Sales...........................	$969,140	1.35	$715,900	.79	$904,045
Cost of Goods Sold..................	615,460	1.41	435.640	.72	608,710
Gross Profit on Sales................	$353,680	1.26	$280,260	.95	$295,335
Selling Expenses:					
Salesmen's Salaries.................	$ 49,890	1.38	$ 36,210	.74	$ 48,645
Traveling Expense..................	20,310	1.04	19,615	.72	27,095
Advertising........................	31,375	1.03	30,600	.88	34,780
Branch Office Expense..............	23,050	.87	26,645	.82	32,610
Dealer Service.....................	25,700	1.04	24,810	1.45	17,065
Freight Out.......................	20,080	1.28	15,700	.75	20,810
Miscellaneous.....................	7,845	.89	8,860	1.07	8,285
Total Selling Expense.............	$178,250	1.10	$162,440	.86	$189,290
Net Profit on Sales..................	$175,430	1.49	$117,820	1.11	$106,045
General and Administrative Expense:					
Officers' Salaries..................	$ 25,000	1.25	$ 20,000	1.00	$ 20,000
Office Salaries.....................	13,750	1.40	9,840	.77	12,810
Rent..............................	4,000	1.00	4,000	.80	5,000
Stationery and Supplies.............	3,600	1.46	2,465	.88	2,800
Telephone and Telegraph............	4,680	1.61	2,910	1.01	2,870
Bad Debts.........................	8,625	1.04	8,295	.61	13,650
Legal and Auditing Expense.........	6,410	1.92	3,330	.91	3,650
Miscellaneous.....................	4,645	1.96	2,375	.48	4,900
Total General and Administrative Expense......................	$ 70,710	1.33	$ 53,215	.81	$ 65,680
Net Profit on Operations..............	$104,720	1.62	$ 64,605	1.60	$ 40,365
Net Financial Expense:					
Discount on Sales..................	$ 17,985	1.32	$ 13,640	.70	$ 19,520
Bond Interest......................	9,000	.88	10,200	.86	11,840
Other Interest.....................	3,075	.60	5,150	.87	5,940
Total...........................	$ 30,060	1.04	$ 28,990	.78	$ 37,300
Discount Received..................	$ 7,420	1.66	$ 4,460	.75	$ 5,980
Interest Received..................	4,030	1.43	2,810	.68	4,160
Miscellaneous.....................	1,395	11.63	120	.09	1,340
Total...........................	$ 12,845	1.74	$ 7,390	.64	$ 11,480
Net Financial Expense...........	$ 17,215	.80	$ 21,600	.84	$ 25,820
Net Profit, before Federal Income Tax..	$ 87,505	2.03	$ 43,005	2.96	$ 14,545
Federal Income Tax..................	12,065	2.12	5,700	3.35	1,700
Net Income.........................	$ 75,440	2.02	$ 37,305	2.90	$ 12,845

different bases, one must be continually on guard to avoid mis-interpretations. For instance, the foregoing statement shows that the gross sales for 1940 were .78 of those for 1939; in other words, the sales decreased 22%. The sales for 1941 were 1.35 of those for 1940; that is, the sales increased 35%.

But what relation does the 35% increase bear to the 22% decrease? There may be some confusion about this matter because the 35% increase was computed on a base of $727,650.00 whereas the 22% decrease was computed on a base of $932,645.00. To avoid this possible confusion, some analysts advocate com-puting both sets of ratios on one base—the figures for the earliest date or period. This procedure is illustrated below:

THE OSBORNE COMPANY
Comparative Profit and Loss Statements
For the Years 1941, 1940, and 1939

	1941		1940		1939
	Amount	Ratio to 1939	Amount	Ratio to 1939	Amount
Gross Sales	$982,400.00	1.05	$727,650.00	.78	$932,645.00
Returned Sales and Allowances	13,260.00	.46	11,750.00	.41	28,600.00
Net Sales	$969,140.00	1.07	$715,900.00	.79	$904,045.00

41

ANALYSIS OF WORKING CAPITAL

Working capital.

The working capital of a business is the excess of its current assets over its current liabilities. The working capital of The Osborne Company (mentioned in Chapter 40) at various dates is shown below:

	December 31			
	1941	1940	1939	1938
Current Assets:				
Cash................................	$ 22,360	$ 21,085	$ 10,740	$ 21,500
Receivables:				
Accounts Receivable..............	$215,420	$168,845	$239,240	$189,880
Notes Receivable................	34,050	41,600	50,095	58,230
Total.........................	$249,470	$210,445	$289,335	$248,110
Less Reserve for Bad Debts.......	11,065	15,430	30,095	20,250
Net Receivables................	$238,405	$195,015	$259,240	$227,860
Inventories:				
Finished Goods..................	$ 50,710	$ 42,300	$ 37,150	$ 49,390
Goods in Process................	30,260	24,860	17,650	28,600
Raw Materials...................	33,430	37,050	25,260	42,750
Total Inventories..............	$114,400	$104,210	$ 80,060	$120,740
Total Current Assets.........	$375,165	$320,310	$350,040	$370,100
Current Liabilities:				
Bank Loans......................	$ 30,000	$ 50,000	$ 85,000	$ 80,500
Accounts Payable.................	68,215	51,350	64,210	78,345
Accrued Salaries and Expenses.......	25,435	22,680	20,490	27,465
Total Current Liabilities......	$123,650	$124,030	$169,700	$186,310
Net Current Assets—Working Capital..	$251,515	$196,280	$180,340	$183,790

Changes indicated by ratios.

The changes in the current assets and current liabilities, over period of time, may be indicated by a statement similar to that in the following page.

This statement shows, among other things, that the current liabilities, at the end of 1941, were only .73 (or 73%) of those at the end of 1939. The cash and the inventories have increased while the receivables have decreased.

	Amounts—December 31			Ratios of Amounts at Ends of Stated Years to Amounts on December 31, 1939	
	1941	1940	1939	1940	1941
Current Assets:					
Cash......................	$ 22,360	$ 21,085	$ 10,740	2.08	1.96
Receivables—Net.............	238,405	195,015	259,240	.92	.75
Inventories:					
Finished Goods.............	50,710	42,300	37,150	1.37	1.14
Goods in Process...........	30,260	24,860	17,650	1.71	1.41
Raw Materials.............	33,430	37,050	25,260	1.32	1.47
Total Current Assets......	$375,165	$320,310	$350,040	1.07	.92
Current Liabilities:					
Bank Loans.................	$ 30,000	$ 50,000	$ 85,000	.35	.59
Accounts Payable.............	68,215	51,350	64,210	1.06	.80
Accrued Salaries and Expenses..	25,435	22,680	20,490	1.24	1.11
Total Current Liabilities...	$123,650	$124,030	$169,700	.73	.73
Working Capital................	$251,515	$196,280	$180,340	1.39	1.09
Net Sales for the Year..........	$969,140	$715,900	$904,045	1.07	.79

In such a statement it is desirable to show the changes in net sales, as these changes should have a bearing on the changes in current assets and current liabilities. For instance, we find that the sales of 1940 were only .79 of those for 1939; the receivables at the end of 1940 were .75 of those at the end of 1939. These conditions indicate that the receivables were of approximately the same age at the two dates. On the other hand, with a considerable decrease in net sales, all of the inventories have increased. Looking at the ratios for 1941, we find that the sales were slightly in excess of those for 1939, as shown by the sales ratio of 1.07 since the receivable ratio is .92, there appears to have been an improvement in the condition of the receivables; however, the investments in finished goods and goods in process have increased more rapidly than the sales have increased, thus suggesting a possible overinvestment in inventories.

Working capital ratio.

The ratio of current assets to current liabilities is regarded a of great significance as a measure of credit position. The amoun of working capital is evidence relative to the size of a loan whic may be made; the working capital ratio is evidence as to th desirability of making any loan.

The significance of the working capital ratio may be shown by an illustration. Assume that two companies have the following current assets and current liabilities:

	Company A	Company B
Total current assets......................	$200,000.00	$1,000.000.00
Total current liabilities...................	100,000.00	900,000.00
Net current assets.......................	$100,000.00	$ 100,000.00

Each company has a working capital of $100,000.00, but Company A's working capital position is relatively more favorable than that of Company B, because Company A has $2.00 of current assets per dollar of current liabilities whereas Company B has only $1.11 of current assets per dollar of current liabilities.

The working capital ratios of The Osborne Company are shown below. They were computed by dividing the current assets by the current liabilities.

	December 31			
	1941	1940	1939	1938
Total current assets....................	$375,165	$320,310	$350,040	$370,100
Total current liabilities.................	123,650	124,030	169,700	186,310
Working capital......................	$251,515	$196,280	$180,340	$183,790
Working capital ratio, or dollars of current assets per dollar of current liabilities....	3.03	2.58	2.06	1.99

Generally a working capital ratio of at least 2 to 1 is considered necessary to indicate a satisfactory current position.

The acid test.

The acid test ratio of The Osborne Company, or the ratio of cash and receivables (quick current assets) to current liabilities, is computed below.

	December 31			
	1941	1940	1939	1938
Quick current assets:				
Cash................................	$ 22,360	$ 21,085	$ 10,740	$ 21,500
Accounts and notes receivable—less reserve for bad debts................	238,405	195,015	259,240	227,860
Total cash and receivables..........	$260,765	$216,100	$269,980	$249,360
Total current liabilities.................	123,650	124,030	169,700	186,310
Excess of quick current assets over current liabilities.......................	$137,115	$ 92,070	$100,280	$ 63,050
Acid test ratio—Dollars of quick current assets per dollar of current liabilities....	2.11	1.74	1.59	1.34

The inventories are relatively much less current than the cash and receivables. The inventories must be sold before their proceeds can be used for the payment of current liabilities; this involves the uncertain factor of the ability to sell the inventories as well as the element of time required for the disposal of finished goods, for the conversion of raw materials and goods in process into finished goods, and for the sale of the finished product.

For these reasons many analysts supplement the working capital ratio by the so-called acid test ratio.

An acid test ratio of at least 1 to 1 is usually regarded as desirable.

Distribution of current assets.

It is obvious from the foregoing discussion of the acid test ratio that the current position of a company is not entirely dependent upon the ratio of total current assets to total current liabilities, but is affected by the kinds of current assets owned. This fact may be further emphasized by the following comparison of a company's financial condition at two dates:

| | December 31 | |
	1941	1940
Current assets:		
Cash...................................	$10,000.00	$30,000.00
Receivables.............................	20,000.00	20,000.00
Inventories.............................	30,000.00	10,000.00
Total current assets....................	$60,000.00	$60,000.00
Current liabilities.........................	30,000.00	30,000.00
Working capital...........................	$30,000.00	$30,000.00

The company had the same working capital ratio (2 to 1) at the two dates. However, its working capital position at the two dates was not the same. From one standpoint its position was much weaker at the end of 1941 than at the end of 1940 because of the shift from the very current asset of cash to the much less current asset of inventories. On the other hand, the amount ultimately to be realized from the current assets may have been increased because there are larger inventories to be converted at a profit. If, for instance, the inventories can be disposed of at 120% of cost, the ultimate realizable values of the current assets at the two dates may be compared as follows:

| | December 31 | |
	1941	1940
Cash.......................................	$10,000.00	$30,000.00
Receivables...............................	20,000.00	20,000.00
Inventories—at 120% of cost................	36,000.00	12,000.00
Total ultimate realizable value.............	$66,000.00	$62,000.00

Notwithstanding the fact that the current assets at the end
1941 may have a greater ultimate realizable value because of
e element of profit in the larger inventories, a shift from the more
rrent assets of cash and receivables to the less current asset of
ventories is usually regarded as undesirable. To determine
1ether any such shift is taking place, a statement similar to the
llowing may be prepared. The per cents are based on the cur-
nt assets of The Osborne Company.

	December 31			
	1941	1940	1939	1938
sh.	5.96%	6.58%	3.07%	5.81%
ceivables—Less Reserve	63.55%	60.88%	74.06%	61.57%
ventories:				
Finished Goods	13.52%	13.21%	10.61%	13.34%
Goods in Process	8.06	7.76	5.04	7.73
Raw Materials	8.91	11.57	7.22	11.55
Total Inventories	30.49%	32.54%	22.87%	32.62%
Total Current Assets	100.00%	100.00%	100.00%	100.00%

eakdown of working capital ratio.

Since any considerable shifts from the relatively more current
sets to the relatively less current assets, or vice versa, will
iterially affect a company's ability to pay its current debts
omptly, it may be desirable to break down the working capital
tio in a manner which will show whether the current liabilities
n be paid from the cash on hand, or whether their payment
ll require all of the cash and part of the proceeds of the receiva-
es, all of the cash and receivables and part of the proceeds of
e finished goods, and so on. The following rather extreme case
used as an emphatic illustration:

	December 31		
	1941	1940	1939
Cash	$30,000.00	$15,000.00	$ 5,000.00
Receivables	20,000.00	10,000.00	10,000.00
Finished goods	15,000.00	20,000.00	15,000.00
Goods in process	10,000.00	30,000.00	20,000.00
Raw materials	5,000.00	5,000.00	30,000.00
Total	$80,000.00	$80,000.00	$80,000.00

The current liabilities at each date were $40,000.00, and the
rking capital ratio at each date was therefore 2 to 1. However,
company's current position changed materially, as shown by
following summary. The ratios are computed on a cumulative
sis; for instance, at the end of 1941: The cash was equal to .75

of the current liabilities; the total cash and receivables were equal
to 1.25 times the current liabilities; and so on.

Table Showing Accumulation of Working Capital Ratio

	December 31		
	1941	1940	1939
Cash..	.750	.375	.125
Receivables.......................................	1.250	.625	.375
Finished goods....................................	1.625	1.125	.750
Goods in process.................................	1.875	1.875	1.250
Raw materials....................................	2.000	2.000	2.000

This table shows the following facts: At the end of 1939 the
cash, receivables, finished goods, and goods in process were required
to obtain a total in excess of the current liabilities; at the end of
1940, only the cash, receivables, and finished goods were required;
and at the end of 1941 only the cash and receivables were required.
The following is a similar tabulation for The Osborne Company.

Table Showing Accumulation of Working Capital Ratio

	December 31			
	1941	1940	1939	1938
Cash...	.18	.17	.06	.12
Receivables—Less reserve.....................	2.11	1.74	1.59	1.34
Finished goods...............................	2.52	2.08	1.81	1.61
Goods in process.............................	2.76	2.28	1.91	1.76
Raw materials...............................	3.03	2.58	2.06	1.99

Working capital turnover.

The adequacy of the working capital is also dependent upon
the frequency with which the current assets are converted. To
determine how rapidly the working capital moves, some analysts
compute a so-called working capital turnover by dividing the sales
for the period by the average working capital used during the
period. Following are the computations of the working capital
turnovers of The Osborne Company:

	1941	1940	1939
Net current assets:			
End of year......................	$251,515.00	$196,280.00	$180,340.00
Beginning of year.................	196,280.00	180,340.00	183,790.00
Average...........................	223,898.00	188,310.00	182,065.00
Net sales for the year................	969,140.00	715,900.00	904,045.00
Working capital turnovers.............	4.33	3.80	4.97

Criticism of working capital turnover.

It is assumed that an increase in the turnover indicates an
improvement. In the author's opinion, however, changes in work-

ing capital turnovers are of practically no significance, since they may result from so many different causes.

In the first place, the sales figure includes a profit; consequently the turnover is affected by the amount of the sales and by the profit thereon. To illustrate, assume the following facts:

	1941	1940
Sales....................................	$500,000.00	$400,000.00
Cost of sales and expenses..................	480,000.00	380,000.00
Net profit.................................	$ 20,000.00	$ 20,000.00
Working capital...........................	$100,000.00	$100,000.00
Working capital turnovers (sales divided by working capital).....................	5	4

The working capital turnover has increased from 4 to 5, but it can scarcely be said that this increase is an improvement; the increase really means that a greater strain was put on the working capital to earn the same profit as before. It would appear desirable, therefore, to make one computation which would show the frequency of the turnover, and another computation which would show the profitability of the turnover, thus:

Frequency of Working Capital Turnover

	1941	1940
Cost of sales and expenses..................	$480,000.00	$380,000.00
Working capital...........................	100,000.00	100,000.00
Number of turnovers....................	4.8	3.8

Profitability of Working Capital Turnover

	1941	1940
Net profit.................................	$ 20,000.00	$ 20,000.00
Working capital...........................	100,000.00	100,000.00
Ratio of profit to working capital.........	20%	20%

It will then be desirable to divide the rate of profit by the number of turnovers, to determine the rate of profit per turnover, thus:

Rate of Profit per Turnover

	1941	1940
Ratio of profit to working capital......................	20%	20%
Number of turnovers.................................	4.8	3.8
Ratio of profit per turnover........................	4.17%	5.26%

But there is still another objection to the working capital turnover, even if it is modified as already suggested. To illustrate the objection, let us assume the same sales, cost of sales, expenses, and net profit in two successive years; the company increased its current liabilities $20,000.00, thus reducing its working capital by the same amount. Turnovers are computed on the next page.

	1941	1940
Sales....................................	$500,000.00	$500,000.00
Cost of sales and expenses..................	450,000.00	450,000.00
Net profit..............................	$ 50,000.00	$ 50,000.00
Current assets...........................	$100,000.00	$100,000.00
Current liabilities........................	70,000.00	50,000.00
Working capital..........................	$ 30,000.00	$ 50,000.00

Frequency of Working Capital Turnover

	1941	1940
Cost of sales and expenses..................	$450,000.00	$450,000.00
Working capital..........................	30,000.00	50,000.00
Number of turnovers.....................	15	9

Profitability of Working Capital Turnover

	1941	1940
Net profit...............................	$50,000.00	$50,000.00
Working capital..........................	30,000.00	50,000.00
Ratio of profit to working capital...........	167%	100%

The changes in the foregoing per cents and turnovers seem to the author to be deceptive. The increase in the turnover from 9 to 15 and the increase in the rate of profit from 100% to 167% indicate an improvement in operations. As a matter of fact, the only change was an increase in the current liabilities, which is a disadvantage.

Ratios based on total current assets.

It would appear, therefore, that a more illuminating statement of the facts would be obtained by making the computations on the basis of the total current assets instead of on the basis of the net current assets. This procedure is illustrated with data of The Osborne Company.

		1941	1940	1939
Net sales..................................		$969,140	$715,900	$904,045
Cost of sales and expenses..................	(a)	893,700	678,595	891,200
Net income................................	(b)	$ 75,440	$ 37,305	$ 12,845
Current assets:				
Beginning of year........................		$320,310	$350,040	$370,100
End of year.............................		375,165	320,310	350,040
Average................................	(c)	$347,738	$335,175	$360,070
Current liabilities:				
Beginning of year........................		$124,030	$169,700	$186,310
End of year.............................		123,650	124,030	169,700
Average................................	(d)	$123,840	$146,865	$178,005
Frequency of current asset turnover (a ÷ c).....	(e)	2.57	2.02	2.48
Profitability of current asset turnover (b ÷ c)...	(f)	21.69%	11.13%	3.57%
Rate of profit per turnover (f ÷ e).............		8.44%	5.51%	1.44%
Working capital ratio (c ÷ d).................		3.03	2.58	2.06

The information furnished by these ratios and per cents may be compared with that shown by the following working capital turnovers, as computed on page 410.

Working capital turnovers.....................   4.33   3.80   4.97

Basing our judgment on the working capital turnovers, conditions in 1941 appear to have been poorer than those in 1939. This conclusion is incorrect; the decrease in the working capital turnover was caused principally by the large decrease in the current liabilities; this decrease in current liabilities increased the working capital used as a divisor in the computation and decreased the quotient, or turnover figure.

Using the other computations, we find improvements all along the line. The number of turnovers of current assets increased slightly—from 2.48 to 2.57; the rate of profit increased from 3.57% to 21.69% of the current assets; the rate of profit per turnover increased from 1.44% to 8.44%; and the working capital ratio increased from 2.06 to 3.03.

There is a slight element of fallacy in the foregoing computations, which should be noted and which can be corrected if greater precision is desired. In making the computation, $893,700.00 (cost of sales and expenses) ÷ $347,738.00 = 2.57, we are attempting to obtain a quotient, 2.57, indicative of the number of times the current assets were used in the payment of costs and expenses. But the costs and expenses included depreciation and amortization charges, which did not involve the use of current assets. If it is desired to eliminate this slight element of fallacy, the current asset turnover may be computed as follows:

	1941	1940	1939
Cost of sales and expenses..........	$893,700.00	$678,595.00	$891,200.00
Less depreciation charges...........	40,855.00	42,830.00	42,240.00
Remainder...................... (a)	$852,845.00	$635,765.00	$848,960.00
Current assets.................. (b)	347,738.00	335,175.00	360,070.00
Current asset turnovers (a ÷ b).....	2.45	1.90	2.36

Turnovers of various current assets.

The foregoing computations determine the frequency with which the total current assets are turned during a period. One may also determine the time required for the conversion of:

(1) Raw materials into finished goods.
(2) Finished goods into accounts receivable.
(3) Receivables into cash.

Raw material turnovers.

The method of computing the raw material turnovers is illustrated below, with the use of the data in the annual statements of The Osborne Company.

		1941	1940	1939
Cost of raw materials used (per statement of cost of goods manufactured)	(a)	$279,620	$185,490	$256,590
Raw material inventories:				
Beginning of year		$ 37,050	$ 25,260	$ 42,750
End of year		33,430	37,050	25,260
Average	(b)	$ 35,240	$ 31,155	$ 34,005
Number of raw material turnovers (a ÷ b)	(c)	7.93	5.95	7.55
Days per turnover (365 ÷ c)		46	61	48

This computation assumes a steady flow of production through the year and no great variations in the inventories during the year. If these conditions do not exist, the turnovers and turnover periods are misstated.

Finished goods turnovers.

The following computations, also, are based on assumptions of uniformity; it is assumed that monthly sales and monthly inventories are uniform during the year.

		1941	1940	1939
Cost of goods sold (per profit and loss statement)	(a)	$615,460	$435,640	$608,710
Finished goods inventories:				
Beginning of year		$ 42,300	$ 37,150	$ 49,390
End of year		50,710	42,300	37,150
Average	(b)	$ 46,505	$ 39,725	$ 43,270
Finished goods turnovers (a ÷ b)	(c)	13.23	10.97	14.07
Days per turnover (365 ÷ c)		28	33	26

Accounts receivable conversion periods.

Assuming an even flow of sales and a uniformity of collectibility during the year, the time required for the collection of receivables may be computed as follows:

		1941	1940	1939
Sales	(a)	$969,140	$715,900	$904,045
Trade receivables at end of year	(b)	249,470	210,445	289,335
Per cent of year's sales uncollected at end of year (b ÷ a)	(c)	25.74%	29.40%	32.00%
Average number of days' sales uncollected (365 × c)		94	107	117

Sum of turnover periods.

The average days required for one complete conversion of raw materials into finished goods, finished goods into receivables, and receivables into cash, are shown below:

	1941	1940	1939
Raw materials into finished goods.............	46	61	48
Finished goods into accounts receivable.......	28	33	26
Accounts receivable into cash.................	94	107	117
Total..	168	201	191

The 2-to-1 rule of thumb.

The working capital position of a company depends upon:

(1) The amount of working capital.

(2) The working capital ratio.

(3) The liquidity of the current assets; there are two factors of liquidity:

(a) The distribution of current assets. (For instance, referring to page 409, we find that The Osborne Company's current assets were somewhat more liquid at the end of 1941 than at the end of 1940, because the per cent of receivables to total current assets had increased and the per cent of total inventories to current assets had decreased.)

(b) The rapidity with which the current assets are turned. (For instance, as shown above, the number of days required for the conversion of each class of current assets was less in 1941 than in 1940.)

It is obvious that the working capital ratio alone is not an adequate measure of the working capital position; consideration must be given to the two factors of liquidity: distribution and rapidity of movement. Since this is true, it is apparent that setting up as a general standard a 2-to-1 working capital ratio is rather blindly following a rule of thumb. A 2-to-1 ratio might be a wholly inadequate ratio for a company with an unliquid distribution and slow movement of current assets; and it is equally possible that a lower ratio might be compensated by good distribution and movement.

Ratio of accounts payable to purchases.

It is desirable to determine, if possible, whether the current liabilities are being paid more promptly or less promptly than in the past. Some light may be thrown on this question by computing the ratio of accounts payable to purchases; an increase in the ratio indicates that a larger percentage of the accounts payable remains unpaid than in the past, and a decrease in the ratio indicates that a smaller percentage remains unpaid.

	1941	1940	1939
Accounts payable—end of year..................	$ 68,215	$ 51,350	$ 64,210
Raw material purchases during the year..........	276,000	197,280	239,100
Ratio of accounts payable to purchases...........	24.72%	26.03%	26.85%

If bank loans appear in the balance sheet, the ratio of accounts payable to purchases is not very significant because decreases in the accounts payable may be offset by increases in the bank loans, and vice versa. Nor is it of great value to determine the ratio of the total accounts payable and bank loans to purchases, since the bank loans may have been incurred for the payment of other expenses.

Fluctuations in operations and working capital.

In many businesses the sales fluctuate greatly from month to month; production also may vary from month to month, either because of the fluctuations in sales or because raw materials are available at only certain periods of the year.

In all businesses subject to considerable seasonal fluctuations in sales or production, the working capital varies from month to month. If we looked at a company's balance sheet a few months after the close of its heavy selling season and before the beginning of a heavy production season, we would probably find the inventories small, the receivables well realized, and the accounts payable and bank loans reduced to a minimum; the working capital ratio would be relatively high because of the small amount of current liabilities. A few months later, after a heavy production season and before the next heavy selling season, we might find the inventories large in anticipation of coming business, the receivables small because recent sales have been small, and the accounts payable and bank loans large as the result of large recent production; the working capital ratio then would be relatively low because of the abnormally large current liabilities.

The effect of seasonal operations on the working capital ratio throughout an annual cycle is illustrated by the following statement. To simplify the illustration, a trading company is used instead of a manufacturing company.

Current Assets and Current Liabilities
At Month Ends from December 31, 1940, to December 31, 1941

	Current Assets				Current Liabilities			Net Current Assets	Ratio
	Cash	Accounts Receivable	Inventories	Total	Accounts Payable	Bank Loans	Total		
1940—December 31	$13,000	$65,000	$50,000	$128,000	$60,000	$20,000	$80,000	$48,000	1.60
1941—January 31	15,000	53,000	52,000	120,000	48,000	20,000	68,000	52,000	1.76
February 28	18,500	41,000	46,000	105,500	33,000	20,000	53,000	52,500	1.99
March 31	18,500	33,000	38,500	90,000	28,000	10,000	38,000	52,000	2.37
April 30	18,000	26,000	30,500	74,500	26,500	—	26,500	48,000	2.81
May 31	24,000	21,000	27,000	72,000	27,500	—	27,500	44,500	2.62
June 30	22,000	33,000	24,500	79,500	35,500	—	35,500	44,000	2.24
July 31	24,000	32,000	27,000	83,000	40,500	—	40,500	42,500	2.05
August 31	19,500	47,000	40,000	106,500	61,500	—	61,500	45,000	1.73
September 30	7,000	54,000	46,500	107,500	58,500	—	58,500	49,000	1.84
October 31	11,000	71,000	51,500	133,500	67,500	10,000	77,500	56,000	1.72
November 30	9,000	90,000	49,000	148,000	70,500	10,000	80,500	67,500	1.84
December 31	21,000	68,000	50,500	139,500	57,000	10,000	67,000	72,500	2.08
Average	$17,000	$48,700	$41,000	$106,700	$47,200	$7,700	$54,900	$51,800	1.94

The natural business year.

From the foregoing illustration it is apparent that a balance sheet at the end of the calendar year is not indicative of the working capital position throughout the year if the operations are subject to any seasonal fluctuations. It is probable that the end of some month during the year marks the end of the company's natural business year—that is, the end of the cycle, when inventories, receivables, and payables are down.

From the standpoint of a businessman presenting a report to the bank for the purpose of obtaining credit, it seems a wise course to adopt a fiscal year corresponding with the natural business year, since the working capital position at the close of the natural business year usually is more attractive than that shown by the balance sheet at any other month end.

The banker also should be interested in knowing at what time during the year, and how well, the prospective borrower can "clean up." Since the end of the natural business year is the end of the clean-up period, a balance sheet as of that date would appear to be more informative than one prepared as of some arbitrary date such as December 31st, which may be the date when, because of seasonal requirements, the current position is the worst extended.

42

MISCELLANEOUS RATIOS

....

Ratio of net worth to total debt.

A company may improve its working capital position by converting a portion of its current liabilities into funded debt. Although this conversion will increase the working capital ratio, it will not improve the ratio of net worth to total debt; in fact, the latter ratio may suffer because of the expenses involved in the funding operations.

If the working capital ratio has increased, it is desirable to know whether the improvement was caused by profitable operations or merely by a change in the nature of the liabilities. If it was caused by profitable operations, the improvement may be expected to continue. If it was caused by a funding operation, the question naturally arises whether the improved working capital position can be maintained or whether the working capital will again become impaired and another, but perhaps impossible, funding program thus be required.

The computation of the ratio of net worth to total debt is illustrated below, using the data of The Osborne Company appearing in Chapter 40. It will be noted that an improvement in the ratio indicates an improvement in the condition.

	December 31			
	1941	1940	1939	1938
Net Worth:				
Capital stock:				
Preferred......................	$100,000	$ 90,000	$ 90,000	$ 90,000
Common.......................	250,000	200,000	200,000	200,000
Surplus.........................	141,050	132,610	103,840	115,045
Total net worth...............	$491,050	$422,610	$393,840	$405,045
Liabilities:				
Current liabilities.................	$123,650	$124,030	$169,700	$186,310
Fixed liabilities..................	150,000	150,000	180,000	200,000
Total liabilities...............	$273,650	$274,030	$349,700	$386,310
Ratio of net worth to total debt.......	1.79	1.54	1.13	1.05

Ratio of security to fixed liabilities.

Since the fixed liabilities are directly secured by mortgages on fixed assets, the mortgage holders are interested in the ratio of the security to the liability. If obtainable, market values of the mortgaged property should be used in the computation; if these values are not available, depreciated book values may be used, as in the following illustration which is based on the assumption that the bonds are secured by a mortgage on all of the fixed assets.

| | December 31 | | | |
	1941	1940	1939	1938
Land..............................	$ 30,500	$ 30,500	$ 30,500	$ 30,500
Buildings..........................	156,570	133,680	139,470	145,260
Machinery and equipment...........	184,200	195,900	207,970	226,890
Total.........................	$371,270	$360,080	$377,940	$402,650
Fixed liabilities....................	$150,000	$150,000	$180,000	$200,000
Ratio of security to fixed liabilities.....	2.48	2.40	2.10	2.01

If a sinking fund is being maintained for the redemption of the fixed liabilities, the method of computing the ratio of security to debt will depend upon the nature of the sinking fund. To illustrate, assume that a company has fixed liabilities of $500,000.00, a sinking fund of $100,000.00, and mortgaged fixed assets of $700,000.00.

If the sinking fund is invested in the company's own bonds, which are being held alive until their maturity, the ratio should be computed as follows:

Fixed assets...	$700,000.00
Bonds outstanding ($500,000.00 minus $100,000.00 in the fund).......	400,000.00
Ratio of security to bonds outstanding............................	1.75

But if the sinking fund is invested in other securities, the ratio should be computed as follows:

Fixed assets..	$700,000.00
Sinking fund..	100,000.00
Total...	$800,000.00
Bonds outstanding......................................	500,000.00
Ratio of security to bonds outstanding....................	1.60

Book value per share of stock.

An increase in the total capital stock and surplus of a company indicates that the aggregate net worth has increased, but this does not necessarily mean an increase in the value of the individual stockholdings; the increase in net worth may have been caused by the issuance of additional stock. It is therefore desirable to determine the book value of each share of stock.

If there is only one class of stock, the book value per share is mputed by dividing the total net worth (capital stock and surus, including all appropriated surplus reserves) by the number shares of stock outstanding. If common and preferred stocks e outstanding, the question arises concerning the apportionment the surplus between the two classes of stock. If the preferred ock is non-participating and if no dividends are in arrears, the tire surplus should be allocated to the common stock. If the eferred stock is fully participating, the surplus must be apporned ratably between the two classes of stock.

Following is the computation of the book value per share of mmon stock of The Osborne Company, on the assumption that e preferred stock is non-participating. It will be noted that, hereas the common stock and surplus increased during 1941, e book value per share of common stock decreased because of the suance of 500 additional common shares.

| | December 31 | | | |
	1941	1940	1939	1938
mmon stock	$250,000	$200,000	$200,000	$200,000
rplus	141,050	132,610	103,840	115,045
Total	$391,050	$332,610	$303,840	$315,045
mber of shares outstanding	2,500	2,000	2,000	2,000
ok value per share	$156.42	$166.30	$151.92	$157.52

atio of net worth to fixed assets.

Is there a tendency toward overinvestment in fixed assets? To tain a partial answer to this question, we may compute the ratio net worth to fixed assets.

| | | December 31 | | | |
		1941	1940	1939	1938
et worth	(a)	$491,050	$422,610	$393,840	$405,045
xed assets—less depreciation	(b)	371,270	360,080	377,940	402,650
atio of net worth to fixed assets (a ÷ b)		1.32	1.17	1.04	1.01

atio of sales to fixed assets.

Additional light can be thrown on this question by computing e ratio of sales to fixed assets, a ratio which is indicative of the e made of the fixed assets.

		1941	1940	1939
les for the year	(a)	$969,140	$715,900	$904,045
xed assets—end of year	(b)	371,270	360,080	377,940
atio of sales to fixed assets (a ÷ b)		2.61	1.99	2.39

Ratio of cost of goods manufactured to fixed assets.

Ratios of sales to fixed assets are affected by the profit o the sale, an element which should be eliminated to determin the relative use made of the fixed assets in production. Fo this reason, and also to eliminate the element of finished good inventory variation, it is preferable to use the cost of goods manu factured instead of the sales. Ratios based on the cost of manu facture will still include the disturbing element of variation i manufacturing costs due to changes in the price level.

		1941	1940	1939
Cost of goods manufactured....................	(a)	$623,870	$440,790	$596,47
Fixed assets—end of year.....................	(b)	371,270	360,080	377,94
Ratio of cost of goods manufactured to fixed assets				
(a ÷ b)..................................		1.68	1.22	1.58

Disposition of manufacturing costs.

The ratio of cost of goods manufactured to fixed assets is not conclusive measure of the effectiveness of the use of the fixed assets Manufacturing costs may have been incurred in an attempt t keep the fixed assets in operation, but, because of less effectiv planning, larger amounts may be tied up in work in process; ol because of decreases in sales, larger amounts may be tied up i finished goods inventories. For these reasons, it may be desirabl to determine the disposition of the manufacturing costs, by com putations similar to the following:

	1941	1940	1939
Manufacturing costs:			
Goods in process—beginning of year............	$ 24,860	$ 17,650	$ 28,60
Raw materials used..........................	279,620	185,490	256,59
Direct labor................................	199,690	136,700	187,33
Manufacturing expense.......................	149,960	125,810	141,60
Total.................................	$654,130	$465,650	$614,12
Disposition of manufacturing costs:			
Goods in process—end of year.................	$ 30,260	$ 24,860	$ 17,65
Goods sold.................................	573,160	398,490	559,32
Finished goods—end of year..................	50,710	42,300	37,15
Total.................................	$654,130	$465,650	$614,12
Percentage distribution of costs:			
Goods in process—end of year.................	4.63%	5.34%	2.87
Goods sold.................................	87.62	85.58	91.08
Finished goods—end of year..................	7.75	9.08	6.05
Total.................................	100.00%	100.00%	100.00

The amounts shown above as the cost of goods sold do no represent the cost of all goods sold, but only the cost of the good sold during the year which were manufactured during the year, determined on the first-in first-out theory, as follows:

	1941	1940	1939
Cost of goods sold	$615,460	$435,640	$608,710
Inventory at beginning of year—regarded as first goods sold	42,300	37,150	49,390
Goods manufactured and sold during year	$573,160	$398,490	$559,320

Ratio of net income to net worth.

The computation of the ratio of net income to capital investment is illustrated below:

	1941	1940	1939
Net worth—end of year:			
Capital stock:			
Common	$250,000.00	$200,000.00	$200,000.00
Preferred	100,000.00	90,000.00	90,000.00
Surplus	141,050.00	132,610.00	103,840.00
Total net worth	$491,050.00	$422,610.00	$393,840.00
Net income for the year	$ 75,440.00	$ 37,305.00	$ 12,845.00
Ratio of net income to net worth	15.36%	8.83%	3.26%

It is somewhat more accurate to determine the ratio of income by using the average net worth for the year, thus:

	1941	1940	1939
Net worth:			
Beginning of year	$422,610.00	$393,840.00	$405,045.00
End of year	491,050.00	422,610.00	393,840.00
Average	$456,830.00	$408,225.00	$399,443.00
Net income	$ 75,440.00	$ 37,305.00	$ 12,845.00
Ratio of net income to net worth	16.51%	9.14%	3.22%

Net income per share of common stock.

If the preferred stock is non-participating, the income per share of common stock is directly affected by the dividend requirements on the preferred stock. To illustrate, the average earnings of The Osborne Company per share of common and preferred stock are shown below:

	1941	1940	1939
Net income for the year	$75,440.00	$37,305.00	$12,845.00
Total common and preferred shares outstanding	3,500	2,900	2,900
Average earnings per share of common and preferred stock	$ 21.55	$ 12.86	$ 4.43

In 1939, the average income of $4.43 per share (net income divided by total preferred and common shares) was less than the $7.00 per share dividend requirement on the preferred stock therefore the income per share of common stock was less tha $4.43. In 1940 and 1941, the average income per share of commo and preferred was more than the $7.00 preferred dividend require ment; therefore the income per share of common was more tha $12.86 in 1940 and more than $21.55 in 1941. The rates of incom per share of common stock are shown below:

	1941	1940	1939
Net income for the year....................	$75,440.00	$37,305.00	$12,845.0
Dividend requirements on preferred stock at $7.00 per share.........................	7,000.00	6,300.00	6,300.0
Net income applicable to common stock......	$68,440.00	$31,005.00	$ 6,545.0
Shares of common stock outstanding at end of year...................................	2,500	2,000	2,00
Income per share of common stock........... $	27.38 $	15.50 $	3.2

Ratio of returns to gross sales.

In the analysis of the profit and loss statement to account fo variations in net profit, the returns and allowances may be con sidered first. Material increases in the ratio of returns an allowances to gross sales indicate increasing customer dissatisfac tion and an increasing expense in adjustments thereof.

	1941	1940	1939
Gross sales....................................	$982,400	$727,650	$932,64
Returns and allowances.......................	13,260	11,750	28,60
Ratio of returns and allowances to gross sales.....	1.35%	1.61%	3.07

Causes of change in gross profit.

The amounts of gross profit of The Osborne Company durin three years, and the ratios based on the gross profits of the prece ing year, are shown below:

	1941	1940	1939
Gross profit on sales.....................	$353,680.00	$280,260.00	$295,335.0
Ratio to gross profit of preceding year.....	126.197+%	94.895+%	

The changes in gross profits are caused by changes in th volume of sales and in the rates of gross profit on the sales. Th changes in net sales are shown below:

	1941	1940	1939
Net sales.............................	$969,140.00	$715,900.00	$904,045.0
Ratio to preceding year...............	135.373+%	79.188+%	

The changes in the rates of gross profit are shown below:

	1941	1940	1939
ᴀte of gross profit	36.494+%	39.147+%	32.668+%
ᴀtio to preceding year	93.221+%	119.835+%	

The foregoing figures show that the amount of gross profit for ᴵ41 was 126.197% of that for 1940. This increase was the result ᴛwo factors: The sales for 1941 were 135.373% of those for 1940, ᴵt the rate of gross profit in 1941 was only 93.221% of that for ᴵ40. These factors may be marshalled as follows:

	Ratio of	
	1941 to 1940	1940 to 1939
Ratio of net sales	135.373%	79.188%
Multiply by ratio of gross profit rates	93.221	119.835
Ratio of gross profit amounts	126.197%	94.895%

ᴴhanges in manufacturing costs.

From the data available in a profit and loss statement and in ᴤ supporting statement showing the cost of goods manufactured, ᴵ is usually impossible to determine whether a change in the rate ᴵ gross profit was caused by a change in the cost of goods sold or a ᴧange in the selling prices.

Some analysts believe that information can be obtained with ᴤspect to changes in manufacturing costs by computing the ratios ᴵ materials, labor, and manufacturing expenses to the total ᴸereof, as follows:

	1941	1940	1939
ᴀnounts:			
Raw materials used	$279,620.00	$185,490.00	$256,590.00
Direct labor	199,690.00	136,700.00	187,330.00
Manufacturing expense	149,960.00	125,810.00	141,600.00
Total	$629,270.00	$448,000.00	$585,520.00
ᴀrcentage distribution:			
Raw materials	44.44%	41.41%	43.82%
Direct labor	31.73	30.51	31.99
Manufacturing expenses	23.83	28.08	24.19
Total	100.00%	100.00%	100.00%

It appears to the author that the changes in the ratios, as ᴸustrated above, disclose no conclusive information. A compari-ᴨn of the per cents for 1941 and 1940 shows that the manufactur-ᴵg expense per cent has decreased whereas the material and labor ᴇr cents have increased. This information might lead to the con-ᴧusion that the unit costs of materials and labor had increased:

but when we note that the total manufacturing costs increase
materially in 1941, it appears more likely that the decrease in th
manufacturing expense per cent was caused by the fact that th
manufacturing expenses are fairly constant in amount and tha
any large increase in production will therefore reduce the per cen
of such expenses to the total production costs.   The increases i
the material and labor per cents may therefore mean nothing s
far as unit costs are concerned, because the decrease in the expens
per cent must be offset by percentage increases elsewhere to mak
up the 100% total.

Ratios of expenses to sales.

In the analysis of the profit and loss statement, it is customar
to determine the ratios of expenses to net sales.   This analysi
may be carried to the extent of determining the per cent of eacl
item of expense to the net sales.   The following illustration show
the per cents of certain classes of expense:

	1941	1940	1939
Net sales.............................	$969,140.00	$715,900.00	$904,045.0
Selling expenses:			
Amount...........................	$178,250.00	$162,440.00	$189,290.0
Per cent of net sales.................	18.39%	22.69%	20.94%
General and administrative expenses:			
Amount...........................	$ 70,710.00	$ 53,215.00	$ 65,680.0
Per cent of net sales.................	7.30%	7.43%	7.26%
Net financial expenses:			
Amount...........................	$ 17,215.00	$ 21,600.00	$ 25,820.0
Per cent of net sales.................	1.77%	3.02%	2.86%

It is doubtful whether such per cents are of great analytica
value, because they are affected by changes in the net sales as wel
as in the expenses.   For instance, it may appear, at first glance
that a decrease in the selling expense ratio from 22.69% to 18.37%
is indicative of a better control over the selling expenses.   But thi
decrease in the rate was caused by a large increase in the net sales
which more than offset (in the percentage computation) th
increase in the selling expenses.   It therefore appears to the autho
that a clearer picture is given by computing the following per cents

Net sales:	
1941..	$969,140.00
1940..	715,900.00
Per cent of increase....................................	35.37%
Selling expenses:	
1941..	$178,250.00
1940..	162,440.00
Per cent of increase.....................................	9.73%

This data presents the following question to the management: s a 9.73% increase in selling expenses justified in view of the 5.37% increase in net sales?   Such a question would not be so kely to arise if the management merely noted that the selling xpenses were 22.69% of the sales in 1940 and 18.37% of the sales i 1941, as the increase in expenses would not be made apparent.

ad debt ratios.

Relative increases or decreases in bad debt losses may be dislosed by determining the ratio of bad debts to net sales, thus:

	1941	1940	1939
[et sales	$969,140.00	$715,900.00	$904,045.00
ad debts	8,625.00	8,295.00	13,650.00
:atio of bad debts to sales	.89%	1.16%	1.51%

This ratio is frequently meaningless because the bad debt xpense shown in the profit and loss statement is the provision for)ss (rather than the amount of accounts written off) and because he provision may be estimated as an arbitrary and perhaps tandardized percentage of the sales.

)iscount ratios.

Are customers taking greater or less advantage of the cash disount privilege?   The answer to this question is indicated by the)llowing ratios:

	1941	1940	1939
[et sales	$969,140.00	$715,900.00	$904,045.00
'ash discounts on sales	17,985.00	13,640.00	19,520.00
:atio of discounts to sales	1.86%	1.90%	2.16%

These ratios are not conclusive, however, since they may be ffected by changes in discount rates and in the sales distribution mong commodities subject to different rates.

Subject to much the same qualifications, the changes in the)llowing ratios are indicative of the extent to which the company s taking advantage of its discount opportunities.

	1941	1940	1939
'urchases	$276,000.00	$197,280.00	$239,100.00
'urchase discounts	7,420.00	4,460.00	5,980.00
:atio of discounts to purchases	2.69%	2.26%	2.50%

)uestionnaire grouping of ratios.

The interpretation of ratios may be facilitated by assembling hem as answers to a questionnaire.   When this is done all ratios

should be computed in such a manner that increases in the ratio
will be indicative of improvements. This may require some
modification of the procedures already explained; such a modification is discussed in the note following the tabulation. The ratio
are those of The Osborne Company; the numbers in parentheses
indicate the pages on which the computations of the ratios are
shown.

	Page	1941	1940	1939
Is the working capital position improving?				
Working capital ratio—end of year	(407)	3.03	2.58	2.06
Acid test ratio..................	(407)	2.11	1.74	1.59
Current asset turnovers per year..	(412)	2.57	2.02	2.48
Raw material turnovers per year..	(414)	7.93	5.95	7.55
Finished goods turnovers.........	(414)	13.23	10.97	14.07
Ratio of sales to receivables......	(Note)	3.88	3.40	3.12
Is the stockholders' equity increasing?				
Ratio of net worth to total debt..	(419)	1.79	1.54	1.13
Book value per share of common stock.......................	(421)	$156.42	$166.30	$151.92
Is the security for the fixed liabilities increasing?				
Ratio of security to fixed liabilities.	(420)	2.48	2.40	2.10
Is there any tendency toward overinvestment in fixed assets?				
Ratio of net worth to fixed assets.	(421)	1.32	1.17	1.04
Ratio of cost of goods manufactured to fixed assets..........	(422)	1.68	1.22	1.58
Is the net income increasing?				
Per cent of net income to net worth	(423)	15.36%	8.83%	3.26
Net income per share of common stock.......................	(423)	$ 21.55	$ 12.86	$ 4.43
Per cent of net income to sales...	(398)	7.78%	5.21%	1.42
Per cent of gross profit to sales...	(398)	36.49%	39.15%	32.67

Note.—On page 414 the condition of the accounts receivable
was determined by computing the following per cents and turnover periods:

	1941	1940	1939
Per cent of year's sales uncollected..................	25.74%	29.40%	32.00
Average number of days' sales uncollected............	94	107	117

Improvements are indicated by decreases, as it is better to have
only 25.74% of the year's sales uncollected than to have 29.40%
These per cents were obtained by dividing the receivables by the
sales. The ratios (3.88, 3.40, and 3.12) shown in the tabulation
above were obtained by dividing the sales by the receivables
in order that increases in the ratios would indicate improved
conditions.

43

PROFIT AND LOSS ANALYSIS

··

Unit cost and profit statements.

Adequate managerial control of manufacturing and selling operations requires more detailed information than is shown by the profit and loss statement of the business as a whole.

If the business is divided into departments, a profit and loss statement for each department is desirable, so that the unprofitable departments can be determined and steps can be taken, if possible, to remedy the conditions which cause the unsatisfactory results.

It is desirable to prepare statements showing the cost and gross profit on each product; such statements may disclose products which are being sold at an inadequate gross profit or even at a loss. The preparation of such statements necessitates the keeping of adequate and reliable records of manufacturing costs.

If these records are available, a statement can be prepared showing, in detail as to material, labor, and overhead, the per-unit costs of goods manufactured and sold. Such a statement is more informative if it covers two years.

The statement on page 430 shows, among other things, the following changes in unit costs:

The raw material costs decreased from \$28.17 to \$27.25; the direct labor costs increased from \$35.32 to \$37.41; the manufacturing expenses increased from \$13.51 to \$15.34; the total cost of manufacture increased from \$77.00 to \$80.00; the cost of goods sold increased from \$76.66 to \$79.34.

To determine the unit cost of goods sold, the opening and closing inventories of finished goods must be taken into consideration. For instance, in 1941:

The 3995 units manufactured cost..............	\$319,600 or \$80 per unit
The 900 units in the opening inventory cost....	69,300 or \$77 per unit
The 4895 units available for sale cost...........	\$388,900
The 825 units on hand at the end of the year are assumed to be part of those manufactured during the year for.............	66,000 or \$80 per unit
The 4070 units sold cost.......................	\$322,900 or \$79.34 per unit

THE *A B C* COMPANY

Comparative Statements of Cost of Goods Manufactured and Sold
In Total and Per Unit
For the Years Ended December 31, 1941 and 1940

	Year Ended December 31, 1941					Year Ended December 31, 1940				
	Units	Material	Direct Labor	Manu-facturing Expense	Total	Units	Material	Direct Labor	Manu-facturing Expense	Total
In Process, January 1...............	40	$ 800	$ 740	$ 310	$ 1,850	50	$ 1,050	$ 940	$ 360	$ 2,350
Put Into Process During Year...............	4,000	108,975	149,500	61,525	320,000	5,000	140,900	176,750	67,620	385,270
Total...............	4,040	$109,775	$150,240	$61,835	$321,850	5,050	$141,950	$177,690	$67,980	$387,620
In Process, December 31...............	45	920	780	550	2,250	40	800	740	310	1,850
Manufactured During Year...............	3,995	$108,855	$149,460	$61,285	$319,600	5,010	$141,150	$176,950	$67,670	$385,770
Manufacturing Cost per Unit...............		$ 27.25	$ 37.41	$15.34	($80.00)		$ 28.17	$ 35.32	$13.51	($77.00)
Finished Goods Inventory, January 1.....	900	at $77.00			69,300	850	at $75.00	(1931 cost)		63,750
Total...............	4,895				$388,900	5,860				$449,520
Finished Goods Inventory, December 31..	825	at $80.00			66,000	900	at $77.00			69,300
Sold...............	4,070	at $79.34			$322,900	4,960	at $76.66			$380,220

If a company manufactures and sells only one commodity, such a statement may be prepared for the business as a whole. If several commodities are dealt in, a separate statement might be prepared for each commodity.

Profit and loss and expense statements.

The following statements illustrate a total and per-unit profit and loss statement and expense schedule. If several commodities are dealt in, a profit and loss statement carried only to the gross profit line might be prepared for each commodity.

THE _A B C_ COMPANY　　　　　　　　　Exhibit C
Comparative Profit and Loss Statement
In Total and Per Unit Sold
For the Years Ended December 31, 1941 and 1940

	1941 Total	1941 Per Unit	1940 Total	1940 Per Unit	Increase Decrease* Per Unit
Number of Units Sold..........		4,070		4,960	
Gross Sales....................	$468,050	$115.00	$620,000	$125.00	$10.00*
Less Returned Sales and Allowances......................	5,700	1.40	6,800	1.37	.03
Net Sales.....................	$462,350	$113.60	$613,200	$123.63	$10.03*
Cost of Goods Sold (Exhibit D)...	322,900	79.34	380,220	76.66	2.68
Gross Profit on Sales...........	$139,450	$ 34.26	$232,980	$ 46.97	$12.71*
Less Selling Expense (Schedule 1)..	62,635	15.39	76,200	15.36	.03
Net Profit on Sales.............	$ 76,815	$ 18.87	$156,780	$ 31.61	$12.74*
Less General Expense (Schedule 2)	49,785	12.23	68,750	13.86	1.63*
Net Profit on Operations........	$ 27.030	$ 6.64	$ 88,030	$ 17.75	$11.11*
Less Net Financial Expense (Exhibit G)......................	4,235	1.04	5,540	1.12	.08*
Net Income...................	$ 22,795	$ 5.60	$ 82,490	$ 16.63	$11.03*

THE _A B C_ COMPANY　　　　　　Exhibit C
Comparative Statement of Selling Expenses　　Schedule 1
In Total and Per Unit Sold
For the Years Ended December 31, 1941 and 1940

	1941 Total	1941 Per Unit	1940 Total	1940 Per Unit	Increase Decrease* Per Unit
Number of Units Sold..............		4,070		4,960	
Advertising.......................	$20,000	$ 4.92	$30,000	$ 6.05	$1.13*
Salesmen's Salaries................	25,000	6.14	25,000	5.04	1.10
Salesmen's Expenses...............	9,130	2.24	10,300	2.08	.16
Freight and Cartage Out...........	5,670	1.39	6,400	1.29	.10
Miscellaneous Selling Expense.......	2,835	.70	4,500	.90	.20*
Totals.......................	$62,635	$15.39	$76,200	$15.36	$ .03

Departmental Operations

Basis of illustration.

Let us assume that a company's statements for three years showed the following facts:

	1941	1940	1939
Net Sales............................	$412,250.00	$380,600.00	$390,550.00
Less Cost of Goods Sold................	207,662.00	223,166.00	212,675.00
Gross Profit on Sales..................	$204,588.00	$157,434.00	$177,875.00
Rate of Gross Profit..................	49.63%	41.36%	45.54%

This business operates three departments. In accounting for the changes in the net sales and in the rates of gross profit, it is very desirable to deal with the departments individually.

Changes in volume of sales.

The increases and decreases in the departmental sales are shown below.

	1941		1940		
	Amount	Ratio to 1940	Amount	Ratio to 1939	1939
Department A..........	$285,600.00	239%	$119,375.00	58%	$204,370.00
Department B..........	76,350.00	41	185,325.00	147	125,900.00
Department C..........	50,300.00	66	75,900.00	126	60,280.00
Total...............	$412,250.00	108	$380,600.00	97	$390,550.00

This statement shows that, although the sales of the business as a whole did not increase or decrease greatly (the sales of 1940 were 97% of those for 1939, and the sales for 1941 were 108% of those for 1940), there were radical fluctuations within the individual departments.

Changes in rates of gross profit.

The changes in the gross profit rates of the three departments and of the business as a whole are shown below.

	1941	1940	1939
Department A:			
Sales............................	$285,600.00	$119,375.00	$204,370.00
Cost of Goods Sold..................	121,740.00	53,370.00	94,725.00
Gross Profit.......................	$163,860.00	$ 66,005.00	$109,645.00
Rate of Gross Profit................	57.38%	55.29%	53.65%
Department B:			
Sales............................	$ 76,350.00	$185,325.00	$125,900.00
Cost of Goods Sold..................	51,190.00	117,460.00	76,132.00
Gross Profit.......................	$ 25,160.00	$ 67,865.00	$ 49,768.00
Rate of Gross Profit................	32.95%	36.62%	39.53%

Department C:

Sales...............................	$ 50,300.00	$ 75,900.00	$ 60,280.00
Cost of Goods Sold..................	34,732.00	52,336.00	41,818.00
Gross Profit........................	$ 15,568.00	$ 23,564.00	$ 18,462.00
Rate of Gross Profit................	30.95%	31.05%	30.63%

Total:

Sales...............................	$412,250.00	$380,600.00	$390,550.00
Cost of Goods Sold..................	207,662.00	223,166.00	212,675.00
Gross Profit on Sales...............	$204,588.00	$157,434.00	$177,875.00
Rate of Gross Profit................	49.63%	41.36%	45.54%

This statement shows that the rate for Department *A* is steadily increasing; the rate for Department *B* is steadily decreasing; and the rates for Department *C* and for the business as a whole are varying.

Effect of changes in departmental volume and rates.

Viewing the business as a whole, we find the following changes in sales and amounts of gross profit:

	Sales		Gross Profit	
	Amount	Per Cent of 1939	Amount	Per Cent of 1939
1941....................	$412,250.00	106%	$204,588.00	115%
1940....................	380,600.00	97	157,434.00	88
1939....................	390,550.00		177,875.00	

Why should the gross profit of 1940 have been only 88% of that for 1939, when the 1940 sales were 97% of those for 1939? And why should an increase of 6% in the sales for 1941 have caused a 15% increase in the gross profit? The answer, of course, lies in the variation in the average rate of gross profit for the business as a whole.

This variation in the average rate of gross profit for the business as a whole was, of course, partly caused by the variation in the departmental gross profit rates, shown on this and the preceding page.

But the change in the average rate was also caused by changes in the relative amounts of business done by each department. It will be noted that the rate for Department *A* is very high (varying from 53.65% to 57.38%), whereas the rates for the other two departments are in the thirties. Obviously, the average rate of gross profit for the business as a whole will increase if the sales of Department *A* become an increasing percentage of the total sales, and the average rate will decrease if the sales of Department *A* become a decreasing percentage of the total sales. It will therefore be of interest to note the relative amounts of business done by the three departments.

	Amount of Sales			Per Cent of Total		
	1941	1940	1939	1941	1940	1939
Department A.......	$285,600	$119,375	$204,370	69.28%	31.36%	52.33%
Department B.......	76,350	185,325	125,900	18.52	48.69	32.24
Department C.......	50,300	75,900	60,280	12.20	19.95	15.43
Total..............	$412,250	$380,600	$390,550	100.00%	100.00%	100.00%

It is obvious that the decrease in the average rate of gross profit from 45.54% in 1939 to 41.36% in 1940 was largely due to the decrease in the percentage of business done by Department A, the high gross profit rate department. And the increase in the average rate from 41.36% in 1940 to 49.63% in 1941 was largely due to the fact that the sales in Department A increased from 31% to 69% of the total.

The combined effect of changes in the departmental rates and changes in the per cent of total business done in each department may be shown by a computation similar to the following.

	Per Cent of Total Sales	Departmental Rate of Gross Profit	Components of the Average Rate of Gross Profit		
			1941	1940	1939
Department A..............	69.28% ×	57.38% =	39.75%		
	31.36% ×	55.29% =		17.34%	
	52.33% ×	53.65% =			28.08%
Department B..............	18.52% ×	32.95% =	6.10		
	48.69% ×	36.62% =		17.83	
	32.24% ×	39.53% =			12.74
Department C..............	12.20% ×	30.95% =	3.78		
	19.95% ×	31.05% =		6.19	
	15.43% ×	30.63% =			4.72
Average Gross Profit Rate of the Business			49.63%	41.36%	45.54%

Departmental merchandise turnovers.

The foregoing statement shows that the gross profit rate of the business as a whole was very adversely affected in 1940 by the large decrease in sales in Department A, where the highest rate of gross profit is earned. The following statement shows that the turnover in Department A also suffered in 1940.

The foregoing statement also shows that Departments B and C are relatively less valuable than Department A from the standpoint of volume of sales and rate of gross profit. The following statement shows that Departments B and C are losing ground in the matter of inventory turnovers.

Departmental Finished Goods Inventory Turnovers

	Dept. A	Dept. B	Dept. C	Total
Finished Goods Inventories—				
December 31:				
1941.........................	$ 37,570	$ 15,655	$ 9,395	$ 62,620
1940.........................	36,850	17,210	4,490	58,550
1939.........................	29,360	14,450	2,885	46,695
1938.........................	34,975	20,300	3,355	58,630
Average Inventories:				
1941.........................(a)	$ 37,210	$ 16,433	$ 6,942	$ 60,585
1940.........................(b)	33,105	15,830	3,687	52,622
1939.........................(c)	32,167	17,375	3,120	52,662
Cost of Sales:				
1941.........................(d)	$121,740	$ 51,190	$34,732	$207,662
1940.........................(e)	53,370	117,460	52,336	223,166
1939.........................(f)	94,725	76,132	41,818	212,675
Turnovers:				
1941.................(d ÷ a)	3.27	3.12	5.00	3.43
1940.................(e ÷ b)	1.61	7.42	14.19	4.24
1939.................(f ÷ c)	2.94	4.38	13.40	4.04

Fixed and Variable Expenses

The break-even point.

Assume that a company's profit and loss statement may be summarized as follows:

Sales..	$500,000.00
Less Cost of Sales and Expenses.........................	475,000.00
Net Profit...	$ 25,000.00

To what extent can the sales decrease before the company begins to lose money? The costs and expenses, amounting to $475,000.00, are 95% of the sales. If the costs and expenses remained in that proportion to sales, regardless of increases or decreases in sales, the company would always make some profit, no matter how small the sales might be.

But some of the expenses are fixed in amount, regardless of the amount of sales, whereas others vary more or less directly in proportion to sales. The so-called "break-even point" computations are based on the assumption that the expenses can be divided into two classes:

(1) Fixed expenses, which are not affected by changes in the amount of sales.

(2) Variable expenses, which vary in direct proportion to the sales.

If we assume that the $475,000.00 of costs and expenses are divisible as follows:

Fixed expenses.. $200,000.00
Variable expenses....................................... 275,000.00

the break-even point can be computed as follows:

Let S = the sales at the break-even point.
The variable expenses incurred in making $500,000.00 of sales are $275,-000.00, or 55% of the sales. Since the variable expenses always vary in proportion to sales, they will be 55% of any sales volume.
Since the sales at the break-even point will exactly equal the fixed and variable expenses,
$$S = \$200,000.00 \text{ (fixed expenses)} + .55S \text{ (variable expenses)}$$
$$S - .55S = \$200,000.00$$
$$.45S = \$200,000.00$$
$$S = \$444,444.44, \text{ the break-even point; if the sales fall below}$$
this amount, the company will incur losses.

Relation of fixed expenses to break-even point.

The smaller the fixed expenses, the lower the break-even point. To illustrate, assume the following division of the $475,000.00 total of costs and expenses:

Fixed expenses.. $100,000.00
Variable expenses—75% of net sales..................... 375,000.00

Let S = the sales at the break-even point.
Then $S = \$100,000.00$ (fixed expenses) + $.75S$ (variable expenses).
$$S - .75S = \$100,000.00.$$
$$.25S = \$100,000.00.$$
$$S = \$400,000.00, \text{ the break-even point.}$$

Use of break-even computations in management.

Guidance in the solution of management problems may often be obtained by the use of the break-even computation. One problem will be presented as an illustration. A company's profit and loss statement is summarized as follows:

Net Sales.. $1,000,000.00

Costs and Expenses:
   Fixed.. $ 300,000.00
   Variable (64% of sales).............................. 640,000.00
   Total.. $ 940,000.00
Net Profit... $ 60,000.00

The company is considering increasing its investment in land, buildings, and machinery; if it does so, the fixed expenses will be increased from $300,000.00 to $400,000.00 per year. Is the increase in fixed assets expedient?

In the first place, let us determine what will happen to the break-even point.

Under present conditions:

$$S = \$300,000.00 \text{ (fixed)} + .64S \text{ (variable)}$$
$$.36S = \$300,000.00$$
$$S = \$833,333.33$$

Under the proposed conditions:

$$S = \$400,000.00 \text{ (fixed)} + .64S \text{ (variable)}$$
$$.36S = \$400,000.00$$
$$S = \$1,111,111.11$$

It thus becomes apparent that the sales must be increased $111,111.11 from their present level before the company will begin to make any profits.

In the second place, let us determine what sales must be made to produce the same profits, $60,000.00, as at the present time. Since the sales must provide for the fixed expenses, the variable expenses, and the $60,000.00 profit,

$$S = \$400,000.00 \text{ (fixed)} + .64S \text{ (variable)} + \$60,000.00$$
$$.36S = \$460,000.00$$
$$S = \$1,277,777.77$$

In the third place, let us consider the probable limits of profit under the two conditions. With the present plant facilities, the maximum production is estimated at an amount which would enable the company to make sales of $1,200,000.00. The increased production with the additional facilities would permit the company to make sales of $1,600,000.00. The probable limits of profits may therefore be estimated as follows:

	Without Plant Additions	With Plant Additions
Sales..	$1,200,000.00	$1,600.000.00
Fixed Expenses.................................	$ 300,000.00	$ 400,000.00
Variable Expenses—64% of sales................	768,000.00	1,024,000.00
Total Expenses.............................	$1,068,000.00	$1,424,000.00
Limits of Profit...............................	$ 132,000.00	$ 176,000.00

These findings may be summarized in the manner shown on the following page.

	Present	Prospective	Difference
Break-even point.................. $	833,333.33	$1,111,111.11	$277,777.77
Sales to make the same profit as at present......................	1,000,000.00	1,277,777.77	* 277,777.77
Limits of profit..................	132,000.00	176,000.00	44,000.00
Sales for limits of profit............	1,200,000.00	1,600,000.00	400,000.00

The management should now estimate the sales possibilities to determine the wisdom of the proposed expenditures. If the company makes the expenditures, but the sales remain at the present level of $1,000,000.00, it will lose $40,000.00 instead of making $60,000.00, because it will have increased its fixed expenses $100,000.00 without changing its variable expenses. With the additional plant, the break-even point will be advanced $277,-777.77, and the sales must be increased the same amount to make the $60,000.00 profit now earned. Against these disadvantages may be set off the possibility of making $44,000.00 more profit than is possible under present conditions, but the earning of this additional profit will depend upon the company's ability to obtain sales of $1,600,000.00.

Classification of expenses.

Break-even computations are predicated on the assumption that all expenses can be grouped into two classes: those which are absolutely fixed in amount, regardless of sales; and those which vary in direct proportion to the sales.

Such an assumption is scarcely justified. Some expenses may be fixed to the extent that they will not vary up to a certain sales limit; if the sales are increased above that limit, these expenses will increase, but may remain fixed at the higher amount within certain new sales limits. Moreover, some expenses may vary in exact proportion to sales, whereas the increases and decreases in other expenses will not be in exact proportion to the increases and decreases in sales.

The rudiments of the break-even computation have been discussed because the computation is becoming increasingly of interest to accountants and executives. The application of the theory requires a recognition of the fact that expenses cannot be rigidly classified as fixed and variable.

44

STATEMENT OF APPLICATION
OF FUNDS

···

First illustration.

The usual purpose of a statement of application of funds is to account for the increase or decrease in working capital between two dates. If the working capital of the business has increased during the period, this improvement is due to the fact that additional funds or resources have come into the business from some source, and that at least a portion of these funds have been used to increase the current assets and/or decrease the current liabilities.

The first illustration is a simple one in which additional funds were provided from a single source: profits.

THE *X Y* COMPANY
Statement of Application of Funds
For the Year Ended December 31, 1941

Funds Provided:	
By Net Profits..	$9,500.00
Funds Applied:	
To the Purchase of Fixed Assets:	
Land and Buildings.....................................	$5,000.00
To the Increase in Working Capital—Per Schedule..........	4,500.00
	$9,500.00

THE *X Y* COMPANY
Schedule of Working Capital

	December 31		Changes in Working Capital	
	1941	1940	Increase	Decrease
Current Assets:				
Cash.....................	$ 3,500.00	$ 2,000.00	$1,500.00	
Accounts Receivable.........	12,500.00	12,000.00	500.00	
Merchandise.................	9,000.00	8,000.00	1,000.00	
Total Current Assets.......	$25,000.00	$22,000.00		
Current Liabilities:				
Accounts Payable...........	4,500.00	6,000.00	1,500.00	
Working Capital..............	$20,500.00	$16,000.00		
Increase in Working Capital.....				$4,500.00
			$4,500.00	$4,500.00

439

Relation to comparative balance sheet.

All of the facts required for the foregoing statement of application of funds were obtained from a comparative balance sheet, which appears below:

THE *X Y* COMPANY
Balance Sheet

	December 31	
	1941	1940
Assets		
Cash..	$ 3,500.00	$ 2,000.00
Accounts Receivable..........................	12,500.00	12,000.00
Merchandise.................................	9,000.00	8,000.00
Land and Buildings...........................	55,000.00	50,000.00
	$80,000.00	$72,000.00
Liabilities and Net Worth		
Accounts Payable.............................	$ 4,500.00	$ 6,000.00
Capital Stock................................	50,000.00	50,000.00
Surplus.....................................	25,500.00	16,000.00
	$80,000.00	$72,000.00

No dividends were paid during the year, and the profits were exactly equal to the increase in surplus, or $9,500.00; this was the only source of funds. Funds were applied in two ways: to an increase in fixed assets, and to an increase in the working capital.

Second illustration.

The next illustration is based on the following comparative balance sheet. The items marked "P" are shown in the statement on page 441 as funds provided; the items marked "A" are shown as funds applied. The unmarked items are current assets and current liabilities, and appear in the schedule of working capital.

THE *P. Q.* COMPANY
Comparative Balance Sheet
December 31, 1941 and 1940

	December 31		Increase	
	1941	1940	Decrease*	
Assets				
Cash...............................	$ 5,500.00	$ 4,000.00	$ 1,500.00	
Accounts Receivable................	2,650.00	3,100.00	450.00*	
Notes Receivable...................	2,500.00	2,000.00	500.00	
Merchandise........................	8,800.00	7,000.00	1,800.00	
Stock of *O. P.* Company.............	—	10,000.00	10,000.00*	P
Land...............................	20,000.00	30,000.00	10,000.00*	P
Buildings..........................	80,000.00	60,000.00	20,000.00	A
	$119,450.00	$116,100.00	$ 3,350.00	

Liabilities and Net Worth				
Accounts Payable...................	$ 2,300.00	$ 2,500.00	$ 200.00*	
Notes Payable.....................	5,000.00	4,000.00	1,000.00	
6% Bonds Payable.................	—	15,000.00	15,000.00*	A
5% Bonds Payable.................	10,000.00	—	10,000.00	P
Capital Stock—Preferred...........	—	25,000.00	25,000.00*	A
Capital Stock—Common...........	80,000.00	50,000.00	30,000.00	P
Surplus..........................	22,150.00	19,600.00	2,550.00	P
	$119,450.00	$116,100.00	$ 3,350.00	

The statement of application of funds and the supporting schedule of working capital appear below:

THE *P. Q.* COMPANY

Statement of Application of Funds

For the Year Ended December 31, 1941

Funds Provided:

By Sale of Stock of *O. P.* Company.....................	$10,000.00
By Sale of Land.......................................	10,000.00
By Issuance of 5% Bonds.............................	10,000.00
By Issuance of Common Stock.........................	30,000.00
By Profits..	2,550.00
Total Funds Provided.............................	$62,550.00

Funds Applied:

To Additions to Buildings............................	$20,000.00
To Retirement of 6% Bonds...........................	15,000.00
To Retirement of Preferred Stock......................	25,000.00
To Increase in Working Capital (per Schedule)...........	2,550.00
Total Funds Applied..............................	$62,550.00

THE *P. Q.* COMPANY

Schedule of Working Capital

	December 31		Changes in Working Capital	
	1941	1940	Increase	Decrease
Current Assets:				
Cash...............................	$ 5,500	$ 4,000	$1,500	
Accounts Receivable.................	2,650	3,100		$ 450
Notes Receivable....................	2,500	2,000	500	
Merchandise........................	8,800	7,000	1,800	
Total Current Assets...............	$19,450	$16,100		
Current Liabilities:				
Accounts Payable....................	$ 2,300	$ 2,500	200	
Notes Payable......................	5,000	4,000		1,000
Total Current Liabilities............	$ 7,300	$ 6,500		
Working Capital.....................	$12,150	$ 9,600		
Increase in Working Capital............				2,550
			$ 4,000	$4,000

Provision for depreciation.

Depreciation is an expense, but the provision for depreciation does not represent an expenditure of funds. Therefore, to find the funds provided by the profits, it is necessary to add the net profits for the period and the depreciation provisions made during the period.

To illustrate, assume that a man began business on January 1, with the following balance sheet:

Assets		Net Worth	
Machine	$500.00	Capital	$600.00
Cash	100.00		
	$600.00		$600.00

He did a cash business, selling all goods for cash and paying cash for all purchases and expenses. He had no inventory at the end of the year, and his Cash account and profit and loss statement at that time were:

Cash Account

Opening Balance	100.00	Purchases	800.00
Sales	2,000.00	Expenses	200.00
		Balance	1,100.00
	2,100.00		2,100.00

Profit and Loss Statement

Sales		$2,000.00
Deduct Cost of Goods Sold		800.00
Gross Profit on Sales		$1,200.00
Deduct: Expenses	$200.00	
Depreciation	50.00	250.00
Net Profit		$ 950.00

The profit and loss statement shows that the net profit was $950.00, but the Cash account shows that the funds of the business were increased $1,000.00 by the profits. Therefore, the amount of funds provided by the profit is equal to the net profit of $950.00 and the depreciation provision of $50.00.

Other reductions in profits not requiring funds.

Book entries charging Profit and Loss with such items as stock discount, bond discount, and organization expense reduce the profits but not the funds provided by the profits. Hence the amounts thus written off should also be added back to the net profits, to determine the funds provided by the profits.

Reserve for bad debts.

The provision made during the period for bad debts might be added back to the profits in a similar manner, but a more correct statement of working capital is produced by deducting the reserve at the beginning of the year from the accounts receivable at that date, and deducting the reserve at the end of the year from the accounts receivable at that date, thus showing in the schedule of working capital only the net amounts or book values of the accounts receivable at the two dates.

It is obvious that this treatment of the provision for bad debts is not consistent with the treatment of the provision for depreciation. Both provisions reduce the net profits without requiring an expenditure of funds. But the inconsistency appears necessary to avoid misstating the working capital at the beginning and end of the year, as shown in the schedule of working capital.

Illustration.

There is submitted below a comparative balance sheet in which there are two items representing deductions from profits which did not require funds, and which therefore are added to the net profits to determine the funds provided by profits. These two items are the increase in the reserve for depreciation and the decrease in bond discount.

THE _R. S._ COMPANY
Comparative Balance Sheet
December 31, 1941 and 1940

	December 31 1941	December 31 1940	Increase Decrease*	
Assets				
Cash	$ 4,000.00	$ 3,000.00	$1,000.00	
Accounts Receivable	7,000.00	7,300.00	300.00*	
Notes Receivable	2,500.00	3,000.00	500.00*	
Merchandise	9,000.00	7,800.00	1,200.00	
Stock of _L. M._ Company	10,000.00	13,000.00	3,000.00*	P
Land	5,000.00	5,000.00	—	
Buildings	15,000.00	13,000.00	2,000.00	A
Bond Discount	900.00	1,000.00	100.00*	P
	$53,400.00	$53,100.00	$ 300.00	
Liabilities and Net Worth				
Accounts Payable	$ 3,100.00	$ 4,000.00	$ 900.00*	
Notes Payable	5,000.00	6,000.00	1,000.00*	
Bonds Payable	20,000.00	20,000.00	—	
Capital Stock	9,000.00	8,000.00	1,000.00	P
Surplus	9,550.00	9,100.00	450.00	P
Reserve for Depreciation	6,750.00	6,000.00	750.00	P
	$53,400.00	$53,100.00	$ 300.00	

The statement of application of funds appears on the following page. The supporting schedule of working capital is not given.

THE *R. S.* COMPANY
Statement of Application of Funds
For the Year Ended December 31, 1941

Funds Provided:
By Profits:
Net Profit...................................... $450.00
Add Charges to Profit and Loss Not Requiring
Funds:
Depreciation.............................. 750.00
Amortization of Bond Discount.............. 100.00 $1,300.00
By Sale of Investment in *L. M.* Stock.................... 3,000.00
By Sale of Capital Stock............................... 1,000.00
Total Funds Provided......................... $5,300.00
Funds Applied:
To Increase in Buildings.............................. $2,000.00
To Increase in Working Capital......................... 3,300.00
Total Funds Applied......................... $5,300.00

Working papers.

The working papers on page 445 (based on the preceding illustration) are a convenient device for assembling the information required for the statement of application of funds and the supporting schedule of working capital. Observe how all items to be added to determine the funds provided by profits are transferred to a special Funds Provided by Profits section at the bottom of the working papers.

Adjustments.

In the preceding illustration, every item of increase or decrease shown in the Year's Excess Debits and Credits columns of the working papers found its way into the schedule of working capital or the statement of application of funds. But this is not always the case, and adjustments may be necessary for three reasons:

(1) Some increases and decreases may be the result of mere book entries which did not record transactions either providing or applying funds; for instance:
(a) The Land account may have been written up $5,000.00 with an offsetting credit to Surplus.
(b) The Goodwill account may have been written down $10,000.00, with an offsetting debit to Surplus.
Adjustments should be made eliminating such increases and decreases, since they had no effect upon the funds.

THE *R. S.* COMPANY
Application of Funds Working Papers
For the Year Ended December 31, 1941

	December 31		Year's Excess		Adjustments		Working Capital		Funds	
Assets	1941	1940	Debits	Credits	Debits	Credits	Increase	Decrease	Applied	Provided
Cash	4,000	3,000	1,000				1,000			
Accounts Receivable	7,000	7,300		300				300		
Notes Receivable	2,500	3,000		500				500		
Merchandise	9,000	7,800	1,200				1,200			
Stock of *L. M.* Company	10,000	13,000		3,000						3,000
Land	5,000	5,000								
Buildings	15,000	13,000	2,000						2,000	
Bond Discount	900	1,000		100	100(c)					
	53,400	53,100								
Liabilities and Net Worth										
Accounts Payable	3,100	4,000	900				900			
Notes Payable	5,000	6,000	1,000				1,000			
Bonds Payable	20,000	20,000								
Capital Stock	9,000	8,000		1,000						1,000
Surplus	9,550	9,100		450	450(a)					
Reserve for Depreciation	6,750	6,000		750	750(b)					
	53,400	53,100	6,100	6,100						
Funds Provided by Profits:										
Net Profit						450(a)				
Depreciation						750(b)				
Bond Discount Amortized						100(c)				
					1,300	1,300				1,300
Increase in Working Capital								3,300	3,300	
							4,100	4,100	5,300	5,300

(2) Some increases or decreases may indicate that funds have been provided or applied, but the increase or decrease in the balance of the account may not represent the true amount of the funds provided or applied; for instance:

(c) Suppose that delivery trucks costing $3,000.00 were sold for $2,400.00, and that the sale was recorded by the following entry:

```
Cash................................. 2,400.00
Surplus..............................   600.00
        Delivery Trucks................          3,000.00
```

The Delivery Trucks account was reduced $3,000.00 but only $2,400.00 of funds were provided.

Adjustments should be made to show the true amount of funds provided or applied.

(3) The increase or decrease in the balance of an account may be the result of several entries, some of which represent funds provided, some of which represent funds applied, and some of which were mere book entries having no relation to funds; for instance, the Surplus account may contain the following entries during the year:

Surplus

(b) Goodwill written down.	10,000	Opening balance...........	18,000
(c) Loss on delivery trucks.	600	(a) Land account written up....	5,000
(d) Cash dividends........	3,000	(e) Net profit.................	5,900
Closing balance........	15,300		
	28,900		28,900

The balance of the Surplus account has decreased $2,-700.00, but this net figure cannot appear in the statement of application of funds; it must be analyzed to determine what entries represent funds provided, what entries represent funds applied, and what entries have no relation to funds.

These adjustments are made in a pair of Adjustment columns in the working papers, as illustrated on page 447. The adjustments are explained below and on page 448.

(a) The Land account was written up $5,000.00 during the year, by a credit to Surplus. As this entry did not affect the funds, it is reversed in the working papers by the adjustment:

Debit Surplus, $5,000.00
Credit Land, $5,000.00

THE *E F* COMPANY
Application of Funds—Working Papers
For the Year Ended December 31, 1941

	December 31		Year's Excess		Adjustments		Working Capital		Funds	
	1941	1940	Debits	Credits	Debits	Credits	Increase	Decrease	Applied	Provided
Assets										
Cash	3,400	2,900	500				500			
Accounts Receivable	5,100	4,500	600				600			
Merchandise	12,300	12,000	300				300			
Land	15,000	10,000	5,000			5,000(a)				
Buildings	48,000	40,000	8,000						8,000	
Delivery Trucks	5,000	8,000		3,000	600(c)					2,400
Goodwill		10,000		10,000	10,000(b)					
	88,800	87,400								
Liabilities and Net Worth										
Accounts Payable	3,500	4,400	900				900			
Capital Stock	70,000	65,000		5,000	5,000(a)					5,000
Surplus	15,300	18,000	2,700		5,900(e)	10,000(b) 600(c) 3,000(d)				
	88,800	87,400	18,000	18,000						
Funds Provided by Profits:										
Net Profit						5,900(e)				5,900
Cash Dividends Paid					3,000(d)				3,000	
					24,500	24,500				
Increase in Working Capital								2,300	2,300	
							2,300	2,300	13,300	13,300

447

(b) The $10,000.00 balance in the Goodwill account was written off during the year. As this write-off did not affect the funds, it is reversed in the working papers by the adjustment:

> Debit Goodwill, $10,000.00
> Credit Surplus, $10,000.00

(c) Delivery trucks costing $3,000.00 were sold during the year for $2,400.00. The $600.00 loss was charged to Surplus. The $3,000.00 decrease in the balance of the Delivery Trucks account is reduced to $2,400.00, the true amount of funds provided by the sale, by the adjustment

> Debit Delivery Trucks, $600.00
> Credit Surplus, $600.00

(d) Surplus was charged during the year with $3,000.00 for cash dividends paid. This item is transferred to a separate line in the working papers by the adjustment:

> Debit Cash Dividends Paid, $3,000.00
> Credit Surplus, $3,000.00

(e) The Surplus account was credited at the end of the year with a net profit of $5,900.00. This item is transferred to a separate line in the working papers by the entry:

> Debit Surplus, $5,900.00
> Credit Funds Provided by Profits, $5,900.00

The adjusted balances are then extended to the Working Capital and Funds columns.

The Surplus adjustments should fully account for the net change in Surplus during the year. Proof of the Surplus adjustments may be made as follows:

Total adjustments crediting Surplus............................... $13,600.00
Total adjustments debiting Surplus............................... 10,900.00
Net credit to Surplus in the adjustment columns of the working papers—
 equal to net debit to the Surplus account during the year........... $ 2,700.00

Extended illustration.

The working papers on page 449 and the statement on page 451 illustrate the method of preparing a statement of application of funds when numerous adjustments must be made.

The adjustments of the working papers on page 449 are explained on page 450.

THE S T COMPANY
Application of Funds—Working Papers
For the Year Ended December 31, 1941

	December 31		Year's Excess		Adjustments		Working Capital		Funds	
	1941	1940	Debits	Credits	Debits	Credits	Increase	Decrease	Applied	Provided
Assets										
Cash	4,100	3,600	500				500			
Accounts Receivable	3,600	4,000		400				400		
Merchandise	18,000	16,000	2,000				2,000			
Land	10,000	10,000								
Buildings	25,000	20,000	5,000						5,000	
Machinery	23,000	18,000	5,000						5,000	
Patents	6,000	7,000		1,000	1,000(b)					
Treasury Stock	10,000		10,000		300(c)				10,300	
Discount on Bonds	400		400		100(e)	500(d)				
Organization Expense	3,500	5,000		1,500	1,500(f)					
	103,600	83,600								
Liabilities and Net Worth										
Accounts Payable	2,800	2,500		300				300		
Notes Payable		3,000	3,000				3,000			
Bonds Payable	10,000			10,000	500(d)					9,500
Reserve for Bad Debts	325	370	45				45			
Reserve for Depreciation—Buildings	3,700	2,500		1,200	1,200(g)					
Reserve for Depreciation—Machinery	5,400	2,600		1,800	1,800(h)					
Capital Stock	60,000	60,000								
Surplus	21,375	11,630		9,745	14,545(a)	300(c) / 1,500(f) / 3,000(i)				
	103,600	83,600	25,945	25,945						
Dividends Paid					3,000(i)				3,000	
Funds Provided by Profits:										
Net Profit for the Year						14,545(a)				18,645
Amortization of Patents						1,000(b)				
Bond Discount Written Off						100(e)				
Depreciation of Buildings						1,200(g)				
Depreciation of Machinery						1,800(h)				
					23,945	23,945				
Increase in Working Capital								4,845	4,845	
							5,545	5,545	28,145	28,145

(a) The net operating profit for the year was $14,545.00. This amount is transferred to the Funds Provided by Profits section by the adjustment:

Debit Surplus, $14,545.00
Credit Funds Provided by Profits, $14,545.00

(b) Amortization of patents was provided during the year in the amount of $1,000.00, by a credit to the Patents account and a debit to operations.

Debit Patents, $1,000.00
Credit Funds Provided by Profits, $1,000.00

(c) Treasury stock of a par value of $10,000.00 was purchased for $10,300.00; the $300.00 premium was charged to Surplus. To show the true amount of funds applied to the purchase of this stock:

Debit Treasury Stock, $300.00
Credit Surplus, $300.00

(d) Bonds of a par value of $10,000.00 were issued for $9,500.00; the discount was charged to Discount on Bonds. To show the true amount of funds provided by the issuance of the bonds:

Debit Bonds Payable, $500.00
Credit Discount on Bonds, $500.00

(e) Bond discount in the amount of $100.00 was written off.

Debit Discount on Bonds, $100.00
Credit Funds Provided by Profits, $100.00

(f) Organization expense in the amount of $1,500.00 was written off by a direct charge to Surplus.

Debit Organization Expense, $1,500.00
Credit Surplus, $1,500.00.

(g) Depreciation of buildings in the amount of $1,200.00 was provided by a credit to the Reserve for Depreciation.

Debit Reserve for Depreciation—Buildings, $1,200.00
Credit Funds Provided by Profits, $1,200.00

(h) Depreciation of machinery was provided in the amount of $1,800.00.

Debit Reserve for Depreciation—Machinery, $1,800.00
Credit Funds Provided by Profits, $1,800.00

(i) Cash dividends of $3,000.00 were paid during the year. These are set out as a separate item by the adjustment:

Debit Dividends Paid, $3,000.00
Credit Surplus, $3,000.00

The following statement of application of funds, and its supporting schedule of working capital, were prepared from the working papers on page 449.

THE *S T* COMPANY
Statement of Application of Funds
For the Year Ended December 31, 1941

Funds Provided:
By Profits:

Net Profit for the Year............................		$14,545.00	
Add Charges to Profits Not Requiring Funds:			
Depreciation—Buildings...............	$1,200.00		
Depreciation—Machinery..............	1,800.00		
Amortization—Patents................	1,000.00		
Bond Discount Written Off...........	100.00	4,100.00	$18,645.00
By Issuance of Bonds at 95.................................			9,500.00
Total Funds Provided........................			$28,145.00

Funds Applied:
To Increases in Fixed Assets:

Buildings...................................	$ 5,000.00	
Machinery...................................	5,000.00	$10,000.00
To Purchase of Treasury Stock at 103.........................		10,300.00
To Payment of Dividend......................................		3,000.00
To Increase in Working Capital (per Schedule)..................		4,845.00
Total Funds Applied..		$28,145.00

THE *S T* COMPANY
Schedule of Working Capital
December 31, 1941 and 1940

	December 31		Changes in Working Capital	
	1941	1940	Increase	Decrease
Current Assets:				
Cash...............................	$ 4,100	$ 3,600	$ 500	
Accounts Receivable—Less Reserve.....	3,275	3,630		$ 355
Merchandise........................	18,000	16,000	2,000	
Total Current Assets...............	$25,375	$23,230		
Current Liabilities:				
Accounts Payable....................	$ 2,800	$ 2,500		300
Notes Payable......................		3,000	3,000	
Total Current Liabilities............	$ 2,800	$ 5,500		
Working Capital.......................	$22,575	$17,730		
Increase in Working Capital............				4,845
			$5,500	$5,500

Deferred charges.

The deferred charges at the beginning of the period, those a the end of the period, and the increases and decreases therein during the period are usually shown in the schedule of working capita and deferred charges, in the manner illustrated below:

Schedule of Working Capital and Deferred Charges

| | December 31 | | Changes In Working Capital | |
	1941	1940	Increase	Decrease
Current Assets:				
Cash...............................	$10,100	$ 9,050	$1,050	
Accounts Receivable..................	5,400	6,000		$ 600
Merchandise.........................	27,500	25,000	2,500	
Total Current Assets...............	$43,000	$40,050		
Current Liabilities:				
Accounts Payable.....................	$ 2,750	$ 3,000	250	
Notes Payable.......................	4,200	4,000		200
Total Current Liabilities.............	$ 6,950	$ 7,000		
Working Capital.......................	$36,050	$33,050		
Deferred Charges:				
Unexpired Insurance..................	$ 360	$ 325	35	
Prepaid Taxes.......................	155	170		15
Total Deferred Charges.............	$ 515	$ 495		
Increase in Working Capital and Deferred Charges.............................				3,020
			$3,835	$3,835

Loss for the period.

If the operations of the business result in a loss, adding bacl the provisions for depreciation and the other expenses not requirin; funds may change the debit to a credit. In other words, there ma; have been a profit before provision was made for non-fund-requir ing expenses. The statement of application of funds will ther show that funds were provided by operations, as follows:

```
Funds Provided:
  By Operations:
    Charges to Profit and Loss Not Requiring Funds:
      Depreciation—Buildings.......................... $ 3,800.00
      Depreciation—Machinery..........................   6,000.00
      Amortization—Patents............................   2,500.00
        Total.........................................  $12,300.00
    Less Net Loss for the Year..........................   7,500.00
    Funds Provided by Operations................................ $4,800.0
```

But if a debit still remains after the depreciation provision and the other non-fund-requiring expenses are added back, th question arises as to how this loss should be shown in the statement of application of funds. Two methods may be used: (1) the loss may be shown in the Funds Applied section, on the theory that the funds provided by sales of assets, additions to stock, and so forth were used in covering the loss; (2) the Funds Provided section may be added and the net loss deducted, to determine the net funds provided, thus:

Funds Provided:
By Sale of Stock		$50,000.00
By Sale of Fixed Assets		25,000.00
Total		$75,000.00
Deduct Loss for the Period:		
Net Loss per Profit and Loss Statement	$7,000.00	
Less Depreciation on Machinery	1,000.00	6,000.00
Net Funds Provided		$69,000.00

The latter is the preferable method.

Decrease in working capital.

If the schedule of working capital and deferred charges shows a decrease, the decrease may be shown in the Funds Provided section of the statement of application of funds, on the theory that funds were provided out of working capital in order to make the expenditures shown in the Funds Applied section.

It is perhaps preferable to reverse the usual sequence of the statement of application of funds in order that the decrease in working capital will be shown as a final balance, thus:

Funds Applied:
Purchase of Fixed Assets	$20,000.00
Payment of Dividend	5,000.00
Total	$25,000.00
Funds Provided:	
By Profits	22,000.00
Decrease in Working Capital	$ 3,000.00

45

AN ACCOUNTING DETECTIVE STORY

···

Purpose of the chapter.

There are two requisites for accounting data which are to serve as reliable bases for conclusions: accuracy and adequacy.

Chapter 39 indicated that it is unwise to rely implicitly on accounting statements, because they may not have been properly drawn to reflect the facts.

The present chapter is intended to emphasize the warning: Don't act on conclusions reached on the basis of inadequate data.

Analysis of a single balance sheet.

Below is a balance sheet which we shall assume was submitted to a bank's loaning officer in support of a request for a loan. For the time being, it will be assumed that the balance sheet contained the only information submitted, and we shall see what conclusions might be reached from an analysis of it.

A B COMPANY

Balance Sheet—December 31, 1941

Assets

CURRENT ASSETS:			
Cash		$ 15,000	
Accounts Receivable	$106,000		
Less Reserve for Bad Debts	3,000	103,000	
Inventories:			
Finished Goods	$135,000		
Goods in Process	18,000		
Raw Materials	30,000	183,000	
Total Current Assets			$301,000
FIXED ASSETS:			
Land		$ 15,000	
Buildings	$200,000		
Less Reserve for Depreciation	30,000	170,000	
Machinery and Equipment	$ 86,000		
Less Reserve for Depreciation	12,000	74,000	
Total Fixed Assets			259,000
			$560,000

Liabilities and Net Worth

CURRENT LIABILITIES............................... $100,000
FIXED LIABILITIES:
First Mortage, Real Estate, 6%, Bonds Payable.... 75,000
    Total Liabilities................................. $175,000
NET WORTH:
Capital Stock—$100.00 Par Value................ $250,000
Surplus:
    Balance, Beginning of Year........... $119.000
    Surplus for the Year, Before Dividends. 31,000
      Total........................... $150,000
    Less Dividends..................... 15,000 135,000
      Total Net Worth.................................. 385,000
        $560,000

A working capital ratio of 2 to 1 is usually regarded as adequate. The *A B* Company has a working capital ratio of 3 to 1.

Current Assets:
  Cash... $ 15,000.00
  Accounts Receivable..................... $106,000.00
    Less Reserve........................... 3,000.00 103,000.00
  Inventories:
    Finished Goods......................... $135,000.00
    Goods in Process....................... 18,000.00
    Raw Materials......................... 30,000.00 183,000.00
    Total... $301,000.00
  Current Liabilities..................................... 100,000.00
  Working Capital....................................... $201,000.00
  Ratio—Current Assets to Current Liabilities.............. 3.01 to 1

The *A B* Company's acid test ratio meets the 1 to 1 requirement set up by some analysts.

Cash.. $ 15,000.00
Accounts receivable—net.............................. 103,000.00
  Total... $118,000.00
Current liabilities... $100,000.00
Acid test ratio... 1.18 to 1

The ratio of net worth to debt shows that there is a considerable investment to protect the liabilities.

Net worth:
  Capital stock....................................... $250,000.00
  Surplus.. 135,000.00
    Total.. $385,000.00
Liabilities:
  Current... $100,000.00
  Fixed... 75,000.00
    Total.. $175,000.00

Ratio of net worth to debt = 385 ÷ 175 =................ 2.20 to 1

The following computation of the ratio of net worth to fixed assets shows that the proprietorship investment is not tied up in fixed assets to the starvation of the working capital.

Net worth...	$385,000.00
Fixed assets—Less depreciation:	
Land...	$ 15,000.00
Buildings...	170,000.00
Machinery and equipment.............................	74,000.00
Total..	$259,000.00

Ratio of net worth to fixed assets = 385 ÷ 259 =.......... 1.49 to 1

The ratio of net worth to inventories, as determined below, appears also to be a favorable one, indicating that an excessive portion of the capital is probably not tied up in inventories.

Net worth...	$385,000.00
Inventories:	
Finished goods.......................................	$135,000.00
Goods in process.....................................	18,000.00
Raw materials..	30,000.00
Total..	$183,000.00

Ratio of net worth to inventories = 385 ÷ 183 =.......... 2.10 to 1

The following ratio indicates that the security behind the mortgage bonds is adequate.

Land...	$ 15,000.00
Buildings—Less depreciation...........................	170,000.00
Total..	$185,000.00
Bonds payable.......................................	$ 75,000.00

Ratio of security to bonded debt = 185 ÷ 75 =........... 2.47 to 1

The Net Worth section of the balance sheet contains some details accounting for the change during the year. One of the items is "Surplus for the Year, Before Dividends—$31,000.00." Tentatively accepting this amount as representing the net income for the year, the following ratios can be computed:

Earnings to bond interest requirements:	
Surplus for the year, before dividends..................	$ 31,000.00
Add back bond interest—6% of $75,000.00..............	4,500.00
Surplus for the year available for bond interest...........	$ 35,500.00
Bond interest requirements............................	$ 4,500.00

Ratio = $35,500 ÷ $4,500 =.......................... 7.89 to 1

Earnings per share of stock:	
Surplus for the year, before dividends..................	$ 31,000.00
Capital stock:	
Par value...	$250,000.00
Number of shares....................................	2,500

Earnings per share = $31,000.00 ÷ 2,500 =............. $ 12.40

The company has only one class of stock; the book value per share of stock at the end of 1941 is computed below.

Capital stock...	$250,000.00
Surplus..	135,000.00
Total...	$385,000.00
Number of shares of stock.............................	2,500
Book value per share..................................	$ 154.00

Comparative balance sheet analysis.

An analysis of financial condition based on a single balance sheet may be very deceptive. Such an analysis will indicate a status on a given date, but it will not disclose trends; that is, it will not show whether the condition is getting better or worse. Consequently, it is always advisable to examine at least two balance sheets.

A comparative balance sheet of the *A B* Company and a statement of application of funds, with a supporting schedule of working capital, are presented below and are subjected to analysis on subsequent pages.

A B COMPANY
Comparative Balance Sheet, December 31, 1941 and 1940

Assets	December 31 1941	1940	Increase Decrease*
CURRENT ASSETS:			
Cash.....................................	$ 15,000	$ 40,000	$ 25,000*
Accounts Receivable.......................	$106,000	$ 74,000	$ 32,000
Less Reserve for Bad Debts...............	3,000	3,000	—
Accounts Receivable—Net..............	$103,000	$ 71,000	$ 32,000
Inventories:			
Finished Goods..........................	$135,000	$110,000	$ 25,000
Goods in Process.......................	18,000	13,000	5,000
Raw Materials...........................	30,000	25,000	5,000
Total Inventories......................	$183,000	$148,000	$ 35,000
Total Current Assets.................	$301,000	$259,000	$ 42,000
FIXED ASSETS:			
Land.....................................	$ 15,000	$ 15,000	$ —
Buildings................................	$200,000	$135,000	$ 65,000
Less Reserve for Depreciation............	30,000	20,000	10,000
Remainder—Depreciated Value..........	$170,000	$115,000	$ 55,000
Machinery and Equipment..................	$ 86,000	$ 65,000	$ 21,000
Less Reserve for Depreciation............	12,000	10,000	2,000
Remainder—Depreciated Value..........	$ 74,000	$ 55,000	$ 19,000
Total Fixed Assets—Depreciated Value..	$259,000	$185,000	$ 74,000
	$560,000	$444,000	$116,000

Liabilities and Net Worth
CURRENT LIABILITIES:

Accounts Payable..........................	$100,000	$ 70,000	$ 30,000

FIXED LIABILITIES:

Bonds Payable............................	$ 75,000	$ 55,000	$ 20,000

NET WORTH:

Capital Stock.............................	$250,000	$200,000	$ 50,000

Surplus:

Balance at Beginning of Year..............	$119,000	$ 95,200	$ 23,800
Surplus for Year, Before Dividends.........	31,000	35,800	4,800*
Total..................................	$150,000	$131,000	$ 19,000
Less Dividends..........................	15,000	12,000	3,000
Balance at End of Year...................	$135,000	$119,000	$ 16,000
Total Net Worth.....................	$385,000	$319,000	$ 66,000
	$560,000	$444,000	$116,000

A B COMPANY
Statement of Application of Funds
For the Year Ended December 31, 1941

Funds Provided:
By Operations:

Surplus for the Year, Before Dividends.....	$31,000.00	
Add Depreciation Provisions:		
Buildings.............................	10,000.00	
Machinery and Equipment..............	2,000.00	$ 43,000.00
By Sale of Bonds.....................................		20,000.00
By Issuance of Stock....................,............		50,000.00
Total Funds Provided.........................		$113,000.00

Funds Applied:

To Payment of Dividends.............................		$ 15,000.00
To Additions to Fixed Assets:		
Buildings (48% increase).....	$65,000.00	
Machinery (32% increase).................	21,000.00	86,000.00
To Increase in Working Capital........................		12,000.00
Total Funds Applied..........................		$113,000.00

Comparative Schedule of Working Capital

	December 31			
	1941		1940	
	Amount	Per Cent	Amount	Per Cent
Current Assets:				
Cash.......................	$ 15,000.00	4.98%	$ 40,000.00	15.45%
Receivables—Net............	103,000.00	34.22	71,000.00	27.41
Inventories:				
Finished Goods............	135,000.00	44.85	110,000.00	42.47
Goods in Process./..........	18,000.00	5.98	13,000.00	5.02
Raw Materials...........	30,000.00	9.97	25,000.00	9.65
Total.................	$301,000.00	100.00%	$259,000.00	100.00%
Current Liabilities.............	100,000.00		70,000.00	
Working Capital...............	$201,000.00		$189,000.00	
Ratio.......................	3.01		3.70	

The statement of application of funds and the comparative schedule of working capital disclose several matters of considerable significance:

(1) *Large additional investments in fixed assets.* Whether or not these increases in plant facilities have been accompanied by corresponding increases in volume of business, cannot be determined in the absence of a comparative profit and loss statement. It is a matter which should be investigated. The comparative balance sheet does disclose the fact that the "Surplus for the Year, Before Dividends" decreased from $35,800.00 in 1940 to $31,-000.00 in 1941.

(2) *The working capital increased $12,000.00.* This is approximately a 6 per cent increase over the working capital of $189,000.00 at the end of 1940. Since the per cents of increase in fixed assets were much larger, doubt immediately arises as to whether sufficient additional working capital has been provided to take care of the requirements of the additional volume which will be required to make the added plant a profitable investment.

(3) *The working capital ratio has materially decreased.*

(4) *The current assets appear to be relatively less current at the end of 1941 than they were at the end of 1940,* as indicated by the percentage increases in the inventories. This change in liquidity is further evidenced by the decrease in the acid test ratio.

	December 31	
	1941	1940
Quick current assets:		
Cash..	$ 15,000.00	$ 40,000.00
Receivables—Net........................	103,000.00	71,000.00
Total...................................	$118,000.00	$111,000.00
Current liabilities.........................	$100,000.00	$ 70,000.00
Acid test ratio............................	1.18	1.59

A number of ratios were computed in the analysis of the balance sheet at the end of 1941. Following are computations of comparative ratios as of December 31, 1941 and 1940. The numbers in parentheses indicate the ratio of the December 31, 1941, amount to that on December 31, 1940. For instance: the net worth has increased 21 per cent while the liabilities have increased 40 per cent; as a consequence, the ratio of worth to debt has decreased.

Worth to Debt

| | December 31 | |
	1941	1940
Net worth:		
Capital stock............................	$250,000.00	$200,000.00
Surplus..................................	135,000.00	119,000.00
Total......................... (1.21)	$385,000.00	$319,000.00
Liabilities:		
Current.................................	$100,000.00	$ 70,000.00
Fixed..................................	75,000.00	55,000.00
Total......................... (1.40)	$175,000.00	$125,000.00
Ratio....................................	2.20	2.55

Worth to Fixed Assets

| | December 31 | |
	1941	1940
Net worth..................... (1.21)	$385,000.00	$319,000.00
Fixed assets—Less depreciation:		
Land....................................	$ 15,000.00	$ 15,000.00
Buildings...............................	170,000.00	115,000.00
Machinery..............................	74,000.00	55,000.00
Total......................... (1.40)	$259,000.00	$185,000.00
Ratio....................................	1.49	1.72

Worth to Inventories

| | December 31 | |
	1941	1940
Net worth..................... (1.21)	$385,000.00	$319,000.00
Inventories:		
Finished goods..........................	$135,000.00	$110,000.00
Goods in process........................	18,000.00	13,000.00
Raw materials..........................	30,000.00	25,000.00
Total......................... (1.24)	$183,000.00	$148,000.00
Ratio....................................	2.10	2.16

Mortgaged Property to Bonds

| | December 31 | |
	1941	1940
Land....................................	$ 15,000.00	$ 15,000.00
Buildings—Less depreciation.............	170,000.00	115,000.00
Total......................... (1.42)	$185,000.00	$130,000.00
Bonds payable................... (1.36)	$ 75,000.00	$ 55,000.00
Ratio....................................	2.47	2.36

Earnings to Bond Interest Requirements

	1941	1940
Surplus for year, before dividends...........	$ 31,000.00	$ 35,800.00
Add bond interest.........................	4,500.00	3,300.00
Total available for interest........ (.91)	$ 35,500.00	$ 39,100.00
Bond interest.................... (1.36)	$ 4,500.00	$ 3,300.00
Ratio....................................	7.89	11.85

Earnings per Share of Stock

	1941	1940
Surplus for year, before dividends	$ 31,000.00	$ 35,800.00
Number of shares outstanding at end of year	2,500	2,000
Earnings per share	$ 12.40	$ 17.90

Book Value per Share of Stock

		December 31	
		1941	1940
Net worth:			
Capital stock		$250,000.00	$200,000.00
Surplus		135,000.00	119,000.00
Total	(1.21)	$385,000.00	$319,000.00
Shares of stock outstanding	(1.25)	2,500	2,000
Book value per share		$ 154.00	$ 159.50

Summary.

The following summary shows unsatisfactory trends in all of the ratios except that indicating the security to the bonded debt. The numbers in parentheses provide a measure of relative declines. For instance, the working capital ratio at the end of 1941 was only .81 of the ratio at the end of 1940; the acid test ratio was only .74 of that at the end of 1940.

		1941	1940
Ratios:			
Working capital	(.81)	3.01	3.70
Acid test	(.74)	1.18	1.59
Worth to debt	(.86)	2.20	2.55
Worth to fixed assets	(.87)	1.49	1.72
Worth to inventories	(.97)	2.10	2.16
Mortgaged property to bonds	(1.05)	2.47	2.36
Earnings to interest requirements	(.67)	7.89	11.85
Earnings per share	(.69)	$ 12.40	$ 17.90
Book value per share	(.97)	154.00	159.50

Results of operations.

The foregoing analyses of the comparative balance sheet disclosed many evidences of a weakening in the company's financial condition. They strongly suggest the possibility that the plant additions are not being used with an effectiveness equal to that of the old plant.

Let us examine the comparative operating statement on page 463 and see what answers we can get to the question: Is the company benefiting or suffering from its plant expansion?

With a 48 per cent increase in buildings and a 32 per cent increase in machinery, the company's gross sales increased only 4 per cent. Obviously, the plant additions have not yet justified themselves by an increased volume of business.

Comparative Profit and Loss Statement
For the Years Ended December 31, 1941 and 1940

| | Year | | Increase | Ratio 1941 |
	1941	1940	Decrease*	to 1940
Gross Sales..................	$862,000.00	$828,000.00	$34,000.00	1.04
Returns.....................	12,000.00	8,000.00	4,000.00	1.50
Net Sales...................	$850,000.00	$820,000.00	$30,000.00	1.04
Cost of Sales...............	595,000.00	557,600.00	37,400.00	1.07
Gross Profit................	$255,000.00	$262,400.00	$ 7,400.00*	.97
Selling Expenses............	148,000.00	132,000.00	16,000.00	1.12
Net Profit on Sales.........	$107,000.00	$130,400.00	$23,400.00*	.82
General Expense.............	96,000.00	94,600.00	1,400.00	1.01
Net Operating Profit........	$ 11,000.00	$ 35,800.00	$24,800.00*	.31
Profit on Securities........	20,000.00	—	20,000.00	
Increase in Surplus, before Dividends....................	$ 31,000.00	$ 35,800.00	$ 4,800.00*	

With a 4 per cent increase in gross sales, there was a 50 per cent increase in returns; this suggests the possibility that the new plant is not producing satisfactory merchandise.

The 4 per cent increase in net sales was accompanied by a 7 per cent increase in the cost of goods sold. Just what caused this relative increase is, of course, not determinable from the data. But it is not unlikely that the additional fixed assets caused additional fixed charges which had to be absorbed by approximately the same volume of production, and which consequently are reflected in higher unit manufacturing costs.

Because the increase in the cost of goods sold was relatively greater than the increase in net sales, there was a decline in the gross profit.

The selling expenses increased 12 per cent. This suggests the probability that sales promotion efforts and expenditures were increased in an attempt to obtain orders for the additional merchandise which could be produced in the added plant; the fact that the sales increased only 4 per cent indicates that this additional sales effort was relatively unsuccessful.

Finally, and of extreme significance, the fact is disclosed that the net operating profit decreased from $35,800.00 in 1940 to $11,-000.00 in 1941, and that most of the 1941 increase in surplus resulted from an extraneous profit on the sale of securities.

Analysis of manufacturing costs.

We shall now assume that we have obtained a statement showing the cost of goods manufactured and sold, and have abstracted from it the data relative to manufacturing costs during the two years presented below:

	1941	1940	Ratio 1941 to 1940
Materials...........................	$180,000.00	$172,000.00	1.05
Labor..............................	225,000.00	213,000.00	1.06
Overhead...........................	220,000.00	194,600.00	1.13
Total...........................	$625,000.00	$579,600.00	1.08
Ratio of 1941 sales to 1940 sales...................................			1.04

The foregoing data appear to support our earlier surmise that the plant additions resulted in an increase in overhead expenses which were not absorbed by an equivalent increase in production. The increases in materials and labor used were 5 and 6 per cent, respectively; the increase in overhead was 13 per cent. Naturally, the application of 13 per cent more overhead to only 5 per cent more materials and labor caused an increase in unit costs, with a resulting decrease in the rate of gross profit.

Production and inventories.

The following data relative to manufacturing costs and inventories were obtained from a statement of cost of goods manufactured and sold; the data relative to sales were obtained from the profit and loss statement.

	1941	1940	Per Cent Increase
Cost of goods manufactured........	$620,000.00	$577,600.00	7.34%
Net sales..........................	850,000.00	820,000.00	3.66
Inventories—End of year:			
Finished goods..................	$135,000.00	$110,000.00	22.73%
Goods in process................	18,000.00	13,000.00	38.46
Raw materials..................	30,000.00	25,000.00	20.00

The foregoing analysis seems to disclose a matter of major significance: an increase in the cost of goods manufactured out of proportion to the increase in sales, and a consequent increase in inventories. This immediately suggests the question: Is the management trying to keep down the unit manufacturing costs by increasing the quantity of production, and finding itself unable to sell the increased merchandise, with the result that it is merely piling up slow-moving inventories? The large per cents of increase in the inventories certainly suggest this possibility.

Let us measure the effect of these inventory increases on the turnovers.

Finished Goods Turnovers

	1941	1940
Cost of sales.............................	$595,000.00	$557,600.00
Inventories:		
December 31, 1939...............................		$ 90,000.00
December 31, 1940.....................	$110,000.00	110,000.00
December 31, 1941.....................	135,000.00	
Total..............................	$245,000.00	$200,000.00
Average............................	$122,500.00	$100,000.00
Turnovers...............................	4.85	5.58
Days per turnover (365 ÷ turnovers).........	75	65

Raw Material Turnovers

	1941	1940
Materials used..........................	$180,000.00	$172,000.00
Inventories:		
December 31, 1939...............................		$ 20,000.00
December 31, 1940.....................	$ 25,000.00	25,000.00
December 31, 1941.....................	30,000.00	
Total..............................	$ 55,000.00	$ 45,000.00
Average............................	$ 27,500.00	$ 22,500.00
Turnovers...............................	6.55	7.64
Days per turnover........................	56	48

The analysis of working capital has already disclosed a decrease in the working capital ratio and a decrease in the acid-test ratio resulting from the increase in inventories. Another weakening of the working capital now appears: the inventories seem to move less rapidly.

Analysis of receivables.

Attention already has been directed to the increase in selling expenses as indicating a campaign to increase sales in order to dispose of the additional merchandise produced by the additional plant. It was also observed that this campaign did not appear to have had satisfactory results.

The following analysis of the accounts receivable seems to indicate that more old accounts were on the books at the end of 1941 than at the end of 1940.

Accounts Receivable Conversion

	1941	1940
Sales for year—Net........................	$850,000.00	$820,000.00
Accounts receivable—End of year...........	106,000.00	74,000.00
Per cent of year's sales uncollected...........	12.47%	9.02%
Days' sales uncollected (365 × per cent)......	46	33

We now face this question: Has the company, in a further attempt to find a market for its product, relaxed its credit requirements, with the result that goods are being sold to customers from whom it is more difficult to obtain collections?

Summary.

The principal features in the foregoing analysis are summarized below:

(1) During the year the company made extensive additions to fixed assets:

Buildings...................................... 48%
Machinery..................................... 32%

(2) These increases were accompanied by a 13 per cent increase in manufacturing overhead.

(3) The increases in fixed assets and in manufacturing overhead were not accompanied by proportionate increases in the volume of sales. It therefore seems doubtful whether the plant expansion was justified.

(4) The 13 per cent increase in manufacturing overhead, spread over 5 per cent more material and 6 per cent more labor, increased the unit manufacturing costs.

(5) Consequently there was a decrease in the rate of gross profit.

(6) Since the decrease in the rate of gross profit was not compensated by an increase in sales volume, there was a decrease in the amount of gross profit.

(7) The selling expenses increased $16,000.00, or 12 per cent —evidently as the result of a promotional program to obtain markets for the additional product. However, the sales increased only 4 per cent.

(8) The net operating profit decreased from $35,800.00 in 1940 to $11,000.00 in 1941.

(9) In an effort to keep the factory busy and reduce unit costs, it appears that goods have been manufactured in excess of sales requirements, with a resulting increase in the inventories.

(10) And in an effort to dispose of the inventories, it appears that sales have been made to poorer credit risks, with the result that there are more old accounts on the books than heretofore, and larger bad debt losses may be in prospect. However, there has been no increase in the reserve for bad debts.

(11) The working capital ratio has decreased from 3.70 to
3.01.

(12) The working capital position has been further weakened
by the less liquid distribution of current assets: less
cash and more receivables and inventories—particularly
the latter.

(13) The working capital position has been still further
weakened because the current assets are being converted
less rapidly than in the past, as shown by the following
statement of conversion periods:

	1941	1940
Materials to finished goods	56 days	48 days
Finished goods to receivables	75 "	65 "
Receivables to cash	46 "	33 "
Total	177 "	146 "

(14) This weakening of the current position is evidently making
it more difficult for the company to pay its current
debts, as indicated by the increase in current liabilities
from $70,000.00 to $100,000.00—an increase of 43
per cent.

Sequel.

The following sentence appeared at the beginning of this
chapter: "The present chapter is intended to emphasize the
warning: Don't act on conclusions reached on the basis of inadequate data."

Another warning is now in order: Comparative balance sheets,
profit and loss statements, and statements of cost of goods manufactured and sold do not always contain all of the information
required for a conclusive analysis. They may perhaps only suggest
fields for further inquiry.

After the analyses shown in this chapter were completed, the
loaning officer had a conference with the president of the *A B*
Company. At this conference, the loaning officer was informed
that:

The plant additions were made in the latter part of 1941, and
were in operation only during a part of December.

The large returns in 1941 were the result of unsatisfactory
goods sold to one customer. The cause of the defect in the
merchandise has been corrected.

The 13 per cent increase in manufacturing overhead, compared
with increases of 5 per cent in material and 6 per cent in

labor, resulted from the fact that operations were charged with some expenses during the construction period which could have been capitalized.

During 1942 it will be possible to keep the plant sufficiently busy to cut down the unit overhead costs to about the 1940 figure.

The president feels optimistic about being able to increase the sales materially, because there are already on hand numerous orders which resulted from the extensive (and expensive) sales campaign conducted toward the end of 1941, and which caused the increase in selling expenses.

The increases in inventories and in receivables are temporary conditions. The receivables are large because of heavy sales late in December, after the plant was in operation and the product was available. Similarly, the inventories are high in anticipation of the filling of orders now held and expected to be received.

The unfavorable working capital position and profit record will be corrected, now that the plant is in full operation and orders can be filled.

46

BRANCH ACCOUNTING

....

Reciprocal current accounts.

A branch is a device for projecting the sales organization into territory at a distance from the home office and setting up a permanent sales establishment in the customers' territory.

A branch keeps a complete set of books in which to record goods received from the home office, purchases from outsiders, sales, accounts receivable, accounts payable, and expenses. The ledger contains an account called Home Office Current, which is credited with everything received from the home office and charged with everything sent to the home office. The Home Office Current account is thus a proprietorship (or net worth) account; therefore, when the books are closed the balance in the Profit and Loss account is transferred to the Home Office account; a profit causes an increase in the net worth, which is reflected by a credit in the Home Office account; a loss causes a decrease, which is reflected by a transfer of the debit balance in the Profit and Loss account to the Home Office account.

A reciprocal Branch Current account is kept on the home office books. It is debited with everything sent to the branch and credited with everything received from the branch. Its debit balance represents the net assets at the branch. Since a branch profit increases the branch net assets, the home office takes up a branch profit by debiting the current account and crediting an income account; and, since a branch loss decreases the branch net assets, the home office takes up a branch loss by debiting a loss account and crediting the current account.

Illustration.

Assume the following transactions:

    (1) Cash sent to the branch, $500.00.
    (2) Merchandise sent to the branch, $5,000.00.

(3) Merchandise purchased by the branch from outsiders on account
$1,000.00.

(4) Sales by the branch:

Cash... $2,000.00.
On account....................................   5,000.00.

(5) Collections from accounts receivable, $4,200.00.
(6) Payments to accounts payable, $750.00.
(7) Expenses paid, $1,200.00.
(8) Cash sent to the home office, $4,000.00.

The following journal entries show the accounts debited an
credited by the home office and the branch:

Branch Books			Home Office Books		
(1) Cash...............	500		Branch Current..........	500	
H. O. Current...		500	Cash..............		5(
(2) Mdse. from H. O......	5,000		Branch Current..........	5,000	
H. O. Current...		5,000	Shipments to Branch		5,0(
(3) Purchases...........	1,000		(to be closed to		
Accounts Payable		1,000	Purchases)		
(4) Cash...............	2,000				
Accounts Receivable..	5,000				
Sales...........		7,000			
(5) Cash...............	4,200				
Accounts Rec....		4,200			
(6) Accounts Payable.....	750				
Cash...........		750			
(7) Expenses............	1,200				
Cash...........		1,200			
(8) H. O. Current........	4,000		Cash.................	4,000	
Cash...........		4,000	Branch Current.......		4,0(

The branch is now ready to close its books. Assuming th
its inventory is $1,500.00, the closing entries on the branch bool
are:

Profit and Loss.................................... 7,200.00
Merchandise from Home Office................   5,000.00
Purchases.....................................   1,000.00
Expenses......................................   1,200.00

Inventory... 1,500.00
Sales... 7,000.00
Profit and Loss...............................   8,500.00

Profit and Loss.................................... 1,300.00
Home Office Current...........................   1,300.00

After closing its books, the branch draws off the following balance sheet:

Branch Balance Sheet

Cash	$ 750.00	Accounts Payable	$ 250.00
Accounts Receivable	800.00	Home Office Current	2,800.00
Inventory	1,500.00		
	$3,050.00		$3,050.00

The home office takes up the profit by the following entry:

Branch Current Account	1,300.00	
Branch Profit and Loss		1,300.00

The Branch Current account on the home office books now appears as follows:

Branch Current

Cash (sent to branch)	500	Cash (received from branch)	4,000
Merchandise (sent to branch)	5,000	Balance	2,800
Net Profit of Branch	1,300		
	6,800		6,800
Balance—down	2,800		

Combined statements.

At the end of the period, statements should be made combining the profit and loss statements of the branch and the home office, and combining the balance sheets of the branch and the home office.   Using assumed figures for the home office, these statements are illustrated below:

THE *X Y* COMPANY
Profit and Loss Statement
For the Year Ended December 31, 1941

	Branch		Home Office		Total	
Sales		$7,000		$18,000		$25,000
Less Cost of Goods Sold:						
Inventory—January 1			$ 4,000		$ 4,000	
Purchases and Shipments from Home Office	$6,000		13,000		19,000	
Total	$6,000		$17,000		$23,000	
Inventory—December 31	1,500	4,500	5,000	12,000	6,500	16,500
Gross Profit on Sales		$2,500		$ 6,000		$ 8,500
Less Expenses		1,200		2,700		3,900
Net Profit		$1,300		$ 3,300		$ 4,600

In the following working papers the balance sheets of the home office and the branch are combined by adding the amounts of similar assets and liabilities and eliminating the reciprocal current accounts.   The current accounts are eliminated because they represent only relationships within the organization, and not relationships of the organization with the outside world.

Combined Balance Sheet Working Papers
December 31, 1941

	Home Office	Branch	Eliminations	Balance Sheet
Assets				
Cash................................	3,200.00	750.00		3,950.00
Accounts Receivable................	2,900.00	800.00		3,700.00
Inventory.........................	5,000.00	1,500.00		6,500.00
Branch Current....................	2,800.00		2,800.00	
	13,900.00	3,050.00	2,800.00	14,150.00
Liabilities and Net Worth				
Accounts Payable..................	1,400.00	250.00		1,650.00
Home Office Current...............		2,800.00	2,800.00	
Capital Stock.....................	7,500.00			7,500.00
Surplus...........................	5,000.00			5,000.00
	13,900.00	3,050.00	2,800.00	14,150.00

The following balance sheet was prepared from the foregoing working papers.

THE X Y COMPANY
Balance Sheet
December 31, 1941

Assets		Liabilities and Net Worth	
Cash.....................	$ 3,950.00	Accounts Payable..........	$ 1,650.00
Accounts Receivable.......	3,700.00	Capital Stock.............	7,500.00
Inventory................	6,500.00	Surplus...................	5,000.00
	$14,150.00		$14,150.00

47

CONSOLIDATED BALANCE SHEETS

··

Parent and subsidiary companies.

A parent company is a corporation which owns all of, or a controlling interest in, the stock of another company, which is called a subsidiary. The parent and subsidiary relationship serves many purposes and finds extensive application in the organization of modern businesses.

It is, for instance, an extremely convenient device for effecting a unified control of a group of previously independent companies. They may be non-competitive corporations, such as public utility companies operating in different cities, which it is desired to consolidate under one management. They may be competing companies which desire to combine in order to reduce the disadvantages of competition. They may be companies conducting a series of related activities—a coal mine, a railroad, a blast furnace, a steel mill, a factory.

It is not always necessary to have recourse to the parent-subsidiary relationship. A single company conducting all operations is sometimes sufficient. But the retention of separate corporate entities, or the establishment of subsidiaries for special purposes, may be desirable or even necessary. Because of legal restraints it may be necessary to set up a separate corporation for the conduct of certain activities. Or operations may be so extensive and diverse in nature that management is made more effective by the retention or establishment of separate corporate entities. Or minority owners of stocks in companies proposing to merge may refuse to consent to a sale of corporate assets, and control can be obtained only through the purchase of a majority of the voting stock. Or the retention of company names may be desirable for the purpose of preserving goodwill. Or it may be desired to give certain individuals interests in the capital and earnings of particular elements of the total enterprise. Or certain activities may involve extraordinary hazards of losses or contingent liabilities, and it may be desired to isolate and limit the risk.

The parent-subsidiary device also has been extensively used for obtaining control of large-capital enterprises through relatively small investments. Assume, for instance, that a man wishes to obtain control of six companies with capitals of $100,000.00 each. Instead of purchasing all of the stock at a cost of $600,-000.00, he may purchase 51 per cent of the stock of each company, at a total cost of $306,000.00. If he wishes to limit his investment further, he may organize a parent company to acquire the stocks at a cost of $306,000.00; acquire a controlling interest in the parent company by an investment of, say, $156,000.00 in its stock; and obtain the remaining required funds of $150,000.00 by sales of the parent company stock to others. To reduce his investment still further, he can pyramid parent companies. A second parent company can be organized to hold the controlling interest of $156,000.00 of stock of the first parent company; if he acquires 51 per cent of the stock of the second parent company, at a cost of, say, $80,000.00, this investment in the "grandfather" company will enable him to control the "father" company, which in turn controls the six "children" companies with their total capitals of $600,000.00.

Such pyramiding of companies is often accompanied by the issuance of preferred stock, mortgage bonds, and collateral trust obligations which further reduce the management's investment and at the same time give it a "leverage" on earnings. As a simple illustration of the procedure, let us assume that a company has net assets of $1,200,000.00, represented by common stock, with no outstanding long-term indebtedness. It earns $96,000.00 annually, or 8% on its stock. The capital structure of the company is changed to provide for the following bond and stock issues

> First mortgage bonds of $300,000.00, bearing 5% interest; annual interest requirements, $15,000.00.
>
> Preferred stock, $300,000.00, entitled to 6% non-participating dividends; annual dividend requirements, $18,000.00.
>
> Common stock, $600,000.00.

The interest and preferred dividend requirements use $33,-000.00 of the former $96,000.00 of net profit, leaving $63,000.00 for the common stock. The leverage has raised the rate of return on the common stock from 8% to slightly more than 10%.

A parent company is organized to hold the $600,000.00 of common stock. The funds which it requires for the acquisition of the common stock are obtained by issuance of collateral trust notes and stock as follows:

> Collateral trust notes of $300,000.00; bearing 6%, due in ten years, secured by deposit of the $600,000.00 of subsidiary common stock; interest requirements, $18,000.00.
> Preferred stock, $100,000.00, entitled to 7% non-participating dividends; dividend requirements, $7,000.00.
> Common stock, $200,000.00.

The parent company will be presumed to receive $63,000.00 annually as a dividend on the common stock of the operating company; the parent company's interest and preferred dividend requirements will use $25,000.00 of this income, leaving $38,000.00 as income applicable to the $200,000.00 of common stock—or a return of 19%.

The use of the leverage device does not, of course, require the existence of the parent-subsidiary relationship, but the two devices have often been used together for the purposes of (1) minimizing the investment necessary to exercise control and (2) increasing the rate of return on the management's investment.

Leverage, of course, works both ways. Assume, for instance, that the operating company should earn only $62,000.00 before interest on its bonds. The rights of the various security holders would be:

```
Operating company:
  Total.................................................   $62,000.00
  Bond interest...............................  $15,000.00
  Preferred dividends.........................   18,000.00   33,000.00
  Common stock.......................................   $29,000.00
Parent company:
  Collateral trust note interest..............  $18,000.00
  Preferred stock dividends...................    7,000.00   25,000.00
  Common stock—2% on $200,000.00.....................   $ 4,000.00
```

Separate and consolidated statements.

Let us assume that the parent company mentioned in the last preceding illustration owns no other assets and has no other liabilities than those mentioned. Its balance sheet would contain the following items:

Balance Sheet

Assets		Liabilities and Net Worth	
Investment in Subsidiary	$600,000	Collateral Trust Notes	$300,000
		Preferred Stock	100,000
		Common Stock	200,000
	$600,000		$600,000

Its profit and loss statement would show the dividends received from its subsidiary, the interest on the collateral trust notes, and any other expenses.

One cannot deny that such statements would show the financial condition and results of operations of the parent company regarded purely as a separate corporate entity. A possible extender of credit should see such statements in order to know the assets to which the parent company has legal title, the liabilities on which it is directly obligated, the sources of its income, and the nature of its expenses.

But such statements give a wholly inadequate idea of what lies beneath the surface. What kind of assets, owned by the subsidiary, underlie the stock investment? What bond and preferred stock issues and what short-term liabilities of the subsidiary are senior to the common stock owned by the parent company? What is the nature of the subsidiary's operations, from which its earnings and the dividends received by the parent company are derived? How profitable are these operations, and how does the subsidiary's net profit or loss for the year applicable to its common stock compare with the dividends paid by the subsidiary to the parent company during the year?

Because of the importance of these and similar questions, the parent company's separate balance sheet and income statement should be supplemented by other statements. A balance sheet and income statement of the subsidiary may be sufficient supplementary information, but there are at least two disadvantages in attempting to obtain a comprehensive view of the financial condition and operating results of a group of companies by inspection of their separate statements.

(1) It is necessary to determine the totals of similar items in the separate statements; this is somewhat difficult even if there are only two companies; it is more difficult if there are numerous subsidiaries.

(2) Intercompany relationships exist in the form of stock holdings, bond holdings, and current receivables and payables which must be eliminated if one is to obtain a true picture of the group of companies considered as a single unit in relation to the outside world; these relationships may not be disclosed by the separate company balance sheets, and, even if determinable, their elimination from the picture presents something of a difficulty.

For these reasons there has developed a custom of preparing a consolidated balance sheet of the parent company and its subsidiaries in which all similar assets and liabilities are combined, and from which are excluded all account balances of the two companies which reflect mere intercompany relationships such as stock holdings, bond holdings, and other indebtedness. And, similarly, it has become customary to prepare a consolidated profit and loss statement in which all similar items of income and expense are combined, except that intercompany purchases and sales and all items representing income to one company and expense to another are eliminated. In other words, the parent and subsidiary account balances are combined in the statements as though they were the accounts of a company and its unincorporated branch.

Investments in branches and subsidiaries.

Assume that Company P operated branch S, and that the following working papers were prepared for the purpose of combining the balance sheets of the home office and the branch.

COMPANY P AND BRANCH S
Combined Balance Sheet Working Papers
July 31, 1941

Assets	Company P	Branch S	Eliminations	Combined Balance Sheet
Cash...............................	$ 25,000	$10,000		$ 35,000
Accounts Receivable..................	35,000	5,000		40,000
Merchandise Inventory................	60,000	25,000		85,000
Branch Current......................	30,000		$30,000	
	$150,000	$40,000	$30,000	$160,000
Liabilities and Net Worth				
Accounts Payable....................	$ 40,000	$10,000		$ 50,000
Home Office Current.................		30,000	$30,000	
Capital Stock.......................	100,000			100,000
Surplus.............................	10,000			10,000
	$150,000	$40,000	$30,000	$160,000

In these working papers the balances of the two reciprocal current accounts are eliminated because they merely represent relationships between the home office and the branch.

Let us now assume that S was a separate corporation with a capital stock of $30,000.00, and that Company P had purchased all of the stock on July 31, 1941 (the date of the above balance sheet working papers), for $30,000.00.

Although the two companies are separate corporate entities, they constitute a single business organization, and a consolidated balance sheet should be prepared to show their combined assets and liabilities. The following working papers for the consolidation of the balance sheets of this parent company and its subsidiary are the same as the preceding ones for combining the balance sheets of the home office and the branch, except for the change in the names of the reciprocal accounts.

COMPANY P AND SUBSIDIARY S
Consolidated Balance Sheet Working Papers
July 31, 1941

Assets	Company P	Company S	Eliminations	Consolidated Balance Sheet
Cash............................	$ 25,000	$10,000		$ 35,000
Accounts Receivable..................	35,000	5,000		40,000
Merchandise Inventory................	60,000	25,000		85,000
Investment in Stock of Company S......	30,000		$30,000	
	$150,000	$40,000	$30,000	$160,000
Liabilities and Net Worth				
Accounts Payable.....................	$ 40,000	$10,000		$ 50,000
Capital Stock:				
Company P.........................	100,000			100,000
Company S.........................		30,000	$30,000	
Surplus............................	10,000			10,000
	$150,000	$40,000	$30,000	$160,000

The consolidated balance sheet prepared from the foregoing working papers is shown below:

COMPANY P AND SUBSIDIARY S
Consolidated Balance Sheet
July 31, 1941

Assets		Liabilities and Net Worth		
Cash......................	$ 35,000	Accounts Payable............		$ 50 000
Accounts Receivable........	40,000	Net Worth:		
Merchandise Inventory.......	85,000	Capital Stock....	$100,000	
		Surplus.........	10,000	110,000
	$160,000			$160,000

Intercompany eliminations.

The elimination of intercompany accounts in the foregoing working papers may be expressed by the following rule:

Elimination of reciprocals:
Subsidiary's Capital Stock account.
Parent company's Investment account.

Subsidiary surplus or deficit.

Let us now assume that on July 31, 1941, the date of acquisition by Company P, the net worth of Company S was represented by capital stock of $25,000.00 and a surplus of $5,000.00. Company P acquired the stock for $30,000.00.

The reciprocal balances on the books of the parent and subsidiary companies now are:

Debit on books of parent company:
Investment in Stock of Company S............ $30,000.00

Credits on books of subsidiary:
Capital Stock............................... $25,000.00
Surplus.....................................   5,000.00

The working papers for the consolidation of the balance sheets appear below:

COMPANY P AND SUBSIDIARY S
Consolidated Balance Sheet Working Papers
July 31, 1941

Assets	Company P	Company S	Eliminations	Consolidated Balance Sheet
Cash.................................	$ 25,000	$10,000		$ 35,000
Accounts Receivable...................	35,000	5,000		40,000
Merchandise Inventory.................	60,000	25,000		85,000
Investment in Stock of Company S......	30,000		$30,000	
	$150,000	$40,000	$30,000	$160,000
Liabilities and Net Worth				
Accounts Payable.....................	$ 40,000	$10,000		$ 50,000
Capital Stock:				
Company P........................	100,000			100,000
Company S........................		25,000	25,000	
Surplus:				
Company P........................	10,000			10,000
Company S........................		5,000	5,000	
	$150,000	$40,000	$30,000	$160,000

The consolidated balance sheet would be the same as that previously illustrated.

Let us now assume that on July 31, 1941, the date of acquisition by the parent company, the subsidiary's net worth of $30,000.00 was represented by capital stock of $35,000.00 and a deficit of $5,000.00, and that the parent company acquired the stock at its net book value of $30,000.00. The procedure for effecting the elimination of the reciprocal accounts is shown in the working papers on the following page.

COMPANY *P* AND SUBSIDIARY *S*
Consolidated Balance Sheet Working Papers
July 31, 1941

Assets	Company P	Company S	Eliminations	Consolidated Balance Sheet
Cash................................	$ 25,000	$10,000		$ 35,000
Accounts Receivable................	35,000	5,000		40,000
Merchandise Inventory..............	60,000	25,000		85,000
Investment in Stock of Company S.....	30,000		$30,000	
	$150,000	$40,000	$30,000	$160,000
Liabilities and Net Worth				
Accounts Payable...................	$ 40,000	$10,000		$ 50,000
Capital Stock:				
Company P......................	100,000			100,000
Company S......................		35,000	$35,000	
Surplus (Deficit*):				
Company P......................	10,000			10,000
Company S......................		5,000*	5,000*	
	$150,000	$40,000	$30,000	$160,000

Elimination of reciprocals.

It now becomes apparent that the rule for the elimination of reciprocals must be amended by the addition of the words shown below in italics.

> Elimination of reciprocals:
> Subsidiary's Capital Stock *and Surplus or Deficit accounts.*
> Parent company's Investment account.

Minority interest.

If the parent company acquires less than 100 per cent of the stock of the subsidiary, it shares the ownership of the subsidiary with the outsiders whose stock it does not purchase. These outsiders are called the minority stockholders of the subsidiary. The Capital Stock and Surplus (or Deficit) accounts of the subsidiary then include two elements:

The holding company's percentage of the subsidiary stock and surplus (or deficit). These items are reciprocal to the parent company's Investment account, and should therefore be eliminated.

The minority stockholders' interest in the subsidiary stock and surplus (or deficit). These items are not reciprocal to any balances on the parent company's books, and are therefore carried to the consolidated balance sheet.

We must therefore again modify our rule for the elimination of intercompany balances, by the addition of the words shown below in italics:

Elimination of reciprocals:
  Subsidiary's Capital Stock and Surplus or Deficit accounts. *Eliminate reciprocal element—parent company's proportion. Extend non-reciprocal element (minority interest) to Consolidated Balance Sheet column.*
  Parent company's Investment account.

Three illustrations of working papers and consolidated balance sheets are given below. All are based on the parent company and subsidiary used in the foregoing illustrations. In all cases the subsidiary has the same assets and liabilities as before; its net assets in every case are $30,000.00. It is assumed, in each case, that the parent company has just acquired a 90 per cent interest in the subsidiary's stock at its book value of $27,000.00, as shown by the subsidiary's net worth accounts.

First illustration. In this illustration, the net worth of the subsidiary was represented by capital stock of $30,000.00; there was no surplus or deficit.

COMPANY *P* AND SUBSIDIARY *S*
Consolidated Balance Sheet Working Papers
July 31, 1941

Assets	Company P	Company S	Eliminations	Consolidated Balance Sheet
Cash..............................	$ 28,000	$10,000		$ 38,000
Accounts Receivable..................	35,000	5,000		40,000
Merchandise Inventory...............	60,000	25,000		85,000
Investment in Stock of Co. *S*—90%....	27,000		$27,000	
	$150,000	$40,000	$27,000	$163,000
Liabilities and Net Worth				
Accounts Payable....................	$ 40,000	$10,000		$ 50,000
Capital Stock:				
Company *P*......................	100,000			100,000
Company *S*......................		30,000		
Eliminate Co. *P*'s 90%...........			$27,000	
Minority Interest—10%..........				3,000
Surplus..........................	10,000			10,000
	$150,000	$40,000	$27,000	$163,000

The consolidated balance sheet prepared from these working papers appears on the next page. Note how the minority interest is shown.

COMPANY P AND SUBSIDIARY S
Consolidated Balance Sheet
July 31, 1941

Assets		Liabilities and Net Worth		
Cash	$ 38,000	Accounts Payable		$ 50,000
Accounts Receivable	40,000	Minority Interest in Company		
Merchandise Inventory	85,000	S—10%		3,000
		Net Worth:		
		Capital Stock....	$100,000	
		Surplus	10,000	110,000
	$163,000			$163,000

Second illustration. This illustration is the same as the foregoing one, with one exception: The subsidiary's net worth was represented by capital stock of $25,000.00 and a surplus of $5,000.00.

COMPANY P AND SUBSIDIARY S
Consolidated Balance Sheet Working Papers
July 31, 1941

Assets	Company P	Company S	Eliminations	Consolidated Balance Sheet
Cash	$ 28,000	$10,000		$ 38,000
Accounts Receivable	35,000	5,000		40,000
Merchandise Inventory	60,000	25,000		85,000
Investment in Stock of Co. S—90%	27,000		$27,000	
	$150,000	$40,000	$27,000	$163,000
Liabilities and Net Worth				
Accounts Payable	$ 40,000	$10,000		$ 50,000
Capital Stock:				
Company P	100,000			100,000
Company S		25,000		
Eliminate Co. P's 90%			$22,500	
Minority Interest—10%				2,500
Surplus:				
Company P	10,000			10,000
Company S		5,000		
Eliminate Co. P's 90%			4,500	
Minority Interest—10%				500
	$150,000	$40,000	$27,000	$163,000

It will be noted that the amounts in the Consolidated column of these working papers are the same as those in the working papers for the first illustration of this group, with one exception: The minority interest of $3,000.00 is now represented by two items instead of one. But, since the minority interest would in each case be shown in the consolidated balance sheet in one amount of $3,000.00, the consolidated balance sheet for the second illustration would be the same as that for the first.

Third illustration. This illustration is the same as the preceding one except that the net worth of the subsidiary is now represented by a Capital Stock account of $35,000.00, less a deficit of $5,000.00, shown by a debit balance in its Surplus account.

COMPANY *P* AND SUBSIDIARY *S*
Consolidated Balance Sheet Working Papers
July 31, 1941

Assets	Company P	Company S	Eliminations	Consolidated Balance Sheet
Cash...............................	$ 28,000	$10,000		$ 38,000
Accounts Receivable................	35,000	5,000		40,000
Merchandise Inventory..............	60,000	25,000		85,000
Investment in Stock of Co. *S*—90%...	27,000		$27,000	
	$150,000	$40,000	$27,000	$163,000
Liabilities and Net Worth				
Accounts Payable...................	$ 40,000	$10,000		$ 50,000
Capital Stock:				
Company *P*......................	100,000			100,000
Company *S*......................		35,000		
Eliminate Co. *P*'s 90%..........			$31,500	
Minority Interest—10%.........				3,500
Surplus (Deficit*):				
Company *P*......................	10,000			10,000
Company *S*......................		5,000*		
Eliminate Co. *P*'s 90%..........			4,500*	
Minority Interest—10%.........				500*
	$150,000	$40,000	$27,000	$163,000

The balance sheet would be the same as in the two preceding illustrations.

Alternative form of working papers.

Consolidated balance sheets usually can be prepared without such elaborate working papers as those previously illustrated. To show a simpler form, let us repeat the second of the last three cases. The balance sheets of the parent and subsidiary companies are shown below and on the next page.

COMPANY *P* AND SUBSIDIARY *S*
Balance Sheets
July 31, 1941

Assets	Company P	Company S
Cash..	$ 28,000.00	$10,000.00
Accounts Receivable........................	35,000.00	5,000.00
Merchandise Inventory......................	60,000.00	25,000.00
Investment in Stock of Company *S*—90%......	27,000.00	
	$150,000.00	$40,000.00

Balance Sheets—*Continued*

Liabilities and Net Worth	Company P	Company S
Accounts Payable..........................	$ 40,000.00	$10,000.00
Capital Stock.............................	100,000.00	25,000.00
Surplus..................................	10,000.00	5,000.00
	$150,000.00	$40,000.00

Of the above accounts, the following asset and liability accounts do not contain any reciprocal elements:

> Cash.
> Accounts Receivable.
> Merchandise Inventory.
> Accounts Payable.

The following net worth accounts of the parent company do not contain any reciprocal elements:

> Capital Stock.
> Surplus.

The consolidated amounts of these items can be entered directly in a consolidated balance sheet, as shown below.

COMPANY P AND SUBSIDIARY S
Consolidated Balance Sheet
July 31, 1941

Assets		Liabilities and Net Worth		
Cash.......................	$38,000	Accounts Payable...........		$ 50,000
Accounts Receivable..........	40,000			
Merchandise Inventory.......	85,000			
		Net Worth:		
		Capital Stock....	$100,000	
		Surplus..........	10,000	110,000

The eliminations from the reciprocal accounts can be made in simple working papers like the following:

	Subsidiary's Accounts		Parent's Investment Account
	Capital Stock	Surplus	
Balances—per balance sheets.....................	$25,000	$5,000	$27,000
Deduct reciprocal elements—90% of subsidiary's net worth..	22,500	4,500	27,000
Remainder—Non-reciprocal element:			
Minority interest..............................	$2,500	$ 500	

The consolidated balance sheet can now be completed by entering the amount of the minority interest.

COMPANY *P* AND SUBSIDIARY *S*
Consolidated Balance Sheet
July 31, 1941

Assets		Liabilities and Net Worth		
Cash	$ 38,000	Accounts Payable		$ 50,000
Accounts Receivable	40,000	Minority Interest in Company		
Merchandise Inventory	85,000	*S*—10%		3,000
		Net Worth:		
		Capital Stock	$100,000	
		Surplus	10,000	110,000
	$163,000			$163,000

Goodwill.

If one company buys the assets and liabilities of another company (instead of its stock), any payment in excess of the value of the net assets acquired is regarded as goodwill. Similarly, if one company acquires control of another company by purchasing its stock, any payment in excess of the book value of the stock acquired may be regarded as a payment for goodwill.

Therefore, if the stock of a subsidiary is purchased at a price in excess of its book value as shown by the Capital Stock and Surplus or Deficit accounts of the subsidiary, the balance in the Investment account on the parent company's books will consist of two elements:

> The book value of the stock acquired.
> The excess payment, or goodwill.

To illustrate, assume that a company paid $32,000.00 for all of the stock of a subsidiary which had a capital stock of $25,000.00 and a surplus of $5,000.00. The balance in the Investment account consists of the following elements:

$30,000.00—representing the book value of the stock acquired. This element is reciprocal to, and is eliminated against, the Capital Stock and Surplus accounts of the subsidiary.

$2,000.00—representing a payment for goodwill. This element is not reciprocal to any balance on the subsidiary's books and therefore is not eliminated, but is shown in the consolidated balance sheet as goodwill, either as a separate item or added to any goodwill that may appear on the books of either company.

It therefore again becomes necessary to expand our rule for the elimination of intercompany accounts, by adding the words shown below in italics.

Elimination of reciprocals:

Subsidiary's Capital Stock and Surplus or Deficit accounts

Eliminate reciprocal element (parent company's portion)
Include the non-reciprocal element (minority interest in the consolidated balance sheet.

Parent company's Investment account:

Eliminate reciprocal element (parent company's proportion of subsidiary's stock and surplus).

Include the non-reciprocal element in the consolidated balance sheet as goodwill.

Illustrations. The following partial balance sheets show facts which are common to the next three illustrations:

COMPANY P AND SUBSIDIARY S
Partial Balance Sheets
July 31, 1941

Assets	Company P	Company S
Cash	$ 26,000.00	$10,000.00
Accounts Receivable	35,000.00	5,000.00
Merchandise Inventory	60,000.00	25,000.00
Investment in Company S—90%	29,000.00	
	$150,000.00	$40,000.00
Liabilities and Net Worth		
Accounts Payable	$ 40,000.00	$10,000.00
Capital Stock:		
Company P	100,000.00	
Surplus:		
Company P	10,000.00	
	$150,000.00	

The parent company owns 90 per cent of the subsidiary's stock, which it just acquired at a cost of $29,000.00.

In the first of the following illustrations the subsidiary has a capital stock of $30,000.00 and no surplus or deficit. The goodwill and minority interest can be computed as follows:

COMPANY P AND SUBSIDIARY S
Consolidating Working Papers
July 31, 1941

	Subsidiary's Capital Stock Account	Parent's Investment Account
Balances	$30,000.00	$29,000.00
Deduct reciprocal element—90% of subsidiary's net worth	27,000.00	27,000.00
Non-reciprocal elements:		
Minority interest—10%	$ 3,000.00	
Goodwill		$ 2,000.00

COMPANY *P* AND SUBSIDIARY *S*
Consolidated Balance Sheet
July 31, 1941

Assets		Liabilities and Net Worth		
Cash	$ 36,000	Accounts Payable		$ 50,000
Accounts Receivable	40,000	Minority Interest in Company		
Merchandise Inventory	85,000	*S*—10%		3,000
Goodwill	2,000	Net Worth:		
		Capital Stock	$100,000	
		Surplus	10,000	110,000
	$163,000			$163,000

The next illustration is the same as the preceding one except that it is now assumed that the subsidiary's net worth is represented by capital stock of $25,000.00 and a surplus of $5,000.00.

COMPANY *P* AND SUBSIDIARY *S*
Consolidating Working Papers
July 31, 1941

	Subsidiary's Accounts		Parent's Invest-
	Capital Stock	Surplus	ment Account
Balances	$25,000	$5,000	$29,000
Deduct reciprocal element—90% of subsidiary's net worth	22,500	4,500	27,000
Non-reciprocal elements:			
Minority interest—10%	$ 2,500	$ 500	
Goodwill			$ 2,000

The consolidated balance sheet would be the same as that in the immediately preceding illustration.

The next illustration contains only the following change: The subsidiary's net worth is represented by capital stock of $35,000.00 and a deficit of $5,000.00. The working papers for the computation of the minority interest and the goodwill are presented below:

COMPANY *P* AND SUBSIDIARY *S*
Consolidating Working Papers
July 31, 1941

	Subsidiary's Accounts		Parent's Invest-
	Capital Stock	Surplus (Deficit*)	ment Account
Balances	$35,000	$5,000*	$29,000
Deduct reciprocal elements—90% of subsidiary's net worth	31,500	4,500*	27,000
Non-reciprocal elements:			
Minority interest—10%	$ 3,500	$ 500*	
Goodwill			$ 2,000

Book value in excess of cost.

If the subsidiary has a Goodwill account on its books at the date when the parent company acquires its stock interest, and if the parent company pays less than book value for the stock, the presumption is that the parent company does not recognize the subsidiary's goodwill. The deficiency in price should be deducted from the goodwill on the subsidiary's books.

Following are assumed company balance sheets:

Balance Sheets—July 31, 1941

Assets	Company P	Company S
Cash	$ 29,000.00	$ 7,000.00
Accounts Receivable	35,000.00	5,000.00
Merchandise Inventory	60,000.00	25,000.00
Investment in Company S—90%	26,000.00	
Goodwill		3,000.00
	$150,000.00	$40,000.00

Liabilities and Net Worth		
Accounts Payable	$ 40,000.00	$10,000.00
Capital Stock	100,000.00	25,000.00
Surplus	10,000.00	5,000.00
	$150,000.00	$40,000.00

COMPANY P AND SUBSIDIARY S
Consolidating Working Papers
July 31, 1941

	Subsidiary's Accounts		Parent's Investment Account
	Capital Stock	Surplus	
Balances	$25,000	$5,000	$26,000
Deduct reciprocal element—90% of subsidiary's net worth	22,500	4,500	27,000
Non-reciprocal elements:			
Minority interest—10%	$ 2,500	$ 500	
Deduction from goodwill			$ 1,000*

COMPANY P AND SUBSIDIARY S
Consolidated Balance Sheet
July 31, 1941

Assets		Liabilities and Net Worth		
Cash	$ 36,000	Accounts Payable		$ 50,000
Accounts Receivable	40,000	Minority Interest in Company S—10%		3,000
Merchandise Inventory	85,000	Net Worth:		
Goodwill	2,000	Capital Stock	$100,000	
		Surplus	10,000	110,000
	$163,000			$163,000

What should be done with an excess of book value over purchase cost if there is no Goodwill account on the subsidiary's books from which it can be deducted?

If there is a Goodwill account on the books of the parent company or some other subsidiary, or if goodwill was paid for in the acquisition of the stock of some other subsidiary, it usually is regarded as correct procedure to make the deduction from any such goodwill items. This does not seem to be a logical procedure, as it is difficult to see how the acquisition of the stock of one subsidiary at less than its book value has any relation to goodwill purchases in other transactions.

If some other assets are known to be overvalued on the subsidiary's books, it seems logical to make a deduction from the stated book values of these other assets.

If there is no goodwill on the books of the subsidiary whose stock was acquired at less than book value, if none of its assets are overvalued, and if there is no goodwill elsewhere in the consolidated working papers (or if it is not considered proper to make a deduction from such goodwill), the excess of the book value of the subsidiary stock over the cost thereof may be shown in the Surplus section of the consolidated balance sheet as Capital Surplus or Surplus Arising from Consolidation, or with some other descriptive title.

Intercompany receivables and payables.

A consolidated balance sheet shows the financial condition of a group of companies with all intercompany relationships eliminated. Related companies frequently buy from and sell to each other, or make intercompany advances. All such intercompany receivables and payables should be eliminated.* The following illustration shows how such eliminations would be made in consolidated working papers of the form illustrated at the beginning of this chapter.

COMPANY P AND SUBSIDIARY S
Consolidated Balance Sheet Working Papers

Assets	Company P	Company S	Eliminations	Consolidated Balance Sheet
Accounts Receivable..............................	$165,000	$60,000	$12,000	$213,000
Notes Receivable—Company S..............	25,000		25,000	
Liabilities				
Accounts Payable............................	$ 90,000	$30,000	$12,000	$108,000
Notes Payable—Company P................		25,000	25,000	

What companies should be consolidated?

A company is a subsidiary if at least a controlling interest in its voting stock is owned by another (parent) company. However, the ownership of a mere control has not been accepted by all accountants as sufficient justification for the inclusion of the subsidiary's accounts in consolidated statements.

A consolidated balance sheet may be said to be based on the assumption that, if the parent company owns all of the stock of the subsidiary, the assets owned and the liabilities owed by the subsidiary may be regarded, for consolidated-statement purposes, as owned and owed by the parent company; and that, if the minority interest is relatively small, the error in the assumption is of relatively small significance and is indicated by the inclusion of the minority interest on the liability side of the balance sheet. But when the minority interest is 49 per cent, the error in the assumption assumes major importance. Many accountants, therefore, have felt that consolidation of a subsidiary was not justified by mere control of voting stock. Some have said that at least 60 per cent of the voting stock should be owned; others have said 75 per cent; others more. Some have said that the propriety of including a subsidiary's accounts in the consolidated statements should depend, not on the percentage of voting stock owned, but on the percentage of the total stock of all classes owned.

On the other hand, some accountants appear to hold the opinion that if a company's investment represents less than 50 per cent of the voting stock, but control has been maintained by proxies, by leases, or otherwise, consolidation is permissible.

It should not be assumed, however, that ownership of all of a subsidiary's stock necessarily makes the preparation of a consolidated balance sheet desirable. The parent and the subsidiary may be engaged in operations so different in nature that consolidated statements would be almost an unintelligible hodge-podge of unrelated data.

For the reasons indicated in the preceding paragraphs, one who reads a consolidated statement should seek to determine the degrees of ownership of the consolidated subsidiaries; he should also observe whether any stock investments appear on the asset side of the balance sheet and indicate the existence of subsidiaries not consolidated, or the existence of stock investments which, though material in amount, do not represent controlling interests.

48

CONSOLIDATED BALANCE SHEETS
Continued

Basis of illustrations

Each consolidated balance sheet in Chapter 47 was prepared as of the date of acquisition of the subsidiary stock. This chapter will illustrate balance sheets at subsequent dates. As a basis for a series of illustrations, the following balance sheets as of January 1, 1941, show the financial condition of the parent company and the subsidiary on the date when the parent company acquired a 90 per cent interest in the stock of the subsidiary at a cost of $138,000.00.

Balance Sheets—January 1, 1941

Assets	Company *P*	Company *S*
Cash	$ 50,000.00	$ 20,000.00
Accounts Receivable	95,000.00	75,000.00
Inventory	125,000.00	70,000.00
Investment in Stock of Co. *S*—90%	138,000.00	
	$408,000.00	$165,000.00
Liabilities and Net Worth		
Accounts Payable	$ 40,000.00	$ 15,000.00
Capital Stock	300,000.00	100,000.00
Surplus	68,000.00	50,000.00
	$408,000.00	$165,000.00

The working papers to determine the goodwill and minority interest are submitted below:

Consolidating Working Papers
January 1, 1941

	Subsidiary's Accounts		Parent's
	Capital Stock	Surplus	Investment Account
Balances	$100,000	$50,000	$138,000
Deduct reciprocal element—90% of subsidiary's net worth	90,000	45,000	135,000
Non-reciprocal elements:			
Minority interest	$ 10,000	$ 5,000	
Goodwill			$ 3,000

491

The following is the consolidated balance sheet at the date of acquisition:

COMPANY *P* AND SUBSIDIARY *S*
Consolidated Balance Sheet
January 1, 1941

Assets		Liabilities and Net Worth		
Cash...............................	$ 70,000	Accounts Payable............		$ 55,000
Accounts Receivable..........	170,000	Minority Interest in Co. *S*—		
Inventory.......................	195,000	10%.....................		15,000
Goodwill........................	3,000	Net Worth:		
		Capital Stock....	$300,000	
		Surplus..........	68,000	368,000
	$438,000			$438,000

Subsidiary Profits, Losses, and Dividends Recorded Through the Investment Account

Parent company's entries.

Chapter 32 contained a discussion of a parent company's accounting procedure whereby the subsidiary profits, losses, and dividends are recorded through the Investment account by the entries indicated below.

For subsidiary profits:
Debit the Investment account.
Credit an income account or Surplus.

For subsidiary losses:
Debit a loss account or Surplus.
Credit the Investment account.

For dividends received:
Debit Cash.
Credit the Investment account.

Two illustrations will now be presented, based on the assumption that the parent company is applying the above-described procedure.

After a profit. Assume that, during the six months subsequent to the acquisition of the subsidiary stock, the subsidiary made a net profit of $20,000.00. The parent company recorded its 90 per cent interest therein as follows:

Investment in Stock of Co. *S*.................... 18,000.00
Income from Subsidiary (closed to Surplus).....   18,000.00
To take up our 90% of the net profit of the subsidiary during the first six months of 1941.

To simplify the illustration, we shall assume that the parent company conducted no operations of any kind during the six months, and that the only change in its surplus was that resulting rom taking up the subsidiary earnings. And, to simplify the llustration further, we shall assume that there were no changes n the subsidiary's balance sheet except a $20,000.00 increase in ash and in surplus resulting from the profits.

The balance sheets of the two companies on June 30, 1941, are herefore assumed to have been as follows:

Balance Sheets—June 30, 1941

Assets	Company P	Company S
Cash	$ 50,000.00	$ 40,000.00
Accounts Receivable	95,000.00	75,000.00
Inventory	125,000.00	70,000.00
Investment in Stock of Co. S—90%	156,000.00	
	$426,000.00	$185,000.00
Liabilities and Net Worth		
Accounts Payable	$ 40,000.00	$ 15,000.00
Capital Stock	300,000.00	100,000.00
Surplus	86,000.00	70,000.00
	$426,000.00	$185,000.00

The working papers for the computation of the minority inter-st and the goodwill appear below.

Consolidating Working Papers
June 30, 1941

	Subsidiary's Accounts		Parent's
	Capital Stock	Surplus	Investment Account
Balances	$100,000	$70,000	$156,000
Deduct reciprocal element—90% of subsidiary's net worth	90,000	63,000	153,000
Non-reciprocal elements:			
Minority interest—10%	$ 10,000	$ 7,000	
Goodwill			$ 3,000

Observe that the amount shown as goodwill is the same as that shown as of January 1, 1941. Naturally this would be the case, because the goodwill is the excess of the cost of the stock over the book value at the date of acquisition. This excess was determined by facts existing at the date of acquisition, and is not affected by subsequent profits or losses of the subsidiary.

The amount shown as the minority interest is 10 per cent of the net worth of the subsidiary on the date of the consolidated balance sheet.

The consolidated balance sheet appears on the next page.

COMPANY P AND SUBSIDIARY S
Consolidated Balance Sheet
June 30, 1941

Assets		Liabilities and Net Worth		
Cash	$ 90,000	Accounts Payable		$ 55,000
Accounts Receivable	170,000	Minority Interest in		
Inventory	195,000	Co. S—10%		17,000
Goodwill	3,000	Net Worth:		
		Capital Stock	$300,000	
		Surplus	86,000	386,000
	$458,000			$458,000

Observe that the consolidated surplus is the same as the surplus shown by the balance sheet of the parent company. This is because the parent company has already credited its Surplus account with its share of the subsidiary's net profit since acquisition.

After a loss and a dividend. We shall now assume that during the second six months the subsidiary lost $10,000.00, and paid a $5,000.00 dividend out of previously accumulated surplus. The parent company's entries are:

Loss from Subsidiary (closed to Surplus)	9,000.00	
Investment in Stock of Company S		9,000.00
To take up our 90% of the loss of Company S during the second six months of 1941.		

Cash	4,500.00	
Investment in Stock of Company S		4,500.00
To record receipt of a dividend from the subsidiary.		

To simplify the illustration as much as possible, let us assume that the loss and the dividend were the only changes during the six months. Their effect on the books of both companies is summarized below:

	Subsidiary's Accounts		Parent Company's Accounts		
				Investment	
	Cash	Surplus	Cash	Account	Surplus
Balances, June 30	$40,000	$70,000	$50,000	$156,000	$86,000
Loss:					
Total	10,000*	10,000*			
90% to parent				9,000*	9,000*
Dividend:					
Total	5,000*	5,000*			
90% to parent			4,500	4,500*	
Balances, December 31	$25,000	$55,000	$54,500	$142,500	$77,000

The company balance sheets, the consolidating working papers, and the consolidated balance sheet appear on the next page.

Balance Sheets—December 31, 1941

Assets	Company P	Company S
Cash....................................	$ 54,500.00	$ 25,000.00
Accounts Receivable......................	95,000.00	75,000.00
Inventory................................	125,000.00	70,000.00
Investment in Stock of Co. S—90%..........	142,500.00	
	$417,000.00	$170,000.00

Liabilities and Net Worth		
Accounts Payable.........................	$ 40,000.00	$ 15,000.00
Capital Stock.............................	300,000.00	100,000.00
Surplus..................................	77,000.00	55,000.00
	$417,000.00	$170,000.00

Consolidating Working Papers
December 31, 1941

	Subsidiary's Accounts		Parent's
	Capital Stock	Surplus	Investment Account
Balances......................................	$100,000	$55,000	$142,500
Eliminate reciprocal element—90% of subsidiary's net worth.................................	90,000	49,500	139,500
Non-reciprocal elements:			
Minority interest—10% of the subsidiary's present net worth............................	$ 10,000	$ 5,500	
Goodwill—same as before...................			$ 3,000

COMPANY P AND SUBSIDIARY S
Consolidated Balance Sheet
December 31, 1941

Assets		Liabilities and Net Worth		
Cash.......................	$ 79,500	Accounts Payable...........		$ 55,000
Accounts Receivable........	170,000	Minority Interest in		
Inventory..................	195,000	Co. S—10%..............		15,500
Goodwill...................	3,000	Net Worth:		
		Capital Stock....	$300,000	
		Surplus..........	77,000	377,000
	$447,500			$447,500

Investment Carried at Cost

If the parent company followed the procedure of carrying the investment at cost and taking up dividends as income, its accounts on January 1, June 30, and December 31, 1941, were as follows:

Parent Company Balance Sheets
Investment Carried at Cost

Assets	January 1	June 30	December 31
Cash.................................	$ 50,000.00	$ 50,000.00	$ 54,500.00
Accounts Receivable..................	95,000.00	95,000.00	95,000.00
Inventory............................	125,000.00	125,000.00	125,000.00
Investment in Stock of Co. S—90%.....	138,000.00	138,000.00	138,000.00
	$408,000.00	$408,000.00	$412,500.00

Parent Company Balance Sheets—*Continued*

Liabilities and Net Worth	January 1	June 30	December 31
Accounts Payable	$ 40,000.00	$ 40,000.00	$ 40,000.00
Capital Stock	300,000.00	300,000.00	300,000.00
Surplus	68,000.00	68,000.00	72,500.00
	$408,000.00	$408,000.00	$412,500.00

Since the only entries made by the parent company were those to take up as income the dividends received from the subsidiary, there are no changes between the balance sheets of January 1 and June 30. The parent company's recording of the dividend on December 31 increased its cash and surplus $4,500.00.

To show clearly the differences in the results obtained by the two methods of accounting, the balance sheets of the parent company used in the preceding illustrations, in which the parent company took up its share of the subsidiary's profits, losses, and dividends through the Investment account, are shown below.

Parent Company Balance Sheets
Subsidiary Profits, Losses, and Dividends
Recorded Through Investment Account

Assets	January 1	June 30	December 31
Cash	$ 50,000.00	$ 50,000.00	$ 54,500.00
Accounts Receivable	95,000.00	95,000.00	95,000.00
Inventory	125,000.00	125,000.00	125,000.00
Investment in Stock of Co. S	138,000.00	156,000.00	142,500.00
	$408,000.00	$426,000.00	$417,000.00
Liabilities and Net Worth			
Accounts Payable	$ 40,000.00	$ 40,000.00	$ 40,000.00
Capital Stock	300,000.00	300,000.00	300,000.00
Surplus	68,000.00	86,000.00	77,000.00
	$408,000.00	$426,000.00	$417,000.00

A comparison of the balance sheets on the two bases of accounting shows that the only differences are in the Investment and Surplus accounts. Therefore, even if the parent company carries the investment at cost, the consolidated assets and liabilities can be computed as in previous illustrations, by adding the similar items in the balance sheets.

Under the accounting procedure of carrying the investment at cost, the parent company has taken into its own Surplus account only the portion of the subsidiary's earnings that has been received in the form of dividends. It has not taken into its surplus the subsidiary earnings since acquisition not distributed in dividends but reflected by the increase in the subsidiary surplus since acquisition. An adjustment for this increase in subsidiary surplus since acquisition should be made in the working papers, as illustrated below:

June 30—after a profit:

Consolidating Working Papers
June 30, 1941

	Subsidiary's Accounts		Parent's Accounts	
	Capital Stock	Surplus	Investment	Surplus
Balances before adjustment...................	$100,000.00	$70,000.00	$138,000.00	$68,000.00
Adjustment—90% of increase in subsidiary surplus since acquisition:				
Balance—June 30.............. $70,000.00				
Balance—Jan. 1................ 50,000.00				
Increase...................... $20,000.00				
90% thereof............................			18,000.00	18,000.00
Balances after adjustment...................	$100,000.00	$70,000.00	$156,000.00	$86,000.00
Eliminate reciprocal element—90% of subsidiary's net worth..............................	90,000.00	63,000.00	153,000.00	
Non-reciprocal elements:				
Minority interest-10%.....................	$ 10,000.00	$ 7,000.00		
Goodwill..............................			$ 3,000.00	
Consolidated surplus.......................				$86,000.00

Observe that the minority interest, goodwill, and consolidated surplus computed above are the same as those shown in the June 30 consolidated balance sheet prepared from accounts kept on the other basis, as shown on page 494.

December 31—after a loss and a dividend:

Consolidating Working Papers
December 31, 1941

	Subsidiary's Accounts		Parent's Accounts	
	Capital Stock	Surplus	Investment	Surplus
Balances before adjustment...................	$100,000.00	$55,000.00	$138,000.00	$72,500.00•
Adjustment—90% of increase in subsidiary surplus since acquisition:				
Balance—Dec. 31.............. $55,000.00				
Balance—Jan. 1................ 50,000.00				
Increase...................... $ 5,000.00				
90% thereof..............			4,500.00	4,500.00
Adjusted balances...........................	$100,000.00	$55,000.00	$142,500.00	$77,000.00
Eliminate reciprocal element—90% of subsidiary's net worth..............................	90,000.00	49,500.00	139,500.00	
Non-reciprocal elements:				
Minority interest—10%.....................	$ 10,000.00	$ 5,500.00		
Goodwill................................			$ 3,000.00	
Consolidated surplus.......................				$77,000.00

The minority interest, goodwill, and consolidated surplus shown above are the same as those shown by the working papers on page 495 prepared from accounts kept on the other basis of accounting.

Profits in inventories.

When one company sells goods at a profit to a related company, the minority stockholders of the selling company have a right to consider that the profit has been realized, since the goods have been sold to a company in which they have no interest. The parent company, which controls the organization and looks upon the various subsidiaries virtually as departments of the organization, should not regard the profit as realized until the goods have been resold to a purchaser outside of the organization.

Therefore, if, at the date of the consolidated balance sheet, the inventories of any of the related companies contain goods that were purchased from other related companies after the consolidation was effected, the inventories should be analyzed to determine how much of their present carrying value is composed of profits added by the selling companies. After this unrealized profit has been ascertained, a reserve should be created, out of the parent company's surplus, for the parent company's portion of such unrealized profit.

To illustrate, it is assumed that Company P owns 90 per cent of the stock of Company S. Company S has sold goods to Company P during the year at a profit, and the inventory of Company P at the end of the year includes goods purchased from Company S on which the latter company made a profit of $1,000.00. Since Company P, in taking up its share of the profits of Company S has taken up $900.00 of this profit, a reserve should be created by deducting $900.00 from the parent company's surplus and transferring it to a reserve.

The reserve for unrealized profits may be shown on the consolidated balance sheet as a deduction from the inventories. Inventories should be priced at cost (unless market is lower), and cost should not include the organization's share of unrealized profits resulting from transfers from one related company to another. Or the inventories may be shown at the net amount after the intercompany profit has been deducted, without showing the reserve on the balance sheet.

Profits from sales before stock acquisition.

If the inventories contain goods which were sold by one company to another before the parent company acquired control of the selling company, no reserve should be created, because the parent company did not take up a share of such profits and should not be required to reduce its surplus by an amount which has not been included therein.   The companies were not related when the sale took place, and hence the profit was not intercompany profit.

Intercompany profits on fixed assets.

When one company produces fixed assets for another related company and makes a profit on the construction, a reserve should be created to eliminate the parent company's proportion of such profit and reduce the fixed assets to cost.   As already shown in connection with inventories, the cost may properly include the profit applicable to the minority interest of the selling company. The parent company cannot equitably ask the minority stock-holders of its subsidiary to forego their share of the profit on work done for a company in which they have no interest; nor can the parent company reasonably be called upon to set up a $10,000.00 reserve for the total profit made by a subsidiary, if the parent company owns only 90 per cent of the stock and has taken up only $9,000.00 of the profit on the construction.

To illustrate, assume that Company P owns 90 per cent of the stock of Company S.   After the combination is effected, the latter company sells fixed assets to Company P at a profit of $1,000.00. At the end of the year, Company P will take up $900.00 of the profit which Company S made on the sale, and it should therefore create a reserve of $900.00 for unrealized profit in fixed assets.

49

CONSOLIDATED PROFIT AND LOSS AND SURPLUS STATEMENTS

Consolidated profit and loss statement—First illustration.

The consolidated balance sheet is frequently accompanied by a consolidated surplus statement, a consolidated profit and loss statement, and supporting statements such as a consolidated statement of cost of goods sold and consolidated schedules of expenses.

The profit and loss statements of the parent and the subsidiary usually contain some items of income and expense resulting from intercompany transactions. The amounts of income and expense shown in the consolidated profit and loss statement should not include these intercompany items.

In the first illustration, it is assumed that during the year under review the parent company purchased $25,000.00 worth of goods from the subsidiary. This amount is included in the sales of the subsidiary (Company S) and in the purchases of the parent company (Company P). The following consolidated working papers show the elimination.

First illustration:

COMPANY P AND SUBSIDIARY COMPANY S
Consolidated Profit and Loss Statement Working Papers
For the Year Ended December 31, 1941

	Company P	Company S	Eliminations Debit	Credit	Consolidated
Sales	$125,000	$100,000	$25,000(a)		$200,000
Deduct Cost of Goods Sold:					
Inventory, December 31, 1940	$ 25,000	$ 15,000			$ 40,000
Purchases	100,000	80,000		$25,000(a)	155,000
Total	$125,000	$ 95,000			$195,000
Deduct Inventory, December 31, 1941	27,000	16,000			43,000
Cost of Goods Sold	$ 98,000	$ 79,000			$152,000
Gross Profit on Sales	$ 27,000	$ 21,000			$ 48,000
Deduct Expenses	15,000	11,000			26,000
Net Profit	$ 12,000	$ 10,000			$ 22,000
Minority Interest—10% of $10,000.00					1,000
Consolidated Net Income					$ 21,000

The consolidated statement prepared from these working papers is presented below:

COMPANY *P* AND SUBSIDIARY COMPANY *S*
Consolidated Profit and Loss Statement
For the Year Ended December 31, 1941

Sales..		$200,000
Deduct Cost of Goods Sold:		
Inventory, December 31, 1940...................	$ 40,000	
Purchases.....................................	155,000	
Total.......................................	$195,000	
Deduct Inventory, December 31, 1941.............	43,000	
Cost of Goods Sold................................		152,000
Gross Profit on Sales.....................................		$ 48,000
Deduct Expenses...		26,000
Net Income Before Deduction of Minority Interest.............		$ 22,000
Deduct Minority Interest in Net Income of Subsidiary.........		1,000
Consolidated Net Income.................................		$ 21,000

Consolidated profit and loss statement—Second illustration.

This illustration indicates how consolidated operating statements are prepared for manufacturing companies. Three intercompany eliminations are shown:

(a) Intercompany sales.
(b) Rent of equipment charged by parent company to subsidiary.
(c) Interest earned by parent company on investment in bonds of subsidiary.

COMPANY *P* AND SUBSIDIARY COMPANY *S*
Consolidated Working Papers
For the Year Ended December 31, 1941

Cost of Goods Sold	Company P	Company S	Eliminations Debit	Eliminations Credit	Consolidated
Materials:					
Inventory, Dec. 31, 1940.............	$ 40,000	$ 15,000			$ 55,000
Purchases.........................	140,000	95,000		$70,000(a)	165,000
Total........................	$180,000	$110,000			$220,000
Deduct Inventory, Dec. 31, 1941......	50,000	25,000			75,000
Materials Used.....................	$130,000	$ 85,000			$145,000
Direct Labor.......................	85,000	65,000			150,000
Manufacturing Expenses..............	70,000	40,000		3,000(b)	107,000
Total........................	$285,000	$190,000			$402,000
Add Goods in Process, Dec. 31, 1940.....	25,000	30,000			55,000
Total..............................	$310,000	$220,000			$457,000
Deduct Goods in Process, Dec. 31, 1941..	55,000	25,000			80,000
Cost of Goods Manufactured............	$255,000	$195,000			$377,000
Add Finished Goods, Dec. 31, 1940......	35,000	30,000			65,000
Total..............................	$290,000	$225,000			$442,000
Deduct Finished Goods, Dec. 31, 1941....	80,000	50,000			130,000
Cost of Goods Sold...................	$210,000	$175,000			$312,000

Consolidated Working Papers—*Continued*

Profit and Loss	Company P	Company S	Eliminations Debit	Eliminations Credit	Consolidated
Gross Sales...........................	$300,000	$225,000	$70.000(a)		$455,000
Deduct Returned Sales and Allowances...	3,000	2,000			5,000
Net Sales.............................	$297,000	$223,000			$450,000
Deduct Cost of Goods Sold.............	210,000	175,000			312,000
Gross Profit on Sales.................	$ 87,000	$ 48,000			$138,000
Miscellaneous Income:					
Rent of Equipment to Company S.....	3,000	—	3,000(b)		—
Bond Interest from Company S.......	2,000	—	2,000(c)		—
Gross Profit and Income..............	$ 92,000	$ 48,000			$138,000
Deduct Expenses:					
Selling Expenses....................	$ 23,000	$ 22,000			$ 45,000
General Expenses...................	24,000	9,000			33,000
Bond Interest......................	—	2,500		2,000(c)	500
Total Expenses.................	$ 47,000	$ 33,500			$ 78,500
Net Income...........................	$ 45,000	$ 14,500			$ 59,500
Minority Interest—10% of $14,500.00..					1,450
Consolidated Net Income,...					$ 58,050

Consolidated profit and loss statement—Third illustration.

This illustration is the same as the preceding one, with an additional feature: the inventories of the parent company at the end of 1941 contain goods which were acquired from the subsidiary, and on which the subsidiary made a profit.

COMPANY *P* AND SUBSIDIARY COMPANY *S*
Consolidated Working Papers
For the Year Ended December 31, 1941

Cost of Goods Sold	Company P	Company S	Eliminations Debit	Eliminations Credit	Consolidated
Materials:					
Inventory, Dec. 31, 1940.............	$ 40,000	$ 15,000			$ 55,000
Purchases...........................	140,000	95,000		$70,000(a)	165,000
Total...........................	$180,000	$110,000			$220,000
Deduct Inventory, Dec. 31, 1941......	50,000	25,000	$ 4,500(d)		70,500
Materials Used......................	$130,000	$ 85,000			$149,500
Direct Labor........................	85,000	65,000			150,000
Manufacturing Expenses...............	70,000	40,000		3,000(b)	107,000
Total...........................	$285,000	$190,000			$406,500
Add Goods in Process, Dec. 31, 1940.....	25,000	30,000			55,000
Total...........................	$310,000	$220,000			$461,500
Deduct Goods in Process, Dec. 31, 1941..	55,000	25,000	2,700(d)		77,300
Cost of Goods Manufactured...........	$255,000	$195,000			$384,200
Add Finished Goods, Dec. 31, 1940......	35,000	30,000			65,000
Total.................................	$290,000	$225,000			$449,200
Deduct Finished Goods, Dec. 31, 1941....	80,000	50,000	5,400(d)		124,600
Cost of Goods Sold...................	$210,000	$175,000			$324,600

Observe that, in the foregoing consolidated working papers, eliminations (d) are entered to reduce the end-of-year inventories by the amounts of the parent company's 90 per cent interest in the unrealized profits. The total amounts of such subsidiary profits on goods remaining in the parent company's inventories, and the parent company's 90 per cent interests in such subsidiary profits, are shown below:

	Intercompany Profit in Inventories	
	Total	90%
Raw materials	$5,000.00	$4,500.00
Goods in process	3,000.00	2,700.00
Finished goods	6,000.00	5,400.00

Consolidated Working Papers—*Continued*

Profit and Loss	Company P	Company S	Eliminations Debit	Eliminations Credit	Consolidated
Gross Sales	$300,000	$225,000	70,000(a)		$455,00●
Deduct Returned Sales and Allowances	3,000	2,000			5,00●
Net Sales	$297,000	$223,000			$450,00●
Deduct Cost of Goods Sold	210,000	175,000			324,60●
Gross Profit on Sales	$ 87,000	$ 48,000			$125,40●
Miscellaneous Income:					
Rent of Equipment to Company *S*	3,000	—	3,000(b)		—
Bond Interest from Company *S*	2,000	—	2,000(c)		—
Gross Profit and Income	$ 92,000	$ 48,000			$125,40●
Deduct Expenses:					
Selling Expenses	$ 23,000	$ 22,000			$ 45,00●
General Expenses	24,000	9,000			33,00●
Bond Interest	—	2,500		2,000(c)	50●
Total Expenses	$ 47,000	$ 33,500			$ 78,50●
Net Income	$ 45,000	$ 14,500			$ 46,90C
Minority Interest—10% of $14,500.00					1,45●
Consolidated Net Income					$ 45,45C

Consolidated profit and loss statement—Fourth illustration.

This illustration is the same as the immediately preceding one, with an additional feature: It is assumed that the parent company owned the 90 per cent interest in the subsidiary during 1940, and that the inventories of the parent company at the end of that year also contained intercompany profits made by the subsidiary.   The amounts of such intercompany profits and the parent company's 90 per cent interests therein are shown below:

	Intercompany Profit in Inventories End of 1940	
	Total	90%
Raw materials	$4,000.00	$3,600.00
Goods in process	1,000.00	900.00
Finished goods	3,500.00	3,150.00

Observe that, in the following consolidated working papers, eliminations (e) have been added for the purpose of eliminating the parent company's 90 per cent interest in the unrealized profit in the inventories at the beginning of 1941. When the consolidated profit and loss statement was prepared at the end of 1940, the inventories at that date were reduced to the basis of cost, exclusive of unrealized profit; consistency requires that they be reduced to the same basis when used as the opening inventories in the statements for 1941.

COMPANY P AND SUBSIDIARY COMPANY S
Consolidated Working Papers
For the Year Ended December 31, 1941

Cost of Goods Sold	Company P	Company S	Eliminations Debit	Eliminations Credit	Consolidated
Materials:					
Inventory, Dec. 31, 1940	$ 40,000	$ 15,000		$ 3,600(e)	$ 51,400
Purchases	140,000	95,000		70,000(a)	165,000
Total	$180,000	$110,000			$216,400
Deduct Inventory, Dec. 31, 1941	50,000	25,000	$ 4,500(d)		70,500
Materials Used	$130,000	$ 85,000			$145,900
Direct Labor	85,000	65,000			150,000
Manufacturing Expenses	70,000	40,000		3,000(b)	107,000
Total	$285,000	$190,000			$402,900
Add Goods in Process, Dec. 31, 1940	25,000	30,000		900(e)	54,100
Total	$310,000	$220,000			$457,000
Deduct Goods in Process, Dec. 31, 1941	55,000	25,000	2,700(d)		77,300
Cost of Goods Manufactured	$255,000	$195,000			$379,700
Add Finished Goods, Dec. 31, 1940	35,000	30,000		3,150(e)	61,850
Total	$290,000	$225,000			$441,550
Deduct Finished Goods, Dec. 31, 1941	80,000	50,000	5,400(d)		124,600
Cost of Goods Sold	$210,000	$175,000			$316,950
Profit and Loss					
Gross Sales	$300,000	$225,000	70,000(a)		$455,000
Deduct Returned Sales and Allowances	3,000	2,000			5,000
Net Sales	$297,000	$223,000			$450,000
Deduct Cost of Goods Sold	210,000	175,000			316,950
Gross Profit on Sales	$ 87,000	$ 48,000			$133,050
Miscellaneous Income:					
Rent of Equipment to Company S	3,000	—	3,000(b)		—
Bond Interest from Company S	2,000	—	2,000(c)		—
Gross Profit and Income	$ 92,000	$ 48,000			$133,050
Deduct Expenses:					
Selling Expenses	$ 23,000	$ 22,000			$ 45,000
General Expenses	24,000	9,000			33,000
Bond Interest	—	2,500		2,000(c)	500
Total Expenses	$ 47,000	$ 33,500			$ 78,500
Net Income	$ 45,000	$ 14,500			$ 54,550
Minority Interest—10% of $14,500.00					1,450
Consolidated Net Income					$ 53,100

The eliminations of unrealized intercompany profits from the inventories at the beginning of the year result in a reduction of the consolidated cost of goods sold for the year; the eliminations of the unrealized profit from the inventories at the end of the year result in an addition to the consolidated cost of goods sold.

The consolidated statements prepared from the working papers of the fourth illustration are presented on the following page.

COMPANY *P* AND SUBSIDIARY COMPANY *S*   Exhibit C

Consolidated Statement of Profit and Loss

For the Year Ended December 31, 1941

Gross Sales..		$455,000
Deduct Returned Sales and Allowances......................		5,000
Net Sales..		$450,000
Deduct Cost of Goods Sold—Exhibit D......................		316,950
Gross Profit on Sales...		$133,050
Deduct Expenses:		
Selling Expenses..............................	$45,000	
General Expenses..............................	33,000	
Bond Interest....................................	500	
Total Expenses...................................		78,500
Net Income Before Deduction of Minority Interest...........		$ 54,550
Minority Interest in Net Income of Subsidiary...............		1,450
Consolidated Net Income..		$ 53,100

COMPANY *P* AND SUBSIDIARY COMPANY *S*   Exhibit D

Consolidated Statement of Cost of Goods Sold

For the Year Ended December 31, 1941

Materials:		
Inventory, December 31, 1940......................		$ 51,400
Purchases..		165,000
Total..		$216,400
Deduct Inventory, December 31, 1941......................		70,500
Materials Used...		$145,900
Direct Labor...		150,000
Manufacturing Expenses..		107,000
Total..		$402,900
Deduct Increase in Inventory—Goods in Process:		
December 31, 1941..............................	$ 77,300	
December 31, 1940..............................	54,100	
Increase...		23,200
Cost of Goods Manufactured....................................		$379.700
Deduct Increase in Inventory—Finished Goods:		
December 31, 1941..............................	$124,600	
December 31, 1940..............................	61,850	
Increase...		62,750
Cost of Goods Sold..		$316,950

Consolidated surplus statement—First illustration.

On page 507 are working papers for the preparation of a consolidated surplus statement to accompany the consolidated profit and loss statement of the third illustration. (Note that the amounts shown as net income for 1941 are those determined in the working papers of the third profit and loss illustration.)

Company *P* has followed the accounting policy of taking up its share of the profits of the subsidiary; its surplus of $136,000.00 at

COMPANY *P* AND SUBSIDIARY COMPANY *S*
Consolidated Surplus Statement Working Papers
For the Year Ended December 31, 1941

	Company P	Company S	Eliminations Debit	Eliminations Credit	Minority	Consolidated
Balances, Dec. 31, 1940:						
Company P..............................	$136,000					$136,000
Company S..............................		$60,000	$54,000		$6,000	
Net income for the year 1941:						
Own operations........................	45,000	14,500				
Eliminate Company P's interest in intercompany profit in inventories.......			12,600			
Extend minority interest in Company S's earnings.......					1,450	
Remainder—consolidated net income.......			13,050			45,450
90% of subsidiary's net income.......	13,050		13,050			
Total....................	$194,050	$74,500			$7,450	$181,450
Deduct dividends paid:						
Company P....................	6,000					6,000
Company S....................		3,000		$2,700	300	
Balances, Dec. 31, 1941........	$188,050	$71,500			$7,150	$175,450

the beginning of 1941 includes its share of the subsidiary's net income between the date of acquisition of its stock and the end of 1940; and there is a surplus credit of $13,050.00 during 1941 representing the parent company's 90 per cent of the subsidiary's net income for 1941.

Because the parent company's surplus as of December 31, 1940, already includes the parent company's share of the subsidiary's earnings to that date, no portion of the subsidiary's surplus of $60,000.00 on December 31, 1940, is extended to the Consolidated column to be included in the consolidated surplus at the beginning of the period.

And since the consolidated net income of $45,450.00 for 1941 includes the parent company's 90 per cent interest in the subsidiary's earnings for that year (90% of $14,500.00, or $13,050.00), the credit of $13,050.00 taken into the parent company's accounts is eliminated. If it were extended to the Consolidated column, a duplication would result.

The consolidated surplus statement prepared from the foregoing working papers is submitted below:

COMPANY *P* AND SUBSIDIARY COMPANY *S*   Exhibit B

Consolidated Surplus Statement

For the Year Ended December 31, 1941

Consolidated Surplus, December 31, 1940	$136,000.00
Add Consolidated Net Income for the Year—Exhibit C	45,450.00
Total	$181,450.00
Deduct Dividends Paid	6,000.00
Consolidated Surplus, December 31, 1941	$175,450.00

Consolidated surplus statement—Second illustration.

This illustration is like the preceding one, with the following exception: The parent company is now assumed to have followed the alternative accounting procedure of carrying the investment in the subsidiary at its cost, and of having credited Surplus with dividends received from the subsidiary instead of with 90 per cent of the subsidiary's net income.

The subsidiary's surplus at the date when the parent company acquired the 90 per cent interest in its stock is assumed to have been $20,000.00; the parent company's 90 per cent interest therein ($18,000.00) cannot be included in the consolidated surplus, because it was earned by the subsidiary prior to acquisition; it is therefore eliminated.

COMPANY *P* AND SUBSIDIARY COMPANY *S*
Consolidated Surplus Statement Working Papers
For the Year Ended December 31, 1941

	Company *P*	Company *S*	Eliminations Debit	Eliminations Credit	Mi-nority	Con-solidated
Balances, Dec. 31, 1940:						
Company *P*...............................	$100,000					$100,000
Company *S*...............................		$60,000	$18,000			
Eliminate 90% of $20,000 at acquisition.............						
Take up 90% of $40,000 increase since acquisition.......						36,000
Minority—10% of present surplus..........					$6,000	
Consolidated surplus, Dec. 31, 1940..........						$136,000
Add:						
Net income for the year 1941.........	45,000	14,500				
Eliminate Company *P*'s interest in intercompany profit in inventories			12,600			
Extend minority interest in Company *S*'s earnings.......					1,450	
Remainder—consolidated net income.........			2,700			45,450
Dividends received.......	2,700					
Total..........	$147,700	$74,530			$7,450	$181,450
Deduct dividends paid:						
Company *P*...............	6,000					6,000
Company *S*............		3,000		$2,700	300	
Balances, Dec. 31, 1941..........	$141,700	$71,500			$7,150	$175,450

The subsidiary's surplus was $60,000.00 at the beginning of 1941; hence there was a $40,000.00 increase between the date of acquisition and the beginning of the year; the consolidated surplus as of the beginning of the year can properly include 90 per cent of this amount, or $36,000.00, and this amount therefore is extended to the Consolidated column.

The credit in the parent company's surplus for the $2,700.00 of dividends received from the subsidiary is offset against the $3,000.00 debit in the subsidiary's surplus for dividends paid. The $300.00 dividend payment to the minority stockholders of Company S is deducted in the Minority column.

A consolidated surplus statement prepared from the following working papers would be the same as that on page 508.

50
COST ACCOUNTING

....

Purpose of cost accounting.

The primary purpose of cost accounting is the determination, as accurately as practicable, of the cost of manufactured products. One of the incidental advantages lies in the maintenance of perpetual inventories of material, goods in process, and finished goods, which furnish a control over these assets and also make it possible to prepare operating statements and balance sheets without the taking of physical inventories.

It is not practicable to deal with different systems of cost accounting within the limited space of a single chapter. It will be possible, however, to present a brief illustration of a production order cost system which will indicate how perpetual inventories are maintained and how the detailed cost records are operated as subsidiary records controlled by accounts in the general ledger.

We shall first discuss the procedure of keeping perpetual inventories with raw materials, goods in process, and finished goods. In the latter part of the chapter we shall discuss the general ledger accounts.

Raw Materials

Materials purchased.

Let us assume that a company, at the beginning of its operations, purchased an invoice of materials containing the following items:

Kind of Material	Number of Units	Cost per Unit	Amount
A	500	$4.00	$2,000.00
B	1,500	2.00	3,000.00
Total			$5,000.00

The perpetual inventory of raw materials will contain a page or a card for each kind of material. After the invoice has been recorded in the voucher register, it may be used by the perpetual inventory clerk to make the following entries on the cards:

Material __A__

Date		Quantity			Price		Cost		
		In	Out	Balance			In	Out	Balance
1941 Feb.	3	500		500	4	00	2,000	00			2,000	00

Material __B__

Date		Quantity			Price		Cost		
		In	Out	Balance			In	Out	Balance
1941 Feb.	3	1,500		1,500	2	00	3,000	00			3,000	00

Materials used.

Materials should not be taken from the store room for use in the factory without a written order, called a *requisition*, which must be approved by some person in authority. Let us assume that the two following material requisitions were issued during February:

Material Requisition

No.__1__

For Production Order No. __1__   Date__2/5/41__

Material	Number of Units	Cost per Unit		Amount	
A	200	4	00	800	00
B	700	2	00	1,400	00
				2,200	00

Approved__Q.H.F.__

```
                        Material Requisition
                                              No. __2__

For Production Order No. __2__          Date____2/16/41____

|   Material   | Number of Units | Cost per Unit | Amount   |
|              |                 |               |          |
|      A       |      150        |    4 | 00     |  600 | 00 |
|      B       |      100        |    2 | 00     |  200 | 00 |
|              |                 |               |          |
|              |                 |               |  800 | 00 |

Approved____ℐℋℰ____
```

The unit costs and the extended amounts were entered on the requisitions by the perpetual inventory clerk.

The material items shown by these requisitions were entered by the inventory clerk in the Out columns of the perpetual inventory records, and the balances were computed and entered.

The raw materials on hand now consist of:

Material A...	$ 600.00
Material B...	1,400.00
Total...	$2,000.00

Material ___A___

Date		Quantity			Price		Cost				
		In	Out	Balance			In		Out	Balance	
1941											
Feb.	3	500		500	4	00	2,000	00		2,000	00
	5		200	300				800	00	1,200	00
	16		150	150				600	00	600	00

Material ___B___

Date		Quantity			Price		Cost				
		In	Out	Balance			In			Out		Balance	
1941											
Feb.	3	1,500		1,500	2	00	3,000	00			3,000	00
	5		700	800				1,400	00	1,600	00
	16		100	700				200	00	1,400	00

Goods in Process

Production orders.

The perpetual inventory of goods in process is kept on sheets called *production orders*. A separate production order is kept for each job or kind of product going through the factory.

Let us assume that the company whose raw material inventory records have already been illustrated worked on two products during February: Product *X* and Product *Y*. Product *X* was started first, and is represented by production order 1; Product *Y* is represented by production order 2.

Production Order____1____

For____800 Product X____

Date		Raw Materials		Direct Labor		Overhead	
1941							
Feb.	5	2,200	00				
	15			1,000	00	500	00
	28			200	00	100	00
Total		2,200	00	1,200	00	600	00

Summary:
Material	2,200	00
Direct Labor	1,200	00
Overhead	600	00
Total	4,000	00

Unit cost   (Quantity produced ___800___)   5 | 00

Production Order____2____

For____200 Product Y____

Date		Raw Materials		Direct Labor		Overhead	
1941							
Feb.	16	800	00				
	28			800	00	400	00

Product X has been completed; the sheet has been summarized to determine the total and unit cost of the product, and the production order has been removed from the work in process binder.

Product Y is still in process. Since it is the only order in process at the end of February, production order 2 shows the total cost of work in process—$2,000.00.

We shall now consider in detail how the information was obtained for the entries on these production orders.

Raw materials.

The cost of materials used is shown by the material requisitions. Copies of the requisitions are therefore given to cost clerks for entry on the production orders.

Requisition Number 1 (page 512) shows that materials costing $2,200.00 were taken from stock on February 5, for use on production order 1. This amount was therefore entered in the Raw Materials column of production order 1 (page 514).

Requisition Number 2 shows that materials costing $800.00 were taken from stock on February 16, for use on production order 2. This amount was therefore entered in the Raw Materials column of production order 2.

Direct labor.

Each factory workman keeps a record of the time spent on each production order, by punching time cards. He uses a separate

Date	2/20/41		Date	2/20/41
Employee's Number	21		Employee's Number	21
Hour In	8 00		Hour In	1 00
Hour Out	12 00		Hour Out	4 00
Elapsed Time	4:00		Elapsed Time	3:00
Hourly Rate	$ .50		Hourly Rate	$ .50
Amount	$2.00		Amount	$1.50
Production Order	1		Production Order	2

Employee's Time Cards

card each day for each production order on which he is engaged. When the card is turned in to the office, it shows the workman's number, the production order number, and the time worked. Clerks enter the hourly wage rate and compute the total labor cost. On page 515 are shown the two cards turned in by one workman on February 20.

These cards are used in making up the payroll, as they show the total time and wages of each employee. The cards of all workmen are then sorted according to the production order numbers, and a summary is prepared showing the total direct labor cost applicable to each production order. The direct labor cost on each production order during February is shown by the summary below.

The reader should refer to the two production orders on page 514, and note that:

Production order 1 was charged with $1,000.00 of direct labor for the first half of the month, and with $200.00 of direct labor for the second half of the month.

Production order 2 was charged with $800.00 of direct labor for the last half of the month.

These amounts were obtained from the following labor cost summary:

Production Order Direct Labor Cost Summary				
	Payroll Periods			
Production Order	Feb. 1 to 15		Feb. 16 to 28	
1	1,000	00	200	00
2			800	00
	1,000	00	1,000	00

Manufacturing expense, or overhead.

The material and labor costs applicable to each production order can be definitely determined by the methods just explained. Overhead expenses must be estimated. This may be done as follows: If, in the past, the annual manufacturing expense has been about 50 per cent of the annual direct labor cost, it may be assumed that this ratio will continue. Therefore, when the labor cost is entered on the production orders, the manufacturing expense may be estimated as 50 per cent of the labor cost.

It is assumed that 50 per cent is a fair overhead rate for the concern under illustration. By reference to the production orders on page 514, it will be noted that the cost clerk, after entering the labor cost, also entered an overhead charge equal to 50 per cent of the labor.

Bases other than direct labor cost may be used for the apportionment of manufacturing expense.

Finished Goods

Perpetual inventory cards.

The finished goods perpetual inventory is kept on cards ruled like those used for raw materials. Product X is the only product finished by the concern under illustration. The inventory card at the end of February appears as follows:

Date		Quantity			Price		Cost		
		In	Out	Balance.			In	Out	Balance
1941									
Feb.	20	800		800	5	00	4,000 00		4,000 00
	27		500	300				2,500 00	1,500 00

Commodity ___X___

Since Commodity X is the only article of finished goods on hand, this one card shows the total value of the finished goods inventory at the end of February—$1,500.00.

Finished goods into stock.

The February 20 entry on the inventory card for finished goods coming into stock was made from production order 1 (see page 514), which showed that 800 units of Commodity X were manufactured at a total cost of $4,000.00, or a unit cost of $5.00.

Finished goods sold.

On February 27, a sale of 500 units of Commodity X was made. The carbon copy of the invoice is provided with a Cost column at the right of the Selling Price column. This carbon is sent to the inventory clerk, who performs the following operations:

(1) Looks up the unit price on the finished goods inventory card.
(2) Computes the total cost of the goods sold and enters this cost in the Cost column of the carbon of the invoice, thus:

(Heading of the Invoice)							
Number	Description	Unit Price		Amount		Cost	
500	Article X	7	00	3,500	00	*2,500*	*00*

(3) Makes entries in the Out columns of the inventory card, showing the number and the cost of the articles sold, and computes the new quantity and cost balances.
(4) Sends the carbon of the invoice back to the office for entry in the sales book.

Inventory Controlling Accounts

The raw material inventory cards show the cost of raw materials on hand; the production orders show the accumulated costs of goods in process; the finished goods inventory cards show the cost of finished goods on hand.

In a large business there may be thousands of these inventory cards and production orders, and the preparation of monthly statements will be greatly facilitated if the following controlling accounts are kept in the general ledger:

Raw Materials   —with a balance equal to the sum of all of the balances on the raw material inventory cards.

Goods in Process—with a balance equal to the sum of all of the balances on the production orders for goods still in process.

Finished Goods   —with a balance equal to the sum of all the balances on the finished goods inventory cards.

Such controlling accounts not only facilitate the preparation of the monthly profit and loss statements and balance sheets but also serve as checks upon the accuracy of the subsidiary perpetual inventory records of raw materials, goods in process, and finished goods.

We shall now see how such accounts can be produced. For purposes of illustration, we shall begin with expenditures for material, labor, and overhead, and trace the flow of these costs through goods in process into finished goods. The illustration will be based on the same assumed facts as those used on the preceding pages in illustrating the perpetual inventory records.

Material, labor, and overhead accounts.

Assume that the expenditures during February for material, labor, and manufacturing expenses were:

(a) Raw materials.. $5,000.00
(b) Direct labor.. 2,000.00
(c) Manufacturing expenses:
   Indirect labor....................................... 500.00
   Factory supplies..................................... 300.00
   Power.. 220.00

The accounts showing charges for these costs appear below:

Raw Materials	Direct Labor	Indirect Labor
(a) Cost 5,000	(b) Paid 2,000	(c) Paid... 500

Factory Supplies
(c) Cost... 300

Power
(c) Cost... 220

Raw materials used.

The raw materials taken from stock for use in the factory are shown by the material requisitions as on pages 512 and 513. These requisitions are listed in a requisition register, as follows:

Date		Requisition No.	Amount	
1941				
Feb.	5	1	2,200	00
	16	2	800	00
			3,000	00

Requisition Register

The requisition register is footed at the end of the month, and the following journal entry is made:

(d) Goods in Process............................. 3,000.00
    Raw Materials...........................   3,000.00
    To transfer the cost of raw materials used during
    the month out of the Raw Materials account, and
    into Goods in Process.

Direct labor spent on goods in process.

The production order direct labor cost summary (see page 516) shows the amount of direct labor charged to each production order. The totals of the summary show that $2,000.00 of direct labor was charged to the production orders during the month. Therefore, at the end of the month, the following journal entry may be made transferring the labor cost shown by the summary into the Goods in Process account:

(e) Goods in Process............................. 2,000.00
    Direct Labor............................   2,000.00
    To charge Goods in Process with the total direct
    labor cost entered on the production orders.

Manufacturing expenses charged to goods in process.

This company is using an overhead rate of 50%; that is, the estimated overhead charged to each production order is 50 per cent of the direct labor. Since $2,000.00 of direct labor was charged to the production orders, the total overhead charge was $1,000.00. This amount may be charged into Goods in Process by the following journal entry:

(f) Goods in Process............................. 1,000.00
    Manufacturing Expense Applied............   1,000.00
    To charge Goods in Process with the total over-
    head applied to the production orders.

It will be observed that, in the foregoing entries charging Goods in Process with material and labor costs, the offsetting credits were made directly in the Raw Materials and Direct Labor accounts. It will also be observed that a somewhat different procedure is followed with respect to manufacturing expenses; the charge to Goods in Process is not offset by credits to the various manufacturing expense accounts, but by credit to a special account which shows the aggregate amount of all such expenses applied to goods in process.

Ledger accounts after transferring costs into Goods in Process.

After the material, labor, and overhead costs for the month are transferred to the Goods in Process account, the accounts affected will contain the following amounts:

Raw Materials	Direct Labor	Indirect Labor
(a) Cost. 5,000| (d) Used 3,000	(b) Paid. 2,000| (e) Used 2,000	(c) Paid... 500|

Factory Supplies

(c) Cost... 300|

Power

(c) Cost... 220|

Manufacturing Expense Applied

| (f)..... 1,000

The Raw Materials account has a debit balance of $2,000.00, representing the cost of all raw materials on hand at the end of February. The costs of the individual items of raw material are shown by the perpetual inventory cards (see page 513): Material A, $600.00; Material B, $1,400.00.

The Direct Labor account has no balance. All of the direct labor has been applied to the cost of goods in process.

The manufacturing expense accounts have total debit balances of $1,020.00; the Manufacturing Expense Applied account has a credit balance of $1,000.00. Twenty dollars of expense has not been applied because of a slight error in the estimated burden rate of 50%. The disposition of this $20.00 is discussed in a subsequent section.

The following account (produced by posting the three journal entries illustrated) shows the total material, labor, and overhead charged to production during the month:

Goods in Process

(d) Raw materials........... 3,000.00|
(e) Direct labor............. 2,000.00
(f) Manufacturing expenses... 1,000.00|

Cost of goods finished.

When goods are finished, the production order is summarized and the total cost ascertained. When the production orders for finished goods are taken from the goods in process binder, the total cost should be entered in a register of completed production orders.

Only one order (order 1—see page 514) was completed by the company in the illustration. This is entered in the register as follows:

Date		Production Order Number	Total Cost	
1941 Feb.	20	1	4,000	00

Register of Completed Production Orders

At the end of the month, the register is totaled, and the cost of goods finished during the month is transferred out of Goods in Process into Finished Goods by the following journal entry:

```
(g) Finished Goods.............................. 4,000.00
      Goods in Process........................          4,000.00
      Total cost of goods completed during the month.
```

After this entry is posted, the two accounts affected will contain the following amounts:

Goods in Process

(d) Raw materials............	3,000.00	(g) Finished goods...........	4,000.00
(e) Direct labor..............	2,000.00		
(f) Manufacturing expenses...	1,000.00		

Finished Goods

(g) Manufactured............	4,000.00

The Goods in Process account has a debit balance of $2,000.00, representing the cost of goods in process at the end of February. Details are shown on production order 2, which is the only order in process at the end of the month.

Cost of goods sold.

As shown on page 518, the carbons of the invoices are provided with a column in which a clerk enters the cost of the goods sold. Invoices are entered in the sales book as shown below.

Date	✔	Name	Invoice Number	Selling Price		Cost	
1941 Feb.	27 ✔	Henderson & Riley	1	3,500	00	2,500	00
				(10-501)		(903-21)	

Sales Book

At the end of the month the two columns are totaled, and the totals are posted as follows:

Total of Selling Price column:
   (h) Debit Accounts Receivable   (See ledger page numbers at foot of
       controlling account   Selling Price column.)
       Credit Sales
Total of Cost column:
   (i) Debit Cost of Sales   (See ledger page numbers at foot of
       Credit Finished Goods   Cost column.)

The accounts affected (except Accounts Receivable) will contain the following amounts:

Finished Goods

(g) Manufactured........... 4,000.00| (i) Sold.................... 2,500.00

The debit balance of this account shows the cost of finished goods still on hand. Details are shown on the finished goods perpetual inventory cards.

Cost of Sales

(i) .... 2,500.00|

Sales

| (h) 3,500.00

The difference between the debit balance in the Cost of Sales account, and the credit balance in the Sales account, is the gross profit for the month. Thus, the gross profit on sales can be determined from the books, without the necessity of taking physical inventories.

Underabsorbed and Overabsorbed Burden

To illustrate the various methods of dealing with underabsorbed and overabsorbed manufacturing expense, let us assume that the manufacturing expense accounts at the end of the year have the following balances:

Indirect Labor................................ $5,200.00
Factory Supplies............................. 3,450.00
Power.. 2,350.00
Manufacturing Expense Applied................ $10,500.00

The actual expenses, as shown by the three debit balances, totaled $11,000.00; the amount applied to the production orders was only $10,500.00.

The $500.00 balance of unabsorbed burden may be treated in several ways, as follows:

(1) Theoretically, it should be apportioned to finished goods sold, finished goods on hand, and goods in process, by a journal entry similar to the following:

Cost of Sales..................................	425.00	
Finished Goods...............................	60.00	
Goods in Process.............................	15.00	
Manufacturing Expense Applied.............		500.00

(2) If the greater portion of the finished goods manufactured has been sold, it is reasonably correct to charge the entire unabsorbed burden to Cost of Sales, by the following journal entry:

Cost of Sales..................................	500.00	
Manufacturing Expense Applied.............		500.00

(3) In some cases the unabsorbed expense is charged to a deferred expense account by an entry similar to the following:

Deferred Manufacturing Expense...............	500.00	
Manufacturing Expense Applied.............		500.00

When this method is followed, the Deferred Manufacturing Expense appears on the asset side of the balance sheet.

Adjustments for overabsorbed burden may be made similarly; that is, (1) by credits to Cost of Sales, Finished Goods, and Goods in Process; (2) by credit to Cost of Sales; or (3) by setting up a deferred credit account.

Summary

The entries in the general ledger cost control accounts and the subsidiary records under this system of accounting are summarized below.

Summary of Entries in the General Ledger Accounts and in the Subsidiary Records Using the Method of Accounting Described in This Chapter

	GENERAL LEDGER	SUBSIDIARY RECORDS
Purchase of Materials..............	Debit Raw Materials—total of Raw Materials column of voucher register.	Enter details in the In columns of the perpetual inventory cards, using facts shown by suppliers' invoices.
Direct Labor Payments..............	Debit Direct Labor—total of Voucher Register column.	
Payment of Manufacturing Expenses..............	Debit various manufacturing expense accounts—voucher register entries, etc.	
Materials Put Into Process..............	Credit Raw Materials—total of material requisition register.	Enter details in Out columns of raw material inventory cards, from material requisitions.
	Debit Goods in Process—total of material requisition register.	Enter in Material column of production orders, from material requisitions.
Direct Labor on Goods in Process..............	Debit Goods in Process and credit Direct Labor—journal entry using amount shown by direct labor cost summary.	Enter in Labor column of production orders, from direct labor cost summary.
Manufacturing Expense Applied..............	Debit Goods in Process and credit Manufacturing Expense Applied—journal entry, amount being based on labor cost summary.	Enter in Overhead column of production orders, amounts being obtained by multiplying the labor cost on the production order by an overhead rate.

525

GENERAL LEDGER	SUBSIDIARY RECORDS
Finished Goods Completed Credit Goods in Process—total of register of completed production orders.	Foot up the production orders for the completed goods and remove them from the goods in process binder.
Debit Finished Goods—total of register of completed production orders.	Enter in In columns of finished goods perpetual inventory cards, using amounts shown by production orders.
Finished Goods Sold Debit Cost of Sales and credit Finished Goods—total of Cost column of sales book	Enter in Out column of finished goods perpetual inventory record, using information shown by the invoice.
Debit Accounts Receivable and credit Sales—total of Selling Price column of sales book.	

After one of the foregoing entries has been made at the end of the year to bring the credit balance of the Manufacturing Expense Applied account into exact agreement with the total of the debit balances in the manufacturing expense accounts, all of these accounts are closed by an entry similar to the following:

Manufacturing Expense Applied................... 11,000.00
    Indirect Labor...............................   5,200.00
    Factory Supplies.............................   3,450.00
    Power.......................................   2,350.00
    To close the manufacturing expense accounts.

51

INDIVIDUAL PROPRIETORSHIPS
AND PARTNERSHIPS

....

Individual proprietorship—Accounts and statements.

In place of the Capital Stock, Surplus, and Dividends Paid accounts kept by a corporation, the books of an individual proprietorship contain the following accounts:

Proprietor's Capital account—credited with investments.

Proprietor's Drawing account—debited with withdrawals.

The procedure of closing the expense and income accounts to Profit and Loss is exactly the same for an individual proprietorship as for a corporation. The Profit and Loss account is closed by transference of its balance to the proprietor's Capital account. The Drawing account, which is charged with the proprietor's withdrawals during the period, is closed to his Capital account. After the books have been closed, the Capital and Drawing accounts appear as illustrated below:

James Burton, Capital

1941						1941					
Dec.	31	Drawings.......	J13	2,650	00	Jan.	1	Investment......	CR 1	7,500	00
						Feb.	15	Additional			
								Investment....	CR 2	1,500	00
						Dec.	31	Net Profit.......	J12	4,500	00

James Burton, Drawings

1941						1941					
Mar.	25	....	CD 3	900	00	Dec.	31	To Capital			
July	8	....	CD 7	400	00			account.......	J13	2,650	00
Sep.	5	....	CD 9	750	00						
Dec.	17	....	CD12	600	00						
				2,650	00					2,650	00

The profit and loss statement of an individual proprietorship does not necessarily differ from that of a corporation in the same line of business.

The balance sheets of the two businesses do not necessarily differ except in the Net Worth section; the balance sheet of the individual proprietorship shows the proprietor's capital instead of the capital stock and the surplus of the corporation.

Instead of the surplus statement prepared for the corporation, a statement of the proprietor's capital is prepared. James Burton's statements are shown below.

JAMES BURTON
Exhibit C

Statement of Profit and Loss
For the Year Ended December 31, 1941

Gross Sales		$48,000.00
Less Returned Sales and Allowances		1,000.00
Net Sales		$47,000.00
Less Cost of Goods Sold:		
Purchases	$35,000.00	
Less Returned Purchases and Allowances	500.00	
Net Purchases	$34,500.00	
Less Inventory, December 31, 1941	4,000.00	
Remainder—Cost of Goods Sold		30,500.00
Gross Profit on Sales		$16,500.00
Less Expense		12,000.00
Net Profit		$ 4,500.00

JAMES BURTON
Exhibit B

Statement of Proprietor's Capital
For the Year Ended December 31, 1941

Investment, January 1, 1941		$ 7,500.00
Add:		
Additional Investment	$1,500.00	
Net Profit for the Year—Exhibit C	4,500.00	6,000.00
Total		$13,500.00
Deduct Withdrawals		2,650.00
Balance, December 31, 1941		$10,850.00

The investment at the beginning of the year and the additional investments and drawings during the year were determined from the Capital and the Drawing accounts.

JAMES BURTON
Exhibit A

Balance Sheet
December 31, 1941

ASSETS:		LIABILITIES:	
Cash	$ 3,850.00	Accounts Payable	$ 6,000.00
Accounts Receivable	9,000.00	Notes Payable	2,000.00
Notes Receivable	2,000.00	Total Liabilities	$ 8,000.00
Merchandise Inventory	4,000.00	NET WORTH:	
		James Burton, Capital—	
		Exhibit B	10,850.00
	$18,850.00		$18,850.00

Nature of a partnership.

"A partnership," as defined by the Uniform Partnership Act, "is an association of two or more persons to carry on, as co-owners, a business for profit."

A partnership may be spoken of as a firm, but it should not be called a company; that term is properly applied only to corporations. The partnership and the corporation are the two most common forms of organization by which two or more persons can join in a business enterprise. The partnership form is usually employed in comparatively small businesses requiring no more capital than can be contributed by a few partners; or in professional practices, such as law, medicine, and accounting, in which the relations of the firm to its clientele should involve a personal responsibility.

This personal responsibility or liability, however, is one of the chief disadvantages of the partnership as compared with the corporation. Subject to certain exceptions, a stockholder in a corporation is not liable for the payment of corporate debts. But each partner is personally liable for all of the partnership debts. If we remember, therefore, that each partner has the right to bind the partnership on business contracts, and that each partner's private fortune can be levied upon, if necessary, for the payment of the firm's debts, it is obvious that one partner with poor judgment may involve the partnership in losses and liabilities which will exhaust the firm's capital and also encroach upon the private resources of the partners.

The partnership contract.

The partnership relation is created by a contract, which should be in writing. Among the more important points to be covered by the contract, which is called the *articles of partnership*, are the following:

(1) The names of the partners and the name of the partnership.
(2) The date when the contract shall become effective.
(3) The nature and place of business.
(4) The capital to be contributed by each partner.
(5) The duties of each partner.
(6) The dates when the books are to be closed and the profits are to be divided.
(7) The portion of profits to be allotted to each partner.

(8) The drawings to be allowed each partner.
(9) The length of time the partnership is to continue, and the rights of the partners in the event of dissolution.
(10) Provision for arbitration in the event of disputes.

Partnership accounts and statements.

A Capital account and a Drawing account are kept with each partner. When the books are closed, the Profit and Loss account is closed by a journal entry in which Profit and Loss is debited with the total profit and each partner's Capital account is credited with his share thereof. Each partner's Drawing account is then closed to his Capital account.

Statements.

The profit and loss statement of a partnership need not differ from that of an individual proprietorship or a corporation in the same line of business. The balance sheet has only one feature peculiar to the partnership: the net worth may be detailed, as illustrated below:

NET WORTH:
C. L. Kent................................. $11,500.00
R. L. Kennedy............................. 16,500.00 $28,000.00

The changes in net worth during the period are shown in a statement of the partners' accounts similar to that illustrated below:

KENT AND KENNEDY   Exhibit B
Statement of Partners' Capitals
For the Year Ended December 31, 1941

	C. L. Kent	R. L. Kennedy	Total
Original Investments, January 1, 1941......	$ 8,000.00	$12,000.00	$20,000.00
Add:			
Additional Investments................	1,500.00	2,000.00	3,500.00
Net Income for the Year—Exhibit C.....	4,000.00	4,000.00	8,000.00
Total.....................................	$13,500.00	$18,000.00	$31,500.00
Deduct Drawings.......................	2,000.00	1,500.00	3,500.00
Balances, December 31, 1941.............	$11,500.00	$16,500.00	$28,000.00

Bases of division of profits.

If the partners make no agreement regarding the method of dividing profits, the law provides that the profits shall be divided equally, regardless of any differences in capital investments, business ability, or time devoted to the business. The partners may, however, make any agreement they desire. Some of the customary methods of dividing profits are:

(1) Equally.
(2) In an arbitrary ratio.
(3) In the capital ratio.
(4) By allowing interest on capitals and dividing the remaining profit in an agreed ratio.
(5) By allowing salaries to the partners and dividing the remaining profit in an agreed ratio.

Equal division. Assume that A and B make a profit of $11,484.00, and that it is to be divided equally, either because of an agreement to that effect or because of failure to make any agreement. Each will be credited with $5,742.00.

Arbitrary ratio. Arbitrary ratios are usually expressed in terms of fractions or per cents. If the profits of $11,484.00 are to be divided in the ratio of two fifths to A and three fifths to B, the division will be as follows:

Summary of Division of Profit

Partner	Ratio	Amount
A	$\frac{2}{5}$	$ 4,593.60
B	$\frac{3}{5}$	6,890.40
Total		$11,484.00

It is sometimes agreed that a portion of the profits shall be divided in one ratio and the remainder in another. To illustrate, assume that the first $8,000.00 of profit is to be divided in the ratio of two fifths to A and three fifths to B, and that the profits in excess of $8,000.00 are to be divided equally. The division should be made as follows:

Summary of Division of Profit

	A	B	Together
First $8,000.00 in ratio of $\frac{2}{5}$ and $\frac{3}{5}$	$3,200.00	$4,800.00	$ 8,000.00
Remainder equally	1,742.00	1,742.00	3,484.00
Total	$4,942.00	$6,542.00	$11,484.00

Capital ratio. If partners wish to divide their profits in the capital ratio, they should have a definite agreement as to whether the ratio at the beginning of the period or the ratio at the end of the period is to govern. Otherwise, disputes may arise if the partners' investments and drawings during the period have changed the capital ratio.

Assume that *A* and *B* invested $10,000.00 and $20,000.00, and that they agreed to divide profits in the ratio of capitals at the beginning of the period. The division of the profits of $11,484.00 is shown below:

Summary of Division of Profit

Partner	Opening Capital Balance	Ratio	Profit
A.......................	$10,000.00	⅓	$ 3,828.00
B.......................	20,000.00	⅔	7,656.00
Total...			$11,484.00

Interest on capital. When the profits are divided in the capital ratio, the entire profit distribution is based on the capital investments. Since capital is only one of the factors in the production of profits, the partners may wish to divide only a portion of the profits in the capital ratio, by allowing interest on capitals, and to divide the remainder in some other ratio.

To illustrate, assume that *A* and *B* agreed to divide their profits by allowing interest at 6% on their opening capital balances, and to divide the remainder equally. The division of the profits is summarized below.

Summary of Division of Profit

	A	B	Together
Interest on opening capital balances:			
A—6% of $10,000.00.....................	$ 600.00		
B—6% of $20,000.00.....................		$1,200.00	
Total interest.....................			$ 1,800.00
Remainder equally.......................	4,842.00	4,842.00	9,684.00
Total.................................	$5,442.00	$6,042.00	$11,484.00

Interest is not to be credited on partners' capitals unless there has been an agreement to that effect, regardless of any difference between the investments of the partners, and regardless of any difference between the amount of a partner's agreed investment and the amount of his actual investment.

Salaries to partners. Partners may recognize the relative values of one another's services by allowing salaries of differing amounts. Such salaries should be regarded as expenses and should be charged to Profit and Loss when the books are closed.

The partnership agreement should state definitely whether the amounts which partners are allowed to draw during the period are to be considered as salaries or as drawings. This agreement is important because it affects the distribution of the profits, for salaries are chargeable to Profit and Loss whereas drawings are chargeable to the respective Capital accounts. To make the point clear, let us assume that the profits of the firm of X and Y were $10,000.00 and that the partners had taken cash during the year in the respective amounts of $1,200.00 and $3,000.00; let us now consider how much each partner is entitled to receive at the end of the year.

	X	Y
If the amounts taken were drawings, the partners are entitled to receive at the end of the year:		
One half of total profits	$5,000.00	$5,000.00
Less amounts already drawn against their shares of profit	1,200.00	3,000.00
Remainder	$3,800.00	$2,000.00
If the amounts drawn were salaries, each partner is entitled to receive one half of the balance in the Profit and Loss account after closing the Salary accounts to that account, or	$2,900.00	$2,900.00

Obviously, X will prefer to have the amounts drawn during the year regarded as drawings, while Y will prefer to have them regarded as salaries. With such conflicting interests, it is evident that a dispute might easily arise in the absence of a specific agreement.

Interest and/or salaries in excess of profits.

If the partnership agreement provides for interest on capitals without any stipulation as to what shall be done if the profits are less than the interest or if the operations result in a loss, the interest must be charged to Profit and Loss and credited to the partners' Capital accounts in accordance with the agreement, and the resulting debit balance in the Profit and Loss account must be charged to the Capital accounts. The same rule holds with respect to partners' salaries.

Admission of a partner.

When a partner is admitted, adjustments of asset values may be considered in order because an interest in the assets is being sold. The adjustments may be of three classes:

(1) The provisions for bad debts, depreciation, and other shrinkages in asset values made in prior periods may have been excessive or inadequate.

(2) The rules which properly govern the valuation of assets of a going concern may not be proper rules to apply in valuing assets when there is to be a change in ownership. For

instance, in calculating the profits of a going concern, it is a conservative practice to value the inventory at cost or market, whichever is lower; but when a partner is to be admitted, he is virtually buying an interest in the inventory of the old partners, and justice would seem to require that the old partners be given the benefit of any increases in market cost prices which occurred prior to his admission. Similar considerations should apply to increases or decreases in the market value of fixed assets.

(3) The parties may agree that a goodwill has been developed by the old partners and that it should be put on the books by credit to their accounts. ·

A new partner may gain admission to a firm in either of two ways: (1) by purchasing all or a portion of the interest of an old partner or, (2) by making a contribution to the capital of the partnership.

No partner has a right to sell all or a portion of his interest in the capital of the firm without the consent of the other partners; the sale must be made by mutual consent. As the payment is made by the purchasing partner to the selling partner, the cash or the other assets given in payment do not appear on the firm's books. The only entry required is one transferring a capital credit from the account of the old partner to the account of the new one— in other words, a debit to the account of the old partner and a credit to the account of the new one.

An investment by a new partner is recorded on the firm's books by debits to accounts of the assets contributed and a credit to the new partner's Capital account.

Retirement or death of a partner.

When a partner retires, he has a right to be paid the amount of his equity in the business. But his equity may not be fairly measured by the balance of his Capital account. Adjustments of asset values may be required for reasons mentioned above, in connection with the admission of a partner. If a retiring partner is not immediately paid in full, his Capital account should nevertheless be closed, because he is no longer a partner. Any balance in his Capital account should be transferred to a personal account or a note payable account, as the case may be. This account should be given a title which will clearly distinguish it from the trade accounts and notes payable.

The death of a partner automatically dissolves the partnership; it becomes the duty of the surviving partners to wind up the affairs.

They should immediately take an inventory and close the books, to determine the capital interest of the deceased partner, including his share of the profits to the date of his death. As the decedent is no longer a partner, the balance of his Capital account should be transferred to a personal account, pending settlement with the estate.

Incorporation of a partnership.

If a partnership business is incorporated the only required entries are those to close the partners' accounts and set up the corporate capital. To illustrate, assume that partners A and B have capitals of $30,000.00 each.

If capital stock of a par or stated value of $60,000.00 is issued to them, the entry to record the change is:

```
A, Capital..................................... 30,000.00
B, Capital..................................... 30,000.00
      Capital Stock.............................         60,000.00
```

If the net assets of the partnership are transferred to the corporation in exchange for capital stock of a par or stated value of $50,000.00, the entry to record the change is:

```
A, Capital..................................... 30,000.00
B, Capital..................................... 30,000.00
      Capital Stock.............................         50,000.00
      Paid-in Surplus...........................         10,000.00
```

Liquidation.

In its narrower sense, liquidation means the payment of a liability. But in its broader sense, liquidation means the process of winding up a business, converting the assets into cash, paying the liabilities, and distributing the remaining cash among the partners or stockholders. The process of liquidating a partnership involves entries to record the following facts:

> Realization of the assets.
> Division of the loss or gain on realization
>   by charges or credits to the partners'
>   capitals.
> Payment of the liabilities.
> Payment of the partners' interests.

One invariable rule should be followed in all partnership liquidations: *Any loss or gain on realization is recorded in the partners' accounts before any payments are made to the partners.*

The following cases illustrate the application of some of the principles involved in partnership liquidations.

Case 1

Losses not sufficient to exhaust any partner's capital.
No loans from partners.

The following is a condensed trial balance of a partnership before realization and liquidation:

D, Capital..		$20,000.00
E, Capital..		10,000.00
Assets...	$35,000.00	
Liabilities.......................................		5,000.00
	$35,000.00	$35,000.00

Profits and losses are shared equally. The assets are sold for $29,000.00, or at a loss of $6,000.00. The facts with regard to the liquidation are shown in the following statement:

Statement of Liquidation

	Assets	D, Capital	E, Capital	Lia-bilities
Balances before realization.................	$35,000	$20,000	$10,000	$5,000
Loss on realization......................	6,000	3,000	3,000	
Cash for division........................	$29,000			
Capital balances after realization............		$17,000	$7,000	
Payment of creditors.....................	5,000			5,000
Payment to partners.....................	$24,000	17,000	7,000	

Case 2

Losses not sufficient to exhaust any partner's capital.
A loan from a partner.

The following is a condensed trial balance of a partnership prior to dissolution:

G, Capital..		$15,000.00
H, Capital..		10,000.00
G, Loan..		5,000.00
Assets...	$35,000.00	
Liabilities.......................................		5,000.00
	$35,000.00	$35,000.00

The assets are sold for $30,000.00. Since nothing is said concerning the profit and loss ratio, it must be assumed that profits and losses are shared equally. The liquidation is shown on page 539.

Statement of Liquidation

	Lia- bilities	G, Loan	G, Capital	H, Capital
Balances before realization...............	$5,000	$5,000	$15,000	$10,000
Loss on realization......................			2,500	2,500
Capital balances after realization.........			$12,500	$ 7,500
Distribution of cash:				
Liabilities...........................	5,000			
G, Loan..............................		5,000		
Partners' capitals.....................			12,500	7,500

This case illustrates the general rule that cash distributions should be made in the following order of priority: (1) to outside creditors, in payment of liabilities; (2) to partners, in payment of loans from them; and (3) to partners, in liquidation of their capital investments. However, this rule is subject to certain exceptions, as illustrated in Case 4.

Case 3

Partnership solvent and able to pay its creditors in full.

Two partners; one partner has a debit balance in his Capital account after realization; the other partner has a credit balance. No partners' loans.

The illustration is based on the following condensed trial balance showing the condition before the realization of the assets.

I, Capital....................................		$15,000.00
J, Capital....................................		3,000.00
Assets.......................................	$30,000.00	
Liabilities...................................		12,000.00
	$30,000.00	$30,000.00

Profits and losses are shared equally. The assets realize $22,000.00.

Statement of Liquidation

	Liabilities	I, Capital	J, Capital
Balances before realization..............	$12,000.00	$15,000.00	$3.000.00
Loss on realization.....................		4,000.00	4,000.00
Capitals after realization................		$11,000.00	$1,000.00*
Distribution of cash:			
Liabilities...........................	12,000.00		
I, Capital............................		10,000.00	
Balances.............................		$ 1,000.00	$1,000.00*

* Debit balance.

In fulfillment of his agreement to bear one half of any loss, J should pay I the $1,000.00 balance of his account. Otherwise I will bear $5,000.00 of the loss and J will bear only $3,000.00.

Case 4

Partnership solvent and able to pay its creditors in full.

Two partners; one partner has a debit balance in his Capital account after realization; the other partner has a credit balance. Both partners have Loan accounts with credit balances.

The credit balance in a partner's Loan account should not be paid to him in full if there is a debit balance in his Capital account. Enough of the loan should be transferred to the Capital account to make good the debit balance in the Capital account, and only the remainder of the loan should be paid to the partner. This is called exercising the right of offset.

If the entire credit balance in the Loan account were paid to the partner, without an offset being made, the partner might refuse, or be unable, to pay in the debit balance of his Capital account.

X and Y share profits in the ratio of 70% and 30%, respectively. Their trial balance prior to realization was:

X, Capital...............................		$20,000.00
Y, Capital...............................		18,000.00
Assets....................................	$87,000.00	
Liabilities...............................		15,000.00
X, Loan.................................		10,000.00
Y, Loan.................................		24,000.00
	$87,000.00	$87,000.00

The assets were sold for $55,000.00; the settlement is shown in the following statement of liquidation:

Statement of Liquidation

	Assets	Liabilities	X, Loan	Y, Loan	X, Capital	Y, Capital
Balances before realization..............	$87,000	$15,000	$10,000	$24,000	$20,000	$18,000
Loss on realization....	32,000				22,400	9,600
Balances after realization..............	$55,000	$15,000	$10,000	$24,000	$ 2,400*	$ 8,400
Offset against loan....			2,400		2,400	
Balances after offset...	$55,000	$15,000	$ 7,600	$24,000	$ —	$ 8,400
Distribution of cash:						
Liabilities..........	$15,000	15,000				
Partners' loans......	31,600		7,600	24,000		
Partner's capital....	8,400					8,400
Total cash.......	$55,000					

* Capital deficit.

Case 5

Partnership solvent and able to pay its creditors in full.
Three partners, one with a debit balance in his Capital account
after realization.   No partners' loans.

This case is intended to illustrate the procedure to be followed
when there are three or more partners, one of whom has a Capital
account which has been reduced to a debit balance by losses.   In
such a situation, it will be impossible to pay in full the partners
who have credit balances unless the partner with a debit balance
pays in the amount thereof.   But suppose that it is desired to distribute the cash on hand before the partner with a debit balance
pays in the amount thereof, and before it is known whether he will
be able to do so.   The question is: How should the cash be divided?
The important thing to remember is that, if the partner with a
debit balance fails to pay in, this debit balance will have to be
charged off as a loss.   The other partners will have to bear this
loss in their profit and loss ratio.   Therefore the cash on hand
should be distributed in such a way as to leave them with exactly
the right balances to absorb the loss.   In other words, the partners
with credit balances should be paid *down to* the amounts with
which they will be charged if the partner with the debit balance
fails to make good this balance.

To illustrate, R, S, and T share profits in the ratio of 50%,
30%, and 20%, respectively.   After payment of their liabilities
in full, preparatory to liquidation, their trial balance appears as
follows:

R, Capital.....................................		$10,000.00
S, Capital.....................................		26,100.00
T, Capital.....................................		23,900.00
Assets..	$60,000.00	
	$60,000.00	$60,000.00

The assets are sold for $38,000.00.   The following statement
shows how the $38,000.00 should be distributed:

Statement of Capitals

	R	S	T	Together
Capitals before realization...	$10,000.00	$26,100.00	$23,900.00	$60,000.00
Loss on realization..........	11,000.00	6,600.00	4,400.00	22,000.00
Balances after realization....	$ 1,000.00*	$19,500.00	$19,500.00	$38,000.00
Cash distributed............		18,900.00	19,100.00	38,000.00
Balances after distribution...	$ 1,000.00*	$ 600.00	$ 400.00	

* Indicates debit balance.

The payments made to S and T were determined thus: The profit and loss ratio is: R, 50%; S, 30%; and T, 20%. If R fails to pay in his debit balance of $1,000.00, the loss will have to be divided between S and T in their ratio of 30 and 20, or three fifths and two fifths.. Therefore S is paid down to three fifths of $1,000.-00, or $600.00; and T is paid down to two fifths of $1,000.00, or $400.00. If R fails to pay in the $1,000.00, S and T will have balances in their accounts exactly equal to the losses with which they will be charged; if R does pay in the $1,000.00, S will be paid $600.00 and T will be paid $400.00.

52

AN AUDIT

What is an audit?

Accountants are pernaps themselves more to blame than anyone else for the misconceptions which the public seems rather generally to entertain with respect to the nature and purpose of an audit.

I may call at a physician's office for a few minutes to ask him to examine a sore on one of my fingers, or I may spend several days in a hospital while he gives me a complete examination. In each case I am obtaining what might be called a physician's audit, but everyone recognizes that such examinations vary widely in scope.

Audits by public accountants also vary in scope. There are two principal reasons for such variations.

In the first place, the scope of the audit depends upon the purpose. Conceivably, an auditor might be engaged to check every transaction during a year and assume full responsibility for the accuracy of the records, the absence of any misappropriations of cash or other frauds, and the correctness of the balance sheet and operating statements prepared from the books at the end of the year. Many people seem to think that all audits are so broad in scope; actually, such an extensive audit usually would be wholly impracticable and would involve a cost out of all proportion to any benefit to be derived from it.

On the other hand, the scope of the audit might be limited to the verification of the subject company's financial condition on a given date, as shown by a balance sheet prepared from its books, so far as such verification could be accomplished without any examination of the records of transactions during a preceding period to see that they were proper and that no fraud had been committed.

Most audits probably are of a scope somewhere between the two extremes described above, and consist chiefly of a verification

543

of the financial condition at the end of the period, supplemented by some examination of the records of cash transactions and operations during the period.

In the second place, the scope of the audit depends upon the individual auditor's judgment as to the nature and extent of the work which he should do in order to assume responsibility with respect to the matters which he has been engaged to verify. The extent of the work to be done should normally be in inverse ratio to the extent and dependability of the company's system of internal check. If the office routine of the client company is such as to give assurance of the correctness of the records, the auditor is justified in relying upon it to a considerable extent; if the system of internal control and check is weak, the auditor must choose between doing additional work or qualifying his report.

The audit report.

The audit report should indicate clearly the scope of the engagement, but it need not go into detail as to the work which the auditor performed; it should be assumed that the work performed was sufficient to meet the requirements of the engagement.

The audit report usually contains a balance sheet, and it may also contain operating statements. However, because of limitations upon the scope of the engagement, operating statements may be omitted.

The report may also contain comments relative to the assets, liabilities, and net worth shown by the balance sheet, the items of income and expense shown in the operating statement, and any other matters which the auditor considers proper subjects for remarks.

Reports formerly contained a so-called "certificate" in which the auditor very formally expressed his opinion about the statements in his report. Because the words "I hereby certify" carry an implication of fact rather than of opinion, whereas accounting statements are unavoidably expressions of opinion rather than of fact, the use of the word "certificate" has been rather generally discontinued. The auditor now merely expresses his opinion.

The auditor has three choices with respect to the expression of opinion. He may express, without qualification, the opinion that the statements in the report fairly reflect the financial condition on a date and the results of operations during a period. If the scope of his examination has been too limited to be conclusive, or if he regards the statements as substantially accurate subject to certain exceptions, he may state the qualifications or exceptions and express an opinion subject thereto. Or he may decline to express an opinion with respect to the statements prepared from the records, in which case he should state the reasons for the omission of an expression of opinion.

The reader's responsibility.

Auditors feel that the readers of their reports have too often merely read the balance sheet and operating statement without giving due consideration to the accompanying comments.

The report should be carefully read to ascertain the scope of the engagement. Obviously, the extent of the auditor's responsibility for the balance sheet and operating statement is proportionate to the scope of the audit and the extent of the verifications which he was engaged to make. His report should indicate, and the reader of the report should realize the importance of ascertaining, the degree of responsibility which the auditor can rightfully be expected to assume.

If an auditor believes that the statements prepared from the company's books require adjustment to reflect properly the financial condition and the results of operations, he makes his recommendations to the proper representatives of the company. But accountants generally believe that they have no right to insist upon the adjustments; they merely have the right to express their exceptions and qualifications in footnotes on the statements or by comments elsewhere in the report. Readers therefore should not rely implicitly on the statements but should read all that the auditors have to say about them.

Illustrative report.

There is not, and naturally cannot be, a standard form of audit report. The contents of an audit report depend upon the nature of the subject company, on the scope and purpose of the engagement, on the nature of the facts to be disclosed, and on the ability of the auditor. The report submitted on the following pages is purely hypothetical, but it shows what information audit reports may properly contain.

AMERICAN MANUFACTURING COMPANY

Report on Examination of Accounts

For the Year Ended October 31, 1940

Contents

BAUMANN, FINNEY & CO.
Accountants and Auditors
Chicago

November 26, 1940.

The Board of Directors,
American Manufacturing Company,
East River, Illinois.

Gentlemen:

We have made an examination of the accounts of AMERICAN MANUFACTURING COMPANY (an Illinois corporation) for the year ended October 31, 1940; under prior engagements we have examined them for the preceding nine years.

Our examination was directed primarily to the verification of the financial condition of the company on October 31, 1940, and included a general review of the income and expense accounts for the year. In connection therewith, we reviewed the system of internal control and the accounting procedures of the company, and examined or tested accounting records and other supporting evidence by methods and to the extent which we deemed appropriate, but we did not make a detailed audit of the operations or cash transactions.

Prior to November 1, 1939, the company capitalized expenditures for tools and dies which were expected to have a useful life of five years or more. Because it was found that the useful life of the tools and dies could not readily be determined at the time of their acquisition, the company, effective November 1, 1939, adopted the policy of charging all such expenditures to factory expense. As a result of this change in policy, the operations for the year were charged with tool and die expenditures in the approximate amount of $7,500.00, instead of with one year's depreciation on that amount.

Subject to the qualifications and limitations stated above, it is our opinion that the accompanying balance sheet and related statements of income and surplus fairly present, in accordance with accepted principles of accounting maintained consistently during the current and the prior year, the financial condition of

(3)

American Manufacturing Company on October 31, 1940, and the results of its operations for the year then ended.

Data included in this report relative to dates and periods prior to November 1, 1939, were taken, with minor reclassifications, from our previously rendered reports and from those of predecessor auditors.

Yours truly,

BAUMANN, FINNEY & CO.

History of the Business and Nature of Operations

The business was organized as a proprietorship in 1911, and operated as such until 1920, under the name of American Manufacturing Co. On July 1, 1920, American Manufacturing Company was incorporated, in Illinois, to acquire the net assets of the proprietorship. Of the 3,000 shares of $100.00 par value common stock authorized, 2,500 shares were issued in payment for the net assets of the proprietorship; the remaining 500 shares were issued, a number of years later, as a stock dividend; 520 shares were subsequently reacquired at a cost of $62,000.00 and are held in the treasury. During the year ended October 31, 1939, an appraisal surplus was recorded, representing a valuation placed on tangible fixed assets in excess of depreciated cost. The remainder of the company's net worth has arisen from sales of preferred stock for cash and from operating profits.

The company manufactures and sells Commodity X and certain related products. Approximately two thirds of the total sales are made directly to retailers; the remaining one third of the sales are made from consignments placed with wholesale jobbers. The products are nationally marketed, and in 1938, York and Sons, Ltd., a 45%-owned affiliate, undertook distribution in Canada. With respect to about one fourth of the direct sales volume, notes or trade acceptances are taken at the time of sale, or the accounts receivable are converted into trade acceptances in the month following the month of sale; these trade acceptances mature, in general, 60 days from their date, although some mature 30 or 90 days from date. The direct sales not settled for by trade acceptances are made on open account under terms of 2% in 30 days, net within 60 days.

(4)

The numbers at the left of the balance-sheet titles indicate the pages of this report where comments relative to the various items will be found.

Balance Sheet,

Assets

CURRENT ASSETS:
11   Cash:
        Free.......................... $236,341.82
        Restricted—for Mortgage Re-
          demption and Expenses.......   7,613.26 $243,955.08
11   United States Treasury Bonds—at
        cost (market value, $77,000.00)..............   76,584.00
     Trade Receivables:
12   Notes and Acceptances......... $133,406.33
14   Accounts.....................   239,325.80
          Total Trade Receivables...... $372,732.13
15   Less Reserve for Bad Debts.....   11,811.24 360,920.89
16   Other Current Receivables:
        Notes........................ $ 7,140.00
        Sundry.......................   1,009.83   8,149.83
16   Inventories:
        Finished Goods:
          On Hand.................... $152,438.29
          On Consignment............   86,264.21
        Work in Process..............   76,803.90
        Raw Materials................   101,603.31 417,109.71
          Total Current Assets........................... $1,106,719.51
20 PREPAID EXPENSES......................................   14,162.85
   OTHER ASSETS:
20   Land Not Used in Operations.................. $ 13,452.65
21   Investment Securities (cost)....... $ 10,652.60
        Less Reserve to Lower
          of Cost or Market Value......   3,152.60   7,500.00
23   Receivable from Officer.....................   2,235.73
23   Blocked Exchange...........................   1,095.17
          Total Other Assets...............................   24,283.55
23 INVESTMENT IN AND ADVANCES TO YORK AND SONS, LTD........   5,413.36
24 TANGIBLE FIXED ASSETS—LESS RESERVES FOR DEPRECIATION..   347,917.16
25 GOODWILL...   26,152.50
                                                           $1,524,648.93

See comments on page 32 relative to contingent liabilities and commitments.

(5)

October 31, 1940

Liabilities and Net Worth

CURRENT LIABILITIES:

18	Notes Payable—Bank........................		$ 25,000.00
19	Trade Creditors:		
	Notes and Acceptances.........	$145,376.82	
	Accounts.....................	270,839.00	416,215.82
19	Reserve for Taxes:		
	Federal Income................	$ 67,346.58	
	Social Security................	5,269.31	
	Miscellaneous.................	2,613.26	75,229.15
20	Payable to Officers and Stockholders...........		15,725.63
25	First Mortgage Bonds—Current Maturity (due June 30, 1941)............................		15,000.00
20	Sundry Current Liabilities....................		4,305.73

	Total Current Liabilities.............................		$ 551,476.33
25	FIRST MORTGAGE BONDS—5% (serial maturities to June 30, 1948):		
	Total Bonds Outstanding....................	$120,000.00	
	Less Portion Maturing Within One Year—Included in Current Liabilities, above...........	15,000.00	
	Bonds Maturing After One Year..........................		105,000.00
	Total Liabilities.....................................		$ 656,476.33
26	RESERVE FOR EMPLOYEES' DISABILITY BENEFITS..............		18,989.00
26	NET WORTH:		
	Capital Stock Issued:		
	Preferred.....................	$200,000.00	
	Common.....................	300,000.00 $500,000.00	
	Surplus:		
	Earned......................	$255,277.10	
	Paid-in.....................	37,250.00	
	Appraisal...................	118,656.50	411,183.60
	Total................................		$911,183.60
	Less Common Stock in Treasury—520 Shares, at cost (see page 27).........................		62,000.00
	Total Net Worth.................................		849,183.60

$1,524,648.93

(5—*Cont.*)

Condensed Comparative Balance Sheet

Condensed balance sheets of the company on October 31, 1940 and 1939, are compared below:

| | October 31 | | Increase |
	1940	1939	Decrease*
Current Assets........................	$1,106,719.51	$807,057.67	$299,661.84
Current Liabilities...................	551,476.33	400,455.25	151,021.08
Net Current Assets.............	$ 555,243.18	$406,602.42	$148,640.76
Other Assets:			
Prepaid Expenses..................	$ 14,162.85	$ 9,816.22	$ 4,346.63
Land Not Used in Operations........	13,452.65	—	13,452.65
Investment Securities—Market Value	7,500.00	18,687.35	11,187.35*
Receivable from Officer.............	2,235.73	6,430.92	4,195.19*
Blocked Exchange..................	1,095.17	2,410.12	1,314.95*
Investment in and Advances to York and Sons, Ltd..................	5,413.36	7,814.22	2,400.86*
Tangible Fixed Assets—Less Reserves for Depreciation.................	347,917.16	362,052.97	14,135.81*
Goodwill.........................	26,152.50	26,152.50	—
Total Other Assets.............	$ 417,929.42	$433,364.30	$ 15,434.88*
Total Working Capital and Other Assets...............	$ 973,172.60	$839,966.72	$133,205.88
Less:			
First Mortgage Bonds—Portion Maturing After One Year.........	$ 105,000.00	$120,000.00	$ 15,000.00*
Reserve for Employees' Disability Benefits........................	18,989.00	25,413.60	6,424.60*
Total Deductions............	$ 123,989.00	$145,413.60	$ 21,424.60*
Remainder—Net Worth...............	$ 849,183.60	$694,553.12	$154,630.48
Ratios			
Current Assets—to Current Liabilities..	2.01	2.02	.01*
Current Liabilities—to Net Worth.....	.65	.58	.07
Total Liabilities—to Net Worth.......	.77	.76	.01
Tangible Fixed Assets—to Net Worth..	.41	.52	.11*
Net Income—to the Average of Net Worth at the Beginning and End of the Year............................	.31	.46	.15*

The statement of application of funds which follows shows the elements of the changes in financial condition which caused the increase of $148,640.76 in working capital.

(6)

Statement of Application of Funds
Year Ended October 31. 1940

Funds were provided from:
Revenue sources:
Net income for the year (see page 28)............ $265,836.63
Charges to operations not requiring funds:
Provisions for depreciation.................... 16,365.64
Loss on sale of investment securities............ 3,002.03
Adjustments for expenses of prior years.......... 1,940.50* $283,263.80
Capital sources:
Sale of preferred stock...................................... 28,950.00
Miscellaneous sources:
Sale of investment securities.................... $ 17,314.54
Decrease in receivable from officer............... 4,195.19
Sale of tangible fixed assets..................... 3,000.00
Decrease in blocked exchange.................... 1,314.95
Decrease in advances to subsidiary............... 2,400.86   28,225.54
  Total funds provided................................ $340.439.34
Funds were applied to:
Payment of dividends:
Preferred......................... $12,000.00
Common...................... 67,500.00 $ 79,500.00
Purchase of treasury stock, common.............. 48,000.00
Additions to tangible fixed assets:
Machinery and equipment........... $17,885.50
Other........................... 1,197.50   19,083.00
Retirement of bonds............................ 15,000.00
Purchase of land not used in operations............ 13,452.65
Miscellaneous:
Payment of employees' disability benefits $ 6,424.60
Increase in prepaid expenses.......... 4,346.63
Purchase of investment securities..... 5,991.70   16,762.93
  Total funds applied................................ 191,798.58
Increase in working capital—detailed on the following page.......... $148,640.76

 * Deduction.

Working Capital

The current assets and current liabilities on October 31, 1940 and 1939, are detailed below:

	October 31 1940	October 31 1939	Increase Decrease*	Ratio 1940 to 1939
Current Assets:				
Cash:				
Free....................	$ 236,341.82	$ 102,340.00	$134,001.82	2.31
Restricted..............	7,613.26	7,600.00	13.26	1.00
Total Cash.........	$ 243,955.08	$ 109,940.00	$134,015.08	2.22
United States Treasury Bonds—at Cost........	$ 76,584.00	$ 53,210.00	$ 23,374.00	1.44
Trade Receivables:				
Notes and Acceptances...	$ 133,406.33	$ 104,319.46	$ 29,086.87	1.28
Accounts...............	239,325.80	206,054.80	33,271.00	1.16
Total Trade Receivables	$ 372,732.13	$ 310,374.26	$ 62,357.87	1.20
Less Reserve for Bad Debts	11,811.24	10,530.69	1,280.55	1.12
Net Trade Receivables	$ 360,920.89	$ 299,843.57	$ 61,077.32	1.20
Other Current Receivables:				
Notes..................	$ 7,140.00	$ 20,830.00	$ 13,690.00*	.34
Sundry.................	$ 1,009.83	$ 2,612.14	$ 1,602.31*	.39
Inventories:				
Finished Goods:				
On Hand..............	$ 152,438.29	$ 63,613.22	$ 88,825.07	2.40
On Consignment.......	86,264.21	90,631.16	4,366.95*	.95
Work in Process.........	76,803.90	137,632.84	60,828.94*	.56
Raw Materials.........	101,603.31	28,744.74	72,858.57	3.53
Total Inventories....	$ 417,109.71	$ 320,621.96	$ 96,487.75	1.30
Total Current Assets	$1,106,719.51	$ 807,057.67	$299,661.84	1.37
Current Liabilities:				
Notes Payable—Bank......	$ 25,000.00	$ 50,000.00	$ 25,000.00*	.50
Trade Creditors:				
Notes and Acceptances...	145,376.82	97,620.39	47,756.43	1.49
Accounts...............	270,839.00	162,030.48	108,808.52	1.67
Reserve for Taxes:				
Federal Income..........	67,346.58	58,884.86	8,461.72	1.14
Social Security..........	5,269.31	4,819.26	450.05	1.09
Miscellaneous...........	2,613.26	3,148.22	534.96*	.83
Payable to Officers and Stockholders............	15,725.63	4,111.72	11,613.91	3.82
First Mortgage Bonds—Current Maturity..........	15,000.00	15,000.00	—	1.00
Sundry Current Liabilities..	4,305.73	4,840.32	534.59*	.89
Total Current Liabilities..........	$ 551,476.33	$ 400,455.25	$151,021.08	1.38
Net Current Assets..........	$ 555,243.18	$ 406,602.42	$148,640.76	1.37
Gross Sales.................	$4,073,072.03	$3,187,023.65	$886,048.38	1.28

(8)

Acid Test of Current Position

The ratios of total quick assets (cash, current investments, and receivables) to current liabilities on October 31, 1940 and 1939, are shown below:

	October 31 1940	1939	Increase Decrease*
Quick assets:			
Cash...........................	$243,955.08	$109,940.00	$134,015.08
United States Treasury bonds—at cost..	76,584.00	53,210.00	23,374.00
Trade receivables—less reserve for bad debts.........................	360,920.89	299,843.57	61,077.32
Other current receivables:			
Notes..........................	7,140.00	20,830.00	13,690.00*
Sundry.........................	1,009.83	2,612.14	1,602.31*
Total quick assets..............	$689,609.80	$486,435.71	$203,174.09
Current liabilities....................	551,476.33	400,455.25	151,021.08
Excess of quick assets over current liabilities........................	$138,133.47	$ 85,980.46	$ 52,153.01
Ratio of quick assets to current liabilities..	1.25	1.21	.04

Current Position, by Months

The company tries to maintain an even flow of production through the year, although there is a considerable fluctuation in sales. The operations by months during the year, and the current position at month-ends, are shown on page 10. All data other than inventories were taken, without verification, from the company's records. Since the company does not maintain perpetual inventories nor take physical inventories monthly, the total inventories at each month-end were estimated by the so-called gross profit method—that is, on the assumption of a uniform rate of gross profit throughout the year.

Schedules of Working Capital, Certain Income
By Months, During the Year

	1939 November	December	January	February	March
For the Month:					
Net Sales............	$250,728	$274,914	$ 291,575	$ 352,613	$ 408,312
Material Purchases....	220,716	219,428	209,009	226,707	222,009
Direct Labor.........	20,325	21,629	21,413	22,613	19,496
Factory Expenses.....	14,683	14,938	14,113	13,843	14,516
Gross Profit on Sales...	65,540	71,862	76,217	92,173	106,732
Net Income before Provision for Federal Income Taxes.......	12,482	16,869	19,891	30,964	41,067
At End of the Month:					
Current Assets:					
Quick Assets:					
Cash.............	$ 79,992	$ 65,646	$ 57,750	$ 53,668	$ 58,158
Investments......					
Receivables—Net.	340,370	436,818	481,589	555,045	649,034
Total Quick Assets........	$420,362	$502,464	$ 539,339	$ 608,713	$ 707,192
Inventories.........	391,158	444,103	473,282	476,006	430,449
Total Current Assets.....	$811,520	$946,567	$1,012,621	$1,084,719	$1,137,641
Current Liabilities.....	548,905	657,082	608,245	729,380	726,234
Working Capital......	$262,615	$289,485	$ 404,376	$ 355,339	$ 411,407
Working Capital Ratio.	1.48	1.44	1.66	1.49	1.57
Acid Test:					
Excess (deficiency*) of quick assets over current liabilities..	$128,543*	$154,618*	$ 68,906*	$ 120,667*	$ 19,042*
Ratio of quick assets to current liabilities	.77	.76	.89	.83	.97

The amounts shown above were taken from the company's records, and do not include monthly provisions for Federal income taxes for the year ended October 31, 1940. The provision recorded as of October 31, 1940, for the year then ended, was in the amount of $67,346.58; the inclusion of this amount in current liabilities on October 31, 1940, reduces the working capital ratio on that date from 2.29 to 2.01 and reduces the ratio of quick assets to current liabilities from 1.42 to 1.25.

(10)

and Expense Items, and Current Ratios
Ended October 31, 1940

	1940						
	April	May	June	July	August	September	October
$	284,344 $	341,619 $	401,812 $	481,413 $	496,722 $	277,312 $	153,011
	218,727	214,708	223,798	224,718	231,000	217,204	214,689
	21,223	19,862	18,682	20,844	20,114	19,731	18,916
	14,620	15,198	13,643	14,512	15,113	14,513	14,241
	74,327	89,299	105,033	125,841	129,843	72,489	39,995
	18,580	28,969	39,888	54,328	57,112	20,304	7,276*
$	54,536 $	67,368 $	52,423 $	60,317 $	86,448 $	177,729 $	243,955
						54,310	76,584
	564,589	553,054	635,216	756,662	825,751	623,486	369,071
$	619,125 $	620,422 $	687,639 $	816,979 $	912,199 $	855,525 $	689,610
	475,004	472,453	431,799	336,302	235,652	282,278	417,109
$	1,094,129 $	1,092,875 $	1,119,438 $	1,153,281 $	1,147,851 $	1,137,803 $	1,106,719
	694.142	653,918	630,592	620,107	552,564	512,212	484,130
$	399,987 $	438,957 $	488,846 $	533,174 $	595,287 $	625,591 $	622,589
	1.58	1.67	1.78	1.86	2.08	2.22	2.29
$	75,017* $	33,496* $	57,047 $	196,872 $	359,635 $	343,313 $	205,480
	.89	.95	1.09	1.32	1.65	1.67	1.42

(10—*Cont.*)

Comments on Current Assets and Current Liabilities

CASH—$243,955.08

The cash balances on October 31, 1940 and 1939, are compared below:

| | October 31 | | Increase | Ratio 1940 |
	1940	1939	Decrease*	to 1939
Unrestricted:				
In bank:				
Commerce National Bank.....	$186,312.14	$ 32,780.08	$153,532.06	5.68
First State Bank............	48,048.99	67,527.80	19,478.81*	.71
On hand:				
Undeposited receipts........	1,480.69	1,532.12	51.43*	.97
Petty cash funds............	500.00	500.00	—	1.00
Total unrestricted..........	$236,341.82	$102,340.00	$134,001.82	2.31
Restricted—Commerce National Bank.......................	7,613.26	7,600.00	13.26	1.00
Total...................	$243,955.08	$109,940.00	$134,015.08	2.22

We did not make a detailed audit of the cash transactions for the year; our examination of the cash records consisted principally of the verification of the balances on October 31, 1940, which was accomplished by counting the funds on hand, reconciling the bank accounts, and obtaining confirmations of balances from the depositaries.

The restricted balance of $7,613.26 with Commerce National Bank represents deposits, made in compliance with the terms of the trust indenture for the real estate mortgage, to meet the following requirements:

For redemption of bonds maturing on June 30, 1941 (in the amount of $15,000.00)—monthly provisions of $1,250.00 since July 1, 1940... $5,000.00
For bond interest accrued to October 31, 1940............... 2,000.00
For payment of the current year's real estate taxes........... 613.26
    Total... $7,613.26

UNITED STATES TREASURY BONDS—$76,584.00

This amount represents the cost of United States Treasury bonds, 2⅞%, due March 15, 1955–1960, of a par value of $75,000.00 and with a market value of $77,000.00 on October 31, 1940.

(11)

NOTES AND ACCEPTANCES RECEIVABLE—TRADE—$133,406.33

The transactions during the year under review with respect to trade notes and acceptances receivable are summarized in the following analysis.

Trade notes and acceptances receivable, October 31, 1939			$ 104,319.46
Add trade notes and acceptances received during the year:			
For sales of merchandise, at the time of sale	$	790,457.07	
In conversion of trade accounts receivable		396,420.88	1,186,877.95
Total			$1,291,197.41
Deduct:			
Collections		$1,152,248.80	
Uncollectible notes, charged to the reserve for bad debts		388.99	
Cancellations occasioned by the return of merchandise for credit		3,832.81	
Miscellaneous net credits (allowances, adjustments, etc.)		1,320.48	1,157,791.08
Trade notes and acceptances receivable, October 31, 1940			$ 133,406.33

(12)

The trade notes and acceptances receivable on October 31, 1940, are classified below according to maturity, class of paper, and month of sale from which the receivable originated:

Maturity	Notes	Trade Acceptances	Total
1940:			
September........................	$ 1,500.00	$ 1,420.93	$ 2,920.93
October..........................	8,000.00	12,008.45	20,008.45
Total past due....................	$ 9,500.00	$13,429.38	$ 22,929.38
November........................	$17,500.00	$31,362.23	$ 48,862.23
December........................	18,526.50	20,527.36	39,053.86
1941:			
January..........................	7,000.00	11,494.95	18,494.95
February.........................	2,065.91	—	2,065.91
March............................	2,000.00	—	2,000.00
Total not due.....................	$47,092.41	$63,384.54	$110,476.95
Total............................	$56,592.41	$76,813.92	$133,406.33

We inspected, or otherwise accounted for, all of the notes and acceptances included in the foregoing schedule.

The trade acceptances are non-interest bearing; the notes bear 4% interest. Accrued interest on the notes to October 31, 1940, is included in Other Current Receivables.

Prior to the completion of our examination, all past due notes and acceptances had been either collected or renewed with reduction in principal, as indicated below:

	Notes and Acceptances Which Matured in		
	September, 1940	October, 1940	Total
Past due on October 31, 1940..............	$2,920.93	$20,008.45	$22,929.38
Collected in full by November 22, 1940......	2,320.93	14,508.45	16,829.38
Remainder...............................	$ 600.00	$ 5,500.00	$ 6,100.00
Partial collections to November 22, 1940.....	200.00	3,000.00	3,200.00
Remainder—uncollected, but renewed, by November 22, 1940....................	$ 400.00	$ 2,500.00	$ 2,900.00

It is the opinion of the management, on the basis of information currently available, that any collection losses on notes and acceptances held on October 31, 1940, will be of inconsequential amount.

(13)

| | Month of Origin | | |
October	September	August	July and Prior
	$ —	$ 806.50	$ 2,114.43
	5,253.45	8,255.00	6,500.00
$ —	$ 5,253.45	$ 9,061.50	$ 8,614.43
$ 8,436.17	$ 6,347.28	$28,078.78	$ 6,000.00
18,009.47	12,544.39	6,000.00	2,500.00
9,948.75	6,546.20	1,500.00	500.00
765.91	800.00	500.00	—
—	2,000.00	—	—
$37,160.30	$28,237.87	$36,078.78	$ 9,000.00
$37,160.30	$33,491.32	$45,140.28	$17,614.43

(13—*Cont.*)

ACCOUNTS RECEIVABLE—TRADE—$239,325.80

Following is an analysis of the accounts receivable transactions during the year under review.

Accounts receivable, October 31, 1939.......................... $ 206,054.80
Add accounts receivable arising from sales of merchandise.......... 3,282,614.96

Total... $3,488,669.76

Deduct:
Collections................................... $2,788,738.87
Notes received in conversion of open accounts....   396,420.88
Charges to reserve for bad debts, for uncollectible
accounts...................................   3,926.13
Sales returns.................................   54,860.21
Miscellaneous—net.............................   5,397.87

Total credits.. $3,249,343.96

Accounts receivable, October 31, 1940.......................... $ 239,325.80

Following is a comparison of the accounts receivable on October 31, 1940 and 1939, analyzed according to age:

| Month of Billing | October 31 | | | | |
| | 1940 | | 1939 | | |
	Amount	Per Cent of Total	Amount	Per Cent of Total	Increase
October..........	$114,617.61	47.89%	$101,321.17	49.17%	$13,296.44
September.......	106,426.13	44.47	91,467.82	44.39	4,958.31
August..........	14,869.77	6.21	10,334.05	5.02	4,535.72
July and prior.....	3,412.29	1.43	2,931.76	1.42	480.53
Total..........	$239,325.80	100.00%	$206,054.80	100.00%	$33,271.00

The October 31, 1940, statements were mailed to the debtors under our supervision with the request that any exceptions be reported to us. The few differences reported, all of minor amount, were referred to the management.

The following summary indicates the collectibility of the receivables as evidenced by collections subsequent to the balance sheet date.

| | October 31 | | | |
| | 1940 | | 1939 | |
	Amount	Per Cent	Amount	Per Cent
Uncollected on November 22, 1940, and November 19, 1939:				
Month of billing:				
October.................	$ 88,418.29	36.94%	$ 89,513.73	43.44%
September...............	63,027.76	26.34	37,383.91	18.14
August..................	3,836.41	1.60	4,229.77	2.05
July and prior...........	629.38	.26	713.46	.35
Total.................	$155,911.84	65.14%	$131,840.87	63.98%
Collected to November 22, 1940, and November 19, 1939......	83,413.96	34.86	74,213.93	36.02
Total—on October 31..........	$239,325.80	100.00%	$206,054.80	100.00%

(14)

The officer in charge of credits prepared the following schedule with respect to the October 31, 1940, receivables which remained uncollected on November 22, 1940:

Month of Billing	Good (Wholly Collectible)	Fair (Partially Uncollectible)	Bad (Probably Uncollectible)	Total
October	$ 85,546.71	$2,620.38	$ 251.20	$ 88,418.29
September	56,856.14	5,613.90	557.72	63,027.76
August	3,332.87	290.43	213.11	3,836.41
July and prior	213.80	95.42	320.16	629.38
Total	$145,949.52	$8,620.13	$1,342.19	$155,911.84

Reserve for bad debts, October 31, 1940 .... $ 11,811.24

RESERVE FOR BAD DEBTS—$11,811.24

Following is an analysis of the reserve for bad debts during the four years ended October 31, 1940:

	Year Ended October 31			
	1937	1938	1939	1940
Balance—Beginning of Year	$ 10,703.42	$ 10,320.67	$ 11,210.91	$ 10,530.69
Additions:				
By Charge to Operations	3,284.41	3,853.67	3,505.72	4,817.25
By Charge to Surplus	1,000.00	—	—	—
Recoveries of Items Charged Off	467.41	198.23	595.66	778.42
Total	$ 15,455.24	$ 14,372.57	$ 15,312.29	$ 16,126.36
Charge-offs:				
Accounts—Trade	$ 4,464.95	$ 2,770.28	$ 3,951.84	$ 3,926.13
Notes and Acceptances—Trade	419.62	291.38	829.76	388.99
Other Receivables	250.00	100.00	—	—
Total Charge-offs	$ 5,134.57	$ 3,161.66	$ 4,781.60	$ 4,315.12
Balance—End of Year	$ 10,320.67	$ 11,210.91	$ 10,530.69	$ 11,811.24
Receivables—End of Year	$206,024.70	$281,272.15	$333,816.40	$380,881.96
Ratio of Reserve to Receivables	5.00%	3.98%	3.15%	3.10%

On the basis of the company's recent loss experience and our review of the receivables with the officer in charge of credits, it is our opinion that the reserve for bad debts, notwithstanding its decrease in ratio to receivables, is an adequate provision for normal collection losses.

(15)

OTHER CURRENT RECEIVABLES—$8,149.83

Notes receivable arising from cash advances to customers are detailed as follows:

Maker	Date of Note	Maturity
J. T. Ashby................	September 30, 1939*	Demand
F. A. Amour................	June 30, 1938	June 30, 1941
I. R. Ogden................	July 15, 1940	A series of $20.00 notes maturing on the 15th of each month to May 15, 1941
Total.......		

* Renewal of a one-year note, dated September 23, 1938.

The notes were presented for our inspection; accrued interest thereon is included in sundry current receivables, below.

Sundry current receivables on October 31, 1940, are detailed as follows:

Vendors' debit balances..................................	$ 584.00
Accrued interest on notes receivable......................	425.83
Total...	$1,009.83

INVENTORIES—$417,109.71

The inventories on October 31, 1940 and 1939, are detailed as follows:

	October 31			
	1940		1939	
	Amount	Per Cent	Amount	Per Cent
Finished goods:				
On hand:				
Current models...........	$126,025.37	30.21%	$ 45,369.53	14.15%
Prior years' models.........	26,412.92	6.34	18,243.69	5.69
On consignment:				
Cost:				
Current models..........	58,646.82	14.06	60,885.76	18.99
Prior year's models.......	24,563.29	5.89	27,426.38	8.55
Expenses of shipment.......	3,054.10	.73	2,319.02	.72
Total finished goods....	$238,702.50	57.23%	$154,244.38	48.10%
Work in process...............	76,803.90	18.41	137,632.84	42.93
Raw materials................	101,603.31	24.36	28,744.74	8.97
Total...............	$417,109.71	100.00%	$320,621.96	100.00%

(16)

Original Amount	Interest Rate	Balance, October 31, 1940	Balances Receivable on Notes, Acceptances, and Open Accounts, October 31, 1940
$4,000.00	4%	$4,000.00	$19,221.68
3,000.00	4	3,000.00	6,314.30
200.00	4	140.00	3,214.62
....		$7,140.00	

(16—*Cont.*)

We were in attendance during, and supervised, the taking of physical inventories of finished goods, work in process, and raw materials on October 31, 1940. Finished goods on consignment were verified by direct confirmation from consignees.

The inventory was priced, by company employees, on bases and from sources indicated below:

Finished goods and work in process—at average cost of materials and direct labor as shown by factory production records.

Materials—at cost or market, whichever was lower, from pricings embodied in the company's perpetual inventory records.

We made extensive tests of the pricings at cost and market and of the accuracy of extensions, footings, and recapitulations.

A certificate was received from officials of the company stating that no obsolete or unusable materials were included in the inventory except at salvage values, and that no portion of the inventory was pledged or otherwise encumbered on October 31, 1940.

The management stated that the large increase in raw materials on hand was the result of a gradual accumulation through the year. Although a balanced supply of raw materials might be maintained at a considerably lower aggregate valuation, officials thought it judicious to increase the available store of materials to the current level, which would provide for approximately two months of normal production without further purchases.

(17)

The turnovers of raw materials and finished goods for the current and for the prior year were as follows:

	Year Ended October 31	
	1940	1939
Raw materials:		
Cost of materials used (page 29)...............	$2,569,858.07	$1,982,603.50
Inventories:		
Beginning of year..........................	$ 28,744.74	$ 53,238.30
End of year...............................	101,603.31	28,744.74
Average...................................	$ 65,174.02	$ 40,991.52
Number of raw material turnovers.............	39.43	48.37
Finished goods:		
Cost of goods sold (page 29)..................	$2,965,021.83	$2,205,060.88
Inventories:		
Beginning of year..........................	$ 154,244.38	$ 123,128.23
End of year...............................	238,702.50	154,244.38
Average...................................	$ 196,473.44	$ 138,686.30
Number of finished goods turnovers...........	15.09	15.90

NOTES PAYABLE—BANKS—$25,000.00

This amount represents two unsecured notes payable, as follows:

Payee	Date of Note	Due Date	Amount
Commerce National Bank...	September 30, 1940	November 29, 1940	$20,000.00
First State Bank...........	April 15, 1940	December 15, 1940	5,000.00
Total..................			$25,000.00

The liabilities were confirmed by the banks. Interest on both notes, at 3% per annum, has been paid to maturity.

Following is a summary of the company's liability on notes payable to banks at month-ends during the year ended October 31, 1940.

End of	Commerce National Bank	First State Bank	Total
1939:			
November...........................	$110,000.00	$15,000.00	$125,000.00
December...........................	190,000.00	20,000.00	210,000.00
1940:			
January............................	240,000.00	20,000.00	260,000.00
February...........................	260,000.00	15,000.00	275,000.00
March..............................	255,000.00	20,000.00	275,000.00
April...............................	210,000.00	15,000.00	225,000.00
May................................	190,000.00	10,000.00	200,000.00
June...............................	170,000.00	5,000.00	175,000.00
July...............................	95,000.00	5,000.00	100,000.00
August.............................	40,000.00	5,000.00	45,000.00
September..........................	30,000.00	5,000.00	35,000.00
October............................	20,000.00	5,000.00	25,000.00

Notes and Acceptances Payable—Trade—$145,376.82

It is the policy of the company to buy from some of its principal suppliers on terms providing for settlement by trade acceptance or note in the month following the month of purchase. Such notes are all payable 90 days from date and the acceptances mature 30, 60, or 90 days from their date.

Notes and acceptances outstanding on October 31, 1940, bore maturities in 1940 and 1941, as follows:

1940:	
November	$ 70,386.24
December	36,962.19
1941:	
January	36,464.87
February	1,563.52
Total	$145,376.82

Requests for confirmations were mailed to the holders of the notes and trade acceptances. Based upon the replies received, it appears that the company's liability is properly stated at the amount shown above.

Accounts Payable—Trade—$270,839.00

We examined available creditors' statements and compared them with the related recorded accounts payable, and we examined the company's records subsequent to October 31, 1940, with respect to liabilities. Requests were mailed to approximately 20% of the creditors of record, for confirmation of the balances shown as owed to them; differences disclosed by the replies received were satisfactorily accounted for. We are of the opinion, based on our examination, that the above-stated amount fairly reflects the company's liability to trade creditors on October 31, 1940.

Reserve for Taxes—$75,229.15

On October 31, 1940, this reserve contained provision for the following taxes:

Federal income—provision for year ended October 31, 1940		$67,346.58
Social security		5,269.31
Miscellaneous:		
Federal capital stock	$1,500.00	
Real estate	613.26	
Personal property	500.00	2,613.26
Total		$75,229.15

The company's Federal income tax returns for the years ended October 31, 1939 and 1940, are subject to review by the Bureau of Internal Revenue.

PAYABLE TO OFFICERS AND STOCKHOLDERS—$15,725.63

The amounts owed to officers and stockholders on October 31, 1940 and 1939, are detailed below:

Name	Nature of Liability	October 31 1940	October 31 1939
G. B. Saxley, President..................	Cash advance	$ 7,500.00	—
O. R. Turner, Vice-president.............	Commissions	4,025.11	3,030.33
P. V. Garver, Vice-president.............	Commissions	2,762.60	—
B. N. White...........................	Commissions	1,437.92	1,081.39
Total..		$15,725.63	$4,111.72

SUNDRY CURRENT LIABILITIES—$4,305.73

The above amount consists of the following:

Credit balances—customers' accounts.......................	$1,713.27
Accrued bond interest.....................................	2,000.00
Accrued interest on notes payable.........................	512.46
Community fund—East River.............................	80.00
Total...	$4,305.73

Comments on Other Assets and Other Liabilities and Reserves

PREPAID EXPENSES—$14,162.85

The following statement shows the amounts of expenses deferred on October 31, 1940 and 1939:

	Deferred on October 31 1940	Deferred on October 31 1939
Insurance....................................	$ 3,563.04	$3,380.42
Supplies.....................................	2,654.33	2,740.69
Sales salaries and commissions................	4,550.00	—
Traveling expenses...........................	3,395.48	3,695.11
Total......................................	$14,162.85	$9,816.22

We tested the company's bases of deferring expenses, and are of the opinion that the amounts shown above were conservatively computed.

LAND NOT USED IN OPERATIONS—$13,452.65

In June 1940, land adjoining the factory site was purchased for prospective plant extension purposes. Income from the rental of the land is included in Other Income, in the accompanying statement of income and expense.

(20)

INVESTMENT SECURITIES—AT COST—$10,652.60
RESERVE FOR DECLINE IN MARKET VALUE—$3,152.60

The cost and market value of investment securities held on October 31, 1940, and the related reserve for decline in market value, are detailed as follows:

	Number of Shares or Par Value	Date of Acquisition
Listed common stocks:		
Bolger Turpentine Company	75	Sept. 23, 1932
Atlas Electric Corporation	25	Nov. 1, 1931
Oliver Bond & Share Co	50	Sept. 16, 1940
American Utilities Corporation	10	Nov. 2, 1939
Railroad bonds:		
Buckingham and Northeastern Railway Company—5's of February 1, 1977	$2,000.00	April 29, 1936
Total		

We inspected stock certificates and bonds representing ownership of all of the securities.

At the close of each year, the reserve for decline in market value is restated, by surplus adjustment, to reduce the carrying value of securities to the lower of cost or market value. When securities are sold, the related reserve for decline in market value is restored to Surplus; and the gain or loss, determined on the basis of cost and selling price, is reflected in the current year's operations.

Cost	Market Value, October 31, 1940	Reserve for Decline in Market Value	Income Received During Year Ended October 31, 1940
$ 5,975.00	$3,134.55	$2,840.45	$ —
1,648.40	1,427.50	220.90	50.00
781.25	690.00	91.25	—
210.45	261.28	—	5.00
2,037.50	2,902.00	—	100.00
$10,652.60		$3,152.60	

(21—*Cont.*)

Following is a summary of the securities transactions and the changes in the reserve account for the year ended October 31, 1940:

	Securities (At Cost)	Reserve for Decline in Market Value	Debit* Credit to Surplus	Profit Loss* on Disposals
Balances, October 31, 1939......	$24,977.47	$6,290.12		
Purchases....................	5,991.70			
Sales:				
Securities held on October 31, 1939:				
Cost........ $15,316.57	15,316.57*			
Selling price.. 11,314.54				
Loss........ $ 4,002.03				$4,002.03*
Reserve—restored to Surplus........		4,104.54*	$4,104.54	
Securities purchased during the year:				
Selling price.. $ 6,000.00				
Cost........ 5,000.00	5,000.00*			
Profit....... $ 1,000.00				1,000.00
Additional reserve required on October 31, 1940:				
For securities held at both the beginning and end of the year....... $ 875.77				
For securities purchased during the year and held on October 31, 1940...... 91.25				
Total.... $ 967.02		967.02	967.02*	
Balances, October 31, 1940......	$10,652.60	$3,152.60		
Net adjustment of reserve—credited to Surplus...........			$3,137.52	
Net loss on disposals—charged to Operations......................				$3,002.03*

RECEIVABLE FROM OFFICER—$2,235.73

The above amount represents the balance receivable from A. R. Weston, Secretary, on open account. The balance receivable from Mr. Weston on October 31, 1939, was $3,750.00.

BLOCKED EXCHANGE—$1,095.17

The above amount represents funds on deposit with the Bank of Erehwon, which remain, as in prior years, blocked by exchange restrictions. A balance of 2,730 wampa was confirmed by the bank. At the current exchange rate of .402 on October 31, 1940, the dollar value was slightly in excess of that stated above.

INVESTMENT IN AND ADVANCES TO YORK AND SONS, LTD.— $5,413.36

The investment in, and advances to, York and Sons, Ltd., the distributor of the company's products in Canada, are detailed below:

Investment (45% ownership):
   Cost of 450 shares of no-par value stock.................... $4,500.00
Advance:
   Represented by an unsecured, one-year, non-interest-bearing
   note, dated August 23, 1940, and due on demand.........   913.36
       Total.. $5,413.36

We have examined a report on an examination of the accounts of York and Sons, Ltd., for the year ended December 31, 1939, rendered under date of February 26, 1940. The subsidiary's operations for that year resulted in a profit of $2,983.11, and the book value of its capital stock on December 31, 1939, was $10.8915 per share.

Dividends received on the stock during the year under review, $225.00, were taken up as income.

The company's sales to York and Sons, Ltd., during the year ended October 31, 1940, totaled $317,019.97.

TANGIBLE FIXED ASSETS—LESS RESERVES FOR DEPRECIATION— $347,917.16

The changes in the fixed asset accounts and depreciation reserves during the year ended October 31, 1940, are summarized below:

	Fixed Assets				
	Balance, October 31, 1939—at Appraisal Values	Additions— at Cost	Deductions		Balance, October 31, 1940
			Disposals	Reversal for Assets Fully De- preciated	
Land (see note 3).....................	$ 86,782.00	$ —	$ —	$ —	$ 86,782.00
Buildings (see note 3):					
A—Factory......................	$152,012.95	$ —			$152,012.95
B—Warehouse...................	75,261.26	—			75,261.26
C—Power Plant..................	16,413.29	1,000.00			17,413.29
Total Buildings................	$243,687.50	$ 1,000.00	$ —	$ —	$244,687.50
Machinery and Equipment:					
Factory........................	$ 84,773.63	$14,964.56	$6,000.00	$3,000.00	$ 90,738.19
Warehouse......................	5,203.83	2,577.77	—	350.00	7,431.60
Power Plant....................	28,325.43	343.17	—	1,500.00	27,168.60
Total Machinery and Equipment..	$118,302.89	$17,885.50	$6,000.00	$4,850.00	$125,338.39
Tools and Dies (see note 4)..........	$ 35,251.26	$ —	$ —	$ —	$ 35,251.26
Furniture and Fixtures..............	$ 12,196.97	$ 197.50	$ —	$ 975.00	$ 11,419.47
Total....................	$496,220.62	$19,083.00	$6,000.00	$5,825.00	$503,478.62

(1) Charged to operations.
(2) Charged to Appraisal Surplus.
(3) Pledged as security to mortgage bonds.
(4) Effective November 1, 1939, the company adopted the policy of charging all expenditures for tools and dies to operations.

The land, buildings, machinery, and other equipment were appraised by The Whipple Appraisal Company as of October 31, 1939. The books were adjusted to the appraisal valuation by credit to Appraisal Surplus in the amount of $132,509.67, representing the excess of the sound value of the assets as shown by the appraisal over the depreciated value shown by the books. This increase is summarized below:

Land...	$ 27,032.00
Buildings...	78,203.50
Machinery and equipment...........................	24,864.85
Tools and dies.....................................	2,293.18
Furniture and fixtures..............................	116.14
Total surplus from appraisal......................	$132,509.67

During the year ended October 31, 1940, the company transferred $13,853.17 of this appreciation to the reserve for depreciation, in accordance with its policy of writing off the appreciation over the remaining lives of the assets.

We examined the additions to the fixed asset accounts during the year and found them to represent properly capitalizable

| | | Reserve for Depreciation | | | | | |
| | | Depreciation Provided | | Deductions | | | |
Rate of Depre- ciation	Balance, October 31, 1939	Of Cost (1)	Of Appre- ciation (2)	For Disposals	Reversal for Assets Fully De- preciated	Balance, October 31, 1940	Net Book Value, October 31, 1940
							$ 86,782.00
5%	$ 39,095.60	$ 2,565.78	$ 4,938.17			$ 46,599.55	$105,413.40
5	16,755.26	1,254.22	2,509.23			20,518.71	54,742.55
4	6,205.64	317.10	372.95			6,895.69	10,517.60
	$ 62,056.50	$ 4,137.10	$ 7,820.35	$ —	$ —	$ 74,013.95	$170,673.55
10	$ 30,624.32	$ 3,339.79	$ 4,335.87	$3,000.00	$3,000.00	$ 32,299.98	$ 58,438.21
8	2,219.15	280.07	84.89	—	350.00	2,234.11	5,197.49
8	11,539.60	1,192.67	442.26	—	1,500.00	11,674.53	15,494.07
	$ 44,383.07	$ 4,812.53	$ 4,863.02	$3,000.00	$4,850.00	$ 46,208.62	$ 79,129.77
20	$ 19,225.54	$ 6,098.05	$ 917.27	$ —	$ —	$ 26,240.86	$ 9,010.40
15	$ 8,502.54	$ 1,317.96	$ 252.53	$ —	$ 975.00	$ 9,098.03	$ 2,321.44
	$134,167.65	$16,365.64	$13,853.17	$3,000.00	$5,825.00	$155,561.46	$347,917.16

(24—Cont.)

charges. As more fully explained on page 3, the company, effective November 1, 1939, adopted the policy of charging to operations all expenditures for tools and dies.

We also examined the depreciation provisions for the year, and found that they were made at the same rates as in prior years and that they appear to be adequate.

GOODWILL—$26,152.50

This intangible was recorded at the time of the organization of the company, in connection with the issuance of its capital stock. There has been no change in the Goodwill account since it was established.

FIRST MORTGAGE BONDS—5%—SERIAL MATURITIES TO JUNE 30, 1948

As of July 1, 1938, the company issued first mortgage bonds in the amount of $150,000.00. The bonds are secured by a mortgage on the company's land and buildings.

The indenture provides that the bonds shall be redeemed in annual installments of $15,000.00, maturing on June 30, 1939 to 1948, inclusive, with interest at the rate of 5% per annum. The interest coupons are payable June 30 and December 31.

The above amount of $120,000.00, representing bonds outstanding on October 31, 1940, is classified in the accompanying balance sheet as follows:

As a current liability—serial maturity due June 30, 1941..... $ 15,000.00
As a non-current liability—bonds maturing after October 31,
    1941... 105,000.00
       Total... $120,000.00

Accrued interest on the bonds is included in Sundry Current Liabilities.

Provisions of the trust indenture requiring cash deposits for the redemption of bonds maturing currently, and for the payment of bond interest and real estate taxes, have been complied with; the amount required on October 31, 1940, $7,613.26, is included in the accompanying balance sheet as a restricted cash balance.

Under the terms of the indenture, the entire outstanding balance of the bond issue becomes immediately due and payable if, at any monthly closing, the net worth (capital stock plus paid-in and earned surplus, less treasury stock) falls below three times the outstanding balance on the bond principal. On October 31, 1940, net worth as defined by the indenture aggregated $730,527.10; unpaid principal on the bonds amounted to $120,000.00.

(25)

RESERVE FOR EMPLOYEES' DISABILITY BENEFITS—$18,989.00

In lieu of carrying workmen's compensation insurance, the company assumes its own liability under a permit received from the Illinois Industrial Commission in 1936.

Below is an analysis of the reserve for the five years ended October 31, 1940:

	1936	1937	1938	1939	1940
		Year Ended October 31			
Balance—beginning of year............... $	—	$21,378.57	$23,378.57	$25,378.57	$25,413.60
Provisions charged to operations........	—	2,000.00	2,000.00	1,000.00	1,000.00
Provision charged to surplus...........	25,000.00	—	—	—	—
Total...........	$25,000.00	$23,378.57	$25,378.57	$26,378.57	$26,413.60
Benefit payments....	3,621.43	—	—	964.97	7,424.60
Balance—end of year.	$21,378.57	$23,378.57	$25,378.57	$25,413.60	$18,989.00

The balance of the reserve on October 31, 1940, was deemed adequate by the management.

Net Worth

The changes in net worth during the year ended October 31, 1940, are summarized below:

	October 31 1940	1939	Increase Decrease*
Capital stock:			
Preferred......................	$200,000.00	$175,000.00	$ 25,000.00
Common......................	300,000.00	300,000.00	—
Surplus:			
Earned......................	255,277.10	67,743.45	187,533.65
Paid-in......................	37,250.00	33,300.00	3,950.00
Appraisal......................	118,656.50	132,509.67	13,853.17*
Treasury stock, common—at cost....	62,000.00*	14,000.00*	48,000.00*
Total net worth...............	$849,183.60	$694,553.12	$154,630.48

These changes are accounted for in the following comments.

PREFERRED STOCK

The preferred stock has a par value of $100.00 per share, and is entitled to cumulative dividends at the rate of 6% per annum; it is non-participating and does not carry voting rights unless dividends are one year or more in arrears.

Of the 5,000 shares authorized, 2,000 were outstanding on October 31, 1940.

(26)

During the year, the company issued 250 shares for $28,950.00 in cash. The difference between the aggregate par value and the issuing price of the shares was credited to Paid-in Surplus. Dividends on preferred stock have been paid to March 1, 1940.

COMMON STOCK
TREASURY STOCK, COMMON

The common stock has a par value of $100.00 per share. Of the 5,000 shares authorized, 3,000 had been issued, 520 were in treasury, and 2,480 were outstanding on October 31, 1940. The shares in treasury were carried at cost. The 400 shares taken into the treasury during the year under review were acquired at a cost of $48,000.00; the remaining 120 shares were acquired in the preceding year at a cost of $14,000.00.

EARNED SURPLUS

The sources of the $187,533.65 increase in earned surplus during the year under review are detailed below:

Increases:
Net income for the year ended October 31, 1940 (page 28).......... $265,836.63
Adjustments for over-provision for prior years' taxes:
    Federal income—1938........................... $ 1,868.74
    Personal property—1938........................ 246.62   2,115.36
Adjustment of reserve for decline in market value of investment
    securities... 3,137.52
      Total.. $271,089.51
Decreases:
Payment of prior years' expenses:
    Advertising....................................... $ 2,134.11
    Salesmen's traveling expense...................... 1,921.75
      Total.. 4,055.86
Net increase before dividends................................. $267,033.65
Dividends paid:
    Preferred... $12,000.00
    Common.. 67,500.00   79,500.00
Net increase after dividends.................................. $187,533.65

Surplus in the amount of $62,000.00, representing the cost of stock held in treasury, is not available for dividends because of statutory limitation.

PAID-IN SURPLUS

The $3,950.00 increase in paid-in surplus represents the premium on the preferred stock sold during the year.

(27)

APPRAISAL SURPLUS

The origin of the appraisal surplus is set forth in detail on page 24.

The $13,853.17 decrease in the balance of the account during the year represents the year's depreciation of appreciation, which was recorded by a deduction from the appraisal surplus and an addition to the reserve for depreciation.

Comparative Statement of Income and Expense
For the Years Ended October 31, 1940 and 1939

	Year Ended October 31 1940	1939	Increase Decrease*	Ratio 1940 to 1939
Gross Sales................	$4,073,072.03	$3,187,023.65	$886,048.38	1.28
Sales Returns and Allowances	58,693.02	39,489.52	19,203.50	1.49
Net Sales.................	$4,014,379.01	$3,147,534.13	$866,844.88	1.28
Cost of Goods Sold (page 29)..	2,965,021.83	2,205,060.88	759,960.95	1.34
Gross Profit on Sales.......	$1,049,357.18	$ 942,473.25	$106,883.93	1.11
Per cent of net sales.......	(26.14%)	(29.94%)	(3.80%*)	
Selling Expenses (page 30)...	479,350.15	429,228.91	50,121.24	1.12
Net Profit on Sales..........	$ 570,007.03	$ 513,244.34	$ 56,762.69	1.11
Per cent of net sales.......	(14.20%)	(16.31%)	(2.11%*)	
General Expenses (page 31)..	219,938.70	169,423.45	50,515.25	1.30
Net Profit on Operations.....	$ 350,068.33	$ 343,820.89	$ 6,247.44	1.02
Add Other Income—Interest, Discount, etc. (page 32)...	23,204.49	22,152.97	1,051.52	1.05
Net Profit on Operations, and Other Income.............	$ 373,272.82	$ 365,973.86	$ 7,298.96	1.02
Deduct Other Expenses—Interest, Discount, etc. (page 32).....................	40,089.61	23,960.93	16,128.68	1.67
Net Income Before Provision for Federal Income Taxes..	$ 333,183.21	$ 342,012.93	$ 8,829.72*	.97
Provision for Federal Income Taxes...................	67,346.58	58,884.86	8,461.72	1.14
Net Income...............	$ 265,836.63	$ 283,128.07	$ 17,291.44*	.94
Per cent of net sales.......	(6.62%)	(9.00%)	(2.38%*)	

Comparative Statement of Cost of Goods Sold

Year Ended

	1940	
	Amount	Per Cent of Manufacturing Cost
Materials:		
Inventory—Beginning of Year....................	$ 28,744.74	
Purchases.......................................	2,635,596.65	
Freight In......................................	7,119.99	
Total......................................	$2,671,461.38	
Less Inventory—End of Year...................	101,603.31	
Cost of Materials Used...................	$2,569,858.07	85.99%
Direct Labor....................................	$ 244,854.00	8.19
Factory Expenses:		
Salaries and Wages:		
Engineering.................................	$ 19,889.07	
Executive...................................	12,936.50	
Inspection...................................	10,236.89	
Stock Room and Receiving....................	8,488.44	
Porters and Watchmen......................	6,195.50	
Supervision.................................	5,382.52	
Machine Shop...............................	4,547.69	
Total.....................................	$ 67,676.61	
Tool and Die Expense......................	29,414.89	
Experimental Expense......................	24,971.14	
Factory Expense and Supplies..................	15,751.64	
Depreciation..................................	15,047.68	
Maintenance and Repairs......................	5,083.45	
Light and Power..............................	4,245.65	
Social Security Taxes.........................	3,904.50	
Laboratory Expense and Supplies...............	3,557.15	
Insurance.....................................	2,286.23	
Provision for Employees' Disability Benefits.......	2,000.00	
Total Factory Expenses...................	$ 173,938.94	5.82
Total Manufacturing Cost........................	$2,988,651.01	100.00%
Add Work in Process—Beginning of Year...........	137,632.84	
Total......................................	$3,126,283.85	
Deduct Work in Process—End of Year.............	76,803.90	
Cost of Goods Manufactured......................	$3,049,479.95	
Add Finished Goods—Beginning of Year............	154,244.38	
Total......................................	$3,203,724.33	
Deduct Finished Goods—End of Year..............	238,702.50	
Cost of Goods Sold.............................	$2,965,021.83	

(29)

For the Years Ended October 31, 1940 and 1939

October 31

	1939			Ratio
	Amount	Per Cent of Manufac- turing Cost	Increase Decrease*	1940 to 1939
$	53,238.30		$ 24,493.56*	.54
	1,949,842.41		685,754.24	1.35
	8,267.53		1,147.54*	.86
$2,011,348.24			$660,113.14	1.33
	28,744.74		72,858.57	3.53
$1,982,603.50		86.81%	$587,254.57	1.30
$	200,843.37	8.79	$ 44,010.63	1.22
$	9,431.58		$ 10,457.49	2.11
	—		12,936.50	—
	9,375.00		861.89	1.09
	3,682.90		4,805.54	2.30
	2,563.41		3,632.09	2.42
	6,292.75		910.23*	.86
	4,019.33		528.36	1.13
$	35,364.97		$ 32,311.64	1.91
	14,079.53		15,335.36	2.09
	5,138.86		19,832.28	4.86
	13,379.13		2,372.51	1.18
	13,708.28		1,339.40	1.10
	5,246.59		163.14*	.97
	3,022.03		1,223.62	1.40
	2,091.32		1,813.18	1.87
	4,760.84		1,203.69*	.75
	1,739.85		546.38	1.31
	2,000.00		—	1.00
$	100,531.40	4.40	$ 73,407.54	1.73
$2,283,978.27		100.00%	$704,672.74	1.31
	89,831.60		47,801.24	1.53
$2,373,809.87			$752,473.98	
	137,632.84		60,828.94*	.56
$2,236,177.03			$813,302.92	1.36
	123,128.23		31,116.15	1.25
$2,359,305.26			$844,419.07	
	154,244.38		84,458.12	1.55
$2,205,060.88			$759,960.95	1.34

(29—Cont.)

During the year ended October 31, 1940, sales increased 25%
over sales for the prior year; the corresponding increase in cost of
sales was 34%. The disproportionate increase in factory expense,
73%, is primarily attributable to the following factors:

In connection with a factory reorganization, an executive's
salary, in the amount of $12,936.50, was charged to factory
expense for the year ended October 31, 1940. The corresponding expenditure for prior years was classified as a general
expense.

As fully explained on page 3 herein, the company changed its
policy with regard to absorbing the costs of tools and dies.
This resulted in a greater charge for tool and dies expense in
1940 than in prior years.

Abnormal expenditures during 1940 in connection with special
research work resulted in an increase of $19,832.28 in experi-
mental expense.

We were informed by company officials that the general level of
prices of materials and labor during the year 1940 was slightly in
excess of the level for the prior year.

Comparative Schedule of Selling Expenses
For the Years Ended October 31, 1940 and 1939

	Year Ended October 31 1940	1939	Increase Decrease*	Ratio 1940 to 1939
Advertising	$162,871.20	$153,313.95	$ 9,557.25	1.06
Sales Salaries and Commissions	111,050.16	87,802.03	23,248.13	1.26
Salesmen's Traveling Expenses	47,725.83	53,903.62	6,177.79*	.89
Sales Office Salaries	32,639.30	29,431.59	3,207.71	1.11
Executive Salaries	21,000.00	17,800.00	3,200.00	1.18
Shipping Salaries	18,694.72	15,325.54	3,369.18	1.22
Freight on Sales	16,256.20	12,297.07	3,959.13	1.32
Licenses	15,250.00	17,126.37	1,876.37*	.89
Warehousing Expense	10,124.08	8,369.52	1,754.56	1.21
Entertainment	9,781.16	6,237.14	3,544.02	1.57
Samples	7,464.27	4,874.51	2,589.76	1.53
Shipping Supplies	5,900.05	3,453.24	2,446.81	1.71
Insurance	5,827.55	5,804.06	23.49	1.00
Social Security Taxes	5,409.61	2,926.51	2,483.10	1.85
Printing, Stationery, and Supplies	3,725.87	4,283.09	557.22*	.87
Promotion	2,946.65	4,351.80	1,405.15*	.68
Taxes—Other	2,683.50	1,928.87	754.63	1.39
Total Selling Expenses	$479,350.15	$429,228.91	$50,121.24	1.12
Net Sales				1.28

Comparative Schedule of General Expenses
For the Years Ended October 31, 1940 and 1939

	Year Ended October 31		Increase Decrease*	Ratio 1940 to 1939
	1940	1939		
Executive Salaries................	$103,050.00	$ 81,000.00	$22,050.00	1.27
Office Salaries...................	53,107.96	43,284.42	9,823.54	1.23
Travel..........................	9,376.22	6,100.10	3,276.12	1.54
Telephone and Telegraph.........	6,355.67	4,522.19	1,833.48	1.41
Office Supplies and Expense.......	6,302.52	5,641.65	660.87	1.12
Insurance.......................	6,291.35	5,064.33	1,227.02	1.24
Taxes—Other than Social Security.	6,164.13	5,848.08	316.05	1.05
Legal and Accounting.............	8,957.02	2,520.78	6,436.24	3.55
Bad Debts......................	4,038.83	2,910.06	1,128.77	1.39
Postage.........................	3,307.09	2,086.59	1,220.50	1.58
Miscellaneous...................	2,165.53	1,293.12	872.41	1.67
Light...........................	1,773.09	1,760.69	12.40	1.01
Social Security Taxes.............	1,527.83	956.46	571.37	1.60
Watch Service..................	1,343.77	1,560.00	216.23*	.86
Depreciation....................	1,317.96	1,281.60	36.36	1.03
Automobile Allowances...........	1,075.26	949.76	125.50	1.13
Entertainment..................	978.46	893.69	84.77	1.09
Dues and Subscriptions...........	970.62	774.40	196.22	1.25
Charity and Donations...........	850.00	244.68	605.32	3.47
Carfare and Messenger...........	547.04	519.92	27.12	1.05
Maintenance and Repairs.........	438.35	210.93	227.42	2.08
Total General Expenses.........	$219,938.70	$169,423.45	$50,515.25	1.30
Net Sales...				1.28

Approximately $5,000.00 of the $6,436.24 increase in legal and accounting fees was represented by the cost of an unsuccessful suit for patent infringement which the company brought against a competitor.

(31)

Comparative Schedule of Other Income and Expenses
For the Years Ended October 31, 1940 and 1939

| | Year Ended October 31 | | Increase | Ratio 1940 to |
	1940	1939	Decrease*	1939
Income:				
Purchase Discount............	$21,095.82	$19,683.27	$ 1,412.55	1.07
Interest and Dividends........	1,808.67	2,469.70	661.03*	.73
Rent—Land.................	300.00	—	300.00	—
Total Other Income.........	$23,204.49	$22,152.97	$ 1,051.52	1.05
Expenses:				
Sales Discount................	$26,891.69	$10,343.43	$16,548.26	2.60
Interest and Exchange.........	10,195.89	12,386.54	2,190.65*	.82
Loss on Sale of Securities......	3,002.03	1,230.96	1,771.07	2.44
Total Other Expenses........	$40,089.61	$23,960.93	$16,128.68	1.67

In December, 1939, the company changed the terms of sale on open account from 1/30, n/60 to 2/30, n/60. The granting of more advantageous terms to customers largely accounts for the increase of $16,548.26 in sales discount shown above.

General

CONTINGENT LIABILITIES

On October 29, 1940, the company received notice that it had been named co-defendant with one of its suppliers in an action for damages in which each was being sued for $100,000.00, and that this action resulted from injury sustained by an individual in the use of an accessory produced by the supplier and furnished by the company as equipment for Commodity X. From our examination of insurance policies, it appears that the company was insured, in the amount of $50,000.00, against loss which might arise from judgment in a lawsuit of this nature, and we were so informed by the company's attorney.

On October 31, 1940, dividends on the company's preferred stock were in arrears since March 1, 1940, in the amount of $6,000.00.

A certificate was furnished us by the officers to the effect that they knew of no other contingent liabilities to which the company was subject on October 31, 1940.

COMMITMENTS

The company entered into a contract during October, 1939, providing for the erection of an additional factory building at a cost of $150,000.00. Work on this contract was not started until November, 1940.

(32)

INSURANCE

The company is protected by insurance coverage, with 80%
coinsurance, on its buildings, equipment, and inventories as follows:

Fire.. $700,000.00
Tornado...   300,000.00

The company does not carry any fidelity bonds on its employees
and officers.

OFFICERS AND DIRECTORS

Officers and directors of the company on October 31, 1940,
were:

Officers:
  G. B. Taxley...................... President
  A. R. Turner...................... Vice-president
  P. V. Garver...................... Vice-president
  A. R. Weston...................... Secretary
  A. O. Andersen.................... Treasurer

Directors:
  G. B. Taxley
  A. R. Turner
  P. V. Garver

Historical Information

NET WORTH

The growth of the company's net worth since the time of incorporation is summarized below:

	Capital Stock	
	Preferred	Common
July 1, 1920—date of incorporation....................		$250,000.00
October 31:		
1922..		250,000.00
1927..	$ 50,000.00	250,000.00
1932..	100,000.00	300,000.00
1935..	125,000.00	300,000.00
1936..	150,000.00	300,000.00
1937..	175,000.00	300,000.00
1938..	175,000.00	300,000.00
1939..	175,000.00	300,000.00
1940..	200,000.00	300,000.00

All of the preferred stock was sold for cash at varying prices in excess of par; the paid-in surplus represents the premiums on the preferred stock.

Except for a stock dividend of $50,000.00 par value issued in 1931, the common stock was issued in payment for the net assets of the predecessor proprietorship.

The common stock in the treasury consists of 520 shares, purchased in 1939 and 1940 at a total cost of $62,000.00.

The source of the appraisal surplus is discussed on page 24.

Following is a summary of the Earned Surplus account since the date of incorporation:

	2¼	5	5
Number of years..................	2¼	5	5
End of period—October 31........	1922	1927	1932
Balance—beginning of period.............		$ 11,592.36	$ 14,274.67
Net income (loss*).....................	$26,592.36	112,820.19	390,613.80
Miscellaneous credits—charges* (net)......	—	1,862.12	1,413.60*
Total before dividends..............	$26,592.36	$126,274.67	$403,474.87
Dividends:			
Preferred.............................		$ 72,000.00	$ 60,000.00
Common...........................	$15,000.00	40,000.00	100,000.00
Stock dividend—common.............			50,000.00
Total dividends....................	$15,000.00	$112,000.00	$210,000.00
Balance—end of period.................	$11,592.36	$ 14,274.67	$193,474.87

(34)

Earned	Surplus Paid-in	Appraisal	Treasury Stock (At Cost)	Net Worth
				$250,000.00
$ 11,592.36				261,592.36
14,274.67	$10,000.00			324,274.67
193,474.87	21,500.00			614,974.87
49,401.57	24,300.00			498,701.57
54,010.36	26,700.00			530,710.36
40,312.89	33,300.00			548,612.89
18,733.61	33,300.00			527,033.61
67,743.45	33,300.00	$132,509.67	$14,000.00*	694,553.12
255,277.10	37,250.00	118,656.50	62,000.00*	849,183.60

3 1935	1 1936	1 1937	1 1938	1 1939	1 1940
$193,474.87	$49,401.57	$ 54,010.36	$ 40,312.89	$ 18,733.61	$ 67,743.45
67,313.80*	39,620.97	88,230.40	156,320.19	283,128.07	265,836.63
3,240.50	11,012.18*	15,072.13	5,899.47*	7,118.23*	1,197.02
$129,401.57	$78,010.36	$157,312.89	$190,733.61	$294,743.45	$334,777.10
$ 60,000.00	$12,000.00	$ 12,000.00	$ 12,000.00	$ 12,000.00	$ 12,000.00
20,000.00	12,000.00	105,000.00	160,000.00	215,000.00	67,500.00
$ 80,000.00	$24,000.00	$117,000.00	$172,000.00	$227,000.00	$ 79,500.00
$ 49,401.57	$54,010.36	$ 40,312.89	$ 18,733.61	$ 67,743.45	$255,277.10

(34—Cont.)

WORKING CAPITAL

The changes in working capital during several recent years are summarized below:

	1936	1937	October 31 1938	1939	1940
Current assets	$638,422.60	$786,238.41	$912,433.29	$807,057.67	$1,106,719.51
Current liabilities....	312,819.50	403,822.39	410,630.17	400,455.25	551,476.33
Working capital.......	$325,603.10	$382,416.02	$501,803.12	$406,602.42	$ 555,243.18
Working capital ratio...	2.04	1.95	2.22	2.02	2.01

RESULTS OF OPERATIONS

The results of operations during the past five years are briefly summarized below:

Year ended October 31:	Net Sales	Gross Profit on Sales	Net Income Before Federal Income Taxes	Federal Income Taxes	Net Income
1936......	$2,012,413.62	$ 527,913.66	$ 44,233.98	$ 4,613.01	$ 39,620.97
1937......	1,914,677.34	541,633.97	101,449.86	13,219.46	88,230.40
1938......	2,814,631.43	768,313.99	182,540.31	26,220.12	156,320.19
1939......	3,147,534.13	942,473.25	342,012.93	58,884.86	283,128.07
1940......	4,014,379.01	1,049,357.18	333,183.21	67,346.58	265,836.63

The stock is closely held. We therefore state below the salaries paid to the principal stockholders as officers, and the net income both before and after such salaries:

Year ended October 31:	Net Income (After Salaries)	Officers' Salaries to Principal Stockholders	Net Income Before Salaries
1936................................	$ 39,620.97	$45,000.00	$ 84,620.97
1937................................	88,230.40	40,000.00	128,230.40
1938................................	156,320.19	60,000.00	216,320.19
1939................................	283,128.07	50,000.00	333,128.07
1940................................	265,836.63	55,000.00	320,836.63

(35)

INDEX

INDEX